A PEOPLE
& A NATION

A History of The United States

VOLUME I: TO 1877

BRIEF TENTH EDITION

Mary Beth Norton
Cornell University

Jane Kamensky
Brandeis University

Carol Sheriff
College of William and Mary

David W. Blight
Yale University

Howard P. Chudacoff
Brown University

Fredrik Logevall
Cornell University

Beth Bailey
Temple University

Debra Michals
Merrimack College

CENGAGE
Learning·

Australia • Brazil • Canada • Mexico • Singapore • United Kingdom • United States

CENGAGE
Learning·

A People and A Nation, Volume I: To 1877,
Brief Tenth Edition

Mary Beth Norton, Jane Kamensky,
Carol Sheriff, David W. Blight,
Howard P. Chudacoff, Fredrik Logevall,
Beth Bailey, Debra Michals

Product Director: Suzanne Jeans

Senior Product Manager: Ann West

Content Developer: Lauren Floyd

Associate Content Developer:
  Megan Chrisman

Product Assistant: Liz Fraser

Senior Media Developer: Laura Hildebrand

Marketing Manager: Valerie Hartman

Market Development Manager:
  Kyle Zimmerman

Senior Content Project Manager: Jane Lee

Senior Art Director: Cate Rickard Barr

Manufacturing Planner: Sandee Milewski

Senior Rights Acquisition Specialist:
  Jennifer Meyer Dare

Production Service:
  Integra Software Services

Cover Designer: Dutton & Sherman Design

Cover Image: Johnson, Eastman
  (1824–1906). *Barn Swallows,* 1878. Oil on
  canvas, 27 3/16 × 22 3/16 inches (69.1 ×
  56.4 cm). Gift of Mrs. John Wintersteen
  in memory of John Wintersteen,
  1953. Philadelphia Museum of Art,
  Philadelphia, USA. Photo Credit:
  © The Philadelphia Museum of Art/
  Art Resource, NY.

Compositor: Integra Software Services

For product information and technology assistance, contact us at
Cengage Learning Customer & Sales Support, 1-800-354-9706

For permission to use material from this text or product,
submit all requests online at **www.cengage.com/permissions**.
Further permissions questions can be emailed to
permissionrequest@cengage.com.

Library of Congress Control Number: 2013944018

Student Edition:

ISBN-13: 978-1-285-43085-0

ISBN-10: 1-285-43085-9

Cengage Learning
200 First Stamford Place, 4th Floor
Stamford, CT 06902
USA

Cengage Learning is a leading provider of customized learning solutions with office locations around the globe, including Singapore, the United Kingdom, Australia, Mexico, Brazil and Japan. Locate your local office at **www.cengage.com/global**.

For your course and learning solutions, visit **www.cengage.com**.

Purchase any of our products at your local college store or at our preferred online store **www.cengagebrain.com**.

Instructors: Please visit **login.cengage.com** and log in to access instructor-specific resources.

Printed at CLDPC, USA, 11-21

Brief Contents

Maps   *ix*

Figures   *xi*

Tables   *xiii*

Preface   *xv*

1 Three Old Worlds Create a New, 1492–1600   *1*

2 Europeans Colonize North America, 1600–1650   *29*

3 North America in the Atlantic World, 1650–1720   *57*

4 Becoming America? 1720–1760   *82*

5 The Ends of Empire, 1754–1774   *109*

6 American Revolutions, 1775–1783   *137*

7 Forging a Nation, 1783–1800   *163*

8 Defining the Nation, 1801–1823   *198*

9 The Rise of the South, 1815–1860   *232*

10 The Restless North, 1815–1860   *264*

11 The Contested West, 1815–1860   *299*

12 Politics and the Fate of the Union, 1824–1859   *327*

13 Transforming Fire: The Civil War, 1860–1865   *363*

14 Reconstruction: An Unfinished Revolution, 1865–1877   *403*

Appendix   *A-1*

Index   *I-2*

Brief Contents

Maps xiv

Figures xx

Tables xxi

Preface xxii

1 Three Old Worlds Create a New, 1492–1600   1

2 Europeans Colonize North America, 1600–1650   29

3 North America in the Atlantic World, 1650–1720   57

4 Becoming America? 1720–1760   82

5 The Ends of Empire, 1754–1774   109

6 American Revolution, 1775–1783   137

7 Forging a Nation, 1783–1800   163

8 Defining the Nation, 1801–1823   193

9 The Rise of the South, 1815–1860   237

10 The Restless North, 1815–1860   264

11 The Contested West, 1815–1860   299

12 Politics and the Fate of the Union, 1824–1859   332

13 Transforming Fire: The Civil War, 1860–1865   362

14 Reconstruction: An Unfinished Revolution, 1865–1877   401

Appendix   A-1

Index   I-1

Contents

Maps   *ix*

Figures   *xi*

Tables   *xiii*

Preface   *xv*

About the Authors   *xxvii*

1 Three Old Worlds Create a New, 1492–1600   *1*

American Societies   *2*

North America in 1492   *5*

African Societies   *8*

European Societies   *10*

Early European Explorations   *12*

Voyages of Columbus, Cabot, and Their Successors   *14*

VISUALIZING THE PAST: **Naming America**   *16*

Spanish Exploration and Conquest   *17*

The Columbian Exchange   *20*

LINKS TO THE WORLD: **Maize**   *22*

Europeans in North America   *23*

LEGACY FOR A PEOPLE AND A NATION: **Revitalizing Native Languages**   *25*

Summary   *25*

2 Europeans Colonize North America, 1600–1650   *29*

Spanish, French, and Dutch North America   *31*

VISUALIZING THE PAST: **Acoma Pueblo**   *35*

England's America   *36*

The Founding of Virginia   *38*

Life in the Chesapeake   *40*

The Founding of New England   *43*

LINKS TO THE WORLD: **Turkeys**   *45*

Life in New England   *48*

The Caribbean   *50*

LEGACY FOR A PEOPLE AND A NATION: **"Modern" Families**   *53*

Summary   *54*

3 North America in the Atlantic World, 1650–1720   *57*

The Growth of Anglo-American Settlements   *58*

VISUALIZING THE PAST: **The Pine Tree Shilling**   *65*

A Decade of Imperial Crises: The 1670s   *66*

The Atlantic Trading System   *68*

LINKS TO THE WORLD: **Exotic Beverages**   *72*

Slavery in North America and the Caribbean   *73*

Forging and Testing the Bonds of Empire   *76*

LEGACY FOR A PEOPLE AND A NATION: **Americans of African Descent**   *79*

Summary   *79*

4 Becoming America? 1720–1760   *82*

Geographic Expansion and Ethnic Diversity   *84*

VISUALIZING THE PAST: **Slaves' Symbolic Resistance**   *88*

Economic Growth and Development in British America   *90*

"Oeconomical" Households: Families, Production, and Reproduction   *93*

Provincial Cultures   *95*

LINKS TO THE WORLD: **Smallpox Inoculation**   *99*

A Changing Religious Culture   *100*

Stability and Crisis at Midcentury   *102*

LEGACY FOR A PEOPLE AND A NATION: **"Self-Made Men"**   *106*

Summary   *106*

5 The Ends of Empire, 1754–1774   109

From the Ohio Country to Global War   111
1763: A Turning Point   115
The Stamp Act Crisis   118
Resistance to the Townshend Acts   122

LINKS TO THE WORLD: **Writing and Stationery Supplies**   123

VISUALIZING THE PAST: **Phillis Wheatley, Enslaved Poet in the Cradle of Liberty**   126

Confrontations in Boston   127
Tea and Turmoil   129
The Unsettled Backcountry   130
Government by Congress and Committee   131

LEGACY FOR A PEOPLE AND A NATION: **Women's Political Activism**   133

Summary   134

6 American Revolutions, 1775–1783   137

Toward War   139
Forging an Independent Republic   141
Choosing Sides   146

LINKS TO THE WORLD: **New Nations**   147

The Struggle in the North   150
Battlefield and Home Front   153

VISUALIZING THE PAST: **Frontier Refugees**   155

The War Moves South   156
Uncertain Victories   158

LEGACY FOR A PEOPLE AND A NATION: **Revolutionary Origins**   160

Summary   160

7 Forging a Nation, 1783–1800   163

Trials of the Confederation   165
From Crisis to the Constitution   170
Promoting a Virtuous Citizenry   175
Building a Workable Government   176
Building a Nation Among Nations   180

VISUALIZING THE PAST: **Newspapers of the Early Republic**   181

The West in the New Nation   185
Created Equal?   187

LINKS TO THE WORLD: **Haitian Refugees**   192

"Revolutions" at the End of the Century   192

LEGACY FOR A PEOPLE AND A NATION: **Dissent During Wartime**   194

Summary   194

8 Defining the Nation, 1801–1823   198

Political Visions   199
Continental Expansion and Indian Resistance   204
The Nation in the Orbit of Europe   208

LINKS TO THE WORLD: **Emigration to Liberia**   212

The War of 1812   214

VISUALIZING THE PAST: **Selling War**   216

Early Industrialization   219
Sectionalism and Nationalism   221

LEGACY FOR A PEOPLE AND A NATION: **States' Rights and Nullification**   228

Summary   228

9 The Rise of the South, 1815–1860   232

The "Distinctive" South   233
Southern Expansion, Indian Resistance, and Removal   238

LINKS TO THE WORLD: **The Amistad Case**   240

Social Pyramid in the Old South   245
The Planters' World   248
Slave Life and Labor   252
Slave Culture and Resistance   254

VISUALIZING THE PAST: **Imaging Nat Turner's Rebellion**   259

LEGACY FOR A PEOPLE AND A NATION: **Reparations for Slavery**   260

Summary   260

10 The Restless North, 1815–1860 *264*

Or Was the North Distinctive? *265*

The Transportation Revolution *267*

Factories and Industrialization *270*

LINKS TO THE WORLD: **Internal Improvements** *272*

Consumption and Commercialization *274*

Families in Flux *276*

The Growth of Cities *278*

Revivals and Reform *286*

VISUALIZING THE PAST: **Engaging Children** *289*

Utopian Experiments *290*

Abolitionism *292*

LEGACY FOR A PEOPLE AND A NATION:
P. T. Barnum's Publicity Stunts *295*

Summary *296*

11 The Contested West, 1815–1860 *299*

The West in the American Imagination *300*

Expansion and Resistance in the
Trans-Appalachian West *304*

The Federal Government
and Westward Expansion *308*

LINKS TO THE WORLD: **Gold in California** *312*

The Southwestern Borderlands *313*

VISUALIZING THE PAST: **Paintings and
Cultural Impressions** *316*

Cultural Frontiers in the Far West *320*

Summary *324*

LEGACY FOR A PEOPLE AND A NATION:
Descendants of Early Latino Settlers *324*

**12 Politics and the Fate of
the Union, 1824–1859** *327*

Jacksonianism and Party Politics *329*

Federalism at Issue: The Nullification and Bank
Controversies *333*

The Second Party System *336*

Women's Rights *338*

The Politics of Territorial Expansion *339*

The War with Mexico and Its Consequences *341*

VISUALIZING THE PAST: **The Mexican War
in Popular Imagination** *345*

1850: Compromise or Armistice? *347*

Slavery Expansion and Collapse of the
Party System *350*

LINKS TO THE WORLD: **William Walker and
Filibustering** *354*

Slavery and the Nation's Future *356*

LEGACY FOR A PEOPLE AND A NATION:
Coalition Politics *359*

Summary *359*

**13 Transforming Fire:
The Civil War, 1860–1865** *363*

Election of 1860 and Secession Crisis *365*

America goes to War, 1861–1862 *369*

War Transforms the South *375*

Wartime Northern Economy and Society *378*

The Advent of Emancipation *382*

The Soldiers' War *385*

1863: The Tide of Battle Turns *387*

VISUALIZING THE PAST: **Black Soldiers
in the Civil War** *388*

Disunity: South, North, and West *390*

1864–1865: The Final Test of Wills *394*

LINKS TO THE WORLD: **The Civil War in Britain** *396*

Summary *399*

LEGACY FOR A PEOPLE AND A NATION:
Abraham Lincoln's Second Inaugural Address *400*

**14 Reconstruction: An Unfinished
Revolution, 1865–1877** *403*

Wartime Reconstruction *405*

The Meanings of Freedom *407*

Johnson's Reconstruction Plan *410*

VISUALIZING THE PAST: **Sharecropping:
Enslaved to Debt** *411*

The Congressional Reconstruction Plan *413*

Politics and Reconstruction in the South   *419*

Retreat from Reconstruction   *424*

LINKS TO THE WORLD: **The "Back to Africa"**
Movement   *427*

LEGACY FOR A PEOPLE AND A NATION:
The Lost Cause   *430*

Summary   *430*

Appendix   *A-1*

Index   *I-2*

Features

MAPS

MAP 1.1 Native Cultures of North America   6

MAP 1.2 European Explorations in America   15

MAP 1.3 Major Items in the Columbian Exchange   20

MAP 2.1 European Settlements and Indian Tribes in Eastern North America, 1650   34

MAP 2.2 Caribbean Colonies ca. 1700   51

MAP 3.1 The Anglo-American Colonies in the Early Eighteenth Century   60

MAP 3.2 Atlantic Trade Routes   70

MAP 4.1 Louisiana, ca. 1720   85

MAP 4.2 Major Origins and Destinations of Africans Enslaved in the Americas   87

MAP 4.3 Non-English Ethnic Groups in the British Colonies, ca. 1775   91

MAP 5.1 European Settlements and Indians, 1754   114

MAP 5.2 European Claims in North America   115

MAP 5.3 Colonial Resistance to the Stamp Act   121

MAP 6.1 The War in the North, 1775–1778   150

MAP 6.2 The War in the South   157

MAP 7.1 Western Land Claims and Cessions, 1782–1802   167

MAP 7.2 Cession of Tribal Lands to the United States, 1775–1790   168

MAP 7.3 African American Population, 1790: Proportion of Total Population   190

MAP 8.1 Louisiana Purchase   205

MAP 8.2 Major Campaigns of the War of 1812   214

MAP 8.3 Missouri Compromise and the State of the Union, 1820   225

MAP 8.4 Latin American Independence, 1840   227

MAP 9.1 Cotton Production in the South   235

MAP 9.2 Removal of Native Americans from the South, 1820–1840   243

MAP 10.1 Major Roads, Canals, and Railroads, 1850   270

MAP 10.2 Major American Cities in 1820 and 1860   279

MAP 11.1 Westward Expansion, 1800–1860   302

MAP 11.2 Settlement in the Old Southwest and Old Northwest, 1820 and 1840   305

MAP 11.3 Western Indians and Routes of Exploration   309

MAP 11.4 Mexico's Far North   314

MAP 11.5 The California Gold Rush   323

MAP 12.1 Presidential Election, 1824   331

MAP 12.2 Presidential Election, 1828   332

MAP 12.3 American Expansion in Oregon   342

MAP 12.4 The War with Mexico   343

MAP 12.5 The Kansas-Nebraska Act and Slavery Expansion, 1854   351

MAP 13.1 The Divided Nation—Slave and Free Areas, 1861   367

MAP 13.2 McClellan's Campaign   370

MAP 13.3 The War in the West   372

MAP 13.4 Battle of Gettysburg   389

MAP 13.5 Sherman's March to the Sea   397

MAP 13.6 The War in Virginia   398

MAP 14.1 The Reconstruction Act of 1867   416

MAP 14.2 Presidential Election of 1876 and the Compromise of 1877   429

FIGURES

FIGURE 2.1 Population of Virginia, 1625   *42*

FIGURE 4.1 Atlantic Origins of Migrants to Thirteen Mainland Colonies of British North America, 1700–1775   *89*

FIGURE 4.2 Trade Revenue from the British Colonies in 1769   *92*

FIGURE 6.1 The Changing Value of the Continental Dollar, 1777–1781   *145*

FIGURE 10.1 Major Sources of Immigration to the United States, 1831–1860   *282*

FIGURE 13.1 Comparative Resources, Union and Confederate States, 1861   *371*

TABLES

TABLE 2.1 The Founding of Permanent European Colonies in North America, 1565–1638   *32*

TABLE 2.2 Tudor and Stuart Monarchs of England, 1509–1649   *38*

TABLE 3.1 Restored Stuart Monarchs of England, 1660–1714   *59*

TABLE 3.2 The Founding of English Colonies in North America and the West Indies, 1655–1681   *61*

TABLE 4.1 The Colonial Wars, 1689–1763   *104*

TABLE 5.1 British Ministries and Their American Policies   *124*

TABLE 7.1 Ratification of the Constitution by State Conventions   *174*

TABLE 12.1 New Political Parties   *346*

TABLE 12.2 The Vote on the Kansas-Nebraska Act   *351*

TABLE 13.1 Presidential Vote in 1860   *366*

TABLE 14.1 Plans for Reconstruction Compared   *417*

Preface

Published originally in 1982, *A People and A Nation* was the first U.S. history survey textbook to move beyond a political history to tell the story of the nation's people—the story of *all* its people—as well. That commitment remains. Our text encompasses the diversity of America's people, the changing texture of their everyday lives, and the country's political narrative. But as historical questions have evolved over the years and new authors have joined the textbook team, we have asked new questions about "a people" and "a nation." The *A People and A Nation* that appear in the book's title are neither timeless nor stable. European colonists and the land's indigenous inhabitants did not belong to this "nation" or work to create it, and Americans have struggled over the shape and meaning of their nation since its very beginning. The people about whom we write thought of themselves in various ways that changed over time. Thus we emphasize not only the ongoing diversity of the nation's people, but their struggles, through time, over who belongs to that "people" and on what terms.

In the tenth edition, we emphasize the changing global and transnational contexts within which the American colonies and the United States have acted. We discuss the ways that an evolving market economy shaped the nation and the possibilities for its different peoples. We show how the meaning of personal, regional, and familial identity changes over time, and we find the nation's history in the contact and collision of its peoples. We think about the role of the state and the expanding reach of the federal government; we emphasize historical contests between federal power and local authority. We examine the consequences of America's expansion and rise to unprecedented world power. And we focus on the meaning of democracy and equality in American history, most particularly in tales of Americans' struggles for equal rights and social justice.

About *A People and A Nation*, Brief

This brief tenth edition, as with earlier brief editions, aims to preserve the integrity of the complete work—along with its unique approach—while condensing it. This edition reflects the scholarship, readability, and comprehensiveness of the full-length version. It also maintains the integration of social, cultural, political, economic, and foreign relations history that has been a hallmark of *A People and A Nation*.

Dr. Debra Michals has worked with us again, along with Dr. Robert Heinrich, to ensure that the changes in content and organization incorporated in the full-length tenth edition were retained in the condensation. The authors attained reductions by paring down details rather than deleting entire sections. The brief tenth edition thus contains fewer statistics, fewer quotations, and fewer examples than the unabridged edition. The brief edition also includes more pedagogy than the unabridged edition: each main heading has a marginal question to give students a preview of the key topics covered. These questions are answered at the end of the chapter in the "Chapter Review." Throughout the chapters, students get assistance from key terms that are boldfaced in the text and defined in the margins.

What's New in This Edition

A primary goal of the revision of *APAN* 10e was to streamline coverage, reducing the number of chapters and so making the book easier to use in an academic semester. The Brief edition follows this new chapter organization and is built on *A People and A Nation*'s hallmark themes, giving increased attention to the global perspective on American history that has characterized the book since its first edition. From the "Atlantic world" context of European colonies in North and South America to the discussion of international terrorism, the authors have incorporated the most recent globally oriented scholarship throughout the volume. We have stressed the incorporation of different peoples into the United States through territorial acquisition as well as through immigration. At the same time, we have integrated the discussion of such diversity into our narrative so as not to artificially isolate any group from the mainstream.

Chapter-by-Chapter Changes

We reduced the number of chapters in the complete book by four—two in each volume. We achieved this reduction by taking a hard look at the areas where the same topics were covered in multiple chapters or where combining material in new ways allowed us to explain historical events more clearly. The list that follows indicates where content has been combined or reworked and which chapter in the ninth edition that content corresponds to (where there has been a change in chapter number). Other chapter-by-chapter changes and additions (including new scholarship) are outlined below as well.

1. **Three Old Worlds Create a New, 1492–1600**
   - New chapter opening vignette on Doña Marina establishes a major theme of cross-cultural communication and miscommunication
   - Increased emphasis on a world in motion: the circulation of goods, peoples, ideas, and money around the Atlantic basin, with new content on African history and the African diaspora
   - New Visualizing the Past, "Naming America"
   - New Legacy for A People and A Nation, "Revitalizing Native Languages"

2. **Europeans Colonize North America, 1600–1650**
   - Chapter-opening vignette reshaped to emphasize the growth of slavery, which receives increased attention in the chapter
   - Expanded coverage of the "sugar revolution" in the Caribbean colonies, their economic importance to Europe, and their role in the growth of new world slavery
   - New Legacy for A People and A Nation, "'Modern' Families"
   - New map, "Caribbean Colonies ca. 1700" (Map 2.2), offers more detail on the economically central colonies of the English, French, Spanish, and Dutch Caribbean

3. **North America in the Atlantic World, 1650–1720**
   - New chapter-opening vignette on the "Indian Kings"
   - Revised and increased coverage of Atlantic slavery, with new statistical foundation in the authoritative Trans-Atlantic Slave Trade Database
   - New Visualizing the Past, "The Pine Tree Shilling"

- Revised map, "The Anglo-American Colonies in the Early Eighteenth Century" (Map 3.1), with increased attention to England's non-mainland colonies
- Revised map, "Atlantic Trade Routes" (Map 3.2)

4. **Becoming America? 1720–1760**
   - New chapter-opening vignette on the 1744 progress of Dr. Hamilton through the colonies
   - New central problem framed: are Britain's North American colonies becoming more like or more unlike Britain in the mid-eighteenth century?
   - Increased coverage of imperial warfare, including the capture and subsequent return of Louisbourg by colonial troops fighting for Britain
   - New Figure 4.1, showing the origins of immigrants to North America in the eighteenth century; shows increasing ethnic diversity of the colonies and overwhelming dominance of African forced migration
   - New Figure 4.2, showing the value of exports and imports by colony, demonstrating the economic dominance of Britain's Caribbean possessions

5. **The Ends of Empire, 1754–1774**
   - Combines material from the ninth edition's Chapters 4 , 5, and 6
   - New chapter-opening vignette on Boston's "Day of General Rejoicing," celebrating Britain's capture of Quebec
   - Increased attention to the *dis*unity of the British colonies on the eve of revolution
   - New coverage of slavery and emergent antislavery in the context of the imperial crisis
   - New section, "The Unsettled Backcountry," pulls together material fragmented across three chapters in earlier editions and extends discussion of the Regulator movement in the Carolinas
   - New Links to the World, "Writing and Stationery Supplies," tied to the Stamp Act protests
   - New Visualizing the Past, "Phillis Wheatley, Enslaved Poet in the Cradle of Liberty"
   - Revised map, "Colonial Resistance to the Stamp Act" (Map 5.3), showing more locations in continental North America and the Caribbean where the Stamp Act inspired crowd actions

6. **American Revolutions, 1775–1783**
   - Combines material from the ninth edition's Chapters 6 and 7
   - New chapter-opening vignette on Mohawk leader Konwatsitsiaenni (Molly Brant) establishes the Revolution as a multisided, multicausal conflict featuring multiple perspectives
   - Expands coverage of loyalists, black and white, and neutrals
   - New treatment of the Revolution as a global war
   - New focus on the logic behind British tactics in prosecuting the American war, and on the relationship between war aims in the Caribbean and the shape of the conflict in North America
   - New section on funding the Revolution, including the hyperinflation of the Continental dollar
   - New concluding section on the ambivalent endings of the conflict for Britons and Americans in the new United States

7. Forging a Nation, 1783–1800
- Combines material from the ninth edition's Chapters 7 and 8
- New chapter-opening vignette on the journey to freedom of former slave Harry Washington, which took him from George Washington's Mount Vernon to Halifax to Sierra Leone
- Introduces new concept of the "revolutionary settlement," which continues in subsequent chapters: winning of the War of Independence marks one formal revolution in American society; the "settlement" of the revolution between 1783 and 1815 involved numerous other contests. Stresses tensions between the broad promises of the Declaration and the bounded world of American citizenship, and the extent to which domestic political and economic visions are forged among other nations, especially Britain and France, but also Iroquoia
- Expanded coverage of the role of culture and the arts in the creation of a national identity to encompass a highly pluralistic and divided society

8. Defining the Nation, 1801–1823
- Combines material from the ninth edition's Chapters 9, 11, and 12
- New section on religious revivals
- Material on early abolitionism and colonization has been moved here from the ninth edition's Chapter 12, which allows us to consider its southern as well as its northern manifestations
- Includes material on preindustrial farms, preindustrial artisans, and early industrialization from the ninth edition's Chapter 11, which allows us to consider southern as well as northern aspects of these topics
- Reorganizes some material so that it now more closely follows a chronological order (e.g., the Missouri Compromise of 1820 now comes before the Monroe Doctrine of 1823)
- New Links to the World, "Emigration to Liberia"

9. The Rise of the South, 1815–1860
- Chapter 10 in the ninth edition
- Adds new material to reflect recent scholarship on slavery and capitalism

10. The Restless North, 1815–1860
- Combines material from the ninth edition's Chapters 11 and 12
- Material on religion, reform, engineering and science, utopianism, and post-1820s abolitionism and the Liberty Party has been moved to this chapter
- Visualizing the Past, "Engaging Children," has been moved here from the ninth edition's Chapter 12

11. The Contested West, 1815–1860
- Chapter 13 in the ninth edition
- Adds section on "War of a Thousand Deserts" (southwestern borderlands warfare), helping to set the stage for war with Mexico in Chapter 12

12. Politics and the Fate of the Union, 1824–1859
- Combines material from the ninth edition's Chapters 12 and 14
- New chapter-opening vignette on Harriet Beecher Stowe's *Uncle Tom's Cabin*
- Includes section on "The Politics of Territorial Expansion" from the ninth edition's Chapter 13

- Now ends with John Brown's raid on Harpers Ferry in 1859
- New Legacy for A People and A Nation, "Coalition Politics"

13. **Transforming Fire: The Civil War, 1860–1865**
   - Chapter 15 in the ninth edition
   - Chapter now begins with the election of 1860, secession, and Fort Sumter
   - Updates death numbers for the Civil War

14. **Reconstruction: An Unfinished Revolution, 1865–1877**
   - Chapter 16 in the ninth edition
   - New material reflects recent scholarship on southerners' dependence on the state for goods and services well after the traditional end of Reconstruction

15. **The Ecology of the West and South, 1865–1900**
   - Combines material from the ninth edition's Chapters 17 and 20
   - New chapter-opening vignette on Nannie Stillwell Jackson's diary entries about everyday life in rural Arkansas in the late nineteenth century
   - New theme of ecology (interactions between humans and the environment)
   - New and expanded coverage of the South from the ninth edition's Chapter 20

16. **Building Factories, Building Cities, 1877–1920**
   - Combines material from the ninth edition's Chapters 18 and 19
   - New chapter-opening vignette on Coney Island
   - Streamlines and reorganizes material

17. **Gilded Age Politics, 1877–1900**
   - Chapter 20 in the ninth edition
   - New chapter-opening vignette on William Graham Sumner, champion of individual liberties
   - New content on influence of police power (government intervention), especially at state and local levels, to balance traditional interpretations that the Gilded Age was an era of laissez-faire

18. **The Progressive Era, 1895–1920**
   - Chapter 21 in the ninth edition
   - Expanded and reorganized material on foreign influences
   - New Links to the World, "Toynbee Hall, London"

19. **The Quest for Empire, 1865–1914**
   - Chapter 22 in the ninth edition
   - Tightens some sections and adds new material to reflect recent scholarship

20. **Americans in the Great War, 1914–1920**
   - Chapter 23 in the ninth edition

21. **The New Era, 1920–1929**
   - Combines material from the ninth edition's Chapters 24 and 26
   - Reorganized to integrate economic expansion abroad

22. **The Great Depression and the New Deal, 1929–1939**
   - Combines material from the ninth edition's Chapters 25 and 26

- Integrates material on the international causes and effects of the Great Depression, better situating the United States in the global economic crisis and growing global struggles
- Incorporates the section "The Approach of War" from the ninth edition's Chapter 26, newly connecting 1930s foreign policy to the domestic economic crisis Tightens domestic sections and eliminates some detail

23. The Second World War at Home and Abroad, 1939–1945
- Combines material from the ninth edition's Chapters 26 and 27
- New chapter-opening vignette on Hawai'i and the Pearl Harbor attack
- Includes material leading up to America's entry into the war, showing more clearly that America's role did not begin when Japan attacked Pearl Harbor
- Condenses coverage of the war into a single chapter

24. The Cold War and American Globalism, 1945–1961
- Chapter 28 in the ninth edition
- Provides new detail pertaining to Eisenhower's Cold War, in particular relating to the Third World
- Updates the map, "The Rise of the Third World: Newly Independent Nations Since 1943" (Map 24.3)

25. America at Midcentury, 1945–1960
- Chapter 29 in the ninth edition
- Expands discussion of the role of popular opinion in the civil rights struggle
- Adds an emphasis on how African American leaders focused on the international context in their ongoing struggle for social justice and civil rights
- Provides new comparative statistics on family life
- Revises discussion of the GI Bill

26. The Tumultuous Sixties, 1960–1968
- Chapter 30 in the ninth edition
- Reorganizes the section on "Liberalism and the Great Society"
- Provides new information on the growth of federal spending

27. A Pivotal Era, 1969–1980
- Chapter 31 in the ninth edition
- New chapter title conveys significant reinterpretation based on recent scholarship
- New section titled "Rights, Liberation, and Nationalism" incorporates and recasts material from the ninth edition's "The New Politics of Identity" and "The Women's Movement and Gay Liberation"
- Emphasizes the growing importance of marketplace solutions and development of debates about government regulation and the marketplace, as well as giving greater attention to government deficits—to help students understand the historical origins of current political debates
- Revises and reorganizes discussion of affirmative action to reflect recent scholarship
- Clarifies explanation of the causes of economic crises
- Emphasizes the original bipartisan support for the ERA
- Includes new comments on Nixon's domestic role

28. **Conservatism Revived, 1980–1992**
   - Chapter 32 in the ninth edition
   - Significantly revises and reorganizes previous material to show the broader social forces/shifts that helped to forge the new conservative coalition, in keeping with current scholarship
   - Gives more attention to regulation and the economy
   - Provides new material on the role and tactics of ACT UP
   - Reorganizes the section on "The End of the Cold War and Global Disorder" to clarify the role of the George Bush (Sr.) administration and the relationship between international and domestic material

29. **Into the Global Millennium: America Since 1992**
   - Chapter 33 in the ninth edition
   - Tightens and reorganizes domestic material on the 1990s; replaces "Violence and Anger in American Society" with "Domestic Terrorism"
   - New section on "Violence, Crime, and Incarceration" draws on recent scholarship on mass incarceration and its impact on American society, including discussion of gun violence
   - Updates information on demographics, population diversity and race/ethnicity, immigration, health, and the changing American family in "Americans in the New Millennium"
   - Substantially adds to treatment of the war in Afghanistan and significantly revises Iraq War treatment, including the drawdown of U.S. troops
   - Includes a new section on the death of bin Laden
   - Adds information about the election of 2012, Obama's first term, congressional deadlock and partisan conflict, the tea party, Obamacare, and DADT
   - Discusses tensions with Iran under Obama, and foreign policy in the 2012
   - New Visualizing the Past, "American War Dead"
   - New Legacy for A People and A Nation, "Twitter Revolution"
   - Updated figures, tables, and maps

Chapter Features: Legacies, Links to the World, and Visualizing the Past
The features in *A People and A Nation, Brief,* tenth edition, illustrate key themes of the text and give students alternative ways to experience historical content.

Legacy for A People and A Nation features appear toward the end of each chapter and offer compelling and timely answers to students who question the relevance of historical study by exploring the historical roots of contemporary topics. New Legacies in this edition include "Revitalizing Native Languages," "'Modern' Families," "Coalition Politics," and "Twitter Revolution."

Links to the World examine ties between America (and Americans) and the rest of the world. These brief essays detail the often little-known connections between developments here and abroad, vividly demonstrating that the geographical region that is now the United States has never been isolated from other peoples and countries. Essay topics range broadly over economic, political, social, technological, medical, and cultural history, and the feature appears near relevant discussions in each chapter. This edition includes new Links on emigration to Liberia and on Toynbee Hall, London. Each Link feature highlights global interconnections with unusual and lively examples that will both intrigue and inform students.

Visualizing the Past offers striking images along with brief discussions intended to help students analyze the images as historical sources and to understand how visual materials can reveal aspects of America's story that otherwise might remain unknown. New to this edition are features about the naming of America, the pine tree shilling, and poet Phillis Wheatley.

A People and A Nation Versions and Platforms

A People and A Nation is available in a number of different versions and formats, so you can choose the learning experience that works best for you and your students. The options include downloadable and online ebooks, Aplia™ online homework, and MindTap™, a personalized, fully online digital learning platform with ebook and homework all in one place. In addition, a number of useful teaching and learning aids are available to help you with course management/presentation and students with course review and self-testing. These supplements have been created with the diverse needs of today's students and instructors in mind.

CengageBrain eBook. An easy-to-use ebook version of *A People & A Nation, Brief* is available for purchase in its entirety or as individual chapters at www.Cengage Brain.com. This ebook has the same look and pagination as the printed text and is fully searchable, easy to navigate, and accessible online or offline. Students can also purchase the full ebook from our partner, CourseSmart, at www.CourseSmart.com.

MindTap Reader **for** *A People and A Nation, Brief* is an interactive ebook specifically designed for the ways in which students assimilate content and media assets in online—and often mobile—reading environments. MindTap Reader combines thoughtful navigation, advanced student annotation support, and a high level of instructor-driven personalization through the placement of online documents and media assets. These features create an engaging reading experience for today's learners. The MindTap Reader eBook is available inside MindTap and Aplia online products. (See below.)

MindTap™: The Personal Learning Experience. MindTap for *A People and A Nation, Brief* is a personalized, online digital learning platform providing students with the full content from the book and related interactive assignments—and instructors a choice in the configuration of coursework and curriculum enhancement. Through a carefully designed chapter-based Learning Path, students work their way through the content in each chapter, aided by dynamic author videos, reading in the ebook (MindTap Reader), robust Aplia™ assignments built around the text content, primary sources, and maps and frequent Check Your Understanding quizzes. A set of web applications known as MindApps helps students in many aspects of their learning and range from ReadSpeaker (which reads the text out loud), to Kaltura (which allows instructors to insert online video and audio into the ebook), to ConnectYard (which allows instructors to create digital "yards" through social media—all without "friending" their students). To learn more, ask your Cengage Learning sales representative to demo it for you—or go to www.Cengage.com/MindTap.

Aplia™ is an online homework product that improves comprehension and outcomes by increasing student effort and engagement. Founded by a professor to enhance his own courses, Aplia provides automatically graded assignments with detailed, immediate explanations on every question. The assignments developed for *A People & A Nation* address the major concepts in each chapter and are designed to promote critical thinking. Question types include questions built around animated maps, primary sources such as newspaper extracts and cartoons, or imagined scenarios, like engaging in a conversation with Benjamin Franklin; images, video clips, and audio clips are incorporated into many of the questions. More in-depth primary source question sets built around larger topics, such as "Native American and European Encounters" or "The Cultural Cold War," promote deeper analysis of historical evidence. Students get immediate feedback on their work (not only what they got right or wrong, but *why*), and they can choose to see another set of related questions if they want to practice further. A searchable **MindTap Reader ebook** is available inside the course as well, for easy reference. Aplia's simple-to-use course management interface allows instructors to post announcements, upload course materials, host student discussions, e-mail students, and manage the gradebook. Personalized support from a knowledgeable and friendly support team also offers assistance in customizing assignments to the instructor's course schedule. For a more comprehensive, all-in-one course solution, Aplia assignments may be found within the MindTap Personal Learning platform (see previous page). To learn more, ask your Cengage Learning sales representative to provide a demo—or view a specific demo for this book at www.aplia.com.

Instructor Resources

Instructor Companion Site. Instructors will find here all the tools they need to teach a rich and successful U.S. history survey course. The protected teaching materials include the *Instructor's Resource Manual*, a set of customizable Microsoft® PowerPoint® lecture slides, and a set of customizable Microsoft® PowerPoint® image slides, including all of the images (photos, art, and maps) from the text. Also included is Cognero®, a flexible, online testing system that allows you to author, edit, and manage test bank content for *A People and A Nation, Brief*. You can create multiple test versions instantly and deliver them through your LMS from your classroom, or wherever you may be, with no special installations or downloads required. The test items include multiple-choice, identification, geography, and essay questions. Go to login.cengage.com to access this site.

eInstructor's Resource Manual. This manual (found on the Instructor Companion site), authored by Chad William Timm of Grand View University, contains a set of learning objectives, a comprehensive chapter outline, ideas for classroom activities, discussion questions, suggested paper topics, and a lecture supplement for each chapter in *A People and A Nation, Brief*.

Student Resources

cengagebrain.com. Save your students time and money. Direct them to www.cengagebrain.com for choice in formats and savings and a better chance to succeed in class. Students have the freedom to purchase à la carte exactly what they need when they need it. Students can purchase or rent their text or purchase access to a downloadable ebook version of *A People and A Nation, Brief*. eAudio modules from *The History Handbook*, or other useful study tools.

Companion Website. The *A People & A Nation, Brief* Student Companion website, available on CengageBrain.com, offers a variety of free learning materials to help students review content and prepare for class and tests. These materials include flashcards, primary source links, and quizzes for self-testing.

Additional Resources

Reader Program

Cengage Learning publishes a number of readers, some devoted exclusively to primary or secondary sources, and others combining primary and secondary sources—all designed to guide students through the process of historical inquiry. Visit www.cengage.com/history for a complete list of readers or ask your sales representative to recommend a reader that would work well for your specific needs.

CourseReader

Cengage Learning's CourseReader lets instructors create a customized electronic reader in minutes. Instructors can choose exactly what their students will be assigned by searching or browsing Cengage Learning's extensive document database. Sources include hundreds of historical documents, images, and media, plus literary essays that can add additional interest and insight to a primary source assignment. Or instructors can start with the "Editor's Choice" collection created for *A People and A Nation*—and then update it to suit their particular needs. Each source comes with all the pedagogical tools needed to provide a full learning experience, including a descriptive headnote that puts the reading into context as well as critical thinking and multiple-choice questions designed to reinforce key points. Contact your local Cengage Learning sales representative for more information and packaging options.

Rand McNally Atlas of American History, 2e

This comprehensive atlas features more than eighty maps, with new content covering global perspectives, including events in the Middle East from 1945 to 2005, as well as population trends in the United States and around the world. Additional maps document voyages of discovery; the settling of the colonies; major U.S. military engagements, including the American Revolution and World Wars I and II; and sources of immigrations, ethnic populations, and patterns of economic change.

Custom Options

Nobody knows your students like you, so why not give them a text tailored to their needs? Cengage Learning offers custom solutions for your course—whether it's making a small modification to *A People and A Nation, Brief* to match your syllabus or combining multiple sources to create something truly unique. You can pick and choose chapters, include your own material, and add additional map exercises along with the Rand McNally Atlas (including questions developed around the maps in the atlas) to create a text that fits the way you teach. Ensure that your students get the most out of their textbook dollar by giving them exactly what they need. Contact your Cengage Learning representative to explore custom solutions for your course.

Acknowledgments

The authors would like to thank David Farber and John Hannigan for their assistance with the preparation of this edition.

We also want to thank the many instructors who have adopted *A People and A Nation* over the years and whose syllabi provided powerful insights leading to the tenth edition's chapter reduction. Also, we have been very grateful for the comments from the historian reviewers who read drafts of our chapters. Their suggestions, corrections, and pleas helped guide us through this momentous revision. We could not include all of their recommendations, but the book is better for our having heeded most of their advice. We heartily thank:

Sara Alpern, Texas A&M University
Mary Axelson, Colorado Mountain College
Friederike Baer, Temple University
Jennifer Bertolet, The George Washington University
Troy Bickham, Texas A&M University
Robert Bionaz, Chicago State University
Victoria Bynum, Texas State University, San Marcos
Randall Couch, Tulane University
Julie Courtwright, Iowa State University
Anthony Edmonds, Ball State University
Mario Fenyo, Bowie State University
Judy Gordon-Omelka, Friends University
Kathleen Gorman, Minnesota State University, Mankato
Michael Harkins, Harper College
Walter Hixson, University of Akron
B.T. Huntley, Front Range Community College
Edith Macdonald, University of Central Florida
Thomas Martin, Sinclair Community College
Allison McNeese, Mount Mercy College
David Montgomery, North Central Michigan College
Steve O'Brien, Bridgewater State College
Paul O'Hara, Xavier University
John Putman, San Diego State University
Thomas Roy, University of Oklahoma
Manfred Silva, El Paso Community College
Laurie Sprankle, Community College of Allegheny County
Michael Thompson, University of Tennessee at Chattanooga
Chad Timm, Grand View University
Jose Torre, College at Brockport, SUNY
Michael Vollbach, Oakland Community College
Kenneth Watras, Paradise Valley Community College
Jeffrey Williams, Northern Kentucky University

The authors thank the helpful Cengage people who designed, edited, produced, and nourished this book. Many thanks to Ann West, senior sponsoring editor; Margaret McAndrew Beasley, senior development editor; Megan Chrisman, associate content developer; Pembroke Herbert, photo researcher; Charlotte Miller, art editor; and Jane Lee, senior content project manager.

M. B. N.
J. K.
C. S.
D. B.
H. C.
F. L.
B. B.
D. M.

About the Authors

Mary Beth Norton

Born in Ann Arbor, Michigan, Mary Beth Norton received her BA from the University of Michigan (1964) and her PhD from Harvard University (1969). She is the Mary Donlon Alger Professor of American History at Cornell University. Her dissertation won the Allan Nevins Prize. She has written *The British-Americans* (1972); *Liberty's Daughters* (1980, 1996); *Founding Mothers & Fathers* (1996), which was one of three finalists for the 1997 Pulitzer Prize in History; and *In the Devil's Snare* (2002), one of five finalists for the 2003 *L.A. Times* Book Prize in History and won the English-Speaking Union's Ambassador Book Award in American Studies for 2003. Her most recent book is *Separated by Their Sex* (2011). She has coedited three volumes on American women's history. She was also general editor of the *American Historical Association's Guide to Historical Literature* (1995). Her articles have appeared in such journals as the *American Historical Review, William and Mary Quarterly*, and *Journal of Women's History*. Mary Beth has served as president of the Berkshire Conference of Women Historians, as vice president for research of the American Historical Association, and as a presidential appointee to the National Council on the Humanities. She has appeared on Book TV, the History and Discovery Channels, PBS, and NBC as a commentator on early American history, and she has lectured frequently to high school teachers. She has received four honorary degrees and is an elected member of both the American Academy of Arts and Sciences and the American Philosophical Society. She has held fellowships from the National Endowment for the Humanities; the Guggenheim, Rockefeller, and Starr Foundations; and the Henry E. Huntington Library. In 2005–2006, she was the Pitt Professor of American History and Institutions at the University of Cambridge and Newnham College.

Jane Kamensky

Born in New York City, Jane Kamensky earned her BA (1985) and PhD (1993) from Yale University. She is now Harry S Truman Professor of American Civilization at Brandeis University, where she has taught since 1993 and has won two university-wide teaching prizes. She is the author of *The Exchange Artist: A Tale of High-Flying Speculation and America's First Banking Collapse* (2008), a finalist for the 2009 George Washington Book Prize; *Governing the Tongue: The Politics of Speech in Early New England* (1997); and *The Colonial Mosaic: American Women, 1600–1760* (1995); and coeditor of *The Oxford Handbook of the American Revolution* (2012). With Jill Lepore, she is the coauthor of the historical novel *Blindspot* (2008), a *New York Times* editor's choice and *Boston Globe* bestseller. In 1999, she and Lepore also cofounded *Common-place* (www.common-place.org), which remains a leading online journal of early American history and life. Jane has also served on the editorial boards of the *American Historical Review*, the *Journal of American History*, and the *Journal of the Early Republic*; as well as on the Council of the American Antiquarian Society and the Executive Board of the Organization of American Historians. Called on frequently as an adviser to public history projects, she has appeared on PBS, C-SPAN, the History Channel, and NPR, among other media outlets. Jane has won numerous major grants and fellowships to support her scholarship. In 2007–2008, a grant from the Andrew W. Mellon Foundation allowed her to pursue advanced training in art history at the Courtauld Institute of Art in London. Her next book, a history of painting and politics in the age of revolution, centered on the life of John Singleton Copley, will be published by W. W. Norton.

Carol Sheriff

Born in Washington, D.C., and raised in Bethesda, Maryland, Carol Sheriff received her BA from Wesleyan University (1985) and her PhD from Yale University (1993). Since 1993, she has taught history at the College of William and Mary, where she has won the Thomas Jefferson Teaching Award; the Alumni Teaching Fellowship Award; the University Professorship for Teaching Excellence; The Class of 2013 Distinguished Professorship for Excellence in Scholarship, Teaching, and Service; and the Arts and Sciences Award for Teaching Excellence. Her publications include *The Artificial River: The Erie Canal and the Paradox of Progress* (1996), which won the Dixon Ryan Fox Award from the New York State Historical Association and the Award for Excellence in Research from the New York State Archives; and *A People at War: Civilians and Soldiers in America's Civil War, 1854–1877* (with Scott Reynolds Nelson, 2007). In 2012, she won the John T. Hubbell Prize from *Civil War History* for her article on the state-commissioned Virginia history textbooks of the 1950s, and the controversies their portrayals of the Civil War era provoked in ensuing decades. Carol has written sections of a teaching manual for the New York State history curriculum, given presentations at Teaching American History grant projects, consulted on an exhibit for the Rochester Museum and Science Center, and appeared in The History Channel's Modern Marvels show on the Erie Canal, and she is engaged in several public-history projects marking the sesquicentennial of the Civil War. At William and Mary, she teaches the U.S. history survey as well as upper-level classes on the Early Republic, the Civil War Era, and the American West.

David W. Blight

Born in Flint, Michigan, David W. Blight received his BA from Michigan State University (1971) and his PhD from the University of Wisconsin (1985). He is now professor of history and director of the Gilder Lehrman Center for the Study of Slavery, Resistance, and Abolition at Yale University and will be Pitt Professor of American History and Institutions at the University of Cambridge in the United Kingdom, 2013–2014. For the first seven years of his career, David was a public high school teacher in Flint. He has written *Frederick Douglass's Civil War* (1989) and *Race and Reunion: The Civil War in American Memory, 1863–1915* (2000). His most recent books are *American Oracle: The Civil War in the Civil Rights Era* (2011) and *A Slave No More: The Emancipation of John Washington and Wallace Turnage* (2007), and he is currently writing a new full biography of Frederick Douglass. His edited works include *When This Cruel War Is Over: The Civil War Letters of Charles Harvey Brewster* (1992), *Narrative of the Life of Frederick Douglass* (1993), W. E. B. Du Bois, *The Souls of Black Folk* (with Robert Gooding Williams, 1997), *Union and Emancipation* (with Brooks Simpson, 1997), and *Caleb Bingham, The Columbian Orator* (1997). David's essays have appeared in the *Journal of American History* and *Civil War History,* among others. A consultant to several documentary films, David appeared in the 1998 PBS series, *Africans in America.* In 2012, he was elected to the American Academy of Arts and Sciences, and he is currently serving on the Executive Board of the Organization of American Historians. David also teaches summer seminars for secondary school teachers, as well as for park rangers and historians of the National Park Service. His book, *Race and Reunion: The Civil War in American Memory, 1863–1915* (2000), received many honors in 2002, including the Bancroft Prize, Abraham Lincoln Prize, and the Frederick Douglass Prize. From the Organization of American Historians, he has received the Merle Curti Prize in Social History, the Merle Curti Prize in Intellectual History, the Ellis Hawley Prize in Political History, and the James Rawley Prize in Race Relations.

Howard P. Chudacoff

Howard P. Chudacoff, the George L. Littlefield Professor of American History and Professor of Urban Studies at Brown University, was born in Omaha, Nebraska. He earned his AB (1965) and PhD (1969) from the University of Chicago. He has written *Mobile Americans* (1972), *How Old Are You?* (1989), *The Age of the Bachelor* (1999), *The Evolution of American Urban Society* (with Judith Smith, 2004), and *Children at Play: An American History* (2007). His current book project is *Game Changers: Major Turning Points in the History of Intercollegiate Athletics.* He has also coedited with Peter Baldwin *Major Problems in American Urban History* (2004). His articles have appeared in such journals as the *Journal of Family History, Reviews in American History,* and *Journal of American History.* At Brown University, Howard has cochaired the American Civilization Program and chaired the Department of History, and serves as Brown's faculty representative to the NCAA. He has also served on the board of directors of the Urban History Association and the editorial board of *The National Journal of Play.* The National Endowment for the Humanities, Ford Foundation, and Rockefeller Foundation have given him awards to advance his scholarship.

Fredrik Logevall

A native of Stockholm, Sweden, Fredrik Logevall is John S. Knight Professor of International Studies and Professor of History at Cornell University, where he serves as vice provost and as director of the Mario Einaudi Center for International Studies. He received his BA from Simon Fraser University (1986) and his PhD from Yale University (1993). His most recent book is *Embers of War: The Fall of an Empire and the Making of America's Vietnam* (2012), which won the Pulitzer Prize in History and the Francis Parkman Prize, and which was named a best book of the year by the *Washington Post* and the *Christian Science Monitor.* His other publications include *Choosing War* (1999), which won three prizes, including the Warren F. Kuehl Book Prize from the Society for Historians of American Foreign Relations (SHAFR); *America's Cold War: The Politics of Insecurity* (with Campbell Craig; 2009); *The Origins of the Vietnam War* (2001); *Terrorism and 9/11: A Reader* (2002); and, as coeditor, *The First Vietnam War: Colonial Conflict and Cold War Crisis* (2007); and *Nixon and the World: American Foreign Relations, 1969–1977* (2008). Fred is a past recipient of the Stuart L. Bernath article, book, and lecture prizes from SHAFR, and a past member of the Cornell University Press faculty board. He serves on numerous editorial advisory boards and is coeditor of the book series, "From Indochina to Vietnam: Revolution and War in a Global Perspective" (University of California Press).

Beth Bailey

Born in Atlanta, Georgia, Beth Bailey received her BA from Northwestern University (1979) and her PhD from the University of Chicago (1986). She is now a professor of history at Temple University. Her research and teaching fields include war and society and the U.S. military, American cultural history (nineteenth and twentieth centuries), popular culture, and gender and sexuality. Beth served as the coordinating author for this edition of *A People and A Nation*. She is the author, most recently, of *America's Army: Making the All-Volunteer Force* (2009). Her other publications include *From Front Porch to Back Seat: Courtship in 20th Century America* (1988), a historical analysis of conventions governing the courtship of heterosexual youth; *The First Strange Place: The Alchemy of Race and Sex in WWII Hawaii* (with David Farber, 1992), which analyzes cultural contact among Americans in wartime Hawai'i; *Sex in the Heartland* (1999), a social and cultural history of the post–WWII "sexual revolution"; and *The Columbia Companion to America in the 1960s* (with David Farber, 2001). She is also coeditor of *A History of Our Time* (with William Chafe and Harvard Sitkoff, 6th ed., 2002; 7th ed., 2007; 8th ed., 2011). Beth has served as a consultant and/or on-screen expert for numerous television documentaries developed for PBS and The History Channel. She has received grants or fellowships from the ACLS, the NEH, and the Woodrow Wilson International Center for Scholars, and was named the Ann Whitney Olin scholar at Barnard College, Columbia University, where she was the director of the American Studies Program, and Regents Lecturer at the University of New Mexico. She has been a visiting scholar at Saitama University, Japan; at the University of Paris Diderot; and at Trinity College at the University of Melbourne, and a senior Fulbright lecturer in Indonesia. She teaches courses on sexuality and gender and war and American culture.

Debra Michals

Born in Boston, Massachusetts, Debra Michals received her BS from Boston University (1984) and her PhD from New York University (2002). She is an instructor of women's history and women's and gender studies at Merrimack College, where in 2008 she also served as acting chair of the Women's and Gender Studies Program. In 2013, Debra coauthored a permanent exhibit for the National Women's History Museum entitled "From Ideas to Independence: A Century of Entrepreneurial Women" (http://entrepreneurs.nwhm.org/). She is currently completing a book on the emergence of women entrepreneurs and the growing number of female breadwinners since World War II, and she has also begun research for a book about gender and modern fatherhood. Debra has been a visiting scholar to Northeastern University (2003), and served as the Acting Associate Director of Women's Studies at New York University (1994–1996), where she helped obtain and administer a Ford Foundation Grant in Women's and Area Studies and earned the university's President's Leadership Service Award. She has contributed to several anthologies, including *Sisterhood Is Forever* (2003); *Image Nation: American Countercultures in the 1960s and '70s* (2002); and *Reading Women's Lives* (2003), as well as the encyclopedia *Notable American Women* (2004). Debra has served as a consultant/editor for The History Channel and has written for the *History Channel Magazine*. She was the content director for The Women's Museum: An Institute for the Future (1998–2000), a consultant to the Elizabeth Cady Stanton Trust, and currently sits on the advisory board for the International Museum of Women. In addition to her own research, Debra is a frequent editor and adviser for scholarly books and pedagogical materials on U.S. history.

Three Old Worlds Create a New

A generation after Columbus crossed the Atlantic, a Spanish soldier named Hernán Cortés traded words with the ruler of the Aztec empire. Motecuhzoma II was among the most powerful men in the Americas. Thousands of loyal courtiers accompanied him to the gates of Tenochtitlán, the capital, one of the largest cities in the world. Cortés, his Spanish troops, and their native allies approached on horseback. The conquistador and the Aztec ruler bowed to each other, and spoke. "Montezuma bade him welcome," recalled Bernal Díaz del Castillo, a soldier on the expedition. "We have come to your house in Mexico as friends," Cortés told his host.

This mixture of ceremony, half-truths, and outright lies was among the first exchanges between two great civilizations from two sides of a great ocean. It was not an easy conversation to have. Motecuhzoma spoke Nahuatl; Cortés spoke Spanish. (The Spanish could not even pronounce the Aztec emperor's name, garbling "Motecuhzoma" as "Montezuma.") But in fact the conversation between Cortés and Motecuhzoma was not a dialogue but a three-way exchange. As Bernal Díaz explains, Cortés addressed the Aztec emperor "through the mouth of Doña Marina."

Who was Doña Marina? Born to Nahuatl-speaking nobles around the year 1500, she grew up at the margins of Aztec and Maya territories. As a child, she was either stolen from her family or given by them to indigenous slave traders. She wound up in the Gulf Coast town of Tabasco. In 1519, the leaders of Tabasco gave Marina to Cortés as one of many offerings they hoped would persuade the Spanish to continue west, into the heart of their enemies' territory. Marina learned Spanish quickly, and her fluency proved vital to the success of the Spaniards' expedition.

Marina was a young woman in whom worlds met and mingled. The Spanish signaled their respect by addressing her as "Doña," meaning lady. Nahuatl speakers rendered *Marina* as *Malintzin*, using the suffix *–tzin* to denote her high status. Spaniards stumbled over the Nahuatl *Malinztin* and often called her *La Malinche*: a triple name, from a double mistranslation.

The legacy of Doña Marina/Malintzin/La Malinche remains as ambiguous as her name. Her fluency helped the invaders to

Chapter Outline

American Societies
Ancient America | *Mesoamerican Civilizations* | *Pueblos and Mississippians* | *Aztecs*

North America in 1492
Gendered Division of Labor | *Social Organization* | *War and Politics* | *Religion*

African Societies
West Africa (Guinea) | *Complementary Gender Roles* | *Slavery in Guinea*

European Societies
Gender, Work, Politics, and Religion | *Effects of Plague and Warfare* | *Political and Technological Change* | *Motives for Exploration*

Early European Explorations
Sailing the Mediterranean Atlantic | *Islands of the Mediterranean Atlantic* | *Portuguese Trading Posts in Africa* | *Lessons of Early Colonization*

Voyages of Columbus, Cabot, and Their Successors
Columbus's Voyage | *Columbus's Observations* | *Norse and Other Northern Voyagers* | *John Cabot's Explorations*

VISUALIZING THE PAST *Naming America*

Spanish Exploration and Conquest
Cortés and Other Explorers | *Capture of Tenochtitlán* | *Spanish Colonization* | *Gold, Silver, and Spain's Decline*

The Columbian Exchange
Smallpox and Other Diseases | *Sugar, Horses, and Tobacco*

LINKS TO THE WORLD *Maize*

Europeans in North America
*Trade Among Indians and
Europeans | Contest Between
Spain and England | Roanoke |
Harriot's Briefe and True Report*

LEGACY FOR A PEOPLE AND A NATION
Revitalizing Native Languages

SUMMARY

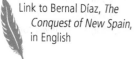

Link to Bernal Díaz, *The
Conquest of New Spain,*
in English

triumph—a catastrophe for the Aztecs and other indigenous peoples. Their descendants consider Doña Marina their foremother and their betrayer, at once a victim and a perpetrator of the Spanish conquest. Marina continues to embody the ambiguities of colonial history, in which power was shifting and contested, and much was lost in translation.

For thousands of years before 1492, human societies in the Americas developed in isolation from the rest of the world. That isolation ended in the Christian fifteenth century. As Europeans sought treasure and trade, peoples from two sides of the globe came into regular contact for the first time. Their interactions involved curiosity and confusion, trade and theft, enslavement and endurance. The history of the colonies that became the United States must be seen in this context of European exploration and exploitation, of native resistance, and of African enslavement and survival. In the Americas of the fifteenth and sixteenth centuries, three old worlds came together to produce a new.

The continents that European sailors reached in the late fifteenth century had their own histories, internal struggles that the intruders sometimes exploited and often ignored. The indigenous residents of what came to be called *the Americas* were the world's most skillful plant breeders; they developed crops more nutritious and productive than those grown in Europe, Asia, or Africa. They had invented systems of writing and mathematics. As in Europe, their societies rose and fell as leaders succeeded or failed. But the arrival of Europeans altered the Americans' struggles with one another.

After 1400, European nations tried to acquire valuable colonies and trading posts worldwide. Initially interested in Asia and Africa, Europeans eventually focused mostly on the Americas. Their designs changed the course of history on four continents.

As you read this chapter, keep the following questions in mind:

- **What were the key characteristics of the three worlds that met in the Americas?**

- **What impacts did their encounter have on each of them?**

- **What were the crucial initial developments in that encounter?**

American Societies

*What led to the development of
major North American civilizations
in the centuries before Europeans
arrived?*

Human beings originated on the continent of Africa, where human-like remains about 3 million years old have been found in what is now Ethiopia. Over many millennia, the growing population dispersed to the other continents. Because the climate was then far colder than it is now, much of the earth's water was concentrated in huge rivers of ice called glaciers. Sea levels were lower, and landmasses covered a larger

Chronology

12,000–10,000 BCE	Paleo-Indians migrate from Asia to North America across the Beringia land bridge
7000 BCE	Cultivation of food crops begins in America
ca. 2000 BCE	Olmec civilization appears
ca. 300–600 CE	Height of influence of Teotihuacán
ca. 600–900 CE	Classic Mayan civilization
1000 CE	Ancient Pueblos build settlements in modern states of Arizona and New Mexico
1001	Norse establish settlement in "Vinland"
1050–1250	Height of influence of Cahokia
	Prevalence of Mississippian culture in modern midwestern and south-eastern United States
14th century	Aztec rise to power
1450s–80s	Portuguese colonize islands in the Mediterranean Atlantic
1477	Marco Polo's *Travels* describes China
1492	Columbus reaches Bahamas
1494	Treaty of Tordesillas divides land claims in Africa, India, and South America between Spain and Portugal
1497	Cabot reaches North America
1513	Ponce de León explores Florida
1518–30	Smallpox epidemic devastates Indian population of West Indies and Central and South America
1519	Cortés invades Mexico
1521	Aztec Empire falls to Spaniards
1524	Verrazzano sails along Atlantic coast of North America
1534–35	Cartier explores St. Lawrence River
1539–42	De Soto explores southeastern North America
1540–42	Coronado explores southwestern North America
1587–90	Raleigh's Roanoke colony vanishes
1588	Harriot publishes *A Briefe and True Report of the New Found Land of Virginia*

proportion of the earth's surface. Scholars long believed the earliest inhabitants of the Americas crossed a land bridge known as Beringia (at the site of the Bering Strait) approximately 12,000 to 14,000 years ago. Yet new archaeological discoveries suggest that parts of the Americas may have been settled much earlier, possibly in three successive waves beginning roughly 30,000 years ago. About 12,500 years ago, when the climate warmed and sea levels rose, Americans were separated from the connected continents of Asia, Africa, and Europe.

Ancient America

The first Americans, called **Paleo-Indians**, were nomadic hunters of game and gatherers of wild plants. They spread throughout North and South America, probably as bands of extended families. By about 11,500 years ago, the Paleo-Indians were making fine stone projectile points, which they attached to wooden spears and used to kill and butcher bison (buffalo), woolly mammoths, and other large mammals. As the Ice Age ended and the human population increased, all the large American mammals except the bison disappeared.

Paleo-Indians The earliest peoples of the Americas.

Consequently, by approximately nine thousand years ago, the residents of what is now central Mexico began to cultivate food crops, especially maize (corn), squash, beans, avocados, and peppers. In the Andes Mountains of South America, people started to grow potatoes. As knowledge of agricultural techniques improved, vegetables and maize proved a more reliable source of food than hunting and gathering.

Most Paleo-Indians started to stay longer in one place, so that they could tend fields regularly. Some established permanent settlements; others moved several times a year. They used controlled burning to clear forests, which created cultivable lands by killing trees and fertilizing the soil with ashes, and also opened meadows that attracted deer and other wildlife. Although they traded such items as shells, flint, salt, and copper, no society became dependent on another group for items vital to its survival.

Wherever agriculture dominated, complex civilizations flourished. Assured of steady supplies of food, such societies could accumulate wealth, trade with other groups, produce ornamental objects, and create elaborate rituals and ceremonies. In North America, the successful cultivation of nutritious crops seems to have led to the growth and development of all the major civilizations: first the large city-states of Mesoamerica (modern Mexico and Guatemala) and then the urban clusters known collectively as the Mississippian culture (in the present-day United States). Each reached its height of population and influence only after achieving success in agriculture. Each later collapsed after reaching the limits of its food supply.

Mesoamerican Civilizations

Scholars know little about the first major Mesoamerican civilization, the Olmecs, who about four thousand years ago lived in cities near the Gulf of Mexico. The Mayas and Teotihuacán, which developed approximately two thousand years later, are better recorded. Teotihuacán, founded in the Valley of Mexico about 300 BCE (Before the Common Era), became one of the largest urban areas in the world, housing perhaps 100,000 people in the fifth century CE (Common Era). Teotihuacán's commercial network extended hundreds of miles. Pilgrims traveled long distances to visit Teotihuacán's pyramids and the great temple of Quetzalcoatl—the feathered serpent, primary god of central Mexico.

On the Yucatan Peninsula, in today's eastern Mexico, the Mayas built urban centers containing tall pyramids and temples, studied astronomy, and created an elaborate writing system. Their city-states engaged in near-constant battle with one another. Warfare and an inadequate food supply caused the collapse of the most powerful cities by 900 CE, ending the classic era of Mayan civilization.

Pueblos and Mississippians

Ancient native societies in what is now the United States learned to grow maize, squash, and beans from Mesoamericans. The Hohokam, Mogollon, and ancient Pueblo peoples of the modern states of Arizona and New Mexico subsisted by combining hunting and gathering with agriculture in an arid region. Hohokam villagers constructed extensive irrigation systems. Between 900 and 1150 CE, Chaco Canyon, at the junction of perhaps four hundred miles of roads, served as a major trading and processing center for turquoise. Yet the sparse and unpredictable rainfall caused the Chacoans to migrate to other sites.

Almost simultaneously, the unrelated Mississippian culture flourished in what is now the midwestern and southeastern United States. Relying largely on maize, squash, nuts, pumpkins, and venison, the Mississippians lived in hierarchically organized settlements. Their largest urban center was the **City of the Sun** (now called Cahokia), near modern St. Louis. Located on rich farmland near the confluence of the Illinois, Missouri, and Mississippi rivers, Cahokia, like Teotihuacán and

City of the Sun (Cahokia)
Area located near modern St. Louis, Missouri, where about twenty thousand people inhabited a metropolitan area.

Chaco Canyon, served as a focal point for religion and trade. At its peak (in the eleventh and twelfth centuries CE), the City of the Sun covered more than five square miles and had a population of about twenty thousand—small by Mesoamerican standards but larger than London in the same era.

The sun-worshipping Cahokians developed an accurate calendar, and the tallest of the city's 120 pyramids, today called Monks Mound, remains the largest earthwork in the Americas. Yet following 1250 CE, the city was abandoned. Archaeologists believe that climate change and the degradation of the environment, caused by overpopulation and the destruction of nearby forests, contributed to its collapse.

Aztecs

Far to the South, the Aztecs (also called Mexicas) migrated into the Valley of Mexico during the twelfth century CE. Their chronicles record that their primary deity, Huitzilopochtli—a war god represented by an eagle—directed them to establish their capital on an island where they saw an eagle eating a serpent, the symbol of Quetzalcoatl. That island city became Tenochtitlán, the nerve center of a rigidly stratified society composed of warriors, merchants, priests, common folk, and slaves.

The Aztecs conquered their neighbors, forcing them to pay tribute in textiles, gold, foodstuffs, and humans who could be sacrificed to Huitzilopochtli. In the Aztec year Ten Rabbit (the Christian 1502), at the coronation of Motecuhzoma II, thousands of people were sacrificed by having their still-beating hearts torn from their bodies.

North America in 1492

What were the gender dimensions of labor in native cultures?

Over the centuries, the Americans who lived north of Mexico adapted their once-similar ways of life to very different climates and terrains, thus creating the diverse culture areas (ways of subsistence) that the Europeans encountered (see Map 1.1). Scholars often delineate such culture areas by language group (such as Algonquian or Iroquoian). Bands that lived in environments not suited to agriculture followed a nomadic lifestyle typified by the Paiutes and Shoshones, who inhabited the Great Basin (now Nevada and Utah). Because finding sufficient food was difficult, such hunter-gatherer bands were small, usually composed of one or more related families. The men hunted small animals, and women gathered seeds and berries.

In more favorable environments, larger groups, like the Chinooks who lived near the seacoasts of present-day Washington and Oregon, combined agriculture with gathering, hunting, and fishing. Residents of the interior (for example, the Arikaras of the Missouri River valley) hunted large animals while also cultivating maize, squash, and beans. The peoples of what is now eastern Canada and the northeastern United States also combined hunting, fishing, and agriculture. They used controlled fires both to open land for cultivation and to assist in hunting.

Trade routes linked distant peoples. For instance, hoe and spade blades manufactured from stone mined in modern southern Illinois have been found as far northeast as Lake Erie and as far west as the Plains. Commercial and other interactions among disparate groups speaking different languages were aided by the universally understood symbol of friendship—the calumet, a feathered tobacco

MAP 1.1

Native Cultures of North America

The natives of the North American continent effectively used the resources of the regions in which they lived. As this map shows, coastal groups relied on fishing, residents of fertile areas engaged in agriculture, and other peoples employed hunting (often combined with gathering) as a primary mode of subsistence. Source: Copyright © Cengage Learning 2015

pipe offered to strangers at initial encounters. Across the continent, native groups sought alliances and waged war against their enemies when diplomacy failed.

Gendered Division of Labor

Societies that relied on hunting large animals, such as deer and buffalo, assigned that task to men, allotting food preparation and clothing production to women. Agricultural societies assigned work in divergent ways. The Pueblo peoples defined agricultural labor as men's work. In the east, peoples speaking Algonquian, Iroquoian, and Muskogean languages allocated most agricultural chores to women, although men cleared the land.

Everywhere in North America, women cared for young children, while older youths learned adult skills from their same-sex parent. Children had a great deal of

Collection of Mary Beth Norton

Jacques Le Moyne, an artist accompanying the French settlement in Florida in the 1560s (see page 31), produced some of the first European images of North American peoples. His depiction of native agricultural practices shows the gendered division of labor: men breaking up the ground with fishbone hoes before women drop seeds into the holes. But Le Moyne's version of the scene cannot be accepted uncritically: unable to abandon a European view of proper farming methods, he erroneously drew plowed furrows in the soil.

freedom. Young people commonly chose their own marital partners, and in most societies couples could easily divorce. Infants and toddlers nursed until the age of two or even longer, and taboos prevented couples from having sexual intercourse during that period.

Social Organization   Southwestern and eastern agricultural peoples also lived in villages, sometimes with a thousand or more inhabitants. The Pueblos resided in multistory buildings constructed on terraces along the sides of cliffs or other easily defended sites. Northern Iroquois villages (in modern New York State) were composed of large, rectangular, bark-covered structures, or longhouses; the name Haudenosaunee, which the Iroquois called themselves, means "People of the Longhouse." In the present-day southeastern United States, Muskogeans and southern Algonquians lived in large thatch houses.

In all the agricultural societies, each dwelling housed an extended family defined matrilineally (through a female line of descent). Mothers, their married daughters, and their daughters' husbands and children all lived together. Matrilineal descent did not imply matriarchy, or the wielding of power by women, but rather denoted kinship and linked extended families into clans. The nomadic bands of the Prairies and Great Plains, by contrast, were most often related patrilineally (through the male line).

War and Politics

Long before Europeans arrived, residents of the continent fought one another for control of hunting and fishing territories, fertile agricultural lands, or the sources of essential items, such as salt (for preserving meat) and flint (for making knives and arrowheads). Native warriors protected by wooden armor engaged in face-to-face combat, since their clubs and throwing spears were effective only at close quarters. They began to shoot arrows from behind trees only when they confronted European guns. War captives were sometimes enslaved, but slavery was never an important source of labor in pre-Columbian America.

Political structures varied considerably. Among Pueblos, the village council, composed of ten to thirty men, was the highest political authority; no larger organization connected multiple villages. The Iroquois had an elaborate hierarchy incorporating villages into nations and nations into a confederation. A council of representatives from each nation made crucial decisions of war and peace. Women more often assumed leadership roles among agricultural peoples. Female sachems (rulers) led Algonquian villages in what is now Massachusetts, but women never became heads of hunting bands. Iroquois women did not become chiefs, yet clan matrons exercised political power, including the power to start and stop wars.

Religion

All the continent's native peoples were polytheistic, worshipping a multitude of gods. The major deities of agricultural peoples like the Pueblos and Muskogeans were associated with cultivation, and their festivals centered on planting and harvest. The most important gods of hunters like those living on the Great Plains were associated with animals, and their major festivals were related to hunting.

A wide variety of cultures, comprising more than 10 million people who spoke over one thousand languages, inhabited America north of Mexico when Europeans arrived. They did not consider themselves one people or "Americans," nor did they think of uniting to repel the invaders who washed up on their shores beginning in 1492.

African Societies

What were the chief characteristics of West African societies in the fifteenth century?

Fifteenth-century Africa, like America, housed a variety of cultures with complex histories of their own. In the north, along the Mediterranean Sea, lived the Berbers, who were Muslims—followers of the Islamic religion. On the east coast of Africa, Muslim city-states traded with India, the Moluccas (part of modern Indonesia), and China. Sustained contact and intermarriage among Arabs and Africans created the Swahili language and culture. Through the East African city-states passed the Spice Route, the conduit of waterborne commerce between the eastern

Mediterranean and East Asia; the rest followed the Silk Road, the long land route across Central Asia.

South of the Mediterranean coast in the African interior lie the great Saharan and Libyan deserts. The introduction of the camel in the fifth century CE made long-distance travel possible, and as Islam expanded after the ninth century, commerce controlled by Muslim merchants helped to spread similar religious and cultural ideas. Below the deserts, the continent is divided between tropical rain forests (along the coasts) and grassy plains (in the interior). South of the Gulf of Guinea, the grassy landscape came to be dominated by Bantu-speaking peoples, who left their homeland in modern Nigeria about two thousand years ago.

West Africa (Guinea)   West Africa was a land of tropical forests and savanna grasslands where fishing, cattle herding, and agriculture had supported the inhabitants for at least ten thousand years before Europeans arrived. The northern region of West Africa, or Upper Guinea, was heavily influenced by Mediterranean Islamic culture. Trade via camel caravans between Upper Guinea and the Muslim Mediterranean connected sub-Saharan Africa to Europe and West Asia. Africans sold ivory, gold, and slaves to northern merchants to obtain salt, dates, silk, and cotton cloth.

Upper Guinea runs northeast-southwest from Cape Verde to Cape Palmas. The people of its northernmost region, the so-called Rice Coast (present-day Gambia, Senegal, and Guinea), fished and cultivated rice in coastal swamplands. The Grain Coast, to the south, was thinly populated and had only one good harbor (modern Freetown, Sierra Leone). Its inhabitants farmed and raised livestock.

In Lower Guinea, south and east of Cape Palmas, most Africans were farmers who practiced traditional religions, rather than Islam. They believed spirits inhabited particular places, and they developed rituals intended to ensure good harvests. Individual villages composed of kin groups were linked into hierarchical kingdoms. At the time of initial European contact, decentralized political and social authority characterized the region.

Complementary Gender Roles   In the societies of West Africa, as in those of the Americas, men and women pursued different tasks. In general, both sexes shared agricultural duties. Men also hunted, managed livestock, and fished. Women were responsible for child care, food preparation, manufacture, and trade. They managed the local and regional networks through which families, villages, and small kingdoms exchanged goods.

Lower Guinea had similar social systems organized according to what anthropologists have called the dual-sex principle. Each sex handled its own affairs: male political and religious leaders governed men, and females ruled women. Many West African societies practiced polygyny (one man's having several wives, each of whom lived separately with her children). Thus, few adults lived permanently in marital households, but the dual-sex system ensured that they were monitored by their own sex.

Throughout Guinea, both women and men served as heads of the cults and secret societies that directed the spiritual life of the villages. Young women were initiated into the Sandé cult, young men into Poro. Neither cult was allowed to reveal its secrets to the opposite sex. Unlike some of their Native American contemporaries, West African women rarely held formal power over men. Yet female religious leaders did govern other members of their sex, enforcing conformity to accepted norms of behavior and overseeing their spiritual well-being.

Slavery in Guinea

West African law recognized individual and communal landownership, but men seeking wealth needed laborers—wives, children, or slaves—who could work the land. West Africans enslaved for life were therefore central elements of the economy. Enslavement was sometimes used to punish criminals, but more often slaves were enemy captives or people who voluntarily enslaved themselves or their children to pay debts. Slaveholders had a right to the products of their bondspeople's labor, although slave status did not always descend to the next generation. Some slaves were held as chattel; others could engage in trade, retaining a portion of their profits; and still others achieved prominent political or military positions. All, however, could be traded at any time.

West Africans, then, were agricultural peoples accustomed to a relatively egalitarian relationship between the sexes. Carried as captives to the Americas, they became essential to transplanted European societies that used their labor but had little respect for their cultures.

European Societies

What were the motives behind fifteenth- and sixteenth-century European explorations?

In the fifteenth century, Europeans, too, were agricultural peoples. Split into numerous small, warring countries, the continent of Europe was divided linguistically, politically, and economically. Yet the daily lives of ordinary people exhibited many similarities. In most European societies, a few families wielded autocratic power over the majority. Although Europeans were not subjected to perpetual slavery, Christian doctrine permitted the enslavement of "heathens" (non-Christians), and some Europeans' freedom was restricted by serfdom, which tied them to the land or to specific owners. In short, Europe's kingdoms resembled those of Africa or Mesoamerica but differed greatly from the more egalitarian societies found in America north of Mexico.

Gender, Work, Politics, and Religion

Most Europeans, like Africans and Americans, lived in small villages. European farmers, called peasants, owned or leased separate landholdings, but they worked the fields communally. Men did most of the fieldwork; women helped at planting and harvesting. In some regions men concentrated on herding livestock while women cared for children, prepared and preserved food, milked cows, and kept poultry. A woman married to a city artisan or storekeeper might assist her husband in business. Because Europeans kept domesticated animals for meat, hunting had little economic importance.

Men dominated all areas of life in Europe. A few women—notably Queen Elizabeth I of England—achieved power by birthright, but most were excluded from positions of authority. European women also held inferior social, religious, and economic positions, yet they wielded power over children and servants.

Christianity was the dominant European religion. In the West, authority rested in the Catholic Church, based in Rome. Although Europeans were nominally Catholic, many adhered to local belief systems that the church deemed heretical. Still, Europe's Christian nations from the twelfth century on publicly united in a goal of driving nonbelievers (especially Muslims) not only from the European continent but also from the holy city of Jerusalem, triggering wars known as the Crusades. Nevertheless, in the fifteenth century, Muslims dominated the commerce and geography of the Mediterranean, especially after they conquered Constantinople (capital of the Christian Byzantine empire) in 1453.

Effects of Plague and Warfare

When the fifteenth century began, European nations were recovering from the devastating Black Death epidemic, which traders seem to have brought from China in 1346. The disease recurred with severity in the 1360s and 1370s, and the best estimate is that one-third of Europe's people died from the epidemic. A precipitous economic decline followed—as did social, political, and religious disruption.

As plague ravaged the population, England and France waged the Hundred Years' War (1337–1453), initiated because English monarchs claimed the French throne. The war interrupted overland trade routes connecting England and Antwerp (in modern Belgium) to Venice, and thence to India and China. Needing a new way to reach their northern trading partners, eastern Mediterranean merchants forged a maritime route to Antwerp. Using a triangular, or lateen, sail (rather than then-standard square rigging) improved the maneuverability of ships, enabling vessels to sail out of the Mediterranean and north around the European coast. Maritime navigation also improved through the acquisition of a Chinese invention, the compass, and the perfection of instruments like the astrolabe and the quadrant, which allowed sailors to estimate their latitude by measuring the relationship of the sun, moon, or certain stars to the horizon.

Political and Technological Change

After the Hundred Years' War, European monarchs consolidated their political power and raised revenues by taxing an already hard-pressed peasantry. The military struggle

Daily life in early sixteenth-century Portugal, as illustrated in a manuscript prayer book. At top a prosperous family shares a meal being served by an African slave. Other scenes show male laborers clearing land and hunting birds (left) and chopping wood (right), while at bottom a woman plants seeds in a prepared bed and in the top background female servants work in the kitchen.

De Agostini Picture Library / G. Dagli Orti / The Bridgeman Art Library inspired new pride in national identity, which eclipsed regional and dynastic loyalties. In England, Henry VII in 1485 founded the Tudor dynasty and began uniting a divided land. Most successful were Ferdinand of Aragón and Isabella of Castile, the Catholic monarchs of Spain. In 1492, they defeated the Muslims who had lived in Spain and Portugal for centuries, and expelled all Jews and Muslims from their domain.

The fifteenth century also brought technological change to Europe. **Movable type** and the **printing press**, invented in Germany in the 1450s, made information more accessible, creating a market for books about fabled lands across the sea. The most important such works were Ptolemy's *Geography*, a description of the known world written in ancient times, first published in 1475; and Marco Polo's *Travels*, published in 1477. The *Travels* recounted a Venetian merchant's adventures in thirteenth-century China and described that nation as bordered on the east by an ocean. The book led many Europeans to believe they could reach China by sea. A transoceanic route would allow Europeans to circumvent the Muslim and Venetian merchants who controlled their access to Asian goods.

movable type Type in which each character is cast on a separate piece of metal.

printing press A machine that transfers lettering or images by contact with various forms of inked surface onto paper or similar material fed into it in various ways.

Motives for Exploration

In the fifteenth and sixteenth centuries, European countries craved easy access to African and Asian goods—silk, dyes, perfumes, jewels, sugar, gold, and especially spices, which were desirable for seasoning food and as possible medicines. The allure of pepper, cinnamon, and cloves stemmed largely from their rarity, extraordinary cost, and mysterious origins. Acquiring these products directly would improve a nation's balance of trade and its standing relative to other countries.

A concern for spreading Christianity around the world supplemented economic motives. Fifteenth-century Europeans saw no conflict between material and spiritual goals. Explorers and colonizers sought to convert "heathen" peoples while at the same time establishing direct trade with Africa, China, India, and the Moluccas.

Early European Explorations

What sailing innovation ultimately facilitated the widespread exploration of the Atlantic and Pacific?

To establish that trade, European mariners first had to explore the oceans. Seafarers needed not just maneuverable vessels and navigational aids but also knowledge of the sea, its currents, and its winds. But where would Atlantic breezes carry their square-rigged ships, which needed the wind directly behind the vessel?

Sailing the Mediterranean Atlantic

Europeans learned the answer to this question in the Mediterranean Atlantic, the expanse of ocean located south and west of Spain and bounded by the Azores (on the west) and the Canaries (on the south), with the Madeiras in their midst. Europeans reached all three sets of islands during the fourteenth century. Sailing to the Canaries from Europe was easy, because strong Northeast Trade Winds blow southward along the Iberian and African coastlines. The voyage took about a week.

The Iberian sailor attempting to return home, however, faced winds that blew directly at him. Instead of waiting for the wind to change, mariners developed a new technique: sailing "around the wind." That meant sailing as directly against the wind as was possible without changing course. In the Mediterranean Atlantic, a mariner would head northwest into the open ocean, until—weeks later—he reached the winds that would carry him home, the so-called Westerlies. This solution became the key to successful exploration of both the Atlantic and the Pacific oceans.

Islands of the Mediterranean Atlantic

During the fifteenth century, Iberian seamen regularly visited the three island groups. The uninhabited Azores were soon settled by Portuguese migrants, who raised wheat for sale in Europe and sold livestock to passing sailors. By the 1450s Portuguese colonists who settled the uninhabited Madeiras were employing slaves (probably Jews and Muslims brought from Iberia) to grow sugar for export. By the 1470s, Madeira had developed a colonial **plantation** economy. For the first time in history, a region was settled explicitly to cultivate a valuable crop to be sold elsewhere. Because the work was so backbreaking, only a supply of enslaved laborers (who could not quit) could ensure the system's success.

plantation A large-scale agricultural enterprise growing commercial crops and usually employing coerced or slave labor.

The Canaries had indigenous residents—the Guanche people, who traded animal skins and dyes with Europeans. After 1402, the French, Portuguese, and Spanish sporadically attacked the islands. The Guanches resisted but were weakened by European diseases. The seven islands eventually fell to Europeans who then carried off Guanches as slaves to the Madeiras or Iberia. Spain conquered the last island in 1496 and devoted it to sugar plantations.

Portuguese Trading Posts in Africa

Other Europeans viewed the Mediterranean Atlantic islands as stepping-stones to Africa. In 1415, Portugal seized control of Ceuta, a Muslim city in North Africa. Prince Henry the Navigator, son of King John I of Portugal, dispatched ships southward along the African coast, attempting to discover an oceanic route to Asia. But not until after Prince Henry's death did Bartholomew Dias round the southern tip of Africa (1488) and Vasco da Gama finally reach India (1498).

Although West African states successfully resisted European penetration of the interior, they let Portugal establish coastal trading posts. The African kingdoms charged traders rent and levied duties on imports. The Portuguese profited by transporting African gold, ivory, and slaves to Europe. By bargaining with African masters to purchase slaves and carrying those bondspeople to Iberia, the Portuguese introduced black slavery into Europe.

Lessons of Early Colonization

Portugal's success grew after it colonized São Tomé, located in the Gulf of Guinea, in the 1480s. With Madeira at its sugar-producing capacity, São Tomé proved an ideal new locale for raising the valuable crop. Planters imported slaves to work in the cane fields, creating the first economy based primarily on the bondage of black Africans.

By the 1490s, Europeans had learned three key lessons of colonization in the Mediterranean Atlantic. First, they learned how to transplant crops and livestock to exotic locations. Second, they discovered that the native peoples of those lands could be conquered or exploited. Third, they developed a model of plantation slavery. The stage was set for a pivotal moment in world history.

Voyages of Columbus, Cabot, and Their Successors

What three themes in Columbus's log about his explorations would come to mark much of the future settlement of Europeans in the Americas?

Christopher Columbus
Italian explorer who claimed the island of San Salvador in the Bahamas for the king and queen of Spain.

Christopher Columbus understood the lessons of the Mediterranean Atlantic. Born in 1451 in the Italian city-state of Genoa, this largely self-educated son of a wool merchant was by the 1490s an experienced sailor and mapmaker. Drawn to Portugal and its islands, he sailed to the Portuguese outpost on Africa's Gold Coast, where he became obsessed with gold and witnessed the economic potential of the slave trade.

Like all accomplished seafarers, Columbus knew the world was round. But he thought that China lay only three thousand miles from Europe's southern coast. Thus, he argued, it would be easier to reach Asia by sailing west. Experts scoffed, accurately predicting that the two continents lay twelve thousand miles apart. When Columbus in 1484 asked the Portuguese rulers to back his plan to sail west to Asia, they rejected what appeared to be a crazy scheme.

Columbus's Voyage

Jealous of Portugal's successes in Africa, Ferdinand and Isabella of Spain agreed to finance most of the risky voyage—Columbus himself would have to pay a quarter of the costs—in part because they hoped the profits would pay for a new expedition to conquer Muslim-held Jerusalem. On August 3, 1492, Columbus set sail from the Spanish port of Palos in command of three ships—the *Pinta*, the *Niña*, and the *Santa Maria*.

On October 12, the vessels found land approximately where Columbus thought Cipangu (Japan) was located (see Map 1.2). He and his men anchored off an island in the Bahamas, called Guanahaní by its inhabitants. Columbus claimed the territory for Spain and renamed Guanahaní San Salvador. Later, he explored the islands now known as Cuba and Hispaniola, which the native Taíno people called Colba and Bohío. Because he thought he had reached the East Indies (the Spice Islands), Columbus referred to the inhabitants as "Indians." The Taínos thought the Europeans had come from the sky, and crowds gathered to meet and exchange gifts with Columbus.

Columbus's Observations

Three themes predominate in Columbus's log. First, he insistently asked the Taínos where he could find gold, pearls, and spices. His informants replied (via signs) that such products could be obtained on other islands or on the mainland. He came to mistrust such answers, noting, "they will tell me anything I want to hear."

Second, Columbus wrote of the strange and beautiful plants and animals. His interest was not only aesthetic. "I believe that there are many plants and trees

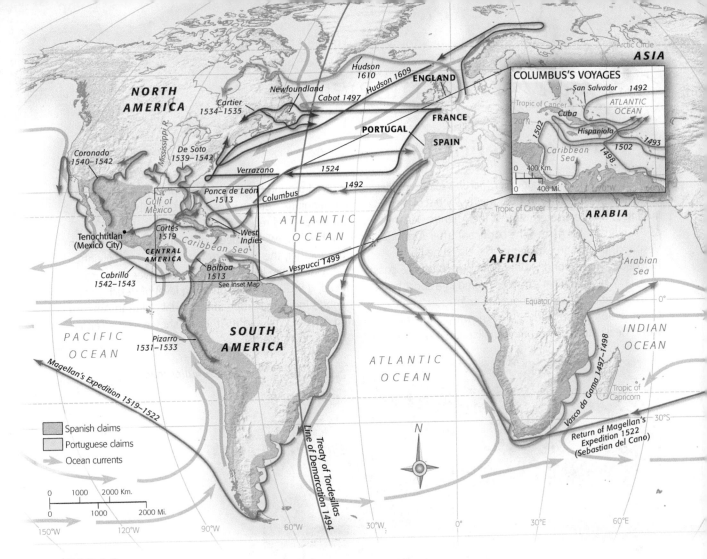

MAP 1.2

European Explorations in America

In the century following Columbus's voyages, European adventurers explored the coasts and parts of the interior of North and South America.

Source: Copyright © Cengage Learning 2015

here that could be worth a lot in Spain for use as dyes, spices, and medicines," he observed, adding that he was carrying home samples for experts to examine.

Included in his cargo of curiosities were some of the islands' human residents, whom Columbus also evaluated as resources to answer European needs. The Taínos were, he said, handsome, gentle, and friendly, though they told him of the fierce Caniba (today called Caribs) who lived on other islands, raided their villages, and ate some captives (hence today's word *cannibal*). Columbus saw the Taínos as likely converts to Catholicism as well as "good and skilled servants."

Columbus made three more voyages, exploring most of the major Caribbean islands and sailing along the coasts of Central and South America. Until the day he died, in 1506 at the age of fifty-five, he believed he had reached Asia.

Others knew better. The Florentine merchant Amerigo Vespucci, who explored the South American coast in 1499, was the first to publish that a new continent had been discovered. By then, Spain, Portugal, and Pope Alexander VI had signed the Treaty of Tordesillas (1494), confirming Portugal's dominance in Africa—and later Brazil—in exchange for Spanish preeminence in the rest of the Western Hemisphere.

Link to the journal of Christopher Columbus

Link to Christopher Columbus's letter to the king and queen of Spain

Naming America

In 1507, German cartographer Martin Waldseemüller created the first map to label the newly discovered landmass on the western side of the Atlantic Ocean as "America." He named the continent after Amerigo Vespucci, the Italian explorer who realized he had reached a "new world" rather than islands off the coast of Asia. Waldseemüller's map appeared in a short book called *Cosmographiae Introductio*, or *Introduction to Cosmography*—the study of the known world. The world he illustrated was both familiar and new. The sun revolved around the earth, as scholars had believed for a millennium. Yet the voyages of Columbus, Vespucci, and others had reconfigured the globe.

When the twelve sheets of Waldseemüller's map are put together, the image stretches nearly five by eight feet. One of the largest printed maps ever then produced, it includes an astonishing level of detail. What symbols indicate European territorial claims in America and Africa? Why might Africa be shown as the center of the known world?

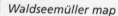

Waldseemüller map

Library of Congress

America

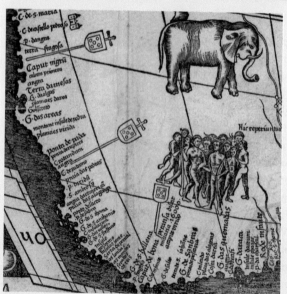

Library of Congress

African peoples

Library of Congress

Norse and Other Northern Voyagers

Five hundred years before Columbus, about the year 1001, a **Norse** expedition under Leif Ericsson sailed to North America across the Davis Strait, which separated Greenland from Baffin Island (located northeast of Hudson Bay; see Map 1.1) by just 200 nautical miles. They settled at a site they named "**Vinland**," but attacks by local residents forced them out after just a few years. In the 1960s, archaeologists determined that the Norse had established an outpost at what is now L'Anse aux Meadows, Newfoundland. Vinland was probably located farther south.

Norse Also known as Vikings, they were a warrior culture from Scandinavia.

Vinland The site of the first known attempt at European settlement in the Americas.

John Cabot's Explorations

The European generally credited with "discovering" North America is Zuan Cabboto, known today as **John Cabot**. Cabot brought to Europe the first formal knowledge of the northern continental coastline and claimed the land for England. Like Columbus, Cabot was a master mariner from the Italian city-state of Genoa; the two men probably knew each other. Calculating that England—which traded with Asia only through intermediaries—would be eager to sponsor exploratory voyages, he gained financial backing from King Henry VII. He set sail from Bristol in May 1497, reaching North America about a month later. After exploring the coast of modern Newfoundland for a month, Cabot rode the Westerlies back to England, arriving in fifteen days.

John Cabot Italian explorer who established English claims to the New World

The voyages of Columbus, Cabot, and their successors brought the Eastern and Western Hemispheres together. Portuguese explorer Pedro Álvares Cabral reached Brazil in 1500; John Cabot's son Sebastian arrived in North America in 1507; France financed Giovanni da Verrazzano in 1524 and Jacques Cartier in 1534; and in 1609 and 1610, Henry Hudson explored the North American coast for the Dutch West India Company (see Map 1.2). All were searching primarily for an easy water route to the riches of Asia—the legendary, nonexistent "Northwest Passage" through the Americas. But in a sign of what was to come, Verrazzano observed that "the [American] countryside is, in fact, full of promise and deserves to be developed for itself."

Spanish Exploration and Conquest

What model of colonization did Spain establish that other nations would later attempt to follow?

Only Spain began colonization immediately. On his second voyage in 1493, Columbus brought to Hispaniola seventeen ships loaded with twelve hundred men, seeds, plants, livestock, chickens, and dogs—as well as microbes, rats, and weeds. The settlement he named Isabela (in the modern Dominican Republic) and its successors became the staging area for the Spanish invasion of America.

Cortés and Other Explorers

At first, Spanish explorers fanned out around the Caribbean basin. In 1513, Juan Ponce de León reached Florida, and Vasco Núñez de Balboa crossed the Isthmus of Panama to the Pacific Ocean, followed by Pánfilo de Narváez and others who traced the coast of the Gulf of Mexico. In the 1530s and 1540s, **conquistadors** explored other regions claimed by Spain: Francisco

conquistadors Spanish conquerors or adventurers in the Americas.

Vásquez de Coronado journeyed through the southwestern portion of what is now the United States, while Hernán de Soto explored the Southeast. Francisco Pizarro, who ventured into western South America, acquired the richest silver mines in the world by conquering the Incas. But the most important conquistador was Hernán Cortés. In 1519, he led a force of roughly six hundred men from Cuba to the Mexican mainland to search for rumored wealthy cities.

Capture of Tenochtitlán

As he traveled toward the Aztec capital, Cortés, speaking through Doña Marina and other interpreters, recruited peoples whom the Aztecs had long subjugated. The Spaniards' strange beasts and noisy weapons awed their new allies. Yet the Spaniards, too, were awed. Years later, Bernal Díaz del Castillo recalled his first sight of Tenochtitlán, built on islands in Lake Texcoco: "We were amazed … on account of the great towers and cues [temples] and buildings rising from the water, and all built of masonry."

The Spaniards also brought smallpox to Tenochtitlán. The disease peaked in 1520, fatally weakening Tenochtitlán's defenders. Largely as a consequence, Tenochtitlán surrendered in 1521, and the Spaniards built Mexico City on its site. Cortés and his men seized a treasure of gold and silver. Thus, the Spanish monarchs controlled the richest, most extensive empire Europe had known since ancient Rome.

Spanish Colonization

Spain established the model of colonization that other countries later imitated, a model with three major elements. First, the Crown sought tight control over the colonies, imposing a hierarchical government that allowed little autonomy to American jurisdictions. That control included carefully vetting prospective emigrants and limiting their number. The Crown insisted that colonists import all their manufactured goods from Spain. Roman Catholic priests attempted to ensure colonists' conformity with orthodox religious views.

Second, men comprised most of the first colonists. Although some Spanish women later immigrated to America, the men took primarily Indian—and, later, African—women as their wives or concubines, a development usually encouraged by colonial administrators. They thereby began creating the racially mixed population that characterizes much of Latin America today.

Third, the colonies' wealth was based on the exploitation of the native population and slaves from Africa. Spaniards took over the role once assumed by native leaders who had exacted labor and tribute from their subjects. Cortés established the **encomienda system**, which granted Indian villages to conquistadors as a reward for their services, thus legalizing slavery in all but name.

encomienda system
Grants by the Spanish which awarded Indian labor to wealthy colonists.

In 1542, after criticism from colonial priest Bartolomé de las Casas, the monarch formulated a new code of laws forbidding the conquerors from enslaving Indians while still allowing them to collect money and goods from tributary villages. These laws, combined with the declining Indian population, led the *encomenderos* to import kidnapped Africans as their controlled labor force. They employed Indians and Africans primarily in gold and silver mines, on sugar plantations, and on huge ranches. African slavery was more common on the larger Caribbean islands than on the mainland.

An image from the Codex Azcatitlan, an account of the Aztec (Mexica) people's history from their arrival in the Valley of Mexico through the conquest by Cortés. Printed European-style in the late sixteenth century—that is, about seven decades after the conquest—the codex nonetheless presents a native viewpoint on the cataclysmic events. Here Cortés and his men are preceded by Malinche, his interpreter and mistress, and followed by their native allies bearing food supplies. Also in the crowd is Cortés's black slave.

Many demoralized residents of Mesoamerica accepted the Christian religion brought to New Spain by Franciscan and Dominican friars—men who had joined religious orders bound by vows of poverty and celibacy. Spaniards leveled cities, constructing cathedrals and monasteries on sites once occupied by Aztec, Incan, and Mayan temples. Indians were exposed to European customs and religious rituals designed to assimilate Catholic and pagan beliefs. Friars juxtaposed the cult of the Virgin Mary with that of the corn goddess, and the Indians melded aspects of their worldview with Christianity, in a process anthropologists call *syncretism*. Thousands of Indians embraced Catholicism, at least partly because it was the religion of their new rulers.

Gold, Silver, and Spain's Decline

The new world's gold and silver, initially a boon, ultimately brought about the decline of Spain as a major power. China, a huge country with silver coinage, gobbled up about half of the total output of new world mines. In the 1570s, the Spanish dispatched silver-laden galleons annually from Acapulco (on Mexico's west coast) to trade at their new settlement at Manila, in the Philippines. This gave Spaniards easy access to luxury Chinese goods such as silk and Asian spices.

The influx of wealth led to rapid inflation, which caused Spanish products to be overpriced in international markets and imported goods to become cheaper in Spain. The Spanish textile industry collapsed. The seemingly endless income from American colonies also emboldened Spanish monarchs to spend lavishly on wars against the Dutch and the English. Late sixteenth- and early seventeenth-century monarchs repudiated the state debt, wreaking havoc on the nation's finances.

When the South American gold and silver mines faltered in the mid-seventeenth century, Spain's economy crumbled, and the nation lost much of its international importance.

The Columbian Exchange

What were the results of contact between native populations and European settlers and explorers?

Columbian Exchange
The widespread exchange of animals, plants, germs, and peoples between Europe, Africa, and the Americas.

A mutual transfer of diseases, plants, and animals (called the **Columbian Exchange** by historian Alfred Crosby; see Map 1.3) resulted from the European voyages of the fifteenth and sixteenth centuries and from Spanish colonization. Many large mammals, such as cattle and horses, were native to the connected continents of Europe, Asia, and Africa, but not the Americas. The Americas' vegetable crops—particularly maize, beans, squash, cassava, and potatoes—were more nutritious and produced higher yields than Europe's and Africa's wheat, millet, and rye. Native peoples learned to raise and consume European livestock, and Europeans and Africans planted and ate American crops. (About three-fifths of all crops cultivated in the world today were first grown in the Americas.) The diets of all peoples were enriched, helping the world's population to double over the next three hundred years. Increased population in Europe fueled further waves of settler colonists, keeping the exchange in motion.

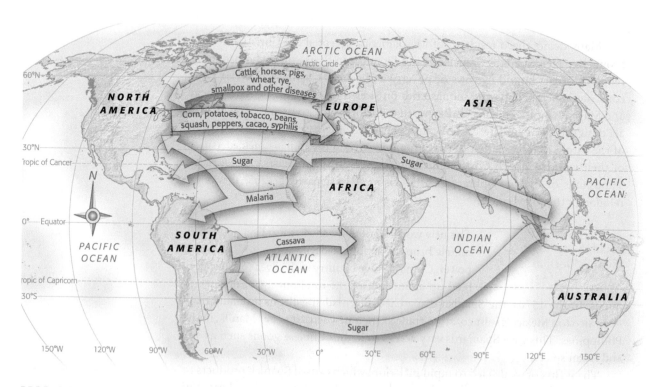

MAP 1.3
Major Items in the Columbian Exchange
As European adventurers traversed the world in the fifteenth and sixteenth centuries, they initiated the "Columbian Exchange" of plants, animals, and diseases. These events changed the lives of the peoples of the world forever, bringing new foods and new pestilence to both sides of the Atlantic. Source: Copyright © Cengage Learning 2015

Smallpox and Other Diseases

Diseases carried from Europe and Africa devastated the Americas. Indians fell victim to microbes that had long infested other continents, killing hundreds of thousands but also leaving survivors with some immunity. When Columbus landed on Hispaniola in 1492, approximately half a million people resided there. Fifty years later, there were fewer than two thousand native inhabitants.

Although measles, typhus, influenza, malaria, and other illnesses severely afflicted the native peoples, the greatest killer was smallpox. Historians estimate that the long-term effects of the alien microorganisms could have reduced the pre-contact American population by as much as 90 percent. Large numbers of deaths further disrupted societies already undergoing severe strains caused by colonization, rendering native peoples more vulnerable to droughts, crop failures, and European invaders.

Even far to the north, where smaller American populations encountered only a few Europeans, disease ravaged the countryside. A great epidemic, probably viral hepatitis, swept through the villages along the coast north of Cape Cod from 1616 to 1618. Again, the mortality rate may have been as high as 90 percent. Just a few years after this dramatic depopulation of the area, English colonists were able to establish settlements virtually unopposed. Disease made a powerful if accidental ally.

The Americans, though, probably gave the Europeans syphilis, a virulent sexually transmitted disease. The first recorded European case occurred in 1493 in Spain, shortly after Columbus's return from the Caribbean. Carried by soldiers, sailors, and prostitutes, it spread quickly through Europe and Asia, reaching China by 1505.

Sugar, Horses, and Tobacco

The exchange of three commodities had significant impacts on Europe and the Americas. European demand for sugar led Columbus to take Canary Island sugar canes to Hispaniola in 1493. By the 1520s, Greater Antilles plantations worked by African slaves regularly shipped sugar to Spain. Half a century later, Portugal's Brazil colony (founded 1532) was producing sugar for the European market on an even larger scale. After 1640, sugar cultivation became the crucial component of English and French colonization in the Caribbean.

Through trade and theft, horses—which, like sugar, were brought to America by Columbus in 1493—spread among the peoples of the Great Plains by 1750. Lakotas, Comanches, and Crows, among others, used horses for transportation and hunting, calculated their wealth in number of horses owned, and waged war on horseback. After acquiring horses, these Indians' mode of subsistence shifted from hunting combined with gathering and agriculture, to one focused almost wholly on hunting buffalo.

In America, Europeans encountered tobacco, which at first they believed was medicinal. Smoking and chewing the "Indian weed" became a fad in Europe in the sixteenth century. Despite the efforts of King James I of England, who in 1604 pronounced smoking "hatefull to the Nose, harmfull to the brain, [and] dangerous to the Lungs," tobacco's popularity soared.

Maize

Mesoamericans believed that maize was a gift from Quetzalcoatl. Cherokees told of an old woman whose blood produced the prized stalks after her grandson buried her body in a field. For the Abenakis, the crop began when a beautiful maiden ordered a youth to drag her by the hair through a burned-over field. The long hair turned into silk, the flower on corn stalks. Both tales' symbolic association of corn and women supports archaeologists' recent suggestion that—in eastern North America at least—female plant breeders substantially improved the productivity of maize.

Sacred to the Indians who grew it, maize was a major dietary staple. They dried the kernels; ground into meal, maize was cooked as a mush or baked as flat cakes, the forerunners of modern tortillas. Although European invaders initially disdained maize, they soon learned it could be cultivated in a wide variety of conditions. So Europeans, too, came to rely on corn, growing it in their American settlements and their homelands.

Maize cultivation spread to Asia and Africa. Today, China is second only to the United States in corn production. In Africa, corn is grown more widely than any other crop. Still, the United States produces over 40 percent of the world's corn, and it is the nation's largest crop. More than half of American corn is consumed by livestock. Much of the rest is processed into syrup, which sweetens carbonated beverages and candies, or into ethanol, a gasoline additive that reduces both pollution and dependence on fossil fuels. Of the ten thousand products in a modern American grocery store, about one-fourth rely on corn.

Today, this crop provides one-fifth of all the calories consumed by the earth's peoples. The gift of Quetzalcoatl has linked the globe.

The LuEsther T. Mertz Library, NYBG / Art Resource, NY

The earliest known European drawing of maize, the American plant that was to have such an extraordinary impact on the entire world.

Europeans in North America

How did England's rivalry with Spain shape its North American colonization efforts during the sixteenth century?

Europeans were initially more interested in exploiting North America's natural resources than in establishing colonies. John Cabot had reported that fish were plentiful near Newfoundland, so French, Spanish, Basque, and Portuguese sailors rushed to take advantage. In the early 1570s, the English joined the Newfoundland fishery. England became dominant in the region, which by the end of the sixteenth century was the focal point of a European commerce more valuable than that with the Gulf of Mexico.

Trade Among Indians and Europeans

Fishermen quickly realized they could increase profits by exchanging cloth and metal goods, such as pots and knives, for native trappers' beaver pelts, used to make fashionable hats in Europe. Initially, Europeans traded from ships sailing along the coast, but later male adventurers set up outposts on the mainland.

Indians similarly desired European goods that could make their lives easier and establish their tribal superiority. Some bands concentrated so completely on trapping for the European market that they abandoned their traditional economies and became partially dependent on others for food. The intensive trade in pelts also had serious ecological consequences. In some regions, beavers were wiped out. The disappearance of their dams led to soil erosion, which later increased when European settlers cleared forests for farmland.

Contest Between Spain and England

The English watched enviously as Spain was enriched by its American possessions. In the mid-sixteenth century, English "sea dogs" like John Hawkins and Sir Francis Drake raided Spanish treasure fleets sailing home from the Caribbean. Their actions helped foment a war that in 1588 culminated in the defeat of a huge Spanish invasion force—the Armada—off the English coast. English leaders started to consider planting colonies in the Western Hemisphere, thereby gaining better access to trade goods while preventing their enemy from dominating the Americas. By the late sixteenth century, world maps designated vast territories "New Spain" and "New France." The glaring absence of a region called "New England" would have been a sore spot for Queen Elizabeth I and her courtiers.

Encouraging the queen to fund increased exploration was Richard Hakluyt, an English clergyman. He translated and published numerous accounts of discoveries, insisting on England's preeminent claim to North America. In *Divers Voyages* (1582) and especially *Principall Navigations* (1589), he argued for the benefits of English colonization.

The first English colonial planners hoped to reproduce Spanish successes by dispatching to America men who would exploit the native peoples for their own and their nation's benefit. A group that included Sir Walter Raleigh promoted a scheme to establish outposts that could trade with the Indians and serve as bases for attacks on Spain's possessions. Queen Elizabeth authorized Raleigh to colonize North America.

A watercolor by John White, an artist with Raleigh's second preliminary expedition (and who later was governor of the ill-fated 1587 colony). He identified his subjects as the wife and daughter of the chief of Pomeioc, a village near Roanoke. Note the woman's elaborate tattoos and the fact that the daughter carries an Elizabethan doll, obviously given to her by one of the Englishmen.

Link to Thomas Harriot's "The Algonquian Peoples of the Atlantic Coast" from *A Briefe and True Report* ...

Roanoke

After two preliminary expeditions, in 1587 Raleigh sent 118 colonists to the territory that tens of thousands of native peoples called Ossomocomuck. Raleigh renamed it Virginia, after Elizabeth, the "Virgin Queen." The group established a settlement on Roanoke Island, in what is now North Carolina. But in August 1590, resupply ships found the colonists had vanished, leaving only the word *Croatoan* (the name of a nearby island as well as one of the area's powerful native groups) carved on a tree. Tree-ring studies show that the North Carolina coast experienced a severe drought between 1587 and 1589, which could have led colonists to abandon Roanoke.

England's first effort at planting a permanent settlement on the North American coast failed, as had earlier ventures by Portugal on Cape Breton Island (early 1520s), Spain in modern Georgia (mid 1520s), and France in South Carolina and northern Florida (1560s). All three enterprises collapsed because of the hostility of neighboring peoples and colonists' inability to be self-sustaining in foodstuffs.

Harriot's Briefe and True Report

The reasons for such failings become clear in Thomas Harriot's *A Briefe and True Report of the New Found Land of Virginia*, published in 1588. Harriot, a noted scientist who sailed with the second of the preliminary voyages to Roanoke, revealed that, although the explorers depended on nearby villagers for food, they antagonized their neighbors by killing some of them for what Harriot admitted were unjustifiable reasons.

Harriot advised later colonizers to deal more humanely with native peoples. But his book also reveals why that advice would rarely be followed. *A Briefe and True Report* examined the possibilities for economic development in America, stressing three points: the availability of valuable commodities, the potential profitability of American products, and the relative ease of manipulating the native population.

Harriot's *Briefe and True Report* depicted a bountiful land full of opportunities for quick profit. The native people residing there would, he thought, "in a short time be brought to civilitie" through conversion or conquest—if they did not die from disease. But European dominance of North America never was fully achieved, in the sense Harriot and his compatriots intended.

Revitalizing Native Languages

If knowledge is power, then language is power. Words make us human, and languages carry the DNA of cultures. From one generation to the next, humans use language as a tool to maintain the distinct identities of individuals and groups. Like peoples, languages evolve, and they are fragile. Their lives depend upon the regular nourishment that new speakers provide.

On the eve of European contact, continental North America was home to the speakers of as many as 1,200 distinct tongues, grouped into over a dozen major language families. (For comparison, linguists sort the languages of Europe into just four main families.) Over the last five centuries, many of those languages—a crucial part of the biodiversity of humankind—have been silenced by the violence of colonialism, by dispersal and disease, by informal pressures to assimilate to increasingly dominant European cultures, and by formal campaigns to suppress their usage. Today an estimated 139 native languages are spoken in the United States; the fluent speakers of perhaps 70 of these tongues are elderly, leaving those languages at risk.

Since the 1970s, however, a native language revitalization movement has grown in strength and visibility across the United States. Cultural survival activists have created immersion schools and nests, language camps, computer programs, even video games to preserve and transmit indigenous languages. Such efforts have trained many fluent speakers of languages once endangered, such as Hawai'ian, for example: in 1984, there were fewer than thirty fluent speakers of Ōlelo Hawai'i under the age of twelve. Today, there are tens of thousands.

One of the most extraordinary language reclamation programs instructs students in Wôpanâak, the Algonquian-family language of the Wampanoag nation of Massachusetts. Founded in 1993 by Jessie Little Doe Baird (Mashpee) and the late Helen Manning, the Wôpanâak Language Reclamation Project (WLRP) faced formidable obstacles: although Wôpanâak was the first indigenous American language to be expressed in alphabetic characters, its last speakers had died in the mid-nineteenth century. Using a range of documents—including sermons and scripture printed in Wôpanâak in the seventeenth century by English missionaries, and colonial land records using the language well into the eighteenth—the WLRP has created a dictionary of over 11,000 words, as well as first- and second-language curricula, an apprenticeship program, and immersion camps. A young Mashpee girl fluent in Wôpanâak and English is the language's first native speaker in seven generations. A Wôpanâak-immersion elementary school is scheduled to open in 2015.

Summary

Initial contact among Europeans, Africans, and Americans began in the fourteenth century, when Portuguese sailors first explored the Mediterranean Atlantic and the West African coast. Those seamen established commercial ties that brought African slaves first to Iberia and then to the islands the Europeans conquered. The Mediterranean Atlantic and its island sugar plantations nurtured the ambitions of mariners. Except for the Spanish, early explorers regarded the Americas primarily as a barrier keeping them from an oceanic route to the riches of China and the Moluccas. European fishermen were the first to realize that the northern coasts had valuable fish and furs.

The Aztecs experienced hunger after Cortés's invasion, and their great temples fell as Spaniards used their stones (and Indian laborers) to construct cathedrals.

The conquerors coerced natives and, later, enslaved Africans to till the fields, mine the precious metals, and herd the livestock that earned immense profits.

The first contacts of old world and new devastated the Western Hemisphere's native inhabitants. European diseases killed millions; European livestock, along with other imported animals and plants, forever modified the environment. Europe, too, was changed: American foodstuffs improved nutrition, and American gold and silver first enriched, then ruined, the Spanish economy.

A century after Columbus landed, many fewer people resided in North America than had lived there in 1491. And the people who did live there—Indian, African, and European—together made a world that was indeed new, a world engaged in the unprecedented process of combining religions, economies, ways of life, and political systems that had developed separately for millennia.

Chapter Review

American Societies

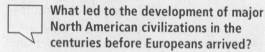
What led to the development of major North American civilizations in the centuries before Europeans arrived?

Agricultural success facilitated the rise of North American civilizations in the era before Europeans arrived. After the Ice Age ended and the prevalence of large mammals decreased, many native peoples in what is now central Mexico about 9000 years ago shifted from hunting to cultivating food crops for survival, including maize (corn), squash, beans, avocados, and peppers. As agricultural methods improved, vegetables became a reliable and nutritious food source, and native people established more permanent settlements. Early Americans began developing trade, accumulating wealth, creating elaborate cultural ceremonies and rituals, and building urban centers. But food supply was so keenly linked to a civilization's success that the first large city-states of Mesoamerica and Mississippian culture ultimately collapsed when food sources became scarce.

North America in 1492

What were the gender dimensions of labor in native cultures?

Like Europeans, Native American societies assigned various tasks and responsibilities to members along gender lines. Native societies that were predominantly hunting assigned women to making food and clothing and carrying their families' possessions whenever they moved. Agricultural peoples had different patterns of the gendered division of labor; some, like the Pueblos, defined farming as men's work, while others, like the Algonquian, Iroquoian, and Muskogean, gave women most agricultural chores, and men hunted and cleared the land. Women just about everywhere raised children, gathered wild foods, and prepared all of what people ate. Agricultural families were defined matrilineally, through the female line of descent, and women assumed more leadership roles than in nomadic hunter peoples. They rarely became chiefs, but older Iroquois women chose chiefs and could start or stop wars.

African Societies

What were the chief characteristics of West African societies in the fifteenth century?

People in West Africa made their living fishing, cattle herding, or farming, depending on where they lived. Those in Upper Guinea fished and grew rice; those in Lower Guinea farmed. Upper Guinea was also the region's overland trade link to Europe and Asia. Islamic culture influenced life in Upper Guinea, while people in the lower region practiced more traditional religions. Like other cultures around the world, West Africans designated tasks according to gender, although their roles were seen as complementary. Both sexes farmed; men hunted and managed livestock and fished, while women cared for children, prepared the food, and managed trade networks. In Lower Guinea, male political and religious leaders ruled men, while women ruled women. Polygyny was common throughout West Africa. So was slavery. In West Africa, a person could be enslaved for committing a crime, to repay debts, or as an enemy's captive, but slave status did not automatically transfer to the next generation, and some slaves could engage in trade and keep some of the profits or rise to important military or political positions.

European Societies

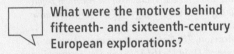

What were the motives behind fifteenth- and sixteenth-century European explorations?

The driving force behind early European explorations was the quest for a transoceanic trade route—the Northwest Passage—that would provide direct access to desirable African and Asian goods such as silks, dyes, jewels, sugar, gold, and spices. If such a route existed, it would allow northern Europeans to bypass the Muslim and Venetian merchants who served as middlemen for these items. Rulers also believed that the more they controlled access to these much-desired products, the better their nation's standing would be relative to other countries. Another, secondary motivation was to spread Christianity and convert those they considered to be heathen peoples.

Early European Explorations

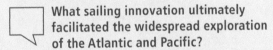

What sailing innovation ultimately facilitated the widespread exploration of the Atlantic and Pacific?

The new technique of "sailing around the wind" made travel faster and less arduous for Atlantic explorers, which ultimately made them increasingly inclined to take on such expeditions. While sailors would travel with the wind in one direction, returning home had previously meant rowing against the wind or waiting for the wind to change, so trips back across the Atlantic were difficult and took weeks longer. But sailing around the wind sped up the journey; when mariners met with a difficult wind, they would now literally sail around it until they could find a wind that would easily and quickly carry them on their way. The same technique could be applied elsewhere under similar conditions; consequently, more and more mariners set out to explore the Atlantic and Pacific.

Voyages of Columbus, Cabot, and Their Successors

What three themes in Columbus's log about his explorations would come to mark much of the future settlement of Europeans in the Americas?

First, Columbus's log notes his quest for gold and other riches. Second, he wrote that the region's resources could be exploited to generate profits for his host country of Spain. In particular, he described the vast potential value of the dyes, spices, and medicines that could be made from plants found in the Americas. Third, Columbus wrote that the inhabitants could be easily converted to Catholicism and remade into servants. His and other explorers' discoveries inspired further exploration by European nations, though for most, colonization would lag for generations.

Spanish Exploration and Conquest

What model of colonization did Spain establish that other nations would later attempt to follow?

Spain developed a model of colonization in the Americas based on three key concepts. First, Spain's monarchy maintained firm control over its colonies with virtually no autonomy granted to American colonies. Second, men made up the majority of early colonists, taking first Indian, and later African, women as wives or concubines. Third, the development of the colonies and the exploitation of their resources were based on exploiting native people and African slaves as labor.

The Columbian Exchange

What were the results of contact between native populations and European settlers and explorers?

Native Americans and Europeans exchanged diseases, plants, and animals when they came into contact in North and South America in the fifteenth and sixteenth centuries. Native American vegetable crops were more nutritious than those in Europe and Africa, while Europeans brought livestock that helped enrich Indians' diets, too. The Spanish also brought horses to their American territories, which aided the shift in native society of the Great Plains from hunting combined with some farming and gathering, to almost exclusively hunting buffalo as the main form of subsistence. Europeans brought many diseases, from typhus to malaria to hepatitis, all of which devastated tribal populations, but none as much as smallpox. Europeans, meanwhile, acquired syphilis from Native Americans, which was debilitating, but not usually fatal.

Europeans in North America

 How did England's rivalry with Spain shape its North American colonization efforts during the sixteenth century?

The English recognized that Spain gained great riches from its American possessions. English sea dogs, such as John Hawkins and Sir Francis Drake, began to raid Spanish treasure ships as they returned to Europe from the Caribbean. These raids led to a war in 1588 in which the English defeated the Spanish Armada. After this victory, the English looked to start new colonies in America in order to gain better access to trade goods and to blunt Spanish influence in the Western Hemisphere.

Suggestions for Further Reading

David Abulafia, *The Discovery of Mankind: Atlantic Encounters in the Age of Columbus* (2008)

Alfred W. Crosby, *The Columbian Exchange: Biological and Cultural Consequences of 1492* (1972)

John H. Elliott, *Empires of the Atlantic World: Britain and Spain in America, 1492–1830* (2006)

Alison Games, *The Web of Empire: English Cosmopolitans in an Age of Expansion, 1560–1660* (2008)

James Horn, *A Kingdom Strange: The Brief and Tragic History of the Lost Colony of Roanoke* (2010)

Peter C. Mancall, *Hakluyt's Promise: An Elizabethan's Obsession for an English America* (2007)

Charles C. Mann, *1491: New Revelations of the Americas Before Columbus (2005); 1493: Uncovering the New World Columbus Created* (2011)

Samuel Eliot Morison, *The European Discovery of America: The Southern Voyages, A.D. 1492–1616 (1974); The Northern Voyages, A.D. 1500–1600* (1971)

Daniel K. Richter, *Before the Revolution: America's Ancient Pasts* (2011)

John K. Thornton, *Africa and Africans in the Making of the Atlantic World, 1400–1680* (1992)

2

Europeans Colonize North America

1600–1650

Captain William Rudyerd seemed like the sort of man any colony in the Americas would prize, so when his older brother urged the planners of the new settlement to appoint him as its muster master general, they agreed. A veteran of wars on the European continent, Rudyerd followed the new dissenting English faith, as did the planners and many of the settlers. Those who mocked these zealous Protestants called them "Puritans."

At first, Rudyerd proved to be a vigorous soldier who worked hard to train the new colony's settlers to defend themselves from attack. But he also quarreled continually with those who failed to show him respect as a gentleman of noble birth. And he was no kinder to those who worked his new land. He beat a servant named Floud, whom scurvy had weakened. When Floud complained to the authorities, Rudyerd had him tied to a tree and whipped. Some weeks later, Floud died.

Such conflicts occurred in all the Anglo-American settlements. But in this colony the disputes were especially dangerous. Rudyerd lived on Providence Island, an isolated Puritan outpost off the coast of modern Nicaragua.

Providence Island, founded by Puritan adventurers in 1630—the same year as Massachusetts Bay—was designed as an Engl[ish] beachhead in the tropics. Labor shortages plagued the colo[ny] from the beginning. Planters wanted to grow and export tobac[co], so they brought poor young people—mostly men—from Lond[on] and the countryside, paying their passage across the ocean [in] exchange for a set number of years in service. But too few migra[nts] took the bait. Those who did, when they didn't die of ill treatm[ent] or hunger or disease, eventually became free—demanding rat[her] than supplying labor.

There were other bound laborers on Providence Island fr[om] the beginning, too: black slaves, brought from Africa via B[er]muda. As the colony's servant troubles increased, the Puri[tan] planters came to rely increasingly on slaves, bound to servic[e in] perpetuity. By the end of the decade, there were several hund[red]

Chapter Outline

Spanish, French, and Dutch North America
New Mexico | Quebec and Montreal | Jesuit Missions in New France | New Netherland

VISUALIZING THE PAST *Acoma Pueblo*

England's America
Social and Economic Change | English Reformation | Puritans, Separatists, and Presbyterians | Stuart Monarchs

The Founding of Virginia
Jamestown and Tsenacommacah | Algonquian and English Cultural Differences | Tobacco Cultivation | Opechancanough's Rebellion | End of Virginia Company

Life in the Chesapeake
Demand for Laborers | Conditions of Servitude | Standard of Living | Chesapeake Politics

The Caribbean
Sugar Cultivation

LEGACY FOR A PEOPLE AND A NATION
"Modern" Families

SUMMARY

bondsmen and bondswomen on Providence Island—more Africans than English.

Despite adopting slavery, the Providence Island planters failed to establish a viable economy in a volatile region. In the end, the colony's desperate attempts to prosper by serving as a base for English privateers caused its downfall. In May 1641, a fleet of seven Spanish ships carrying two thousand soldiers captured the island.

By then, Spain no longer predominated in the Americas. France, the Netherlands, and England all had permanent colonies in North America by the 1640s. Like the conquistadors, French and Dutch merchants and planters hoped to make a quick profit and then perhaps return to their homelands.

Unlike other Europeans, most English colonists came to America intending to stay. When they succeeded, they permanently displaced native populations. In the area that came to be known as New England, settler-colonists arrived in family groups. They re-created the European agricultural economy and family life to an extent impossible in colonies where single men predominated, as they did in the colonies of the Chesapeake region and the Caribbean, which focused on the large-scale production of cash crops for export.

English settlers prospered only after adapting to the alien environment. They had to learn to grow such unfamiliar American crops as maize and squash. They also had to develop extensive trading relationships with native peoples and with other English and European colonies. Needing field laborers, they first used English indentured servants. But like the Providence Islanders, they soon imported African slaves. The early history of England's America is best understood as a series of complex negotiations among European, African, and American peoples.

As you read this chapter, keep the following questions in mind:

- **Why did different groups come to the Americas? Which people came by choice, and which were forced to migrate?**

- **How did different native peoples react to their presence?**

- **In what ways did the English colonies in North America and the Caribbean differ, and in what ways were they alike?**

Chronology

1558	Elizabeth I becomes queen of England
1565	Founding of St. Augustine (Florida), oldest permanent European settlement in present-day United States
1598	Oñate conquers Pueblos in New Mexico for Spain
1603	James I becomes king of England
1607	Jamestown founded, first permanent English settlement in North America
1608	Quebec founded by the French
1610	Santa Fe, New Mexico, founded by the Spanish
1614	Fort Orange (Albany) founded by the Dutch
1619	Virginia House of Burgesses established, first representative assembly in the English colonies
1620	Plymouth colony founded, first permanent English settlement in New England
1622	Powhatan Confederacy rebels against Virginia
1624	Dutch settle on Manhattan Island (New Amsterdam)
	James I revokes Virginia Company's charter
	St. Kitt's founded, England's first Caribbean colony
1625	Charles I becomes king of England
1627	English colonize Barbados
1630	Massachusetts Bay colony founded
1634	Maryland founded
1636	Roger Williams expelled from Massachusetts Bay, founds Providence, Rhode Island
	Connecticut founded
1637	Pequot War in New England
1638	Anne Hutchinson expelled from Massachusetts Bay
1642	Montreal founded by the French
1646	Treaty ends hostilities between Virginia and Powhatan Confederacy

Spanish, French, and Dutch North America

How did the Jesuits' treatment of Native Americans differ from that of explorers and other settlers?

Spaniards established the first permanent European settlement within the boundaries of the modern United States, but others had tried previously. Twice in the 1560s Huguenots (French Protestants) escaping persecution planted colonies on the south Atlantic coast. A passing ship rescued the starving survivors of the first colony, located in present-day South Carolina. The second, near modern Jacksonville, Florida, was destroyed in 1565 by a Spanish expedition commanded by Pedro Menéndez de Avilés. Menéndez set up a fortified outpost named St. Augustine—now the oldest continuously inhabited European settlement in the United States.

The local Guale and Timucua nations initially allied themselves with the Spanish and welcomed Franciscan friars into their villages, but they soon resisted the imposition of Spanish authority. Still, the Franciscans offered the Indians spiritual solace for the diseases and troubles besetting them after the Europeans' invasion, and eventually gained numerous converts at missions that stretched westward across Florida and northward into the islands along the Atlantic coast.

New Mexico

In 1598, more than thirty years after the founding of St. Augustine, Juan de Oñate, a Mexican-born adventurer whose *mestiza* wife descended from both Cortés and Motecuhzoma, led about five hundred soldiers and settlers to New Mexico seeking riches. The Pueblo peoples greeted them cordially. But when the Spaniards used torture, murder, and rape to extort supplies from the villagers, the residents of Acoma killed several soldiers, including Oñate's nephew. The invaders responded ferociously, killing more than eight hundred people and capturing the remainder. All captives above the age of twelve were enslaved for twenty years, and men older than twenty-five had one foot amputated. Horrified, the other Pueblo villages surrendered.

Oñate's bloody victory proved illusory. New Mexico held little wealth and was too far from the Pacific to protect Spanish sea-lanes. The Spanish maintained a small military outpost and a few Christian missions in the area, with the capital at Santa Fe (founded 1610). As in regions to the south, Spanish leaders were granted *encomiendas,* giving them control over Pueblo villagers' labor. In the absence of mines or fertile agricultural lands, however, such grants yielded small profit.

Quebec and Montreal   The French focused on the area that Jacques Cartier had explored in the 1530s. They tried to establish permanent bases along Canada's Atlantic coast but failed until 1605, when they founded Port Royal. In 1608, Samuel de Champlain set up a trading post at an interior site that the Iroquois called Stadacona. Champlain renamed it Quebec. It was the most defensible spot in the St. Lawrence River valley, a stronghold that controlled access to the continent's heartland. In 1642, the French established a second post, Montreal, at the falls of the St. Lawrence, a place the Indians knew as Hochelaga.

The new posts quickly took over the lucrative trade in beaver pelts (see Table 2.1). The colony's leaders granted land along the river to wealthy *seigneurs*

TABLE 2.1   The Founding of Permanent European Colonies in North America, 1565–1638

Colony	Founder(s)	Date	Basis of Economy
Florida	Pedro Menéndez de Avilés	1565	Farming
New Mexico	Juan de Oñate	1598	Livestock
Virginia	Virginia Co.	1607	Tobacco
New France	France	1608	Fur trading
Bermuda	English sailors	1609	Tobacco, ship-building
New Netherland	Dutch West India Co.	1614	Fur trading
Plymouth	Separatists	1620	Farming, fishing
Maine	Sir Ferdinando Gorges	1622	Fishing
St. Kitts, Barbados, et al.	European immigrants	1624	Sugar
Massachusetts Bay	Massachusetts Bay Company	1630	Farming, fishing, fur trading
Maryland	Cecilius Calvert	1634	Tobacco
Rhode Island	Roger Williams	1636	Farming
Connecticut	Thomas Hooker	1636	Farming, fur trading
New Haven	Massachusetts migrants	1638	Farming
New Hampshire	Massachusetts migrants	1638	Farming, fishing

(nobles), who imported tenants to work their farms. Only a few Europeans resided in New France; most were men, some of whom married Indian women. More than twenty-five years after its founding, Quebec had just sixty-four resident families, along with traders and soldiers. Northern New France never grew much beyond the river valley between Quebec and Montreal (see Map 2.1).

Jesuit Missions in New France

French missionaries of the Society of Jesus (Jesuits), a Roman Catholic order dedicated to converting nonbelievers to Christianity, first arrived in Quebec in 1625. The Jesuits, whom the Indians called Black Robes, tried to persuade indigenous peoples to live near French settlements and adopt European agricultural methods. When that effort failed, they attempted to introduce Catholicism without insisting that Indians fundamentally alter their traditions. The Black Robes learned Indian languages and traveled to remote regions, where they lived among the Huron, Iroquois, and Abenaki peoples.

Jesuits sought to undermine the authority of traditional religious leaders. Immune to smallpox (having survived it already), they explained epidemics as God's punishment for sin, their arguments aided by the ineffectiveness of traditional remedies against the pestilence. Jesuits predicted eclipses and amazed villagers by communicating with each other over long distances through marks on paper. The Indians' desire to harness the power of literacy made them receptive to the missionaries.

Jesuits slowly gained thousands of converts. Catholicism offered women the inspiring role model of the Virgin Mary, personified in Montreal and Quebec by Ursuline nuns who ministered to Indian women and children. Many converts cast off native customs allowing premarital sex and easy divorce, which Catholic doctrine prohibited. In the late 1670s, one convert, a young Mohawk named Kateri Tekakwitha, inspired thousands with her celibacy and other ascetic devotional practices. Known as "the Lily of the Mohawks," her grave was said to be the site of miracles. In October 2012, the Roman Catholic Church made her the first Native American saint.

If they embraced some Christian doctrine, most native converts resisted strict European child-rearing methods. Jesuits recognized that such aspects of native culture could be compatible with Christianity. Their conversion efforts were further aided by their lack of interest in labor tribute or land.

New Netherland

In 1614, five years after Henry Hudson explored the river that now bears his name, his sponsor, the Dutch West India Company, established an outpost (Fort Orange) at present-day Albany, New York. The Dutch sought beaver pelts, and their presence so close to Quebec threatened France's regional domination. The Netherlands, the world's dominant commercial power, sought trade rather than colonization. Thus **New Netherland** remained small. The colony's southern anchor was **New Amsterdam**, founded in 1624 on Manhattan Island.

New Netherland was a small outpost of a vast commercial empire that extended to Africa, Brazil, and modern-day Indonesia. Autocratic directors-general ruled the colony, and settlers felt little loyalty to their nominal leaders. Few migrants

New Netherland Dutch colony in America.

New Amsterdam Dutch colony that would become New York.

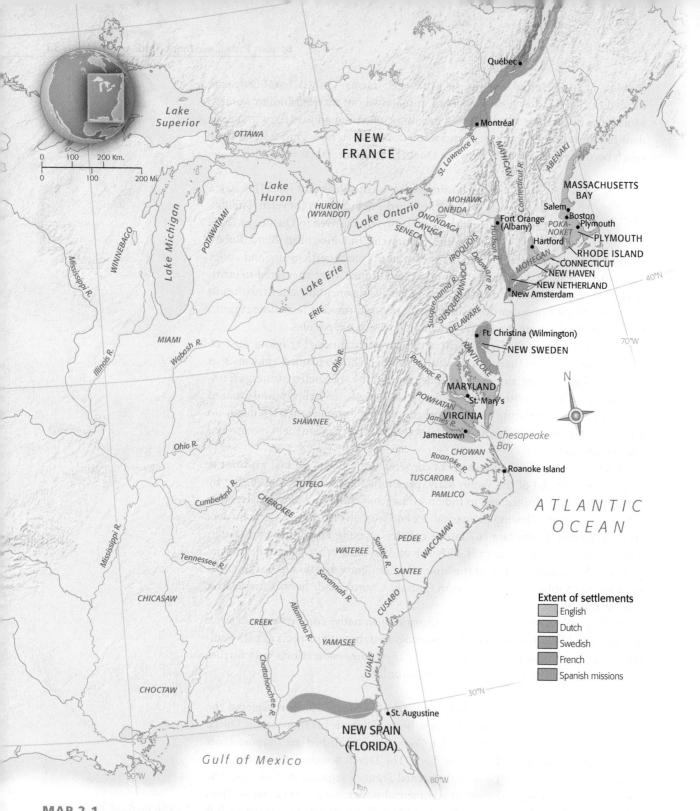

MAP 2.1

European Settlements and Indian Tribes in Eastern North America, 1650

The few European settlements established in the East before 1650 were widely scattered, hugging the shores of the Atlantic Ocean and the banks of its major rivers. By contrast, America's native inhabitants controlled the vast interior expanse of the continent, and Spaniards had begun to move into the West. Source: Copyright © Cengage Learning 2015

Visualizing THE PAST

Acoma Pueblo

Today, as in the late sixteenth century when it was captured by the Spanish, the Acoma Pueblo sits high atop an isolated mesa. The Ancient Pueblo selected the location, 365 feet above the valley floor, because they could easily defend it. Building the complex was a massive undertaking. Its rooms alone required over forty tons of sandstone to be cut from the surrounding cliffs and pulled up the mesa. Much of the labor was likely provided by other natives enslaved by the Ancient Pueblos. The buildings for which they gave their labor and their lives endured; some structures dating to the eleventh century still stand in the middle of the village.

In addition to making construction difficult, situating the city so high above the plains created problems with water supply. To this day there is no source of water in the village. Acoma's residents had to carry water up a steep set of stairs cut into the mesa's side (today there is an almost equally steep road). The women of Acoma were and are accomplished potters. Some pots, like the one shown here, were designed with a low center of gravity. How would that design help women to reach the top of the mesa with much-needed water? How would they carry such pots?

© Kevin Fleming/CORBIS

Acoma Pueblo today. The village is now used primarily for ritual purposes; few people reside there permanently, because all water must be trucked in.

Richard A. Cooke/CORBIS

A pot designed for carrying water to the top of the mesa.

arrived; as late as the mid-1660s, New Netherland had only about five thousand European inhabitants. Some were Swedes and Finns in the former colony of New Sweden (founded in 1638 on the Delaware River; see Map 2.1), which the Dutch seized in 1655.

Indian allies of New France and New Netherland clashed partly because of fur-trade rivalries. In the 1640s the Iroquois, who traded chiefly with the Dutch and lived in modern upstate New York, warred with the Huron, who traded primarily with the French and lived in present-day Ontario. With guns supplied by the Dutch, the Iroquois virtually exterminated the Huron, whose population had been decimated by smallpox. The Iroquois thus established themselves as a major force in the region.

England's America

What two developments prompted England to consider North American colonization in the early seventeenth century?

The failure of Raleigh's Roanoke colony ended English efforts to settle North America for nearly two decades. When the English decided in 1606 to try once more, they found success using a model unlike those of Spain, France, or the Netherlands. England sent large numbers of men and women to establish agriculturally based colonies on the mainland. Two major developments prompted approximately 200,000 ordinary English men and women to move to North America in the seventeenth century.

Social and Economic Change

The first development was the onset of dramatic social and economic change. In the 150-year period after 1530, largely due to the importation of American crops, England's population doubled. Those additional people competed for food, clothing, and other goods, which led to inflation. The increased number of workers caused a simultaneous fall in wages, and many laborers fell into poverty. When landowners raised rents, seized lands that peasants had long used in common (enclosure), or combined smallholdings into large units, they displaced their tenants. England's cities swelled to bursting. Approximately 75,000 people lived in London in 1550. A century later, nearly 400,000 people packed its narrow alleys and cramped buildings.

As "masterless men"—the landless and homeless—crowded the streets, officials came to believe that colonies in North America could siphon off what they viewed as England's "surplus population." Similarly, many ordinary people decided they could improve their circumstances by migrating to the new world.

English Reformation

The sixteenth century also witnessed a religious transformation that eventually led many English dissenters to leave. In 1533 Henry VIII, wanting a male heir and infatuated with Anne Boleyn, asked the pope to annul his nearly twenty-year marriage to the Spanish-born Catherine of Aragón. When the pope refused, Henry founded the Church of England and—with Parliament's concurrence—proclaimed himself its head.

At first, the Church of England differed little from Catholicism. Under Henry's daughter, Elizabeth I (child of his second marriage, to Anne Boleyn), though, new currents of religious belief dramatically affected England's recently established church.

These currents constituted the **Protestant Reformation**, led by Martin Luther, a German monk, and **Jean Calvin**, a French cleric and lawyer. Challenging the Catholic doctrine that priests were intermediaries between laypeople and God, Luther and Calvin insisted that people could interpret the Bible for themselves. Both rejected Catholic rituals and elaborate church hierarchy. They also asserted that the key to salvation was faith in God, rather than the Catholic combination of faith and good works. Calvin went further, stressing the need for total submission to God's will.

Protestant Reformation
Split of reformers from Roman Catholic church; triggered by Martin Luther.

Jean Calvin Early Protestant theologian who believed in "predestination."

Puritans, Separatists, and Presbyterians

During the long reign of Elizabeth I (1558–1603), Calvin's ideas gained influence in England, Wales, and especially Scotland. (In Ireland, Catholicism remained dominant.) The Scottish church eventually adopted Presbyterianism, which eliminated bishops and placed religious authority in bodies of clerics and laymen called presbyteries. By the late sixteenth century, though, many Calvinists—including those called Puritans (because they wanted to purify the church), or Separatists (because they wanted to leave it entirely)—believed that reformers in England and Scotland had not gone far enough. Henry had simplified the church hierarchy, and the Scots had altered it; Puritans and Separatists wanted to abolish it. Henry and the Scots had subordinated the church to the state; the dissenters wanted a church free from political interference. The established churches of England and Scotland continued to encompass all residents of the realm. Calvinists wanted to confine church membership to those God had chosen for salvation.

Paradoxically, dissenters insisted that people could not know if they were "saved." Mere mortals could not comprehend or affect their predestination to heaven or hell. Thus, pious Calvinists confronted serious dilemmas: if the saved (or "elect") could not be identified with certainty, how could proper churches be constituted? And if you could not alter fate, why attend church or respect civil law? Calvinists admitted that their judgments about church membership only approximated God's unknowable decisions. They reasoned that God gave the elect the ability to accept salvation and to lead a moral life. Though good works would not earn you a place in heaven, pious behavior might signal that you belonged there.

Stuart Monarchs

Elizabeth I's Stuart successors, her cousin James I (1603–1625) and his son Charles I (1625–1649), exhibited little tolerance for Calvinists (see Table 2.2). As Scots, they also had little respect for the traditions of representative government that had developed in England. James I publicly declared the divine right of kings, the notion that a monarch's power came directly from God and that his subjects had a duty to obey him.

Both James I and Charles I wanted to enforce religious conformity. Because Calvinists—and remaining Catholics in England and Scotland—challenged many important precepts of the Church of England, the Stuart monarchs authorized the

TABLE 2.2   Tudor and Stuart Monarchs of England, 1509–1649

Monarch	Reign	Relation to Predecessor
Henry VIII	1509–1547	Son
Edward VI	1547–1553	Son
Mary I	1553–1558	Half-sister
Elizabeth I	1558–1603	Half-sister
James I	1603–1625	Cousin
Charles I	1625–1649	Son

removal of dissenting clergymen. In the 1620s and 1630s, some Puritans, Separatists, Presbyterians, and Catholics decided to move to America, where they hoped to practice their beliefs freely. Some fled to avoid arrest and imprisonment.

The Founding of Virginia

How did English cultural traditions clash with those of Native Americans in Virginia?

joint-stock company Business corporation that amasses capital through sales of stock to investors.

Jamestown First successful English colony, established in 1607.

The impetus for England's first permanent colony in the Western Hemisphere was both religious and economic. The newly militant English Protestants wanted to combat "popery" at home and in the Americas. Accordingly, in 1606, a group of merchants and wealthy gentry—some of them aligned with religious reformers—obtained a royal charter for the Virginia Company, organized as a **joint-stock company**. Such forerunners of modern corporations pooled the resources of many small investors through stock sales. Although Virginia Company investors anticipated great profits, neither settlement the company established—one in Maine that collapsed within a year, and **Jamestown**—earned much.

Jamestown and Tsenacommacah

In 1607, the Virginia Company dispatched 108 men and boys to a region near Chesapeake Bay called Tsenacommacah by its native inhabitants. That May, the colonists established a settlement called Jamestown on a swampy peninsula in a river they also named for their monarch. The colonists fell victim to dissension and disease. The gentlemen and soldiers at Jamestown expected to rely on local Indians for food and tribute, yet the residents of Tsenacommacah refused to cooperate. Moreover, the settlers arrived in the midst of a severe drought. The arrival of hundreds more colonists over the next several years only added to the pressure on scarce resources.

John Smith Colonial leader of Jamestown who established order, good relations with Indians.

The weroance (chief) of Tsenacommacah, Powhatan, had inherited rule over six Algonquian villages and later controlled some twenty-five others (see Map 2.1). Late in 1607, Powhatan tentatively agreed to an alliance negotiated by colonial leader Captain **John Smith**. In exchange for foodstuffs, Powhatan wanted guns, hatchets, and swords, which would give him a technological advantage over his enemies.

The fragile relationship soon foundered on mutual mistrust. The weroance relocated his primary village in early 1609 to a place the newcomers could not access easily. Without Powhatan's assistance, Jamestown experienced a "starving time" (winter 1609–1610). Hundreds perished and at least one survivor resorted to digging up corpses for food. When spring came, barely 60 of the 500 colonists who had come to Jamestown remained alive. They left on a newly arrived ship, but en route up the James River encountered ships carrying a new governor, additional settlers, and supplies, so they returned to Jamestown.

Link to John Smith's description of the "starving time" in Jamestown

To gain the upper hand with the Indians, the settlers in 1613 kidnapped Powhatan's daughter, Pocahontas. In captivity, she converted to Christianity and married a colonist, John Rolfe. Their union initiated a period of peace between the English and her people. Funded by the Virginia Company, she and Rolfe sailed to England to promote the colony. Pocahontas died at Gravesend in 1616, leaving an infant son who returned to Virginia as a young adult.

Algonquian and English Cultural Differences

English settlers and Algonquian natives focused on their cultural differences, although both groups held deep religious beliefs, subsisted primarily through agriculture, accepted social and political hierarchy, and observed well-defined gender roles. English men regarded Indian men as lazy because they did not cultivate crops and spent their time hunting (a sport, not work, in English eyes). Indian men thought English men effeminate because they did the "woman's work" of cultivation. English political and military leaders tended to rule autocratically, whereas Algonquian leaders (even Powhatan) had more limited authority.

Furthermore, Algonquian and English concepts of property differed. Most Algonquian villages held their land communally. Land could not be bought or sold outright, although certain rights to use it (for example, for hunting or fishing) could be transferred. Enclosures in the previous century had made English villagers accustomed to individual farms. The English also refused to accept Indians' claims to traditional hunting territories, insisting that only cultivated land could be owned or occupied. Ownership of such "unclaimed" property, the English believed, lay with the English monarchy, whose flag **John Cabot** had planted in North America in 1497.

John Cabot Italian explorer who established English claims to North America.

The English believed in the superiority of their civilization, and they expected native peoples to adopt English customs and to convert to Christianity. They showed little respect for the Indians when they believed English interests were at stake, as was demonstrated once the settlers found a salable commodity.

Tobacco Cultivation

That commodity was tobacco. In 1611, John Rolfe planted seeds of a variety from the Spanish Caribbean, which was superior to the strain Indians grew. Nine years later, Virginians exported 40,000 pounds of cured leaves; by the late 1620s, annual shipments had jumped to 1.5 million pounds.

Tobacco cultivation made Virginia prosper and altered life for everyone. It required abundant land because a field could produce only about three good crops before it had to lie fallow for several years to regain its fertility. Virginians therefore established farms along both sides of the James River at some distance from one another—a settlement pattern convenient for tobacco cultivation but dangerous for defense.

Opechancanough's Rebellion

Opechancanough, Powhatan's brother and successor, watched the English colonists' expansion and their attempts to convert natives to Christianity. Recognizing the danger, he launched attacks along the James River on March 22, 1622. By day's end, 347 English colonists (about one-quarter of the population) lay dead. Only a warning from two Christian converts saved Jamestown from destruction.

Reinforced by shipments of migrants and arms from England, the settlers repeatedly attacked Opechancanough's villages. A peace treaty was signed in 1632, but in April 1644 the elderly Opechancanough assaulted the invaders one last time. In 1646, survivors of the Powhatan Confederacy formally subordinated themselves to England.

End of Virginia Company

The 1622 assault killed the Virginia Company, which had remained unprofitable due to internal corruption and the heavy costs of settlement. But before its demise, the company developed two precedent-setting policies. First, to attract settlers, it established the "headright" system in 1617. Every new arrival paying his or her own way was promised fifty acres; those who financed the passage of others received similar headrights. To English farmers who owned little or no land, the headright system offered a powerful incentive to move to Virginia. To wealthy gentry, it promised the possibility of vast agricultural enterprises. Two years later, the company authorized the landowning men of the major Virginia settlements to elect representatives to an assembly called the **House of Burgesses**. Just as they had at home, English landholders expected to elect members of Parliament and control local governments.

House of Burgesses First elected representative legislature in North America that first met in 1619.

When James I revoked the charter in 1624, transforming Virginia into a royal colony, he continued the company's headright policy but abolished the assembly. Virginians protested, and by 1629 the House of Burgesses was functioning again. The colonists successfully insisted on governing themselves; thus, the political structure of England's American possessions differed from that of the Spanish, Dutch, and French colonies.

Life in the Chesapeake

What were the myths and realities of indentured servitude in the Chesapeake?

By the 1630s, tobacco was the chief source of revenue in Virginia and in the second English Chesapeake colony: Maryland. Given by Charles I to George Calvert, first Lord Baltimore, as a personal possession (proprietorship), Maryland was colonized in 1634. (Virginia and Maryland border Chesapeake Bay—see Map 2.1—and are referred to collectively as "the Chesapeake.") The Calvert family intended the colony as a haven for their persecuted fellow Catholics. Cecilius Calvert, second Lord Baltimore, became the first colonizer to offer freedom of religion to all Christian settlers, codified in Maryland's Act of Religious Toleration (1649). In everything but religion, the two Chesapeake colonies resembled each other.

Demand for Laborers

Above all else, successful Chesapeake farms required workers. Powhatans, their numbers reduced by war and disease, could not supply such needs. Nor were enslaved Africans widely available: traders could more easily and profitably sell slaves to Caribbean planters. By 1650, only about seven hundred blacks lived in Virginia and Maryland.

At first, Chesapeake tobacco farmers looked primarily to England to supply their labor needs. The headright system (which Maryland also adopted) allowed a tobacco planter to obtain both land and labor by importing English workers. He could use his profits to pay for the passage of more workers, thereby gaining more land, and even movement into the ranks of the emerging planter gentry.

Male laborers, along with a few women, immigrated to America as **indentured servants**, paying their passage by contracting to work from four to seven years. Indentured servants accounted for 75 to 85 percent of the approximately 130,000 English immigrants to Virginia and Maryland during the seventeenth century.

Males between the ages of fifteen and twenty-four composed roughly three-quarters of the servants; only one immigrant in five or six was female. Most of these young men came from farming or laboring families.

indentured servants
Young men and women, usually unemployed and poor, who were given free passage to America, plus basic needs such as food, shelter, and clothing, in exchange for labor, usually for four to seven years.

Conditions of Servitude

From a distance at least, the Chesapeake seemed to offer such people chances for advancement unavailable in England. Servants who fulfilled the terms of their indenture earned "freedom dues" of clothes, tools, livestock, corn, tobacco, and sometimes even land. Yet servants typically worked six days a week, ten to fourteen hours a day—often in starvation conditions—in a disease-riddled semitropical climate.

Servants faced severe penalties for running away. But laws did require masters to supply servants with sufficient food, clothing, and shelter, and they were not to be beaten excessively. Cruelly treated servants could turn to the courts, sometimes winning verdicts that transferred them to more humane masters or released them from their indentures.

Servants and their owners alike first had to survive the process the colonists called "seasoning," a bout with disease (probably malaria) that usually occurred during their first Chesapeake summer. About 40 percent of male servants did not survive long enough to become freedmen. Young men of twenty-two who successfully weathered their seasoning could expect to live only another twenty years.

For those who survived, the opportunities for advancement were real. Until the late seventeenth century, former servants often became independent farmers ("freeholders"). But in the 1670s, tobacco prices entered a fifty-year period of stagnation and decline, while good land grew scarce and expensive. In 1681, Maryland dropped its requirement that servants receive land as part of their freedom dues, forcing many freed servants to live as wage laborers or tenant farmers. By 1700, the Chesapeake was no longer the land of opportunity it once had been.

Standard of Living

Life in the early Chesapeake was hard for everyone, regardless of sex or status. The imbalanced sex ratio

Age and Sex Composition

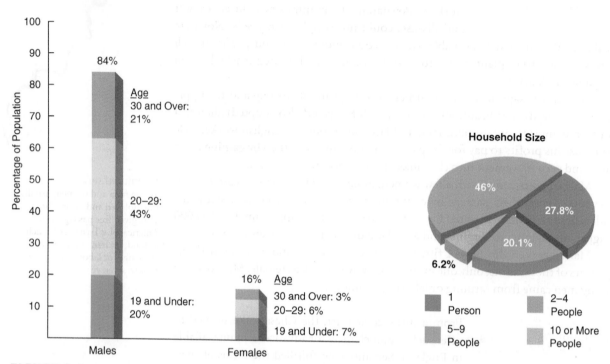

FIGURE 2.1
Population of Virginia, 1625

The only detailed census taken in the English mainland North American colonies during the seventeenth century was prepared in Virginia in 1625. It listed a total of 1,218 people, constituting 309 "households" and living in 278 dwellings—so some houses contained more than one family. The chart shows, on the left, the proportionate age and gender distribution of the 765 individuals for whom full information was recorded, and, on the right, the percentage variation in the sizes of the 309 households. The approximately 42 percent of the residents of the colony who were servants were concentrated in 30 percent of the households. Nearly 70 percent of the households had no servants at all.

(Source: Wells, Robert V., *The Population of the British Colonies in America Before 1776.* © 1975 Princeton University Press, 2003 renewed PUP. Reprinted by permission of Princeton University Press.)

(see Figure 2.1), the incidence of servitude, and the high rates of mortality combined to produce small and fragile households.

Farmers (and sometimes their wives) toiled in the fields alongside servants. Because hogs needed little tending, Chesapeake households subsisted mainly on pork and corn, a filling but not nutritious diet. Families supplemented with fish, wildfowl, and vegetables they grew in small gardens. The difficulty of preserving food for winter consumption magnified the health problems caused by epidemic disease.

Few households had many possessions beyond farm implements, bedding, and basic cooking and eating utensils. Ramshackle houses commonly had just one or two rooms. Rather than making clothing or tools, families imported them from England.

Chesapeake Politics   Throughout the seventeenth century, immigrants made up a majority of the Chesapeake population. Most members of Virginia's House of Burgesses and

Maryland's House of Delegates (established in 1635) were immigrants; they also dominated the governor's council, which simultaneously served as the highest court, part of the legislature, and executive adviser to the governor. A native-born ruling elite emerged only in the early eighteenth century.

In the seventeenth-century Chesapeake, most property-owning white males could vote, and they chose as their legislators (burgesses) the local elites who seemed to be their natural leaders. But because most such men were immigrants lacking strong ties to one another or to the region, the assemblies remained unstable and contentious.

The Founding of New England

What were John Winthrop's expectations for the Massachusetts Bay Company colony?

Economic and religious motives also drew people to New England. Environmental factors and the Puritans' organization of the New England colonies meant that the northern settlements developed very differently from their southern counterparts.

Contrasting Regional Demographic Patterns Royal bureaucrats in late 1634 ordered port officials in London to collect information on travelers departing for the colonies. The records for 1635 document the departure of 53 vessels—20 to Virginia, 17 to New England, 8 to Barbados, 5 to St. Christopher, 2 to Bermuda, and 1 to Providence Island. Almost 5,000 people sailed on those ships—2,000 for Virginia, about 1,200 for New England, and the rest for island destinations. Nearly three-fifths of the passengers were between 15 and 24 years old.

But among those bound for New England, such youths constituted less than one-third of the total. Whereas women made up 14 percent of those headed to Virginia, they were almost 40 percent of New England–bound passengers. New England migrants often traveled in family groups and with others from the same towns. They also brought more goods and livestock with them than their Chesapeake counterparts.

Contrasting Regional Religious Patterns Puritan congregations became key institutions in colonial New England, whereas spread-out settlement patterns made it difficult to organize a church in the Chesapeake. Not until the 1690s did the Church of England plant deeper roots in Virginia; by then, it had also replaced Catholicism as the established church in Maryland.

In both New England and the Chesapeake, religion affected the lives of pious Calvinists who were expected to reassess the state of their souls regularly. Because even the most pious could never be certain they were among the elect, anxiety troubled them. This anxiety lent a special intensity to their beliefs and to their concern with proper behavior—their own and that of others.

Separatists Separatists who thought the Church of England too corrupt to be salvaged became the first religious dissenters to move to New England. In 1609, a Separatist congregation relocated to Leiden, in the Netherlands, where they found freedom of worship but also toleration of religions and behaviors they abhorred. Hoping to isolate themselves from worldly temptations, these people, known today as Pilgrims, received permission from the Virginia Company to colonize the northern part of its territory.

Plymouth Colony established by Pilgrims in Massachusetts.

In September 1620, more than one hundred people, only thirty of them Separatists, set sail from England on the *Mayflower*. In November, they landed on Cape Cod, farther north than intended. They moved across Massachusetts Bay to a fine harbor (named **Plymouth** by John Smith, who had visited it in 1614) and into the empty dwellings of a Pawutuxet village whose inhabitants had died in the epidemic of 1616–1618.

Pilgrims and Pokanokets

Because they landed outside the jurisdiction of the Virginia Company, some non-Separatists questioned the authority of the colony's leaders. In response, the **Mayflower Compact**, signed in November 1620 on shipboard, established a "Civil Body Politic" as a temporary substitute for a charter. Male settlers elected a governor and made decisions at town meetings. Later, Plymouth created an assembly to which landowning male settlers elected representatives.

Mayflower Compact
Agreement signed by *Mayflower* passengers to establish order in their new settlement.

Link to the Mayflower Compact

Only half of the *Mayflower*'s passengers lived until spring. Survivors owed much to the Pokanokets (a branch of the Wampanoags) who controlled the area. Pokanoket villages had suffered terrible losses in the recent epidemic, so to protect themselves from the powerful Narragansetts of the southern New England coast, the Pokanokets allied themselves with the newcomers. In the spring of 1621, their leader or sachem, Massasoit, agreed to a treaty, and the Pokanokets supplied the settlers with foodstuffs. The colonists also relied on Tisquantum (or Squanto), a Pawutuxet who served as a conduit between native peoples and Europeans. Captured by fishermen in the early 1610s and taken to Europe, Tisquantum had learned to speak English. He returned to find that the epidemic had wiped out his village. Caught between worlds, Tisquantum became the settlers' interpreter and a source of information about the environment.

Massachusetts Bay Company

Before the 1620s ended, another group of Puritans (Congregationalists, who hoped to reform the Church of England from within) launched the colonial enterprise that would come to dominate New England. Charles I, who became king in 1625, attempted to suppress Puritan practices. Some Congregationalist merchants, concerned about their long-term prospects in England, dispatched colonists to Cape Ann (north of Cape Cod) in 1628. The following year, the merchants obtained a royal charter, constituting themselves as the Massachusetts Bay Company.

The new joint-stock company quickly attracted Puritans who feared they no longer would be able to practice their religion freely in their homeland. They looked toward New England, where they could handle their affairs—secular and religious—as they pleased.

Turkeys

Near the end of their first year in North America, the Plymouth colonists held a traditional English feast to celebrate the harvest. Famously, they invited Massasoit's Pokanokets, and they probably consumed turkey. But why was this bird, originally from America and enjoyed at Thanksgiving today, named for a region of the then–Ottoman Empire? The native peoples of the Americas had named the fowl in their own languages; Aztecs, for example, called a male bird *huexoloti* and a female *totolin*.

When Columbus carried the birds back to Spain after his first voyage, the Iberian Peninsula was a focal point for Mediterranean commerce, and Spanish mariners sailed frequently to the Middle East. One Spanish vessel took some *huexoloti* and *totolin* to the Ottoman Empire. There, farmers familiar with distant Asian relatives of the bird improved the breed, ultimately producing a plumper, tamer version. By the end of the century "turkeys" were widely consumed throughout the British Isles.

When Thomas Harriot in his 1588 *Briefe and True Report* mentioned the wild North American version of the birds, he termed them "Turkie cockes and Turkie hennes." He failed to give the names native peoples used because these birds were not new to his audience.

Jamestown and Plymouth settlers recognized the birds in their new homelands as relatives of the fowls they had consumed in England. But they regarded the wild American birds as inferior since they ravaged young crops and were viewed as pests. So the settlers in both Virginia and New England soon imported English turkeys to raise for meat.

Were the "turkeys" consumed at the so-called First Thanksgiving the wild American birds or the tame Ottoman-English variety? No matter; that they were termed "turkeys" linked these fowls of American origin to the Mediterranean, Europe, and the Middle East as a prime example of animals in the Columbian Exchange.

Victoria & Albert Museum; London; UK/The Bridgeman Art Library

Turkeys from the Americas quickly traveled around the world, as is illustrated by this Mughal painting from the Islamic empire in India. The local artist Ustad Mansur painted a "turkey-cock" brought to the emperor Jahangir in 1612 from Goa—a Portuguese enclave on the west coast of the Indian subcontinent. Presumably the turkey had been transported from the Iberian Peninsula to that European outpost, whence the fowl made its way to Jahangir's court—where it was immortalized by an artist to whom it was an unusual sight.

The South part of New-England, as it is Planted this yeare, 1634.

William Wood's "The South Part of New-England," which appeared in his book New Englands Prospect *(London, 1634), was the first printed map of the region by an Englishman who had settled there. English place names—the Charles River, Elizabeth Isle, Cape Ann, New Ipswich—dot the map, illustrating the colonists' desire to remake the territory in the image of their homeland. But Wood also records many Algonquian place names—including Massachusetts Bay itself—reminding the viewer of the power of local native groups and their proximity to English settlement.*

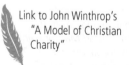

Link to John Winthrop's "A Model of Christian Charity"

Governor John Winthrop

In October 1629, the Massachusetts Bay Company elected **John Winthrop**, a member of the lesser English gentry, as its governor. Winthrop organized the initial segment of the great Puritan migration. In 1630, more than one thousand English men and women moved to Massachusetts—most of them to Boston. By 1643, nearly twenty thousand more had followed.

Caught up in the currents of European utopian thought, the colony's backers envisioned a utopia across the ocean—a new Jerusalem. Some time before the colonists embarked, Winthrop set down his expectations for the new colony in an essay called "Christian Charitie." Winthrop stressed the communal nature of the colonists' endeavor. Differences in status or wealth—though retained—would not imply differences in worth. On the contrary, God had planned the world so that "every man might have need of others, and from hence they might be all knit more nearly together in the bond of brotherly affection." In New England, Winthrop warned, "we shall be as a city upon a hill, the eyes of all people are upon us." If the Puritan experiment failed, "the Lord will surely break out in wrath against us."

Winthrop's essay became famous two centuries later. In 1838, one of his descendants published it for the first time, under its now-familiar title, "A Model of Christian Charity," recasting the discourse as a sermon preached en route to New England, and a parable about uniquely American virtues.

Covenant Ideal

The Puritans expressed their communal ideal in the doctrine of the covenant. They believed God had made a contract with them when they were chosen for the special mission to America. In turn, they covenanted with one another to work together. Founders of churches, towns, and even colonies in Anglo America often drafted documents setting forth the principles on which their institutions would be based. The Pilgrims' Mayflower Compact was a covenant, as was the Fundamental Orders of Connecticut (1639), which defined the basic law for the settlements along the Connecticut River valley.

The leaders of Massachusetts Bay likewise transformed their joint-stock company charter into the basis for a covenanted community based on mutual consent. They gradually changed the General Court—the company's small governing body—into a colonial legislature. They also granted the status of freeman, or voting member, to property-owning adult male church members. Less than two decades after its founding, the colony had a functioning system of self-government composed of a governor and a two-house legislature.

New England Towns

In Massachusetts groups of men—often from the same English village—applied for grants of land on which to establish towns (novel governance units that did not exist in England). The grantees copied the villages from whence they had come. First, they laid out lots for houses and a church. Then they gave each family parcels of land around the town center, reserving the best and largest plots for the most distinguished residents, including the minister. The "lower sort" received smaller and less desirable allotments. Still, every man and even a few single women obtained land.

Town centers developed quickly, evolving in three distinct ways. Isolated agricultural settlements in the interior tried to sustain Winthrop's vision of community life based on diversified family farms. Coastal towns, like Boston and Salem, became bustling seaports. And commercialized agricultural towns grew up in the Connecticut River valley, where easy water transportation enabled farmers to sell surplus goods.

Pequot War and Its Aftermath

Migration into the Connecticut Valley ended the Puritans' relative freedom from clashes with nearby Indians. Relocating under the direction of their minister, Thomas Hooker, their new settlements were within the territory of the powerful Pequot nation.

Pequot War Clash in 1637 that resulted as English colonists moved to settle in the Connecticut Valley on land inhabited by the Pequot Indians. The colonists were victorious and took over the Indians' land.

The arrival of English settlers ended the Pequots' monopoly over regional trading networks. Clashes between Pequots and English colonists had begun earlier, but the establishment of settlements in the Connecticut Valley moved them toward war. After two English traders were killed (not by Pequots), the English raided a Pequot village. In return, Pequots attacked Wethersfield, Connecticut, in April 1637, killing nine and capturing two. The following month, Englishmen and their Narragansett allies burned the main Pequot town on the Mystic River, slaughtering at least four hundred Pequots, mostly women and children, and enslaving the survivors.

For the next four decades, New England Indians accommodated themselves to the European invasion. They traded with the newcomers and sometimes worked for them, but they resisted incorporation into English society. The one European practice they consistently adopted was keeping livestock, for domesticated animals provided excellent sources of meat once hunting territories became English farms and wild game disappeared.

Missionary Activities

Only a few Massachusetts clerics, most notably John Eliot and Thomas Mayhew, seriously undertook missionary work among the Algonquin. Eliot insisted that converts farm the land in English fashion, take English names, and discard a wide range of their own customs. He met with little success. Only eleven hundred

Indians (out of many thousands) lived in the fourteen "Praying Towns" he established, and just 10 percent of the town residents had been baptized.

The missions in New France were more successful. Puritan services lacked Catholicism's beautiful ceremonies and special appeal for women, and Calvinists could not promise believers a heavenly afterlife. Yet on the island of Martha's Vineyard, Thomas Mayhew converted many Indians to Calvinist Christianity by allowing Wampanoag Christians to lead traditional lives and by training their men as ministers.

What attracted Indians to such religious ideas? Many must have turned to European religion to cope with the dramatic changes the intruders had wrought. The combination of disease, alcohol, new trading patterns, and loss of territory disrupted customary ways of life. Shamans had little success restoring traditional ways. Many natives must have concluded that the Europeans' ideas could help them survive.

Life in New England

What was the impact of religion on colonial life in New England?

New England's colonizers lived differently than their Algonquian neighbors and Chesapeake counterparts. Algonquian bands usually moved four or five times each year to maximize their environment. In spring, women planted the fields, but once crops were established, they gathered wild foods while men hunted and fished. Villagers returned to their fields for harvest, separated again for fall hunting, and wintered together in a sheltered spot.

English people lived year-round in the same location. Household furnishings and house sizes resembled those in the Chesapeake, but New Englanders' houses were sturdier. Their diets were also more varied. They replowed fields, employing manure as fertilizer rather than clearing new fields every few years. They fenced croplands to keep out the cattle, sheep, and hogs that were their chief meat sources.

Cradle, from Barnstable or Yarmouth, Massachusetts, 1665-85 (red oak & white pine), American School, (17th century)/Historic New England, Boston, Massachusetts, USA/The Bridgeman Art Library

Cradles like this one, made by a joiner living in the English plantations on Cape Cod in the third quarter of the seventeenth century, would have seen a lot of use in New England, where an even ratio of male to female settlers, early marriages, and relatively long life expectancies meant that large families—of five or more surviving children—quickly became the norm.

New England Families   Because Puritans often moved to America in family groups, the age range in early New England was wide; and because many more women migrated to New England than to the tobacco colonies, the population could immediately begin to reproduce itself. New England was also healthier. Where Chesapeake population patterns gave rise to few, mostly small families, New England families were numerous, large, and long-lived. Most men married; immigrant women married young (at age twenty, on the average); and marriages lasted longer and produced more children, who were more likely to live to maturity. New England women could anticipate raising five to seven healthy children.

The presence of so many children, combined with Puritans' stress on reading the Bible, led to concern for education. Schooling in the spread-out Chesapeake was haphazard. Living in towns, New Englanders could establish small schools. Whereas early Chesapeake parents commonly died before their children married, New England parents exercised much control over their adult offspring. Young men needed acreage from their fathers before they could marry. Daughters, too, needed a dowry of household goods supplied by their parents. These needs sometimes led to conflict between the generations.

Labor in a New Land

Early New England farms produced chiefly for subsistence and local sale; the region's climate generally did not support the production of staple crops. Family labor was the norm. Sons took up the callings of their fathers, and daughters, their mothers.

The prevalence of family labor should not blind us to the presence of slavery in New England. As the planters of Providence Island demonstrated, Puritan principles did not rule out chattel slavery. John Winthrop kept a Narragansett man and his wife as slaves; upon his death, he bequeathed them to one of his sons. One Salem captain, William Pierce, sold a consignment of captured Pequots in the Caribbean and used the proceeds to buy African slaves.

Like cotton, tobacco, and salt, African men, women, and children were Atlantic commodities, bought and sold in ports around the ocean's rim. By mid-century, roughly four hundred people of African descent lived in New England, the great majority enslaved. Their number hovered around two in every hundred New Englanders for most of the colonial era, with higher concentrations in seaports like Boston and, later, Newport, Rhode Island. In 1650, the scale of New England's black population, and the legal status of those forced migrants, closely resembled that of the Chesapeake.

Impact of Religion

Puritans controlled the governments of the early northern colonies. In Massachusetts Bay and New Haven, church membership was a prerequisite for voting. All the early English colonies, north and south, taxed residents to build churches and pay ministers' salaries, but only New England based criminal codes on the Old Testament. New Englanders were required to attend religious services. Their leaders also believed the state was obliged to support the one true church—theirs.

Puritan legal codes dwelled heavily on moral conduct. Laws forbade drunkenness, card playing, dancing, or even cursing—yet the frequency of such offenses demonstrates that New Englanders regularly engaged in these banned activities. Couples who had sex before marriage (as revealed by the birth of a baby less than nine months after their wedding) faced fines and public humiliation. Nonetheless, roughly one bride in ten was pregnant. Sodomy, usually defined as sex between men, was punishable by death. Yet only two men were executed for the crime in the seventeenth century.

It is easy to think of the Puritans as killjoys and hypocrites, as many people did at the time. But New England's social conservatism stemmed from its radical views on the nature of true religion and its relationship to just government. A central irony of Puritan dissent—and a central dilemma of the early New England colonies—was that their godly experiment attracted people more radical than the colonies' leaders. New England preachers and magistrates refused to grant freedom of worship to those who held different beliefs.

Roger Williams A minister who advocated complete separation of church and state and religious to leration.

| Roger Williams |

Roger Williams, a young minister trained at Cambridge, England, migrated to Massachusetts in 1631. Williams preached that the Massachusetts Bay Company had no right to land already occupied by Indians, that church and state should be separate, and that Puritans should not impose their ideas on others.

Called before the General Court in October 1635, Williams refused to retract his claim that the colony's churches were "full of Antichristian pol[l]ution," among other statements. Fearful that his beliefs tended to anarchy, the magistrates banished him from the colony. When soldiers came to escort him to a ship back to England, they discovered that he had fled.

Williams trekked through the hard winter of 1636 to the head of Narragansett Bay, where he founded the town of Providence on land he obtained from the Narragansetts and Wampanoags. Providence and other towns in what became Rhode Island tolerated all faiths, including Judaism, and became a haven for other dissenters.

Anne Hutchinson Dissenter feared not only for her theology but also because she challenged gender roles; banished from Massachusetts.

| Anne Hutchinson |

A skilled medical practitioner popular with the women of Boston, **Anne Hutchinson** greatly admired John Cotton, a minister who emphasized the covenant of grace, or God's free gift of salvation. (By contrast, most Puritan clerics stressed the need for believers to engage in good works in preparation to receive God's grace.) Hutchinson held religious meetings in her home. Proclaiming that the faithful could communicate directly with God, she questioned the importance of the institutional church and its ministers. Such ideas—along with Hutchinson's model of female authority—threatened Puritan orthodoxy.

In November 1637, officials charged her with maligning the colony's ministers. After two days of holding her own in debate during her trial, she boldly declared that God had spoken to her directly. That assertion ensured her banishment. The clergy also excommunicated her. "You have stepped out of your place," one preacher told her; "you have rather been a Husband than a Wife and a preacher than a Hearer; and a Magistrate than a Subject." Civil authorities exiled Hutchinson, her family, and some of her followers to Rhode Island in 1638.

The Caribbean

What made the Caribbean islands initially desirable for colonization?

New England and the Chesapeake often dominate histories of colonial America. But if we look forward from the seventeenth century instead of backward from 1776, or if we imagine ourselves in the countinghouses of London rather than the meetinghouses of Boston, New England and the Chesapeake recede in importance, and the Caribbean looms large. In many respects, the island colonies of the West Indies lay at the center of what Europeans meant by "America."

France, the Netherlands, and England collided repeatedly in the Caribbean. The Spanish concentrated their colonization efforts on the Greater Antilles—Cuba, Hispaniola, Jamaica, and Puerto Rico. The tiny islands Spain ignored attracted other European powers seeking bases from which to attack Spanish ships loaded with American gold and silver.

England was the first northern European nation to establish a permanent foothold in the smaller Caribbean islands (the Lesser Antilles), colonizing St. Christopher (St. Kitts) in 1624, then later other islands, such as Barbados (1627), Providence (1630), and Antigua (1632). France colonized Guadeloupe and Martinique, and the Dutch gained control of tiny St. Eustatius (strategically located near St. Christopher). Like Providence Island, many colonies changed hands during the seventeenth century. For example, the English drove the Spanish out of Jamaica in 1655, and the French soon thereafter took over half of Hispaniola, creating the colony of St. Domingue (modern Haiti).

MAP 2.2
Caribbean Colonies ca. 1700

English, Spanish, French, Dutch, and other European powers fought for territory in the Caribbean basin throughout the colonial period. At stake were prized shipping routes and the high value of the cash crops produced on the islands, especially sugar, which brought in far more revenue than any other colonial product. Sugar demanded a huge labor force, and so the Caribbean was also the center of the transatlantic slave trade. Many of the enslaved people in mainland English North America were first brought in chains to Jamaica or Barbados. Source: Copyright © Cengage Learning 2015

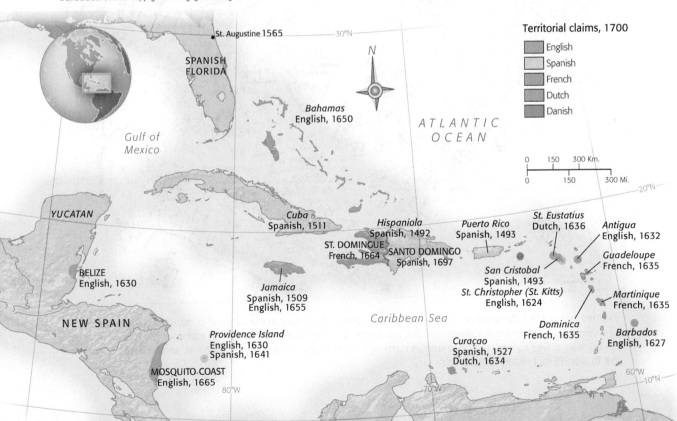

Sugar Cultivation

Beginning in the 1630s, what historians call a "sugar revolution" remade the West Indies and changed the center of gravity in England's America. Entering Europe in substantial quantities at approximately the same time as coffee and tea—stimulating, addictive, and bitter Asian drinks—sugar quickly became crucial to the European diet. By 1700, the English were consuming four pounds of sugar per person each year—a figure that would more than quadruple by the end of the century.

The first sugar grown in the West Indies reached Spain in 1517. By the 1530s, some thirty-four sugar mills operated on the island of Hispaniola alone. These were factory-like complexes staffed by round-the-clock workforces. The work was backbreaking, even lethal. The island's sugar was processed by large numbers of enslaved Africans—perhaps 25,000 of them by 1550.

By 1600, Brazil had come to dominate the West Indies sugar trade. Connections between Portuguese planters there and the Portuguese merchants who controlled the slaving forts of Angola gave Brazilian sugar growers a competitive advantage. Eager to seize that advantage for themselves, the Dutch conquered both ends of this supply chain in the 1630s.

©Topham/The Image Works

First printed in 1657, Richard Ligon's map of Barbados depicts the colony in the midst of its transition to a sugar-growing monoculture. English plantations line the island's Leeward Coast. At the top left corner of the map, a planter on horseback fires his musket at two African runaways. Ligon had seen such cruelty firsthand, and he wrote about it in his True and Exact History of Barbados.

"Modern" Families

Since the late twentieth century, "family values" has been a catchphrase in American politics. Organizations such as Focus on the Family and the American Family Association (both founded by Christian evangelicals in 1977) lobby Washington to protect so-called traditional families from what they see as the modern plagues of premarital sex, fatherless households, and easy divorce. But not much about the "traditional" American family is in fact traditional. In many ways, the families created by seventeenth-century English migrants to the Chesapeake look remarkably modern.

English women were scarce in early Virginia and Maryland. In the first decades of colonization, men outnumbered women by as much as six to one; by mid-century, there were still as many as three male settlers for every female. Young women who made the journey typically migrated as indentured servants. By law, they could not marry during that time; masters did not want to lose working hands to pregnancy. Roughly one in five servant women became pregnant while under indenture nonetheless. Marriage itself could be informally contracted. With few ministers around to solemnize their vows, some couples simply declared themselves wed—or, on occasion, divorced.

Women in the Chesapeake had their pick of husbands. But indenture delayed marriage, and the region's high rates of endemic disease meant that families were easily broken. Only one marriage in three lasted as long as a decade before a spouse died—typically the man. Widows remarried quickly, often within a few months of a husband's death. Men planned for this eventuality, giving their wives an unusual degree of control over their property and their children.

What did early Chesapeake families look like, then? With two or three children, they were smaller than American families in the post–World War II era. Households formed when parents remarried and combined the remnants of previous families and so included a motley array of blood kin and step-kin. Children routinely grew up with orphaned cousins, half-siblings, and stepparents.

As the region's demography slowly stabilized, these decidedly modern households of English descent began to police family boundaries more zealously—especially as African slaves were brought to the Chesapeake. Those boundaries, too, were modern innovations, not time-honored traditions. Then as now, new worlds made extraordinary demands on families, and tradition was a luxury few could afford.

The English colonizers of Barbados discovered in the early 1640s that the island's soil and climate were ideal for cultivating sugar cane. In the 1640s and 1650s, Barbadian tobacco growers and other small farmers sold out to sugar planters, who amassed enormous landholdings. The sugar planters staffed their fields and furnaces with large gangs of bound laborers—African slaves, English and Irish servants, Portuguese convicts—any man who could be bought and worked for six or eight years, till sugar used him up.

But as the Atlantic trade in Africans grew cheaper and more efficient, race-based slavery came to prevail. By the last quarter of the seventeenth century, 175 large planters, each of whom owned more than 100 acres and 60 slaves, controlled the economy of Barbados, which, like the West Indies more broadly, had become a slave society. The island's English population fell from 30,000 in the 1640s to less than 20,000 in 1680, while the number of the enslaved rose from 6,000 to more than 46,000. By then, Barbados had become the most valuable colony in English America. Its sugar exports were worth more than all of the exports from the rest of English America—*combined.*

Summary

By the mid-seventeenth century, Europeans had come to North America and the Caribbean to stay, indelibly altering not only their own lives but also those of native peoples. Europeans killed Indians with weapons and diseases and had varying success in converting them to Christianity. Indigenous peoples taught Europeans to eat new foods and recognize—however reluctantly—other cultures. The prosperity and survival of many of the European colonies depended on the cultivation of American crops (maize and tobacco) and an Asian crop (sugar), thus attesting to the importance of post-Columbian ecological exchange.

To a greater extent than their European counterparts, the English transferred the society and politics of their homeland to a new environment. Their sheer numbers, coupled with their hunger for vast quantities of land, brought them into conflict with their Indian neighbors. New England and the Chesapeake differed in the structure of their populations, the nature of their economies, their settlement patterns, and their religious culture. Yet they resembled each other in the conflicts their expansion engendered, and in their tentative experiments with the use of slave labor. In years to come, both regions would become embroiled in increasingly fierce rivalries besetting the European powers

Chapter Review

Spanish, French, and Dutch North America

How did the Jesuits' treatment of Native Americans differ from that of explorers and other settlers?

Spanish and other settlers typically sought to dominate the native populations, controlling their labor and often enslaving them, sometimes through the use of violence. The French Jesuits who settled New France (Montreal and Quebec) initially tried to convert Indians to Christianity and convince them to farm in the European style. When that failed, missionaries introduced Catholicism without insisting that Indians abandon their traditions. Missionaries learned Indian languages and lived among potential converts, and while they tried to undermine the authority of shamans, Jesuits also recognized the compatibility of some aspects of native culture with Christianity. This somewhat flexible approach, combined with their lack of interest in land or tribute, made at least some Indians receptive to conversion.

England's America

What two developments prompted England to consider North American colonization in the early seventeenth century?

First, dramatic population growth in England, partly as a result of more nutritious foods of American origin, increased competition for food, clothing, shelter, and jobs. That, in turn, spurred inflation; wages also fell. Some profited, but those at the lower end of the socioeconomic spectrum—those with little or no land—lapsed into poverty and homelessness. Cities became overcrowded, leading officials to see colonizing North America as a way to reduce England's "surplus" population and related woes. Others hoped to improve their lot in the land-rich colonies. Second, the Protestant Reformation sparked new forms of Christianity that diverged from the Church of England, and while Elizabeth I tolerated such dissent, her successors, the Stuart monarchs, did not. Ultimately, seeking to practice freely their religious beliefs (and avoid imprisonment), some English Puritans, Separatists, and Catholics fled to America.

The Founding of Virginia

How did English cultural traditions clash with those of Native Americans in Virginia?

While both were religious, Englishmen considered Indian men lazy because they let women cultivate crops while they hunted, which the English regarded as a sport and not work. Native Americans thought Englishmen were effeminate because they farmed, which Indians considered women's work. English political and military leaders tended to rule autocratically, whereas Algonquian leaders had more limited authority. Most importantly, where the English believed in individual farms and private landownership, the Algonquians held land communally as a village.

Life in the Chesapeake

What were the myths and realities of indentured servitude in the Chesapeake?

Chesapeake tobacco farmers filled their extensive demand for labor with indentured servants from England—typically young men who worked for four to seven years in exchange for their passage. Indentured servitude for these young men represented a chance at upward mobility. Most gained "freedom dues" at the completion of their contract, including clothes, tools, livestock, casks of corn and tobacco, and sometimes land. But they worked long hours, six or seven days a week, doing intense physical labor in hot climates. Masters could discipline or sell them, and if indentured servants fled, they faced extreme penalties, although some did win verdicts against cruel masters calling for their transfer or release from indenture. Exposure to disease combined with intense labor so that only 60 percent of indentured men lived to become freedmen, and many who did lived only another twenty years.

The Founding of New England

What were John Winthrop's expectations for the Massachusetts Bay Company colony?

First elected governor in 1629, John Winthrop was instrumental in organizing the first Puritan migration from England to the colony. In his essay "Christian Charitie," Winthrop called for the new colony to serve as a moral and spiritual example for the rest of the world, a "city upon a hill." He urged colonists of varying ranks to work together, to mediate status differences, and to unite around their communal interests. He envisioned a true commonwealth, where people put the common good ahead of their own and were governed by Christian brotherhood.

Life in New England

What was the impact of religion on colonial life in New England?

Although Puritans fled England to practice their faith freely in New England, they offered no such freedom of worship to those who dissented from their beliefs. Puritans controlled the government in many early northern colonies and made Congregationalism the only recognized religion, with church membership and voting rights linked. Colonists were punished with fines or whippings for missing religious services. In addition, strict behavioral codes meant colonists were tried for drunkenness, card playing, dancing, or idleness. Couples who had sex during their engagement were fined and publicly humiliated. People who behaved in ways that today would be called homosexual were sometimes executed. Dissenters such as Roger Williams or Anne Hutchinson, who challenged Puritan orthodoxy, were tried and banished—Williams founded Providence, Rhode Island, based on religious tolerance and was subsequently joined by Hutchinson. Beyond challenging church authority, Hutchinson violated gender norms by preaching.

The Caribbean

What made the Caribbean islands initially desirable for colonization?

European colonizers had different reasons for being drawn to the Caribbean islands. Spain, which focused on larger islands, saw them as offering the potential for greater wealth with less effort than smaller islands might. Other countries saw the smaller islands as a base to attack Spanish vessels transporting gold, silver, and other valuable commodities from the Americas. The second reason for settling on the smaller islands was sugar cultivation. Sugar was in high demand in Europe, particularly since the sweetener improved the taste of coffee and tea and provided a sweet, yet quick, energy boost.

Suggestions for Further Reading

Richard S. Dunn, *Sugar and Slaves: The Rise of the Planter Class in the English West Indies, 1624–1713* (1972)

Alison Games, *Migration and the Origins of the English Atlantic World* (1999)

David D. Hall, *A Reforming People: Puritanism and the Transformation of Public Life in New England* (2011)

Jane Kamensky, *Governing the Tongue: The Politics of Speech in Early New England* (1997)

Karen O. Kupperman, *The Jamestown Project* (2007)

C. S. Manegold, *Ten Hills Farm: The Forgotten History of Slavery in the North* (2010)

Mary Beth Norton, *Founding Mothers & Fathers: Gendered Power and the Forming of American Society* (1996)

Stephan Palmié and Francisco Scarano, eds., *The Caribbean: A History of the Region and Its Peoples* (2011)

Christopher L. Tomlins, *Freedom Bound: Law, Labor, and Civic Identity in Colonizing English America, 1580–1865* (2010)

David J. Weber, *The Spanish Frontier in North America* (1992)

North America in the Atlantic World

3

1650–1720

Their journey began in Mohawk country, where western New York met eastern Iroquoia. As European settlements in the region grew in size and power, each of the four men had sought a new birth under the Christian God. Tejonihokarawa, from the Wolf Clan, became Hendrick. Sagayenkwaraton, whose Mohawk name meant Vanishing Smoke, would be called Brant. Onigoheriago was baptized John. Etowaucum, a Mohican, took the name Nicholas. If they found solace in their adopted faith, they also found in the English new allies against old enemies.

Now, during Queen Anne's War—part of England's decades-long struggle to wrest the heart of North America from the French—those new English allies tapped the four Christian Indians for a diplomatic mission. Hendrick, Brant, John, Nicholas, and their retinue traveled overland from Albany to Boston. At Boston's Long Wharf, they boarded one of the vessels that regularly sailed the Atlantic, carrying English manufactures to New England and returning east loaded with timbers, fish, and furs. Six weeks later, after what they called "a long and tedious Voyage," the delegation arrived in London.

In the teeming metropolis, the go-betweens were gr[...] their task. Scarlet cloaks trimmed in gold replaced thei[...] Their feet were encased in soft yellow slippers and their[...] tucked beneath turbans. They were given grand new title[...] their elaborate costumes: the four men became Indian K[...]

Finally, on the morning of April 19, 1710, they [...] St. James Palace. The diplomats presented Queen Ann[...] Scotland and England, newly unified as Great Britain—[...] of wampum, pledged their help against "her Enemies th[...] and asked her to commit more men and materiel to pro[...] war at the western edges of her dominion.

The Four Indian Kings stayed in London for two we[...] ing a royal progress. They sat for state portraits that wo[...] in Kensington Palace; they dined with dukes and adm[...] watched plays and cockfights. Crowds trailed them ev[...] and thousands more read about them in the newspape[...]

Chapter Outline

The Growth of Anglo-American Settlements
New York | New Jersey | Pennsylvania | Carolina | Jamaica | Chesapeake | New England | Colonial Political Structures

VISUALIZING THE PAST *The Pine Tree Shilling*

A Decade of Imperial Crises: The 1670s
New France and the Iroquois | Pueblo Peoples and Spaniards | King Philip's War | Bacon's Rebellion

The Atlantic Trading System
Why African Slavery? | Atlantic Slave Trade | West Africa and the Slave Trade | New England and the Caribbean | Slaving Voyages

LINKS TO THE WORLD *Exotic Beverages*

Why did New York's development lag behind that of other British colonies in the seventeenth century?

they left, the Four Kings sailed down the Thames to Greenwich, where they toured the dockyards that made the ships that were knitting together the Crown's growing blue water empire.

Hendrick, Brant, John, and Nicholas were hardly the first Native Americans to cross the Atlantic, but the Four Indian Kings came as tributaries from a *new* new world. England's tentative plantations overseas had become an empire. Oceangoing vessels now crisscrossed the globe, carrying European goods to America and Africa, Africans to the Americas, Caribbean sugar to New England and Europe, and New England fish and wood products (and occasionally Indian slaves) to the Caribbean. The North American colonies expanded their territorial claims and diversified their economies after the mid-seventeenth century. Mohawk country was closer to the British metropolis than ever before.

Three developments shaped life in the mainland English colonies between 1650 and 1720: escalating conflicts with Indians and with other European colonies; the expansion of slavery; and changes in the colonies' relationships with England.

The explosive growth of the slave trade significantly altered the Anglo-American economy. At first involving primarily Indians and already enslaved Africans from the Caribbean, the trade soon came to focus on men and women kidnapped in Africa and brought directly to the Americas. The large influx of West African slaves expanded agricultural productivity, fueled the international trading system, and dramatically reshaped colonial society.

The burgeoning North American economy attracted new attention from English administrators. After 1660, London bureaucrats attempted to supervise the American settlements to ensure that the mother country benefited from their economic growth.

As English settlements expanded, they came into conflict not only with powerful Indian nations but also with the Dutch, the Spanish, and especially the French. By 1720, war—between Europeans and Indians, among Europeans, and among Indians allied with different colonial powers—had become an all-too-familiar feature of American life. The people and products of the North American colonies had become integral to the world trading system and enmeshed in its conflicts.

As you read this chapter, keep the following questions in mind:

- **What were the consequences of the transatlantic slave trade in North America and Africa?**
- **How did English policy toward the colonies change from 1650 to 1720?**
- **What were the causes and results of new friction between Europeans and native peoples?**

The Growth of Anglo-American Settlements

Between 1642 and 1646, civil war between supporters of King Charles I and the Puritan-dominated Parliament engulfed England. Parliament triumphed, leading to the execution of the king in 1649 and interim rule by the parliamentary army's leader, Oliver Cromwell, during the so-called ommonwealth period. But after Cromwell's death, Parliament restored

Chronology

1642–46	English Civil War
1649	Charles I executed
1651	First Navigation Act passed to regulate colonial trade
1660	Stuarts (Charles II) restored to throne
1663	Carolina chartered
1664	English conquer New Netherland; New York founded
	New Jersey established
1672	England's Royal African Company chartered; becomes largest single slave-trading enterprise
1675–76	Bacon's Rebellion disrupts Virginia government; Jamestown destroyed
1675–78	King Philip's War devastates New England
1680–1700	Pueblo revolt temporarily drives Spaniards from New Mexico
1681	Pennsylvania chartered
1685	James II becomes king
1686–88	Dominion of New England established, superseding charters of colonies from Maine to New Jersey
1688–89	James II deposed in Glorious Revolution; William and Mary ascend English throne
1689	Glorious Revolution in America; Massachusetts, New York, and Maryland overthrow royal governors
1688–99	King William's War fought on northern New England frontier
1691	New Massachusetts charter issued
1692	Witchcraft crisis in Salem; nineteen people hanged
	Earthquake ravages Port Royal, Jamaica
1696	Board of Trade and Plantations established to coordinate English colonial administration
	Vice-admiralty courts established in America
1701	Iroquois Confederacy adopts neutrality policy toward France and England
1702–13	Queen Anne's War fought by French and English
1710	Four "Indian Kings" visit London
1711–13	Tuscarora War (North Carolina) leads to capture or migration of most Tuscaroras
1715	Yamasee War nearly destroys South Carolina

the monarchy once Charles I's son and heir, Charles II, agreed to restrictions on his authority (see Table 3.1).

The Restoration, as the period following the coronation of Charles II was known, transformed the British empire. Assuming the throne in 1660, the new king rewarded nobles and other supporters with vast tracts of land on the North American continent and in the West Indies. The colonies thereby established six of the thirteen polities that eventually would form the United States—New York, New Jersey, Pennsylvania (including Delaware), and North and South Carolina (see Map 3.1)—as

TABLE 3.1   Restored Stuart Monarchs of England, 1660–1714

Monarch	Reign	Relation to Predecessor
Charles II	1660–1685	Son
James II	1685–1688	Brother
Mary	1688–1694	Daughter
William	1688–1702	Son-in-law
Anne	1702–1714	Sister, Sister-in-law

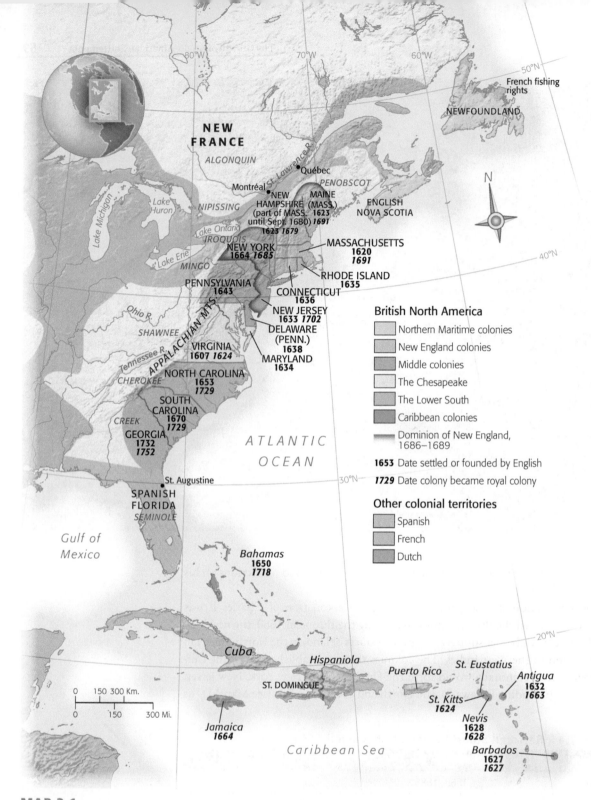

MAP 3.1

The Anglo-American Colonies in the Early Eighteenth Century

By the early eighteenth century, the English colonies nominally dominated the Atlantic coastline of North America. But the colonies' formal boundary lines are deceiving because the western reaches of each colony were still largely unfamiliar to Europeans and because much of the land was still inhabited by Native Americans. Source: Copyright © Cengage Learning 2015

well as Jamaica, the richest of the thirteen colonies that would remain loyal to the Crown. Collectively, these became known as the Restoration colonies.

New York

In 1664, Charles II deeded the region between the Connecticut and Delaware rivers, including the Hudson Valley and Long Island, to his younger brother James, the duke of York. That the Dutch had settled there mattered little. In August, James's warships anchored off Manhattan Island, demanding New Netherland's surrender. The colony complied without resistance. Although in 1672 the Netherlands briefly retook the colony, the Dutch permanently ceded it in 1674.

In New Netherland, James acquired a heterogeneous possession, which he renamed after himself, as New York (see Table 3.2). In 1664, a significant minority of English people (mostly Puritan New Englanders on Long Island) already lived there, along with the Dutch, Algonquians, Mohawks, Mohicans, Iroquois, Africans, Germans, Scandinavians, and a smattering of other Europeans. In addition, the Dutch West India Company had imported slaves into the colony. At the time of the English conquest, almost one-fifth of Manhattan's approximately fifteen hundred inhabitants were of African descent. Slaves then made up a higher proportion of New York's urban population than of the Chesapeake's rural people.

James's representatives moved cautiously in establishing English authority over this diverse population. The Duke's Laws, a 1665 legal code, applied solely to the English settlements on Long Island and was only later extended to the entire colony. James initially allowed Dutch residents to maintain their local government, land titles, and customary legal practices. Each town could choose which church (Dutch Reformed, Congregational, or Anglican) to support with its taxes. But James distrusted legislative bodies, and not until 1683 did he agree to the colonists' requests for an elected legislature.

The duke did not promote migration, so the colony's population grew slowly, barely reaching eighteen thousand by 1698. Until the second decade of the eighteenth century, Manhattan remained a commercial backwater within the orbit of Boston.

New Jersey

In 1664, the duke of York regranted the land between the Hudson and Delaware rivers—East and West Jersey—to his friends Sir George Carteret and John

TABLE 3.2 The Founding of English Colonies in North America and the West Indies, 1655–1681

Colony	Founder(s)	Date	Basis of Economy
Jamaica	Oliver Cromwell, Charles II	1655/1661	Cacao, indigo, beef, sugar
New York (formerly New Netherland)	James, duke of York	1664	Farming, fur trading
New Jersey	Sir George Carteret, John Lord Berkeley	1664	Farming
North Carolina	Carolina proprietors	1665	Tobacco, forest products
South Carolina	Carolina proprietors	1670	Rice, indigo
Pennsylvania (incl. Delaware)	William Penn	1681	Farming

Lord Berkeley. The Jersey proprietors quickly attracted settlers, promising generous land grants, limited freedom of religion, and—without authorization from the Crown—a representative assembly. Many Puritan New Englanders migrated to the Jerseys, along with Barbadians, Dutch New Yorkers, and eventually Scots. By 1726, New Jersey had 32,500 inhabitants, only 8,000 fewer than New York.

Within twenty years, members of the Society of Friends, also called **Quakers**, purchased Carteret's share (West Jersey) and portions of Berkeley's (East Jersey). Quakers rejected earthly and religious hierarchies. With no formally trained clergy, the small radical sect allowed men and women to speak in meetings and become "public Friends" who traveled throughout the Atlantic world to preach God's word. Authorities did not welcome the Quakers' radical egalitarianism, and Friends encountered persecution everywhere.

Quakers Members of a religious sect that embraced egalitarianism and rejected traditional religious hierarchies. They believed that the Holy Spirit or the "inner light" could inspire every soul.

Pennsylvania

In 1681, Charles II granted the region between Maryland and New York to his friend **William Penn**, a prominent Quaker. Penn held the colony as a personal proprietorship, one that earned profits for his descendants until the American Revolution. But Penn also saw his province as a haven for persecuted coreligionists. In widely distributed promotional tracts printed in German, French, and Dutch, Penn touted fertile land available to all comers on liberal terms. He promised to tolerate all religions—although only Christian men could vote—and to establish a representative assembly. He guaranteed such legal protections as the right to bail and trial by jury, prized and ancient rights known throughout England's American realm as "English liberties."

William Penn The proprietor of the last unallocated tract of American territory at the king's disposal, which would become Pennsylvania.

By mid-1683, more than three thousand people—among them Welsh, Irish, Dutch, and Germans—had moved to Pennsylvania. Within five years the population reached twelve thousand. Philadelphia, sited on the easily navigable Delaware River, drew merchants and artisans from throughout the English-speaking world. Pennsylvania's plentiful and fertile lands enabled its residents to export surplus flour and other foodstuffs to the West Indies. Practically overnight Philadelphia acquired more than two thousand citizens and challenged Boston's commercial dominance.

Penn attempted to treat native peoples fairly. He learned the language of the Delawares (or Lenapes), from whom he purchased land to sell to European settlers. Penn also established strict trade regulations and forbade the sale of alcohol to Indians. Yet the same toleration that attracted Tuscarora, Shawnee, and Miami peoples to Pennsylvania also brought non-Quaker Europeans—Scots-Irish (Irish Protestants), Germans, and Swiss—who clashed repeatedly over land with the Indians.

Carolina

The southernmost proprietary colony, granted by Charles II in 1663, stretched from the southern boundary of Virginia to Spanish Florida. Strategically, a successful English settlement there would prevent Spaniards from pushing farther north. The fertile, semitropical land also promised to yield valuable figs, olives, wines, and silk. The proprietors named their new province Carolina in honor of Charles (whose Latin name was Carolus). The "Fundamental Constitutions of Carolina," which they asked the political philosopher John Locke to draft, outlined

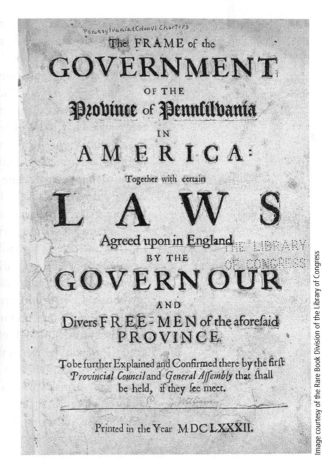

William Penn, later the proprietor of Pennsylvania, as he looked during his youth in Ireland. In numerous pamphlets (right) printed in the late seventeenth century, Penn spread the word about his new colony to thousands of readers in England and its other colonial possessions.

a colony governed by landholding aristocrats and characterized by a structured distribution of political and economic power.

But Carolina failed to follow this plan. Instead, it quickly developed two distinct population centers, which in 1729 split into separate colonies under royal rule. Virginia planters settled the Albemarle region that became North Carolina. They established an economy based on cultivating tobacco and exporting forest products. The other population center, which eventually formed the core of South Carolina, developed at Charles Town, founded in 1670. Many of its early residents migrated from Barbados, where land was increasingly consolidated as the sugar revolution advanced.

Carolina settlers raised corn and cattle, which they sold to Caribbean planters to feed their slaves. They also depended on trade with nearby Indians for commodities they could sell elsewhere, especially deerskins and enslaved Indians. Before 1715, Carolinians exported an estimated thirty thousand to fifty thousand Indian slaves.

Jamaica

Like Carolina, Jamaica absorbed numerous migrants from Barbados in the late seventeenth century. First colonized by Spain in 1494, the enormous island— at nearly 4,500 square miles, it is twenty-six times the size of Barbados—was still thinly settled when English troops seized it in 1655. Intended as a base from which to plunder Spanish treasure ships, the English garrison fared poorly at first. After the Restoration, however, powerful merchants in London convinced Charles II to convert Jamaica to a royal colony. In those early years, Jamaica was a haven for privateers, transported convicts, and smugglers.

But for all its anarchic tendencies, the colony soon began to grow and even flourish. A census taken in 1673 put Jamaica's population at 17,272, more than ten times what it had been when the English captured it. More than half the inhabitants—some 9,504—were enslaved Africans. As the sugar revolution took hold in Jamaica, the number of slaves soared, reaching 55,000—more than eight times the number of white settlers—by 1713. The enslaved rebelled frequently; six organized revolts rocked the colony before 1693. In the mid-eighteenth century, Jamaica's slave rebellions evolved into full-scale wars.

Jamaica proved as profitable as it was volatile, however. Nowhere was the combustible mixture more visible than in the provincial English boomtown of Port Royal. By 1680, it had nearly three thousand inhabitants. Wealthy planters, privateers, and the merchants lived in opulent brick houses, while their slaves crowded into huts. Taverns and brothels lined the wharves. Those who thought of Port Royal as a new world Sodom saw divine justice when, in 1692, an earthquake buried the city and hundreds of its inhabitants beneath the sea. A devastating fire ravaged the remainder eleven years later.

Yet Port Royal, no less than Boston, and Jamaica, no less than Pennsylvania, epitomized British America. The island recovered from the heavy blows of the late seventeenth century. On the eve of the American Revolution, Jamaica was the most valuable British colony, if not the economic capital of the Anglo-Atlantic world.

Chesapeake

The English Civil War retarded the development of the earlier English settlements. Struggles between supporters of the king and Parliament caused military clashes in Maryland and political upheavals in Virginia in the 1640s. But once the war ended and immigration resumed, the colonies again expanded. Tobacco growers imported increasing numbers of English indentured servants as farms developed into plantations.

Chesapeake tobacco planters continued to acquire small numbers of enslaved workers. At first, almost all came from a population that historian Ira Berlin has termed "Atlantic creoles": people (sometimes of mixed race) who came from other European settlements in the Atlantic world, primarily Iberian outposts. Not all the Atlantic creoles who came to the Chesapeake were bondspeople; some were free or indentured. With their arrival, the Chesapeake became what Berlin calls a "society with slaves," where slavery coexisted with other labor systems.

New England

Migration to New England essentially ceased when the Civil War began in 1642. While English Puritans were challenging the king and then governing England as a commonwealth, they had little incentive to leave their homeland. Yet the Puritan colonies' population grew dramatically by natural increase. By the 1670s, New England's population had more than tripled to approximately seventy thousand, which placed pressure on available land. Colonial settlement spread far into the

Visualizing THE PAST

The Pine Tree Shilling

The early settlers of Massachusetts shipped most of the coins they had brought with them back across the Atlantic, to pay for goods imported from England and Europe. With money always in short supply, they conducted local and regional trade with tokens including musket balls and wampum, the clamshell beads Algonquian and Iroquois peoples prized for ceremonial exchanges. But in the 1640s, the value of wampum collapsed, just as Bostonians entered Caribbean trade.

Long-distance commerce demanded a circulating medium whose value held stable across space and time. That meant coins made from precious metal, whose weight governed their worth. Trade brought silver coins to New England from the Spanish mines at Potosí, but they were often shaved or debased—worth less than their face value. So in 1652, Massachusetts began to mint its own higher-quality coins. Mint master John Hull, a staunch Puritan, designed them without a human face, since the Bible's commandments forbade the worship of graven images. For the usual king's profile, he substituted a tall pine tree.

When Charles II was restored to the throne, he began to question colonial laws that departed from English norms. In 1665, his royal commissioners directed Massachusetts to close its mint. By minting money, Boston was acting like a city-state; the Crown would have it behave like a colony. Yet Massachusetts kept producing silver shillings until the colony's charter was revoked in the late 1680s. What did the pine tree signify in Atlantic commerce? How did the colonists identify themselves on the shilling?

Pine Tree Shilling front

Pine Tree Shilling back

interior of Massachusetts and Connecticut, and many later generations migrated to other colonies to find sufficient farmland. Others learned such skills as blacksmithing or carpentry to support themselves in the growing towns. By 1680, some 4,500 people lived in Boston, which was becoming a genuine city.

New Englanders who remained in the small, yet densely populated and intensely fractious older communities experienced a range of social tensions. Men and women frequently sued their neighbors for slander, debt, and other offenses. After 1650, accusations of witchcraft—roughly 100 in all before 1690—landed suspects in courtrooms across the region. But few of the accused, most of whom were middle-aged women, were convicted, and fewer still were executed.

Colonial Political Structures

By the last quarter of the seventeenth century, almost all the Anglo-American colonies had well-established political and judicial structures. In New England, property-holding men or the legislature elected the governors; in other regions, the king or the proprietor appointed such leaders. A council, elected or appointed, advised the governor and served as the upper house of the legislature. Each colony had a judiciary with local justices of the peace, county courts, and, usually, an appeals court composed of the councilors. Most colonies had local governing bodies as well.

A Decade of Imperial Crises: The 1670s

How did settlers' interests collide with those of Native Americans?

Between 1670 and 1680, New France, New Mexico, New England, and Virginia experienced bitter conflicts as their interests collided with those of America's original inhabitants.

New France and the Iroquois

In the mid-1670s Louis de Buade de Frontenac, the governor-general of Canada, decided to expand New France's reach south and west to establish a trade route to Mexico and to gain direct control of the fur trade. Accordingly, he encouraged the explorations of Father Jacques Marquette, Louis Jolliet, and René-Robert Cavelier de La Salle in the Great Lakes and Mississippi valley regions. Frontenac's goal, however, led to conflict with the powerful Iroquois Confederacy, composed of five Indian nations—the Mohawks, Oneidas, Onondagas, Cayugas, and Senecas. (In 1722, the Tuscaroras became the sixth.)

Link to letter from Father Marquette describing some interactions with Indians

Before the arrival of Europeans, the Iroquois waged wars primarily to acquire captives to replenish their population. Foreigners brought ravaging disease as early as 1633, intensifying the need for captives. The Europeans' presence also created an economic motive for warfare: the desire to dominate the fur trade and to gain unimpeded access to imported goods. Bloody conflict with the Huron in the 1640s initiated a series of conflicts with other Indians known as the **Beaver Wars**, in which the Iroquois fought to control the peltry trade. Iroquois warriors raided other villages for pelts or attacked Indians carrying furs to European outposts. Then the Iroquois traded that booty for European blankets, knives, guns, alcohol, and other items.

Beaver Wars Series of conflicts between the Hurons (and other Indians) and Iroquois in a quest for pelts.

As Iroquois dominance grew, beginning in the mid-1670s, the French repeatedly attacked, seeing the Iroquois as a threat to France's plans to trade with western Indians. Although in 1677 New Yorkers and the Iroquois established a formal alliance known as the Covenant Chain, the English offered little beyond weapons to their trading partners. Without much aid, the Confederacy held its own and even expanded, enabling it in 1701 to negotiate neutrality treaties with France and other Indians. For the next half-century, the Iroquois maintained their power through trade and diplomacy rather than warfare. The mission of the "Indian Kings" to London belonged to this diplomatic tradition.

Pueblo Peoples and Spaniards

In New Mexico, too, events of the 1670s led to a crisis with long-term consequences. Under Spanish domination, the Pueblo peoples had added Christianity to their beliefs while retaining traditional rituals. But as decades passed, Franciscans adopted increasingly violent tactics to eliminate the native religion. Priests and secular colonists who held *encomiendas* placed heavy labor demands on the people, who were also suffering from Apache raids and food shortages. In 1680, the Pueblos revolted under the leadership of **Popé**, a respected shaman, driving the Spaniards out of New Mexico. Although Spain restored its authority by 1700, Spanish governors now stressed cooperation with the Pueblos. The **Pueblo Revolt of 1680** constituted the most successful and longest-sustained Indian resistance movement in colonial North America.

Popé Leader of the Pueblo Revolt against Spanish in 1680.

Pueblo Revolt of 1680 The most successful Indian uprising in American history. Pueblo Indians rebelled against Spanish authority and drove the Spanish from their New Mexico settlements.

King Philip's War

In the more densely settled English colonies, hostilities developed over land. By the early 1670s, the growing settlements in southern New England surrounded Wampanoag ancestral lands on Narragansett Bay. The local chief, Metacom—whom the English called "King Philip"—was troubled by the impact of European culture on his land and people. Philip led attacks on nearby communities in June 1675. Other Algonquian peoples, among them Nipmucks and Narragansetts, joined King Philip's forces. In the fall, they attacked settlements in the northern Connecticut River valley; the war spread to Maine when the Abenakis entered the conflict. In 1676, the Indian allies devastated villages like Lancaster, and even attacked Plymouth and Providence. Altogether, the native alliance wholly or partially destroyed twenty-seven of ninety-two towns and attacked forty others, pushing the line of English settlement back toward the coast.

King Philip's War Major war between Indians and New England settlers.

In summer 1676, the Indian coalition ran short of food and ammunition. On June 12, the Mohawks—ancient Iroquois enemies of New England Algonquians—devastated a major Wampanoag encampment while most of the warriors were away attacking an English town. After King Philip was shot to death that August, the southern alliance crumbled. But fighting on the Maine frontier continued for another two years until the English and Abenakis agreed to end the conflict in 1678.

After the war, hundreds of Wampanoags, Nipmucks, Narragansetts, and Abenakis were captured and sold into slavery; many more died of starvation and disease. New Englanders had broken the power of the southern coastal tribes. Thereafter the southern Indians lived in small clusters, subordinated to the colonists and often working as servants or sailors. Only on the island of Martha's Vineyard did Christian Wampanoags (who had not participated in the war) preserve their cultural identity.

The settlers paid a terrible price for their victory: an estimated one-tenth of New England's adult male population was killed or wounded. Proportional to population, it was the most lethal conflict in American history. The colonists' heavy losses also caused many Puritans to wonder if God had turned against them. New Englanders did not fully rebuild abandoned interior towns for another three decades, and not until the American Revolution did the region's per capita income again reach pre-1675 levels.

Bacon's Rebellion
Uprising that resulted from many conflicts, among them mounting land shortage and settlers' desires for Indian lands.

Link to Nathaniel Bacon's Declaration in the Name of the People

Bacon's Rebellion

Conflict over land simultaneously wracked Virginia. In the early 1670s, ex-servants unable to acquire land greedily eyed the territory reserved by treaty for Virginia's natives. Governor William Berkeley resisted starting a war to further the aims of backcountry settlers. Dissatisfied colonists then rallied behind a recent immigrant, the gentleman Nathaniel Bacon, who shared their frustration that all the desirable land had been claimed. Using as a pretext the July 1675 killing of an indentured servant by Doeg Indians, Bacon and his followers attacked the Doegs and the more powerful Susquehannocks. In retaliation, Susquehannocks raided outlying farms early in 1676.

The governor declared Bacon and his men outlaws. During the chaotic summer of 1676, Bacon alternately pursued Indians and battled the governor. In September, Bacon's forces burned Jamestown to the ground. But when Bacon died of dysentery the following month, the rebellion collapsed. Even so, a new treaty signed in 1677 opened much of the disputed territory to settlement. The end of Bacon's Rebellion thus pushed most of Virginia's Indians west beyond the Appalachians.

The Atlantic Trading System

How was slavery at the center of the expanding trade network between Europe and the colonies?

In the 1670s and 1680s, the prosperity of the Chesapeake rested on tobacco, which depended on an ample labor supply. But fewer English men and women proved willing to indenture themselves. Population pressures had eased in England, and the Restoration colonies and Caribbean sugar boom gave migrants other settlement options. Furthermore, fluctuating tobacco prices and land scarcity made the Chesapeake less appealing. Wealthy Chesapeake planters found the answer to their labor problem in the Caribbean sugar islands, where Dutch, French, English, and Spanish planters purchased African slaves.

Why African Slavery?

Slavery had been practiced in Europe and Islamic lands for centuries. European Christians justified enslaving heathen peoples in religious terms, arguing that slavery might lead to conversion. Muslims, too, enslaved infidels and imported black African bondspeople into North Africa and the Middle East. Others believed that prisoners of war could be enslaved. Consequently, when Portuguese mariners encountered African societies holding slaves, they purchased bondspeople. From the 1440s on, Portugal imported large numbers of slaves into the Iberian Peninsula.

English people had few moral qualms about enslaving other humans. Slavery was sanctioned in the Bible and widely practiced by contemporaries. Yet colonists did not inherit the law and culture of slavery fully formed. Instead, they fashioned the institution of bondage and concepts of "race" to suit their economic and social needs. The 1670 Virginia law that first tried to define which people could be enslaved declared, "all servants not being christians imported into this colony by shipping shal be slaves for their lives." Such awkward, nonracial phrasing reveals that Anglo-American settlers had not yet fully developed the meaning of *race* or the category of *slave*.

Atlantic Slave Trade

North American mainland planters could not have obtained bondspeople without the rapid development of an Atlantic trading system. Although this elaborate system has been called the triangular trade, people and products did not move across the ocean in easily diagrammed patterns (see Map 3.2).

Chesapeake tobacco and Caribbean and Brazilian sugar were shipped to Europe, where they were in demand. The profits paid for African laborers and European manufactured goods. The African coastal rulers took payment for slaves in European manufactures and East Indian textiles. Europeans purchased slaves from Africa for resale in their colonies and acquired sugar and tobacco from America, in exchange dispatching their manufactures everywhere.

European nations fought bitterly to control the Atlantic trade. The Portuguese dominated at first, but were supplanted by the Dutch in the 1630s. Between 1652 and 1674, England and the Netherlands fought three wars—conflicts over naval supremacy that largely centered on the slave trade. The Dutch lost out to the English, who controlled the trade through the Royal African Company, chartered by Charles II in 1672. The company maintained seventeen forts and trading posts, dispatched to West Africa hundreds of ships carrying English goods, and transported thousands of slaves to the Caribbean colonies. Some of its agents made fortunes, yet even before the company's monopoly expired in 1712, independent traders carried most of the Africans imported into the colonies. In the fifty years beginning in 1676, British and American ships transported an estimated 689,600 captured Africans, more than 177,000 of them in vessels owned by the Royal African Company.

By the middle of the eighteenth century, American tobacco had become closely associated with African slavery. An English woodcut advertising tobacco from the York River in Virginia accordingly depicted not a Chesapeake planter but rather an African, shown with a hoe in one hand and a pipe in the other. Usually, of course, slaves would not have smoked the high-quality tobacco produced for export, although they were allowed to cultivate small crops for their own use.

West Africa and the Slave Trade

Most of the enslaved people carried to North America originated in West Africa. Some came from the Rice Coast and Grain Coast, but even more had resided in the Gold Coast, Slave Coast, and the Bight of Biafra (modern Nigeria) and Angola. Certain coastal rulers—for instance, the Adja kings of the Slave Coast—allowed the establishment of permanent slave-trading posts in their territories. Such rulers controlled Europeans' access to bound laborers and simultaneously controlled inland Africans' access to desirable trade goods.

The slave trade affected West African nations unevenly. It helped to create such powerful eighteenth-century kingdoms as Dahomey and Asante (formed from the Akan States), while rulers in parts of Upper Guinea, especially modern Gambia and Senegal, largely resisted involvement with the trade. Traffic in slaves destroyed smaller polities and disrupted traditional economic patterns. Agricultural production intensified, especially in rice-growing areas, to supply hundreds of slave ships with foodstuffs. Because prisoners of war constituted the bulk of the exported slaves, some nations initiated conflicts specifically to acquire valuable captives.

MAP 3.2
Atlantic Trade Routes

By the late seventeenth century, an elaborate trade network linked the countries and colonies bordering the Atlantic Ocean. The most valuable commodities exchanged were enslaved people and the products of slave labor. Source: Copyright © Cengage Learning 2015

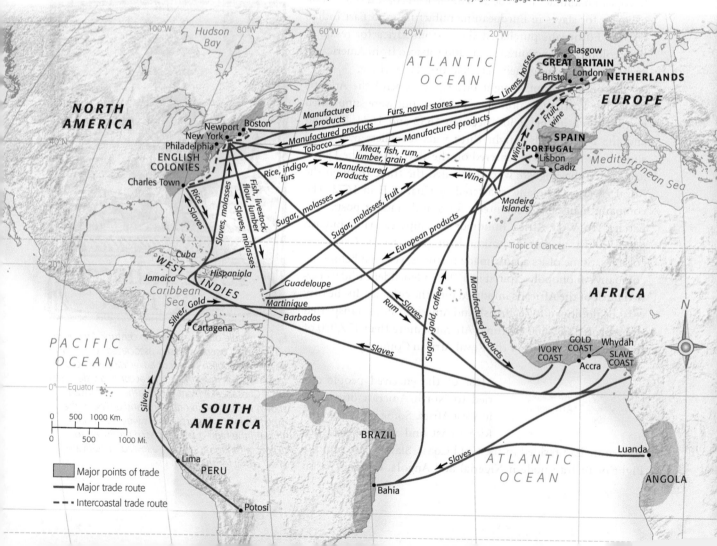

Atlas Blaeu van der Hem

In the fifteenth century, Portuguese explorers renamed the town of Elmina—a trading village on the coast of present-day Ghana—after the gold they exported from the site. (El mina means "the mine.") The construction of the massive fort or "castle" depicted in this watercolor began in 1482. At first, its primary purpose was to protect the precious metal trade along what Europeans called Africa's Gold Coast. But during the seventeenth century, enslaved Africans became the primary exports of ports like Elmina, which the Dutch acquired in 1637. Captive men, women, and children were held in the fortress's dungeons before beginning the long voyage to the Americas. The fort's export gate, facing the sea, came to be known as the Door of No Return.

New England and the Caribbean

New England had a complex relationship to the trading system. The region produced only one item England wanted: tall trees to serve as masts for sailing vessels. To buy English manufactures, New Englanders depended on profits earned in the Caribbean. The Caribbean colonies lacked precisely the items that New England produced: cheap corn and salted fish to feed slaves, and wood for barrels. By the late 1640s, decades before the Chesapeake economy became dependent on *production* by slaves, New England's commerce rested on *consumption* by slaves and owners.

Slaving Voyages

Tying the system together was the voyage (commonly called the **middle passage**) that brought Africans to the Americas. Brought aboard in small groups, drawn from many inland nations, speaking diverse languages, an average of 300 men, women, and children comprised what slave merchants called a "full complement" of human merchandise, though voyages transporting 400 or 500 Africans were not uncommon, and cargoes exceeding 600 were not unheard of.

middle passage The brutal and often fatal journey of slaves from Africa to America.

On shipboard, men were shackled in pairs in the hold except for periods of exercise on deck. Women and children were usually allowed to move around, and to work at such assigned tasks as food preparation and cleaning. Many resisted enslavement by refusing to eat, jumping overboard, or joining in revolts, which rarely succeeded. Their communal singing and drumming, reported by numerous observers, must have lifted their spirits and forged solidarity. But conditions were hellish, as captains packed captives into holds that were hot, crowded, and reeking with smells from vomit and the "necessary tubs."

Links TO THE WORLD

Exotic Beverages

American and European demand for tea (from China), coffee (from Arabia), chocolate (from Mesoamerica), and rum (distilled from sugar, which also sweetened the bitter taste of the other three) helped to reshape the world economy after the mid-seventeenth century. Approximately two-thirds of the people who migrated across the Atlantic before 1776 were involved—primarily as slaves—in the production of tobacco, calico, and these four drinks. As they moved from luxury to necessity, the exotic beverages had a profound impact on custom and culture.

Each beverage had its own pattern of consumption. Chocolate, brought to Spain from Mexico, became the preferred drink of aristocrats, who took it hot, at intimate gatherings. Coffee became the morning beverage of English and colonial businessmen, who praised it for keeping drinkers sober and focused. Coffee was served in new public coffeehouses, patronized chiefly by men. The English called them "penny universities";

government leaders thought coffeehouses were nurseries of subversion. The first coffeehouse opened in London in the 1660s; Boston had several by the 1690s. By the mid-eighteenth century, though, tea—consumed in the afternoon at tea tables presided over by women—had supplanted coffee in England and America. Where tea embodied genteel status and polite conversation, rum was imbibed by free working people.

The American colonies played a vital role in the production, distribution, and consumption of these beverages. Chocolate originated in America, and cacao plantations in the tropics multiplied to meet the rising demand. Coffee and tea were avidly consumed in the colonies. And rum involved Americans in every phase of its production and consumption. The sugar grown on Caribbean plantations was transported to the mainland in barrels and ships made from North American wood. There the syrup was turned into rum at 140 distilleries. Americans drank an estimated four gallons per person each year. Much of the rest they transported to Africa, where the rum purchased more slaves, beginning the cycle again.

Library of Congress

The frontispiece of Peter Muguet, Tractatus De Poto Caphe, Chinesium The et de Chocolata, 1685. *Muguet's treatise visually linked the three hot, exotic beverages recently introduced to Europeans. The drinks are consumed by representatives of the cultures in which they originated: a turbaned Turk (with coffeepot in the foreground), a Chinese man (with teapot on the table), and an Indian drinking from a hollowed, handled gourd (with a chocolate pot and ladle on the floor in front of him).*

The traumatic voyage brought heavy fatalities to captives and crew. An average of 10 to 20 percent of the newly enslaved died en route. Another 20 percent or so died either before the ships left Africa or shortly after their arrival in the Americas. Merchants tallied lost lives in pounds sterling. Sailors also died at high rates—one in four or five—chiefly through exposure to diseases.

Slavery in North America and the Caribbean

What skills did African slaves bring to America that proved vital to the development of colonial South Carolina?

Barbados, America's first "slave society" (an economy wholly dependent on enslavement), spawned others. As the island's population expanded, about 40 percent of the early English residents dispersed to other colonies. Migrants carried their laws, commercial contacts, and slaveholding practices with them. A large proportion of the first Africans imported into North America came via Barbados. In addition to the many Barbadians who settled in Carolina, others moved to the southern regions of Virginia, New Jersey, and New England.

African Enslavement in the Chesapeake

Newly arrived Africans in the Chesapeake tended to be assigned to outlying parts of plantations (called quarters) until they learned some English and the routines of American tobacco cultivation. Mostly men, they lived in groups of ten to fifteen workers housed together in one or two buildings and supervised by an Anglo-American overseer. Each man was expected to cultivate about two acres of tobacco a year. Their lives must have been filled with toil and loneliness, for few spoke the same language, and all worked six days a week. Many used their Sunday off to cultivate their own gardens or to hunt or fish to supplement their meager diet. Only rarely could they form families because of the scarcity of women.

Slaves usually cost about two and a half times as much as indentured servants, but they supplied a lifetime of service, assuming they survived—which large numbers did not. Planters with enough money could acquire slaves and accumulate greater wealth, whereas the less affluent could not even afford indentured servants. The introduction of large numbers of Africans into the Chesapeake therefore widened the gap between rich and poor planters in Anglo-American society.

So many Africans were imported into Virginia and Maryland that by 1710 people of African descent composed one-fifth of the population. Even so, a decade later American-born slaves outnumbered their African-born counterparts in the Chesapeake, a trend that continued thereafter.

Link to Colonial Virginia Laws Pertaining to Slaves and Servants

African Enslavement in South Carolina

Africans came with their owners from Barbados to South Carolina in 1670, composing one-quarter to one-third of the colony's early population. The Barbadian slave owners quickly discovered that African-born slaves had skills well suited to South Carolina's semitropical environment. African-style dugout canoes became the chief means of transportation in the colony. Fishing nets copied from African models proved efficient. Africans also adapted their cattle herding techniques. Because meat and hides were early exports, Africans contributed to South Carolina's prosperity.

In 1693, as slavery was taking firm root in South Carolina, officials in Spanish Florida began offering freedom to runaways who would convert to Catholicism. Over the years, hundreds of South Carolina fugitives took advantage of the offer, although not all won their liberty.

After 1700, South Carolinians started to import slaves directly from Africa. From about 1710 until midcentury, the African-born constituted a majority of the enslaved population in the colony, and by 1750, bondspeople composed a majority of its residents. The similarity of the South Carolinian and West African environments, coupled with the substantial African-born population, ensured the survival of more aspects of West African culture than elsewhere on the North American mainland. Only in South Carolina did enslaved parents continue to give their children African names; only there did a dialect develop that combined English words with terms from Wolof, Bambara, and other African languages. (Known as Gullah, it has survived to the present day in isolated areas.) African skills remained useful, so techniques lost in other regions when the migrant generation died were instead passed down to the migrants' children.

Rice and Indigo

Slave importation coincided with the successful introduction of rice in South Carolina. English people knew nothing about producing rice, but captives taken from Africa's Rice Coast had long worked with the crop.

On rice plantations, which were far larger than Chesapeake tobacco quarters, every field worker was expected to cultivate three to four acres a year. Most were female because many enslaved men were assigned to jobs like blacksmithing or carpentry. Planters also expected slaves to grow part of their own food. By the early eighteenth century, a "task" system of predefined work assignments prevailed. After bondspeople had finished their set tasks for the day, they could rest or work their own garden plots or undertake other projects. One scholar has suggested that the **task system** resulted from negotiations between slaves familiar with rice cultivation and masters who needed their expertise.

task system Each slave had a daily or weekly quota of tasks to complete.

Developers of South Carolina's second cash crop also used the task system and drew on slaves' specialized skills. Indigo, the only source of blue dye for the growing English textile industry, was much prized. In the early 1740s, Eliza Lucas, a young woman born in Antigua, drew on the knowledge of slaves and overseers from the West Indies and developed planting and processing techniques for the precious commodity.

Indian Enslavement in North and South Carolina

In 1708, Indian bondspeople accounted for as much as 14 percent of the South Carolina population. The trade in Indian slaves began when the Westos (originally known as the Eries), migrated south from the Great Lakes region in the mid-1650s, after the Beaver Wars. The Westos raided Spain's lightly defended Florida missions and sold Indian captives to Virginians. The Carolina proprietors monopolized trade with the Westos, which infuriated settlers shut out of the commerce in slaves and deerskins.

Carolina planters secretly financed attacks on the Westos, wiping them out by 1682. Southeastern Indians reacted to such slave raids—continued by other native peoples after the defeat of the Westos—by trying to protect themselves through subordination to the English or Spanish, or by coalescing into new, larger political units, such as those known later as Creeks, Chickasaws, or Cherokees.

At first, the Carolinians did not clash with neighboring Indians. But in 1711 the Tuscaroras, an Iroquoian people, attacked a Swiss-German settlement at New Bern, North Carolina, which had expropriated their lands, which ignited the **Tuscarora War**. South Carolinians and their Indian allies then combined to defeat the Tuscaroras in a bloody war. Afterward, more than a thousand Tuscaroras were enslaved. The remainder migrated northward and joined the Iroquois Confederacy.

Tuscarora War War in the Carolinas from 1711 through 1713 that pitted Tuscarora Indians against colonists and their Indian allies.

Four years later, the Yamasees, who had helped Carolina to conquer the Tuscaroras, enlisted the Creeks and other Muskogean peoples to attack outlying English settlements. The Yamasee-Creek offensive was thwarted only when reinforcements arrived from the north, colonists hastily armed their African slaves, and Cherokees joined the fight. After the war, Carolina's involvement in the Indian slave trade ceased, because the Creeks, Yamasees, and Tuscaroras had all moved away for self-protection. The native peoples who remained were able to rebuild their strength, for they were no longer subjected to slavers' raids.

Enslavement in the North

Atlantic creoles from the Caribbean and native peoples from the Carolinas and Florida, along with Indians enslaved for crime or debt, composed the bound laborers in the northern mainland colonies. Some bondspeople resided in urban areas, especially New York. Yet even in the North most bondspeople worked in the countryside on farms and large estates. Some bondsmen toiled in new rural enterprises, such as ironworks, alongside hired laborers and indentured servants. Slavery made its most dramatic contribution to the northern economy at one remove, through the West Indies provision trade. But although relatively few northern colonists owned slaves, some individual slaveholders benefited directly from the institution and wanted to preserve it.

Slave Resistance

As slavery grew, so too did slaves' resistance. Usually resistance took the form of work slowdown or escape, but occasionally bondspeople planned rebellions. Seven times before 1713, the English Caribbean experienced

This advertisement for a sale of slaves of African descent appeared in the New York Journal in 1768. The expertise of two of the people described would have appealed to urban buyers: a cooper would have been useful to a barrelmaker or shipper, and the seamstress might have attracted attention from dressmakers. The other bondspeople mentioned could have been purchased by people who wanted house servants or laborers.

major revolts involving at least fifty slaves and causing the deaths of both whites and blacks.

The first slave revolt in the mainland English colonies occurred in New York in 1712. The rebels set a fire and then ambushed those who tried to put it out, killing eight and wounding another twelve. Some rebels committed suicide to avoid capture; of those caught and tried, eighteen were tortured and executed. Their decapitated bodies were left to rot outdoors as a warning to others.

Forging and Testing the Bonds of Empire

How did mercantilism benefit some colonies economically and hurt others?

English officials seeking new sources of revenue focused on the expanding Atlantic trade in slaves and the products of slave labor. Parliament and the Stuart monarchs drafted laws to harness the proceeds of the trade for the mother country.

Colonies Into Empire

Like other European nations, England based its commercial policy on *mercantilism*, the theory that viewed the economic world as a collection of countries whose governments competed for shares of a finite amount of wealth. What one nation gained, another lost. Each nation sought economic self-sufficiency while maintaining a favorable balance of trade by exporting more than it imported. Colonies played an important role, supplying the mother country with valuable raw materials and serving as a market for the parent country's manufactured goods.

Parliament's Navigation Acts—passed between 1651 and 1673—established three principles of mercantilist theory. First, only English or colonial merchants could legally trade in the colonies. Second, certain valuable American products could be sold only in the mother country or in other English colonies. At first, these "enumerated" commodities included wool, sugar, tobacco, indigo, ginger, and dyes; later acts added rice, naval stores (masts, spars, pitch, tar, and turpentine), copper, and furs. Third, foreign goods destined for sale in the colonies had to be shipped through England, paying English import duties. Years later, new laws established a fourth principle: the colonies could not export items that competed with English manufactures.

These laws adversely affected Chesapeake planters who could not seek foreign markets for their staple crops. The statutes initially helped English Caribbean sugar producers by driving Brazilian sugar out of the home market, but later prevented English planters from selling sugar elsewhere. Others benefited. The laws stimulated the creation of a lucrative shipbuilding industry in New England. And the northern and middle colonies produced many unenumerated goods—fish, flour, meat and livestock, and barrel staves—that could be traded directly to the French, Spanish, or Dutch Caribbean islands if carried in English or American ships.

Mercantilism and Navigation Acts

English authorities soon learned that enforcing mercantilist legislation would be difficult. Smuggling was widespread, and colonial officials often looked the other way when illegally imported goods were sold.

Because American juries tended to favor local smugglers, Parliament in 1696 established American vice-admiralty courts, which operated without juries and adjudicated violations of the Navigation Acts.

The Navigation Acts imposed regulations on Americans' international trade, but by the early 1680s the mainland colonies had become accustomed to a considerable degree of political autonomy. Massachusetts, Plymouth, Connecticut, and Rhode Island operated as independent entities, subject neither to the direct authority of the king nor to a proprietor. Virginia was a royal colony and New Hampshire (1679) and New York (1685) gained that status, but all other mainland settlements were proprietorships, over which the Crown exercised little control. In the English colonies, free adult men who owned property expected to have a voice in their governments, especially in decisions concerning taxation.

James II, who became king in 1685, and his successors sought to tighten the reins of government and reduce the colonies' political autonomy. English officials targeted New England, which they saw as a hotbed of smuggling. Moreover, Puritans denied freedom of religion to non-Congregationalists and maintained laws incompatible with English practice. The charters of all the colonies from New Jersey to Maine were revoked, and a royal Dominion of New England was established in 1686. (For the boundaries of the Dominion, see Map 3.1) Sir Edmund Andros, the Dominion's governor, had immense power: Parliament dissolved the assemblies, and Andros needed only the consent of an appointed council to make laws and levy taxes.

Glorious Revolution in America

New Englanders had endured Andros's **autocratic** rule for more than two years when they learned that James II's power was crumbling. The king had angered his subjects by levying taxes without parliamentary approval and by converting to Catholicism. In April 1689, Boston's leaders jailed Andros and his associates. The following month, they received news of the bloodless coup known as the Glorious Revolution, in which James had been replaced in late 1688 by his daughter Mary and her husband, the Dutch prince William of Orange.

autocratic Absolute or dictatorial rule.

The Glorious Revolution affirmed the supremacy of Protestantism and Parliament. The new monarchs acceded to Parliament's Declaration of Rights "vindicating and asserting their ancient rights and liberties," which confirmed citizens' entitlement to free elections, fair trials, and petition, and specified that no monarch could ignore acts of Parliament on issues of taxation and defense. In 1776, the American Declaration of Independence would borrow heavily from Parliament's 1689 Declaration of Rights.

Link to the 1689 English Bill of Rights

Across the mainland colonies, the Glorious Revolution inspired revolt. In Maryland, the Protestant Association overturned the government of the Catholic proprietor, and in New York a militia officer of German origin, Jacob Leisler, assumed control of the government.

But like James II, William and Mary believed England should exercise tighter control over its unruly American possessions. Consequently, only the Maryland rebellion received royal sanction, primarily because of its anti-Catholic thrust. In New York, Leisler was hanged for treason. Massachusetts became a royal colony with an appointed governor. Its new 1691 charter eliminated the religious test for voting and office holding. A parish of the Church of England appeared in Boston. The **"city upon a hill"** as John Winthrop had envisioned it, had fallen.

"city upon a hill" John Winthrop's vision of the Puritan settlement in New England as a model for the world.

King William's War

A war with the French and their Algonquian allies compounded New England's difficulties. After King Louis XIV of France allied himself with the deposed James II, England declared war on France in 1689. (This war is today known as the Nine Years' War, but the colonists called it King William's War.) Even before war broke out in Europe, Anglo-Americans and Abenakis clashed over settlements in Maine that colonists had reoccupied after the 1678 truce. Abenaki attacks wholly or partially destroyed several towns, and colonial expeditions against Montreal and Quebec in 1690 failed. The Peace of Ryswick (1697) formally ended the war in Europe but failed to bring much respite to North America's northern frontiers.

The 1692 Witchcraft Crisis

For eight months in 1692, witchcraft accusations spread through Essex County, Massachusetts, a heavily populated area directly threatened by the Indian attacks to the north. Before the outbreak ended, fourteen women and five men were hanged, one man was pressed to death with heavy stones, fifty-four people confessed to being witches, and more than 140 suspects were jailed. The worst phase of the crisis concluded when the governor dissolved the special court established to try the accused. During the final trials, which took place in regular courts, judges and juries discounted so-called spectral evidence, offered by witnesses who claimed to be afflicted by witches in the form of specters. Almost all the defendants were acquitted, and the governor quickly reprieved the few found guilty. If frontier warfare and political turmoil had created an environment where witch fears could become epidemic, the imposition of a new imperial order on the colony helped to cure the plague.

Link to Ann Putnam's Confession

New Imperial Measures

In 1696, England created the fifteen-member Board of Trade and Plantations, the chief government organ concerned with the American colonies. The board gathered information, reviewed Crown appointments in America, scrutinized colonial legislation, supervised trade policies, and advised ministries on colonial issues. Still, it had no enforcement powers. Although the Board of Trade improved colonial administration, supervision of the American provinces remained decentralized and haphazard.

Most colonists resented English "placemen" who arrived to implement the policies of king and Parliament, but they adjusted to their demands and to the restrictions imposed by the Navigation Acts. They fought another of Europe's wars—the War of the Spanish Succession, called Queen Anne's War in the colonies—from 1702 to 1713.

Colonists who allied with the royal government received patronage in the form of offices and land grants and composed "court parties" that supported English officials. Others, who were either less fortunate in their friends or defended colonial autonomy, made up the opposition, or "country" interest.

Americans of African Descent

People of African descent composed only a tiny proportion of the population of the mainland North American colonies before 1650. But the rise of southern economies based largely on the enslavement of Africans, coupled with the widespread employment of enslaved Africans in northern colonies, dramatically altered the American population. By 1775, some 280,000 Africans had been imported into the territory that later became the United States; they and their descendants constituted about 20 percent of the population at that time.

According to the 2010 census, 13.6 percent of the American people now claim descent from African ancestors. Because the legal importation of African slaves ended in 1808, and because the United States attracted relatively few voluntary migrants from Africa until the twentieth century, most of today's African Americans have colonial ancestors—a claim few Americans of European descent can make.

The modern African American population includes people with many different skin colors, reflecting a long history of interracial sexual relationships (both coerced and voluntary). African Americans have had children with Europeans and Indians since the colonial period; more recently, they have intermarried with Asian and Latino immigrants. In part, the mingling of different peoples of color resulted from state laws that for centuries forbade legal marriages between Americans of European descent and those of other races. In 1967, the Supreme Court ruled in *Loving v. Virginia* that such laws violated the rights to due process and equal protection enshrined in the Fourteenth Amendment to the U.S. Constitution.

In the year 2000, the census for the first time recognized the children of interracial unions by allowing Americans to define themselves as members of more than one race. By 2010, the number of black Americans identifying as mixed race had reached 3.1 million, increasing at a higher rate than those identifying as black alone.

Beginning in the late twentieth century, the number of black Americans whose origins lie in modern Africa increased substantially. In 2005, the annual number of voluntary migrants from Africa to the United States passed the number of Africans brought to this country against their will during any of the peak years of the slave trade. No historic figure better represents this emerging face of black America than Barack Hussein Obama II. In 2008, this Hawai'ian-born son of a man from Kenya and a woman from Kansas became the forty-fourth president of the United States.

Summary

The years from 1650 to 1720 established economic and political patterns that would structure subsequent changes in mainland colonial society. England's first attempt to regulate colonial trade, the Navigation Act of 1651, was quickly followed by others. By 1720, the essential elements of the imperial administrative structure that would govern the English colonies until 1775 had been put in place.

In 1650, just two isolated centers of English population, New England and the Chesapeake, existed along the seaboard, along with the Dutch New Netherland. In 1720, nearly the entire East Coast of North America was in English hands, and Indian control east of the Appalachian Mountains had largely been broken by warfare. West of the mountains, Iroquois power reigned. What had been an immigrant population was now mostly American-born, except for the African-born people in South

Carolina and the Chesapeake; economies originally based on trade in fur and skins had become more complex and more closely linked with the mother country; and political structures had become more uniform. Yet at the same time the adoption of large-scale slavery and cash crop agriculture in the Chesapeake, the Carolinas, and the West Indies differentiated these true slave societies from the colonies to the north.

Yet the economies of the northern colonies also rested on profits from the Atlantic trading system, the key element of which was traffic in slaves. New England sold foodstuffs and wood products to the West Indies. Pennsylvania and New York, too, found in the Caribbean a ready market for their livestock, grains, and flour. Atlantic slavery drove all the English colonial economies in these years. The West Indies colonies, especially Barbados and Jamaica, were the empire's economic engine. In 1720, their exports to Britain—chiefly 705,000 tons of sugar—were worth more than double what the combined mainland colonies produced.

Spanish settlements in America north of Mexico remained largely centered on Florida missions and on New Mexican military outposts (*presidios*) and missions during these years. The French had explored the Mississippi Valley but had not yet planted many settlements in the Great Lakes or the west. Both nations' colonists depended on indigenous people's labor and goodwill. Yet the Spanish and French presence to the south and west of the English settlements ensured future conflicts among the European powers in North America.

Chapter Review

The Growth of Anglo-American Settlements

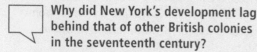 **Why did New York's development lag behind that of other British colonies in the seventeenth century?**

Granted to James the duke of York in 1664, New York remained a shadow of Boston until well into the 1720s largely because James, unlike William Penn of Pennsylvania and other proprietors, did not encourage migration with offers of land grants and religious freedom to would-be colonists. Instead, migrants traveled to New Jersey and Pennsylvania. In addition James refused a legislative assembly—which many English colonists wanted—until 1683.

A Decade of Imperial Crises: The 1670s

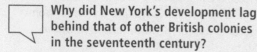 **How did settlers' interests collide with those of Native Americans?**

Settlers' and Native Americans' interests clashed in two pivotal areas: control of trade and desire for more land. New France and the Iroquois Confederacy clashed over control of the valuable fur trade, which the Iroquois had fought hard to attain. Bitter battles and attacks lasted for twenty years, before culminating in a neutrality treaty. Similarly, in the densely settled New England colonies in the 1670s, hostilities developed as Wampanoags led by King Philip felt threatened by the Anglo-American communities that surrounded their territory. And in Virginia Nathaniel Bacon and his followers also focused on seizing desirable interior land from Indians, ultimately attacking them and pushing them farther west.

The Atlantic Trading System

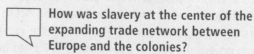 **How was slavery at the center of the expanding trade network between Europe and the colonies?**

First, the Chesapeake developed around tobacco farming, which required a vast supply of workers. Fewer English workers were available as population pressures in England eased and Restoration colonies offered land and other opportunities to would-be settlers. Tobacco growers instead turned to slave labor, as did other plantation colonies, thereby expanding the sale and transport of slaves. In addition, commodities produced by slave labor helped boost exports and trade networks, while the need to feed and clothe slaves stimulated new business opportunities for other colonies. New England, for example, profited by selling foodstuffs to feed slaves. The slave trade itself created a global economic network and tensions among European nations seeking to control the lucrative trade.

Slavery in North America and the Caribbean

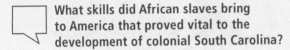

What skills did African slaves bring to America that proved vital to the development of colonial South Carolina?

African-born slaves had several skills that were crucial to the economic development of South Carolina. From a similarly semitropical climate, these slaves adapted dugout canoes from their homeland to create a key means of transportation in the many rivers of the Carolinas. Their fishing nets also proved more efficient. African cattle herding techniques aided in producing the meat and hides that were an early export from the region. Some slaves, particularly women, also knew how to cultivate rice, which was rapidly becoming a staple crop in South Carolina. The area's other cash crop—indigo (the only source of blue dye for the growing English textile industry)—similarly drew on the knowledge of slaves transported to South Carolina from the Caribbean, where indigo plantations flourished.

Forging and Testing the Bonds of Empire

How did mercantilism benefit some colonies economically and hurt others?

Mercantilism was grounded in the notion that the world contained a finite amount of wealth, and that if one nation gained, another had to lose. For England, that meant controlling colonial trade and development in ways that benefited the mother country. England passed the Navigation Acts between 1651 and 1673, which allowed only English merchants to trade in the colonies, permitted certain American products to be sold only to England or other English colonies, and required foreign goods bound for the colonies to be shipped through England so it could collect related duties. Later, England additionally prevented colonists from exporting anything that competed with English goods. For Chesapeake planters, these policies had a negative effect, preventing them from selling staple crops in foreign markets. English sugar producers in the Caribbean were initially helped, as their Brazilian competitors were driven from the market, but later suffered when they were prevented from selling their sugar elsewhere. New England benefited from the emergence of a lucrative shipbuilding industry, while the northern and middle colonies gained from trading goods not included in the Navigation Acts such as fish, flour, meat, livestock, and barrels.

Suggestions for Further Reading

Ned Blackhawk, *Violence Over the Land: Indians and Empires in the Early American West* (2006)

David Eltis and David Richardson, *Atlas of the Transatlantic Slave Trade* (2010)

Alan Gallay, *The Indian Slave Trade: The Rise of the English Empire in the American South, 1670–1717* (2002)

Eric Hinderaker, *The Two Hendricks: Untangling a Mohawk Mystery* (2010)

Andrew Knaut, *The Pueblo Revolt of 1680* (1995)

Jill Lepore, *The Name of War: King Philip's War and the Origins of American Identity* (1998)

Edmund S. Morgan, *American Slavery, American Freedom: The Ordeal of Colonial Virginia* (1975)

Mary Beth Norton, *In the Devil's Snare: The Salem Witchcraft Crisis of 1692* (2002)

Marcus Rediker, *The Slave Ship: A Human History* (2007)

Stephanie E. Smallwood, *Saltwater Slavery: A Middle Passage From Africa to American Diaspora* (2007)

Owen Stanwood, *The Empire Reformed: English America in the Age of the Glorious Revolution* (2011)

Becoming America?

4

1720–1760

D r. Alexander Hamilton was a learned man. The son of a theologian, he studied medicine at the University of Edinburgh, which boasted the best medical school in the world. But if Edinburgh was crowded with genius, it was hardly brimming with opportunity. In 1739, Hamilton lit out for the colonies, settling in Annapolis, where his older brother preached.

Dr. Hamilton quickly established himself among the town's elite, but like many migrants to the Chesapeake, he sickened in the climate. He thought travel might improve his health. In May 1744, he and a slave named Dromo set off on a four-month tour of the countryside from Maryland to Maine. An avid reader of polite literature including the new books called *novels* then flooding British presses, the doctor recorded his impressions in a journal to which he gave the Latin title *Itinerarium*.

The diversity of the colonists astonished Hamilton. In one Philadelphia tavern, he dined with "Scots, English, Dutch, Germans, and Irish; there were Roman Catholicks, Church [of England] men, Presbyterians, Quakers, Newlightmen, Methodists, Seventh day men, Moravians, Anabaptists, and one Jew," all talking politics, while a "knott of Quakers" debated the price of flour. He met rich planters from Jamaica, Antigua, and Barbados. He saw Africans everywhere. In Boston, he watched "a parade of Indian chiefs." Their leader, the Mohawk sachem Hendrick Theyanoguin, urged the assembled natives to "brighten the chain with the English, our friends, and take up the hatchet against the French, our enemies."

Hendrick, Hamilton wrote, was a "bold, intrepid fellow." In Scotland, a better man commanded deference from his inferiors. Here, there was little respect on offer. He and Dromo watched "a boxing match between a master and his servant," who had called the master a "shitten elf." These "infant countrys of America" bred "aggrandized upstarts," Hamilton wrote. About the "different ranks of men in polite nations" they knew little, and cared less.

But for all their "nastiness, impudence, and rusticity," there was a strange worldliness about "the American providences."

Chapter Outline

Geographic Expansion and Ethnic Diversity
Spanish and French Territorial Expansion | France and the Mississippi | Involuntary Migrants from Africa | Newcomers from Europe | Scots-Irish, Scots, and Germans | Maintaining Ethnic and Religious Identities

VISUALIZING THE PAST *Slaves' Symbolic Resistance*

Economic Growth and Development in British America
Commerce and Manufacturing | Wealth and Poverty | City Life | Regional Economies

"Oeconomical" Households: Families, Production, and Reproduction
Indian and Mixed-Race Families | European American Families | African American Families | Forms of Resistance

Provincial Cultures
Oral Cultures | Rituals on the "Middle Ground" | Civic Rituals | Rituals of Consumption | Tea and Madeira | Polite and Learned Culture | The Enlightenment

LINKS TO THE WORLD *Smallpox Inoculation*

A Changing Religious Culture
George Whitefield | Impact of the Awakening | Virginia Baptists

Stability and Crisis at Midcentury
Colonial Political Orders | Slave Rebellions and Internal Disorder | European Rivalries in North America | The Fall of Louisbourg | The Ohio Country | Iroquois Neutrality

LEGACY FOR A PEOPLE AND A NATION *"Self-Made Men"*

SUMMARY

Farmers' wives wore fine imported cloth, and tradesmen talked philosophy. Hamilton viewed botanical engravings in rural Maryland and a plaster copy of the Venus de Medici in Boston. He drank tea in every hamlet, coffee in every town, and rum at every crossroads. Always, there was talk of international politics, especially "the dreaded French war"—King George's War—that once again drew the raw edges of the empire into the maelstrom of European rivalries.

As many travelers to North America in the eighteenth century noticed, they did things differently in the colonies. People didn't stay within their stations. Property was held more widely, and opinions voiced more readily, in more languages, than anywhere in Europe. After 1720, a massive migration of European and African peoples changed the North American landscape. Ethnic diversity became especially pronounced in the cities. The British colonies south of New England drew the largest number of newcomers, whose arrival swelled the population, altered political balances, and introduced new religious sects. Unwilling immigrants (slaves and transported convicts) likewise clustered in the middle and southern colonies. The rough equality Hamilton witnessed among whites was everywhere built upon the bondage of Africans and their descendants.

This polyglot population hardly resembled the places from which its peoples had been drawn. But in some ways, the America Hamilton encountered was more British than ever. A flood of European and especially British goods allowed genteel and middling folks to fashion themselves in the image of fashionable Britons. Educated colonists participated in transatlantic intellectual life. Yet most colonists, whether free or enslaved, worked with their hands daily from dawn to dark. The social and economic distance among different ranks of Anglo-Americans had widened noticeably.

In 1720, much of North America remained under Indian control. Four decades later, indigenous peoples still dominated the interior, yet their lives had been indelibly altered by the expansion of European settlements. France extended its reach from the St. Lawrence to the Gulf of Mexico. Spanish outposts spread east and west from a New Mexican heartland. The British colonies stretched from the Atlantic coast to the Appalachian Mountains, where they threatened French and Indian claims. North America's resources were worth fighting for, and as European conflicts crossed the Atlantic once again during the 1740s (see Table 4.1 on page 104), many colonists in British North America defended King George II's empire against other nations jockeying for control of the continent.

As you read this chapter, keep the following questions in mind:

- **What were the effects of demographic, geographic, and economic changes on Europeans, Africans, and Indian nations alike?**

- **What were the key elements of eighteenth-century provincial cultures?**

- **In what ways was North America becoming less like Britain at midcentury? In what ways were colonists *more* British than before?**

Chronology

1690	Locke's *Essay Concerning Human Understanding* published, a key example of Enlightenment thought
1718	New Orleans founded in French Louisiana
1721–22	Smallpox epidemic in Boston leads to first widespread adoption of inoculation in America
1732	Founding of Georgia
1733	Printer John Peter Zenger tried for and acquitted of "seditious libel" in New York
1737	"Walking Purchase" of Delaware and Shawnee lands in Pennsylvania
1739	Stono Rebellion (South Carolina)

	George Whitefield arrives in America; Great Awakening broadens
1739–48	King George's War affects American economies
1740s	Black population of the Chesapeake begins to grow by natural increase
1741	New York City "conspiracy" reflects whites' continuing fears of slave revolts
1745	Fall of Louisbourg to New England troops; returned to France in 1748
1751	Franklin's *Experiments and Observations on Electricity* published, important American contribution to Enlightenment science
1760–75	Peak of eighteenth-century European and African migration to English colonies

Geographic Expansion and Ethnic Diversity

What spurred population growth in the British colonies in the thirty years before 1775?

In the mid-eighteenth century, dramatic population growth, along with geographic expansion, characterized the British mainland colonies. In 1700, only about 250,000 European Americans and African Americans resided in the colonies. Thirty years later, that number had more than doubled, reaching 2.5 million by 1775.

Migration from Scotland, Ireland, England, Germany, and especially Africa contributed to the growth, but most of the gain stemmed from natural increase. Once the difficult early decades of settlement had passed, the population of Britain's mainland colonies doubled approximately every twenty-five years. A chief cause of this growth was women's youthful age at first marriage (early twenties for Euro-Americans, late teens for African Americans). Married women became pregnant every two to three years and normally bore five to ten children. Since the colonies, especially those north of Virginia, were relatively healthful places to live, a large proportion of children who survived infancy reached maturity and began families of their own. The result was a young, rapidly growing population; about half the people in Anglo America were under sixteen years old in 1775. (By contrast, less than one-quarter of the U.S. population is currently under sixteen.)

Spanish and French Territorial Expansion

British North America's growing population was sandwiched between the Atlantic coast (on the east) and Appalachian Mountains (on the west). By contrast, Spanish and French territories expanded across the continent while their populations increased only modestly. Nevertheless, French and Spanish geographic expansion had far-reaching effects on native peoples.

Venturing into the Mississippi Valley in the early eighteenth century, the French and Spanish encountered powerful Indian nations like the Quapaws,

Osages, and Caddos. A few Europeans—priests, soldiers, farmers, traders, ranchers—met native peoples who wanted access to manufactured goods, and who accordingly sought friendly relations. The Spanish and French invaders had to adapt to Indian diplomatic and cultural practices. French officials, for example, often complained of being forced to endure lengthy calumet ceremonies; Spaniards, unaccustomed to involving women in diplomacy, had to accede to Texas Indians' use of female representatives. The European nations established neighboring outposts in the lower Mississippi region in 1716—the French at Natchitoches (west of the Mississippi), the Spaniards at nearby Los Adaes (see Map 4.1). France had already settled Biloxi Bay (in the modern state of Mississippi) in 1699, and strengthened its presence near the Gulf of Mexico by establishing New Orleans in 1718.

Spaniards focused first on Texas (establishing San Antonio in 1718), and later on the region they called Alta (upper) California. After learning that Russians were planning to colonize the region, they sent expeditions north from their missions in Baja California. From a base at San Diego, where the Franciscan Junipero Serra set up the first mission in Alta California in 1769, they traveled to Monterey Bay. There, in 1770, they claimed Alta California for Spain. Over the next decades, they established presidios and missions along the coast from modern San Francisco to San Diego.

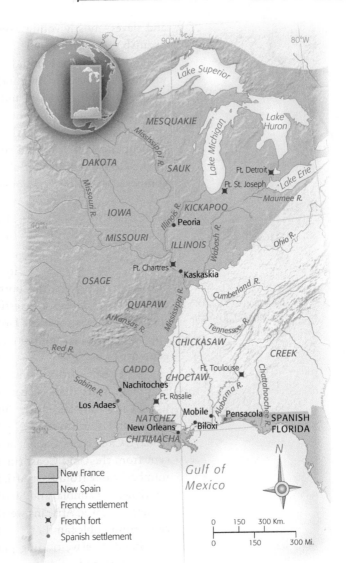

MAP 4.1
Louisiana, ca. 1720
By 1720, French forts and settlements dotted the Mississippi River and its tributaries in the interior of North America. Two isolated Spanish outposts were situated near the Gulf of Mexico. Source: Copyright © Cengage Learning 2015

France and the Mississippi

French settlements north of New Orleans served as the glue of empire. *Coureurs de bois* (literally, "forest runners") used rivers and lakes to carry goods between Quebec and the new Louisiana territory. Indians traded furs and hides for guns, ammunition, and other items. The population of the largest French settlements, known collectively as *le pays de Illinois* ("the Illinois country"), never totaled much above three thousand.

French expansion reshaped native alliances elsewhere. For example, the equestrian Comanches of the Plains, now able to trade with the French, no longer needed Spanish goods—or their previous allies, the Utes. Deprived of powerful partners, the Utes negotiated peace with New Mexico in 1752. Once enslaved by Spaniards, Utes enslaved Paiutes and other nonequestrian peoples. They exchanged hides and slaves—mostly young women—for horses and metal goods until the end of Spanish rule in the region.

In French officials' minds, Louisiana's paramount goals were protection of the valuable Caribbean islands and prevention of Spanish and British expansion. But the profit-seeking farmers and Indian traders who settled there demanded slaves from the French government. In 1719 officials acquiesced, dispatching more than six thousand Africans, mostly from Senegal, over the next decade. Yet Louisiana's residents never developed a successful plantation economy. They did raise some tobacco and indigo, which, along with skins and hides obtained from the Indians, composed the colony's major exports.

Involuntary Migrants from Africa

Elsewhere in the Americas, slavery took hold more firmly during the eighteenth century. In all, more Africans than Europeans came to the Americas, the majority of them as slaves and about half between 1700 and 1800. Most were transported to Brazil or the Caribbean, primarily in British or Portuguese vessels. The estimated 280,000 people imported before 1780 into the region that became the United States amounted to less than 3 percent of the approximately 12.3 million enslaved people brought to the Americas during the existence of slavery.

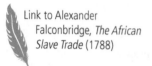

Link to Alexander Falconbridge, *The African Slave Trade* (1788)

Slaves came from many different ethnic groups and regions of Africa (see Map 4.2). More than 40 percent embarked from West Central Africa (modern Congo and Angola), nearly 20 percent from the Bight of Benin (modern Togo, Benin, and southwestern Nigeria), about 13 percent from the Bight of Biafra (today's Cameroon, Gabon, and southeastern Nigeria), and approximately 9 percent from the Gold Coast (modern Ghana and neighboring countries). Smaller numbers came from East Africa, the Windward Coast, and the Rice Coast (modern Senegal, Gambia, and Sierra Leone). Thousands, possibly tens of thousands, of these enslaved Africans were Muslims. Some were literate in Arabic, and some came from noble families.

Standard slave-trading practice, in which a vessel loaded its human cargo at one port and sold it in another, meant that people from the same broad area tended to arrive in the Americas together. That tendency was heightened by planter partiality for particular ethnic groups. Virginians, for example, purchased primarily Igbos from the Bight of Biafra, whereas South Carolinians and Georgians selected Senegambians and people from West Central Africa. Rice planters' desire to purchase Senegambians, who cultivated rice in their homeland, is easily explained, but historians disagree about the reasons underlying the other preferences.

Especially after 1740, American-born people of African descent came to dominate the mainland enslaved population because of natural increase. Although about 40 percent of the Africans were male, women and children together composed a majority of slave imports; planters valued girls and women for their reproductive and productive capacities. All the colonies passed laws to ensure that the children of enslaved women were born into slavery. A planter who owned adult female slaves could engineer the growth of his labor force without additional major purchases of workers.

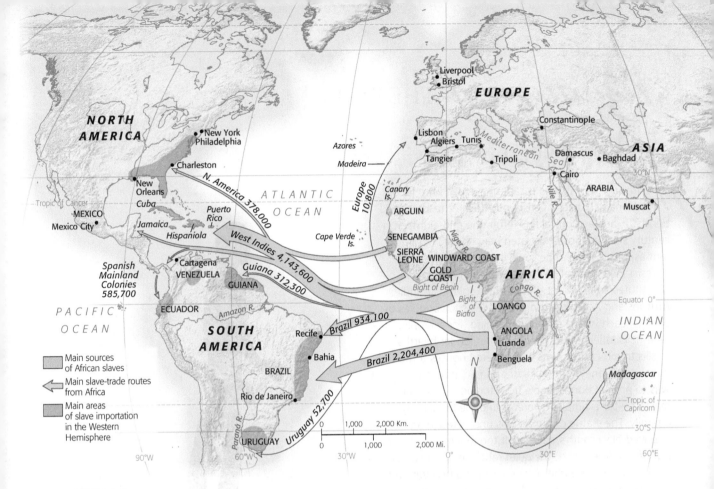

MAP 4.2

Major Origins and Destinations of Africans Enslaved in the Americas

As this schematic map shows, enslaved Africans were drawn from many regions of western Africa (with some coming from the interior of the continent) and were shipped to areas throughout the Americas. Source: Copyright © Cengage Learning 2015

Newcomers from Europe

About 350,000 Europeans moved to mainland British North America between 1700 and 1780, most of them after 1730. Influenced by mercantilist thought, British authorities had come to regard a large, industrious population at home as an asset. Thus, they discouraged emigration, except for the deportation of such "undesirables" as vagabonds and Jacobite rebels (supporters of the deposed Stuart monarchs). Instead, they recruited German and French Protestants to the colonies by offering free land, religious toleration, and, after 1740, relaxed citizenship (naturalization) requirements.

The most successful migrants came well prepared, having learned from earlier arrivals that land and resources were abundant, but that they would need capital. Penniless bound laborers, who constituted approximately 40 percent of the newcomers, did less well.

Worst off were the 50,000 or so migrants who arrived as convicted felons sentenced to transportation for two to fourteen years. Typically unskilled and perhaps one-third female, they were dispatched most often to Maryland to work in tobacco fields, as ironworkers, or as household servants.

Visualizing THE PAST

Slaves' Symbolic Resistance

Although revolts and escapes have been the focus of many studies of enslaved Africans' resistance to bondage, archaeological finds from the mid-eighteenth century such as those illustrated here reveal important aspects of slaves' personal lives and other forms of resistance. The set of objects found in Annapolis constitutes a *minkisi,* or West African spiritual bundle. Africans and African Americans placed such bundles of objects, each with a symbolic meaning (for example, bent nails reflected the power of fire), under hearths or sills to direct the spirits who entered houses through doors or chimneys. The *minkisi's* primary purpose was to protect bondspeople from the power of their masters—for example, by preventing the breakup of a family. The statue of a man was uncovered in an enslaved blacksmith's quarters. It too reflects resistance, but of a different sort: the quiet rebellion of a talented craftsman who used his master's iron and his own time and skill to create a remarkable object. What can we learn about enslaved people's lives from such artifacts as these, even though the illiterate bondspeople left no written records?

Artifact found in an excavation in Alexandria, Virginia.

A minkisi *from the eighteenth century found under the floor of the Charles Carroll house in Annapolis, Maryland.*

Scots-Irish, Scots, and Germans

One of the largest groups of immigrants—about 143,000—came from Ireland or Scotland, largely as families. About 66,000 Scots-Irish, descendants of Presbyterian Scots who had settled in the north of Ireland during the seventeenth century, joined some 35,000 people who came to America from Scotland (see Figure 4.1). Another 42,000 Protestants and Catholics migrated from southern Ireland. High rents, poor harvests, and religious discrimination (in Ireland) combined to push people from their homelands.

Irish immigrants usually landed in Philadelphia or New Castle, Delaware. Many moved into the Pennsylvania backcountry. Later migrants moved to the backcountry of Maryland, Virginia, and the Carolinas, where they squatted on land belonging to Indians, land speculators, or colonial governments. They gained a reputation for lawlessness, drinking, and fighting.

Migrants from Germany and German-speaking areas of Switzerland numbered about 85,000 between 1730 and 1755. They, too, usually came in family groups and landed in Philadelphia. Like earlier English indentured servants, many paid for their passage by contracting to work as servants for a specified period. Germans tended to settle together when they could. Many moved west into Pennsylvania and then south into the backcountry of Maryland and Virginia. Others landed in Charles Town and settled in the Carolina interior. The Germans belonged to a

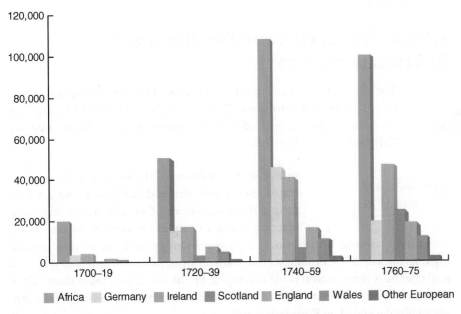

FIGURE 4.1

Atlantic Origins of Migrants to Thirteen Mainland Colonies of British North America, 1700–1775

Immigrants from Ireland, Scotland, and Germany significantly outnumbered those from England throughout the eighteenth century. But as this figure shows, forced migrants from Africa comprised by far the largest number of new arrivals in the mainland British colonies. In the Caribbean colonies, the pattern would be yet more pronounced.

(Source for European numbers: Aaron Fogelman, "Migrations to the Thirteen British North American Colonies, 1700–1775: New Estimates," *The Journal of Interdisciplinary History,* vol. 22, no. 4 (Spring 1992), pp. 691–709. Source for African numbers: The Trans-Atlantic Slave Trade Database, available online at: http://www.slavevoyages.org. Accessed August 1, 2012.)

variety of Protestant sects—primarily Lutheran, German Reformed, and Moravian— and added to the religious diversity of Pennsylvania.

The most concentrated period of colonial immigration fell between 1760 and 1775, when more than 125,000 free migrants and 100,000 enslaved people arrived— nearly 10 percent of the population of British North America. Late-arriving free immigrants had to crowd into the cities or move to the edges of settlement; land elsewhere was occupied (see Map 4.3).

Maintaining Ethnic and Religious Identities

Huguenots French Calvinist dissenters from that country's dominant Catholicism.

These migration patterns made British North America one of the most diverse places on earth. How readily migrants assimilated into Anglo-American culture depended on patterns of settlement, group size, and migrants' cultural ties. The French Protestants (**Huguenots**) who migrated to Charles Town or New York City were unable to sustain their language or their religious practices for more than two generations, whereas Huguenots who settled in the Hudson Valley remained recognizably French and Calvinist for a century. Small groups of colonial Jews maintained a distinct identity wherever they settled. In places like New York City, Newport, Savannah, and Kingston, Jamaica, they established synagogues and worked actively to preserve their faith and culture. Larger groups of migrants (Germans, Irish, and Scots) found it easier to sustain European ways.

Economic Growth and Development in British America

How were the colonies' economic fates increasingly linked to world markets?

The dramatic increase in the population of British America caused colonial economies to grow. By contrast, New Spain's northern borderlands stagnated, and of France's American possessions, only the Caribbean islands flourished.

Commerce and Manufacturing

In British North America, the rising population generated ever-greater demand for goods and services, fueling the development of small-scale colonial manufacturing and a complex network of internal trade. Iron making became British America's largest industry, with production surpassing England's by 1775. Colonists built roads, bridges, mills, and stores to serve new settlements. A lively coastal trade developed; by the late 1760s, more than half of the vessels leaving Boston sailed to other mainland colonies. The colonies no longer wholly depended on European goods.

Settlers' prosperity nevertheless depended heavily on overseas demand for tobacco, rice, indigo, fish, and timber products. Selling such items earned the colonists the credit they needed to buy English and European goods. Between 1700 and 1775, colonists' purchases of British manufactures increased from 5 percent to 25 percent of Britain's total exports. But when British demand for American products slowed, the colonists' income and purchasing power dropped, leading to economic downswings.

Wealth and Poverty

Despite fluctuations, the American economy grew during the eighteenth century. That growth produced better standards of living for all property-owning Americans. Early in the century, as the price of British manufactures fell, more households acquired amenities such as chairs and earthenware dishes. Diet also improved as trade brought more varied foodstuffs. After 1750, luxury items could be found in the homes of the wealthy, and the "middling sort" imported English ceramics. Even the poorest property owners had better household goods.

While wealthy Americans improved their position relative to other colonists, new arrivals had less opportunity for advancement than their predecessors. Even so, few free settlers in rural areas (where about 95 percent of the colonists lived) appear to have been truly poor. By 1750, at least two-thirds of rural householders owned their own land.

City Life

Nowhere was the maturation of the colonial economy more evident than in the port cities of British North America. By 1760, Boston (with a population around 15,600), New York (18,000), and fast-growing Philadelphia (nearly 24,000) had become provincial British cities on the scale of Bristol and Liverpool. Unlike rural colonists, city dwellers purchased their food and wood. They lived by the clock rather than the sun, and men's jobs frequently took them away from their households.

Early American cities also saw growing extremes of wealth and poverty. By the last quarter of the eighteenth century, some of the largest merchant families—such as the Hancocks in Boston—had amassed fortunes their forebears could not have imagined. Yet roughly one-fifth of Philadelphia's workforce was enslaved, and blacks comprised nearly 15 percent of the population of New York City. White or black, the families of urban laborers lived on the edge of destitution.

Even some of the poorest city people—common sailors, prostitutes—had extensive contact with worlds far beyond their homes. By 1760,

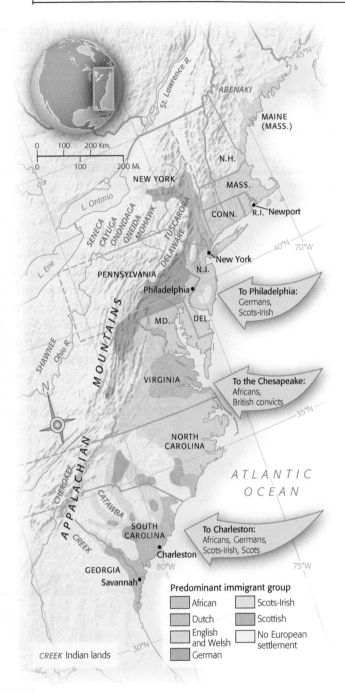

MAP 4.3

Non-English Ethnic Groups in the British Colonies, ca. 1775

Non-African immigrants arriving in the years after 1720 were pushed to the peripheries of settlement, as is shown by these maps. Scottish, Scots-Irish, French, and German newcomers had to move to the frontiers. The Dutch remained where they had originally settled in the seventeenth century. Africans were concentrated in coastal plantation regions.

Source: Copyright © Cengage Learning 2015

most substantial towns had at least one weekly newspaper. The press offered the latest "advices from London" (usually two to three months old), news from other colonies, and local reports. Newspapers were available (and often read aloud) at taverns and coffeehouses, so people who could not afford or read them could learn the news.

King George's War Also known as the War of Austrian Succession, started out as a conflict between Britain and Spain, but then escalated when France sided with Spain.

Regional Economies

Within this overall picture, broad regional patterns emerged, heightened by **King George's War**, also called the War of the Austrian Succession (1739–1748). The war created strong demand for ships and sailors, thus invigorating the economy of New England. But when the shipbuilding boom ended, the economy stagnated.

The war and its aftermath brought prosperity to the middle colonies and the Chesapeake, where fertile soil and a long growing season produced an abundance of grain. After 1748, when several poor harvests in Europe caused flour prices to rise, Philadelphia and New York took the lead in the foodstuffs trade. In the Chesapeake, the beginnings of grain cultivation changed settlement patterns by encouraging the development of port towns (like Baltimore) where merchants and shipbuilders established businesses to handle the new trade.

In South Carolina, rice and indigo fields were periodically devastated by hurricanes, causing hardship and bankruptcies. Yet after 1730, when Parliament removed rice from the list of products enumerated by the Navigation Acts, South Carolinians prospered by trading directly with Europe. The outbreak of war disrupted that trade. The colony entered a depression that did not end until the 1760s. Overall, though, South Carolina experienced rapid economic growth. By the time of the Revolution,

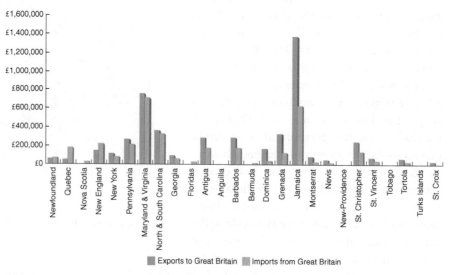

FIGURE 4.2

Trade Revenue from the British Colonies in 1769

As this figure shows, the different regions of the British mainland colonies had distinct trading patterns with Britain. New England imported more than it exported; much of its export trade was with the Caribbean. The exports of the Chesapeake colonies (especially tobacco) and the Carolinas (rice and indigo) were more significant, but the value of sugar from Jamaica dwarfed the produce of all the other British colonies.

(Source: David MacPherson, *Annals of Commerce, Manufactures, Fisheries and Navigation, with Brief Notices of the Arts and Sciences Connected with them, Containing the Commercial Transactions of the British Empire and Other Countries* (1805), volume III, p. 495.)

its freeholders had the highest average wealth in continental Anglo America, though the wealth of Barbadian and Jamaican planters dwarfed even theirs.

The newest British settlement, Georgia, was chartered in 1732 as a haven for English debtors released from prison. Its founder, **James Oglethorpe**, envisioned Georgia as a garrison whose farmers would defend the southern flank of English settlement against Spanish Florida. To ensure that all adult men could serve as the colony's armed protectors, Georgia's charter prohibited slavery. But Carolina rice planters won the removal of the restriction in 1751. Thereafter, Georgia developed into a rice-planting slave society.

James Oglethorpe Founder of Georgia colony.

"Oeconomical" Households: Families, Production, and Reproduction

How did European American families differ from those of Indians or African Americans?

Throughout the colonial era and well into the nineteenth century, the household was the basic unit of economic production, and economic production was the overriding concern of American families. Indeed, the Greek word *oikos*, meaning "household," is also the root of the English word *economy*. Seventeenth-century English writers often used *oeconomie* to discuss household and family matters. Families constituted the chief mechanisms for both production and consumption, yet family forms and structures varied widely.

Indian and Mixed-Race Families

Once Europeans established dominance in any region, Indians there could no longer pursue traditional modes of subsistence. That led to unusual family structures as well as new economic strategies. In New England, Algonquian husbands and wives often could not live together, for adults supported themselves by working separately (perhaps wives as domestic servants, husbands as sailors). Some native women married African American men, unions encouraged by sexual imbalances in both populations. And in New Mexico, detribalized Navajos, Pueblos, Paiutes, and Apaches employed as servants by Spanish settlers clustered in small borderlands towns. Known as *genizaros*, they lost contact with Indian cultures, instead living on the fringes of Latino society.

Wherever the population contained relatively few European women, sexual liaisons occurred between European men and Indian women. The resulting mixed-race people, whom Spanish colonists called *mestizos* and French settlers designated *métis*, often served as go-betweens, navigating the intersection of two cultures. In New France and the Anglo-American backcountry, many of the children of such families became Native American leaders. By contrast, in the Spanish borderlands, the offspring of Europeans and *genizaros* were considered inferior. Often denied legal marriage, they bore generations of "illegitimate" children of various racial mixtures, giving rise in Latino society to multiple labels describing precise degrees of skin color.

European American Families

Eighteenth-century Anglo-Americans referred to all the people who occupied one household (including servants or slaves) as a family. In 1790, the average home in the United States contained 5.7 free people. Few included grandparents or other extended kin. The head of the household represented it to the outside world, voting in elections, managing the finances, and holding legal authority over the rest of the family—his wife, children, and servants or slaves. In the eyes of the law, wives were *femes covert*, their personhood "covered" by their husbands.

In English, French, and Spanish America, the vast majority of European families supported themselves through farming and raising livestock. Household tasks were allocated by sex. The mistress took responsibility for what Anglo-Americans called "indoor affairs." She and her female helpers prepared food, cleaned the house, and washed and made clothing. Women's work—often performed while pregnant, nursing, or sometimes both—was unremitting.

The husband and his male helpers, responsible for "outdoor affairs," planted and cultivated fields, built fences, chopped wood, harvested and marketed crops, tended livestock, and butchered cattle and hogs. Farmwork was so extensive that no married couple could do it alone. If childless, they hired servants or purchased slaves.

African American Families

Most African American families lived as components of European American households. More than 95 percent of colonial African Americans were held in bondage. In South Carolina, a majority of the population was of African descent; in Georgia, about half; and in the Chesapeake, 40 percent. Portions of the Carolina low country were nearly 90 percent African American by 1790.

In the North, the scarcity of other blacks made it difficult for bondspeople to form households. In the Chesapeake, men and women who regarded themselves as married (slaves could not legally wed) frequently lived in different quarters or on different plantations. On large Carolina and Georgia rice plantations, enslaved couples usually lived together and accumulated property by working for themselves after completing daily "tasks." Everywhere, slave family ties were forged against the threat of separation by sale.

Forms of Resistance

Because all British colonies permitted slavery, bondspeople had few options for escaping servitude other than fleeing to Florida, where the Spanish offered protection. Some recently arrived Africans stole boats or ran off to join the Indians or establish independent communities. Others made their way to cities like Philadelphia, where they might melt into small communities of free black laborers and artisans.

Among American-born slaves, family ties strongly affected the decision to "steal" oneself by running away. Many owners therefore kept families together for practical reasons. Most escaped slaves advertised in the newspapers were young men; it was harder for women with children to escape.

Although colonial slaves rarely rebelled collectively, they resisted in other ways. Bondspeople rejected owners' attempts to commandeer their labor on Sundays without compensation. Links among families also helped to ameliorate the uncertainties of existence under slavery. If parents and children were separated by sale, other relatives helped with child rearing.

Most slave families carved out some autonomy, especially in their working and spiritual lives, and particularly in the Lower South. Some African Americans preserved traditional beliefs or Islamic faith. Others converted to Christianity (often retaining some African elements), comforted by the Bible's promise that all would be free and equal in heaven. Slaves in South Carolina and Georgia jealously guarded their customary ability to control their time after completing their "tasks." On Chesapeake tobacco plantations, slaves planted their own gardens, trapped, and fished to supplement their minimal diet. Late in the century, some Chesapeake planters began to hire slaves out to others, often allowing the workers to keep a small part of their earnings.

Provincial Cultures

How did rituals function in colonial America?

The early American household was a nursery of culture, a term with many, sometimes competing definitions. When anthropologists speak of culture, they typically mean the customs and rituals that define a community—its folkways, in other words. Where folkways belong to the many, learned or "high" culture—art, literature, philosophy, and science—may be the realm of the few. Yet folkways interact with the life of the mind, and cultures are always plural. In some respects, diverse, increasingly stratified North American cultures grew more British as the colonies became more fully integrated provinces of empire. But in other ways, as Dr. Hamilton learned, the ragged outer margins of the British realm fashioned very distinctive cultures indeed.

Oral Cultures

Most people in North America were illiterate. Those who could read often could not write. Parents, older siblings, or widows who needed extra income taught youngsters to read; middling boys and genteel girls might learn to write in private schools. Few Americans other than some Anglican missionaries tried to instruct enslaved children; masters feared literate slaves, who could forge documents to pass as free. And few Indian converts learned European literacy skills.

Thus, the everyday cultures of colonial North America were primarily oral and—at least through the first half of the eighteenth century—intensely local. Household and public rituals served as the chief means through which the colonists forged cultural identities and navigated the boundaries among them.

Rituals on the "Middle Ground"

Particularly important rituals developed on what the historian Richard White has termed the "middle ground"—the psychological and geographical space in which Indians and Europeans encountered each other, primarily via trade or warfare.

When Europeans sought to trade with Indians, they encountered indigenous systems of exchange that stressed gift giving rather than buying and selling. Successful bargaining required French and English traders to present Indians with gifts (cloth, rum, gunpowder, and other goods) before negotiating for pelts and skins. Only after those gifts were reciprocated could formal trading proceed.

Civic Rituals

Ceremonial occasions reinforced identities within as well as boundaries between cultures. New England governments proclaimed days of thanksgiving (for good harvests, military victories, and other "providences") and days of fasting and prayer (to lament war, drought, or epidemic). Everyone was expected to participate. Because able-bodied men between the ages of sixteen and sixty were required to serve in local militias, monthly musters also brought townsfolk together.

In the Chesapeake, widely spaced farms meant that communities came together less frequently. Ritual life centered on court and election days. When the county court met, men came to file lawsuits, appear as witnesses, or serve as jurors. Court attendance provided civic education; men watched to learn what their neighbors expected of them. Elections served a similar purpose, for property-holding men voted in public. An election official, often flanked by the candidates for office, called each man forward to declare his preference. The gentleman for whom the ballot was cast would then thank the voter. Later, the candidates treated their supporters to rum.

Throughout colonial North America, the punishment of criminals reminded the community of proper behavioral standards. Public hangings and whippings, along with orders to sit in the stocks, expressed a community's outrage and restored harmony.

Elizabeth Murray, the subject of this 1769 painting by John Singleton Copley, was the wife of James Smith, a wealthy rum distiller. Her fashionable dress and pose would seem to mark her as a lady of leisure, yet both before and during her marriage this Scottish immigrant ran a successful dry goods shop in Boston. She thus simultaneously catered to and participated in the new culture of consumption.

Rituals of Consumption

By 1770, Anglo-Americans spent roughly one-quarter of their household budgets on consumer goods. Since similar British imports flooded shop counters from Maine to Georgia, such purchases established cultural links among the residents of North America, creating what historians have termed "an empire of goods."

Seventeenth-century settlers had acquired necessities by bartering with neighbors or ordering from a home-country merchant. By the middle of the eighteenth century, specialized shops proliferated in colonial towns and cities. Colonists would take time to "go shopping," a novel and pleasurable leisure activity. Buyers confronted a dazzling array of possibilities and fashioned their identities by choosing among them. Some historians have termed this shift a "consumer revolution."

The purchase of an object—for example, a mirror or some beautiful imported fabric—initiated a series of consumption rituals. Consumers proudly deployed their purchases (and thus their status and taste): hanging the mirror prominently on a wall, sewing the fabric into a special piece of clothing. A prosperous man might hire an artist to paint his family using imported objects and wearing fine clothing, thereby creating a pictorial record to be admired and passed down as a kind of cultural inheritance.

Poor and rural people similarly took pleasure even in inexpensive purchases. Backcountry storekeepers accepted bartered goods; one Virginia woman traded hens and chickens for a pewter dish. Slaves exchanged cotton they grew in their free time for ribbons and hats.

Tea and Madeira

Tea drinking, a consumption ritual largely controlled by women, played an important role throughout Anglo America. Households with aspirations to genteel status purchased pots, cups, strainers, sugar tongs, even special tables. Tea provided a focal point for socializing and, because of its cost, served as a marker of cosmopolitan status. Poor households consumed tea as well, but without the fancy equipment used by their better-off neighbors.

Madeira wine, imported from the Portuguese islands, had also become a favored drink of the elite by 1770. Serving the wine required specialized accoutrements and elaborate ceremony; purchasing it involved considerable expense. In 1784, one Philadelphia merchant's spending on Madeira and other exotic liquors equaled the combined annual budgets of two artisan families.

Polite and Learned Culture

Wealthy colonists spent their money ostentatiously. They built large brick homes of the neoclassical style newly fashionable in England, with columns, symmetrical floor plans, and an array of specialized rooms.

Built in 1730, William Byrd's grand home, which he called Westover, reflects the genteel aspirations of a new generation of British Americans. Byrd, one of Virginia's wealthiest planters, had spent time in London, and he designed his James River plantation according to the most current English tastes, with an emphasis on symmetry and a highly theatrical entrance. Byrd's diaries reveal the uneasy combination of cosmopolitan refinement and slaveholding barbarism that marked the daily lives of elites in the southern colonies.

Andre Jenny/Alamy

The grandest houses in the colonies would barely have qualified as outbuildings of England's great country houses, yet they were far more elaborate than the homes of earlier settlers. Sufficiently well-off to enjoy "leisure" time (a first for North America), genteel Euro-Americans also cultivated polite manners, adopting stylized forms of address and paying attention to "proper" comportment.

Although the effects of accumulated wealth were most pronounced in British America, elite families in New Mexico, Louisiana, and Quebec also fashioned genteel cultures that distinguished them from the "lesser sort." One historian has termed these processes "the refinement of America."

Refined gentlemen prided themselves not only on their possessions, but also on their education and on their intellectual connections to Europe. Many had been tutored by private teachers; some attended college. (Harvard, the first colonial college, founded in 1636, was joined by William and Mary in 1693, Yale in 1701, and later by several others, including Princeton in 1747.) By the 1740s, aspiring colonial gentlemen regularly traveled to London and Edinburgh to complete their educations in law or medicine, and to Italy to become connoisseurs of art and antiquities.

American women were largely excluded from advanced education, with the exception of devout women who joined nunneries in Canada or Louisiana. Instead, genteel daughters perfected womanly accomplishments like French (rather than Latin), needlework, and musicianship. Even relatively educated women including John Adams's wife Abigail and Benjamin Franklin's sister Jane bemoaned their scant learning and poor spelling.

Yet women, like men, were part of a burgeoning world of print in Anglo America. There were more than a thousand private libraries in seventeenth-century Virginia. In Boston, the Mather family's collection numbered several thousand titles by 1700. Booksellers in cities and towns offered a wide selection of titles imported from England and an increasing number printed in the colonies. The number of newspapers grew rapidly as well, from three journals in 1720 to 31 in 1770. Those who could not afford to buy newspapers perused them in coffeehouses, and those who could not afford to buy books might read them in new civic institutions called libraries. Benjamin Franklin, a candle-maker's son who made his living as a printer, founded the Library Company of Philadelphia, the first subscription library in North America, in 1731.

The Enlightenment

Enlightenment Intellectual revolution that elevated reason, science, and logic.

Spreading through travel and print and polite conversation, the intellectual currents known as the **Enlightenment** deeply affected American provincials. Around 1650, some European thinkers began to analyze nature to determine the laws governing the universe. They conducted experiments to discover general principles underlying phenomena like the motions of planets. Enlightenment philosophers sought knowledge through reason and challenged previously unquestioned assumptions. **John Locke**'s *Essay Concerning Human Understanding* (1690), for example, disputed the notion that human beings are born imprinted with innate ideas. All knowledge, Locke asserted, derives from observations.

John Locke British philosopher and major Enlightenment thinker; known for his emphasis on the power of human reasoning.

The Enlightenment supplied educated Europeans and Americans with a common vocabulary and a unified worldview, one that insisted the enlightened eighteenth century was better, and wiser, than ages past. A prime example of America's

Smallpox Inoculation

Smallpox, the world's greatest killer of human beings, repeatedly ravaged North American colonists and Indians. Thus, when the vessel *Seahorse* arrived in Boston from the Caribbean in April 1721 carrying smallpox-infected passengers, authorities quarantined the ship. But it was too late: smallpox escaped into the city, and by June several dozen were afflicted.

The Reverend Cotton Mather, a member of London's Royal Society (an Enlightenment organization), had read years earlier of a medical technique unknown to Europeans but widely employed in North Africa and the Middle East. Called inoculation, it involved taking pus from the pustules (or poxes) of an infected person and inserting it into a small cut on the arm of a healthy individual. With luck, that person would experience a mild case of smallpox, followed by lifetime immunity. Mather's interest was further piqued by his slave, Onesimus, a North African who had been inoculated as a youth and who described the procedure in detail.

Mather promoted inoculation as a solution to the smallpox epidemic, but nearly all the city's doctors ridiculed his ideas. Mather won only one major convert, Zabdiel Boylston, a physician and apothecary. The two men inoculated their own children and about two hundred others, despite bitter opposition. After the epidemic ended, Bostonians could see the results: of those inoculated, just 3 percent had died; among the thousands who took the disease "in the natural way," mortality was 15 percent. Even Mather's most vocal opponents thereafter supported inoculation.

Thus, through transatlantic links forged by the Enlightenment and enslavement, American colonists learned how to combat the deadliest disease.

Today, thanks to a successful vaccination campaign by the World Health Organization, smallpox has been eradicated.

An Historical
ACCOUNT
OF THE
SMALL-POX
INOCULATED
IN
NEW ENGLAND,

Upon all Sorts of Persons, *Whites, Blacks,* and of all Ages and Constitutions.

With some Account of the Nature of the Infection in the NATURAL and INOCULATED Way, and their different Effects on HUMAN BODIES.

With some short DIRECTIONS to the UNEXPERIENCED in this Method of Practice.

Humbly dedicated to her Royal Highness the Princess of WALES, by *Zabdiel Boylston,* Physician.

LONDON:
Printed for S. CHANDLER, *at the* Cross-Keys *in the* Poultry.
M.DCC.XXVI.

Private Collection/Picture Research Consultant & Archives

Several years after he and Cotton Mather combated a Boston smallpox epidemic by employing inoculation, Zabdiel Boylston published this pamphlet in London to spread the news of their success. The dedication to the Princess of Wales was designed to indicate the royal family's support of the procedure.

participation in the Enlightenment was **Benjamin Franklin**, who retired from his successful printing business in 1748 at age forty-two, thereafter devoting himself to scientific experimentation and public service. His *Experiments and Observations on Electricity* (1751) established the terminology and basic theory of electricity still used today.

Enlightenment rationalism affected politics as well. Locke's *Two Treatises of Government* (1691) and works by French and Scottish philosophers challenged a

Benjamin Franklin American who embodied Enlightenment ideas.

divinely sanctioned, hierarchical political order originating in the power of fathers over families. Men created governments and so could alter them, Locke declared. A ruler who broke the social contract and failed to protect people's rights could legitimately be ousted—peacefully or violently. Enlightenment theorists proclaimed that God's natural laws governed even monarchs. The rough and tumble political philosophy Dr. Hamilton found on his 1744 journey through the colonies offers evidence of a vernacular Enlightenment bubbling up from the lower orders as well.

A Changing Religious Culture

What was the social and political impact of the Great Awakening?

Religious observance was perhaps the most pervasive facet of eighteenth-century provincial culture. In Congregational (Puritan) churches, church leaders assigned seating to reflect standing in the community. By midcentury, wealthy men and their wives sat in privately owned pews; children, servants, slaves, and the less fortunate still sat in sex-segregated fashion in the rear, sides, or balcony of the church. Seating in Virginia's Church of England parishes also mirrored the local status hierarchy. By contrast, Quaker meetinghouses in Pennsylvania and elsewhere used an egalitarian but sex-segregated seating system.

The religious culture of the colonies began to change significantly in the mid-eighteenth century. From the mid-1730s through the 1760s, waves of revivalism—today known as the First **Great Awakening**—swept over British America, especially New England (1735–1745) and Virginia (1750s–1760s). Orthodox Calvinists sought to combat Enlightenment rationalism, which denied innate human depravity. Simultaneously, the uncertainty accompanying King George's War made colonists receptive to **evangelists'** messages.

Great Awakening Protestant revival movement that emphasized each person's urgent need for salvation by God.

evangelist A preacher or minister who enthusiastically promotes the Christian gospels.

America's revivals began in New England. In the mid-1730s, the Reverend Jonathan Edwards, a preacher and theologian in Northampton, Massachusetts, gained new youthful followers with the Calvinist message that sinners could attain salvation only by recognizing their depraved nature and surrendering completely to God's will. Parishioners of both sexes experienced an emotional release from sin, which came to be seen as a moment of conversion, a new birth.

Link to excerpts from Jonathan Edwards' "A Faithful Narrative of the Surprising Work of God, in the Conversion of Many Hundred Souls, in Northampton...."

George Whitefield English preacher who toured the colonies and played a major role in the Great Awakening.

George Whitefield

Such ecstatic conversions remained isolated until 1739, when **George Whitefield**, an Anglican clergyman already celebrated for leading revivals in Britain, crossed the Atlantic. For fifteen months, he toured the British colonies, concentrating his efforts in the major cities. One historian has termed Whitefield "the first modern celebrity" because of his skillful self-promotion. Everywhere he traveled, his fame preceded him. Thousands of free and enslaved folk turned out to listen—and to experience conversion. Whitefield's tour created new interconnections among far-flung colonies.

Established clerics initially welcomed Whitefield and his American-born imitators. Soon, however, many concluded that the "revived" religion challenged their approach to doctrine and practice. They disliked the emotional style of the revivalists, whose itinerancy also disrupted normal patterns of church attendance.

Particularly troublesome to the orthodox were the female exhorters who publicly proclaimed their right to expound God's word.

Impact of the Awakening

Opposition to the Awakening splintered congregations. "Old Lights"—orthodox clerics and their followers—engaged in bitter disputes with "New Light" evangelicals. American Protestantism fragmented further as Congregationalists and Presbyterians split into factions, and as new evangelical sects—Methodists and Baptists—gained adherents. Paradoxically, the proliferation of distinct denominations eventually fostered a willingness to tolerate religious pluralism. Where no sect could monopolize orthodoxy, denominations had to coexist if they were to exist at all.

The Awakening challenged traditional modes of thought. Revivalists' emphasis on emotion over learning undermined received wisdom about society and politics as well as religion. Some New Lights defended the rights of people to dissent from a community consensus, thereby challenging one of the fundamental tenets of colonial political life.

Virginia Baptists

The egalitarian themes of the Awakening tended to attract ordinary folk and repel the elite. By the 1760s, Baptists had gained a secure foothold in Virginia;

George Whitefield preaching, Collet, John (c.1725–80)/Private Collection/The Bridgeman Art Library

This painting by John Collet shows the charismatic evangelist George Whitefield preaching out of doors in Britain, but the same scene would have been repeated many times in the colonies, especially after the clergy of established churches denied him access to their pulpits, deeming him too radical for their liking. Note the swooning woman in the foreground; women were reputed to be especially susceptible to Whitefield's message. Is the worker offering him a mug of ale derisively or devotedly? The answer is not clear, except that the gesture underscores the diversity of Whitefield's audience—not all were genteel or middling folk.

inevitably, their beliefs and behavior clashed with the refined lifestyle of the plantation gentry.

Strikingly, almost all Virginia Baptist congregations included free and enslaved members, and some had African American majorities. Church rules applied equally to all members; interracial sexual relationships, divorce, and adultery were proscribed for all. In addition, congregations forbade masters' breaking up slave couples through sale. Yet it is easy to overstate the racial egalitarianism of Virginia evangelicals and the attractiveness of the new sects to black members. Masters censured for abusing their slaves were quickly readmitted, and African Americans totaled only 1 percent of southern evangelicals.

The Great Awakening had important social and political consequences. In some ways, the evangelicals were profoundly conservative, preaching an old-style theology. In other respects, the revivalists were recognizably modern, using the techniques of Atlantic commerce, and calling into question habitual modes of behavior in the **secular** as well as the religious realm.

secular Not specifically relating to religion or to a religious body.

Stability and Crisis at Midcentury

What were the myths and realities of colonial assemblies?

The Great Awakening points to the unsettled nature of provincial life in the mid-eighteenth century. A number of other crises—ethnic, racial, economic, and military—exposed lines of fracture within North America's diverse society. In the 1740s and 1750s, Britain expanded its claims to North American territory and to the obligations of provincials. At the same time, Anglo-American colonists felt more strongly entitled to the liberties of British subjects. And Britain and France alike came to see North America as increasingly central to their economic, diplomatic, and military strategies in Europe.

Colonial Political Orders

Men from genteel families dominated political structures, for voters (free male property holders) tended to defer to their "betters" on election days. These political leaders sought to increase the powers of elected assemblies relative to the powers of governors and other appointed officials. Assemblies began to claim privileges associated with the British House of Commons, such as initiating tax legislation and controlling the militia. Assemblies also influenced Crown appointees by threatening to withhold their salaries.

To win hotly contested elections, New York's leaders began competing openly for votes. Yet in 1735, the colony's government imprisoned newspaper editor **John Peter Zenger**, who had too vigorously criticized its actions. Defending Zenger against the charge of "seditious libel," his lawyer argued that the truth could not be defamatory, thus helping to establish a free-press principle later found in American law.

John Peter Zenger Central figure in a trial that opened the way for freedom of the press.

Assemblymen saw themselves as thwarting encroachments on colonists' British liberties—for example, by preventing governors from imposing oppressive taxes. By midcentury, they often compared the structure of their governments to Britain's mixed polity, equating their governors with the monarch, their councils with the aristocracy, and their assemblies with Britain's House of Commons. But Anglo-Americans increasingly viewed royal governors and appointed councils as potential threats to colonial ways of life. Many colonists saw the assemblies as the people's protectors. In reality, however, colonial assemblies, often controlled by dominant families, rarely responded to poorer constituents' concerns.

At midcentury, the political structures that had stabilized in a period of relative calm confronted a series of crises. Significantly, these upheavals demonstrated that the political accommodations forged in the aftermath of the **Glorious Revolution** had become inadequate to govern Britain's American empire.

Glorious Revolution Overthrow of James II in favor of William and Mary.

Stono Rebellion A slave uprising in 1739 in South Carolina.

Slave Rebellions and Internal Disorder

Early on Sunday, September 9, 1739, about twenty enslaved men, most likely Catholics from Kongo, gathered near the Stono River south of Charles Town. September fell in the midst of South Carolina's rice harvest (and thus at a time of great pressure for male Africans), and September 8 was, to Catholics, the birthday of the Virgin Mary. Seizing guns and ammunition, the rebels killed storekeepers and nearby planter families. Joined by other local bondsmen, they then headed toward Florida in hopes of finding refuge. That afternoon, however, a troop of militia attacked the fugitives, who numbered about a hundred, killing some and dispersing the rest. The colony quickly captured and executed the survivors, but rumors about escaped renegades haunted the colony for years.

News of the **Stono Rebellion** reverberated far beyond South Carolina. The press frequently reported on slave uprisings in the West Indies, but on the mainland, where slaves did not so vastly outnumber their masters, such an organized revolt was remarkable, and terrifying. Throughout British America, laws governing the behavior of African Americans were stiffened after Stono. In New York City, which had witnessed the first mainland slave revolt in 1712, the news from the South, coupled with fears of Spain generated by the outbreak of King George's War, set off a reign of terror in 1741. Thirty-one blacks and four whites were executed—gruesomely—for allegedly plotting a slave uprising under the guidance of a Spanish priest. The Stono Rebellion and the New York "conspiracy" confirmed Anglo-Americans' deepest fears about the dangers of slaveholding and revealed the assemblies' inability to prevent internal disorder.

A *James Parker*

JOURNAL
OF THE
PROCEEDINGS
IN
The Detection of the Conspiracy
FORMED BY
Some *White* People, in Conjunction with *Negro* and other *Slaves*,

FOR

Burning the City of *NEW-YORK* in AMERICA,
And Murdering the Inhabitants.

Which Conspiracy was partly put in Execution, by Burning His Majesty's House in Fort GEORGE, within the said City, on Wednesday the Eighteenth of *March*, 1741. and setting Fire to several Dwelling and other Houses there, within a few Days succeeding, And by another Attempt made in Prosecution of the same infernal Scheme, by putting Fire between two other Dwelling-Houses within the said City, on the Fifteenth Day of *February*, 1742 ; which was accidentally and timely discovered and extinguished.

CONTAINING,

I. A NARRATIVE of the Trials, Condemnations, Executions, and Behaviour of the several Criminals, at the Gallows and Stake, with their *Speeches* and *Confessions*; with Notes, Observations and Reflections occasionally interspersed throughout the Whole.
II. AN APPENDIX, wherein is set forth some additional Evidence concerning the said Conspiracy and Conspirators, which has come to Light since their Trials and Executions.
III. LISTS of the several Persons (Whites and Blacks) committed on Account of the Conspiracy ; and of the several Criminals executed; and of those transported, with the Places whereto.

By the Recorder of the City of NEW-YORK.

Quid facient Domini, audent cum talia Fures? Virg. Ecl.

NEW-YORK:
Printed by *James Parker*, at the New Printing-Office, 1744.

Daniel Horsmanden played a leading role in the prosecution of alleged conspirators who had so terrified white inhabitants of New York City in 1741. He expected many buyers for his Journal of the Proceedings in the Detection of the Conspiracy, *an exacting and often sensationalist account of the trials that had resulted in the execution of thirty-five people, thirteen of whom were burned at the stake. But by 1744, public opinion had begun to turn against the trials, which some compared to the Salem witchcraft hysteria. Horsmanden was mocked in the newspapers, and in 1748 the* Journal's *printer slashed its price, noting, "as he has been a considerable Loser by printing that Book, he proposes to sell 'em very cheap."*

European Rivalries in North America

In addition to their internal divisions, Britain's mainland colonies were surrounded by hostile, or potentially hostile, neighbors: Indians everywhere, the Spanish in Florida and along the Gulf coast, the French along the rivers and lakes that stretched from the St. Lawrence to the Mississippi. The Spanish posed little direct threat; the French were another matter. In none of the three Anglo-French wars fought between 1689 and 1748 was Britain able to shake France's hold on the American frontier (see Table 4.1 and Map 5.1).

The Fall of Louisbourg

In the North American theater of King George's War, hostilities largely played out along the northern border between British and French America. The massive French fortress at Louisbourg, on Cape Breton Island, quickly became the largest French town on the continent, with more than 4,000 settlers and some 1,500 soldiers. Privateers based at Louisbourg regularly menaced New England merchants and fishermen. In 1744, William Shirley, the royal governor of Massachusetts, hatched a scheme to seize the fort for the Crown.

Many thought Shirley's plan to conquer Louisbourg foolhardy, but in June 1745, after a two-month-long siege, the fort fell to ragtag regiments of some 4,000 colonial soldiers, most of them from Massachusetts. But when the war ended in 1748, Britain returned the fortress to France in exchange for concessions in India and the Low Countries, the imperial priorities of the moment. Massachusetts was left with staggering debt, hundreds of new widows and orphans, and needy soldiers crippled in the futile fight.

The Ohio Country

By the time King George's War ended, the crucible of North America's imperial rivalries could be found farther south, in lands west of the Appalachians and

TABLE 4.1   The Colonial Wars, 1689–1763

American Name	European Name	Dates	Participants	American Sites	Dispute
King William's War	Nine Years' War	1689–97	England, Holland versus France, Spain	New England, New York, Canada	French power
Queen Anne's War	War of Spanish Succession	1702–13	England, Holland, Austria versus France, Spain	Florida, New England	Throne of Spain
King George's War	War of Austrian Succession	1739–48	England, Holland, Austria versus France, Spain, Prussia	West Indies, New England, Canada	Throne of Austria
French and Indian War	Seven Years' War	1756–63	England versus France, Spain	Ohio Country, Canada	Possession of Ohio Country

east of the Mississippi that came to be known as the Ohio Country. The trouble started in the 1730s, as Anglo-American traders pushed west and challenged French power beyond the Appalachians. French officials' fear of British incursions increased when the Delawares and Shawnees ceded large tracts of land to Pennsylvania. In 1737, two sons of William Penn and their Iroquois allies persuaded the Delawares to sell off as much land as a man could walk in a day and a half. Then the Pennsylvania negotiators sent trained runners down prepared trails to multiply the acreage. Delawares derided the deceitful Walking Purchase as "ye Running Walk." The agreements reached by the Penn family and the Iroquois ignored the claims of both the local Indians and Scots-Irish and German squatters, all of whom were told to move. Disgruntled Delawares and Shawnees migrated west, where they joined other displaced eastern Indians who nursed similar grievances.

Claimed by both Virginia and Pennsylvania, the region to which they migrated was coveted by wealthy Virginians. In 1745, a group of land speculators organized as the Ohio Company of Virginia received a grant of nearly a third of a million acres from the House of Burgesses. The company's agents established trading posts in the crucial area where the Allegheny and Monongahela rivers join to form the Ohio. But that region was also strategically vital to the French, because the Ohio River offered access by water to French posts along the Mississippi. By the early 1750s, Pennsylvania fur traders, Ohio Company representatives, the French military, Scots-Irish and German squatters, Iroquois, Delawares, and Shawnees all jostled for position in the region.

Iroquois Neutrality Maintaining the policy of neutrality they developed in 1701, the Iroquois Confederacy manipulated the European rivals and consolidated their control over the vast regions north of Virginia and south of the Great Lakes. During Queen Anne's War and again in King George's War, they refused to commit warriors exclusively to either side, and so were showered with gifts by both. Conflict with Cherokees and Catawbas in the South gave young Iroquois warriors combat experience and replenished their population with new captives. They also cultivated peaceful relationships with Pennsylvania and Virginia; their role in treaties like the Walking Purchase furthered Iroquois domination of the Shawnees and Delawares. And they forged friendly ties with French-allied Algonquians of the Great Lakes region. But even the Iroquois could not fully control the Ohio Country, and by the late 1750s, conflict there would spread to Europe, and then around the globe.

When he traveled the colonies in 1744, Dr. Hamilton never once referred to the people who lived there as *Americans*. Nor did colonial settlers much use that term at the time. But after King George's War, and especially after the next and most convulsive of the century's Anglo-French wars, colonists began increasingly to imagine themselves as a group with shared and distinct concerns. Colonial writers began occasionally to refer to "Americans," "American colonists," or "continentals." These newly labeled Americans continued to pledge their allegiance to Britain, but some of them began to wonder whether Parliament and the Crown understood their needs and their rights.

"Self-Made Men"

American culture celebrates the "self-made man" (always someone explicitly *male*) of humble origins who gains wealth or prominence through extraordinary effort. Those most commonly cited include the nineteenth-century businessmen Andrew Carnegie (once a poor immigrant from Scotland) and John D. Rockefeller (born on a hardscrabble farm in upstate New York).

The first exemplars of this tradition lived in the eighteenth century. Benjamin Franklin's *Autobiography* chronicled his method for achieving success after beginning life as the seventeenth child of a Boston candle-maker. From such humble origins Franklin became a wealthy, influential man active in science, politics, education, and diplomacy. Yet Franklin's tale is rivaled by that of a slave who became one of the eighteenth century's leading antislavery activists. He acquired literacy, purchased his freedom, married a wealthy Englishwoman, and published a popular autobiography that predated Franklin's. His first master called him Gustavus Vassa, but when publishing his *Interesting Narrative* in 1789, he called himself Olaudah Equiano.

In that *Narrative*, Equiano said he was born in Africa in 1745, kidnapped at age eleven, and transported to Barbados and then to Virginia, where a British naval officer purchased him. For years, scholars have relied on that account for its insights into the middle passage. But evidence recently uncovered by Vincent Carretta, although confirming much of Equiano's autobiography, shows that Equiano twice identified his birthplace as Carolina and was three to five years younger than he claimed. Carretta speculates that the *Narrative* gained part of its credibility from Equiano's African birth and that admitting his real age would have raised questions about the account of his early life.

Equiano, or Vassa, thus truly "made himself," just as Benjamin Franklin and many others have done. (Franklin tended to omit, rather than alter, inconvenient parts of his personal history—for example, his illegitimate son and his ownership of slaves.) Equiano used information undoubtedly gleaned from acquaintances who *had* experienced the middle passage to craft an accurate depiction of its horrors. In the process, he became one of the first Americans to explicitly remake himself.

Summary

The decades before 1760 transformed North America. French and Spanish settlements expanded, and newcomers from Germany, Scotland, Ireland, and Africa brought their languages, customs, and religions with them to the British colonies. European immigrants were concentrated in the growing cities and in the backcountry, while most enslaved migrants from Africa lived and worked within one hundred miles of the Atlantic coast. In many areas of the colonial South, 50 to 90 percent of the population was of African origin. In the West Indies, the enslaved black majority was far larger.

The economic life of Europe's mainland North American colonies proceeded simultaneously on local and transatlantic levels. On the farms, plantations, and ranches where most colonists resided, arduous labor dominated people's lives while providing goods for consumption and sale. Simultaneously, an international trade network affected colonial economies. The wars fought by European nations during the eighteenth century created new opportunities for overseas sales and disrupted traditional markets. The fortunate few who reaped the profits of international commerce comprised the wealthy class of merchants and landowners who dominated colonial life.

A century and a half after European peoples first settled in North America, the colonies mixed diverse European, American, and African traditions into a novel cultural blend. Yet at the same time, colonists continued to identify themselves as French, Spanish, or British rather than as Americans. That did not change in the West Indies, Canada, Louisiana, or in the Spanish territory, but in the 1760s some Anglo-Americans began to realize that their interests did not necessarily coincide with those of Great Britain.

Chapter Review

Geographic Expansion and Ethnic Diversity

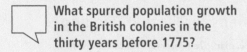 **What spurred population growth in the British colonies in the thirty years before 1775?**

Immigration—particularly of Scots-Irish and Germans—contributed to the population growth among European Americans, but the largest single factor was natural increase (live births). Once the difficult years of early settlement passed and the sex ratio evened out in the South, the population doubled every twenty-five years. Natural increase also boosted the African American enslaved population after 1740, and in some regions the slave population was further augmented by new imports of enslaved people.

Economic Growth and Development in British America

How were the colonies' economic fates increasingly linked to world markets?

As colonies became more entwined in overseas trade, their fortunes were increasingly tied to the ups and downs of those economies. Although colonists developed small-scale manufacturing and broader trade networks to meet increased local demand for goods and services, they nonetheless required external markets for their products—tobacco, rice, indigo, fish, and timber. They used the money made from these items to purchase European and English imports. If demand for American goods fell, so did colonists' income, causing economic downturns. The outbreak of King George's War, for example, increased overseas demand for grain grown in the Chesapeake and led tobacco farmers to convert more of their acreage to the crop, while New England suffered when the shipbuilding boom of the war years ended.

"Oeconomical" Households: Families, Production, and Reproduction

How did European American families differ from those of Indians or African Americans?

Anglo Americans used the word "family" to describe everyone in a household: parents, children, extended kin, and slaves. Families typically supported themselves by farming, with each member assigned a task according to gender norms. (Women did indoor work and related tasks; men did outdoor work.) After contact, extended kin became more important to Native families, particularly as they were decimated by disease. Shortages of European women in French and Spanish colonies led to increased intermarriages, with children raised in Indian villages rather than among settlers. Most African Americans were enslaved, and their families subsumed under European American households. In the Chesapeake, slaves couples who considered themselves married (despite laws prohibiting slave marriage) often lived apart, in different quarters or plantations, with children residing with mothers. On large Carolina and Georgia rice plantations, enslaved couples usually lived together and accumulated property by working for themselves after completing daily "tasks." All slave families could be destroyed by sale at any time.

Provincial Cultures

> **How did rituals function in colonial America?**

Cultural rituals played a central role in colonial life, both to create community and to reinforce social status. Civic rituals generated community involvement and revealed the behavior communities expected of their members. In New England, everyone was required to participate in official holidays or local militia musters; in the Chesapeake, rituals centered on court or election days; and public punishment of criminals throughout North America was designed to reinforce behavioral standards. Even simple rituals, such as tea-drinking, reinforced gender norms and distinctions of wealth and status. Colonists adapted rituals to facilitate trade with Indians, who had vastly different customs. Europeans seeking to trade with Indians engaged in the gift-giving system typical of native cultures before trade could begin.

A Changing Religious Culture

> **What was the social and political impact of the Great Awakening?**

Socially, the Great Awakening challenged traditional norms and patterns. A few women, for example, began to claim a right to preach, and Protestant denominations further split into the "Old Lights"—who followed traditional teachings and ministers—and the "New Light" evangelicals. While initially sparking animosity, ultimately the rise of new denominations promoted greater tolerance for religious diversity. The Great Awakening's egalitarianism also challenged the colonial tradition of deference, in which people knew their place and respected their so-called "betters." New Lights attracted ordinary people as followers and preachers and argued that the world was divided into the saved and the damned without respect to gender, age, or status.

Stability and Crisis at Midcentury

> **What were the myths and realities of colonial assemblies?**

Anglo-American assemblymen believed they safeguarded colonists' liberties from encroachments by the British government, such as oppressive taxation. Regarding Britain's appointed councils and governors as potential threats, colonists looked to assemblies as their protectors. In truth, elite, wealthy families dominated the assemblies and paid little regard to poorer constituents' concerns, nor did they reapportion themselves so that new settlements would gain representatives, which angered backcountry residents and non-English immigrants.

Suggestions for Further Reading

Richard R. Beeman, *The Varieties of Political Experience in Eighteenth-Century America* (2004)

William E. Burns, *Science and Technology in Colonial America* (2005)

Richard Bushman, *The Refinement of America: Persons, Houses, Cities* (1992)

Kathleen DuVal, *The Native Ground: Indians and Colonists in the Heart of the Continent* (2006)

Ellen Hartigan-O'Connor, *The Ties That Buy: Women and Commerce in Revolutionary America* (2009)

Rhys Isaac, *The Transformation of Virginia, 1740–1790* (1982)

Jill Lepore, *New York Burning: Liberty, Slavery, and Conspiracy in Eighteenth-Century Manhattan* (2005)

Paul W. Mapp, *The Elusive West and the Contest for Empire, 1713–1763* (2011)

Harry S. Stout, *The Divine Dramatist: George Whitefield and the Rise of Modern Evangelicalism* (1991)

David Waldstreicher, *Runaway America: Benjamin Franklin, Slavery, and the American Revolution* (2004)

The Ends of Empire

1754–1774

5

A spectacular victory demanded a stirring celebration, and the capture of Quebec from the French in September 1759 was indeed a spectacular victory. When news of this latest British triumph reached Boston, in October, town fathers proclaimed a "Day of general Rejoicing." Church bells started ringing at dawn and pealed through the day. Troops paraded down King Street, pausing to blast "Rejoicing Fires" from their muskets. As night fell, a feast for the eyes joined the sounds of celebration. Public buildings blazed with candlelight. The hills surrounding the town glowed with "large bonfires formed in a pyramidal manner." An "abundance of extraordinary Fire-Works were play'd off in almost every Street," the *Boston Gazette* reported. In the seaport's lanes and alleys, "Persons of all Ranks" joined in the revelry.

Boston's "Rejoicing" was "the greatest ever known an universal Joy," the *Gazette* declared. As word of Britain's stunning victory spread through the colonies in the waning days of 1759, similar festivities took place across Anglo America.

The celebratory mood would not last. Within months, the war in North America would be over, and the wartime business boom would go bust. By the end of the 1760s, many provincials would come to suspect King George II's grandson, George III, had turned tyrant. From Nova Scotia to Antigua, protestors against the Crown's new taxes—taxes designed to pay for costly British victories like the one at Quebec—would flood the streets. But the inhabitants of Anglo America knew none of this in the fall of 1759. Proud subjects living on the western edge of His Majesty's empire, they had little reason to anticipate that "this country" would ever be anything but British.

The American Revolution required a thorough transformation in consciousness: a shift of political allegiance from Britain to a polity that was called, at first, the United Colonies. "The Revolution was effected before the war commenced," John Adams later wrote. The true Revolution was not the war, he said, but a fundamental change "in the minds and hearts of the people."

Chapter Outline

From the Ohio Country to Global War
Albany Congress | *Seven Years' War*

1763: A Turning Point
Neolin and Pontiac | *Proclamation of 1763* | *George III* | *Theories of Representation* | *Real Whigs* | *Sugar and Currency Acts*

The Stamp Act Crisis
James Otis's Rights of the British Colonies | *Patrick Henry and the Virginia Stamp Act Resolves* | *Continuing Loyalty to Britain* | *Anti–Stamp Act Demonstrations* | *Americans' Divergent Interests* | *Sons of Liberty* | *Opposition and Repeal*

LINKS TO THE WORLD *Writing and Stationery Supplies*

Resistance to the Townshend Acts
John Dickinson's Letters | *Rituals of Resistance* | *Daughters of Liberty* | *Divided Opinion over Boycotts*

VISUALIZING THE PAST *Phillis Wheatley, Enslaved Poet in the Cradle of Liberty*

Confrontations in Boston
Boston Massacre | *A British Plot?* | *Samuel Adams and Committees of Correspondence*

Tea and Turmoil
Reactions to the Tea Act | *Coercive and Quebec Acts*

The Unsettled Backcountry
Land Riots in the North | *"Regulators" in the South* | *Renewed Indian Warfare*

Government by Congress and Committee

First Continental Congress |
Continental Association | *Committees of
Observation* | *Provincial Conventions*

LEGACY FOR A PEOPLE AND A NATION
Women's Political Activism

SUMMARY

Between 1760 and 1775, huge numbers of ordinary Americans transferred their obligations and affections from their mother country to their sister colonies. Yet Adams spoke of a singular Revolution, when in fact there were many. Rich and poor, free and enslaved, indigenous and European, urban and rural, mainland and Caribbean, even male and female Americans experienced the era's upheavals differently.

In the 1750s, a series of events began to draw colonists' attention from domestic matters to their relations with Great Britain. It started with the conflict in which Britain captured Quebec: the Seven Years' War. Britain's overwhelming victory dramatically altered the balance of power in North America. Anglo-Americans no longer had to fear the French, who were ousted from the continent, or the Spanish, who were ejected from Florida. Indians, who had become expert at playing European powers against one another, found one of their major diplomatic tools blunted.

The victory also transformed Great Britain's colonial policy. Britain's massive war-related debt needed to be paid. Parliament saw the colonies as the chief beneficiaries of British success, and for the first time imposed revenue-raising taxes on the North American territories, in addition to the customs duties that had long regulated trade. That decision exposed differences in the political thinking of Britons in mainland America and Britons in the home islands and the West Indies—differences long obscured by a shared political vocabulary centered on English liberties.

During the 1760s and early 1770s, a broad coalition of the residents of Anglo America, men and women alike, resisted the new tax levies and attempts by British officials to tighten their control over provincial governments. They laid aside old antagonisms to coordinate responses to the new measures, and they slowly began to reorient their political thinking. As late as the summer of 1774, though, most continued to seek a solution within the framework of the empire.

As you read this chapter, keep the following questions in mind:

- **What were the causes and consequences of the Seven Years' War?**

- **What British policies did Americans protest, and what theories and strategies did they develop to support those protests?**

- **Why did the Tea Act of 1773 dramatically heighten tensions between the mainland colonies and Great Britain?**

Chronology

1754	Albany Congress fails to forge colonial unity
	George Washington defeated at Fort Necessity, Pennsylvania
1755	Braddock's army routed in Pennsylvania
1756	Britain declares war on France; Seven Years' War officially begins
1759	British take Quebec
1760	American phase of war ends with British capture of Montreal
	George III becomes king
1763	Treaty of Paris ends Seven Years' War
	Pontiac's allies attack forts and settlements in American West
	Proclamation of 1763 attempts to close land west of Appalachians to settlement
1764	Sugar Act lays new duties on molasses, tightens customs regulations
	Currency Act outlaws colonial paper money
1765	Stamp Act requires stamps on all printed materials in colonies
	Sons of Liberty forms
1765–66	Hudson River land riots pit tenants and squatters against large landlords
1766	Parliament repeals Stamp Act
	Declaratory Act insists that Parliament can tax the colonies
1767	Townshend Acts lay duties on trade within the empire, send new officials to America
1767–69	Regulator movement (South Carolina) tries to establish order in backcountry
1768–70	Townshend duties resisted; boycotts and protests divide merchants and urban artisans
1770	Townshend duties repealed except for tea tax
	Boston Massacre: five colonial rioters killed by British regulars
1771	North Carolina Regulators defeated by eastern militia; six executed for treason
1772	Boston Committee of Correspondence formed
1773	Tea Act aids East India Company, spurs protest in Boston
1774	Coercive Acts punish Boston and Massachusetts
	Quebec Act reforms government of Quebec
	"Lord Dunmore's War" between Shawnees and backcountry settlers in Virginia
	First Continental Congress convenes in Philadelphia, adopts Articles of Association
1774–75	Provincial conventions replace collapsing colonial governments

From the Ohio Country to Global War

What was at stake in the Seven Years' War?

In the early 1750s, British officials drafted plans better to coordinate what one writer called "the Interior Government" of their American territories. Imperial reformers were concerned because the disunity of the colonies made it hard to construct an effective bulwark against the French, who were once again on the march in the continent's interior. The unchecked incursions of backcountry traders and squatters had alienated native allies vital to the British colonies' defense. In the summer of 1753, as the French erected a chain of forts in the Ohio Country, the Mohawk leader Hendrick Theyanoguin declared the Covenant Chain binding his people to the English broken. When news of the Iroquois breakdown and the French buildup reached London, the Board of Trade directed the colonies to assemble in conference and bury the hatchet.

This engraving, labeled "The brave old Hendrick, the Great Sachem or Chief of the Mohawk Indians . . . now in Alliance with & Subject to the King of Great Britain," was sold in London in late 1755, just after the war chief Hendrick Theyanoguin died fighting for the British at the Battle of Lake George. Though he holds a hatchet and a wampum belt, Hendrick wears a fine English-style coat edged with gold braid, and elegant ruffled linens. This costume matches the finery Alexander Hamilton described when he saw Hendrick parade through the streets of Boston a decade before. (See Chapter 4)

Albany Congress In response to the board's instructions, twenty-five delegates from the seven northern and middle colonies and more than two hundred Indians from the Six Nations of the Iroquois Confederacy gathered in Albany, New York, in June 1754. The colonists sought to forge a stronger alliance with the Iroquois and to coordinate plans for intercolonial defense. They failed on both counts. Hendrick's Mohawks renewed their support for the British, but the rest of the Iroquois nations reaffirmed their neutrality policy. The colonists, too, remained divided. Connecticut land speculators battled the Pennsylvania proprietors; New England commissioners refused funds to defend western New York; New York's delegates fought even among themselves.

Before they dispersed in July, the Congress endorsed the Plan of Union crafted by Pennsylvania's Benjamin Franklin. The plan proposed the creation of an elected intercolonial legislature with the power to tax and outlined strategies for a common defense. It met with quick and universal rejection in the provincial legislatures, which wanted to safeguard their autonomy more than their citizens.

While the Albany Congress deliberated, the war had already begun. In the fall of 1753, Governor Robert Dinwiddie of Virginia had dispatched a small militia troop to build a palisade at the forks of the Ohio River. Reinforcements quickly followed. When a substantial French force arrived the following April, the Virginia militia surrendered. The French then constructed Fort Duquesne. Learning of the confrontation, the inexperienced young major who commanded more Virginia reinforcements

Benjamin Franklin published this cartoon, labeled "Join, or Die," in his newspaper, The Pennsylvania Gazette, in May 1754. The woodcut depicts the British provinces from South Carolina to New England as segments of a snake that had perished because of its violent division. The cartoon promoted Franklin's Plan of Union, which would have created an intercolonial legislature. Though the Albany Congress endorsed the plan, it was roundly rejected by the legislatures of those colonies that considered it.

soon engaged a French detachment. Hoping to start a war that would force the British to defend the Ohio Country against the French, Tanaghrisson, the leader of the major's Ohio Indian scouts, murdered the French commander. Pursuing French troops then trapped the Virginians and their Indian allies in the crudely built Fort Necessity at Great Meadows, Pennsylvania. After a day-long battle during which more than one-third of his men were killed or wounded, twenty-two-year-old Major George Washington surrendered on July 3, 1754.

Seven Years' War

Tanaghrisson's attack, and Washington's blunder, ignited what became the first global war—a testament to the increasing centrality of North America in European nations' struggles for dominance. The fighting at the forks of the Ohio helped to reinvigorate a conflict between Austria and Prussia that sent European nations scrambling for allies. Eventually England, Hanover, and Prussia lined up against France, Austria, and Russia, joined by Sweden, Saxony, and, later, Spain.

Seven Years' War Major French-English conflict that was the first worldwide war.

The war began disastrously for the British. In July 1755, French and Indian warriors attacked Major General Edward Braddock's troops as they prepared for a renewed assault on Fort Duquesne. Braddock was killed and his forces decimated. Many Ohio Indians subsequently joined the French. Delaware warriors repeatedly attacked the Pennsylvania frontier for two more years. Settlers felt betrayed because the Indians attacking them had once been (one observer noted) "familiars at their houses [who] eat drank cursed and swore together were even intimate play mates."

Britain declared war on France in 1756, thus formally beginning the Seven Years' War. Even before then, Britons and New Englanders feared that France would try to retake Nova Scotia, where most of the population was descended from seventeenth-century French settlers who had intermarried with local M'ikmaqs. Afraid that the approximately twelve thousand settlers, known as Acadians, would abandon their posture of neutrality, British commanders in 1755 forced about seven thousand of them from their homeland—the first large-scale modern deportation, now called ethnic cleansing. Ships crammed with Acadians sailed to each mainland colony. Many families were separated, some forever. After 1763, the survivors relocated: some returned to Canada, others traveled to France or its Caribbean colonies. Many settled in Louisiana, where they became known as Cajuns (derived from *Acadian*).

British officers met with scant success coercing the colonies to supply men and materiel to the army. When William Pitt, the Member of Parliament placed in charge of the Crown's war effort in 1757, agreed to reimburse the colonies' wartime expenditures and placed recruitment in local hands, he gained greater American support. Even so, Virginia's burgesses appropriated more funds to defend against slave insurrections than to fight the French and Indians. Many colonial militiamen served, not always happily, alongside equally large numbers of red-coated regulars from Britain.

Eventually, Pitt's strategy turned the tide. In July 1758, British forces recaptured the fortress at Louisbourg, thus severing the major French supply artery down the St. Lawrence River. In the fall, the Delawares and Shawnees accepted British peace overtures, and the French abandoned Fort Duquesne. Then, in September 1759,

MAP 5.1

European Settlements and Indians, 1754

By 1754, Europeans had expanded the limits of the English colonies to the eastern slopes of the Appalachian Mountains. Few independent Indian nations still existed in the East, but beyond the mountains they controlled the countryside. Only a few widely scattered English and French forts maintained the Europeans' presence there. Source: Copyright © Cengage Learning 2015

MAP 5.2
European Claims in North America

The dramatic results of the British victory in the Seven Years' (French and Indian) War are vividly demonstrated in these maps, which depict the abandonment of French claims to the mainland after the Treaty of Paris in 1763. Source: Copyright © Cengage Learning 2015

General James Wolfe's forces defeated the French and took Quebec. A year later, the British captured Montreal, and the American phase of the war ended.

In the **Treaty of Paris** (1763), France surrendered to Britain its major North American holdings (excepting New Orleans), as well as several Caribbean islands, its slave-trading posts in Senegambia, and all of its possessions in India. Spain, an ally of France toward war's end, gave Florida to the victors. France ceded Louisiana west of the Mississippi to Spain, in partial compensation for its ally's losses elsewhere (see Map 5.2).

Treaty of Paris Treaty by which France ceded most of its holdings to Great Britain and some smaller amounts to Spain.

1763: A Turning Point

Indigenous peoples of the interior first felt the impact of Britain's victory. After Britain gained the upper hand in the American theater of war in 1758, the Creeks and Cherokees lost their ability to force concessions by threatening to turn to France or Spain. In desperation, and in retaliation for British atrocities, Cherokees attacked the Carolina and Virginia frontiers in 1760. Though initially victorious, the Indians were defeated the following year. Late in 1761, a treaty allowed the construction of British forts in their territories and opened a large tract to European settlement.

How did colonists' ideas about government differ from those of the British in the 1760s?

Neolin and Pontiac

In the Ohio Country, the Ottawas, Chippewas, and Potawatomis reacted angrily when Great Britain, no longer facing French competition, raised prices on trade goods and ended traditional gift-giving practices. As settlers surged into the Monongahela and Susquehanna valleys, a shaman named Neolin (also known as the Delaware Prophet) urged Indians to oppose European incursions on their lands and cultures. Contending that Indians were destroying themselves through dependence on European goods (especially alcohol), Neolin advocated resistance, both peaceful and armed. If all Indians west of the mountains united against the invaders, he declared, the Master of Life would once again look kindly upon his people. Ironically, Neolin's reference to a single Master of Life bore traces of his people's encounter with European Christianity.

Heeding Neolin's call in spring 1763, the Ottawa war chief Pontiac forged an unprecedented alliance among Hurons, Chippewas, Potawatomis, Delawares, Shawnees, and Mingoes (Pennsylvania Iroquois). Pontiac's forces besieged Fort Detroit while war parties attacked other British outposts in the Great Lakes. Detroit withstood the siege, but by late June the other forts west of Niagara and north of Fort Pitt (the renamed Fort Duquesne) had fallen to Pontiac's alliance. Indians raided the Virginia and Pennsylvania frontiers throughout the summer, killing at least two thousand settlers. Still, they could not take Niagara, Fort Pitt, or Detroit. In early August, colonial militiamen soundly defeated a combined Indian force at Bushy Run, Pennsylvania. Pontiac broke off the siege of Detroit in late October, and a treaty ending the war was finally negotiated three years later.

For nearly eighty years, European settlers and Indians who lived in "Penn's Woods" had avoided major conflicts. But the Indian attacks and the settlers' responses—especially the massacre of several families of defenseless Conestoga Indians in December 1763 by Scots-Irish vigilantes known as the Paxton Boys—revealed that violence in the region would become endemic.

Proclamation of 1763

London officials had no experience managing an area as vast as the territory Britain acquired from France, which included French settlers along the St. Lawrence, many Indian communities, and growing numbers of settlers and speculators. In October, George III's ministry issued the **Proclamation of 1763**, which designated the headwaters of rivers flowing into the Atlantic from the Appalachians as the western boundary for colonial settlement (see Map 5.1). Its promulgators expected the proclamation line to prevent clashes by forbidding colonists to move onto Indian lands. Instead, it infuriated land speculators and settlers who had already squatted west of the line.

Proclamation of 1763
England's attempt to end Indian problems by preventing westward movement by colonists.

After 1763, the speculators (who included George Washington, Thomas Jefferson, Patrick Henry, and Benjamin Franklin) lobbied vigorously to have their claims validated by colonial governments and London administrators. At a treaty conference in 1768 at Fort Stanwix, New York, they negotiated with Iroquois representatives to push the boundary line farther west and south. Still claiming to speak for the Delawares and the Shawnees, the Iroquois agreed to the deal, which brought them valuable trade goods and did not affect their own territories. Yet even though the Virginia land companies eventually gained the support of the House of Burgesses, they never made any headway in London because administrators worried that western expansion would require funds they did not have.

George III

The British national debt doubled during the Seven Years' War, to £137 million. Financing Britain's war debt—and defending newly acquired territories—bedeviled King George III, who succeeded his grandfather, George II, in 1760. During the crucial years between 1763 and 1770, when the rift with the colonies widened, the king replaced cabinet ministers rapidly. Although determined to assert the power of the monarchy, George III stubbornly regarded adherence to the status quo as the hallmark of patriotism.

Selected as prime minister in 1763, George Grenville had to find new sources of funds, and the British people were already heavily taxed. Because the colonists had benefited greatly from wartime outlays, Grenville concluded, Anglo-Americans should shoulder a larger share of the empire's costs.

Theories of Representation

Americans believed they could be represented only by men who lived nearby and for whom they or their property-holding neighbors actually voted. Grenville and his English contemporaries, by contrast, believed that Parliament—king, lords, and commons acting together—represented all British subjects, wherever they resided and whether or not they could vote. In Parliament, the particular constituency that chose a member of the House of Commons had no special claim on that member's vote, nor did the member have to live near his constituents. According to this theory, called *virtual representation*, all Britons—including colonists—were represented in Parliament. Their consent to its laws could thus be presumed.

In the colonies, however, members of the lower houses of the assemblies were viewed as *actually* representing the regions that elected them. Voters cast their ballots for those they believed would advance the particular interests of a given district and province. Events of the 1760s revealed the incompatibility of these two understandings of representation.

Real Whigs

The colonists had grown accustomed to a faraway central government. They believed a good government was one that largely left them alone, a view in keeping with the theories of British writers known as the Real Whigs or Commonwealth thinkers. Drawing on a tradition of dissent that reached back to the English Civil War, the Real Whigs stressed the dangers inherent in a powerful government, particularly a monarchy. Some even favored republicanism, which proposed to eliminate monarchs and vest political power more directly in the people. Real Whig writers warned people to guard constantly against government's attempts to encroach on their liberty and seize their property.

As Britain tightened the reins in the 1760s and early 1770s, many Americans saw parallels in their circumstances and Real Whig ideology. Excessive and unjust taxation, they believed, could destroy their freedoms.

Sugar Act Act passed by British Parliament that sought to raise revenues by taxing colonial imports, notably the sugar trade.

Sugar and Currency Acts

In 1764, Parliament passed the **Sugar Act** and Currency Act. The Sugar Act (also known as the Revenue Act) revised existing customs regulations and laid new duties on some imports into the colonies. Influential Caribbean sugar planters lobbied for the act, which protected their commerce by preventing mainland rum distillers from smuggling molasses from the French islands. The act also established a vice-admiralty court at Halifax, Nova Scotia, to adjudicate violations of the law. Unlike the Navigation Acts, which the colonies considered legitimate, the Sugar Act was explicitly designed to raise revenue, not to channel American trade through Britain. The Currency Act outlawed most colonial paper money, because British merchants had complained that Americans paid their debts in inflated local currencies.

The Sugar Act and Currency Act were imposed on an already depressed economy. A business boom accompanied the Seven Years' War, but prosperity ended in 1760, when the fighting moved overseas. Urban merchants found fewer buyers for imported goods, and the loss of military demand for foodstuffs hurt American farmers. The bottom dropped out of the European tobacco market, threatening the livelihood of Chesapeake planters. Thus, the prospect of increased import duties and inadequate currency panicked merchants.

Without precedent for a campaign against acts of Parliament, eight colonial legislatures in 1764 sent separate petitions to Parliament requesting the Sugar Act's repeal. They argued that its commercial restrictions would hurt Britain as well as the colonies and that they had not consented to its passage. The protests had no effect.

The Stamp Act Crisis

How did James Otis and Patrick Henry offer different ways to address the Stamp Act crisis?

Stamp Act Obliged colonists to purchase and use special stamped (watermarked) paper for newspapers, customs documents, various licenses, college diplomas, and legal forms used for recovering debts, buying land, and making wills.

The **Stamp Act** (1765), Grenville's most important proposal, required tax stamps on most printed materials, placing the heaviest burden on members of the colonial elite, who used printed matter more intensively than did ordinary folk. Anyone who purchased a newspaper, made a will, transferred land, earned a diploma, bought dice or playing cards, applied for a license, accepted a government post, or took a loan would have to buy a stamp. It also required that scarce sterling coin be used to purchase tax stamps. The act broke with the colonial tradition of self-imposed taxation. Violators would be tried by vice-admiralty courts, in which judges alone rendered decisions, leading Americans to fear the loss of their right to trial by jury. And since the revenues would pay for British peacekeepers in North America, the tax also mobilized long-established fears of a standing army.

James Otis's *Rights of the British Colonies*

The most important colonial pamphlet protesting the Sugar Act and the proposed Stamp Act was *The Rights of the British Colonies Asserted and Proved*, by James Otis Jr., a brilliant young Massachusetts attorney. Otis exposed the dilemma that confounded the colonists for the next decade. How could they oppose certain acts of Parliament without questioning Parliament's authority over them? Colonists, he asserted, were "entitled to all the natural, essential, inherent, and inseparable rights" of Britons, including the right not to be taxed without their consent. But Otis also accepted the prevailing theory of British government: Parliament was the supreme authority in the empire. Even its wrongheaded laws had to be obeyed until repealed. To resolve the dilemma, Otis proposed colonial representation in Parliament, an idea that was never taken seriously on either side of the Atlantic.

Like many Enlightenment thinkers, Otis reasoned from natural rights. But like very few writers at the time, he extended this natural rights logic to the enslaved. "The Colonists are by the law of nature free born, as indeed are all men, white or black," he wrote. It was common, in the 1760s, for colonists to protest that Britain's tyranny enslaved them. To receive the stamps "is Death—is worse than Death—it is slavery!" said Pennsylvania's John Dickinson. James Otis went further, warning "It is a clear truth, that those who every day barter away other mens liberty, will soon care little for their own." Slowly, the era's talk of liberty would begin to erode the intellectual foundations of human bondage.

Otis published his pamphlet before the Stamp Act was passed. When Americans first learned of the act's adoption in the spring of 1765, they reacted indecisively. Few colonists publicly favored the law, but colonial petitions had failed to prevent its adoption. Perhaps Otis was correct: Americans had to pay the tax, reluctantly but loyally.

Patrick Henry and the Virginia Stamp Act Resolves

Patrick Henry, a young Virginia attorney serving his first term in the House of Burgesses, was appalled by his fellow legislators' complacency. Near the end of the legislative session, when many burgesses had already departed, Henry introduced seven proposals against the Stamp Act. The few burgesses remaining adopted five of Henry's resolutions by a bare majority. But some colonial newspapers printed Henry's original resolutions as if the House had passed them all, even though one was rescinded and two others were never debated or voted on.

The four propositions adopted by the burgesses echoed Otis's arguments about taxation, asserting that colonists had never forfeited the rights of British subjects. The other three resolutions went much further. The repealed resolution claimed for the burgesses "the only exclusive right" to tax Virginians, and the two never considered asserted that Virginians need not obey tax laws passed by other legislative bodies—namely, Parliament.

Link to Patrick Henry, Resolutions Against the Stamp Act (1765)

Continuing Loyalty to Britain

Though willing to fight for their liberties as Britons within the empire, the colonists did not seek independence. Over the next decade, colonial leaders searched for a formula that would let them control their internal affairs, especially taxation, while remaining under British rule. But the British theory of government insisted that Parliament held absolute authority over all colonial possessions. In effect, the American rebels wanted British leaders to revise their fundamental understanding of how government worked. That was simply too much to expect.

The effectiveness of Americans' opposition to the Stamp Act rested on more than ideological arguments over parliamentary power. The battle was waged on the streets as well as on the page.

Anti–Stamp Act Demonstrations

In August, the Loyal Nine, a Boston artisans' social club, organized a protest against the Stamp Act. Hoping to show that people of all ranks opposed the act, they convinced rival labor associations, composed of workers and poor tradesmen, to lay aside their differences for the demonstration.

On August 14, the demonstrators hung an effigy of Andrew Oliver, the province's stamp distributor, from a tree on Boston Common. That night a large crowd led by a group of about fifty well-dressed tradesmen paraded the effigy around the city. Demonstrators then built a bonfire near Oliver's house and fed the effigy to the flames. They broke most of Oliver's windows and threw stones at officials. The Loyal Nine achieved success when Oliver publicly renounced the duties of his office. One Bostonian jubilantly wrote, "I believe people never was more Universally pleased."

Twelve days later, another crowd action—aimed this time at Oliver's brother-in-law, Lieutenant Governor Thomas Hutchinson—drew no praise from Boston's respectable citizens. On the night of August 26, a mob destroyed Hutchinson's elegant townhouse. The lieutenant governor reported that by the next morning, nothing was left of his mansion "but the bare walls and floors."

Link to Thomas Hutchinson Recounts the Reaction to the Stamp Act in Boston (1765)

Americans' Divergent Interests

The differences between the two Boston mobs of August 1765 exposed divisions that would characterize subsequent protests. Skilled craftsmen as well as merchants, lawyers, and other educated elites preferred orderly demonstrations centered on political issues. For the city's laborers, economic grievances were paramount. Certainly, their "hellish Fury" as they wrecked Hutchinson's house suggests resentment of his ostentatious display of wealth.

The Stamp Act controversy for the first time drew ordinary folk into transatlantic politics. Matters that previously had been of concern only to an elite few were now discussed in every tavern and coffeehouse. Anti–Stamp Act demonstrations took place from Nova Scotia to the West Indies (see Map 5.3).

But though the act placed the heaviest tax burden on the Caribbean colonies—levying double or triple duty on large island land transfers, for example—protests there were notably tepid. On the largest, most populous, and richest islands—Jamaica and Barbados—planters complied with the tax. Since the wealthiest sugar barons were sojourners more than settlers, they had strong personal ties to Britain. They also depended on mercantilist legislation to favor their sugar exports. Finally, they relied upon British military might to protect them from their enslaved workforces. Over three-quarters of the revenues collected during the Stamp Act's brief life came from the West Indies.

On the mainland, street protests were so successful that by November 1, when the law was scheduled to take effect, not one stamp distributor on the mainland

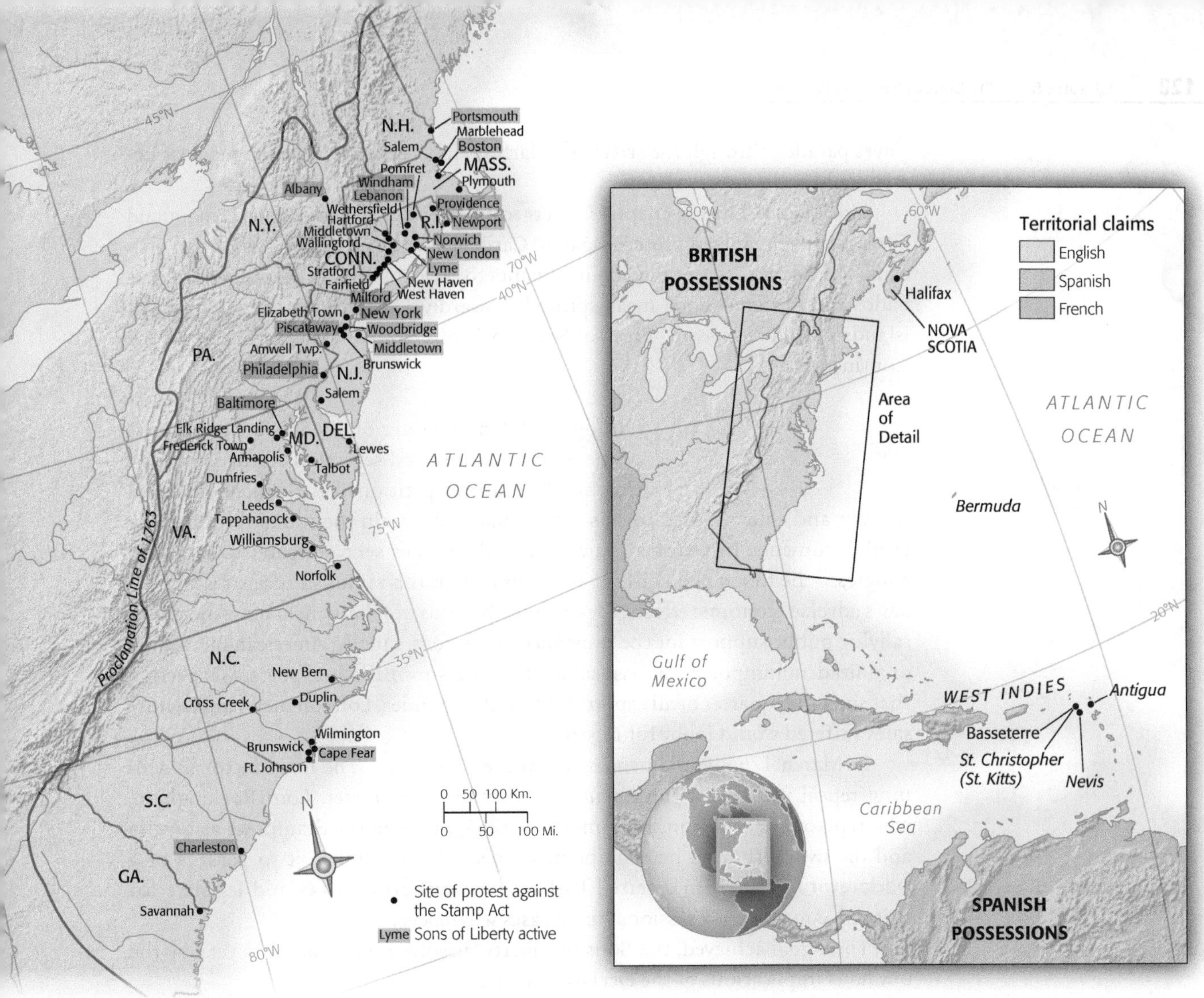

MAP 5.3
Colonial Resistance to the Stamp Act

All of the towns and islands labeled on this map witnessed crowd actions protesting the Stamp Act of 1765; British colonies outside the eventual United States joined in the nearly universal opposition to the hated measure. Source: Copyright © Cengage Learning 2015

was willing to enforce the act. Yet wealthy men recognized that mobs composed of the formerly powerless could endanger their dominance of society.

| Sons of Liberty | Elites attempted to channel resistance into acceptable forms by creating an intercolonial association, the **Sons of Liberty**. Composed of merchants, lawyers, prosperous tradesmen, and tavern owners, the Sons of Liberty by early 1766 linked protest leaders from Charleston, South Carolina, to Portsmouth, New Hampshire. |

Sons of Liberty Groups formed to resist the Stamp Act.

The Sons of Liberty could influence events but not control them. In Charleston (formerly Charles Town) in October 1765, a crowd shouting, "Liberty Liberty and stamp'd paper" forced the resignation of the South Carolina stamp distributor. But the Charleston Sons of Liberty were horrified when in January 1766 local slaves paraded through the streets similarly crying, "Liberty!" The language of liberty could easily slip its channels.

No Sons of Liberty chapters emerged in the West Indies. Indeed, mainland Sons groups organized protests against Caribbean colonists as well as British officials. The *Boston Gazette* called on merchants to boycott "the SLAVISH Islands of Barbados and Antigua—Poor, mean spirited, Cowardly, Dastardly Creoles." The sugar islands should receive no "Fresh or Salt Provisions from any Son of liberty on the Continent."

Opposition and Repeal

During the fall and winter of 1765–1766, opponents of the Stamp Act pursued several different strategies. Colonial legislatures petitioned Parliament to repeal the law, and courts closed because they could not obtain the stamps required for legal documents. In October, nine mainland colonies sent delegates to a general congress—the first since 1754—in New York to draft a remonstrance stressing the law's adverse economic effects. Meanwhile, the Sons of Liberty held mass meetings, rallying public support for the resistance movement. Finally, American merchants organized nonimportation associations to pressure British exporters, expecting that since one-quarter of all exports went to the colonies, London merchants whose sales suffered would lobby for repeal.

In March 1766, Parliament repealed the Stamp Act. The main factor in winning repeal was the appointment of a new prime minister. Lord Rockingham, who replaced Grenville in the summer of 1765, opposed the Stamp Act as unwise and divisive. Although he championed repeal, he also linked it to passage of a **Declaratory Act**, which asserted Parliament's authority to tax and legislate for Britain's American possessions "in all cases whatsoever."

Declaratory Act Affirmed parliamentary power to legislate its colonies "in all cases whatsoever."

Their goal achieved, the Sons of Liberty dissolved. Few colonists yet saw the ominous implications of the Declaratory Act.

Resistance to the Townshend Acts

How did the American population become politicized in the late 1760s?

In summer 1766, another change in the ministry in London revealed how fragile the colonists' victory had been. The new prime minister, William Pitt, had fostered cooperation between the colonies and Britain during the Seven Years' War. But Pitt fell ill, and Charles Townshend became the dominant force in the ministry. An ally of Grenville, Townshend renewed efforts to obtain badly needed funds from Britain's American possessions (see Table 5.1).

The duties Townshend proposed in 1767 seemed to extend the Navigation Acts by focusing on trade goods like paper, glass, and tea. But they differed, first by applying to British imports, not to those from foreign countries. Second, the revenues would pay some colonial officials, thereby eliminating assemblies' ability to threaten to withhold salaries from uncooperative officials. Additionally, Townshend's scheme established an American Board of Customs Commissioners and created vice-admiralty courts at Boston, Philadelphia, and Charleston. Both moves angered merchants, whose profits would be threatened by more vigorous enforcement of the Navigation Acts. Significantly, Townshend exempted the West Indies

Links TO THE WORLD

Writing and Stationery Supplies

In the seventeenth century, colonists stressed the importance of teaching children to read the Bible; writing was not seen as nearly so necessary. Yet as the eighteenth century progressed, and especially during the era of the American Revolution, writing skills acquired new significance. Family members parted by the war needed to communicate with each other, and new opportunities arose for merchants who could deal with distant correspondents.

Writing drew on a wide range of items from around the world. Paper was either imported from Britain or manufactured at an increasing number of American paper mills. The quill pens (goose feathers) that Americans used as writing implements often originated in Germany or Holland. Penknives, needed to sharpen blunt quills, and inkpots (made of brass, glass, or pewter, among other materials), also largely came from Britain. But the Americans could not write readily without additional items obtained from international trade.

For example, to absorb ink properly, paper needed to be treated with pounce, a powder made from a combination of gum sandarac (a tree resin from North Africa) and pumice, a powdered volcanic glass. Lacking envelopes, eighteenth-century writers folded their sheets of paper, addressed them on the outside, and sealed them with wax made in Holland or Britain from a combination of lac (a resinous secretion of insects, still used today for shellac) from India and cinnabar, a red quartz-like crystal, from Spain. Ink was manufactured from oak galls from Aleppo (in Syria), gum arabic (sap from acacia trees) from Sudan, and alum and copperas (derived from different stones) from Britain. Most ink was shipped from Britain in powdered form; in America, another key ingredient, urine, would be added to cause the alum to blend properly with the other substances to create the liquid ink.

When colonial elites drafted petitions against the Stamp Act, the implements they employed connected them to a long commercial chain stretching to Great Britain, the European continent, North Africa, and the Middle East.

Desk and Bookcase, c.1762 (mahogany, white cedar, yellow poplar, yellow pine, silvered glass & gilded brass), American School, (18th century) / Philadelphia Museum of Art, Pennsylvania, PA, USA / Purchased with the Mr. and Mrs. Walter H. Annenberg Fund for Major Acquisitions, and with supporting funds from the Henry P. McIlhenny Fund in memory of Frances P. McIlhenny, funds contributed by H. Richard Dietrich, Jr., and other private donors / The Bridgeman Art Library

This writing desk, made in Pennsylvania in the mid-to-late eighteenth century, would have been owned by a well-to-do family from the mid-Atlantic states. The pigeonholes would hold incoming and outgoing letters; the many drawers could store paper, ink, seals and sealing wax, and other supplies. The new importance of writing thus produced a perceived need for novel types of furniture.

TABLE 5.1   British Ministries and Their American Policies

Head of Ministry	Major Acts
George Grenville	Sugar Act (1764)
	Currency Act (1764)
	Stamp Act (1765)
Lord Rockingham	Stamp Act repealed (1766)
	Declaratory Act (1766)
William Pitt/ Charles Townshend	Townshend Acts (1767)
Lord North	Townshend duties (except for the tea tax) repealed (1770)
	Tea Act (1773)
	Coercive Acts (1774)
	Quebec Act (1774)

from key provisions of the new duties, a divide-and-conquer tactic revealing that Parliament had learned from the Stamp Act protests.

John Dickinson's *Letters*

Passage of the Townshend Acts drew a quick response from the colonies. One series of widely published essays in particular, *Letters from a Farmer in Pennsylvania*, by the prominent lawyer John Dickinson, expressed a broad consensus. Dickinson contended that Parliament could regulate colonial trade but could not raise revenue. By distinguishing between regulation and taxation, Dickinson avoided the sticky issue of the colonies' relationship to Parliament.

The Massachusetts assembly responded to the Townshend Acts by drafting a letter to the other colonial legislatures, suggesting a joint protest petition. When Lord Hillsborough, recently named to the new post of secretary of state for America, learned of the Massachusetts circular letter, he ordered the colony's governor, Francis Bernard, to demand that the assembly recall it. He also directed other governors to prevent their assemblies from discussing it. Hillsborough's order motivated colonial assemblies to unite against this new threat to their prerogatives. In late 1768, the Massachusetts legislature resoundingly rejected Bernard's recall order. Bernard dissolved the assembly, and other governors similarly responded.

Rituals of Resistance

The number of votes cast against recalling the circular letter—92—assumed ritual significance in the resistance movement. The number 45 already had symbolic meaning because **John Wilkes**, a radical Londoner sympathetic to the American cause, had been jailed for publishing a pamphlet entitled *The North Briton*, No. 45. In Boston, the silversmith Paul Revere made a punchbowl weighing 45 ounces that held 45 gills (half-cups) and was engraved with the names of the "glorious 92" opposition legislators; James Otis, John Adams, and others publicly drank 45 toasts from it.

John Wilkes British opponent of King George III who became a hero to American colonists.

Such public rituals familiarized common people with the terms of the argument. For example, when the Charleston Sons of Liberty held their meetings in public, crowds gathered to watch and listen. Songs supporting the American cause also helped to spread the word. American leaders urged colonists of all ranks and both sexes to sign agreements not to purchase or consume British products. The consumer revolution that had previously linked colonists culturally and economically now supplied them with a ready method of displaying their allegiance.

Daughters of Liberty
As the primary purchasers of textiles and household goods, women played a central role in the nonconsumption movement. More than three hundred Boston matrons publicly promised not to buy or drink tea, "Sickness excepted." The women of Wilmington, North Carolina, burned their tea after walking through town in a solemn procession. Women exchanged recipes for tea substitutes or drank coffee instead. The best known of the protests, the so-called Edenton Ladies Tea Party, was actually a meeting of prominent North Carolina women who pledged to work for the public good and to support resistance to British measures.

In many towns, young women calling themselves Daughters of Liberty met to spin in public squares to encourage colonists to end the colonies' dependence on British cloth by wearing homespun. These patriotic displays served the same purpose as the male rituals involving the numbers 45 and 92. When young ladies from well-to-do families sat outdoors at spinning wheels all day, eating only American food, drinking local herbal tea, and listening to patriotic sermons, they served as political instructors.

Divided Opinion Over Boycotts
The Stamp Act boycotts had helped revive a depressed economy by creating a demand for local products and reducing merchants' inventories. But by 1768 and 1769, merchants were again enjoying boom times and had no incentive to support boycotts. In contrast, artisans, who recognized that the absence of British goods would increase demand for their own manufactures, formed the core of the crowds that picketed importers' stores, publicized offending merchants' names, and sometimes destroyed property.

Such tactics were effective: colonial imports from England dropped dramatically in 1769. But the tactics also aroused heated opposition. Even some Americans who supported resistance to British measures questioned the use of violence to enforce the boycott. The threat to private property inherent in the campaign frightened wealthier and more conservative men and women.

Colonists were relieved when news arrived in April 1770 that the Townshend duties had been repealed, except for the tea tax. A new prime minister, Lord North, persuaded Parliament that duties on trade within the empire were ill advised. The other Townshend Acts remained in force, but repealing the duties made the provisions for paying officials' salaries and tightening customs enforcement appear less objectionable.

Visualizing THE PAST

Phillis Wheatley, Enslaved Poet in the Cradle of Liberty

In July 1761, the *Phillis* docked at Boston's Long Wharf after a long voyage during which nearly a quarter of its human cargo died. The captain placed an advertisement in the papers hawking "prime young slaves, from the Windward Coast." One of the least valuable among them was a little girl still missing her two front teeth. A merchant named John Wheatley purchased her as a gift for his wife, naming the child after the boat that brought her from Africa.

Phillis Wheatley grew up in a genteel house on King Street. The Wheatleys, influenced by the ideas of the Great Awakening, recognized her talents and educated her beyond the station of nearly all slaves and, indeed, of most white girls and women. She began to write poetry. In 1770, her elegy on the death of George Whitefield made her famous in evangelical circles on both sides of the Atlantic. In 1773, a volume of her poems was published in London.

Wheatley's *Poems on Various Subjects* included an "elegant engraved likeness of the Author." Printed in an era when books seldom featured portraits of female authors and almost never bore the likenesses of people of African descent, Wheatley's image—probably based on a painting by the black Boston artist Scipio Moorhead—is a striking exception. What attributes does the portrait give the poet? How do the title page and the frontispiece represent her race, age, gender, and genius?

Wheatley frontispiece

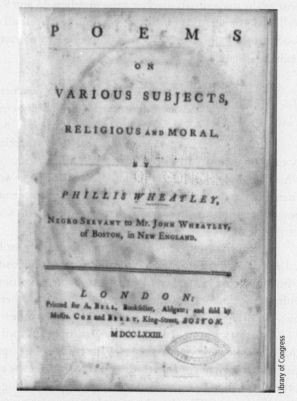

Wheatley title page

Library of Congress

Library of Congress

Confrontations in Boston

The decision to base the American Board of Customs Commissioners in Boston helped lead to the confrontation that patriots labeled the "**Boston Massacre**." Mobs targeted the customs officials from the day they arrived in November 1767. In June 1768, their seizure of the patriot leader John Hancock's sloop *Liberty* on suspicion of smuggling caused a riot. The ministry sent troops to maintain order. That October, two regiments of British regulars—about 700 men—marched up Long Wharf toward the Common. They served as constant visible reminders of the oppressive potential of British power. Patrols roamed the streets at all hours. Parents feared for the safety of their daughters, whom soldiers subjected to coarse sexual insults. Additionally, many redcoats sought employment in their off-duty hours, competing for unskilled jobs with the city's workingmen. The two groups brawled repeatedly in taverns and on the streets.

How did Samuel Adams's Committees of Correspondence mark a turning point in Americans' political thinking?

Boston Massacre Confrontation between colonists and British troops in which five colonists where shot and killed.

Boston Massacre

On the evening of March 5, 1770, a crowd of laborers threw hard-packed snowballs at troops guarding the Customs House. Against orders, the sentries fired on the crowd, killing four and wounding eight, one of whom died a few days later. Reportedly, the first to fall was Crispus Attucks, a sailor of mixed Nipmuck and African ancestry. Rebel leaders idealized Attucks and the other dead rioters as martyrs for liberty, holding a solemn funeral and later commemorating March 5 with patriotic orations.

Link to a description of the Boston Massacre from the *Boston Gazette* (March 12, 1770)

Despite the political benefits the patriots derived from the massacre, they probably did not approve of the crowd action that provoked it. Since the destruction of Hutchinson's house in August 1765, the Sons of Liberty had expressed distaste at uncontrolled riots. When the soldiers were tried for the killings, John Adams and Josiah Quincy Jr., both unwavering patriots, acted as their defense attorneys. Almost all the accused were acquitted, and the two men convicted were released after being branded on the thumb.

A British Plot?

The favorable outcome of the soldiers' trials persuaded London officials not to retaliate against Boston, and for more than two years after the massacre, the imperial crisis seemed to quiet. But the most outspoken newspapers, including the *Boston Gazette*, the *Pennsylvania Journal*, and the *South Carolina Gazette*, continued to publish essays pointing to the stationing of troops in Boston and the growing number of vice-admiralty courts as evidence of plans to enslave the colonists. Indeed, patriot writers played repeatedly on the word *enslavement*—though they rarely questioned the institution of slavery, as James Otis had in 1764. And none of them yet advocated American independence.

In fall 1772, the North ministry began to implement the Townshend Act that paid governors and judges from customs revenues. In early November, voters at a Boston town meeting established a **Committee of Correspondence** to publicize the decision by exchanging letters with other Massachusetts towns. Heading the committee was Samuel Adams.

Committee of Correspondence Local committees established throughout colonies to coordinate anti-British actions.

Shortly after the Boston Massacre, Paul Revere engraved this illustration of the confrontation near the Customs House on March 5, 1770. Offering visual support for the patriots' version of events, Revere depicted British soldiers firing on an unresisting crowd (instead of the aggressive mob described at the soldiers' trial) and—even worse—a gun firing from the building itself, which has been labeled "Butcher's Hall."

Samuel Adams and Committees of Correspondence

Aged fifty-one in 1772, Samuel Adams was about a decade older than other American resistance leaders, including his distant cousin John. He had been a Boston tax collector, a clerk of the Massachusetts assembly, and one of the Sons of Liberty. His Committee of Correspondence sought to create an informed consensus among the residents of Massachusetts. Such committees, which were eventually established throughout the colonies, broadened the protest movement beyond the seacoast and major cities and towns (see Map 5.3).

The statement prepared by the Boston Committee declared, "All persons born in the British American Colonies" had natural rights to life, liberty, and property. Grievances included taxation without representation, the increased presence of troops and customs officers on American soil, the expanded jurisdiction of vice-admiralty courts, and the nature of the instructions given to American governors by their superiors in London. No longer did resistance leaders—at least in Boston—mention the necessity of obedience to Parliament. They placed colonial rights first, loyalty to Britain a distant second.

Tea and Turmoil

The tea tax was the only Townshend duty still in effect by 1773. After 1770, some Americans had continued to boycott English tea; others resumed drinking it. Tea figured prominently in the colonists' diet and their cultures, so the boycott meant forgoing a favorite beverage and altering everyday rituals.

How did the Tea Act push the colonies to the brink of revolution?

Reactions to the Tea Act

In May 1773, Parliament passed the **Tea Act** to save the East India Company from bankruptcy. The company held a monopoly on British trade with the East Indies and was vital to the British economy. According to the Tea Act, only the East India Company's agents could sell tea in America. This enabled the company to avoid intermediaries and to price its tea competitively with that sold by smugglers. The net result would be cheaper tea for American consumers. Resistance leaders, however, interpreted the measure as designed to make them admit Parliament's right to tax them. Others saw the Tea Act as the first step in an East India Company monopoly on all colonial trade. Residents of the four cities designated to receive the first tea shipments prepared to respond to this perceived new threat to their freedom.

Tea Act England's attempt to bail out East India Company that heightened tensions between the British and the colonies.

A tea ship sent to New York City never arrived. In Philadelphia, Pennsylvania's governor persuaded the captain to return to Britain. Tea bound for Charleston was unloaded; some was destroyed, the rest sold in 1776 by the new state government.

The only confrontation occurred in Boston. The first of three tea ships, the *Dartmouth*, entered Boston harbor on November 28. Customs laws required cargo to be landed and duty paid within twenty days of a ship's arrival; otherwise, customs officers would seize the cargo. After several mass meetings, Bostonians voted to post guards on the wharf to prevent the tea from being unloaded. Governor Thomas Hutchinson refused to permit the three vessels to leave the harbor.

On December 16, one day before the cargo was to be confiscated, more than five thousand people crowded into Old South Church. The meeting, chaired by Samuel Adams, made a final attempt to convince Hutchinson to return the tea to England. But he refused. In the early evening Adams reportedly announced "that they had now done all they could for the Salvation of their Country." Cries rang out from the crowd: "Boston harbor a tea-pot tonight! The Mohawks are come!" Within a few minutes, about sixty men crudely disguised as Indians assembled at the wharf. They boarded the three ships and dumped their cargo into the harbor. By 9 PM, 342 chests of tea worth approximately £10,000 floated in splinters.

Coercive and Quebec Acts

The North administration reacted with outrage. In March 1774, Parliament adopted the first of four laws that colonists referred to as the **Coercive, or Intolerable, Acts**. It ordered the port of Boston closed until the tea was paid for, prohibiting all but coastal trade in food and firewood. Later that spring, Parliament passed three other punitive measures. The Massachusetts Government Act altered the province's charter, substituting an appointed council

Coercive, or Intolerable, Acts A series of restrictive laws comprised of the Boston Port Bill, the Massachusetts Government Act, the Justice Act, the Quartering Act, plus the unrelated Quebec Act. Intended by the British Parliament to primarily punish Massachusetts, the acts instead pushed most colonies to the brink of rebellion.

for the elected one, increasing the governor's powers, and forbidding most town meetings. The Justice Act allowed a person accused of committing murder while suppressing a riot or enforcing the laws to be tried outside the colony where the incident had occurred. Finally, the Quartering Act permitted military officers to commandeer privately owned buildings to house their troops.

Parliament then turned to reforming Quebec's government. The Quebec Act granted greater religious freedom to Catholics, alarming Protestant colonists who equated the Church of Rome with despotism. It also reinstated French civil law and established an appointed council (rather than an elected legislature). Finally, to protect northern Indians against Anglo-American settlement, the act annexed to Quebec the area west of the Appalachians, east of the Mississippi River, and north of the Ohio River—thereby removing the region from the jurisdiction of seacoast colonies. Wealthy speculators who hoped to develop the Ohio Country would now have to deal with officials in Quebec.

Resistance leaders saw the Coercive Acts and the Quebec Act as proof that Britain had embarked on a deliberate plan to oppress them. The Boston Committee of Correspondence urged all colonies to join an immediate boycott of British goods. But other provinces hesitated to take such a drastic step. In the British West Indies, even opponents of Parliament's evolving American policy thought the "Boston firebrands" had gone too far and hoped the Coercive Acts might restore order. Rhode Island, Virginia, and Pennsylvania each suggested convening another intercolonial congress. Even the most ardent patriots remained loyal Britons and hoped for reconciliation. So the colonies agreed to send delegates to Philadelphia in September to attend a Continental Congress.

The Unsettled Backcountry

What internal struggles plagued the backcountry during the 1760s and 1770s?

In the same years that residents of British North America wrestled over deepening divisions between the colonies and the mother country, they contended over divisions *within* colonial society. Along the western edges of British settlement in the 1760s and 1770s, these internal struggles sometimes verged on civil war.

Land Riots in the North

By midcentury, with most fertile land east of the Appalachians purchased or occupied, conflicts over land escalated. The most serious land riots occurred along the Hudson River in 1765–1766. Late in the seventeenth century, the governor of New York had granted huge tracts in the lower Hudson Valley to prominent families. The proprietors in turn divided these estates into small farms, which they rented chiefly to poor Dutch and German migrants who regarded tenancy as a step toward independence. But in the eighteenth century, New Englanders and Europeans increasingly migrated to the region, resisting tenancy and often squatting. In the mid-1760s, the Philipse family sued farmers who had lived on Philipse land for two decades. The courts ordered squatters to make way for tenants with valid leases. Instead, farmers rebelled, terrorizing proprietors and tenants, and on one occasion battling a county sheriff and his posse. The rebellion lasted nearly a year, ending only when British troops captured its leaders.

"Regulators" in the South

The Regulator movements of the late 1760s (South Carolina) and early 1770s (North Carolina) pitted backcountry farmers against wealthy eastern planters who controlled the colonial governments. In South Carolina, Scots-Irish settlers protested their lack of an adequate voice in colonial political affairs. For months, they policed the countryside in vigilante bands known as Regulators, complaining of lax and biased law enforcement. North Carolina Regulators objected primarily to heavy taxation by the colonial legislature. In September 1770, they dragged a justice from the Rowan County Courthouse and then ransacked his house. The following May, several thousand Regulators fought and lost a battle with eastern militiamen at Alamance. A month later, six of the insurgents were hanged for treason.

Renewed Indian Warfare

In 1774, Virginia, headed by a new royally appointed governor, **Lord Dunmore**, asserted its title to the developing backcountry. Tensions mounted as Virginians surveyed land on the south side of the Ohio River—territory claimed by the Shawnees. In April, settlers attacked a Shawnee canoe carrying women and children as well as one man, murdering and scalping all nine. John Logan, a Mingo leader whose kin died in the attack, gathered warriors to retaliate against frontier settlements. When the governor dispatched some two thousand troops, these skirmishes escalated into a conflict known as **Lord Dunmore's War**. When the peace was finally settled in October, the Shawnee leader Cornstalk ceded the enormous territory that became the state of Kentucky to Dunmore's forces.

Lord Dunmore Royal governor of Virginia who promised freedom to slaves who fought to restore royal authority.

Lord Dunmore's War Confrontation between Virginians and the Shawnee Indians in 1774. During the peace conference that followed, Virginia gained uncontested rights to lands south of the Ohio country in exchange for its claims on the northern side.

Government by Congress and Committee

How did the First Continental Congress redefine America's relationship to England?

In the summer of 1774, while the Virginia backcountry bled and Boston suffered, fifty-six delegates from the mainland colonies readied for a "Grand **Continental Congress**" in Philadelphia. Because colonial governors had forbidden regular assemblies to conduct formal elections, most of the delegates had been chosen by extralegal conventions. The lawyer John Adams, one of four delegates from Massachusetts, anticipated that the Congress would serve as "a School of Political Prophets I Suppose—a Nursery of American Statesmen."

But what were American statesmen and what, indeed, was America? New England merchants and southern planters shared little common culture. So distinct were the interests of the British West Indies that those thirteen colonies sent no delegates at all—nor did Georgia. Even in the fall of 1774, as tavern talk throughout the colonies turned to the imminence of civil war, Great Britain remained the only nation the congressmen shared. They pledged their fealty to George III and pressed their claims not for American freedom but for "English liberty."

Continental Congress Group of representatives appointed by conventions in most of the North American colonies of Great Britain.

First Continental Congress

The colonies' leading political figures—mostly lawyers, merchants, and planters—attended the Philadelphia Congress. In addition to John Adams, the

Massachusetts delegation included his elder cousin Samuel Adams. Among others, New York sent John Jay, a talented young attorney. From Pennsylvania came the conservative Joseph Galloway and his longtime rival, John Dickinson. Virginia elected Richard Henry Lee, Patrick Henry, and George Washington.

The congressmen faced three tasks when they convened at Carpenters' Hall on September 5: defining American grievances, developing a resistance plan, and articulating their constitutional relationship with Great Britain. Radical congressmen, like Lee of Virginia, argued that colonists owed allegiance only to George III, not Parliament. The conservatives—Galloway and his allies—proposed a plan of union that would require Parliament and a new American legislature jointly to consent to laws governing the colonies. Delegates narrowly rejected Galloway's proposal, but they were not prepared to embrace the radicals' position either. Finally, they accepted wording proposed by John Adams. The crucial clauses in the Congress's Declaration of Rights and Grievances asserted that Americans would obey Parliament, but only voluntarily, and would resist all taxes in disguise.

Continental Association

The delegates agreed on the laws they wanted repealed (notably the Coercive Acts) and decided to implement an economic boycott while petitioning the king for relief. They adopted fourteen Articles of Association calling for nonimportation of British goods (effective December 1, 1774), nonconsumption of British products (effective March 1, 1775), and nonexportation of American goods to Britain and the British West Indies (effective September 10, 1775).

The Articles of Association (also known as the Continental Association) were designed to appeal to different groups and regions. The nonimportation agreement banned commerce in slaves as well as manufactures, which accorded with a long-standing desire of the Virginia gentry, whose members worried that slave importations discouraged skilled Europeans from immigrating. Delaying nonconsumption for three months after implementing nonimportation gave merchants time to sell items they acquired before December 1. In 1773, many Virginians had vowed to stop exporting tobacco in order to raise prices in a then-glutted market. So they welcomed an association that banned exportation while permitting them to profit from higher prices for their current crop. Postponing the nonexportation agreement also gave northern exporters of wood and foodstuffs to the Caribbean a final season of sales before the embargo.

West Indian grandees worried about the Articles of Association. Severing their supply lines from North America could bring famine, which could provoke widespread slave insurrection. The *Antigua Gazette* chided the mainland colonists for "their folly, madness, and ingratitude" in adopting the new resolutions.

Committees of Observation

To enforce the Continental Association, Congress recommended that every mainland locale elect committees of observation and inspection. By specifying that committee members be chosen by all men qualified to vote, Congress guaranteed the committees a broad popular base. The seven to eight thousand committeemen became local leaders of American resistance.

Women's Political Activism

In the twenty-first century, female citizens of the United States participate at every level of American public life. Nancy Pelosi was elected Speaker of the House, third in line for the presidency, in January 2007; Hillary Rodham Clinton ran for president in 2008; Elena Kagan became the Supreme Court's third current female member in late 2010. The 2012 elections brought a record number of women to the 113th Congress: twenty sit in the Senate, and eighty-one in the House. Many women also serve as governors and in state offices. But before the 1760s, American women were seen as having no legitimate public role. A male essayist expressed the consensus in the mid-1730s: "Poli[ti]cks is what does not become them; the Governing Kingdoms and Ruling Provinces are Things too difficult and knotty for the fair Sex."

That changed when colonists resisted new British taxes and laws in the 1760s. Because women made household purchasing decisions, and because their labor in spinning and textile manufacture could replace imported clothing, it was vital for them to participate in the cause. For the first time in American history, women began to take formal political stands, deciding whether to boycott British goods. The groups they established to promote home manufactures—dubbed "Daughters of Liberty"—constituted the first American women's political organizations.

By the mid-nineteenth century, women's political involvement would begin to coalesce into a national "woman movement." In 1848, the leaders of a woman's rights convention at Seneca Falls, New York, drafted a Declaration of Sentiments, closely modeled on the language of the Declaration of Independence. The legacy of revolutionary-era women for the nation continues today in such groups as Emily's List and Concerned Women for America. Indeed, contemporary Americans would undoubtedly find it impossible to imagine their country without female activists of all affiliations.

Initially charged with overseeing implementation of the boycott, within six months these committees became de facto governments. They examined merchants' records, publicizing those who continued to import British goods. They promoted home manufactures and urged Americans to abandon expensive leisure-time activities, which were believed to reflect vice and corruption.

The committees gradually extended their authority. They attempted to identify opponents of American resistance, developed elaborate spy networks, circulated copies of the Continental Association for signature, and investigated reports of questionable activities. Suspected dissenters were urged to support the colonial cause publicly; if they refused, the committees had them watched, restricted their movements, or even tried to force them into exile.

Provincial Conventions While the committees of observation expanded their power during the winter and early spring of 1775, the regular colonial governments edged toward collapse. In most colonies, popularly elected provincial conventions took over the government, sometimes replacing the legislatures or holding concurrent sessions. In late 1774 and early 1775, these conventions approved the Continental Association, elected delegates to a Second Continental Congress (scheduled for May), organized militias, and gathered arms. Royal officials suffered repeated humiliation. Courts were prevented from meeting, and militiamen mustered only when committees ordered. During the six months preceding the battles at Lexington and Concord, ordinary Americans forged independence at the local level, even though the vast majority of them still proclaimed loyalty to Great Britain.

Summary

At the outbreak of the Seven Years' War in the Ohio Country, no one could have predicted such dramatic change in Britain's mainland colonies. Yet that conflict simultaneously removed France from North America and created a huge debt that Britain had to repay, developments with major implications for the imperial relationship.

After the war ended in 1763, the number of mainland colonists who considered themselves political actors increased substantially, and they began to develop an American identity. Their concept of the political process differed from that of the mother country, and they held a different definition of what constituted representation and consent to government actions. They also came to understand that their economic interests were sometimes distinct from those of Great Britain. Colonial political leaders reached such conclusions only after a long train of events, some of them violent. While many colonists questioned the imperial relationship with Britain, bloodshed in the backcountry revealed persistent divisions *within* American society, including battles between frontier settlers and displaced Indians.

In late 1774, Americans were committed to resistance but not to independence. During the next decades, they would forge a new American nationality.

Chapter Review

From the Ohio Country to Global War

What was at stake in the Seven Years' War?

The Seven Years' War was ultimately a contest over land between the British, French, Native Americans, and some settlers. All parties vied for control of large tracts of western land. France sought to hold and expand its possessions along the Ohio River, which it relied on for trade. After battling with Indians, France continued to push southward in its land grabbing, and Anglo-American colonists gathered in Albany, New York, to address the French threat. The colonists sought to forge a stronger alliance with the Iroquois and to coordinate plans for intercolonial defense, but they failed on both counts. England declared war in 1756 and, after winning the protracted battle, the issue of land between European nations was settled when France ceded most of its North American territories to Britain.

1763: A Turning Point

How did colonists' ideas about government differ from those of the British in the 1760s?

British authorities believed that Parliament—which included the king, lords, and commons—represented *all* British subjects regardless of where they lived. In this system of virtual representation, the people's consent to Parliament's actions was assumed. Americans, on the other hand, increasingly believed in direct representation, that they could only be represented by men who lived nearby and whom they elected. Moreover, they understood the lower houses as representing the regions that elected them. Living on the other side of the ocean, colonists were also accustomed to a central government with limited authority and embraced the Real Whig notion that good government was one that left them alone to manage their affairs. As England imposed taxes and greater control over the colonies beginning in 1763, many colonists believed their freedom was endangered and questioned whether authority should lie with the monarchy or the people.

The Stamp Act Crisis

 How did James Otis and Patrick Henry offer different ways to address the Stamp Act Crisis?

Angry about the heavy taxes and questioning Britain's right to impose them, colonists began to wonder how they might resist Parliament yet remain British subjects. At issue for essayists such as James Otis was how to oppose certain acts of Parliament while at the same time recognizing that Parliament was a supreme authority to which they must yield. He argued that Americans had to pay the tax, reluctantly but loyally. In contrast, Patrick Henry introduced seven proposals against the stamp act to the Virginia House of Burgesses. The four propositions adopted by the burgesses echoed Otis's arguments about taxation, but the other three argued that local governments rather than Parliament should have the right to raise taxes. Some colonial newspapers printed all seven resolutions as though they were passed, thus contributing to the spread of these ideas.

Resistance to the Townshend Acts

 How did the American population become politicized in the late 1760s?

Ordinary Americans were not accustomed to being involved in political affairs, which they understood as handled by elites. The Sons of Liberty made a conscious effort to draw people from all ranks into their anti-Townshend campaign, partly because they needed widespread participation for their boycott of British products designed in protest to the act. Although colonial leaders created rituals that would teach illiterate Americans about the reasons for resistance, including celebrations commemorating previous demonstrations and political songs, the people too were involved in the process. Women helped by spinning yarn outdoors in public, symbolically displaying their patriotism for all to see.

Confrontations in Boston

 How did Samuel Adams's Committees of Correspondence mark a turning point in Americans' political thinking?

An original member of the Sons of Liberty, Adams wanted to widen the movement's scope beyond its stronghold in New England cities and seacoast towns and create consensus among Massachusetts residents for the cause of liberty. The pamphlet he produced for the Boston Committee of Correspondence in 1772 was widely distributed. It stated the rights of colonists to life, liberty, and property, and it outlined complaints against England for taxation without representation, unnecessary troops and customs officers on American soil, the use of imperial revenues to pay colonial officials, and the expanded jurisdiction of vice-admiralty courts. Far more radical than earlier documents, this one did not seek to define the limits of parliamentary authority but instead declared colonists' allegiance to America first and England a distant second.

Tea and Turmoil

 How did the Tea Act push the colonies to the brink of revolution?

When Parliament imposed the Tea Act on the colonies in May 1773, it was attempting to save the East India Company from bankruptcy, but colonists recognized it was designed in part to make them admit Parliament's right to tax them. Citizens in several cities wanted to prevent the tea from being unloaded from ships; in Boston, that led to a protest in which the tea was dumped in the harbor by men dressed as Indians. Parliament responded with punitive laws, known as the Coercive or Intolerable Acts, ordering the city to pay for the tea and closing the port until it did. Other acts reorganized the state's government, banned town meetings, and allowed officers to commandeer private buildings to house troops. Colonists saw such measures as proof that Britain would oppress them and sent delegates to a Continental Congress in Philadelphia in 1774 to decide how to respond.

The Unsettled Backcountry

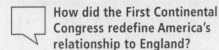

What internal struggles plagued the backcountry during the 1760s and 1770s?

In the North, conflicts over land escalated. In 1765–1766, land riots erupted along the Hudson River, as New Englanders and Europeans who migrated to the region squatted on claimed land. When the court ordered the squatters to clear the land for valid tenants, they rebelled. In the South, Regulator movements formed in South Carolina in the late 1760s and in North Carolina in the early 1770s. Their protests often grew violent, such as in May 1771 when North Carolina Regulators fought and lost a battle with militiamen at Almanace. Additionally, Indian warfare escalated. Lord Dunmore's War resulted in the Shawnee leader Cornstalk ceding the territory that became Kentucky to Dunmore's forces.

Government by Congress and Committee

How did the First Continental Congress redefine America's relationship to England?

Congressmen meeting at the First Continental Congress in September 1774 were not ready for a complete break from England, but they did outline America's grievances, develop a resistance plan, and define America's relationship to Great Britain. Debate covered the spectrum of opinion from the radical call to obey only the king and not Parliament to the more conservative view that would have Parliament and a new American legislature jointly enacting colonial laws. In the end, the group compromised and agreed in the Declaration of Rights and Grievances to obey Parliament on a voluntary basis (rather than as subjects) and resist all taxes imposed by Parliament.

Suggestions for Further Reading

Fred Anderson, *The War That Made America: A Short History of the French and Indian War* (2005)

Bernard Bailyn, *The Ideological Origins of the American Revolution* (1967)

Christopher Leslie Brown, *Moral Capital: Foundations of British Abolitionism* (2006)

Colin G. Calloway, *The Scratch of a Pen: 1763 and the Transformation of North America* (2006)

Vincent Caretta, *Phillis Wheatley: Biography of a Genius in Bondage* (2011)

Benjamin H. Irvin, *Clothed in Robes of Sovereignty: The Continental Congress and the People out of Doors* (2011)

Marjoleine Kars, *Breaking Loose Together: The Regulator Rebellion in Pre-Revolutionary North Carolina* (2002)

Pauline R. Maier, *From Resistance to Revolution: Colonial Radicals and the Development of American Opposition to Britain, 1765–1776* (1972)

Gary B. Nash, *The Unknown American Revolution: The Unruly Birth of Democracy and the Struggle to Create America* (2005)

Andrew Jackson O'Shaughnessy, *An Empire Divided: The American Revolution and the British Caribbean* (2000)

American Revolutions

1775–1783

6

The Mohawks knew her as Konwatsitsiaenni, a leader in the Turtle clan. To the British, she was Molly Brant, common-law wife of the continent's most powerful Indian agent, Sir William Johnson. After the Seven Years' War, Molly Brant became the first lady of Mohawk country, one of the busiest trading regions in the Atlantic world. Her power and influence, wrote one British official, was "far superior to that of all their Chiefs put together."

In the 1760s, people of all nations journeyed to Johnson Hall, the English-style manor that Brant shared with Johnson and their growing biracial family. There visitors might smoke the calumet and drink tea served by African slaves, bury the hatchet and play billiards, view a collection of English silver and Algonquian wampum. Worlds met and mingled at Johnson Hall, and in Molly Brant. She wore Mohawk dress and refused to speak English; Johnson spoke Mohawk and sometimes painted his face in the manner of native warriors. Yet Brant and Johnson named four of their eight mixed-race children after British monarchs: Mary, Elizabeth, Anne, and George.

William Johnson died in 1774, on the eve of a war that would destroy the world he and Molly Brant had built at the western edge of Britain's empire. As Brant returned to her home village of Canajoharie, Mohawk country was transformed into a battleground. When the Americans took up arms against King George, Molly and her younger brother Joseph rallied the Mohawks behind the British. The Oneidas threw in with the patriots, who professed themselves "afraid" that Brant's "influence may give us some trouble."

Through the summer of 1777, Mohawk country burned and bled. Johnson Hall stood abandoned. Tipped off by Brant, pro-British militia and Mohawk warriors ambushed American forces and their native allies at the Oneida village of Oriskany (Oriske) that August. The daylong battle left two hundred patriots and fifty loyalists dead. Joseph Brant's Mohawks torched what remained of Oriskany; Oneida warriors and American troops razed Canajoharie. Soldiers plundered Molly Brant's house. Her people became refugees, hounded and sometimes horsewhipped by patriot forces as they marched north to seek shelter at Fort Niagara.

Chapter Outline

Toward War
Battles of Lexington and Concord | The Siege of Boston | First Year of War | Second Continental Congress | George Washington

Forging an Independent Republic
Varieties of Republicanism | Common Sense | Jefferson and the Declaration of Independence | Colonies to States | Limiting State Governments | Articles of Confederation | Funding a Revolution | Symbolizing a Nation

LINKS TO THE WORLD *New Nations*

Choosing Sides
Patriots | Loyalists | Neutrals | Native Americans | African Americans

The Struggle in the North
New York and New Jersey | Campaign of 1777 | Iroquois Confederacy Splinters | Burgoyne's Surrender | Franco-American Alliance of 1778

Battlefield and Home Front
Militia Units | Continental Army | Officer Corps | Hardship and Disease | Home Front

VISUALIZING THE PAST *Frontier Refugees*

The War Moves South
South Carolina and the Caribbean | Greene and the Southern Campaign | Surrender at Yorktown

Uncertain Victories
Saving Jamaica | Treaty of Paris

LEGACY FOR A PEOPLE AND A NATION
Revolutionary Origins

SUMMARY

After the war, Molly Brant settled in the town of Kingston, in the new British colony of Upper Canada. In compensation for all she had done and for all she had lost, the British government awarded her an annual pension of £100. Her daughters married Canadian officials. Only her surviving son chose to live among the Iroquois, in the new Six Nations reserve on Grand River, north of the new national border dividing what had once been his mother's homeland.

The American Revolution created an enduring republic from thirteen separate colonies. But as Molly Brant's experience shows, it was also a bloody civil war. The fighting uprooted countless families and forced roughly sixty thousand loyalists—black, white, and native—into exile. The rupture of trading relationships between colonies and empire wreaked havoc upon the American economy.

The struggle for independence required revolutionary leaders to accomplish three closely related aims. The first was political and ideological: transforming a loyal resistance into a movement demanding separation from Britain. The colonies' elected officials worked to enlist all European Americans in the patriot cause, and to ensure the neutrality of Indians and slaves.

To win independence, patriot leaders also needed to secure international recognition and aid, particularly from France. They dispatched to Paris the most experienced American diplomat, Benjamin Franklin, who skillfully negotiated the Franco-American alliance of 1778, which proved crucial to the American war effort.

Only the third task directly involved the British. George Washington, named commander-in-chief of the American army in the summer of 1775, soon recognized that his primary goal should be not to win battles so much as to preserve his army to fight another day. Consequently, the story of the Revolutionary War often unfolds in British action and American reaction, British attacks and American defenses and withdrawals.

The challenges the rebellion presented to the British army aided the American war effort. King George's fighting forces—at least 100,000 men over the course of the war—had to cross 3,000 miles of ocean. Over such vast distances, men, materiel, and vital news traveled achingly slowly. The theater of war was itself immense as well. And the United Colonies had no single capital whose conquest would wipe out the rebellion. Against an enemy so various and dispersed, priorities were difficult to assign, especially after the entry of the French on the American side. Faced with such complexities, British military planners made grave errors. In the end, the Americans' improbable triumph owed as much to their geography, their endurance, and their enemy's missteps as to their military prowess.

American victories on the battlefield violently severed the political bonds tying thirteen of the former colonies to Great Britain. But military success does not alone make a nation; that task required profound changes in politics, culture, and society. The triumph of the Continental army only began the long work of creating the United States.

As you read this chapter, keep the following questions in mind:

- **What choices of allegiance confronted residents of North America after 1774? Why did people make the choices they did?**

- **What strategies did the British and American military forces adopt, and why?**

- **How did the United States win independence and forge the outlines of a new national government?**

Chronology

1775	Battles of Lexington and Concord; first shots of war fired
	Siege of Boston begins
	Second Continental Congress begins
	Washington named commander-in-chief of Continental army
	"Olive Branch" petition seeks reconciliation with Britain
	Dunmore's proclamation offers freedom to Virginia patriots' slaves who join British forces
1776	Thomas Paine advocates independence in *Common Sense*
	British evacuate Boston
	Second Continental Congress directs states to draft constitutions
	Declaration of Independence adopted
	New York City falls to British
1777	Articles of Confederation sent to states for ratification
	Philadelphia falls to British
	Burgoyne surrenders at Saratoga
1778	French alliance brings vital assistance to America
	British evacuate Philadelphia
1779	Sullivan expedition destroys Iroquois villages
1780	Charleston falls to British
1781	Articles of Confederation ratified
	Americans take Yorktown; Cornwallis surrenders
1782	British victory over French at Battle of the Saintes secures Jamaica
	Peace negotiations begin
1783	Treaty of Paris grants independence to the United States

Toward War

On January 27, 1775, Lord Dartmouth, Britain's secretary of state for America, wrote to General Thomas Gage in Boston, urging him to act. Opposition could not be "very formidable," Dartmouth wrote.

What were the problems with Great Britain's war strategy?

Battles of Lexington and Concord

Gage, the commander-in-chief of Britain's forces in America and, since the departure of Thomas Hutchinson, also the governor of Massachusetts, received Dartmouth's letter on April 14. He quickly dispatched an expedition to confiscate the stockpile of colonial military supplies at Concord. Boston sent two messengers, William Dawes and Paul Revere (later joined by Dr. Samuel Prescott), to rouse the countryside. When several hundred British regulars approached Lexington at dawn on April 19, they found just seventy militiamen mustered on the common. The Americans' commander ordered his men to withdraw, but as they dispersed, a shot rang out. British soldiers then fired. When they stopped, eight Americans lay dead, and another ten wounded. The British marched on to Concord, five miles away.

There the militia contingents were larger. At the North Bridge, three British soldiers were killed and nine wounded. Then thousands of militiamen hidden in houses and behind trees fired at the British forces as they retreated toward Boston. By day's end, the redcoats had suffered 272 casualties, including 70 deaths. The Americans suffered just 93 casualties.

The Siege of Boston

By April 20, some twenty thousand American militiamen had gathered around Boston. Many soon went home for spring planting, but those who remained were organized into formal units. Boston was thus besieged by patriot militia whose presence effectively contained Gage's forces within the beleaguered town. For nearly a year, the two armies stared at each other across the battlements. The redcoats attacked only once, on June 17, when they drove the Americans from trenches atop Breed's Hill in Charlestown. In that misnamed Battle of Bunker Hill, the British incurred their greatest wartime losses: over 800 wounded and 228 killed. The Americans lost less than half that number.

First Year of War

During the same eleven-month period, patriots captured the British Fort Ticonderoga on Lake Champlain, acquiring much-needed cannon. Trying to bring Canada into the war, they also mounted a northern campaign that ended in disaster at Quebec in early 1776. But the long lull in fighting between the main armies at Boston during the war's first year gave both sides a chance to organize and strategize.

Prime Minister Lord North and his new American secretary, Lord George Germain, made three central assumptions about the war. First, they forecast that patriot forces could not withstand the assaults of trained British regulars. Accordingly, they dispatched Great Britain's largest force ever: 370 transport ships carrying 32,000 troops and tons of supplies, accompanied by 73 naval vessels and 13,000 sailors. Among them were thousands of professional German soldiers (many from the state of Hesse) who had been hired out to Britain. Second, British officials and army officers believed that capturing major cities—a central aim in European warfare—would defeat the rebel army. Third, they assumed that military victory would regain the colonies' allegiance.

All three assumptions proved false. North and Germain vastly underestimated Americans' commitment to resistance. Officials also missed the significance of the American population's dispersal. Although Britain would control each of the largest mainland ports at some time during the war, less than 5 percent of the population lived in those cities. Furthermore, with a vast coastline, commerce was easily rerouted. Capturing cities did relatively little damage to the American cause.

Most of all, London officials did not initially understand that military triumph would not alone bring political victory. Securing the colonies would require Americans to resume their allegiance to the empire. After 1778, King George's ministry determined to achieve that goal by expanding the use of loyalist forces and restoring civilian authority in occupied areas. But the policy came too late. Britain's leaders never fully realized they were fighting an entirely new kind of conflict: not a conventional European war but the first modern war of national liberation.

Second Continental Congress

Britain had a bureaucracy to supervise the war; Americans had only the Second Continental Congress. The delegates who convened in Philadelphia on May 10, 1775, had to assume the mantle of intercolonial government. As spring edged into summer, Congress organized the United Colonies to prosecute the war. The delegates authorized the printing of money, established a committee to supervise foreign relations, strengthened the militia, and ordered ships built for a new Continental navy. In July, Pennsylvania's John Dickinson proclaimed, "We are reduced to the alternative of chusing an unconditional submission to the tyranny of irritated ministers, or resistance by force.—The latter is our choice."

Yet for many delegates, hesitation remained. That same month, Dickinson drafted a petition beseeching the king to halt the growing conflict. Approved by Congress on July 5, 1775, the address, now known as the Olive Branch petition, asserted that its 48 signatories remained "your Majesty's faithful subjects in the colonies."

Even while preparing the Olive Branch petition—which the king would ultimately reject—Congress pursued its most urgent task: creating the Continental army and appointing its leadership. Many delegates recognized the importance of naming a commander-in-chief who was not a New Englander. In mid-June, John Adams proposed the appointment of a fellow delegate to Congress, **George Washington** of Virginia. Congress unanimously concurred.

George Washington
American military leader and the first President of the United States (1789–1797).

George Washington

Devoted to the American cause, Washington was dignified, conservative, and respectable—a man of unimpeachable integrity. The early death of his older brother and his marriage to the wealthy widow Martha Custis had made him one of the wealthiest planters in Virginia. Though a slaveholding aristocrat, Washington was committed to representative government. After his mistakes early in the Seven Years' War, he had repaired his reputation by maintaining a calm demeanor under fire.

Washington took command of the army surrounding Boston in July 1775. In March 1776, the arrival of cannon captured at Ticonderoga finally enabled him to pressure the redcoats, yet an assault on Boston proved unnecessary. Sir William Howe, Britain's new commander, wanted to transfer his men to New York City, where he expected support from **loyalists**. On March 17, the British and more than a thousand of their supporters abandoned Boston forever.

loyalists Colonists who retained a profound reverence for the British crown and believed that if they failed to defend their king, they would sacrifice their personal honor.

Forging an Independent Republic

How did Thomas Paine's Common Sense *help reshape the war's purpose?*

Well before the British fleet (along with many loyalist exiles) sailed north to await reinforcements in Halifax, the colonies were moving inexorably toward independence. By the late summer of 1775, Congress had begun to mold the tenets of republican thought into the structures of republican governments and to fashion the rituals and symbols of a nation.

Varieties of Republicanism

Since its first meeting, in the autumn of 1774, Congress's actions had been strongly influenced by republican thought. Three different definitions of republicanism jockeyed for preeminence in the new United States. Despite their differences, all three strands contrasted the industrious virtue of America with the decadence of Britain and Europe. Most agreed that a virtuous country would be composed of hardworking citizens who would dress simply, live plainly, and elect wise leaders to public office.

Ancient history and political theory informed the first concept, embraced chiefly by members of the educated elite (such as the Adamses of Massachusetts). The histories of Greece and Rome suggested that republics fared best when they were small and homogeneous. Unless a republic's citizens were willing to sacrifice their private interests for the public good, government would collapse. A truly virtuous man, classical republican theory insisted, had the temperament—and the resources—to forgo personal profit and work for the best interests of the nation. Society would be governed by members of a "natural aristocracy," men whose talent elevated them to positions of power. Rank would be founded on merit rather than birth.

A second definition, advanced by other elites and some skilled craftsmen, followed the Scottish thinker Adam Smith, whose treatise entitled *An Inquiry into the Nature and Causes of the Wealth of Nations* was published just weeks before Congress declared American independence. Smith argued that republican virtue would be achieved through the pursuit of private interests, rather than through the subordination of personal profit to communal ideals.

The third notion of republicanism was more egalitarian. Men who advanced this version—including many with scant formal education—wanted government to respond directly to the needs of ordinary folk, and rejected the notion that the "lesser sort" should defer to their "betters." They were democrats in more or less the modern sense, in an era when "democracy" was a term of insult, roughly equivalent to mob rule. For them, the untutored wisdom of the people embodied republican virtue. The most prominent advocate of this concept of republicanism was a radical English printer named Thomas Paine, who sailed to Philadelphia in 1774 bearing letters of introduction from Benjamin Franklin. In 1776, he would be one of the best-known writers in the world.

Common Sense

Common Sense A pamphlet written by Thomas Paine that advocated freedom from British rule.

First printed in January 1776, Thomas Paine's **Common Sense** sold for two shillings—about $15 in today's money. Perhaps one hundred thousand Americans bought copies or read sections reprinted in newspapers. Thousands more heard it read aloud in taverns, coffeehouses, and public squares. An estimated one in five American adults became familiar with Paine's arguments.

Paine's best seller did not create American independence, but it transformed the terms of debate. He wrote with passion verging on rage, in straightforward prose that reflected the oral culture of ordinary folk. *Common Sense* took the Bible—the only book familiar to most Americans—as its primary source of authority. As its title suggested, *Common Sense* aimed to cut through a fog of received wisdom—to see clearly and speak plain.

Paine insisted that America's independence was inevitable. Just as all children one day grow up, the "authority of Great Britain over this continent, is a form of government, which sooner or later must have an end." He said monarchs were "ridiculous" tyrants, and aristocrats greedy and corrupt. And for the frequently heard assertion that an independent America would be weak and divided, he substituted unlimited confidence in its future: "The sun never shined on a cause of greater worth."

It is unclear how many were converted to the cause by *Common Sense*. But by late spring, towns, grand juries, and provincial legislatures drafted at least

Link to *Common Sense*

ninety different statements demanding American independence. Then, on June 7, Congress confirmed the movement toward separation. Virginia's Richard Henry Lee introduced the crucial resolution: "that these United Colonies are, and of right ought to be, free and independent States…that all political connection between them and the State of Great Britain is, and ought to be, totally dissolved." Congress postponed a vote on Lee's resolution to allow time for consultation and public reaction. In the meantime, they directed a five-man committee—including Thomas Jefferson, John Adams, and Benjamin Franklin—to draft a declaration of independence. The committee assigned primary responsibility for writing the document to Jefferson, a thirty-four-year-old Virginia lawyer known for his eloquence.

Jefferson and the Declaration of Independence

A member of the House of Burgesses, Thomas Jefferson had been educated at the College of William and Mary and in the law offices of a prominent attorney. His broad knowledge of history and political theory was evident in the Declaration and his draft of the Virginia state constitution. An intensely private man, Jefferson loved his home and family deeply. Not until after his wife Martha's death in 1782, from complications following the birth of their sixth (but only third surviving) child, did Jefferson fully commit himself to public service. He would not marry again. In the late 1780s, he began a long-lasting relationship with one of his slaves, Sally Hemings. Hemings was Martha Jefferson's half-sister, born of another relationship between a slave owner and enslaved woman. Between 1790 and 1808, she bore seven children whose father was almost certainly Thomas Jefferson.

Jefferson's draft of the **Declaration of Independence** reached Congress on June 28, 1776. The delegates voted for independence four days later, then refined the wording of the Declaration for two more days, adopting it with some changes on July 4. The Declaration of Independence (see Appendix) concentrated on the actions of George III, accusing him of attempting to destroy representative government in the colonies and of oppressing Americans.

Declaration of Independence Proposed by the Second Continental Congress, this document proclaimed independence of the Thirteen Colonies from British rule.

The Declaration's chief long-term importance lay in the first lines of its second paragraph, ringing statements of principle that have served ever since as the ideal to which Americans aspire: "We hold these truths to be self-evident: That all men are created equal; that they are endowed by their Creator with certain unalienable rights; that among these are life, liberty and the pursuit of happiness; that, to secure these rights, governments are instituted among men, deriving their just powers from the consent of the governed; that whenever any form of government becomes destructive of these ends, it is the right of the people to alter or to abolish it, and to institute new government."

By adopting the Declaration, the congressmen committed treason, a capital offense. When they concluded with the assertion that they "mutually pledge[d] to each other our lives, our fortunes, and our sacred honor," they spoke the truth.

Colonies to States

Shortly before adopting the Declaration, Congress directed the individual provinces to replace their colonial charters with state constitutions. After several years of experimentation with different methods, states eventually decided to elect conventions for the sole purpose of drafting constitutions. In this fashion, states sought authorization directly from the people to establish new governments. Delegates then submitted the constitutions they had drafted to voters for ratification.

Under their colonial charters, Americans learned to fear the power of governors and to see their legislatures as defenders of the people. Accordingly, the first state constitutions typically provided for the governor to be elected annually, mandated term limits, and gave him little independent authority. Pennsylvania's constitution featured no governor or upper legislative house.

The constitutions expanded the legislature's powers. Each state except Pennsylvania and Vermont retained a two-house structure, with members of the upper house serving longer terms and required to own more property than their counterparts in the lower house. But they also redrew electoral districts to more accurately reflect population patterns. Finally, most states lowered property qualifications for voting. Thus, the revolutionary era witnessed the first deliberate attempt to broaden the base of American government.

Limiting State Governments

Seven constitutions contained formal bills of rights, and others had similar clauses. Most guaranteed citizens freedom of the press, fair trials, the right to consent to taxation, and protection against general search warrants; an independent judiciary would uphold such rights. Most states also guaranteed freedom of religion, but seven states required that all officeholders be Christians, and some continued to support churches with tax money.

In general, state constitution makers put greater emphasis on preventing tyranny than on wielding political power effectively. But establishing such weak political units, especially in wartime, all but ensured that the constitutions would need revision. Revised versions increased the powers of the governor and reduced the legislature's authority.

American politicians initially concentrated on drafting state constitutions and devoted little attention to their national government. Not until late 1777 did Congress send the **Articles of Confederation**—which outlined a national government—to the states for ratification.

Articles of Confederation
The first document that sought to create the terms of a national government. It reserved substantial powers for the states, granting to each state its "sovereignty, freedom and independence."

Articles of Confederation

Under the Articles, the chief organ of national government was a unicameral (one-house) legislature in which each state had one vote. Its powers included conducting foreign relations, mediating interstate disputes, controlling maritime affairs, regulating Indian trade, and valuing state and national money. Congress could request but not compel the payment of taxes. (See the Appendix for the text of the Articles of Confederation.)

The Articles required the unanimous consent of state legislatures for ratification or amendment, and a clause concerning western lands proved troublesome. The draft Congress accepted in 1777 allowed states to retain land claims from their original charters. But states with definite western boundaries (such as Maryland and New Jersey) wanted the others to cede to the national government their landholdings west of the Appalachian Mountains. Maryland refused to accept the Articles until 1781, when Virginia finally surrendered its western holdings to national jurisdiction (see Map 7.1).

Funding a Revolution Finance posed the most persistent problem faced by both state and national governments. Congress borrowed what it could at home and abroad, but such mechanisms went only so far. With limited credit and even less power to tax, Congress turned to printing paper money.

Through 1775 and the first half of 1776, these paper dollars—dubbed "Continentals"—passed at face value. But in late 1776, as the American army suffered reverses, prices rose, confidence in the nation's credit fell, and the value of the Continental began to depreciate. State governments tried to prop up the ailing currency by requiring acceptance of paper money on an equal footing with specie (coins). States borrowed funds, established lotteries, and levied taxes. But they also printed their own competing currencies. State currencies—totaling roughly $209 million—funded nearly 40 percent of the cost of the war. But as the conflict dragged on, they too plummeted in value.

By the end of 1780, the Continental had declined so far that it took 100 paper dollars to purchase one Spanish silver dollar (see Figure 6.1). Congress responded

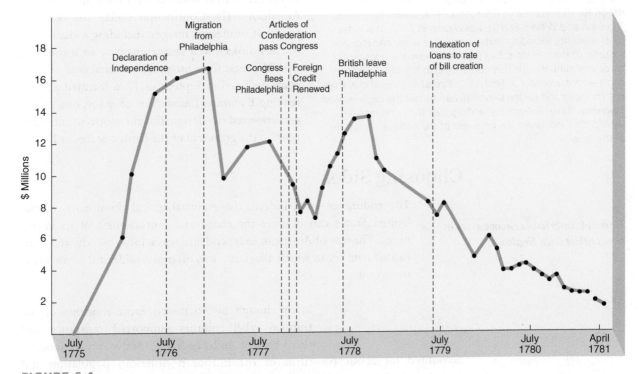

FIGURE 6.1
The Changing Value of the Continental Dollar, 1777–1781
This graph, illustrating the total value in silver coin of congressional bills of credit issued during the Revolution, shows that confidence in the new American currency was high at the beginning of the war. In 1777 and early 1778, the Continental's value sank with American defeats and rose with American victories. But after July 1778, the enormous number of bills in circulation caused their value to plummet. By the end of the war, they were virtually worthless.

(Source: Adapted from Charles W. Calormis, "Institutional Failure, Monetary Scarcity, and the Depreciation of the Continental," *Journal of Economic History,* Vol. 48, No. 1 (March 1988), p. 56.)

National Archives

Congress debated the design of a proper emblem for the new nation for six years before this national seal, drawn by Charles Thomson and William Barton, was chosen in 1782. While many of its elements, including thirteen stripes of white and red, and a cluster of thirteen stars, had surfaced in earlier proposals, the fierce and martial eagle was new. Benjamin Franklin called the eagle—once a symbol of Britain—"a Bird of bad moral character." But Thomson and Barton prevailed. Barton said the eagle evoked "supreme Power & Authority, and signifies the Congress"—wishful thinking, given the weakness of the national legislature at the time.

by devaluing its notes, accepting Continental dollars in payment of taxes at one-fortieth of their face value. This scheme succeeded in retiring much of the "old tenor" paper, at an enormous cost to people who had taken the notes. All told, Congress issued more than $200 million worth of Continental dollars—funding about 40 percent of the cost of the war—before stopping the presses.

Symbolizing a Nation

In addition to passing laws and mustering troops, Congress devised a wide array of symbols and ceremonies to promote a sense of "we" in the everyday interactions of ordinary citizens. The United States shared no common language or lineage. When they printed money, coined medals, invented seals, designed uniforms, and proclaimed festivals, members of Congress worked to create unity from the diversity of former British subjects who must now become Americans. The Continental dollar, for example, tried out numerous images, including a chain with thirteen links and a beaver gnawing an unyielding oak. The crest for a proposed national coat of arms commissioned in September 1776 featured a scroll reading *E Pluribus Unum*: "out of many, one." Congress rejected the design, but the motto would reappear on the great seal of the United States in 1782.

Choosing Sides

How did Americans choose sides in the conflict with England?

The endurance—and, indeed, the eventual global dominance—of the United States can obscure the chaos and tentativeness of its beginnings. The war of American independence was a long, bloody, and multisided conflict in which allegiance was often unstable and virtue often uncertain.

Patriots

Many though by no means most residents of the thirteen rebel colonies supported resistance and then backed independence. Active revolutionaries accounted for about two-fifths of the European American population and included small and middling farmers, members of dominant Protestant sects, Chesapeake gentry, merchants, urban artisans, elected officeholders, and people of English descent. Wives usually, but not always, fell in with their husbands about politics. Although such groups supported the Revolution, some patriots sought more sweeping political reform than others. Many fought for social and economic change instead or as well.

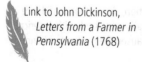

Link to John Dickinson, *Letters from a Farmer in Pennsylvania* (1768)

Links TO THE WORLD

New Nations

The American Revolution created the United States and led to the formation of three other nations: Canada, Sierra Leone, and Australia.

In modern Canada before the Revolution, only Nova Scotia had many English-speaking settlers. Largely New Englanders, they were recruited after 1758 to repopulate the region forcibly taken from the exiled Acadians. During and after the Revolution, loyalist families moved to the region that is now Canada, which remained under British rule. In just a few years, the refugees transformed the former French colony, laying the foundation of the modern Canadian nation.

An early view of the settlement of black loyalists in West Africa, the foundation of the modern nation of Sierra Leone.

Sierra Leone, too, was founded by colonial exiles— African Americans who fled to the British army during the war. Many of them ended up in London. Seeing the refugees' poverty, charitable merchants— calling themselves the Committee for Relief of the Black Poor—developed a plan to resettle the African Americans elsewhere. The refugees rejected the Bahamas, fearing reenslavement there. They accepted a return to their ancestors' homeland. In early 1787, vessels carrying about four hundred settlers reached Sierra Leone in West Africa, where representatives of the Black Poor committee had acquired land. The first years were difficult, and many of the newcomers died of disease and deprivation. But in 1792, several thousand loyalist African Americans left Nova Scotia to join the struggling colony. The influx ensured Sierra Leone's survival; it remained a part of the British empire until achieving independence in 1961.

At the Paris peace negotiations in 1782, American diplomats refused to allow the United States to continue to serve as a dumping ground for British convicts. Britain thus needed another destination for the felons its courts sentenced to transportation. It sent them to Australia, claimed for Britain in 1770. Britain continued this practice until 1868, but voluntary migrants also came. The modern nation was created on January 1, 1901.

Thus, the founding of the United States links the nation to the formation of its northern neighbor and to new nations in West Africa and the Pacific.

Thomas Rowlandson, an English artist, sketched the boatloads of male and female convicts as they were being ferried to the ships that would take them to their new lives in the prison colony of Australia. Note the gibbet on the shore with two hanging bodies— symbolizing the fate these people were escaping.

Loyalists

At least one-fifth of the European American population rejected independence. Their objections to violent protest, their desire to uphold legally constituted government, and their fears of anarchy combined to make them sensitive to its dangers. British-appointed government officials; Anglican clergy everywhere and lay Anglicans in the North; tenant farmers; members of persecuted religious sects; backcountry southerners who had rebelled against eastern rule in the late 1760s and early 1770s; and non-English ethnic minorities, especially Scots: all believed that the colonial assemblies had shown little concern for their welfare in the past. Joined by merchants whose trade depended on imperial connections, and by former British military men who had settled in America after 1763, they formed a loyalist core.

Whole regions of British America continued within the empire. Halifax, Quebec, and St. John (Prince Edward Island) in what became Canada; as well as East and West Florida, the Bahamas, Barbados, Dominica, Grenada, Jamaica, the Leeward Islands, and St. Vincent remained loyal to Britain, while Bermuda steered a precarious neutral course. The unfolding war cannot be understood without accounting for Britain's desire to protect its valuable Caribbean possessions, especially Jamaica.

After the war, roughly sixty thousand American loyalists scattered to different parts of the British empire. Their number included some eight to ten thousand escaped slaves. In addition, slave-owning loyalists carried an estimated fifteen thousand enslaved African Americans along the varied paths of their diaspora from the United States.

Neutrals

Between the patriots and the loyalists, there remained in the uneasy middle perhaps two-fifths of the European American population. Some, such as Quakers, were sincere pacifists. Others shifted their allegiance to whichever side appeared to be winning, or cared little about politics and deferred to those in power. Neutral colonists resisted British and Americans alike when taxes became too high or when calls for militia service came too often. Neutrals made up an especially large proportion of the population in the backcountry, where Scots-Irish settlers had little love for either the patriot gentry or British authorities.

To patriots, apathy or neutrality was as heinous as loyalism. In the winter of 1775–1776, the Second Continental Congress recommended that all "disaffected" persons be disarmed and arrested. State legislatures began to require voters (or, in some cases, all free adult men) to take oaths of allegiance; refusal usually meant banishment to England or extra taxes. The patriots' policies helped to prevent their opponents from banding together to threaten the revolutionary cause.

Native Americans

Their grievances against European American newcomers flooding the backcountry predisposed many Native Americans toward an alliance with Great Britain. Yet some chiefs urged caution: the British abandonment of Fort Pitt (and them) suggested that the Crown might not protect them in the future. Moreover,

British officials understood that neither the Indians' style of fighting nor their war aims necessarily coincided with British goals and methods. Accordingly, they at first sought from Indians only a promise of neutrality.

Patriots also courted Indians' neutrality. In 1775, the Second Continental Congress sent a message to Indian communities, describing the war as "a family quarrel between us and Old England" and requesting that native warriors "not join on either side." The Iroquois Confederacy responded with a pledge of neutrality that would prove short-lived.

The British victory over France in 1763 had destroyed the Indian nations' most effective means of maintaining their independence: playing European powers against one another. Only a few communities (among them the Stockbridge of New England and the Oneidas in New York) unwaveringly supported the American revolt; most native villages either remained neutral or sporadically aligned themselves with the British.

Warfare between settlers and Indians persisted in the backcountry long after fighting between patriot and redcoat armies had ceased. Indeed, the Revolutionary War constituted a brief chapter in the ongoing struggle for control of the region west of the Appalachians, which continued through the next century.

African Americans

So, too, the African Americans' Revolution formed but one battle in an epic freedom struggle that continues in the twenty-first century. African Americans did not need revolutionary ideology to tell them that slavery was wrong, but the pervasive talk of liberty added fuel to their struggle. Above all, the goal of bondspeople was *personal* independence—liberation from slavery.

In New England, where blacks comprised the smallest share of the population, many joined the patriot ranks. But most slaves in most colonies thought they stood a better chance with the British. Groups of bondsmen from Massachusetts to South Carolina offered to assist the British army in exchange for freedom. In April 1775, several Williamsburg, Virginia, slaves sent word to the royal governor, Lord Dunmore, that they were prepared to "take up arms" on his behalf. Dunmore began to formulate the policy he announced in November, with a proclamation offering to free any Virginia slaves and indentured servants who abandoned their patriot masters and joined the British. An estimated 2,500 enslaved Virginians—among them numerous women and children—did so. The surviving men (many perished in a smallpox epidemic) were organized into the British Ethiopian Regiment.

The best recent estimates suggest that some thirty to forty thousand, more than two-thirds of whom were women and children, escaped their bondage during the conflict. Those who survived till the war's end left with the redcoats, joining the global loyalist diaspora.

Patriots could never completely ignore the threats posed by loyalists and neutrals, or the particular aims of Indians and African Americans. But the difficulties of a large-scale slave revolt on the mainland, coupled with dissension in Indian communities and the patriots' successful campaign to neutralize loyalists, generally allowed the revolutionaries to remain in control of the countryside.

The Struggle in the North

What was France's role in the American Revolution?

In late June 1776, the first ships carrying Sir William Howe's troops from Halifax appeared off the coast of New York (see Map 6.1). Taking New York, home to numerous loyalists, would allow the British to consolidate their colonial allies, isolate New England, and, as Howe's successor put it, "gain the hearts & subdue the minds of America." On July 2, redcoats landed on Staten Island, but Howe waited for reinforcements from England before attacking. Washington therefore had time to march his army of seventeen thousand south from Boston to defend Manhattan.

MAP 6.1
The War in the North, 1775–1778

The early phase of the Revolutionary War was dominated by British troop movements in the Boston area, the redcoats' evacuation to Nova Scotia in the spring of 1776, and the subsequent British invasion of New York and New Jersey. Source: Copyright © Cengage Learning 2015

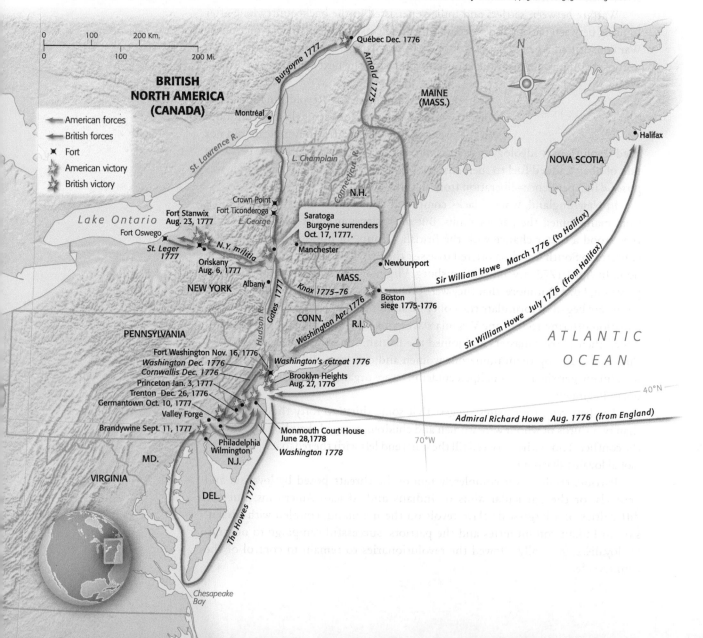

New York and New Jersey

By August, when British forces reached full strength, they comprised some twenty-four thousand men, including at least eight hundred fugitive slaves. Washington and his men, still inexperienced, made major mistakes, losing battles at Brooklyn Heights and on Manhattan Island. In September, New York City fell to the British, who captured nearly three thousand American soldiers.

As Washington and his men slowly retreated into Pennsylvania, British forces took control of most of New Jersey. But Washington determined to strike back. He crossed the Delaware River at night to attack a Hessian encampment at **Trenton** early on December 26. The patriots captured more than nine hundred Hessians and killed another thirty; only three Americans were wounded. Several days later, Washington defeated British forces at Princeton. Having gained command of the field, Washington set up winter quarters at Morristown, New Jersey.

Trenton New Jersey battle where Washington took almost a thousand Hessian prisoners on December 26. It significantly boosted the flailing morale of Washington's troops to fight on.

Campaign of 1777

British strategy for 1777 still aimed to isolate New England from the other colonies. General John Burgoyne would lead redcoat and Indian invaders down the Hudson River from Canada to rendezvous near Albany with a similar force moving east. The combined forces would then presumably link up with Howe's troops in New York City. But Howe was planning to capture Philadelphia. Thus in 1777 this independent operation of British armies in America ultimately resulted in disaster.

Howe delayed beginning the Philadelphia campaign for months, and then took precious weeks to transport his troops by sea. By the time British forces advanced, Washington had had time to prepare his defenses. The two armies clashed at Brandywine Creek in September, and then at Germantown a month later. Although the British won both engagements, the Americans acquitted themselves well. The redcoats captured Philadelphia in late September, forcing Congress to move inland. But the campaign season was nearly over, and the revolutionary army had gained skill and confidence.

Far to the north, Burgoyne was headed toward defeat. He and his men had set out from Montreal in mid-June. An easy British triumph at Fort Ticonderoga in July was followed by two setbacks in August—the redcoats and Mohawks halted their march east after the battle at Oriskany, New York; and in a clash near Bennington, Vermont, American militiamen nearly wiped out eight hundred of Burgoyne's German mercenaries.

The Stockbridge Indians of western Massachusetts were among the only native groups to ally themselves firmly with the Continental army. Johann von Ewald, a Hessian captain whose unit battled the Stockbridge troops at White Plains, New York, drew this sketch of a Stockbridge warrior. Ewald noted that native soldiers marched in deerskin shoes and carried bows, arrows, and battle-axes along with their muskets. "Through the nose and in the ears they wore rings," Ewald wrote in his journal. Elements of traditional Stockbridge culture had survived many years among Christian missionaries.

Iroquois Confederacy Splinters

The August 1777 battle at Oriskany revealed new divisions within the Six Nations of the Iroquois Confederacy, formally pledged to neutrality. The loyalist Mohawk bands led by **Molly and Joseph Brant** won over the Senecas and the Cayugas. The Oneidas—committed to the American side—brought in the Tuscaroras before fragmenting into pro-British, pro-patriot, and neutral factions. At Oriskany, some Oneidas and Tuscaroras fought with patriot militiamen against their Mohawk brethren, shattering a three-hundred-year-old league of friendship.

Molly and Joseph Brant
Mohawk leaders who supported the British.

The collapse of Iroquois unity and the confederacy's abandonment of neutrality had devastating consequences. In 1778, British-allied warriors raided villages in western Pennsylvania and New York. The Americans the following summer dispatched an expedition to burn Iroquois crops and settlements. The devastation forced many bands to seek food and shelter north of the Great Lakes during the winter of 1779–1780. Many Iroquois followed Molly Brant's path into exile, settling permanently in Canada.

Burgoyne's Surrender

After several skirmishes with American soldiers commanded by General Horatio Gates, Burgoyne was surrounded near **Saratoga**, New York. On October 17, 1777, he surrendered his entire force.

Saratoga   A turning point in the American Revolution. The American victory in this battle convinced France that Americans could win the war, leading France to ally with the colonists.

Burgoyne's defeat buoyed patriots and disheartened Britons. Most important, the American victory at Saratoga drew France formally into the conflict. The American Revolution gave the French an opportunity to avenge their defeat in the Seven Years' War. Even before Benjamin Franklin arrived in Paris in late 1776, France covertly supplied the revolutionaries with military necessities. Indeed, 90 percent of the gunpowder used by the Americans during the war's first two years came from France, transported via its Caribbean colony in Martinique.

Franco-American Alliance of 1778

Franklin worked tirelessly to strengthen ties between the two nations. Adopting a plain style of dress, he played on the French image of Americans as virtuous farmers. In February 1778, the countries signed two treaties. In the Treaty of Amity and Commerce, France recognized American independence and established trade ties. In the Treaty of Alliance, France and the United States pledged that neither would negotiate peace with the British without consulting the other. France also abandoned any future claim to Canada and to North American territory east of the Mississippi River.

The French alliance had two major benefits for the patriot cause. First, France began to aid the Americans openly, sending troops, warships, arms, ammunition, clothing, and blankets. Second, Britain now had to fight France in the Caribbean and elsewhere. Spain's entry into the war as an ally of France (but not of the United States) in 1779, followed by Holland's in 1780, turned what had been a colonial rebellion into a global war. The French aided the Americans throughout the conflict, but in its latter half that assistance proved vital.

Battlefield and Home Front

How was the Continental army staffed?

The shooting war remained in the northern and mid-Atlantic colonies through 1778. After France entered the conflict, Britain's attention shifted southward, and the colonies north of Pennsylvania saw little action. Yet the war also extended far beyond the battlefield, and it affected colonists across North America for eight long years. Roughly two hundred thousand men—nearly 40 percent of the free male population over the age of sixteen—served either in state militia units or in the Continental army over the course of the conflict. Their sacrifice and suffering changed their lives, and the lives of everyone in their households.

Militia Units

Only in the first months of the war was the revolutionaries' army manned primarily by the semi-mythical "citizen-soldier," the militiaman who swapped his plow for a musket. After a few months, early arrivals went home. They reenlisted only briefly when the contending armies neared their farms and towns. In such militia units, elected officers and the soldiers who chose them reflected local status hierarchies, yet these units retained a flexibility absent from the Continental army, composed of men in statewide units led by appointed officers.

Continental Army

As in Britain's military, the Continental army's officer corps was composed of gentlemen—men of property—who exercised strict control over soldiers. The soldiers were primarily young, single, or propertyless men. They enlisted for long periods or for the war's duration. Some were ardent patriots; others saw the army as a chance to earn monetary bonuses or land. To meet their quotas, towns and states recruited everyone they could, including recent immigrants. Nearly half of Pennsylvania soldiers were of Irish origin, and about 13 percent were German.

Dunmore's proclamation led Congress in January 1776 to modify an earlier policy prohibiting African Americans in the regular army. Recruiters in northern states turned increasingly to bondsmen, often promising them freedom after the war. Southern states initially resisted, but all except Georgia and South Carolina eventually enlisted black soldiers. Approximately five thousand African Americans served in the Continental army, commonly in racially integrated units. They were assigned tasks that others shunned, such as burying the dead and foraging for food. At any given time they composed about 10 percent of the regular army, but they seldom served in militia units.

American wives and widows of poor soldiers came to the army with their menfolk because they were too impoverished to survive alone. Such camp followers—roughly 3 percent of the total number of troops—worked as cooks, nurses, and launderers.

Officer Corps

Officers in the Continental army lived according to different rules of conduct and compensation than did enlisted men. A colonel earned seven times as much as a common soldier, and a junior officer was paid one and one-half times as much. Officers were discouraged from fraternizing with enlisted men, and sometimes punished for doing so.

Continental officers developed an intense sense of pride and commitment to the revolutionary cause. Officers' wives, too, prided themselves on their and their husbands' service. Unlike poor women, they did not travel with the army but instead made extended visits while the troops were in camp. Martha Washington and other officers' wives, for example, lived at Valley Forge in the winter of 1777–1778. They brought food, clothing, and household furnishings to make their stay more comfortable, and they entertained each other and their menfolk at teas, dinners, and dances. They created friendships later renewed when some of their husbands became the new nation's leaders.

Hardship and Disease

Ordinary soldiers endured great hardship. Wages were low, and often the army could not meet the payroll. Soldiers occasionally hired themselves out as laborers to nearby farmers to augment their meager earnings. Rations (a daily allotment of bread, meat, vegetables, milk, and beer) did not always appear, leaving men to forage for food. When conditions deteriorated, troops threatened mutiny (though only a few carried out that threat) or simply deserted. Punishments for desertion, theft, and assault were harsh; convicted soldiers were sentenced to hundreds of lashes, whereas officers were publicly humiliated, deprived of their commissions, and discharged in disgrace.

Disease—especially dysentery, various fevers, and, early in the war, smallpox—was a constant feature of camp life. Because most British soldiers had already survived smallpox (which was endemic in Europe), it did not pose as significant a threat to redcoat troops. In early 1777, Washington ordered that the entire regular army be inoculated. Inoculation, coupled with the increasing numbers of foreign-born (and mostly immune) men who enlisted, helped to protect Continental soldiers later in the war, contributing significantly to the eventual American victory.

American soldiers and sailors unfortunate enough to be captured by the British endured great suffering, especially those held in makeshift prisons or on prison ships (known as hulks) in or near Manhattan. Redcoat officers regarded the patriots as rebellious traitors rather than as prisoners of war. Fed meager rations and kept in crowded, unsanitary conditions, over half of these prisoners eventually fell victim to disease.

Home Front

Wartime disruptions affected the lives of all Americans. Both American and British soldiers plundered farms and houses. Moreover, troops carried disease wherever they went, including when they returned home. People suffered from shortages of salt, soap, flour, and other necessities. Severe inflation hampered spending (see Figure 6.1). With export markets curtailed, income fell dramatically.

Even such basic social patterns as gender roles were profoundly altered by the war. With men absent from their homes, wives who previously had handled only the "indoor affairs" of their households found themselves responsible for "outdoor affairs" as well. Most white women did not work in the fields themselves, but they supervised field hands and managed their families' finances. These new responsibilities added to the burdens of wives and mothers, but also gave some of them a sense of independence and a connection to the public life of the new nation.

Frontier Refugees

In 1763, following its victory in the Seven Years' War, Great Britain took command of Fort Detroit. Shown here in an eighteenth-century watercolor, the fort was located on the narrow strait connecting Lake Huron to Lake Erie. The strategic site controlled water access to the three westernmost Great Lakes; such water travel was crucial in an era with few and poor frontier roads. Patriot forces tried twice to capture Detroit, from which Indian raiding parties attacked frontier settlements. Britain's native allies defeated the revolutionaries both times.

Throughout the war, Detroit served as a magnet for loyalist refugees. Among them was Marie-Therese Berthelet Lasselle, who fled with her family to the fort from their trading post at what is now Fort Wayne, Indiana. Depicted here is her self-portrait in watercolor on silk, with additional silk embroidery. What can we learn about frontier female refugees from such sources? What does this tell us about her aspirations, as well as her skills?

The Bridgeman Art Library

The artist who painted this watercolor of early Detroit is unknown. The view shows both the village and the fort that protected the residents.

Monroe County Historical Commissions, Monroe, Michigan

Only genteel women learned how to produce such works as these, combining embroidery and watercolor. Great artistic skills contribute to this remarkable self-portrait by Marie-Therese Berthelet Lasselle.

The War Moves South

What events led the British to cease offensive operations and begin peace negotiations in 1782?

In the wake of the Saratoga disaster, British military leaders reassessed their strategy. With France (and soon Spain) in the fight, the North American theater shrank in importance; defending the West Indies, and even England and Ireland, became priorities. Britain's attention shifted toward the southern colonies in large part to create a base of operations from which to sustain and protect its Caribbean dominions. After 1778, Britain continued the American war chiefly to serve the ends of empire in the West Indies and in Europe.

South Carolina and the Caribbean

In June 1778, Sir Henry Clinton, who replaced Howe as Britain's commander, ordered the evacuation of Philadelphia and sent a convoy that captured the French Caribbean island of St. Lucia, thereafter a key British base. Clinton also dispatched a small expedition to Georgia. When Savannah and then Augusta fell into British hands, he became convinced that a southern strategy could succeed. In late 1779, he sailed from New York to besiege Charleston (see Map 6.2). The Americans trapped there held out for months, but on May 12, 1780, General Benjamin Lincoln surrendered the patriots' entire southern army—5,500 men.

The redcoats quickly spread through South Carolina, establishing garrisons at key points in the interior. Hundreds of South Carolinians proclaimed renewed loyalty to the Crown. Thousands of escaped slaves streamed into Charleston, ready to assist the British in exchange for freedom. Clinton began the process of pacifying the south. Because there were three sides in this phase of the conflict—the British army, the Continental army, and over twenty thousand African Americans seeking freedom from bondage—one historian labels the southern campaign a "triagonal war."

The entry of France, Spain, and Holland made the southern campaign a naval as well as a land war. France's powerful navy picked off Britain's Caribbean islands one by one, including Grenada—second only to Jamaica in sugar production—and, in 1781, St. Christopher. The British capture of the Dutch island of St. Eustatius in early 1781 actually cost them dearly, for Admiral Sir George Rodney neglected to pursue the French fleet to Virginia, where it would play a major role in the **battle at Yorktown**.

On land, the fall of Charleston failed to dishearten the patriots; instead, it spurred them to greater exertions. Patriot women in four states formed the Ladies Association, which collected money to purchase shirts for needy soldiers. Recruiting efforts were revitalized. Nevertheless, at Camden in August 1780, forces under **Lord Cornwallis**, the new British commander in the South, defeated a reorganized southern army led by Horatio Gates.

Greene and the Southern Campaign

After the Camden defeat, Washington (who remained in the North to contain the British garrison at New York) appointed General Nathanael Greene to command the southern campaign.

battle at Yorktown The battle at Yorktown, Virginia, which resulted in the defeat of British military leader Lord Cornwallis and his surrender to George Washington.

Lord Cornwallis British general whose surrender at York town in 1781 effectively ended the Revolutionary War.

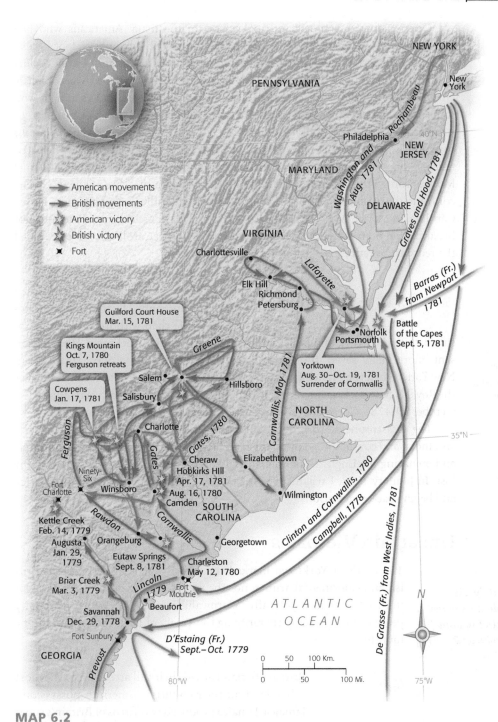

MAP 6.2

The War in the South

The southern war—after the British invasion of Georgia in late 1778—was characterized by a series of British thrusts into the interior, leading to battles with American defenders in both North and South Carolina. Finally, after promising beginnings, Cornwallis's foray into Virginia ended with disaster at Yorktown in October 1781. Source: Copyright © Cengage Learning 2015

Greene adopted a conciliatory policy toward the many Americans who had switched sides. He ordered his troops to treat captives fairly and not to loot loyalist property. He helped the shattered provincial congresses of Georgia and South Carolina reestablish civilian authority in the interior—a goal the British had failed to accomplish. Greene also pursued diplomacy with Indians. Although redcoat invaders initially won some native allies, by war's end, only the Creeks remained allied with Great Britain.

Even before Greene took command in December 1780, the tide had begun to turn. At King's Mountain, in western North Carolina, a backcountry force defeated redcoats and loyalists that October. Then in January 1781, Greene's aide Daniel Morgan routed the British regiment Tarleton's Legion at nearby Cowpens. Greene confronted British troops under Lord Cornwallis at Guilford Court House, North Carolina, in March. Although Cornwallis controlled the field at day's end, most of his army had been destroyed. Greene returned to South Carolina, where he forced the redcoats to retire to Charleston.

Surrender at Yorktown

Cornwallis headed north into Virginia, where he joined forces with redcoats commanded by the American traitor Benedict Arnold. He then withdrew to the peninsula between the York and James rivers, where he fortified Yorktown. Washington sent more than seven thousand French and American troops south from New York. When the French fleet arrived from the Caribbean just in time to defeat the Royal Navy vessels sent to relieve Cornwallis, the British general was trapped. On October 19, 1781, Cornwallis surrendered.

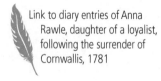

Link to diary entries of Anna Rawle, daughter of a loyalist, following the surrender of Cornwallis, 1781

The catastrophe at Yorktown, coupled with losses in West Florida, Minorca, and India, and compounded by Spanish and French ships then besieging Gibraltar and menacing the English Channel, forced Britain to give up its rebel colonies for lost. In January 1782, Parliament voted to cease offensive operations in America and begin peace negotiations.

Uncertain Victories

What risky—but ultimately wise— move did American diplomats make in negotiating peace with England after the American Revolution?

The Battle at Yorktown marked the last engagement between the British and Continental armies, not the end of the Revolutionary War. Not until more than a year after Cornwallis's surrender were preliminary peace terms agreed upon; ratifying the Treaty of Paris took another nine months.

Saving Jamaica

British officials turned their full attention to the most valuable of all their country's American possessions: Jamaica. Jamaica produced two-fifths of Britain's sugar and nine-tenths of its rum. Its human capital—over two hundred thousand slaves on the eve of revolution—likewise added to the balance sheet of empire. Through the autumn of 1781, Jamaica faced increased threat from France and Spain.

If the patriots' revolution ended in British defeat in Virginia in October 1781, Britain's American war ended in victory over the French at the Battle of the Saintes in April 1782. The win, led by redeemed General George Rodney, helped Britain obtain favorable peace terms from France in the negotiations under way in Paris.

DEA / G. NIMATALLAH/Getty Images

Admiral George Rodney's triumph over the French navy at the Battle of the Saintes in April 1782 preserved Britain's control of Jamaica, an economic cornerstone of the empire. The victory—a crucial success that stood out amidst the broader pattern of British losses in the American War— was celebrated with heroic sculptures and maritime paintings like this one, part of a series of images of the battle that Nicholas Pocock was commissioned to begin in 1782.

Treaty of Paris

Americans rejoiced when they learned of the signing of the preliminary peace **treaty of Paris** in November 1782. The American diplomats—Benjamin Franklin, John Jay, and John Adams—ignored Congress's instructions to let France take the lead and negotiated directly with Great Britain. Their instincts were sound: the French government was more an enemy to Britain than a friend to the United States. (In fact, French ministers worked secretly to try to prevent the establishment of a strong, unified government in America.) Spain's desire to claim the region between the Appalachian Mountains and the Mississippi River further complicated the negotiations. But the American delegates achieved their main goal: independence as a united nation.

Signed on September 3, 1783, the Treaty of Paris granted unconditional independence to the United States of America. Generous boundaries delineated the new nation: to the north, approximately the present-day boundary with Canada; to the south, the 31st parallel (about the northern border of modern Florida); to the west, the Mississippi River. Florida, acquired by Britain in 1763, reverted to Spain (see Map 7.1). In ceding so much land to the United States, Britain ignored the territorial rights of its Indian allies. British diplomats also poorly served loyalists and British merchants, who were disappointed in the outcome.

Some provisions of the treaty rankled in the United States as well. Article Four, which allowed British merchants to recover prewar debts that Americans owed them, and Article Five, which recommended that loyalists be allowed to recover their confiscated property, aroused considerable opposition in America.

treaty of Paris A treaty signed in 1783 when the British recognized American independence and agreed to withdraw all royal troops from the colonies.

Legacy FOR A PEOPLE AND A NATION

Revolutionary Origins

Many historians today contend that the American Revolution was not truly "revolutionary," if *revolution* means overturning an earlier power structure. The nation won its independence and established a republic, both radical events in the eighteenth century. But with the exception of British officials, essentially the same men who had led the colonies also led the new country. In contrast, the nearly contemporary French Revolution witnessed the execution of the monarch and many aristocrats, and a significant redistribution of authority. So the legacy of the American Revolution appears at once radical and conservative.

Throughout the more than two hundred years since the "Revolution," varying groups have claimed to represent its true meaning. People protesting discriminatory policies against women and minorities (usually dubbed "liberals") invoke the "created equal" language of the Declaration of Independence. Left-wing organizations rail against concentrations of wealth and power. Those protesting higher taxes (usually

called "conservatives") often adopt the symbolism of the Boston Tea Party, as in the "tea party" movement that arose in the spring of 2009 to oppose Obama administration policies. Right-wing militias arm themselves, preparing to defend their homes and families against a malevolent government, just as they believe the minutemen did in 1775. Indeed, vigilante groups styling themselves "minutemen" patrol the United States–Mexico border to defend it against illegal aliens. The message of the Revolution can be invoked to support extralegal demonstrations of any description, from invasions of military bases by antiwar protesters to demonstrations outside abortion clinics. But the Revolution can also be invoked to oppose such street protests because—some would argue—in a republic, change should come peacefully, via the ballot box.

Just as Americans in the eighteenth century disagreed over the meaning of their struggle, so the legacy of revolution remains contested in the twenty-first century.

Summary

The war finally over, victorious Americans could contemplate their achievement with satisfaction and even awe. Having forged a working coalition among the disparate mainland colonies, they declared their membership in the family of nations and entered a successful alliance with France. With an inexperienced army, they had defeated the world's greatest military power. They won only a few battles—most notably, at Trenton, Saratoga, and Yorktown—but their army always survived to fight again. Ultimately, the Americans wore down an enemy that had other parts of its empire to shore up.

In winning the war, the Americans reshaped the physical and mental landscapes in which they lived. They excluded from their new nation their loyalist neighbors. They established republican governments and created new national loyalties. They also laid claim to most of the territory east of the Mississippi River and south of the Great Lakes, thereby greatly expanding the land potentially open to their settlements and threatening native dominance of the interior. They had also begun, sometimes without recognizing it, the long national reckoning with slavery that would last nearly another century.

In the future, Americans would face a great new challenge: defining their nation and ensuring its survival in a world dominated by the bitter rivalries among Britain, France, and Spain and threatened by divisions within the American people as well.

Chapter Review

Toward War

What were the problems with Great Britain's war strategy?

Prime Minister Lord North and American Secretary Lord George Germain believed that an unprecedented fighting force would overwhelm the colonists. They targeted major American cities, believing that this typical goal of European warfare would work in America as well. And they reasoned that once the colonists surrendered, they would return their allegiance to Great Britain. But American forces proved more resistant that the British had predicted, even in the face of such a powerful opposing army. The British captured the largest mainland port cities, but less than 5 percent of the colonists lived there. Finally, military victory could not alone restore the authority of the Crown in the colonies. Rather, a British political victory rested upon the Americans' resuming their allegiance to the empire, a step most were not willing to take.

Forging an Independent Republic

How did Thomas Paine's *Common Sense* help reshape the war's purpose?

While Americans had been at war with Great Britain for months, most leaders denied seeking a complete break from England and focused on achieving some autonomy and a redress for various grievances. In January 1776, Paine's widely popular pamphlet called for independence and the establishment of a republic (a government by the people with no king or nobility). He argued that once America broke from European control, it would become strong and prosperous. Within months of its publication, the Second Continental Congress passed a resolution that the colonies should be free and all ties to Great Britain dissolved and charged five men, among them Thomas Jefferson, to write a declaration of independence.

Choosing Sides

How did Americans choose sides in the conflict with England?

Only two-fifths of the European American population of the thirteen colonies were patriots seeking to separate from England—among them small and middling farmers, Chesapeake gentry, merchants, city artisans, elected officeholders—and even then, their specific goals varied. Loyalists who opposed the break with England represented one-fifth of the population and included Anglican clergy; parishioners in the North; tenant farmers; members of persecuted religious sects; backcountry southerners; ethnic minorities, especially Scots; and merchants who relied on British trade. Two-fifths of the population remained neutral, including pacifist groups such as the Quakers. Only a few Indian communities supported the American revolt; most native villages either remained neutral or sporadically aligned themselves with the British. Finally, free blacks in the North and in the middle colonies took the patriots' side, while southern bondspeople thought they'd have a better chance at personal freedom by allying with the British, who made such promises to runaway slaves.

The Struggle in the North

What was France's role in the American Revolution?

Initially, France secretly sent military supplies to the Americans and regarded the revolution as a chance to avenge its defeat to Britain in the Seven Years' War. Once Americans won the Battle of Saratoga, the French openly supported them, sending naval vessels, ammunition, and troops. France's assistance proved vital to American victory in the final years of the war. Americans and the French signed two treaties in 1778, the Treaty of Amity and Commerce, which recognized American independence and set up trade relations; and the Treaty of Alliance, which promised neither side would negotiate peace (in conflicts with Britain) without consulting the other. France also abandoned claims to Canada and to North American territory east of the Mississippi River.

Battlefield and Home Front

How was the Continental army staffed?

Only in the war's earliest months were battlefields filled by militiamen, who left their fields to fight. After that, American leaders organized an army comprising young, single, often propertyless men who enlisted for a period of time for money or land. Towns were required to send their quota of soldiers and did so by enlisting everyone, including recent immigrants. Initially, African Americans were banned from the army, but by 1776, that prohibition was lifted, as northern recruiters promised slaves their freedom after the war. About five thousand enlisted, comprising 10 percent of the army. African Americans were typically in integrated units but were often given tasks others rejected, such as burying the dead. Wives and widows of poor soldiers often followed the camps, too, working as cooks, nurses, and launderers for rations or low wages.

The War Moves South

What events led the British to cease offensive operations and begin peace negotiations in 1782?

The British conceded the war after suffering losses both on the mainland and around the world. Beginning in late 1780, American forces began a string of victories in the South. They defeated the British at King's Mountain and Cowpens, and they inflicted heavy losses on Cornwallis's men at Guilford Court House. With the help of the French navy, Americans surrounded Cornwallis at Yorktown, where he surrendered on October 19, 1781. In addition, the British suffered losses in West Florida, Minorca, and India, and they endured Spanish and French ships menacing the English Channel. These worldwide catastrophes led Parliament to cease offensive operations in America in January 1782.

Uncertain Victories

What risky—but ultimately wise—move did American diplomats make in negotiating peace with England after the American Revolution?

During the signing of a preliminary peace treaty in Paris in 1782 ending the American Revolution,

diplomats Benjamin Franklin, John Jay, and John Adams ignored Congress's instructions to let Paris lead the way. Congress wanted them to follow the terms of the 1778 Treaty of Alliance, in which Americans promised not to make peace with England without consulting France first (and vice versa). Instead, the diplomats trusted their instincts and negotiated on their own. Turns out they were right: French ministers had secretly tried to prevent a strong government from taking hold in America. War-weary Britain not only gave America its independence, but also ceded vast tracts of land and unlimited fishing rights off Newfoundland.

Suggestions for Further Reading

Edwin G. Burrows, *Forgotten Patriots: The Untold Story of American Prisoners during the Revolutionary War* (2008)

Colin Calloway, *The American Revolution in Indian Country* (1995)

Emma Christopher, *A Merciless Place: The Fate of Britain's Convicts after the American Revolution* (2011)

Stephen Conway, *The British Isles and the War of American Independence* (2000)

Caroline Cox, *A Proper Sense of Honor: Service and Sacrifice in George Washington's Army* (2004)

David Hackett Fischer, *Paul Revere's Ride* (1995)

Alan Gilbert, *Black Patriots and Loyalists: Fighting for Emancipation in the War for Independence* (2012)

Edward G. Gray and Jane Kamensky, eds., *The Oxford Handbook of the American Revolution* (2012)

Maya Jasanoff, *Liberty's Exiles: American Loyalists in the Revolutionary World* (2011)

Jill Lepore, *The Whites of Their Eyes: The Tea Party's Revolution and the Battle over American History* (2010)

Piers Mackesy, *The War for America, 1775–1783* (1964)

Pauline Maier, *American Scripture: Making the Declaration of Independence* (1997)

Mary Beth Norton, *Liberty's Daughters: The Revolutionary Experience of American Women, 1750–1800* (2nd ed., 1996)

Andrew Jackson O'Shaughnessy, *The Men Who Lost America: British Leadership, the American Revolution, and the Fate of the Empire* (2013)

Forging a Nation

1783–1800

The pullout began in March 1783, when news reached New York City that America and Britain had agreed upon preliminary terms of peace. Twenty thousand British troops had to be shipped to other corners of the empire, and thirty-five thousand loyalist civilians needed to find homes in a new world they had neither imagined nor embraced. Like their counterparts in Savannah and Charleston, most of New York's loyalists would rebuild their shattered lives in exile. In April, transport ships began to depart, bound for Nova Scotia, Quebec, London, and the Bahamas. The fate of thousands of African American loyalists was especially insecure. A British commission met weekly in a tavern on Pearl Street to arbitrate the claims of former bondspeople. Had they served the British cause and spent at least a year behind British lines, thus earning freedom by the terms of the treaty? Or would they be re-enslaved, recovered as lost property by their aggrieved owners?

Each Wednesday, the commissioners granted passage to the lucky ones whose names they recorded in a ledger called the "Book of Negroes." One of the first ships out, called *L'Abondance*, carried 132 free blacks to new lives in Nova Scotia. Among them was a man whom Lord Dunmore had recruited from the workforce of a Virginia patriot when the war began. Harry Washington escaped Mount Vernon and never looked back, not even when his former owner assumed command of the Continental army. His exodus would take him from the Chesapeake to New York to a small settlement south of Halifax and eventually to the African American colony in Sierra Leone, whose capital the former slaves and their patrons named Freetown.

On November 25, 1783, months after *L'Abondance* spirited Harry Washington to lasting freedom, his onetime master rode into New York City in triumph. General George Washington processed to the fort at the southern tip of Manhattan. At one o'clock, a cannon fired as the last British troops in the new United States climbed into longboats and rowed out to ships facing east, toward home.

Chapter Outline

Trials of the Confederation
Foreign Affairs | Order and Disorder in the West | Ordinance of 1785 | Northwest Ordinance | The First American Depression

From Crisis to the Constitution
Annapolis Convention | Shays's Rebellion | Constitutional Convention | Virginia and New Jersey Plans | Slavery and the Constitution | Congressional and Presidential Powers | Federalists and Antifederalists | Bill of Rights | Ratification

Promoting a Virtuous Citizenry
Virtue and the Arts | Educational Reform | Judith Sargent Murray

Building a Workable Government
First Congress | Executive and Judiciary | Washington's First Steps | Alexander Hamilton | National and State Debts | Hamilton's Financial Plan | First Bank of the United States | Whiskey Rebellion

Building a Nation Among Nations
Republicans and Federalists | French Revolution | Democratic Societies | Jay Treaty Debate | Washington's Farewell Address | Election of 1796 | XYZ Affair | Quasi-War with France | Alien and Sedition Acts | The Convention of 1800

VISUALIZING THE PAST *Newspapers of the Early Republic*

The West in the New Nation
War in the Northwest Territory | "Civilizing" the Indians

Created Equal?
Women and the Republic |
Emancipation and Manumission |
Congress Debates Slavery |
Growth of Free Black Population |
Freedpeople's Lives | *Development
of Racist Theory* | *A White Men's
Republic*

LINKS TO THE WORLD *Haitian Refugees*

"Revolutions" at the End of the Century
Fries's Rebellion | *Gabriel's Rebellion* |
Election of 1800

LEGACY FOR A PEOPLE AND A NATION *Dissent
During Wartime*

SUMMARY

The evacuation of New York City marked one ending of the American Revolution. But Americans now confronted urgent questions about their future. How could they create and sustain a virtuous republic? How would that republic take its place "among the powers of the earth," as the Declaration of Independence had put it? And how could the country's leaders foster consensus among a populace so varied in a nation so vast?

Fighting the British dissolved at least some of the boundaries that had long divided American colonists, inspiring new loyalties to the new nation. But throughout the long civil war, Americans had remained a stunningly diverse people. *E Pluribus Unum*, the nation's new Great Seal proclaimed: "from many, one." Making one nation of many peoples—settling the Revolution—was the enormous task of the 1780s and 1790s, and remains unfinished still.

Nation making involved formal politics and diplomacy, as the leading men of the United States set out to fashion a unified government from diverse polities and divergent republican ideals. The country's first such government, under the Articles of Confederation, proved too weak and decentralized. Political leaders tried another approach when they drafted the Constitution in 1787.

Ratifying the Constitution provoked heated and sometimes violent contests in 1787 and 1788. Those battles between Federalists (supporters of the Constitution) and Antifederalists (its opponents) foreshadowed still wider divisions over major questions confronting the republic: the relationship between national power and states' rights, the formulation of foreign policy, the future of Indian nations encompassed within the borders of the United States, and the limits of dissent. Americans could not fully accept the division of the nation's citizens into competing factions known as Federalists and Republicans (or Democratic-Republicans). In republics, they believed, consensus should prevail; the rise of factions signified decay and corruption. Yet political leaders worked actively to galvanize supporters, thereby reworking the nation's political practice, if not its theory.

The hard work of settling the Revolution also took place in the less distinct but more populous realms of culture and ideas. In the early United States, novelists, painters, and educators at every level pursued explicitly moral goals. Women's education became newly important, for the mothers of the republic's "rising generation" were primarily responsible for ensuring the nation's future.

And then there were Thomas Jefferson's soaring words in the Declaration of Independence: "all men are created equal." Given that bold statement of principle, how could white republicans justify holding African Americans in perpetual bondage? During the war, thousands of bondsmen and bondswomen had answered that question by freeing themselves. Some white Americans, too, freed their slaves or voted for state laws that abolished slavery. Others redoubled their defense of the institution.

"We the People of the United States": in their name, and by their power, was the federal Constitution ratified. But who, precisely, were "the People," and how did various groups among them encounter the new nation? Some of the answers were clearer in 1800 than they had been in 1776. But as Thomas Jefferson assumed the presidency, the long work of settling the Revolution had barely begun.

As you read this chapter, keep the following questions in mind:

- **What challenges confronted the new nation's leaders at home and abroad during the 1780s and 1790s?**

- **What were the elements of the new national identity? How did poor farmers, women, Indians, and African Americans fit into that identity?**

- **What disputes divided the nation's citizens, and how did Americans react to those disputes?**

Trials of the Confederation

What was the significance of the Northwest Ordinance?

Under the Articles of Confederation, the unicameral legislature, called the Second Continental Congress until 1781 and the Confederation Congress thereafter, proved inefficient and unwieldy. It was simultaneously a legislative body and a collective executive; there was no judiciary. It had no independent income and no authority to compel the states to accept its rulings. In the 1780s, the limitations of the Articles would become glaring.

Foreign Affairs

Because the Articles denied Congress the power to establish a national commercial policy, foreign trade exposed the new government's weaknesses. After the war, Britain, France, and Spain restricted America's trade with their colonies. Congress watched helplessly as British goods flooded the United States while American produce could no longer be sold in the British West Indies.

The Spanish presence on the nation's southern and western borders caused Congress other difficulties. Spain in 1784 closed the Mississippi River to American navigation. The United States opened negotiations with Spain in 1785, but the talks collapsed when Congress divided. Southerners and westerners insisted on navigation rights, whereas northerners focused on winning commercial concessions in the West Indies.

The refusal of state and local governments to comply with provisions of the Treaty of Paris relating to the payment of prewar debts and the confiscated property of loyalists gave Britain an excuse to maintain military posts on the Great Lakes. Furthermore, Congress's inability to convince states to implement the treaty disclosed its lack of power.

Chronology

1777	Vermont becomes first jurisdiction to abolish slavery
1783	British expelled from New York City
1784	United States signs treaty with Iroquois at Fort Stanwix; Iroquois repudiate it two years later
1785	Land Ordinance of 1785 provides for surveying and sale of national lands in Northwest Territory
1785–86	United States negotiates treaties with Choctaws, Chickasaws, and Cherokees
1786	Annapolis Convention discusses reforming government
1786–87	Shays's Rebellion in western Massachusetts raises questions about future of the republic
1787	Constitutional Convention drafts new form of government
1788	Hamilton, Jay, and Madison urge ratification of the Constitution in *The Federalist*
	Constitution ratified
1789	Washington inaugurated as first president
	French Revolution begins
1790	Hamilton's *Report on Public Credit* proposes assumption of state debts
1791	First ten amendments (Bill of Rights) ratified
	First national bank chartered
	Haitian Revolution begins
1793	France declares war on Britain, Spain, and the Netherlands
	Washington proclaims American neutrality in Europe's war
	Democratic societies founded, the first grassroots political organizations
1794	Whiskey Rebellion in western Pennsylvania protests taxation
1795	Jay Treaty with Britain resolves issues remaining from the Revolution
	Pinckney's Treaty with Spain establishes southern boundary of the United States
	Treaty of Greenville with Miami Confederacy opens Ohio to settlement
1796	First contested presidential election: Adams elected president, Jefferson vice president
1798	XYZ Affair arouses American opinion against France
	Sedition Act penalizes dissent
1798–99	Quasi-War with France
	Fries's Rebellion in Pennsylvania protests taxation
1800	Gabriel's Rebellion threatens Virginia slave owners
1800–01	Jefferson elected president by the House of Representatives after stalemate in electoral college

Order and Disorder in the West

Beyond the Appalachians, individual states jockeyed over the vague western boundaries indicated by their colonial charters (see Map 7.1). The United States assumed the Treaty of Paris cleared its title to all land east of the Mississippi except the area still held by Spain. Still, recognizing that land cessions should be obtained from powerful tribes, Congress initiated negotiations with northern and southern Indians (see Map 7.2).

At Fort Stanwix, New York, in 1784, American diplomats negotiated a treaty with chiefs who claimed to represent the Iroquois; at Hopewell, South Carolina, in late 1785 and early 1786, they negotiated with emissaries from the Choctaw, Chickasaw, and Cherokee nations. In 1786, the Iroquois repudiated the Fort Stanwix treaty, denying that the negotiators were authorized to speak for the Six Nations. The confederacy threatened new attacks on frontier settlements, but the flawed treaty stood. By 1790, the once-dominant confederacy was confined to a few scattered reservations.

MAP 7.1

Western Land Claims and Cessions, 1782–1802

After the United States achieved independence, states competed with one another for control of valuable lands to which their original charters granted them possible and sometimes overlapping claims. That competition led to a series of compromises among the states or between individual states and the new nation, indicated on this map. Source: Copyright © Cengage Learning 2015

In the South, too, the United States took the treaties as confirmation of its sovereignty. European Americans poured over the southern Appalachians, provoking the Creeks to declare war. In 1790, they came to terms with the United States.

Ordinance of 1785 — Western nations, such as the Shawnees, Chippewas, Ottawas, and Potawatomis, challenged Iroquois hegemony as early as the 1750s. After Iroquois power collapsed, they formed a confederacy and demanded negotiations with the United States. At first, the American government ignored the western confederacy. Shortly after state land cessions were completed, Congress organized the Northwest Territory, bounded by the Mississippi River, the Great Lakes, and the Ohio River

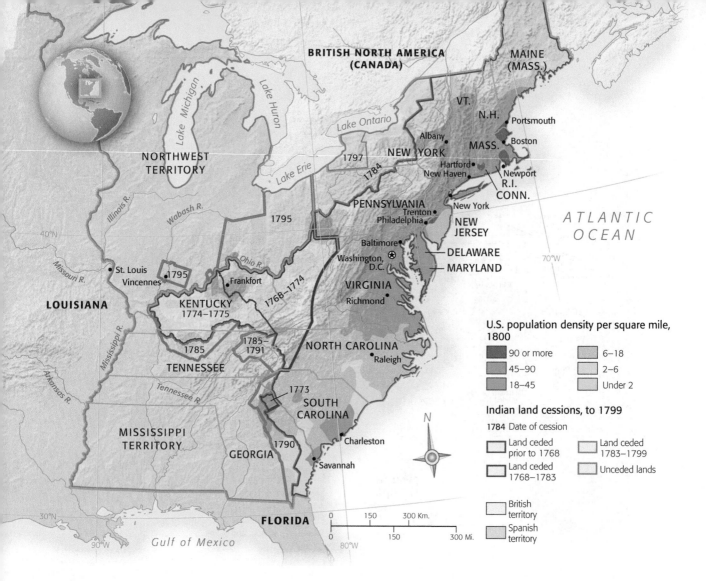

MAP 7.2

Cession of Tribal Lands to the United States, 1775–1790

The land claims of the United States meant little as long as Indian nations still controlled vast territories within the new country's formal boundaries. A series of treaties in the 1780s and 1790s spelled the end of native territorial sovereignty over some lands, which were opened to white settlement. Source: From Lester J. Cappon et al., eds., *Atlas of Early American History: The Revolutionary Era, 1760–1790* Copyright © 1976 by Princeton University Press.

(see Map 7.1). Ordinances passed in 1784, 1785, and 1787 outlined the process through which the land could be sold to settlers and formal governments created. The 1784 law created procedures for settlers to form governments and organize new states that would join the federal union "on an equal footing with the original states." Congress in 1785 directed that the Northwest Territory be surveyed into townships 6 miles square, each divided into thirty-six sections of 640 acres (one square mile). One dollar was the minimum price per acre; the minimum sale was one section. The resulting minimum outlay, $640, lay beyond the reach of small farmers, except veterans who received part of their army pay in land warrants. Proceeds from western land sales constituted the first independent revenues available to the national government.

Northwest Ordinance

The Northwest Ordinance of 1787 contained a bill of rights that guaranteed settlers freedom of religion and the right to jury trial, forbade cruel and unusual punishments, and nominally prohibited slavery. Eventually, that prohibition became an important symbol for antislavery northerners, but at the time it had little effect. Some residents already held slaves, and Congress would not deprive them of their property. The ordinance also allowed slave owners to "lawfully reclaim" runaways who took refuge in the territory—the first national fugitive slave law. Not until 1848 was enslavement abolished throughout the Old Northwest.

The ordinance of 1787 also specified the process by which territorial residents could organize state governments and seek admission to the Union "on an equal footing with the original States." Early in the nation's history, therefore, Congress assured residents of the territories the same rights held by citizens of the original states.

Although the Northwest Ordinance is often viewed as one of the few lasting accomplishments of the Confederation Congress, it remained largely theoretical in 1787. Miamis, Shawnees, and Delawares in the region refused to acknowledge American sovereignty. They opposed settlement violently, attacking pioneers who ventured too far north of the Ohio River. Not until after the Articles of Confederation were replaced with a new constitution could the United States muster sufficient force to implement the ordinance.

The Commissioners, 1778 (litho), American School, (18th century)/Private Collection/Peter Newark Pictures/ The Bridgeman Art Library

A British cartoon ironically reflected Americans' hopes for postwar trade, hopes that were dashed after 1783. The Indian woman symbolizing America sits on a pile of tobacco bales, with rice and indigo casks bound for Europe nearby. The artist was satirizing the failed 1778 British peace commission and Britons' willingness to make concessions to the rebellious colonies, but his image captured Americans' belief in the importance of their produce.

The First American Depression

The Articles were ill equipped to confront the transformation of the American economy. During the war, trade between Europe (especially Britain) and North America ceased almost entirely. As vital sources of income and goods dried up, the plummeting value of the Continental dollar diminished purchasing power. After the peace, exporters of staple crops and importers of manufactured goods suffered from restrictions that European powers imposed on American commerce.

Although recovery began by 1786, the war's effects proved hard to erase. By 1790, per capita income had dropped more than 40 percent from its prewar average, nearly equaling Americans' losses in the early years of the Great Depression.

The near-total cessation of foreign commerce during the war did stimulate domestic manufacturing. Moreover, America's export trade shifted from Europe and toward the West Indies. Foodstuffs shipped to the French and Dutch Caribbean colonies became America's largest single export, replacing tobacco (and thus accelerating the Chesapeake's conversion to grain).

From Crisis to the Constitution

By the mid-1780s, Americans involved in overseas trade, western land speculation, foreign affairs, and finance had become acutely aware of the inadequacies of the Articles of Confederation.

How did the question of slavery become linked to the new U.S. Constitution?

Annapolis Convention

Recognizing the Confederation Congress's inability to deal with commercial matters, representatives of Virginia and Maryland met at George Washington's Mount Vernon in March 1785 to negotiate an agreement about trade on the Potomac River. The meeting prompted an invitation to other states to discuss trade policy more broadly at a convention in Annapolis, Maryland. Although nine states named representatives to the gathering in September 1786, only five delegations attended. Consequently, they issued a call for another convention, to be held in Philadelphia nine months later, "to devise such further provisions as shall appear necessary to render the constitution of the federal government adequate to the exigencies of the Union."

At first, few other states responded. But the nation's economic problems also caused taxation woes. The states had run up huge war debts, issuing securities to pay soldiers, purchase supplies, and underwrite loans. During the hard times of the early 1780s, many veterans and other creditors sold those securities to speculators for pennies on the dollar. In 1785, Congress requisitioned still more taxes from the states to cover national war bonds. When states tried to comply, they succeeded primarily in arousing popular protests. In Massachusetts, which levied heavy taxes at full price in specie, farmers faced with selling their land to pay the new taxes responded furiously. The actions of men from the state's western counties, many of them veterans from leading families, proved that reform was needed.

Shays's Rebellion

Daniel Shays, a former Continental army officer, led the disgruntled westerners. On January 25, 1787, about fifteen hundred troops assaulted the Springfield federal armory. Terming Massachusetts "tyrannical" and styling themselves "Regulators" (like backcountry Carolinians in the 1760s), Shaysites linked their rebellion with the struggle for American independence. The militiamen defending the armory fired on their former comrades in arms, who suffered twenty-four casualties. Some (including Shays) fled the state; two were hanged; most paid fines and took oaths of allegiance to Massachusetts. The state legislature soon reduced the burden on landowners, easing tax collections and enacting new import duties instead.

Constitutional Convention

To political leaders, the rebellion confirmed the need for a stronger federal government. After most states appointed delegates, the Confederation Congress belatedly endorsed the Philadelphia convention, "for the sole and express purpose of revising the Articles of Confederation." In mid-May 1787, fifty-five men, representing all the states but Rhode Island, assembled in the Pennsylvania State House. George Washington was elected presiding officer.

Most delegates to the Constitutional Convention were substantial men of property. Their ranks included merchants, planters, physicians, generals, governors, and especially lawyers. More than half of them had attended college. Most wanted to give the national government new authority, yet they also sought to advance their states' divergent interests.

A dozen men did the bulk of the convention's work. Of those, **James Madison** of Virginia most fully deserves the title "Father of the Constitution." A Princeton graduate from western Virginia, he had served on the local Committee of Safety and was elected to the provincial convention, the state's lower and upper houses, and the Continental Congress (1780–1783).

James Madison Known as the "Father of the Constitution" and was elected President of the United States in 1808.

To prepare for the Philadelphia meeting, Madison ordered more than two hundred books on history and government from Paris, analyzing their accounts of past confederacies and republics. Rejecting the common assertion that republics had to be small to survive, Madison asserted that a large, diverse republic was less likely to succumb to the influence of a particular faction. No one set of interests would be able to control it, and political stability would result from compromises among contending parties.

Virginia and New Jersey Plans

The so-called **Virginia Plan**, introduced on May 29 by that state's governor, Edmund Randolph, embodied Madison's conception of national government. The plan provided for a two-house legislature with the lower house elected directly by the people and the upper house selected by the lower; representation in both houses proportional to property or population; an executive elected by Congress; a national judiciary; and congressional veto over state laws.

Virginia Plan A proposal calling for the establishment of a strong central government rather than a confederation of states. It gave Congress virtually unrestricted rights of legislation and taxation, power to veto any state law, and authority to use military force against the states.

Many delegates believed the Virginia Plan went too far toward national consolidation. After two weeks of debate, disaffected delegates—particularly those from small states—united under William Paterson of New Jersey. The **New Jersey Plan**, presented June 15, proposed retaining a unicameral Congress in which each state had an equal vote, while giving Congress new powers of taxation and regulation.

New Jersey Plan A proposal calling for a single-chamber congress in which each state had an equal vote, just as the Articles, but strengthened the taxing and commercial powers of Congress.

Although the convention initially rejected Paterson's position, he and his allies won several victories in subsequent months.

The delegates agreed that the new government should have a two-house (bicameral) legislature. Further, they concurred that "the people," however defined, should be directly represented in at least one house. But they differed on three key questions: Should representation in both houses of Congress be proportional to population? How was representation in either house to be apportioned among the states? And, finally, how would the members of the two houses be elected?

The last issue proved easiest to resolve. To quote John Dickinson, delegates deemed it "essential" that the lower branch of Congress be elected directly by the people and "expedient" that members of the upper house be chosen by state legislatures. The plan had the virtue of placing the election of one house of Congress a step removed from the "lesser sort," whose judgment the wealthy convention delegates did not trust.

The possibility of proportional representation in the Senate caused greater disagreement. Small states argued for equal representation, which would give them relatively more power at the national level. Large states supported a proportional plan, which would allot them more votes in the upper house. For weeks, the convention deadlocked. A committee appointed to work out a compromise recommended equal representation in the Senate, with a proviso that all appropriation bills originate in the lower house. Only the absence of several opponents of the compromise at the time of the vote averted a breakdown.

Slavery and the Constitution

The question of how to apportion representation in the lower house divided the nation along sectional lines. Delegates concurred that a census should be conducted every ten years to determine the nation's population, and they agreed that Indians, who paid no taxes, should be excluded for purposes of representation. Delegates from states with large slave populations wanted to count African and European inhabitants equally for the purposes of representation (though not for taxation); delegates from states with few slaves wanted to count only free people.

Delegates resolved the dispute by using a formula developed by the Confederation Congress in 1783 to allocate financial assessments among states: three-fifths of slaves would be included in population totals. (The formula reflected delegates' judgment that slaves were less efficient producers of wealth than free people, not that they were three-fifths human and two-fifths property.) What came to be known as the "three-fifths compromise" on representation won unanimous approval.

three-fifths clause Allowed three-fifths of all slaves to be counted for congressional representation and, thereby, in the electoral college that selected the president.

The **three-fifths clause** assured southern voters congressional representation out of proportion to their numbers and a disproportionate influence on the selection of the president. In return for southerners' agreement that Congress could pass commercial regulations by a simple majority vote, New Englanders agreed that Congress could not end the importation of slaves for twenty years. Further, the fugitive slave clause (Article IV, Section 2) required all states to return runaways to their masters. By guaranteeing national assistance to any states threatened with "domestic violence," the Constitution promised aid in putting down future slave revolts and incidents like Shays's Rebellion. Although the words *slave* and *slavery* do not appear in the Constitution (the framers used such euphemisms as "other persons"), eleven of its eighty-four clauses concerned slavery in some fashion. All but one of those protected the institution.

Congressional and Presidential Powers

The delegates concurred that the national government needed the authority to tax and to regulate foreign and interstate commerce. The convention implied but did not explicitly authorize a national judicial veto of state laws. Delegates also drafted a long list of actions forbidden to states, and they stipulated that religious tests could never be required of U.S. officeholders.

The convention placed primary responsibility for foreign affairs with a new official, the president, who was also designated commander-in-chief of the armed forces. With the Senate's consent, the president could appoint judges and other federal officers. To select the president, delegates established the electoral college, whose members would be chosen in each state by legislatures or voters. If a majority of electors failed to unite behind one candidate, the House of Representatives (voting as states, not as individuals) would choose the president, who would serve for four years but be eligible for reelection.

The key to the Constitution was the distribution of political authority (**separation of powers**) among executive, legislative, and judicial branches of the national government, and the division of powers between states and nation (called *federalism*). The president could veto congressional legislation, but that veto could be overridden by two-thirds majorities in both houses, and his treaties and major appointments required the Senate's consent. Congress could impeach the president and federal judges, but courts appeared to have the final say on interpreting the Constitution. Two-thirds of Congress and three-fourths of the states had to concur on amendments. These **checks and balances** would prevent the government from becoming tyrannical, but at times they prevented the government from acting decisively. And the line between state and national powers remained so blurry that the United States fought a civil war in the next century over that issue.

The convention held its last session on September 17, 1787. All but three of the 42 delegates still present then signed the Constitution. (See the appendix for the text of the Constitution.) Congress submitted the document to the states in late September. The ratification clause provided for the new system to take effect after approval by special conventions in at least nine states. Thus, the national Constitution, unlike the Articles of Confederation, would rest directly on popular authority.

separation of powers The establishment of three distinct branches of government each with varying political powers.

federalism System in which states and central governments have distinctive roles and powers.

checks and balances A separation of powers between the various branches of government, designed to prevent one branch from dominating the others.

Federalists and Antifederalists

Every newspaper in the country printed the full text of the Constitution, and most supported its adoption. Although most citizens concurred that the national government needed more power over taxation and commerce, some believed the proposed government held the potential for tyranny. The unprecedented debate frequently spilled into the streets.

Those supporting the Constitution called themselves **Federalists**. They drew upon classical republicanism, promoting a virtuous, self-sacrificing republic led by a manly aristocracy of talent. They argued that the separation of powers among legislative, executive, and judicial branches, and the division of powers between states and nation, would preclude tyranny.

Federalists The name supporters of new Constitution gave themselves during the ratification struggle.

Antifederalists So dubbed by the Federalists, the Antifederalists were opposed to the Constitution because they feared it gave too much power to the central government and it did not contain a bill of rights.

The Federalists termed those who opposed the Constitution **Antifederalists**, thus casting them in a negative light. Antifederalists recognized the need for a national source of revenue. But they saw the states as the chief protectors of individual rights and believed that weakening the states would promote the rise of arbitrary power. Heirs of the Real Whig ideology of the late 1760s and early 1770s, Antifederalists stressed the need for constant popular vigilance to avert oppression. Indeed, some of those who had originally promulgated such ideas—Samuel Adams, Patrick Henry, and Richard Henry Lee—led the opposition to the Constitution. Joining them were small farmers determined to safeguard their property from excessive taxation, backcountry Baptists and Presbyterians, and upwardly mobile men who would benefit from an economic and political system less tightly controlled than that the Constitution envisioned.

Bill of Rights The first ten amendments of the Constitution that guaranteed personal liberties.

Bill of Rights

The Constitution's lack of specific guarantees to protect the rights of the people against the tyranny of a powerful central government troubled Antifederalists, who wanted the document to incorporate a bill of rights, as did Britain's governing documents since the Glorious Revolution. Most state constitutions had done so as well. *Letters of a Federal Farmer*, perhaps the most widely read Antifederalist pamphlet, listed the rights that should be enshrined: freedom of the press and religion, trial by jury, and protection from unreasonable searches.

Ratification

In June 1788, when New Hampshire ratified, the Constitution's requirement of nine states was satisfied. But New York and Virginia had not yet voted, and the new framework could not succeed without those powerful states.

TABLE 7.1 Ratification of the Constitution by State Conventions

State	Date	Vote
Delaware	December 7, 1787	30–0
Pennsylvania	December 12, 1787	46–23
New Jersey	December 18, 1787	38–0
Georgia	January 2, 1788	26–0
Connecticut	January 9, 1788	128–40
Massachusetts	February 6, 1788	187–168
Maryland	April 28, 1788	63–11
South Carolina	May 23, 1788	149–73
New Hampshire	June 21, 1788	57–47
Virginia	June 25, 1788	89–79
New York	July 26, 1788	30–27
North Carolina	November 21, 1789	194–77
Rhode Island	May 29, 1790	34–32

Pro-Constitution forces won by ten votes in the Virginia convention, which, like Massachusetts, recommended that a list of specific rights be added. In New York, James Madison, John Jay, and Alexander Hamilton, writing under the pseudonym "Publius," published *The Federalist*, a series of eighty-five essays explaining the theory behind the Constitution and answering critics. Their arguments, coupled with Federalists' promise to add a bill of rights, helped win the battle there. On July 26, 1788, New York ratified the Constitution by just three votes. Although the last states—North Carolina and Rhode Island—did not join the Union for over a year, the new government was a reality.

Link to James Madison, *The Federalist Papers* (1787–88)

Promoting a Virtuous Citizenry

How were notions of republican virtue engendered in post-revolutionary America?

As citizens of the United States constructed their republic, they sought to embody republican principles of nationalism and virtue not only in their governments but also in their society and culture.

Virtue and the Arts

Republican writers and artists strove to counter the notion that the fine arts signaled luxury and corruption. William Hill Brown's *The Power of Sympathy* (1789), the first novel published in the United States, unfolded a story of seduction as a warning to "the Young Ladies of United Columbia," and promised to "Inspire the Female Mind with a Principle of Self Complacency." Mason Locke Weems published *Life of Washington* in 1800 shortly after George Washington's death. This moralizing biography—with its invented tale of the boy who chopped down the cherry tree and could not tell a lie—became the era's most popular secular work.

Painters, too, used their works to elevate republican taste. Prominent artists Gilbert Stuart and Charles Willson Peale painted portraits of upstanding republican citizens. Stuart's portraits of George Washington—three painted from life, from which the artist made scores of copies, which in turn spawned countless engravings—came to represent the face of the young republic around the world. Stuart's own motives were commercial as well as patriotic. When he returned to the United States in 1793 after nearly two decades in Britain, he told a friend, "I expect to make a fortune by Washington alone."

Bequest of Mrs. Benjamin Ogle Tayloe; Collection of The Corcoran Gallery of Art/Corbis

Gilbert Stuart completed this portrait of George Washington in 1800, after Washington's death renewed the frenzy of interest in the first president's likeness. For this version, Stuart copied his own famed "Athenaeum" portrait, which he had painted when Washington sat for him in 1796. Copies of Stuart's copies—painted as well as engraved—decorated homes throughout the early United States and surfaced as far away as Canton, China.

Educational Reform

Americans' concern for the future of the infant republic focused their attention on children. Education had previously been seen as the concern of families. But if young

Terra Foundation for American, Chicago/Art Resource, NY

Judith Sargent Stevens (later Murray), by John Singleton Copley, ca. 1769. The eventual author of essays advocating improvements in women's education sat for this portrait on the eve of her first marriage, some two decades before she began to publish her work. Her direct gaze and high forehead suggest both her intelligence and her seriousness of purpose.

people were to resist vice and become useful citizens, they would need education. In fact, the very survival of the nation depended on it. Some northern states began using tax money to support public elementary schools.

To instruct their children adequately, mothers would have to be properly educated. Massachusetts insisted that town elementary schools teach girls as well as boys. Throughout the United States, private academies were founded to give teenage girls from well-to-do families advanced schooling. Colleges remained closed to women, but a few fortunate girls could study history, geography, rhetoric, and mathematics along with fancy needlework—the only artistic endeavor considered appropriate for ladies.

Judith Sargent Murray Judith Sargent Murray of Gloucester, Massachusetts, became the chief theorist of women's education in the early republic. In powerful essays published in the 1780s and 1790s, Murray argued that women and men had equal intellects but unequal schooling. Boys and girls should be educated alike, Murray insisted, and girls should be taught to support themselves by their own efforts: "Independence should be placed within their grasp." Murray's writings were part of a general rethinking of women's position that occurred in a climate of political upheaval.

Building a Workable Government

How did the chartering of the Bank of the United States provoke an early constitutional debate?

Only a few Antifederalists ran for office in the congressional elections held late in 1788; even fewer were elected. The drafters of the Constitution had deliberately left many key issues undecided, so the nationalists' domination of the First U.S. Congress meant that their views prevailed.

First Congress Congress faced four immediate tasks when it convened in April 1789: raising revenue, responding to calls for a bill of rights, setting up executive departments, and organizing the federal judiciary. James Madison, representing Virginia in the House of Representatives, persuaded Congress to adopt the Revenue Act of 1789, imposing a 5 percent tariff on certain imports. The First Congress thus achieved an effective national tax law.

Madison also took the lead with respect to constitutional amendments. When introducing nineteen proposed amendments in June, he told his fellow representatives they needed to respond to the people's will, noting that North Carolina had vowed not to ratify the Constitution without a Bill of Rights. After heated debates, Congress approved twelve amendments. The states ratified ten, which became part of the Constitution on December 15, 1791.

The First Amendment prohibited Congress from restricting freedom of religion, speech, the press, peaceable assembly, or petition. The Second Amendment guaranteed the right "to keep and bear arms" because of the need for a "well regulated Militia." The Third Amendment limited the quartering of troops in private homes. The next five pertained to judicial procedures. The Fourth Amendment prohibited "unreasonable searches and seizures," the Fifth and Sixth established the rights of accused persons, the Seventh specified the conditions for jury trials in civil cases, and the Eighth forbade "cruel and unusual punishments." The Ninth and Tenth Amendments reserved to the people and the states other unspecified rights and powers.

Executive and Judiciary

Congress also considered the organization of the executive branch, preserving the three administrative departments established under the Articles of Confederation: War, Foreign Affairs (renamed State), and Treasury. Congress also instituted two lesser posts: the attorney general—the nation's official lawyer—and the postmaster general. Further, the House and Senate agreed that the president could dismiss officials whom he had appointed, making the heads of executive departments accountable solely to the president.

The most far-reaching law, the **Judiciary Act of 1789**, defined the jurisdiction of the federal judiciary and established a six-member Supreme Court, thirteen district courts, and three appellate courts. Its most important provision, Section 25, allowed appeals from state to federal courts when cases raised certain constitutional questions.

Judiciary Act of 1789
Outlined the federal judiciary's jurisdiction and established the Supreme Court, as well as district and appellate courts. How did the chartering of the Bank of the United States provoke an early constitutional debate?

Washington's First Steps

George Washington did not seek the presidency. In 1783, he resigned his army commission and retired to Mount Vernon. Yet after the adoption of the new government, only Washington was thought to have sufficient stature to serve as the first president, an office largely designed with him in mind. The unanimous vote of the electoral college merely formalized that consensus. Symbolically, Washington donned a suit of homespun for the inaugural ceremony in April 1789.

Washington acted cautiously during his first months in office, knowing he would set precedents. His first major task was to choose the heads of the executive departments. For the War Department, he selected an old comrade in arms, Henry Knox of Massachusetts. He chose for the State Department fellow Virginian Thomas Jefferson, who had been minister to France. For secretary of the treasury, the president chose the brilliant, ambitious **Alexander Hamilton**.

Alexander Hamilton Secretary of Treasury under President George Washington.

Alexander Hamilton

The illegitimate son of a Scottish aristocrat, Hamilton—no relation to Dr. Alexander Hamilton who toured the colonies in 1744 (see Chapter 4)—was born in the British West Indies in 1757. He spent his early years in poverty, but in 1773, financial support from friends allowed him to enroll at King's College (later Columbia University) in New York. Hamilton volunteered for service in the American army, where he came to Washington's attention. After the war, Hamilton practiced law in New York City and served as a delegate to the Annapolis Convention and the Constitutional Convention. His contributions to *The Federalist* in 1788 revealed him as one of the republic's chief political thinkers.

Caribbean-born, Hamilton had no natal ties to any state. His primary loyalty lay with the nation. He never feared the exercise of centralized executive authority, and he favored close ties with Britain. Believing people to be motivated primarily by economic self-interest, his notion of republicanism placed little weight on self-sacrifice for the common good. Those beliefs significantly influenced the way he tackled the new nation's tangled finances.

National and State Debts

Hamilton's first task was to deal with the public debt. Americans agreed that their new government could establish its credit only by repaying at full face value the obligations the nation had incurred while winning independence. But the state debts were another matter. Some states—notably, Virginia, Maryland, North Carolina, and Georgia—had largely paid off their war debts. They opposed taxing their citizens so the national government could assume other states' debts. Massachusetts, Connecticut, and South Carolina, by contrast, still had sizable unpaid debts and would welcome national assumption. The possible assumption of state debts also had political implications; such a move would concentrate economic and political power at the national level.

Report on Public Credit
Hamilton's plan to ensure that wealthy merchants, who held the public debt, would be linked to the government's financial survival.

Hamilton's Financial Plan

Hamilton's first **Report on Public Credit**, sent to Congress in January 1790, proposed that Congress assume outstanding state debts, combine them with national obligations, and issue securities covering both principal and accumulated unpaid interest. Hamilton hoped to ensure that holders of the public debt—many of them wealthy merchants and speculators—had a significant financial stake in the new government's survival. Opposition coalesced around James Madison, whose state of Virginia had mostly eliminated its debt, and who wanted to avoid rewarding wealthy speculators who purchased debt certificates at deep discounts from needy veterans and farmers.

The House initially rejected the assumption of state debts. But the Senate adopted Hamilton's plan largely intact. Compromises followed, linking the assumption bill to another controversial issue: the location of the permanent national capital. A southern site on the Potomac River was selected, and the first part of Hamilton's financial program became law in August 1790.

First Bank of the United States

Four months later, Hamilton submitted to Congress a second report on public credit, recommending the creation of a national bank modeled on the Bank of England. The Bank of the United States was to be chartered for twenty years with $10 million of paid-in capital—$2 million from public funds, and the balance from private investors. The bank would collect and disburse moneys for the treasury, and its notes would circulate as the nation's currency. But another issue loomed: did the Constitution give Congress the power to establish such a bank?

Madison thought not. The Constitutional Convention had rejected a clause authorizing Congress to issue corporate charters. Attorney General Edmund Randolph and Secretary of State Thomas Jefferson agreed with Madison. Washington asked Hamilton to reply to his critics. In his *Defense of the Constitutionality of the Bank*, Hamilton argued that Congress could choose any means not specifically prohibited by the Constitution to achieve a constitutional end. Washington concurred, and the bill became law.

The Bank of the United States proved successful, as did the debt program. The new nation's securities became desirable investments at home and abroad. The resulting influx of capital, coupled with the high prices that American grain now commanded in European markets, eased farmers' debt burdens and contributed to a new prosperity.

Hamilton's *Report on Manufactures* (1791) outlined an ambitious plan to promote the United States' industrial development through limited use of protective tariffs. But Congress rejected the report, believing that America's future lay in agriculture and the carrying (shipping) trade and that the mainstay of the republic was the yeoman farmer.

Also controversial was another feature of Hamilton's financial program enacted in 1791: an excise tax on whiskey to provide additional income to the national government. The tax affected a relatively small number of westerners—the farmers who grew corn and the distillers who turned it into whiskey—and might also reduce the consumption of whiskey. (Eighteenth-century Americans consumed about twice as much alcohol per capita as Americans do today.) Moreover, western farmers and distillers tended to support Jefferson, and Hamilton saw the benefits of taxing them rather than his own merchant supporters.

Whiskey Rebellion   News of the tax sparked protests in the West, where residents were upset that the same government that protected them inadequately from Indian attacks was now proposing to tax them disproportionately. For two years, large groups on the frontiers of Pennsylvania, Maryland, and Virginia drafted petitions protesting the tax, imitated crowd actions of the 1760s, and occasionally harassed tax collectors.

President Washington responded with restraint until July 1794, when western Pennsylvania farmers resisted two tax collectors. When about seven thousand rebels convened on August 1 to plot the destruction of Pittsburgh, Washington acted to prevent a repeat of Shays's Rebellion. On August 7, he told insurgents to disperse and summoned nearly thirteen thousand militiamen. Federal forces marched westward in October and November, led at times by Washington himself. The troops met no resistance and arrested only twenty suspects. Two men were convicted of treason; Washington pardoned both.

The suppression of the **Whiskey Rebellion** demonstrated that the national government would not allow violent resistance to its laws. In the republic, people dissatisfied with a given law should try to amend or repeal it.

Whiskey Rebellion Tax protest by western farmers that turned violent. Washington's response, sending in troops, demonstrated that only peaceful protests would be tolerated in a republic.

Building a Nation Among Nations

What was the underlying purpose of the Alien and Sedition Acts of 1798?

By 1794, some Americans were beginning to seek change through electoral politics. In a government of the people, sustained factional disagreement was taken as a sign of corruption, but that did little to check partisanship.

Republicans and Federalists

As early as 1792, Jefferson and Madison became convinced that Hamilton's policies of favoring wealthy commercial interests at the expense of agriculture threatened the United States. Characterizing themselves as the true heirs of the Revolution, they charged Hamilton with plotting to subvert republican principles. They and their followers began calling themselves Republicans. Hamilton likewise accused Jefferson and Madison of attempting to destroy the republic. To link themselves with the Constitution, Hamilton and his supporters called themselves Federalists. Newspapers aligned with each side fanned the flames of partisanship.

The growing controversy persuaded Washington to promote political unity by seeking office again in 1792. But after 1793, developments in Europe magnified the disagreements, as France (America's wartime ally) and Great Britain (America's most important trading partner) resumed hostilities.

French Revolution

In 1789, many Americans welcomed the news of revolution in France. The French people's success in overthrowing an oppressive monarchy enabled Americans to see themselves as the vanguard of a trend that would reshape the world.

But by 1793, the reports from France had grown alarming. Political leaders succeeded each other with bewildering rapidity. Executions mounted; the king was beheaded that January. Although many Americans, including Jefferson and Madison, retained sympathy for the revolution, others—Hamilton among them— began to cite France as a prime example of the perversion of republicanism.

Debates within the United States intensified when republican France declared war on Austria in 1792, and then on Britain, Spain, and Holland the following year. That confronted the Americans with a dilemma. The 1778 Treaty of Alliance with France bound them as allies "forever." Yet the United States remained connected to Great Britain through a shared history, language, and commerce.

Edmond Genêt French minister to the United States

The situation intensified in April 1793, when **Edmond Genêt**, a representative of the French government, landed in Charleston, South Carolina. Genêt's arrival raised troubling questions for President Washington. Should he receive Genêt, thus officially recognizing France's revolutionary government? Should he acknowledge an obligation to aid France under the terms of the 1778 treaty? Washington received Genêt but also issued a proclamation stating that the United States would adopt "conduct friendly and impartial toward the belligerent powers." Federalist newspapers defended the neutrality proclamation, while Republicans who favored assisting France only reluctantly accepted the popular policy.

Visualizing THE PAST

Newspapers of the Early Republic

In the 1790s newspapers did not attempt to present news objectively, and indeed, none of their readers expected them to do so. Instead, newspapers were linked to the rapidly expanding political factions of the new nation—the partisan groupings (not yet political parties in the modern sense) terming themselves *Federalists* and *Republicans*. The "official" paper of the Federalists was *The Gazette of the United States* (colonial papers supported by individual governments too had been called *gazettes*—just as the *London Gazette* was tied to the English government). Among the Republicans' many allied newspapers was *The New-York Journal, and Patriotic Register*. A reader comparing the front pages of any two issues could see at a glance the differences between them. *The Gazette of the United States* filled its first page with sober news articles, whereas the face *The New-York Journal* presented to the world was consumed entirely with advertisements, some headed by intriguing design elements. Which would appeal more directly to America's artisans and forward-thinking yeomen, and why?

Front Page of the New York Journal & Patriotic Register, August 21, 1793 (litho), American School, (18th century)/ © Chicago History Museum, USA/ The Bridgeman Art Library

Front Page of the Gazette of the United States, April 15, 1789 (litho), American School, (18th century)/American Antiquarian Society, Worcester, Massachusetts, USA/Courtesy, American Antiquarian Society/The Bridgeman Art Library

Democratic Societies

Genêt's faction fell from power in Paris, and he subsequently sought political asylum in the United States. But his disappearance from the diplomatic scene did not diminish the impact of the French Revolution in America. More than forty Democratic societies, formed by Americans sympathetic to the French Revolution, organized between 1793 and 1800. Members cast themselves in the mold of the 1760s resistance movement, as defenders of fragile liberty from corrupt and self-serving Federalist rulers.

The rapid spread of citizens' groups outspokenly critical of the administration disturbed Hamilton and Washington. Federalist writers charged that the societies' "real design" was "to involve the country in war, to assume the reins of government and tyrannize over the people." In the fall of 1794, Washington accused the clubs of fomenting the Whiskey Rebellion. As the first organized political dissenters in the United States, the Democratic societies alarmed officials who had not yet accepted the idea that one component of a free government was an organized loyal opposition.

Jay Treaty Debate

In 1794, George Washington dispatched Chief Justice John Jay to London to negotiate unresolved questions in Anglo-American relations. The United States wanted to establish freedom of the seas and to assert its right, as a neutral nation, to unfettered trade with both combatants. Further, Great Britain still held posts in the American Northwest, thus violating the 1783 peace treaty. Southern planters also wanted compensation for the slaves who left with the British army after the war.

Jay had little to offer the British, but Britain agreed to evacuate the western forts and reduce restrictions on American trade to England and the Caribbean. The **Jay Treaty** established two arbitration commissions—one to deal with prewar debts Americans owed to British creditors and the other to hear claims for captured American merchant ships—but Britain adamantly refused to compensate slave owners for their bondspeople. Most Americans, including the president, at first expressed dissatisfaction with the treaty, which was nevertheless ratified by the Senate in secret in late June 1795.

After the treaty was published, Republican newspapers organized rallies and urged Washington to reject it. Federalists countered with gatherings and essays of their own, contending that Jay's treaty was preferable to no treaty at all. Washington signed the pact in mid-August. Just one opportunity remained to prevent it from taking effect: Congress had to appropriate funds to carry out the treaty, and appropriation bills had to originate in the House of Representatives.

Hoping the opposition would dissipate, Washington delayed submitting the treaty to the House until March 1796. Pressure on the House to appropriate the funds to carry out the treaty built quickly. Federalists successfully linked the Jay Treaty with another, more popular pact that Thomas Pinckney of South Carolina had negotiated with Spain the previous year. **Pinckney's Treaty** gave the United States valuable navigation privileges on the Mississippi River and the right to land and store goods at New Orleans tax-free. The overwhelming support it received helped to overcome opposition to the Jay Treaty. In late April, a divided House appropriated the money by a three-vote margin.

Jay Treaty Pact that sought to resolve mounting tensions between Britain and the United States in the years after the Revolution. Britain agreed to relinquish control of its western U.S. posts, establish commissions to receive claims for ships damaged by British seizures, and broaden U.S. access to trade with the West and British.

Pinckney's Treaty Also called the Treaty of San Lorenzo, it won westerners the right of duty-free access to New Orleans and the use of the Mississippi River for commerce.

Ironically, the Federalists' campaign to sway public opinion violated their fundamental philosophy of government—that ordinary people should defer to the judgment of elected leaders. The Federalists won the battle, but in the long run they would lose the war, for Republicans ultimately proved more effective in appealing to the citizenry.

The terms used by Jefferson and Madison ("the people" versus "aristocrats") or by Hamilton and Washington ("true patriots" versus "subversive rabble") do not adequately describe the growing divisions in the electorate. Republicans, especially strong in the southern and middle states, tended to be confident and optimistic. Southern planters foresaw a prosperous future fueled by westward expansion. Republicans employed democratic rhetoric to win over small farmers in southern and mid-Atlantic states. Members of non-English ethnic groups found Republicans' message attractive, as did artisans. Republicans prized America's internal resources and remained sympathetic to France.

Federalists, concentrated among the commercial interests of New England, stressed the need for order, hierarchy, and obedience to authority. In their eyes, the nation's internal and external enemies made alliance with Great Britain essential. The Federalists' vision of international affairs may have been accurate, but it was also unappealing. Federalists offered voters little hope of a better future, and the Republicans prevailed in the end.

Washington's Farewell Address

After the treaty debate, wearied by the criticism, George Washington decided not to seek reelection. In September, Washington published his Farewell Address, most of which Hamilton wrote. The address outlined two principles that guided American foreign policy at least until the late 1940s: to maintain commercial but not political ties to other nations, and to reject permanent alliances. Washington also stressed America's uniqueness—its exceptionalism—and the need for independent action in foreign affairs, today called *unilateralism*.

Some interpret Washington's plea for an end to partisan strife as a call for politicians to consider the good of the whole nation. But in the context of the impending presidential election, the Farewell Address appears rather as an attack on the Republican opposition. Washington advocated unity behind the Federalist banner.

Election of 1796

The presidential **election of 1796** saw the first serious contest for the position. Federalists in Congress put forward Vice President John Adams, with the diplomat Thomas Pinckney as his running mate. Congressional Republicans chose Thomas Jefferson as their presidential candidate; the lawyer, Revolutionary War veteran, and politician Aaron Burr of New York ran for vice president. But the method of voting in the electoral college did not take into account the possibility of party slates. The Constitution's drafters had not foreseen the emergence of competing political organizations, so the document provided no way to express support for one candidate for president and another for vice president. The electors simply voted for two people. The man with the highest total became president; the second highest, vice president.

election of 1796 Federalist John Adams won by three votes and, as the second-highest vote-getter in the electoral college, Thomas Jefferson became vice president.

That procedure was the Federalists' undoing. Adams won the presidency with 71 votes. With 68 votes, the next highest total, Jefferson would become vice president. During the next four years, the new president and vice president, once allies, became bitter enemies.

XYZ Affair

As president, John Adams clung to an outdated notion that the president should remain above politics. Thus, Adams kept Washington's cabinet intact, despite its key members' allegiance to his chief Federalist rival, Alexander Hamilton. Adams was often passive, letting others (usually Hamilton) take the lead. But Adams's detachment did enable him to weather the greatest international crisis the republic had yet faced.

The Jay Treaty improved America's relationship with Great Britain, but it provoked France to retaliate by seizing American vessels carrying British goods. In response, Congress authorized building ships and stockpiling weapons and ammunition. President Adams also sent three commissioners to Paris to negotiate a settlement, but agents of Talleyrand, the French foreign minister, demanded a bribe of $250,000 before negotiations could begin. The Americans refused and reported the incident in dispatches the president received in March 1798. Adams informed Congress and recommended further increases in military spending.

Convinced that Adams had deliberately sabotaged negotiations, Republicans insisted that the dispatches be turned over to Congress. Adams complied, withholding only the names of the French agents, whom he labeled X, Y, and Z. The revelation that the Americans had been treated with contempt stimulated anti-French sentiment in the United States and became known as the **XYZ Affair**. Congress abrogated the Treaty of Alliance and authorized American ships to commandeer French vessels.

XYZ Affair French demand for bribes from American negotiators that triggered great anger.

Quasi-War with France

Thus began an undeclared war with France fought in Caribbean waters between warships of the U.S. Navy and French privateers. Although Americans initially suffered heavy losses, by early 1799 the U.S. Navy had established its superiority, easing the threat to America's vital Caribbean trade.

Republicans, who opposed war and sympathized with France, could not quell anti-French feelings. Because Agent Y had boasted of a "French party in America," Federalists accused Republicans of traitorous designs.

Alien and Sedition Acts

Federalists moved to codify their belief that Republicans were subversive foreign agents. In 1798, the Federalist-controlled Congress adopted four laws known as the **Alien and Sedition Acts**, intended to weaken the Republican faction. Three of the acts targeted recently arrived immigrants, whom Federalists accurately suspected of sympathizing with Republicans. The Naturalization Act lengthened the residency period required for citizenship and ordered resident aliens to register with the federal government. The two Alien Acts provided for the detention of enemy aliens during wartime and gave the president authority to deport any alien he deemed dangerous to national security.

Alien and Sedition Acts A series of laws passed in 1789 under the label of national security but that were intended to suppress dissent and block the rise of the Republican faction.

The fourth statute, the Sedition Act, outlawed conspiracies to prevent the enforcement of federal laws. Violations were punishable by five years in prison and a $5,000 fine. The act also made writing, printing, or uttering "false, scandalous and malicious" statements "with intent to defame" the government or the president a crime punishable by as much as two years' imprisonment and a fine of $2,000. Today, a law punishing political speech would be unconstitutional. But in the eighteenth century, when organized opposition was suspect, many Americans supported such restrictions.

The Sedition Act led to fifteen indictments and ten guilty verdicts. Republican newspaper editors nevertheless continued their criticisms of Federalists, energized rather than quashed by the persecution. Jefferson and Madison combated the acts in another way. Petitioning the Federalist-controlled Congress to repeal the laws would clearly fail, and Federalist judges refused to allow accused individuals to question the Sedition Act's constitutionality. Accordingly, Republican leaders turned to the state legislatures. Concealing their role to avoid being indicted for sedition, Jefferson and Madison drafted resolutions that were introduced into the Kentucky and Virginia legislatures, respectively, in the fall of 1798. Because a compact among the states had created the Constitution, the resolutions contended, people speaking through their states had a right to judge the constitutionality of federal actions. Both legislatures pronounced the Alien and Sedition Acts unconstitutional, thus advancing the doctrine later known as nullification.

Although no other state endorsed them, the **Virginia and Kentucky Resolutions** placed the opposition party squarely in the revolutionary tradition of resistance to tyrannical authority. Jefferson and Madison had identified a key constitutional issue: How far could states go in opposing the national government? This question would not be definitively answered until the Civil War.

Link to the Virginia Resolution

Virginia and Kentucky Resolutions Jefferson's and Madison's response to the Alien and Sedition Acts. The Resolution stressed states' rights and the power of nullification in response to Alien and Sedition Acts.

The Convention of 1800

Just as northern legislatures were rejecting the Virginia and Kentucky Resolutions, Federalists split over France. Hamilton and his supporters called for a declaration legitimizing the undeclared naval war. Adams, though, received private signals that the French government regretted its treatment of the American commissioners. In response, he dispatched William Vans Murray to Paris to negotiate with Napoleon Bonaparte, France's new leader. The United States sought compensation for ships France had seized since 1793 and abrogation of the treaty of 1778. The Convention of 1800, which ended the Quasi-War, conceded only the latter point. Still, it freed the United States to follow the independent course George Washington had urged in his Farewell Address.

The West in the New Nation

How did the new nation begin to expand its boundaries westward?

By 1800, the nation had added three states (Vermont, Kentucky, and Tennessee) and more than 1 million people to the nearly 4 million counted by the 1790 census. It claimed sovereignty east of the Mississippi River and north of Spanish Florida. But the United States had control of the Northwest Territory only after American troops battled a powerful confederacy of eight Indian nations led by the Miamis.

War in the Northwest Territory

In 1789, General Arthur St. Clair, first governor of the Northwest Territory, failed to open more land to settlement through treaty negotiations with the western confederacy. Subsequently, Little Turtle, the confederacy's able war chief, defeated forces led by General Josiah Harmar (1790) and by St. Clair (1791) in battles near the border between modern Indiana and Ohio. In the United States' worst defeat in frontier history, more than six hundred of St. Clair's men died, and scores more were wounded.

The Miami Confederacy declared that peace could be achieved only if the United States recognized the Ohio River as its northwestern boundary. But the national government refused. In August 1794, a newly invigorated army under the command of General Anthony Wayne, a Revolutionary War hero, defeated the confederacy at the Battle of Fallen Timbers, near present-day Toledo, Ohio (see Map 7.2). Eager to avoid a costly and prolonged frontier conflict, the general reached agreement with the confederacy in August 1795.

The resulting Treaty of Greenville gave the United States the right to settle much of what was to become Ohio. In turn, the United States formally accepted the principle of Indian sovereignty, by virtue of residence, over all lands the native peoples had not ceded. Never again would the United States government claim that it had acquired Indian territory solely through negotiation with a European or North American country.

"Civilizing" the Indians

Even Indian peoples who lived independent of federal authority came within the orbit of American influence. The nation's stated goal was to "civilize" them. To promote "a love for exclusive property" among Indian peoples, Henry Knox proposed that the government give livestock and agricultural training to individual natives. Four years later, the **Indian Trade and Intercourse Act of 1793** codified the secretary of war's proposals.

The plan incorrectly posited that Indians' traditional commitment to communal landowning could easily be overcome, and it ignored their centuries-old agricultural practices. Policymakers focused on Indian men: because they hunted, male Indians were "savages" who should be "civilized" by learning to farm. That women traditionally farmed was irrelevant because, to officials, Indian women—like those of European descent—should confine themselves to child rearing, household chores, and home manufacturing.

Many Indian nations responded cautiously to the "civilizing" plan. The Iroquois Confederacy had been devastated by the war. Restricted to small reservations increasingly surrounded by Anglo-American farmlands, men could no longer hunt and often spent their days idle. Quaker missionaries started a demonstration farm among the Senecas to teach men to plow, but women showed greater interest.

Iroquois men became more receptive to the reformers after the spring of 1799, when a Seneca named Handsome Lake experienced remarkable visions. Like earlier prophets, Handsome Lake preached that Indian peoples should renounce alcohol, gambling, and other destructive European customs. He directed followers to reorient men's and women's work assignments as Quakers advocated, as he recognized

Indian Trade and Intercourse Act of 1793 Series of U.S. laws that attempted to "civilize" Indians according to European American standards.

In 1805, an unidentified artist painted Benjamin Hawkins, a trader and U.S. agent to the Indians of the Southeast, at the Creek agency near Macon, Georgia. Hawkins introduced European-style agriculture to the Creeks, who are shown here with vegetables from their fields. Throughout the eastern United States, Indian nations had to make similar adaptations of their traditional lifestyles in order to maintain their group identity.

that only by adopting the European sexual division of labor could the Iroquois retain their autonomy.

Created Equal?

The Constitution distinguished between "persons" and "citizens." All persons inhabiting the United States comprised, in some vague sense, *the people* who were sovereign in a republic. But only *citizens* voted and fully possessed the rights enumerated in the Constitution's first ten amendments. The language of Jefferson's Declaration of Independence, however, was far more sweeping: "all men are created equal." In eighteenth-century parlance, *all men* meant *all persons.* After independence, women, the enslaved, free persons of color, and radical thinkers wrestled anew with the contradictions between such capacious notions of liberty and the laws and customs of the young United States.

What contributed to the growing number of free blacks in America after the Revolution?

Women and the Republic

"I long to hear that you have declared an independancy," wrote **Abigail Adams** to her husband John in March 1776. And "by the way," she continued, "in the new Code of Laws which I suppose it will be necessary for you to make I desire you would Remember the Ladies, and be more generous and favourable to them than your ancestors." She hoped that Congress would "not

Abigail Adams Wife of Revolutionary figure John Adams (and second U.S. President). Influenced by the ideology of the Revolution, her letter to her husband is considered an early effort for greater rights for women.

DEA PICTURE LIBRARY/Getty Images

Mary Wollstonecraft (1759–1797) was one of the most famous thinkers of her day. In her youth she worked as a teacher, governess, and part-time author. In 1792, she published A Vindication of the Rights of Woman, *which argued that the radical equality envisioned by the revolutionaries in France should be extended to relations between the sexes.* Vindication *became an international best seller, with French, German, and American editions printed within the year. Engravings based on this portrait of Wollstonecraft by John Opie served as the frontispiece to later editions of her works, and circulated widely in the United States.*

put such unlimited power into the Hands of the Husbands," who traditionally held near-absolute authority over their wives' property and persons. "If perticuliar care and attention is not paid to the Laidies [sic] we are determined to foment a Rebellion, and will not hold ourselves bound by any Laws in which we have no voice, or Representation." Like many other disfranchised Americans in the age of revolution, Abigail Adams adapted patriot ideology to serve purposes revolutionary leaders had never intended.

Abigail Adams did not ask for woman suffrage, but others did, and some authors began to discuss and define the "rights of women" in general terms. Judith Sargent Murray, Thomas Paine, and James Otis all published essays on the topic, as did many transatlantic radicals. In 1792, Britain's Mary Wollstonecraft inflamed readers throughout the English-speaking world with her tract entitled *A Vindication of the Rights of Woman*.

Nor was the battle for women's rights confined to the page. The New Jersey state constitution in 1776 defined voters as "all free inhabitants"; subsequent state laws explicitly enfranchised female voters. For several decades, women who met the state's property qualifications—as well as free black landowners—voted in New Jersey's elections. That women chose to vote was evidence of their altered perception of their place in the country's political life.

As political contests grew more openly combative, women's role in the public sphere came to seem more threatening—both to the republic and to womanhood itself. Increasingly, thinkers emphasized the differences between men and women rather than their shared humanity. After an election marred by drunken violence, New Jersey's state legislature abolished female voting in 1807. Throughout the nation, as property qualifications for white male voters shrank, the presumed distinction between white men and everyone else grew.

Emancipation and Manumission

How did approximately seven hundred thousand enslaved and free blacks—persons but not citizens, who comprised 20 percent of the American population—fit into the developing nation? In the late 1770s and early 1780s, enslaved men and women in New Hampshire, Connecticut, and Massachusetts petitioned their courts and legislatures for freedom.

Such agitation catalyzed the gradual abolition of slavery in the North, a process now known as "the first emancipation." Vermont banned slavery in its 1777 constitution. Responding to lawsuits filed by enslaved men and women, Massachusetts courts ruled in 1783 that the state constitution prohibited slavery. Other states adopted gradual emancipation laws between 1780 (Pennsylvania) and 1804 (New Jersey). No southern state passed a general emancipation law, but the legislatures of Virginia (1782), Delaware (1787), and Maryland (1790 and 1796) altered statutes that restricted slave owners' ability to free their bondspeople.

Congress Debates Slavery

At the national level, too, the Revolution transformed slavery from an unspoken assumption to an open question. In 1790, three groups of Quakers submitted petitions to Congress calling for the abolition of slavery and the international slave trade. Southerners vigorously asserted that Congress should not even consider the petitions. They insisted that slavery was integral to the Union and that abolition would cause more problems than it solved. Congress accepted a committee report denying it the power to halt slave importations before 1808 or to emancipate slaves at any time, that authority "remaining with the several States alone." The precedent that Congress could not abolish slavery endured until the Civil War.

Revolutionary ideology thus had limited impact on the well-entrenched interests of large slaveholders. Even in the northern states—societies with slaves, not slave societies—lawmakers' concern for the *property* rights of owners led them to favor gradual over immediate emancipation. New York's law freed children born into slavery after July 4, 1799, but only after they reached their mid-twenties. And not until the late 1840s did Rhode Island and Connecticut abolish all vestiges of slavery.

Growth of Free Black Population

The number of free people of African descent grew dramatically after the Revolution. Wartime escapees from plantations, bondsmen who served in the Continental army, and others emancipated by their owners or by new state laws were now free. By 1790, nearly 60,000 free people of color lived in the United States; ten years later, they numbered more than 108,000, more than 10 percent of the African American population.

A sailor of African descent posed proudly for this portrait around 1790. Unfortunately, neither the name of the sailor nor the name of the artist is known today.

Private Collection/Picture Research Consultants & Archives

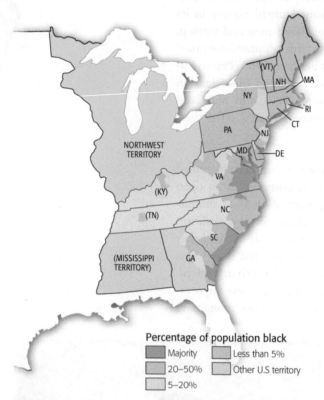

MAP 7.3
African American Population, 1790: Proportion of Total Population

The first national census clearly indicated that the African American population was heavily concentrated in the coastal South. Although there were growing numbers of blacks in the backcountry—presumably taken there by migrating slave owners—most parts of the North and East had few African American residents. But slavery shaped the economy of the entire U.S. in the early republic, and even in the mid-Atlantic and the North, its abolition took place gradually, sometimes over decades. Source: CAPPON, LESTER J.; ATLAS OF EARLY AMERICAN HISTORY, © 1976 Princeton University Press, 2004 renewed PUP. Reprinted by permission of Princeton University Press.

Percentage of population black
- Majority
- 20–50%
- 5–20%
- Less than 5%
- Other U.S territory

In the Chesapeake, manumissions were speeded by the shift from tobacco to grain production. Because grain cultivation was less labor intensive, planters complained about "excess" slaves, and occasionally freed some of their less productive or more favored laborers. The enslaved also negotiated agreements allowing them to live and work independently until they could save enough to purchase themselves. Virginia's free black population more than doubled in the two decades after 1790. By 1810, nearly one-quarter of Maryland's African American population lived outside of legal bondage.

Freedpeople's Lives

Freedpeople from rural areas often headed to port cities, especially Boston, Philadelphia, and the new boomtown of Baltimore. Women outnumbered men among the migrants, for they had better employment opportunities, especially in domestic service. Some freedmen also worked in domestic service, but larger numbers were unskilled laborers and sailors. A few women and a sizable proportion of men (nearly one-third of those in Philadelphia in 1795) were skilled workers or retailers. Many replaced the surnames of former masters with names like Newman or Brown and established independent two-parent families. They also began to occupy distinct neighborhoods, probably due to discrimination.

Even whites who recognized African Americans' right to freedom were unwilling to accept them as equals. Several states—including Delaware, Maryland, and South Carolina—adopted laws denying property-owning black men the vote. South Carolina forbade free blacks from testifying against whites in court. New Englanders used indenture contracts to control freed youths, who were often barred from public schools. Freedmen found it difficult to purchase property and find good jobs.

To survive and prosper, freedpeople came to rely on collective effort. In Charleston, mulattos formed the Brown Fellowship Society, which provided them insurance, financed a school, and helped to support orphans. In 1794, former slaves in Philadelphia and Baltimore, led by the African American clergyman

Richard Allen, founded societies that eventually became the **African Methodist Episcopal (AME) church**. AME congregations—along with African Baptist, African Episcopal, and African Presbyterian churches—became cultural centers of free black communities.

Development of Racist Theory

Their endeavors were especially important because the post-revolutionary years witnessed the development of racist theory in the United States. European Americans had long regarded their slaves as inferior, but the most influential thinkers reasoned that bondspeople's seemingly debased character derived from their enslavement, rather than enslavement's being the consequence of inherited inferiority. After the Revolution, slave owners skirted the contradiction between slaveholding practice and the egalitarian implications of revolutionary theory. They argued that people of African descent were less than fully human and thus the principles of republican equality applied only to European Americans.

Simultaneously, the concept of "race" began to be applied to groups defined by skin color. Egalitarian thinking among European Americans at once downplayed status distinctions within their own group, and distinguished all "whites" from all others. Notions of "whiteness," "redness," and "blackness" developed alongside beliefs in European Americans' superiority.

With this new racial thought came the assertion that, as Thomas Jefferson insisted in 1781, blacks were "inferior to the whites in the endowments both of body and mind." There followed the belief that those with black skin were inherently lazy, even though owners had often argued that slaves made "natural" workers. Another notion was that blacks were sexually promiscuous, and that African American men lusted after European American women. The more common sexual exploitation of enslaved women by their masters generally aroused little concern, though Federalist newspaper editors did not hesitate to use Jefferson's long-standing relationship with Sally Hemings to inflame public opinion against him.

African Americans challenged these racist notions. In 1791, Benjamin Banneker, a free black mathematical genius, sent Jefferson a copy of his latest almanac (which included his astronomical calculations) to show blacks' mental powers. Jefferson admitted Banneker's intelligence but regarded him as exceptional, and said he would need more evidence to change his mind about people of African descent.

A White Men's Republic

Though many men of African descent had served with honor in the Continental army, laws from the 1770s on linked male citizenship rights to "whiteness." Some historians argue that, just as excluding women from the political realm reserved all power for men, so identifying common racial antagonists helped to foster white solidarity across class lines. The division of American society between slave and free was transformed into a division between blacks—some of whom were free—and whites.

Haitian Refugees

Less than a decade after winning independence, the United States confronted its first immigration crisis. Among the approximately 600,000 residents of St. Domingue in the early 1790s were about 100,000 free people, almost all of them slave owners; half were whites, the rest of mixed race. After the French Revolution those free mulattos sought greater social and political equality. Slaves then seized the opportunity to revolt. By 1793, they had triumphed under the leadership of a former bondsman, Toussaint L'Ouverture. In 1804 they ousted the French, establishing the republic of Haiti. Thousands of whites and mulattos, accompanied by as many slaves as they could transport, sought asylum in the United States.

Southern plantation owners worried that refugee slaves so familiar with ideas of freedom and equality would mingle with their own bondspeople. Many were uncomfortable with the arrival of numerous free people of color. Most southern states adopted laws forbidding the entry of Haitian slaves and free mulattos, but the laws were difficult to enforce, as was a similar congressional act. More than fifteen thousand refugees—white, black, and mixed race—flooded into the United States and Spanish Louisiana. Many ended up in Virginia (which did not pass an exclusion law) or in the cities of Charleston, Savannah, and New Orleans.

In both New Orleans and Charleston, the influx of Haitians of mixed race aroused a heightened color consciousness that placed light-skinned people atop a hierarchy of people of color. After the United States purchased Louisiana in 1803, the number of free people of color there almost doubled in three years, largely because of a final surge of immigration from Haiti. And, in Virginia, the Haitian revolt inspired slaves in 1800 to plan the action now known as Gabriel's Rebellion.

The Haitian refugees thus linked European Americans and African Americans to events in the West Indies.

A free woman of color in Louisiana early in the nineteenth century, possibly one of the refugees from Haiti. Esteban Rodriguez Mir, named governor of Spanish Louisiana in 1782, ordered all slave and free black women to wear head wraps rather than hats—which were reserved for whites—but this woman and many others subverted his order by nominally complying, but nevertheless creating elaborate headdresses.

Courtesy of the Collections of the Louisiana State Museum

"Revolutions" at the End of the Century

What gave rise to new potential revolutions in America at the end of the eighteenth century?

Three events in the last two years of the eighteenth century can be deemed real or potential revolutions: Fries's Rebellion, Gabriel's Rebellion, and the election of Thomas Jefferson. Each mirrored the tensions and uncertainties of the young republic.

Fries's Rebellion

The tax resistance movement named for Revolutionary War veteran John Fries arose among German American farmers in Pennsylvania's Lehigh Valley in 1798–1799. To finance the Quasi-War, Congress taxed land, houses, and legal documents. German Americans, imbued with revolutionary ideals (nearly half were veterans), saw in the taxes a threat to their liberties and livelihoods. Asserting their right to resist unconstitutional laws, they raised liberty poles, petitioned Congress, and barred assessors from their homes.

When a federal judge ordered the arrest of twenty resisters, Fries led 120 militiamen to Bethlehem, where they surrounded a tavern temporarily housing the prisoners. President Adams described the militiamen's actions as acts of war. Fries and many of his neighbors were arrested and tried; he and two others were convicted of treason, thirty-two more of violating the Sedition Act. Although Fries and the other "traitors" were sentenced to hang, Adams pardoned them just two days before their scheduled execution. Despite clemency from a Federalist president, the region's residents became, and remained, Republican partisans.

Gabriel's Rebellion

Gabriel, an enslaved Virginia blacksmith who planned the second end-of-the-century revolution, drew on both Haitian and American revolutionary experiences. He first recruited other skilled African American artisans who lived, as he did, under minimal supervision. Next, he enlisted rural slaves. The rebels planned to attack Richmond on the night of August 30, 1800. They would set fire to the city, seize the capitol building, and capture the governor, James Monroe. At that point, Gabriel believed, other slaves and poor whites would join the movement.

Heavy rain forced a postponement. Several planters then learned of the plot. Gabriel avoided arrest for weeks, but militia troops apprehended and interrogated other rebel leaders. Twenty-six rebels, including Gabriel, were hanged. Southern state legislatures responded to the plot by passing increasingly severe laws regulating slavery, which became even more firmly entrenched as an economic institution and way of life in the region.

Election of 1800

The third end-of-the-century revolution was the election of Thomas Jefferson as president and a Congress dominated by Republicans. Leading up to November 1800, Federalists and Republicans openly campaigned for congressional seats and maneuvered to control the electoral college. Republicans again nominated Jefferson and Burr; Federalists named John Adams, with Charles Cotesworth Pinckney of South Carolina as vice president. When the votes were counted, Jefferson and Burr had tied with 73, while Adams garnered 64 and Pinckney 63. Under the Constitution, the existing House of Representatives would decide the election.

Voting in the House continued for six days; in the end, a deal was struck that gave Jefferson the presidency on the thirty-sixth ballot. The bitterly fought election prompted the adoption of the Twelfth Amendment, which provided that electors would thenceforth cast separate ballots for president and vice president.

In an 1820 letter to then-president James Monroe, Jefferson linked "the revolution of 1776" to "that of 1800." Historians debate whether the so-called Revolution

Dissent During Wartime

The Quasi-War with France in 1798–1799 spawned the nation's first attempt to suppress dissent. By criminalizing dissenting speech, the Sedition Act of 1798 tried to mute criticism of the war and President John Adams. Fifteen men were indicted and ten fined and jailed after being convicted under the statute.

Although Americans might assume that their right to free speech under the First Amendment, now more fully accepted than it was two centuries ago, protects dissenters during wartime, history suggests otherwise. Every conflict has stimulated efforts to suppress dissenters. During the Civil War, the Union jailed civilian Confederate sympathizers. During the First World War, the government deported immigrant aliens who criticized the war effort. World War II brought the silencing of those who had opposed American entry into the war. The consequences of antiwar protests in the Vietnam era still affect the nation today, for the American people remain divided over whether the proper course of action in the 1960s and 1970s was dissent from, or acquiescence to, government policy.

The USA PATRIOT Act, adopted after the terrorist attacks of September 11, 2001, removed long-standing restrictions on federal government surveillance of citizens, controversially granting access to library records. Criticism of the wars in Iraq and Afghanistan has raised questions: Do newspapers that publish classified information or pictures of abused prisoners overstep the First Amendment? Can political figures censure the conduct of the wars without being labeled unpatriotic?

Freedom of speech is never easy to maintain, and wartime conditions make it much more difficult. When the nation comes under attack, many argue that dissent should cease. Others contend that people must always have the right to speak freely. Events in the United States since the 9/11 attacks suggest that this legacy remains contentious for the American people.

---

of 1800 deserves the name Jefferson later gave it. Many of the Republicans' promised reforms failed to materialize. The defeated Federalists retained and indeed strengthened their hold on the federal judiciary. But at the very least, Jefferson's inauguration—which marked the first peaceful transfer of power from one faction to another in a modern republic—ushered in a new era in American political culture, one in which republican theory and partisan practice could coexist. "We are all Republicans, we are all Federalists," the new president proclaimed in his first inaugural address. The unifying sentiment was welcome, but hardly accurate.

Summary

During the 1780s, the republic's upheavals convinced many leaders that the United States needed a more powerful central government. Drafted in 1787, the Constitution created that stronger national framework. The document's supporters—called Federalists—contended that their design was just as "republican" as the flawed Articles of Confederation had been. Those labeled Antifederalists argued otherwise, but ultimately lost the fight.

Inhabitants of the early United States faced changed lives and changed politics. Indian peoples east of the Mississippi River found aspects of their traditional cultures under assault. Enslaved African Americans faced increasingly restrictive laws in the southern colonies. In the North, freedom suits, manumissions, and gradual emancipation laws fostered a growing free black community. At the same time, a newly systematic and defensive pro-slavery argument emphasized race (rather than slave or free status) as the determinant of African Americans' standing in the nation. Imagined chiefly as mothers of the next generation and selfless contributors to the nation's welfare, white women played a limited role in American public life. Writers and artists promoted such feminine self-sacrifice and other republican virtues.

The years between 1788 and 1800 established enduring precedents for Congress, the presidency, and the federal judiciary. The United States forged diplomatic independence. The French Revolution prompted debates over foreign and domestic policy. In the 1790s, the United States saw the emergence of organized factionalism and grassroots politicking involving both men and women. In 1801, after more than a decade of struggle, the Jeffersonian view of an agrarian, decentralized republic prevailed over Alexander Hamilton's vision of a centralized economy and a strong national government.

Chapter Review

Trials of the Confederation

What was the significance of the Northwest Ordinance?

The Northwest Ordinance of 1787 included a bill of rights guaranteeing freedom of religion and the right to a jury trial, and it forbade cruel and unusual punishments and nominally prohibited slavery. But its ban on slavery was more symbolic than actual because it did not deny slaveholders living in the territory the right to their human property and included the first fugitive slave law. The Northwest Ordinance also specified the process by which residents of the territories could organize state governments and seek admission to the Union "on an equal footing with the original States." Congress therefore assured territorial residents the same rights held by citizens of the original states.

From Crisis to the Constitution

How did the question of slavery become linked to the new U.S. Constitution?

Slavery came into play at the Constitutional Convention as states debated how their populations should be counted in determining the number of representatives each would get in the lower house of Congress. Slave states wanted their bondspeople fully counted, while those from states with few slaves wanted only free people counted. The dispute was resolved by a formula known as the three-fifths compromise, noting that three-fifths of slaves would be included in population totals used to determine congressional districts. While the words *slave* and *slavery* are not used in the Constitution, it nonetheless included direct and indirect protections for slavery, among them assistance in putting down revolts, returning fugitive slaves to masters, and agreeing not to end the importation of bondspeople for twenty years.

Promoting a Virtuous Citizenry

How were notions of republican virtue engendered in post-revolutionary America?

Republican writers and artists produced works that reinforced republican notions. For example, Mason Locke Weems's *Life of Washington* offered a moralizing tale of honesty and integrity. Americans, especially in the North, began to focus on public education as a means to help children become useful citizens. Some argued that since child rearing was women's role, they, too, would need education to help raise virtuous future citizens. The essaying Judith Sargent Murray argued that women and men had equal intellects but unequal schooling and proposed that boys and girls be educated alike. Her writings were part of a general rethinking of women's position.

Building a Workable Government

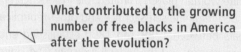

How did the chartering of the Bank of the United States provoke an early constitutional debate?

Treasury Secretary Alexander Hamilton asked Congress to charter a national bank, modeled on England's, which would act as a collecting and disbursing agent for the treasury and the source for national currency. Some political leaders, like James Madison and Thomas Jefferson argued that the Constitution did not give Congress the power to establish the bank. Hamilton, by contrast, stated that Congress could use any means not prohibited by the Constitution to achieve a constitutional end. President Washington agreed, and the bill establishing the Bank of the United States became law.

Building a Nation Among Nations

What was the underlying purpose of the Alien and Sedition Acts of 1798?

Adopted by the Federalist-controlled Congress, these acts were designed to suppress dissent—still seen as dangerous and subversive rather than a natural part of a republic—and weaken the competing Republican faction. Hence, the acts targeted recent immigrants, typically Republican supporters, by lengthening the residency requirement for citizenship, among other rules, as well as allowing the president to detain or deport any alien considered dangerous to national security. The Sedition Act outlawed antigovernment conspiracies and curbed free speech by making the writing or uttering of false, malicious, or scandalous statements against the government illegal. Although the Federalists expected the acts to weaken their critics, the laws only increased dissent.

The West in the New Nation

How did the new nation begin to expand its boundaries westward?

The United States nominally controlled the land east of the Mississippi and north of Spanish Florida, and later, through warfare and treaty, managed to extend its northernmost boundary to the Ohio River. Initially, leaders attempted to negotiate with Indians living there for the land; when that failed, war with eight Indian nations ensued, culminating in 1795 with the Treaty of Greenville. This agreement allowed the United States to settle most of what would become Ohio in exchange for acknowledging the principle of Indian sovereignty—by virtue of residence—over lands that had not been ceded.

Created Equal?

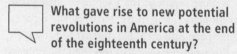

What contributed to the growing number of free blacks in America after the Revolution?

Slaves who escaped plantations during the war, those who served in the military, or those who had been freed by their owners or state laws accounted for many of the 60,000 free people of color in the United States by 1790 and 108,000 by 1800. Northern states, which were less reliant on slave labor, increasingly freed slaves and were more likely to adopt laws abolishing slavery. But even there, many states respected owners' "property rights" and preferred gradual manumission over outright abolition. In the courts, too, blacks challenged the contradictions between forced bondage and the ideology of the Revolution, and while often unsuccessful, their actions forced policymakers to grapple with this issue. Postwar economic changes also spurred manumissions, particularly in the Chesapeake, where the shift from tobacco to grain production meant far fewer slaves were required, doubling the free black population in Virginia between 1790 and 1810, for example.

"Revolutions" at the End of the Century

What gave rise to new potential revolutions in America at the end of the eighteenth century?

Three events revealed unresolved issues—and growing tensions—in the new republic. First, Fries's Rebellion questioned the power of the central government to tax, seeing it—much as early revolutionaries had—as a threat to personal liberties and livelihoods. Second, Gabriel's Rebellion of semifree blacks sought to challenge the slave system in the Chesapeake (but ended up inspiring stricter slave laws in the South). And finally, the hotly contested 1800 presidential election revealed a structural flaw in the Constitution, which required that presidential electors vote for two men without designating one as president and the other as vice president, thus creating the tie between Jefferson and Burr. It led to the Twelfth Amendment, which provided that electors cast separate ballots for presidential and vice presidential candidates.

Suggestions for Further Reading

Annette Gordon-Reed, *The Hemingses of Monticello: An American Family* (2008)

Eliga Gould, *Among the Powers of the Earth: The American Revolution and the Making of a New World Empire* (2012)

Woody Holton, *Unruly Americans and the Origins of the Constitution* (2007)

David Jaffe, *A New Nation of Goods: The Material Culture of Early America* (2010)

Catherine O'Donnell Kaplan, *Men of Letters in the Early Republic: Cultivating Forums of Citizenship* (2008)

Pauline Maier, *Ratification: The People Debate the Constitution, 1787–1788* (2010)

David Andrew Nichols, *Red Gentlemen & White Savages: Indians, Federalists, and the Search for Order on the American Frontier* (2008)

Jeffrey L. Pasley, *"The Tyranny of Printers": Newspaper Politics in the Early American Republic* (2001)

David Waldstreicher, *Slavery's Constitution: From Revolution to Ratification* (2009)

Rosemarie Zagarri, *Revolutionary Backlash: Women and Politics in the Early American Republic* (2007)

8

Defining the Nation

1801–1823

Eager to distinguish himself from the allegedly aristocratic ways of his Federalist predecessors, President Thomas Jefferson displayed impatience for ceremony. But on his first New Year's Day in office, he awaited the ceremonial presentation of a much-heralded tribute to his commitment, as one gift bearer put it, to "defend Republicanism and baffle all the arts of Aristocracy." Crafted in Massachusetts, the belated inaugural gift weighed more than twelve hundred pounds and measured four feet in diameter, bearing the inscription "THE GREATEST CHEESE IN AMERICA—FOR THE GREATEST MAN IN AMERICA."

The "mammoth cheese" was devised the previous July and made by the "Ladies" of Cheshire, a western Massachusetts farming community as Jeffersonian-Republican as it was Baptist. As a religious minority in largely Congregationalist New England, the Cheshire Baptists celebrated a president whose vision featured agrarianism and separation of church and state.

Federalist editors joked that the mammoth cheese's maggot-infested condition upon delivery symbolized the nation under Republican rule. Its size resulted from the excesses of democracy, in which even women and backwoods preachers could play leading roles.

The Federalists' derision of the mammoth cheese inspired further demonstrations of democratic pride. In subsequent months, a Philadelphia baker sold "Mammoth Bread," and two years later, in 1804, a "mammoth loaf" was served in the Capitol to a crowd of Federalist-disparaging Republicans, including President Jefferson.

People excluded from formal political participation—the vote—expressed ideal visions for the nation's future when they petitioned legislatures, marched in parades, debated in taverns—and sent the president a mammoth cheese. Behind such symbolism lay serious political ideologies. Jeffersonians believed virtue derived from agricultural endeavors and thus celebrated the acquisition of the Louisiana Territory. Their efforts to expand

Chapter Outline

Political Visions
Separation of Church and State | Religious Revivals | Political Mobilization | The Partisan Press | Limited Government | Judicial Politics | The Marshall Court | Judicial Review | Election of 1804 | Nationalism and Culture

Continental Expansion and Indian Resistance
New Orleans | Louisiana Purchase | Lewis and Clark Expedition | Divisions Among Indian Peoples | Tenskwatawa and Tecumseh

The Nation in the Orbit of Europe
First Barbary War | Threats to American Sovereignty | The Embargo of 1807 | International Slave Trade | Early Abolitionism and Colonization | Election of 1808 | Women and Politics | Failed Policies | Mr. Madison's War

LINKS TO THE WORLD *Emigration to Liberia*

The War of 1812
Invasion of Canada | Naval Battles | Burning Capitals | War in the South | Treaty of Ghent | American Sovereignty Reasserted | Domestic Consequences

VISUALIZING THE PAST *Selling War*

Early Industrialization
Preindustrial Farms | Preindustrial Artisans | Putting-Out and Early Factories

their agriculturally based "empire of liberty" westward were resisted by Native Americans and their European allies, and sometimes by Federalists. The War of 1812 largely removed such resistance, facilitating the United States' nearly unbridled expansion west. Although that war ended with few issues resolved, it secured the United States' sovereignty, opened much of the West to European Americans and their African American slaves, and helped spur revolutions in transportation and industry.

Contemporary observers hailed postwar nationalism as an "Era of Good Feelings," but when economic boom turned to bust, nationalistic optimism faded. No issue proved more divisive than slavery's future in the West, as Missouri's petition for statehood revealed.

As you read this chapter, keep the following questions in mind:

- **What characterized the two main competing visions for national development?**
- **How did America's relationship with Europe influence political and economic developments?**
- **In what ways did nonvoting Americans—most blacks, women, and Native Americans—take part in defining the new nation?**

Sectionalism and Nationalism

American System | *Early Internal Improvements* | *Panic of 1819* | *Missouri Compromise* | *The Era of Good Feelings* | *Government Promotion of Market Expansion* | *Boundary Settlements* | *Monroe Doctrine*

LEGACY FOR A PEOPLE AND A NATION
States' Rights and Nullification

SUMMARY

Political Visions

In his inaugural address, Jefferson appealed to opponents and supporters as citizens with common republican beliefs: "We are all republicans, we are all federalists.... A wise and frugal government, which shall restrain men from injuring one another, which shall leave them free to regulate their pursuits of industry and improvement, and shall not take from the mouth of labor the bread it had earned. This is the sum of good government."

Outgoing president John Adams missed Jefferson's call for unity, having left Washington before dawn. Former friends, he and Jefferson now disliked each other. Democratic-Republicans—as the Republicans of the 1790s now called themselves—and Federalists bitterly disagreed on how society and government should be organized. Federalists advocated a strong national government to promote economic development. Democratic-Republicans believed that limited government would foster republican virtue. Nearly two decades later, Jefferson would call his election "the revolution of 1800."

Was Jefferson's election and political vision truly "the revolution of 1800"?

Separation of Church and State

On the day he received the overripe cheese, Jefferson reciprocated with a letter to the Baptist association in Danbury, Connecticut, proclaiming that the

Chronology

1801	Marshall becomes chief justice
	Jefferson inaugurated as president
1801–05	United States defeats Barbary pirates
1803	*Marbury v. Madison*
	Louisiana Purchases
1804	Jefferson reelected president
1804–06	Lewis and Clark Expedition
1805	Tenskwatawa emerges as Shawnee leader
1807	Chesapeake affair
	Embargo Act
1808	Congress bans slave importation
	Madison elected president
1808–13	Tenskwatawa and Tecumseh organize Indian resistance
1811	National Road begun
1812	Madison reelected president
1812–15	War of 1812
1813	Tecumseh's death
	Boston Manufacturing Company starts textile mill in Waltham, Massachusetts
1814	Treaty of Ghent
1814–15	Hartford Convention
1815	Battle of New Orleans
1817	Regular steamboat travel begins on Mississippi
1817–25	Erie Canal constructed
1819	*McCulloch v. Maryland*
	Adams-Onís Treaty
1819–early 1820s	First major depression
1820–21	Missouri Compromise
1822	Colonization of Liberia begins (formally established in 1824)
1823	Monroe Doctrine

Constitution's First Amendment supported a "wall of separation between church and state." New England Baptists hailed Jefferson as a hero, but New England Federalists believed their worst fears were confirmed. During the 1800 election, Federalists waged a venomous campaign, incorrectly labeling Jefferson an atheist. Their rhetoric proved so effective that, after Jefferson's election, some New England women hid their Bibles in their gardens to foil Democratic-Republicans allegedly bent on confiscating them.

Religious Revivals

Jefferson became president during a period of religious revivalism, particularly among Methodists and Baptists, whose democratic preaching—all humans, they said, were equal in God's eyes—encouraged a growing democratic political culture. The most famous revival was at Cane Ridge, Kentucky, in August 1801. According to one report, twenty-five thousand men and women, free and enslaved, attended. The call to personal repentance and conversion invigorated southern Protestantism, giving churches an evangelical base. All revivalists believed in individual self-improvement, but northern revivalists also emphasized communal improvement, becoming missionaries for individual salvation and social reform (see Chapter 10).

Emboldened by secular and religious ideologies about equality, society's non-elites articulated their own political visions and worked to reshape the debates. When the Cheshire Baptists sent their cheese to President Jefferson, for example, they pointedly informed the Virginia planter that it had been made "without a single slave to assist."

Political Mobilization

The revolution of 1800, which gave the Democratic-Republicans majorities in both houses of Congress along with the presidency, resulted from an electorate limited largely to property-holding men. Under the Constitution, states regulated voting. Nowhere but New Jersey could property-owning, single women vote; that right was granted inadvertently and revoked in 1807. In 1800, free black men meeting property qualifications could vote everywhere but Delaware, Georgia, South Carolina, and Virginia, though local custom often kept them from exercising that right. Nonetheless, partisan politics captured Americans' imaginations. Political mobilization took place locally, as candidates rallied popular support on militia training grounds, in taverns and churches, at court gatherings, and during holiday celebrations. Voters and nonvoters expressed their views through parades, petitions, songs, and debates. Most important, they devoured a growing print culture of pamphlets, broadsides (posters), almanacs, and newspapers.

The Partisan Press

Read aloud in taverns, artisans' workshops, and homes, newspapers gave national importance to local events. In 1800, the nation had 260 newspapers; by 1810, it had 396—virtually all unabashedly partisan.

Courtesy Winterthur Museum, Museum purchase, 1959.131

Although most places limited the vote to property-owning white men, elections, such as this one in Philadelphia, drew multiracial crowds of men, women, and children.

The parties adopted official organs. After his election, Jefferson persuaded the *National Intelligencer* to move from Philadelphia to Washington, where it became the Democratic-Republicans' voice. In 1801, Alexander Hamilton launched the *New York Evening Post* as the Federalist vehicle. Published six or seven times a week, party papers helped invigorate the growing obsession with partisan politics.

Limited Government

To bring into his administration men sharing his vision of individual liberty, an agrarian republic, and limited government, Jefferson rejected appointments that Adams made in his presidency's last days and dismissed Federalist customs collectors. He awarded treasury and judicial offices to Republicans. Jeffersonians worked to make the government leaner. If Alexander Hamilton had viewed the national debt as the engine of economic growth, Jefferson deemed it the source of government corruption. Secretary of the Treasury Albert Gallatin halved the army budget and reduced the 1802 navy budget by two-thirds. He moved to reduce the national debt from $83 million to $57 million, hoping to retire it by 1817. Jefferson closed two of the nation's five diplomatic missions abroad, at The Hague and in Berlin. And the Democratic-Republican–controlled Congress oversaw the repeal of all internal taxes, including the despised whiskey tax of 1791.

Ideas of liberty also distinguished Democratic-Republicans from Federalists. Opposition to the Alien and Sedition Acts of 1798 had united Republicans. Jefferson now declined to use the acts against his opponents, instead pardoning those convicted of violating them.

Congress let the Sedition Act expire in 1801 and the Alien Act in 1802, and repealed the Naturalization Act of 1798, which required fourteen years of residency for citizenship. The 1802 act that replaced it required only five years of residency, loyalty to the Constitution, and the forsaking of foreign allegiances and titles. It remained the basis of naturalized American citizenship into the twentieth century.

Judicial Politics

To many Democratic-Republicans, the judiciary represented a centralizing and undemocratic force, since judges were appointed, not elected, and served for life. At Jefferson's prompting, the House impeached (indicted) and the Senate convicted Federal District Judge John Pickering of New Hampshire, whose alleged alcoholism made him an easy target. The House impeached Supreme Court Justice Samuel Chase for judicial misconduct. A staunch Federalist, Chase had pushed for prosecutions under the Sedition Act, campaigned for Adams in 1800, and denounced Jefferson's administration. But Democratic-Republicans failed to muster the two-thirds Senate majority necessary for conviction. The failure to remove Chase preserved the Court's independence and established the precedent that criminal actions, not political disagreements, justified removal from office.

The Marshall Court

Although Jefferson appointed three new Supreme Court justices, the Court remained a Federalist stronghold under John Marshall. Even after the Democratic-Republicans achieved a majority of Court seats in 1811, Marshall remained influential as chief justice. Under the Marshall Court (1801–1835), the Supreme Court upheld federal supremacy over the states while protecting commercial interests.

Marshall made the Court an equal branch of government. He strengthened the Court by having it speak with a more unified voice; rather than issuing individual concurring judgments, justices now issued joint majority opinions. From 1801 through 1805, Marshall wrote twenty-four of the Court's twenty-six decisions; through 1810, he wrote 85 percent of the opinions.

Judicial Review

In his last hours as president, Adams named Federalist William Marbury a justice of the peace in the District of Columbia. Jefferson's secretary of state, James Madison, declined to certify the appointment, allowing the new president to appoint a Democratic-Republican. Marbury sued, requesting a writ of mandamus (a court order forcing the president to appoint him). If the Supreme Court ruled in Marbury's favor in **Marbury v. Madison**, the president probably would not comply, and the Court could not force him to do so. Yet by refusing to issue the writ, the Federalist-dominated bench would hand the Democratic-Republicans a victory.

Marbury v. Madison Case in which the Supreme Court's power to determine the constitutionality of laws was established.

Instead, Marshall recast the issue. He ruled that Marbury had a right to his appointment but that the Supreme Court could not compel Madison to honor it because the Constitution did not grant the Court power to issue a writ of mandamus. Without specific mention in the Constitution, Marshall wrote, the section of the Judiciary Act of 1789 authorizing the Court to issue writs was unconstitutional. Thus, the Supreme Court denied itself the power to issue writs of mandamus but established its far greater power to judge the constitutionality of laws. In doing so, Marshall fashioned the theory of judicial review. Because the Constitution was "the supreme law of the land," Marshall wrote, any federal or state act contrary to the Constitution must be null and void. This power of the Supreme Court to determine the constitutionality of legislation and presidential acts permanently enhanced the independence of the judiciary and breathed life into the Constitution.

Election of 1804

In the first election after the Twelfth Amendment's ratification, Jefferson dropped Aaron Burr as his running mate and, to establish a North–South balance, chose George Clinton of New York. They swamped their opponents—South Carolinian Charles Cotesworth Pinckney and New Yorker Rufus King—in the electoral college by 162 votes to 14, carrying fifteen of the seventeen states. The 1804 election escalated the animosity between Burr and Hamilton, who supported Burr's rival in the New York gubernatorial election. When Hamilton called Burr a liar, Burr challenged Hamilton to a duel. Because New York had outlawed dueling, the encounter occurred in New Jersey. Details of the duel remain hazy but Hamilton died after being shot by Burr. New York and New Jersey prosecutors indicted Burr for murder.

Burr fled to the West. While historians disagree about his motives, the "Burr Conspiracy" was understood at the time as a scheme with Brigadier General James Wilkinson to create a new empire by militarily taking what is now Texas and by persuading existing western territories to leave the United States. Tried for treason in 1807, Burr faced a prosecution aided by President Jefferson but overseen by Jefferson's rival Chief Justice Marshall. Prompted by Marshall to interpret treason narrowly, the jury acquitted Burr, who fled to Europe.

Nationalism and Culture

As statesmen bickered, other Americans conveyed their nationalist visions artistically. Painters continued to memorialize great birth scenes of American nationhood, such as the Declaration of Independence's signing, Revolutionary War battles, and the Constitutional Convention. Four of John Trumbull's revolutionary scenes, commissioned in 1817, still hang in the Capitol building rotunda in Washington.

Architecturally, Americans self-consciously constructed a new, independent nation. Designed by Major Pierre Charles L'Enfant, the city of Washington was meant to embody a "reciprocity of sight:" each of the government's three branches—legislative, judicial, and executive—should keep an eye on one another. Across America, wealthier citizens commissioned Federal-style homes, which imitated the simplicity of classical architecture and used indigenous building materials.

The era's best-selling book was Noah Webster's spelling book, which proposed making English more "republican." It sold nearly 100 million copies by the end of the nineteenth century. Webster supported a national language that, unlike "King's English," would not require elite training. Words should be spelled as they sound—for example, "honor" should replace "honour."

Continental Expansion and Indian Resistance

Why was the Louisiana Purchase among Jefferson's most popular decisions as president?

By 1800, hundreds of thousands of white Americans had settled in the rich Ohio River and Mississippi River valleys, intruding on Indian lands. In the Northwest they raised foodstuffs, primarily wheat; in the Southwest they cultivated cotton. During the American Revolution, cotton production was profitable only for the Sea Island planters in South Carolina and Georgia, who grew the long-staple variety. Short-staple cotton, which grew in the interior, was unmarketable because its sticky seeds required removal by hand. After New England inventor **Eli Whitney** designed a cotton gin in 1793, allowing one person to remove the same number of seeds that previously required fifty people, cultivation of short-staple cotton spread rapidly into Louisiana, Mississippi, Alabama, Arkansas, and Tennessee. The cotton gin greatly increased the demand for slaves who seeded, tended, and harvested cotton fields.

Eli Whitney Invented the cotton gin, which made cleaning of southern cotton faster and cheaper.

American settlers depended on free access to the Mississippi River and its Gulf port, New Orleans. Whoever controlled the port of New Orleans had a hand on the American economy's throat.

New Orleans

Spain, which acquired France's territory west of the Mississippi after the Seven Years' War (1763), secretly transferred it back to France in 1800 and 1801.

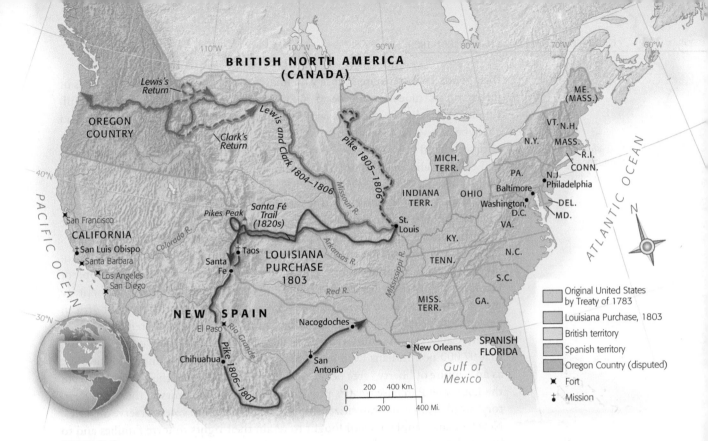

MAP 8.1

Louisiana Purchase

The Louisiana Purchase (1803) doubled the area of the United States and opened the trans-Mississippi West for American settlement. Source: Copyright © Cengage Learning 2015

American officials discovered this in 1802, when Napoleon seemed poised to rebuild a French empire in the New World. American concerns intensified when Spanish officials, on the eve of ceding control to the French, violated Pinckney's Treaty by barring Americans from storing their products at New Orleans prior to transshipment to foreign markets. Western farmers and eastern merchants thought Napoleon had closed the port; they talked war.

To relieve the pressure for war and win western farmers' support, Jefferson urged Congress to authorize the call-up of eighty thousand militiamen. He also sent Virginia's Governor James Monroe to join Robert Livingston in France to buy the port of New Orleans and as much of the Mississippi Valley as possible. Arriving in Paris in April 1803, Monroe learned that France had already offered to sell Louisiana to the United States for just $15 million. With St. Domingue torn from French control by revolution and slave revolt, Napoleon abandoned dreams of a New World empire, and instead now urgently needed money to wage war against Britain. On April 30, Monroe and Livingston signed a treaty to buy the 827,000-square-mile territory (see Map 8.1).

Louisiana Purchase

The **Louisiana Purchase** ensured that the United States would control the Mississippi's mouth, pleasing western settlers who relied on the river to market

Louisiana Purchase The U.S. purchase of the Louisiana Territory (the area from the Mississippi River to the Rocky Mountains) from France in 1803 for $15 million. The purchase virtually doubled the area of the United States.

their goods. It also inspired those who imagined the United States as the nexus of international trade networks between Europe and Asia. Louisiana promised to fulfill easterners' dreams of cheap, fertile lands. Its vast expanse meant, too, that land could be reserved for Indians displaced by white settlers and their black slaves. But critics doubted its constitutionality (even Jefferson agonized over it); others worried that it belied the Democratic-Republicans' commitment to debt reduction. And some New England Federalists complained that it undermined their commercial interests and threatened the republic by spreading the population beyond where it could be controlled. Overall, though, the Louisiana Purchase was the most popular achievement of Jefferson's presidency.

When the United States acquired the territory, hundreds of thousands of people there became American subjects, including Native Americans as well as people of European and African descent. Around New Orleans, Louisiana's colonial heritage was reflected in its people: creoles of French and Spanish descent; slaves of African descent; free people of color; Acadians, or Cajuns (descendants of French settlers in eastern Canada); and some Germans, Irish, and English. The 1810 census reported that 97,000 non-Indians lived in the area. Although Jefferson imagined the West as an "empire of liberty," free people of color soon discovered their exclusion from the Louisiana Purchase treaty's provision that "the inhabitants of the ceded territory" would gain American citizenship. Denied the right to vote and serve on juries, New Orleans' people of color fought to retain their rights to form families and to bequeath property and belongings as they pleased, and some succeeded.

Lewis and Clark Expedition

Jefferson feared that, if Americans did not claim the trans-Mississippi West, the British, who still controlled present-day Canada and parts of the Pacific Northwest, would. He launched a military-style mission to chart the region's commercial possibilities—its water passages to the Pacific and trading opportunities with Indians—while cataloguing its geography, peoples, flora, and fauna.

The Corps of Discovery expedition, headed by Meriwether Lewis and William Clark, began in May 1804 and lasted for more than two years; it traveled up the Missouri River, across the Rockies, and down the Columbia to the Pacific Ocean— and back. The **Lewis and Clark Expedition** members "discovered" (as they saw it) dozens of previously unknown Indian tribes, many of whom had long before discovered Europeans. Although the expedition was prepared for possible conflict, its goal was peaceable: to foster trade relations, win political allies, and tap into Indians' knowledge of the landscape. Lewis and Clark brought twenty-one bags of gifts for Native American leaders to establish goodwill and to stimulate interest in trade. Most of the interactions were cordial, but when Indians were unimpressed by the gifts, tensions arose.

The Corps of Discovery proved democratic in seating enlisted men on courts-martial and allowing Clark's black slave York and the expedition's female guide **Sacagawea** to vote on where to locate winter quarters in 1805. But unlike the expedition's other members, neither York nor Sacagawea drew wages, and when York later demanded his freedom, Clark repaid him with "a severe trouncing."

Link to Thomas Jefferson: Constitutionality of the Louisiana Purchase (1803)

Lewis and Clark Expedition Expedition led by Meriwether Lewis and William Clark to explore the Louisiana Territory.

Sacagawea Female Native American guide who aided Lewis and Clark in exploring the Louisiana Territory.

Lewis and Clark failed to discover a Northwest Passage to the Pacific, but their explorations contributed to nationalist visions of American expansion. Fossils and Native American artifacts they collected were displayed in Charles Willson Peale's museum at Independence Hall in Philadelphia, an institution emphasizing the uniqueness of America's geography and republican experiment.

Nationalists overlooked Indians' land claims. Although Jefferson had more sympathy for Indians than many of his contemporaries—he expressed interest in their cultures and believed Indians to be intellectually equal to whites—he nonetheless lobbied, unsuccessfully, for a constitutional amendment that would transport them west of the Mississippi into Louisiana Territory. He became involved in efforts to pressure the Chickasaws to sell their land, and if legal methods failed, he advocated trickery. Traders, he suggested, might run them into debt, which they would have to repay "by a cessation of lands."

Divisions Among Indian Peoples

Some Indian nations adopted white customs as a means of survival and often agreed to sell their lands and move west. These "accommodationists" (or "progressives") were opposed by "traditionalists," who urged adherence to native ways and refused to relinquish their lands. Distinctions between accommodationists and traditionalists were not always clear-cut, however.

In the early 1800s, two Shawnee brothers, Tenskwatawa (1775–1837) and **Tecumseh** (1768–1813), led a traditionalist revolt against American encroachment by fostering a pan-Indian federation centered in the Old Northwest and reaching into parts of the South. By the 1800s, the Shawnees lost most of their Ohio land, occupying scattered sites there and in the Michigan and Louisiana territories. Despondent, Lalawethika—Tenskwatawa's name as a youth—turned to a combination of European remedies (particularly whiskey) and Native American ones, becoming a shaman in 1804. But when European diseases ravaged his village, he despaired.

Tecumseh The Shawnee leader who sought to unite several tribes from Canada to Georgia against encroachment on their lands by American settlers; allied with the British in the War of 1812.

Tenskwatawa and Tecumseh

Lalawethika emerged from an illness in 1805 as a new man, renamed Tenskwatawa ("the Open Door") or—by whites—"the Prophet." Claiming to have died and been resurrected, he traveled in the Ohio River valley as a religious leader, attacking the decline of moral values among Native Americans, warning against whiskey, and condemning intertribal battles. He urged Indians to return to the old ways and to abandon white ways: to hunt with bows and arrows, not guns; to stop wearing hats; and to give up bread for corn and beans.

By 1808, Tenskwatawa and his older brother Tecumseh had turned their focus to resisting American aggression. They invited all Indians to settle in pan-Indian towns in Indiana, first at Greenville (1806–1808) and then at Prophetstown (1808–1812). This challenged the treaty-making process by denying the claims of Indians who were guaranteed the same land under the 1795 Treaty of Greenville. Younger Indians flocked to Tecumseh, the more political of the two brothers.

Convinced that only an Indian federation could stop white settlement, Tecumseh sought to unify northern and southern Indians from Canada to Georgia. Among southern Indians, only one Creek faction welcomed him, but his efforts alarmed

Russell, Charles Marion (1865–1926)/Peter Newark American Pictures/Bridgeman Art Library

This Charles M. Russell painting of the Lewis and Clark Expedition depicts Sacagawea talking with Chinook Indians. A Shoshone, Sacagawea knew the land and the languages of the mountain Indians, and helped guide the Corps of Discovery.

white settlers and government officials. In November 1811, while Tecumseh was in the South, Indiana governor William Henry Harrison moved against Tenskwatawa and his followers. During the battle of Tippecanoe, the army burned their town; as they fled, the Indians exacted revenge on white settlers. When Harrison vowed reprisals, Tecumseh allied with the British. This alliance in the West, combined with American issues over neutrality rights on the high seas, propelled the United States toward war with Britain.

The Nation in the Orbit of Europe

What led to the War of 1812?

The early republic's economy relied heavily on fishing and the carrying trade, with the American merchant marine transporting commodities between nations. Merchants in Boston, Salem, and Philadelphia traded with China, sending cloth and metal to swap for furs with Chinook Indians on the Oregon coast, and then sailing to China to trade for porcelain, tea, and silk. The slave trade lured American ships to Africa. Not long after Jefferson's first inaugural address, the United States was at war with Tripoli—a state along the Barbary Coast of North Africa—over a principle that would long be a cornerstone of American foreign policy: freedom of the seas. That is, outside national territorial waters, the high seas should be open for free transit.

First Barbary War

In 1801, the bashaw (pasha) of Tripoli declared war on the United States for its refusal to pay tribute for safe passage of its ships through the Mediterranean. Jefferson deployed a naval squadron to protect American ships. After two years of stalemate, Jefferson declared a blockade of Tripoli, but when the American frigate *Philadelphia* ran aground in the harbor, its three hundred officers and sailors were imprisoned. Jefferson refused to ransom them, and a small American force accompanied by Arab, Greek, and African mercenaries marched from Egypt to the "shores of Tripoli" to seize the port of Derne. A treaty ended the war in 1805, but the United States continued to pay tribute to the three other Barbary states—Algiers, Morocco, and Tunis—until 1815. In the intervening years, the United States became embroiled in European conflicts.

At first, Jefferson distanced the nation from European turmoil in the wake of the French Revolution. After the Senate ratified the Jay Treaty in 1795, the United States and Great Britain reconciled. Britain withdrew from its western forts on American soil and interfered less in American trade with France. Then, in May 1803, two weeks after Napoleon sold Louisiana to the United States, France was at war against Britain and, later, Britain's continental allies, Prussia, Austria, and Russia. Initially, the United States benefited, as American merchants gained control of most of the West Indian trade. After 1805, when Britain defeated the French and Spanish fleets at Trafalgar, Britain's Royal Navy tightened its control of the oceans. Two months later, Napoleon crushed the Russian and Austrian armies at Austerlitz. Stalemated, France and Britain launched a commercial war, blockading trade and costing the United States dearly.

Threats to American Sovereignty

To replenish their supply of sailors, British vessels stopped American ships and impressed (forcibly recruited) British deserters, British-born naturalized American seamen, and other sailors suspected of being British. Perhaps six to eight thousand Americans were impressed between 1803 and 1812. Alleged deserters—many of them American citizens—faced British courts-martial. Americans saw the principle of "once a British subject, always a British subject" as a mockery of U.S. citizenship and national sovereignty. Americans also resented the British interfering with their West Indian trade and seizing American vessels within U.S. territorial waters.

In April 1806, Congress responded with the Non-Importation Act, barring British manufactured goods from American ports. Because the act exempted most cloth and metal articles, it had little impact on British trade; instead, it warned the British what to expect if they continued to violate American neutral rights. In November, Jefferson suspended the act while Baltimore lawyer William Pinkney joined James Monroe in London to negotiate a settlement. The treaty they carried home did not mention impressments; hence the president never submitted it for ratification.

Difficult Anglo-American relations came to a head in June 1807 when the USS *Chesapeake*, sailing from Norfolk for the Mediterranean, was stopped by the British frigate *Leopard*, whose officers demanded to search the ship for British deserters. Refused, the *Leopard* opened fire, killing three Americans and wounding eighteen others. The British seized four deserters, three of whom held American citizenship; one was hanged. The incident outraged Americans while exposing American military weakness.

The Embargo of 1807

Jefferson responded with what he called "peaceable coercion." In July, the president closed American waters to British warships and increased military and naval expenditures. In December 1807, Jefferson put economic pressure on Great Britain by invoking the Non-Importation Act, then implementing the **Embargo Act of 1807**. The embargo, which forbade exports from the United States to any country, was a short-term measure to avoid war by pressuring Britain and France to respect American rights and by preventing confrontation between American merchant vessels and European warships.

Embargo Act of 1807 Act that forbade exports from the United States to any country.

The embargo's biggest economic impact, however, fell on the United States. Exports declined by 80 percent in 1808, squeezing New England shippers and workers. Manufacturers received a boost, as the domestic market became theirs exclusively. Merchants began to shift from shipping to manufacturing. In 1807, there were twenty cotton and woolen mills in New England; by 1813, there were more than two hundred.

International Slave Trade

With Jefferson's encouragement, Congress voted in 1807 to abolish the international slave trade as of January 1, 1808—the earliest date permissible under the Constitution. South Carolina still allowed the legal importation of slaves, but most of the state's planters favored a ban, nervous about adding to the black population of a state where whites were outnumbered. The final bill provided that smuggled slaves would be sold according to the laws of the state or territory in which they arrived, underscoring that even illegal slaves were property. Had the bill not done so, threatened one Georgia congressman, the result might have been "resistance to the authority of the Government," even civil war.

During the last four months of 1807, sixteen thousand African slaves arrived at Gadsden Wharf in Charleston, where they were detained by merchants eager to wait out the January 1 deadline. Although hundreds, if not thousands of these slaves died in the disease-ridden holding pens before they could be sold, merchants calculated that the increased value of those who survived would outweigh the losses. Even after January 1, 1808, a brisk and profitable illegal trade emerged. In 1819, Congress authorized the president to use force to intercept slave ships along the African coast, but the small American navy could not have halted the illicit trade.

Early Abolitionism and Colonization

From the nation's earliest days—in Philadelphia, New York, Albany, Boston, and Nantucket—free blacks formed societies to petition legislatures, seek judicial redress, stage marches, and publish tracts chronicling slavery's horrors. By 1830, the nation had fifty African American abolitionist societies.

After the Revolution, white abolitionists also formed antislavery organizations in places like Boston and Philadelphia, with its large population of Quakers, whose religious beliefs emphasized human equality. These reformers pressed for gradual abolition and an end to the international slave trade. Although they aided African Americans seeking freedom through judicial decisions, their assumptions about blacks' racial inferiority kept them from advocating for equal rights. Early white abolitionists were typically wealthy men whose societies excluded women, African Americans, and nonelites.

Elites often supported the colonization movement, which crystallized in 1816 with the organization of the American Colonization Society. Its members planned to purchase and relocate American slaves and free blacks to Africa or the Caribbean. Supporters included Thomas Jefferson, James Madison, James Monroe, and Henry Clay. In 1824, the society founded Liberia, on Africa's west coast, and began a settlement for African Americans who were willing to go. The society had resettled nearly twelve thousand by 1860. Some colonizationists aimed to strengthen slavery by ridding the South of troublesome slaves or to purge the North of African Americans altogether. Others hoped colonization would improve African Americans' conditions. Although some African Americans supported the movement, black abolitionists generally denounced it.

In an effort to win support for measures to end the international slave trade and slavery itself, abolitionists published drawings of the inhumanely cramped slave ships, where each person was allotted a space roughly the size of a coffin. Disease spread rapidly under such conditions, causing many slaves to die before reaching American shores.

Election of 1808

Once congressional discussion of the international slave trade subsided, politicians focused on the embargo, especially as the 1808 presidential election neared. Democratic-Republicans suffered from factional dissent in seaboard states hobbled by trade restrictions. Although nine state legislatures passed resolutions urging Jefferson to run again, the president declined and supported James Madison, his secretary of state. Madison won the endorsement of the party's congressional caucus, but Virginia Democratic-Republicans put forth James Monroe, who later withdrew. Madison and Vice President George Clinton headed the ticket. Charles Cotesworth Pinckney and Rufus King again ran on the Federalist ticket.

The younger Federalists played up widespread disaffection with Democratic-Republican policy, especially the embargo. Pinckney received 47 electoral votes to Madison's 122, but he carried all of New England except Vermont, and won Delaware. Federalists also gained seats in Congress and captured the New York State legislature. Still, the transition from one Democratic-Republican administration to the next went smoothly.

Emigration to Liberia

Even as European immigrants sought republican freedoms in the United States, close to twelve thousand African Americans sought similar opportunities in Liberia—first a colony organized by the American Colonization Society (1822), then an independent nation (1847) along Africa's west coast.

Excluded from the American Revolution's promises of equality, some African Americans advocated resettlement in the Caribbean, Canada, and, especially, Africa. In 1816, Paul Cuffee, an abolitionist and shipping merchant of African American and Native American descent, resettled nine African American families in Sierra Leone, a British colony established for freed slaves. After his death the following year, the American Colonization Society (ACS) continued his work, with such members as President James Monroe and Senator Henry Clay. In 1824, the ACS formally established Liberia, to which it encouraged immigration of freeborn and recently freed African Americans. The ACS's members held wide-ranging views; some saw slavery as a threat to American principles or prosperity, while others aimed primarily to deport free blacks, widely seen as a threat to slavery. Because ACS leaders called blacks "useless and pernicious" (Henry Clay) and reasoned that colonization would secure American slavery, many African Americans denounced ACS-sponsored emigration.

But others saw Liberia as the best opportunity for freedom and as a chance to enlighten native Africans. Initially, American transplants succumbed in large numbers to malaria and struggled to wrestle land and power from indigenous populations. Within a generation, though, the Americo-Liberians had established themselves as elites, subjecting native populations to the second-class citizenship they themselves experienced in the United States.

The Republic of Liberia declared its independence from the ACS in 1847, and today only about 5 percent of its population descends from original settlers. But its constitution is modeled on the U.S. Constitution, its official language is English, its flag resembles the American stars-and-bars, and the American dollar is accepted alongside the Liberian dollar. For the past three decades, the nation has suffered from violent political turmoil over who should rule: the descendants of the nineteenth-century Americo-Liberians or leaders of indigenous ethnic groups. Begun in the 1820s, African American emigration to Liberia forged a link with both immediate and enduring consequences.

CORBIS

Eager to persuade readers of Liberia's success as a colony for former American slaves, colonizationists published images such as this one of the president's house in Monrovia, in which sparsely clad African natives are juxtaposed with genteel American transplants. Even as the image lauds the supposed superiority of African Americans to Africans, it implies that African Americans will themselves fare much better in Africa than they could in the United States.

Women and Politics

Wives of elected and appointed officials played crucial roles in facilitating the transition, fostering conversation and diplomatic negotiation, providing an ear or a voice for unofficial messages, and—in international affairs—standing as surrogates for their nation. Elite women hosted events that muted partisan rivalries. Political wives' interactions among themselves served political purposes, too: when First Lady Dolley Madison visited congressmen's wives, she cultivated goodwill for her husband while collecting recipes so she could serve regional cuisine at White House functions.

Jeffersonians appealed directly for women's support of their embargo. Sympathetic women responded by spurning imported fabric and making (or directing their slaves to make) homespun clothing. Federalists, however, encouraged women to "keep commerce alive," and sympathetic women bought smuggled goods.

Failed Policies

Facing domestic opposition, the embargo collapsed. Instead, the Non-Intercourse Act of 1809 reopened trade with all nations except Britain and France, and authorized the president to resume trade with those two nations once they respected American neutral rights. In June 1809, President Madison reopened trade with Britain after its minister to the United States promised that Britain would repeal restrictions on American trade. But His Majesty's government in London repudiated the minister's assurances, leading Madison to revert to nonintercourse.

When the Non-Intercourse Act expired in 1810, Congress substituted Macon's Bill Number 2, reopening trade with both Great Britain and France but providing that, when either nation stopped violating American commercial rights, the president would suspend American commerce with the other. When Napoleon accepted, Madison declared nonintercourse on Great Britain in 1811. Although the French continued to seize American ships, Britain became the main focus of American hostility because it dominated the seas.

In spring 1812, the British admiralty ordered its ships not to stop, search, or seize American warships, and in June Britain reopened the seas to American shipping. But before word of this policy change reached America, Congress declared war.

Mr. Madison's War

The House voted 79 to 49 for war; the Senate, 19 to 13. Democratic-Republicans favored war by 98 to 23; Federalists opposed it 39 to 0. Those who favored war, including President Madison, pointed to assaults on American sovereignty and honor: impressment, violation of neutral trading rights, and British alliances with western Indians. Others saw an opportunity to conquer and annex British Canada. Most militant were land-hungry southerners and westerners—the "**War Hawks**"—led by John C. Calhoun of South Carolina and first-term congressman and House Speaker Henry Clay of Kentucky. Most representatives from the coastal states, and especially the Northeast, feared trade disruption to commerce and opposed "Mr. Madison's War."

Initially, the Federalists benefited from antiwar sentiment. They joined renegade Democratic-Republicans in supporting New York City mayor DeWitt Clinton for president in 1812. Clinton lost to Madison by 128 to 89 electoral votes, but Federalists gained some congressional seats and carried many local elections. The pro-war South and West remained solidly Democratic-Republican.

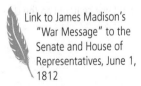

Link to James Madison's "War Message" to the Senate and House of Representatives, June 1, 1812

War Hawks Militant Republicans of the early nineteenth century who demanded more aggressive policies and who wanted war with Britain.

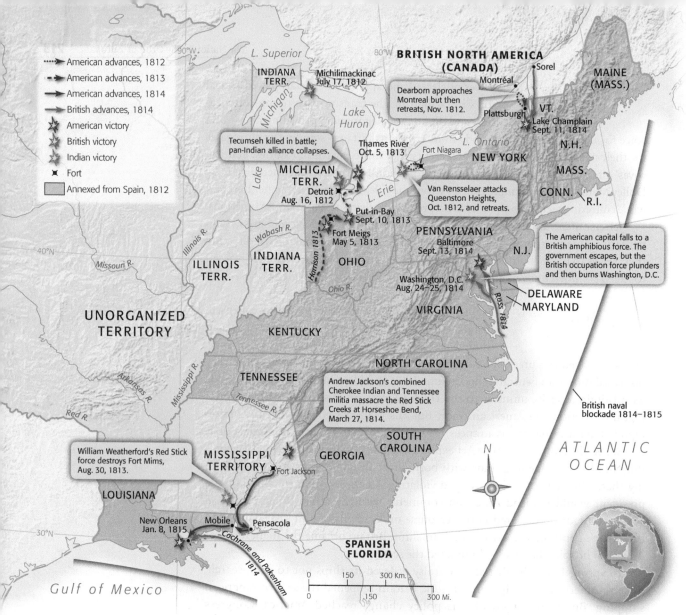

MAP 8.2

Major Campaigns of the War of 1812

The land war centered on the U.S.–Canadian border, the Chesapeake Bay, and the Louisiana and Mississippi territories.

Source: Copyright © Cengage Learning 2015

The War of 1812

What were the consequences of the War of 1812?

Lasting from 1812 to 1815, the war unfolded in skirmishes (see Map 8.2) for which the U.S. armed forces were ill prepared. The U.S. Military Academy at West Point, founded in 1802, produced only eighty-nine regular officers, and campaigns were executed poorly. Although the U.S. Navy had a corps of experienced officers, it proved no match for the Royal Navy.

The government's efforts to lure recruits—with sign-up bonuses and promises of three months' pay and rights to purchase 160 acres of western land—had mixed success. At first, recruitment went well among westerners motivated by civic spirit, desire for land, anti-Indian sentiment, and fears of Tecumseh's pan-Indian organization. But with pay delays and inadequate supplies, recruitment dwindled. In New England, Federalists discouraged enlistments. Militias in New England and New York often refused to fight outside their states. Desperate for soldiers, New York offered freedom to slaves who enlisted and compensation to their owners, and the U.S. Army made the same offer to slaves in the Old Northwest and Canada. But in the Deep South, fear of arming slaves kept them out of the military except in New Orleans, where a free black militia dated back to Spanish control of Louisiana. The British recruited slaves by promising freedom in exchange for service. In the end, British forces outnumbered the Americans.

Invasion of Canada

Despite recruitment problems, Americans expected to take Canada easily. Canada's population was sparse, its army small, and the Great Lakes inaccessible to the Royal Navy in the Atlantic. Americans hoped, too, that French Canadians might welcome U.S. forces.

Americans aimed to split Canadian forces and isolate pro-British Indians, especially Tecumseh, whom the British had promised an Indian nation in the Great Lakes region. In July 1812, U.S. general William Hull, territorial governor of Michigan, marched his troops—who outnumbered those of the British—into Upper Canada (modern Ontario), hoping to conquer Montreal. But by abandoning Mackinac Island and Fort Dearborn, and by surrendering Fort Detroit, he left the Midwest exposed. Captain Zachary Taylor provided the only bright spot, giving the Americans a land victory with his September 1812 defense of Fort Harrison in Indiana Territory. By the winter of 1812–1813, the British controlled half of the Old Northwest.

Naval Battles

Despite victories on the Atlantic by the USS *Constitution* (nicknamed "Old Ironsides"), the USS *Wasp*, and the USS *United States*, the American navy—which began the war with just seventeen ships—could not match the powerful Royal Navy. By 1814, the Royal Navy blockaded nearly all American ports along the Atlantic and Gulf coasts. After 1811, American trade overseas declined by nearly 90 percent, and the lost customs duties threatened to bankrupt the federal government and prostrate New England.

The contest for control of the Great Lakes, the key to the war in the Northwest, evolved as a shipbuilding race. Under Master Commandant Oliver Hazard Perry and shipbuilder Noah Brown, the United States outbuilt the British on Lake Erie and defeated them at the bloody Battle of Put-in-Bay on September 10, 1813, gaining control of Lake Erie.

Burning Capitals

A ragged group of Kentucky militia volunteers, armed with swords and knives, marched 20 to 30 miles a day to join General William Henry Harrison's forces in Ohio. Now 4,500 strong, Harrison's troops took Detroit before crossing into Canada, where at the Battle of the Thames they defeated British, Shawnee, and Chippewa forces in October 1813. Among the dead was Tecumseh. The Americans then razed the Canadian capital of York (now Toronto).

Visualizing THE PAST

Selling War

The War of 1812 was not always a popular war, but afterward many Americans trumpeted the war's successes. To the left, we see a recruitment poster from 1812, in which General William Henry Harrison seeks additional cavalrymen. Hampered partly by transportation difficulties, Harrison is unable to offer much—soldiers are even requested to supply their own bacon and horses—but he promises that the expedition will be short, undoubtedly a concern to men eager to return to the fall harvest. To the right, we see a handkerchief made in 1815, after the Treaty of Ghent and the Battle of New Orleans; it features the United States' victories against the world's greatest naval power, Great Britain. Featuring a decorative border, the kerchief may have been for display. What similar values do we see promoted in the two images, and what factors—such as their intended audiences, their purposes, and when they were created—might account for any differences between them?

> **CIRCULAR.**
>
> *ST. MARY's, September 20th, 1813.*
>
> SIR—As the force which I have collected at this place (of mounted men) is not sufficient to accomplish the object of the expedition, which it was proposed to set out from hence——You are hereby authorised to circulate through the country my wishes to be joined by any number of mounted men, (corps ready organised would be preferred) under the authority heretofore given by Gov. Meigs. Companies which may join me to serve for the expedition and which will furnish their own horses will have credit for a tour of duty, and the expedition is not expected to continue more than thirty days, and will, at any rate, not extend beyond forty.
>
> I am, respectfully,
> your humble servant,
> WM. H. HARRISON.
>
> P. S. The men must bring on as much bacon as possible. Any one who will bring a spare horse, saddle and bridle, shall be allowed fifty cents per day for the use of them—The bearer is authorised to hire horses and give certificates which will be taken up and paid for by the Quarter Master.
> W. H. HARRISO

With a tiny regular army, the United States often had to rely on short-term recruits to wage war on the British.

Made in 1815 from cotton textiles—whose domestic production soared during the War of 1812, with trade cut off from Britain—this handkerchief helps promote American "liberty and independence."

After defeating Napoleon in Europe in April 1814, the British launched a land counteroffensive against the United States, concentrating on the Chesapeake Bay. Royal troops occupied Washington, D.C., in August and set it ablaze. The presidential mansion and parts of the city burned all night. The president and cabinet fled. Dolley Madison stayed to oversee removal of cabinet documents and save a Gilbert Stuart portrait of George Washington.

The British intended the attack on Washington as a diversion. The major battle occurred in September 1814 at Baltimore, where the Americans held firm. Francis Scott Key, detained on a British ship, watched the bombardment of Fort McHenry and later wrote "The Star-Spangled Banner" (which became the national anthem in 1931). The British inflicted heavy damage but achieved little militarily; their offensive on Lake Champlain also failed. The war reached a stalemate.

War in the South

To the south, two wars were happening simultaneously. In the Patriot War, a private army of Americans secretly supported by the Madison administration tried to seize East Florida from Spain. What started as a settlers' rebellion along the Georgia-Florida border—to grab more land, strike at the Spaniards' Indian allies, and later to protest the Spaniards' arming of black soldiers—turned into a war. Federalists condemned the invasion of a neutral territory, and the Senate refused twice (in 1812 and 1813) to support military seizure of Florida. Embarrassed, Madison withdrew his support, and the movement collapsed in May 1814.

In the war with Britain, the southern theater proved more successful. The final campaign began with an American attack on the Red Stick Creeks along the Gulf of Mexico and the British around New Orleans, and it ended with Americans gaining new territory. Responding to Tecumseh's call to resist U.S. expansion, in 1813 the Red Sticks attacked Fort Mims, about forty miles from Mobile, killing hundreds of white men, women, and children. Seeking revenge, General Andrew Jackson of Tennessee rallied his militiamen and Indian opponents of the Red Sticks and crushed them at Horseshoe Bend (in present-day Alabama) in March 1814. This led to the Treaty of Fort Jackson, in which the Creeks ceded 23 million acres, or about half of their holdings, and withdrew to the southern and western Mississippi Territory.

Jackson became a major general and continued south toward the Gulf of Mexico. After seizing Pensacola (in Spanish Florida) and securing Mobile, Jackson's forces marched to New Orleans. Three weeks later, on January 8, 1815, Jackson's poorly trained army held its ground against two British frontal assaults. At day's end, more than two thousand British soldiers lay dead or wounded, while the Americans suffered only twenty-one casualties.

The Battle of New Orleans occurred two weeks after the war's conclusion: word had not yet reached America that British and United States diplomats had signed the **Treaty of Ghent** on December 24, 1814. Still, the Battle of New Orleans catapulted General Andrew Jackson to national political prominence.

Treaty of Ghent Treaty that ended the War of 1812, restoring the prewar status quo.

Treaty of Ghent

The Treaty of Ghent essentially restored the prewar status quo. It provided for an end to hostilities, release of prisoners, restoration of conquered territory, and arbitration of boundary disputes. But the United States received no satisfaction on impressment, blockades, or other maritime rights for neutrals, and the British demands for territorial cessions from Maine to Minnesota went unmet. The British dropped their promise of an independent Indian nation.

Napoleon's defeat allowed the United States to discard its prewar demands because peace in Europe made impressment and interference with American commerce moot issues. Similarly, war-weary Britain stopped pressing for military victory.

American Sovereignty Reasserted

The War of 1812 affirmed the independence of the American republic and ensured Canada's independence from the United States. Trade and territorial disputes with Great Britain continued, but they never again led to war.

The return of peace allowed the United States to again focus on the Barbary Coast, where the dey (governor) of Algiers had declared war on the United States. In the Second Barbary War, U.S. forces held hundreds of Algerians while negotiating a treaty in the summer of 1815 that forever freed the United States from paying tributes for passage in the Mediterranean. The Second Barbary War reaffirmed America's commitment to freedom of the seas.

Domestic Consequences

The War of 1812 had profound domestic consequences. Federalists' hopes of returning to national prominence evaporated with the **Hartford Convention**. New England delegates—frustrated by the stalemated war and the shattered New England economy—met in Hartford, Connecticut, in the winter of 1814–1815 to discuss revising the national compact or pulling out of the republic. Although moderates prevented a secession resolution—withdrawal from the Union—delegates condemned the war and the embargo while endorsing constitutional changes that would weaken the South's power and make it harder to declare war. When news arrived of Jackson's victory in New Orleans and the Treaty of Ghent, the Hartford Convention made the Federalists look wrongheaded, even treasonous. By the 1820s, the party faded from the national scene.

Hartford Convention
Federalist meeting that was perceived as disloyalty during time of war and began the downfall of the party.

With Tecumseh's death, midwestern Indians lost their powerful leader; with the British withdrawal, they lost their strongest ally. Some accommodationists, such as the Cherokees, temporarily flourished, but the war effectively disarmed traditionalists bent on resisting American expansion. Although the Treaty of Ghent pledged the United States to end hostilities with Indians and to restore their prewar "possessions, rights, and privileges," Indians could not make the United States honor the agreement.

For American farmers, the war opened formerly Indian land for cultivating cotton in the Old Southwest and wheat in the Old Northwest. It also stimulated industry, as Americans could no longer rely on overseas imports. The War of 1812 thus fueled demand for raw cotton, and the newly acquired lands in the Southwest beckoned southerners, who migrated there with slaves or hopes of someday owning slaves. The war's conclusion accelerated three trends that would dominate U.S. history for decades: industrial takeoff, slavery's entrenchment, and westward expansion.

Early Industrialization

How did early industrialization bridge older farm/family production with newer systems of production for market?

As a result of the embargo and the War of 1812, the North underwent an accelerated industrial development as the South became more dependent on cotton production (see Chapter 9). Although the two regions' economies followed different paths, they remained interconnected.

Preindustrial Farms   Before the War of 1812, most American farmers practiced mixed agriculture, raising a variety of crops and livestock. When they produced more than they needed, they traded the surplus with neighbors or sold it to local storekeepers. Such transactions often transpired without money; farmers might trade eggs for shoes, or they might work their neighbor's fields in exchange for bales of hay.

Family members provided most farm labor, though some yeoman farmers, North and South, relied on slaves or indentured servants. Men and boys worked in the fields, herded livestock, chopped firewood, fished, and hunted. Women and girls tended gardens, milked cows, spun cloth, processed and preserved food, prepared meals, washed clothes, and tended infants and toddlers.

Farmers lent each other farm tools, harvested each other's fields, bartered goods, and raised their neighbors' barns and husked their corn. Little cash exchanged hands, mostly because money was scarce. Still, New England farmers often kept elaborate account books, whereas southern farmers made mental notes of debts. Years might pass without debts repaid. In the local economy—where farmers exchanged goods with people they knew—a system of "just price" prevailed, in which neighbors calculated value based on how much labor was involved. When farmers engaged in long-distance trade they set prices based on what the market would bear.

Preindustrial Artisans   Farmers who lived near towns often purchased crafted goods from local cobblers, saddlers, blacksmiths, gunsmiths, silversmiths, and tailors. Most artisans, though, lived in the nation's seaports, where master craftsmen (businessmen who owned shops and tools) employed apprentices and journeymen. Although the majority of craftsmen, North and South, were white, free blacks were well represented in some cities' trades, such as tailoring and carpentry in Charleston, South Carolina. Teenage apprentices lived with masters, who taught, lodged, and fed them in exchange for labor. The master's wife and daughters cooked, cleaned, and sewed for the workers. When their apprenticeship expired, apprentices became journeymen who earned wages, hoping to one day own shops. The workplace had little division of labor or specialization. A tailor measured, designed, and sewed an entire suit, for example.

Men, women, and children worked long days on farms and in workshops, but the pace was uneven and unregimented. When busy, they worked dawn to dusk;

work slowed after the harvest or when a large order was completed. Husking bees and barn raisings brought people together to shuck corn and build, and to eat, drink, and dance. Busy periods did not stop artisans from taking grog breaks, from reading the newspaper aloud, or even from attending a political meeting. Journeymen often staggered in late on Monday mornings, if they showed up at all, after carousing on their day off. In this way, workers exerted influence over the workplace.

Putting-Out and Early Factories

Early industry reorganized daily work routines and market relationships. In the late eighteenth and early nineteenth centuries a "putting-out" system developed, particularly in Massachusetts, New Jersey, and Pennsylvania. Women and children continued to produce goods, but now a merchant supplied raw materials, paid them a wage (usually a price for each piece produced), and sold their wares in distant markets, pocketing the profits himself. This "outwork" appealed to women eager for cash, whether to secure economic independence or to save money for land where their children might establish farms. Particularly in New England—where population density, small farms, and tired soil constricted farming opportunities—the putting-out system provided opportunities to earn money with which to buy more fertile western lands.

The earliest factories grew in tandem with the putting-out system. When Samuel Slater helped set up the first American water-powered spinning mill in Rhode Island in 1790—using children to card and spin raw cotton into thread—he sent the spun thread to nearby farm families who were paid to weave it into cloth. Although the work remained familiar, women now operated looms for wages and produced cloth primarily for the market.

Despite their separate identity, Americans relied on British technology to combine the many steps of textile manufacturing—carding (or disentangling) fibers, spinning yarn, and weaving cloth—under one factory roof. Slater, a British immigrant, had reconstructed from memory the complex machines he'd had in England. But Slater's mill only carded and spun yarn; hand-weaving it into cloth was often done by farm women. In 1810, Bostonian Francis Cabot Lowell visited the British textile center of Manchester, touring factories and later sketching from memory what he had seen. In 1813, he and his business associates founded the Boston Manufacturing Company, uniting all phases of textile manufacturing under one roof in Waltham, Massachusetts. A decade later, the Boston Manufacturing Company established its model industrial village—named for its now-deceased founder—along the Merrimack River. At Lowell, Massachusetts, there would be boardinghouses for workers, a healthy alternative to Manchester's tenements and slums.

Northern industrialization was linked to slavery. Much of the capital came from merchants who partly made their fortunes through the slave trade. Two of the most prominent industries—textiles and shoes—expanded alongside a growing southern cotton economy. Southern cotton fed northern textile mills, and northern shoe factories sold "Negro brogans" (work shoes) to southern planters.

Courtesy Gore Place Society, Waltham, Mass.

This contemporary painting shows the Boston Manufacturing Company's 1814 textile factory at Waltham, Massachusetts. All manufacturing processes were brought together under one roof, and the company built its first factories in rural New England to tap roaring rivers as a power source.

Sectionalism and Nationalism

How did the American System mark the triumph of Federalist economic policy?

Following the War of 1812, Madison and the Democratic-Republicans absorbed the Federalist idea that the national government should encourage growth. His agenda, which Henry Clay later called the American System, included a national bank, improved transportation, and a protective tariff—a tax on imported goods to protect American manufacturers from foreign competition. Yet true to his Jeffersonian roots, Madison argued that only a constitutional amendment could authorize the federal government to build local roads and canals. Instead, most internal improvements would fall to the states.

American System

Clay and congressional leaders such as Calhoun of South Carolina believed the American System would ease sectional divides. The tariff would stimulate

New England industry, whose goods would find markets in the South and West. The South's and West's agricultural products—cotton and foodstuffs—would feed New England mills and workers. Manufactured and agricultural products would move along roads and canals that tariff revenues would fund. A national bank would handle the transactions.

In 1816, Congress chartered the Second Bank of the United States (the first bank's charter expired in 1811) to serve as a depository for federal funds and to issue currency, collect taxes, and pay government debts. The Second Bank of the United States would also oversee state and local banks, ensuring that their paper money had backing in specie (precious metals). Like its predecessor, the bank mixed public and private ownership; the government provided one-fifth of the bank's capital and appointed one-fifth of its directors.

Congress also passed the Tariff of 1816, which taxed imported woolens and cottons as well as iron, leather, hats, paper, and sugar. This tariff divided the nation. New England, western, and Middle Atlantic states would benefit from it and thus applauded it, whereas many southerners objected that it raised prices on consumer goods and could prompt Britain to retaliate with a tariff on cotton.

Southerners such as Calhoun promoted roads and canals to "bind the republic together." However, on March 3, 1817, the day before leaving office, President Madison, citing constitutional scruples, vetoed Calhoun's "Bonus Bill," which would have authorized federal funding for such public works.

Early Internal Improvements

Federalists and Democratic-Republicans agreed that improved transportation would promote national prosperity. For Federalists, roads and canals were necessary for commercial development; for Jeffersonians, they would spur western expansion and agrarian growth. In 1806, Congress passed (and Jefferson signed) a bill authorizing funding for the Cumberland Road (later, the National Road), running 130 miles between Cumberland, Maryland, and Wheeling, Virginia (now West Virginia). In 1820, Congress authorized a survey of the National Road to Columbus, Ohio, a project completed in 1833.

Erie Canal Major canal that linked the Great Lakes to the Atlantic seaboard, opening the upper Midwest to wider development.

Most transportation initiatives received funding from states and/or private investors. Between 1817 and 1825, New York constructed the **Erie Canal**, linking the Great Lakes to the Atlantic seaboard. Although southern states constructed modest canals, the South's trade used river-going steamboats after 1817, when steamboats began traveling regularly upriver on the Mississippi. With canals and steamboats, western agricultural products traveled faster and inexpensively, fueling westward expansion. Canals expanded commercial networks into regions without natural waterways and reoriented midwestern commerce through the North.

Panic of 1819

Immediately following the War of 1812, the international demand for (and price of) American commodities soared. Poor weather in Europe led to crop failures, increasing demand for northern foodstuffs and southern cotton, which, in turn, triggered western land speculation. Speculators raced to buy large tracts at modest, government-established prices and then to resell them at hefty profits to would-be settlers.

The young nation's dirt roads meant bumpy and dusty travel for goods as well as passengers, prompting calls for transportation innovations, such as canals and, later, railroads, to spur economic growth.

Prosperity proved short-lived. By the late 1810s Europeans could grow their own food, and Britain's new Corn Laws established high tariffs on imports. Cotton prices fell in England. Wars in Latin America interfered with mining and reduced the supply of precious metals, leading European nations to hoard specie. American banks furiously printed paper money and expanded credit further. Fearful of inflation, the Second Bank of the United States demanded in 1819 that state banks repay loans in specie. State banks then called in the loans and mortgages they had made. Falling commodities prices meant that farmers could not pay their mortgages, and plummeting land values—50 to 75 percent declines in portions of the West—meant they could not meet debts even by selling their farms. The nation's banking system collapsed, triggering a financial panic.

Foreclosures soared and unemployment skyrocketed, reaching 75 percent in Philadelphia. Workers and their families could not make it through the winter without charitable donations of food, clothing, and firewood. Americans everywhere contemplated the virtues and hazards of rapid market expansion, disagreeing on whom to blame for its shortcomings. Even as the nation's economy rebounded in the early 1820s amid a flurry of internal improvements, no one could predict in what region or sector the nation's fortunes would lie.

Missouri Compromise

America also faced a political crisis in 1819 about slavery's westward expansion. Residents of the Missouri Territory petitioned Congress for admission to the Union with a constitution permitting slavery. Missouri's admission would give slaveholding states a two-vote majority in the Senate and set a precedent for new western states created from the Louisiana Purchase.

Following the Louisiana Purchase and after the War of 1812, the American population surged westward, leading five new states to join the Union: Louisiana (1812), Indiana (1816), Mississippi (1817), Illinois (1818), and Alabama (1819). Of these, Louisiana, Mississippi, and Alabama permitted slavery. Because Missouri was on the same latitude as free Illinois, Indiana, and Ohio, its admission as a slave state would push slavery farther westward and northward.

For two and a half years the issue dominated Congress. When Representative James Tallmadge Jr. of New York proposed gradual emancipation in Missouri, some southerners accused the North of threatening to destroy the Union. The House, which had a northern majority, passed the Tallmadge Amendment, but the Senate rejected it.

House Speaker Henry Clay—himself a western slaveholder—offered a compromise in 1820. Maine, carved out of Massachusetts, would enter as a free state, followed by Missouri as a slave state, maintaining the balance between slave and free states. In the rest of the Louisiana Territory north of Missouri's southern border of 36°30', slavery would be prohibited (see Map 8.3).

The compromise carried but almost unraveled when Missouri submitted a constitution barring free blacks from the state. Opponents contended that it violated the federal constitutional provision that citizens of each state were "entitled to all privileges and immunities of citizens in the several States." Proponents countered that many states already barred free blacks. In 1821, Clay proposed a second compromise: Missouri would guarantee that its laws would not discriminate against citizens of other states. (Once admitted to the Union, Missouri twice adopted laws barring free blacks.) For more than three decades, the **Missouri Compromise** governed congressional policy toward admitting new slave states. But it masked rather than suppressed the simmering political conflict over slavery's westward expansion.

The Era of Good Feelings

So, too, did the so-called "**Era of Good Feelings**," as a Boston newspaper dubbed the presidency of James Monroe, which was marked by a lack of partisan political discord. Madison's successor, Monroe was the third Virginian elected president since 1801. A former senator and twice governor of Virginia, he served under Madison as secretary of state and of war and used his association with Jefferson and Madison to attain the presidency. In 1816, he and his running mate, Daniel Tompkins, trounced the last Federalist presidential nominee, Rufus King, garnering all the electoral votes except those of the Federalist strongholds of Massachusetts, Connecticut, and Delaware.

Led by Federalist chief justice John Marshall, the Supreme Court became the bulwark of the nationalist agenda. In ***McCulloch v. Maryland*** (1819), the Court struck down a Maryland law taxing banks that were not chartered by its legislature—a law aimed at hindering the Baltimore branch of the Second Bank

Missouri Compromise
Attempt to end the debate over the number of slave and free states admitted to the Union by admitting Missouri as a slave state and Maine as a free state and banning slavery in the Louisiana Territory north of the 36°30' latitude line.

Era of Good Feelings
Period of one-party politics during administration of James Monroe.

McCulloch v. Maryland
Supreme Court decision that restated national supremacy over the states.

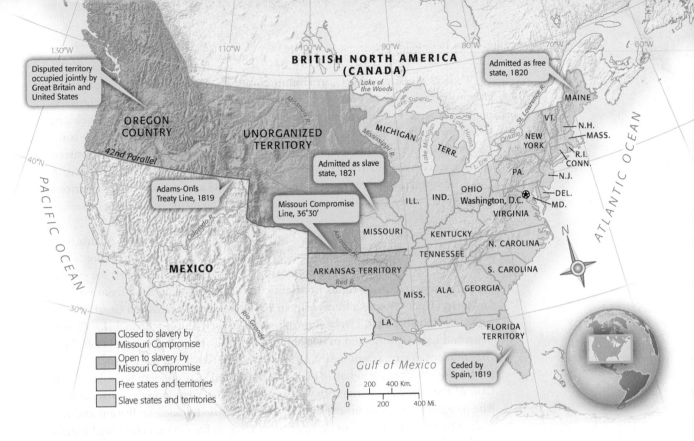

MAP 8.3
Missouri Compromise and the State of the Union, 1820
The compromise worked out by House Speaker Henry Clay established a formula that avoided debate over whether new states would allow or prohibit slavery. In the process, it divided the United States into northern and southern regions. Source: Copyright © Cengage Learning 2015

of the United States. The bank refused to pay the tax and sued. At issue was state versus federal jurisdiction. Writing for a unanimous Court, Marshall asserted the supremacy of the federal government over the states. The Court ruled, too, that Congress had the power to charter banks. The Marshall Court thus supported the Federalist view that the federal government could promote interstate commerce.

Government Promotion of Market Expansion

Later Supreme Court cases validated government promotion of economic development and encouraged business enterprise. In *Gibbons v. Ogden* (1824), the Supreme Court overturned the New York law granting Robert Fulton and Robert Livingston (and their successor, Aaron Ogden) a monopoly on the New York–New Jersey steamboat trade. Chief Justice Marshall ruled that the federal power to license new enterprises took precedence over New York's grant of monopoly rights and declared that Congress's power under the commerce clause of the Constitution extended to "every species of commercial intercourse." Within two years, the number of steamboats in New York increased from six to forty-three. A later ruling in *Charles River Bridge v. Warren Bridge* (1837), encouraged new enterprises and technologies by favoring competition over monopoly, and the public interest over implied privileges in old contracts.

Federal and state courts, in conjunction with state legislatures, encouraged the proliferation of corporations—organizations holding property and transacting business as if they were individuals. Corporation owners, called shareholders, were granted limited liability, or freedom from personal responsibility for the company's debts beyond their original investment. The federal government assisted commercial development, too, by expanding the number of U.S. post offices from three thousand in 1815 to fourteen thousand in 1845 and by protecting inventions through patent laws and domestic industries through tariffs on foreign imports.

Boundary Settlements

Monroe's secretary of state, John Quincy Adams, son of John and Abigail Adams, managed the nation's foreign policy from 1817 to 1825. He pushed for expansion of American fishing rights in Atlantic waters, political distance from Europe, and peace. Under Adams's leadership, in 1817 the United States and Great Britain signed the Rush-Bagot Treaty limiting them to one ship each on Lake Champlain and Lake Ontario and to two ships each on the remaining Great Lakes. This first modern disarmament treaty demilitarized the U.S.-Canadian border. Adams pushed for the Convention of 1818, which fixed the U.S.-Canadian boundary from Lake of the Woods in Minnesota westward to the Rockies along the 49th parallel. The delegates disagreed on the boundary west of the Rockies, so Britain and the United States settled on joint occupation of Oregon for ten years (renewed indefinitely in 1827).

Adams's negotiations also resulted in the Adams-Onís Treaty, in which the United States gained Florida. Although the Louisiana Purchase omitted reference to Spanish-ruled West Florida, the United States claimed the territory as far east as the Perdido River (the present-day Florida-Alabama border). During the War of 1812, the United States seized Mobile and the remainder of West Florida; after the war Adams claimed East Florida. In 1819, Don Luís de Onís, the Spanish minister to the United States, agreed to cede Florida to the United States without payment if the United States renounced its dubious claims to northern Mexico (Texas) and assumed $5 million of claims by American citizens against Spain. The treaty also defined the southwestern boundary of the Louisiana Purchase and divided Spanish Mexico and Oregon Country at the 42nd parallel.

Monroe Doctrine

Adams's desire to insulate the United States and the Western Hemisphere from European conflict inspired his greatest achievement: the **Monroe Doctrine**. Between 1808 and 1822, the United Provinces of Río de la Plata (present-day northern Argentina, Paraguay, and Uruguay), Chile, Peru, Colombia, and Mexico all broke from Spain (see Map 8.4). In 1822, the United States became the first nation outside Latin America to recognize the new states. But with reactionary regimes ascending in Europe and France now occupying Spain, the United States feared that continental powers would attempt to return the new Latin American states to colonial rule.

Monroe's message to Congress in December 1823 became known as the Monroe Doctrine. He announced that the American continents "are henceforth not to be considered subjects for future colonization by any European power." This

Monroe Doctrine Foreign policy statement that proclaimed that the American continents were not to be subjected to European colonization and demanded nonintervention by Europe in New World nations.

OREGON COUNTRY
(Joint U.S.-British occupation)

BRITISH NORTH AMERICA
(CANADA)
(Gr. Br.)

Mississippi R.

New York

Philadelphia
Washington, D.C.

UNITED STATES

40°N

Colorado R.

MEXICO
1821

San Antonio

New Orleans

Charleston

40°W

ATLANTIC
OCEAN

N

Rio Grande

Gulf of Mexico

Mexico City

Veracruz

Havana

CUBA
(Spain)

BAHAMA IS.
(Gr. Br.)

HAITI 1804

PUERTO RICO (Spain)

20°N

BRITISH
HONDURAS (Gr. Br.)

GUATEMALA
Guatemala City

JAMAICA
(Gr. Br.)

Caribbean Sea

UNITED PROVINCES OF
CENTRAL AMERICA
1823–1839

Panama

TRINIDAD (Gr. Br.)

BR. GUIANA (Gr. Br.)

DUTCH GUIANA (Neth.)

FRENCH GUIANA (France)

Caracas

VENEZUELA

Socorro

Bogotá

Magdalena R.

Orinoco R.

GRAN COLOMBIA
1819–1830

Quito

ECUADOR

Galápagos
Islands

Amazon R.

Equator 0°

EMPIRE OF BRAZIL
1822

PACIFIC
OCEAN

Lima

PERU
1824

BOLIVIA
1825

La Paz

Sucre

Salvador

Paraná R.

PARAGUAY
1811

São Paulo

Rio de Janeiro

20°S

CHILE
1817

UNITED
PROVINCES OF
THE RIO DE
LA PLATA
1816

URUGUAY
1828

Valparaíso

Santiago

ARGENTINA

Buenos Aires

Montevideo

Bahía
Blanca

PATAGONIA
(Disputed between
Argentina and Chile)

Islas Malvinas
(Falkland Islands)

80°W

60°W

| 0 | 500 | 1000 Km. |
| 0 | 500 | 1000 Mi. |

1811 Year independence gained

Colony

MAP 8.4
Latin American Independence, 1840

With Central and South American colonies triumphing in their wars of independence against European colonial powers, President Monroe sought to enhance the United States' security by warning European nations against meddling in the region.

Source: Copyright © Cengage Learning 2015

States' Rights and Nullification

Under the Constitution, the exact nature of the relationship between the states and the federal government was ambiguous because Constitutional Convention delegates disagreed on whether states or the nation should prevail in an irreconcilable conflict. The Tenth Amendment offered a slight clarification: powers not delegated to the central government, it said, were reserved to the states or to the people.

When New England Federalists met in Hartford in late 1814 to prepare a list of grievances against "Mr. Madison's War," they drew on the doctrine of nullification, first announced sixteen years earlier in the Kentucky and Virginia Resolutions, written by Thomas Jefferson and James Madison, respectively. Opposing the Alien and Sedition Acts, these founding fathers asserted that, if the national government assumed powers not delegated to it by the Constitution, states could nullify federal actions—that is, declare them inoperative within state borders. Some New England Federalists discussed taking nullification further by seceding. Their formulation of states' rights to nullify federal authority left a legacy for dissent that has recurred in crises up to the present.

In the following decade, South Carolina nullified federal tariffs, and in 1861 southern states threatened by Abraham Lincoln's election as president claimed the right of secession. Although the Civil War supposedly settled the issue—states could neither nullify federal law nor secede—southern states opposing the Supreme Court's 1954 ruling in favor of school integration again claimed the right to nullify "unauthorized" federal policy within their borders. In the early twenty-first century, as the U.S. Congress failed to muster a two-thirds majority to propose a constitutional amendment banning gay marriage, dozens of states ratified their own such constitutional amendments. Symbolically, the threat of secession remains potent. Decrying the 2009 federal stimulus package to jump-start the ailing national economy, Texas governor Rick Perry declared that his state might secede rather than face unwanted spending, taxation, and debt. In 2012, after the Supreme Court affirmed the constitutionality of the Patient Protection and Affordable Care Act ("Obamacare"), opponents renewed grassroots calls for their states' secession. The Hartford Convention's legacy for a people and a nation provides Americans who dissent from national policy with a model for using state governments, and threats of secession, as protest vehicles.

addressed American anxiety about Latin America and Russian expansion beyond Alaska and its settlements in California. Monroe demanded nonintervention by Europe in the affairs of independent New World nations, and he pledged U.S. noninterference in European affairs including Europe's existing New World colonies. European nations stayed out of New World affairs because they feared the British Royal Navy, not the United States' proclamations.

Summary

The partisanship of the 1790s made the early republic a period of vigorous political engagement. With a vision of an agrarian nation that protected individual liberty, Jeffersonians promoted a limited national government—one that stayed out of religious affairs and spent little on military forces, diplomatic missions, and economic initiatives. The rival Federalists, who exerted their influence through the judiciary, declared federal supremacy over states even as the judiciary affirmed its supremacy over other government branches. Federalists hoped a strengthened federal government would promote commerce and industry.

Despite his belief in limited government, Jefferson considered the Louisiana Territory acquisition and the Corps of Discovery his greatest presidential accomplishments. Americans soon streamed into the Louisiana Territory, and more would have gone if not for Indians (and their British allies) and poorly developed transportation routes.

With its economy focused on international shipping, the greatest threats to the United States soon came from abroad. In its wars with the Barbary states, the United States sought to guard its commerce and ships on the high seas. Although the War of 1812 was a military stalemate, it inspired a new sense of nationalism and launched an era of American development.

The Treaty of Ghent reaffirmed American independence; thereafter, the nation settled disputes with Great Britain by negotiation. The war also seriously impaired Indian resistance in the Midwest and Southwest, while accelerating American industrial growth. Federalists' opposition to the war undermined their credibility, and their party faded from the national political scene by 1820. The absence of partisan conflict created what contemporaries called an Era of Good Feelings.

Still, competing visions of America's route to prosperity endured. Under Chief Justice John Marshall, the Supreme Court supported the Federalist agenda, issuing rulings that stimulated commerce and industry. Democratic-Republicans looked, instead, toward the Louisiana Territory. But most Americans agreed on the need for improved transportation, though most improvements took place in the North.

In 1819 the postwar economic boom ended, as congressmen debated whether to admit Missouri as a slave state. Henry Clay's compromise removed slavery's expansion from political center stage, but did not permanently settle the issue.

The United States also acquired Florida. Fearful of European intentions to reassert influence in the Americas and emboldened by the nation's expanding boundaries, President Monroe proclaimed that the United States would not tolerate European intervention in American affairs. But even as its expanding boundaries strengthened the United States' international presence, territorial expansion threatened political unity at home.

Chapter Review

Political Visions

Was Jefferson's election and political vision truly "the revolution of 1800"?

Jefferson considered his election in 1800 a revolution, since it also gave his Democratic-Republican Party a majority in both houses of Congress. That made it easier to enact his vision of limited government, individual liberty (which required the separation of church and state), and an agrarian (versus commercial) republic.

Since Democratic-Republicans viewed national debt as a sign of corruption, he authorized his treasury secretary to cut the federal budget and decrease the national debt (which Federalists saw as a tool to stimulate the economy). Jefferson also pardoned those convicted under the Alien and Sedition Acts, which he regarded as a violation of liberties, and attempted to remove a Supreme Court justice opposed to his brand of politics. (He was ultimately unsuccessful, which maintained the Court's independence.)

Continental Expansion and Indian Resistance

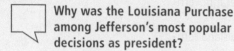 Why was the Louisiana Purchase among Jefferson's most popular decisions as president?

The purchase of 827,000 square miles of land west of the Mississippi from France doubled the size of the United States, secured American interests from potential European incursion at its inland borders, and opened more land for American settlement (even though Native Americans were already living there). Moreover, by purchasing the land on the other side of the river, the United States controlled access to the Mississippi, which appealed to western settlers who relied on it to get their goods to market. Finally, it fed dreams of cheap, fertile lands for would-be settlers.

The Nation in the Orbit of Europe

What led to the War of 1812?

Continuing disputes with Great Britain over the nature of American independence. Ongoing hostilities between European nations spilled over onto American ships, as Great Britain often stopped and seized U.S. ships and forced British deserters and British-born but naturalized American citizens into military service. As many as six to eight thousand Americans were impressed from 1803 to 1812. American trade vessels were also seized. Trade embargoes did little to stop the practice and ultimately hurt American merchants and the U.S. economy. In seeking Congressional support for war, Madison pointed to violation of neutral trading rights, British alliances with western Indians, and affronts to American independence as additional causes, while others saw war as an opportunity to annex British Canada. Although Britain reopened the seas and ordered its ships not to disturb American warships by June of 1812, news of the policy change did not reach America until long after Congress declared war.

The War of 1812

What were the consequences of the War of 1812?

The most important outcome of the war was that it affirmed American independence and autonomy as a nation and guaranteed no future battles with Britain over trade or territory. In other ways, the Treaty of Ghent that ended the fighting, simply restored the prewar status quo: the United States did not get the results it wanted

on impressments, blockades, and maritime rights for neutral parties. On the home front, the war shattered the U.S. economy and led some New England Federalists to threaten secession, which contributed to the party's demise when the war soon ended. Indians who had supported the British lost a major ally. And while Indians had their land and rights restored by the Treaty of Ghent, they had no power to enforce it. With the end of war, three trends emerged that were pivotal for the nation's future: westward expansion, the entrenchment of slavery, and industrial development.

Early Industrialization

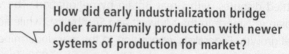 How did early industrialization bridge older farm/family production with newer systems of production for market?

The South continued as an agricultural region and expanded its slave system, while the North transformed quickly into a market economy. With the war cutting off European trade, northern entrepreneurs invested in domestic production and factories. Former artisans and farmers increasingly shifted from producers to wage workers. Early forms of market changes came from piecework or outwork, where manufacturers hired women and children in their homes to produce goods, often paying them for each piece produced. After the first mills were opened in the 1790s, women and children went to work there. People increasingly bought goods—clothes, shoes, and soap—that they once made for themselves. Commercial farming emerged in the North to meet the growing demand for foodstuffs that was created when people shifted from farming to factory jobs. Those farmers who remained in agriculture shifted increasingly to cash crops.

Sectionalism and Nationalism

How did the American System mark the triumph of Federalist economic policy?

Long opposed to big government, Democratic-Republicans amended this philosophy to adopt the Federalist notion that the central government should aid economic growth and encourage the development of commerce and industry. Their program was dubbed the American System, and included a national bank, development of transportation networks, and a protective tariff that would tax imported goods to protect American products from foreign competitors. Advocates of the American System, such as South Carolina leader

John C. Calhoun, believed it could bridge sectional divides and expand the nation. Both parties embraced internal improvements for different reasons: Federalists saw them as spurring commercial development, while Jeffersonians (Democratic-Republicans) thought they would lead to western and agrarian expansion.

Suggestions for Further Reading

Stephen Aron, *American Confluence: The Missouri Frontier from Borderland to Border State* (2006)

Claude A. Clegg III, *The Price of Liberty: African Americans and the Making of Liberia* (2004)

David Edmunds, *Tecumseh and the Quest for Indian Leadership* (2006)

Richard S. Newman, *The Transformation of American Abolitionism: Fighting Slavery in the Early Republic* (2002)

Kent Newmyer, *John Marshall and the Heroic Age of the Supreme Court* (2001)

Jeffrey Ostler, *The Plains Sioux and U.S. Colonialism from Lewis and Clark to Wounded Knee* (2004)

Jeffrey Pasley, Andrew Robertson, and David Waldstreicher, eds., *Beyond the Founders: New Approaches to the Political History of the Early American Republic* (2004)

Alan Taylor, *The Civil War of 1812: American Citizens, British Subjects, Irish Rebels, and Indian Allies* (2010)

Gordon S. Wood, *Empire of Liberty: A History of the Early Republic, 1789–1815* (2009)

The Rise of the South

9

1815–1860

Thomas Jefferson died, as he lived, in debt, on July 4, 1826, the same day his longtime rival John Adams died. At Jefferson's Virginia home, Monticello, anxiety filled his white and black "families."

On January 15, 1827, a five-day estate sale took place at Monticello. Among the paintings, furniture, and mementoes were "130 valuable negroes." Monticello's blacksmith, Joseph Fossett, watched his wife Edith and eight children sold to four different bidders.

Jefferson was reportedly a caring slaveholder, who tried to keep families together. After his wife, Martha (with whom he had two daughters), died in 1782, Jefferson had six children with his slave, Sally Hemings, four of whom lived beyond infancy. Sally was the half sister of Jefferson's wife, and part of an extended family of light-skinned Hemingses.

Joe Fossett, as Jefferson promised, became free one year after his master's death. Jefferson had earlier freed his four children with Hemings: William Beverly Hemings, Harriet Hemings II, James Madison Hemings, and Thomas Eston Hemings. Jefferson never freed Sally; Virginia law would have required him to attain, publicly, a dispensation from the state legislature to free her without removing her from the state, and Jefferson wanted no more salacious publicity about his house servant and mistress. Sally died a slave, in Charlottesville, Virginia, in 1835 at age sixty-two. Monticello itself was sold in 1831. But across the South in the 1820s, the "business" of slavery expansion and cotton production was hardly over.

In 1815, the southern states and territories, with fertile soil and a growing slave labor force, were poised for growth and prosperity. New lands were settled, new states were peopled, and the South emerged as the world's most extensive commercial agricultural economy. The Old South's wealth came from export crops, land, and slaves, and its population was almost wholly rural. Racial slavery affected values, customs, laws, class structure, and

Chapter Outline

The "Distinctive" South
South-North Similarity | South-North Dissimilarity | A Southern Worldview and the Proslavery Argument | A Slave Society

Southern Expansion, Indian Resistance, and Removal
A Southern Westward Movement | Indian Treaty Making | Indian Accommodation | Indian Removal as Federal Policy | Cherokees | Cherokee Nation v. Georgia | Trail of Tears | Seminole Wars

LINKS TO THE WORLD *The Amistad Case*

Social Pyramid in the Old South
Yeoman Farmers | Yeoman Folk Culture | Yeomen's Livelihoods | Landless Whites | Yeomen's Demands and White Class Relations | Free Blacks | Free Black Communities

The Planters' World
The Newly Rich | Social Status and Planters' Values | King Cotton in a Global Economy | Paternalism | Marriage and Family Among Planters

Slave Life and Labor
Slaves' Everyday Conditions | Slave Work Routines | Violence and Intimidation Against Slaves | Slave-Master Relationships

Slave Culture and Resistance
African Cultural Survival | Slaves' Religion and Music | The Black Family in Slavery | The Domestic Slave Trade | Strategies of Resistance | Nat Turner's Insurrection

the region's relationship to the nation and the world. As slaves were increasingly defined as chattel, they struggled to survive and resist, sometimes overtly, but often simply in daily life and culture. By 1860, white southerners asserted the moral and economic benefits of slavery and sought to advance their political power over the national government.

As you read this chapter, keep the following questions in mind:

- **How and why was the Old South a "slave society," with slavery permeating every class and group within it, free or unfree?**

- **How and why did white southerners come to see cotton as "king" of a global economy, and how did the cotton trade's international reach shape southern society from 1815 to 1860?**

- **How did African American slaves build and sustain a meaningful life and a sense of community amid the potential chaos and destruction of their circumstances?**

- **How would you weigh the comparative significance of the following central themes in the history of the Old South: class, race, migration, power, liberty, wealth?**

VISUALIZING THE PAST *Imaging Nat Turner's Rebellion*

LEGACY FOR A PEOPLE AND A NATION *Reparations for Slavery*

SUMMARY

The "Distinctive" South

What made the antebellum South different from the North?

In the first half of the 1800s, slaveholding states from the Chesapeake and Virginia to Missouri, and from Florida across to Texas, came to be designated as the South. Today, many consider it America's most distinctive region. Historians have long examined how the Old South was like and unlike the rest of the nation. Because of its unique history, has the South, in the words of poet Allen Tate, always been "Uncle Sam's other province"? Analyzing why the South seems more religious, conservative, or tragic than other regions has been an enduring practice.

Certain American values, such as materialism, individualism, and faith in progress, have been associated with the North and values such as tradition, honor, and family loyalty, with the South. Stereotype has also labeled the South as static, even "backward," and the North as dynamic in the pre–Civil War decades. In truth, there were many Souths: low-country rice and cotton regions with dense slave populations; mountainous regions of small farmers; semitropical wetlands in the Southeast; **plantation** culture in the cotton belt and Mississippi Valley; Texas grasslands; tobacco- and wheat-growing regions in Virginia and North Carolina; bustling port cities; wilderness areas with rare hillfolk homesteads.

plantation Large landholding devoted to a cash crop such as cotton or tobacco.

Chronology

1810–20	An estimated 137,000 slaves are forced to move from the Upper South to Alabama, Mississippi, and other western regions
1822	Vesey's insurrection plot is discovered in South Carolina
1830s	Vast majority of African American slaves in America are native born
1830s–40s	Cotton trade grows into largest source of commercial wealth and America's leading export
1831	Turner leads a violent slave rebellion in Virginia
1832	Virginia holds the last debate in the South about the future of slavery; gradual abolition is voted down
	Publication of Dew's proslavery tract *Abolition of Negro Slavery*
1836	Arkansas gains admission to the Union as a slave state
1839	Mississippi's Married Women's Property Act gives married women some property rights
1845	Florida and Texas gain admission to the Union as slave states
	Publication of Douglass's *Narrative of the Life of Frederick Douglass, an American Slave, Written by Himself*
1850	Planters' share of agricultural wealth in the South is 90 to 95 percent
1850–60	Of some 300,000 slaves who migrate from the Upper to the Lower South, 60 to 70 percent go by outright sale
1857	Publication of Hinton R. Helper's *The Impending Crisis*, denouncing the slave system
	Publication of George Fitzhugh's *Southern Thought*, an aggressive defense of slavery
1860	There are 405,751 mulattos in the United States, accounting for 12.5 percent of the African American population
	Three-quarters of all southern white families own no slaves
	South produces largest cotton crop ever

South-North Similarity The South shared much in common with the rest of the nation. The geographic sizes of the South and the North were roughly the same. In 1815, white southerners and fellow northerners shared heroes and ideology from the American Revolution and War of 1812. They worshipped the same Protestant God as northerners, lived under the same Constitution, and similarly combined nationalism and localism in their attitudes toward government. But as slavery and the plantation economy expanded (see Map 9.1), the South did not become a land of individual opportunity in the same manner as the North.

Research has shown that, despite enormous cruelties, slavery was a profitable labor system for planters. Southerners and northerners shared an expanding capitalist economy. As it grew, the slave-based economy reflected planters' rational choices. More land and more slaves generally converted into more wealth.

By the eve of the Civil War in 1860, the distribution of wealth and property in the two sections was almost identical: 50 percent of free adult males owned only 1 percent of real and personal property, and the richest 1 percent owned 27 percent of the wealth. North and South had ruling classes. Entrepreneurs in both sections sought their fortunes in an expanding market economy. The southern "master class" was more likely than propertied northerners to move west to make a profit.

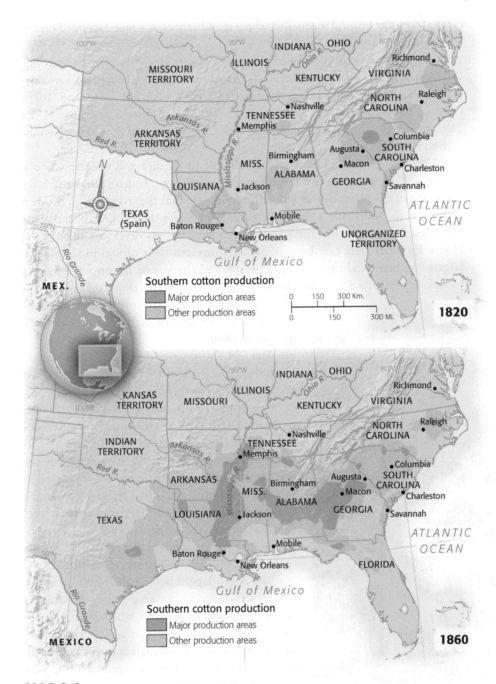

MAP 9.1

Cotton Production in the South

These two maps reveal the rapid westward expansion of cotton production and its importance to the antebellum South. Source: Copyright © Cengage Learning 2015

South-North Dissimilarity

In terms of differences, the South's climate and longer growing season gave it a rural and agricultural destiny. Many great rivers provided rich soil and transportation routes. The South developed as a biracial society of brutal inequality, where the liberty of one race depended on the enslavement of another.

Cotton growers spread over large areas to maximize production and income. Consequently, population density in the South was low; by 1860, there were only 2.3 people per square mile in largely unsettled Texas, 15.6 in Louisiana, and 18.0 in Georgia. The Northeast averaged 65.4 people per square mile—Massachusetts had 153.1 people per square mile, and New York City compressed 86,400 people into each square mile.

Where people were scarce, it was difficult to finance and operate schools, churches, libraries, inns, and restaurants. Similarly, the South's rural character and vision of the plantation as self-sufficient meant that the section spent little on public health. Southerners were strongly committed to their churches, and some embraced universities, but these institutions were far less developed than in the North. Factories were rare because planters invested their capital in slaves. The largest southern "industry" was lumbering, and the largest factories used slaves to make cigars. The South was slower than the North to develop a unified market economy and a regional transportation network and had only 35 percent of the nation's railroad mileage in 1860.

The Old South never developed its own banking and shipping capacity to any degree and relied on the North for both. Most southern bank deposits were in the North, and as early as 1822, one-sixth of all southern cotton cleared for Liverpool or Le Havre from the port of New York. With cotton constituting two-fifths of New York's exports, merchants and bankers there became interested in the fate of slavery and cotton prices. In economic conventions from 1837 to 1839, southern delegates debated foreign trade, dependence on northern importers and financiers, and other alleged threats to their commercial independence.

The South lagged behind the North in industrial growth. Its urban centers were mostly ports like New Orleans and Charleston, which became crossroads of commerce and small-scale manufacturing. In the interior were small market towns dependent on agricultural trade. Lacking manufacturing jobs, the South did not attract immigrants as readily as the North. By 1860, only 13 percent of the nation's foreign-born population lived in slave states.

Like most northerners, antebellum southerners embraced evangelical Christianity. Americans everywhere believed in a personal God and in conversion and piety as the means to salvation. But southern evangelical Baptists and Methodists concentrated on personal rather than social

Library of Congress

America, 1841, lithograph and watercolor by Edward Williams Clay. An idealized portrayal of loyal and contented slaves, likely distributed by northern apologists for slavery. All is well on the plantation as well-dressed slaves dance and express their gratitude to their master and his perfect family. The text includes the old slave saying: "God bless you master! You feed and clothe us. When we are sick you nurse us, and when too old to work, you provide for us!" The master replies piously: "These poor creatures are a sacred legacy from my ancestors and while a dollar is left me, nothing shall be spared to increase their comfort and happiness."

improvement. By the 1830s in the North, evangelicalism was a wellspring of reform movements (see Chapter 10); but in states where blacks were numerous and unfree, religion, as one scholar has written, preached "a hands-off policy concerning slavery." Moreover, distance and sparse population prevented reform-minded women from developing associations with each other. The only reform movements that grew in the emerging southern Bible Belt, such as temperance, focused exclusively on personal behavior.

A Southern Worldview and the Proslavery Argument

In the wake of the American Revolution, Enlightenment ideas of natural rights and equality stimulated antislavery sentiment in the Upper South, produced a brief flurry of manumissions, and inspired hope for gradual emancipation. But that confidence waned in the new nation. As slavery spread, southerners vigorously defended it.

By the 1820s, white southerners justified slavery as a "**positive good**," not merely a "necessary evil." They used the antiquity of slavery, as well as the Bible's many references to slaveholding, to foster a historical argument for bondage. But at the heart of the proslavery rationale was a deep and abiding racism. Whites were the more intellectual race, they claimed, and blacks more inherently physical and therefore destined for labor. In an 1851 proslavery tract, John Campbell declared that "there is as much difference between the lowest tribe of negroes and the white Frenchman, Englishman, or American, as there is between the monkey and the negro."

Some southerners defended slavery in practical terms: their bondsmen were economic necessities. In 1845, James Henry Hammond of South Carolina argued that slaveholding was a matter of property rights protected by the Constitution. The deepest root of the proslavery argument was a hierarchical view of the social order with slavery prescribed by God. Southerners cherished tradition, believing social change should come slowly, in increments, if at all. As Nat Turner's slave rebellion compelled the Virginia legislature to debate the gradual abolition of slavery in 1831–1832, Thomas R. Dew, a slaveholder and professor at the College of William and Mary, contended that "that which is the growth of *ages* may require ages to remove." Dew's widely read *Abolition of Negro Slavery* (1832) ushered in an outpouring of proslavery writing that would intensify over the next thirty years. As slavery expanded westward and fueled national prosperity, Dew cautioned that gradual abolition threatened the South's "irremediable ruin." Dew declared black slavery the "order of nature" and the basis of the "well-ordered, well-established liberty" of white Americans. Dew's well-ordered society also included the proper division of men and women into separate spheres and functions.

Proslavery advocates invoked natural-law doctrine, arguing that the natural state of humankind was inequality of ability and condition, not equality. Proslavery writers believed that people were born to certain stations in life; they stressed dependence over autonomy and duty over rights as the human condition. As Virginia writer George Fitzhugh put it in 1854, "Men are not born entitled to equal rights. It would be far nearer the truth to say, that some were born with saddles on their backs, and others booted and spurred to ride them." Given the persistence

positive good Southern justification for slavery as beneficial to the larger society, both to white owners and their black slaves.

of modern racism throughout the U.S., it is especially important to comprehend antebellum southerner's rationalizations for slavery.

Many slaveholders saw themselves in a paternal role, as guardians of a familial relationship between masters and slaves. Although contradicted by countless examples of slave resistance and escape, and by slave sales, planters needed to believe in and exerted great energy in constructing the idea of the contented slave.

| A Slave Society |

Slavery and race affected everything in the South. There, whites and blacks were socialized, married, reared children, worked, conceived of property, and honed their habits of behavior under the influence of slavery. This was true of slaveholding and nonslaveholding whites and of enslaved and free blacks. Slavery shaped the South's social structure, fueled its economy, and dominated its politics.

Still, the South was interdependent with the North, West, and Europe in a growing capitalist market system. For its cotton trade, southerners relied on northern banks, steamship companies, and merchants. But there were elements of this system that southerners increasingly disliked, especially urbanism, wage labor, a broadening right to vote, and threats to their racial and class order. Distinctive or national, the South's story begins in what we have come to call the Old South, a term only conceivable after the eviction of native peoples from the region.

Southern Expansion, Indian Resistance, and Removal

How did Native Americans living in western territories respond to increasing migration by southern whites?

When the trans-Appalachian frontier opened in the wake of the War of 1812, 5 to 10 percent of the population moved annually, usually westward. In the first two decades of the century, they poured into the Ohio Valley; by the 1820s, they were migrating into the Mississippi River valley and beyond. By 1850, two-thirds of Americans lived west of the Appalachians.

| A Southern Westward Movement |

After 1820, the heart of cotton cultivation and the slave-based plantation system shifted from the coastal states to Alabama and the newly settled Mississippi Valley—Tennessee, Louisiana, Arkansas, and Mississippi. Southern slaveholders took slaves with them to the newer areas of the South, and **yeoman** farmers followed, hoping for new wealth through cheap land and slaves.

yeoman Independent small farmer, usually nonslaveholding.

A wave of migration was evident everywhere in the Southeast. As early as 1817, a Charleston, South Carolina, newspaper reported that migration out of that state had reached "unprecedented proportions." Almost half of the white people born in South Carolina after 1800 left the state, most for the Southwest.

The way to wealth for southern seaboard planters was to go west to grow cotton for the booming world markets, by purchasing more land and slaves. Mississippi's population soared from 73,000 in 1820 to 607,000 in 1850, with African American slaves in the majority. Across the Mississippi River, Arkansas' population went from

14,000 in 1820 to 210,000 in 1850. By 1835, the American immigrant population in Texas reached 35,000, including 3,000 slaves, outnumbering Mexicans two to one. American settlers declared Texas's independence from Mexico in 1836, spurring further American immigration into the region. By 1845, "Texas fever" boosted the Anglo population to 125,000. Statehood that year opened the floodgates to more immigrants and to a confrontation with Mexico that would lead to war.

As the **cotton kingdom** grew to what southern political leaders dreamed would be national and world dominion, this westward migration, fueled initially by optimistic nationalism, ultimately made migrant planters more sectional and southern. By the 1840s, these capitalist planters, fearful that their slave-based economy was under attack, sought to protect and expand their system. Increasingly, they saw themselves, as one historian has written, less as "landowners who happened to own slaves" than as "slaveholders who happened to own land."

cotton kingdom A broad swath of territory where cotton was a mainstay that stretched from South Carolina, Georgia, and northern Florida in the east through Alabama, Mississippi, central and western Tennessee, and Louisiana, and from there on to Arkansas and Texas.

For most white Americans, the Indians were in the way of their growing empire. Before 1830, large swaths of upper Georgia belonged to the Cherokees, and huge regions of Alabama and Mississippi were Creek, Choctaw, or Chickasaw land. Indians were also on the move, but in forced migrations. Taking Indian land, so the reasoning went, merely reflected the natural course of progress: the "civilizers" had to displace the "children of the forest." National leaders provided the rhetoric and justification needed. As president in 1830, Andrew Jackson explained why the Indians must go. "What good man would prefer a country," he asked, "covered with forests and ranged by a few thousand savages to our extensive Republic, studded with cities, towns, and prosperous farms?"

Indian Treaty Making

In theory, under the U.S. Constitution, the federal government recognized Indian sovereignty and treated Indian peoples as foreign nations. Agreements between Indian nations and the United States were signed and ratified like other international treaties. In practice, however, fraud dominated the government's approach to treaty making and Indian sovereignty. As the country expanded, new treaties would shrink Indian landholdings.

Although Indian resistance persisted against such pressure after the War of 1812, it only slowed the process. In the 1820s, native peoples in the middle West, Ohio Valley, Mississippi Valley, and other parts of the cotton South ceded 200 million acres for a pittance.

Indian Accommodation

Increasingly, Indian nations east of the Mississippi sought to survive through accommodation. In the first three decades of the century, the Choctaw, Creek, and Chickasaw peoples in the lower Mississippi became suppliers and traders. Under treaty provisions, Indian commerce took place through trading posts and stores that provided Indians with supplies, and purchased or bartered Indian-produced goods. The trading posts extended credit to chiefs, who increasingly fell into debt that they could pay off to the federal government only by selling their land.

By 1822, the Choctaw nation had sold 13 million acres but still carried a $13,000 debt. The Indians struggled, increasing agricultural production and hunting, working as farmhands and craftsmen, and selling produce at market stalls in

Links TO THE WORLD

The Amistad Case

In April 1839, a Spanish slave ship, *Tecora*, sailed from Lomboko, the West African region that became Sierra Leone. On board were Mende people, sold by their African enemies. In June, they arrived in Havana, Cuba, a Spanish colony. Two Spaniards purchased fifty-three of the Mende and sailed aboard *La Amistad* for their plantations elsewhere in Cuba. After three days at sea, the Africans revolted. Led by a man the Spaniards called Joseph Cinque, they killed the captain and took control. They ordered the two Spaniards to return them to Africa, but the slaveholders tried to reach the American South. Far off course, *La Amistad* was seized by the USS *Washington* in Long Island Sound and brought ashore in Connecticut.

The "Amistad Africans" soon became a cause for abolitionists and slaveholders, as well as an issue in U.S.–Spanish relations. The Africans were imprisoned in New Haven, and a dispute ensued: Were they slaves and murderers, and the property of Cuban owners, or were they free people exercising their natural rights? Were they Spanish property, seized on the high seas in violation of a 1795 treaty? If a northern state could "free" captive Africans, what did it mean for enslaved African Americans in the South? Connecticut abolitionists went to court, where a U.S. circuit court judge dismissed the mutiny and murder charges but refused to release the Africans because their Spanish owners claimed them as property.

Meanwhile, a Yale professor of ancient languages, Josiah Gibbs, visited the captives and learned their words for numbers. In New York, he walked along the docks repeating the Mende words until an African seaman, James Covey, responded. Covey journeyed to New Haven, conversed with the jubilant Africans, and soon their tale garnered sympathy throughout New England.

In a new trial, the judge ruled that the Africans were illegally enslaved and ordered them returned to their homeland. Slave trade between Africa and the Americas had been outlawed in a treaty between Spain and Great Britain. Spain's lawyers demanded the return of their "merchandise." Needing southern votes to win reelection, President Martin Van Buren supported Spanish claims.

The administration appealed to the Supreme Court in February 1841. Arguing the abolitionists' case, former president John Quincy Adams pointed to a copy of the Declaration of Independence on the court wall, invoked the natural rights to life and liberty, and chastised Van Buren. In a 7-to-1 decision, the Court ruled that the Africans were "free-born."

On November 27, 1841, thirty-five survivors and five American missionaries embarked for Africa, arriving in Sierra Leone on January 15, 1842. The Amistad case showed how intertwined slavery was with freedom, and the United States with the world. It poisoned diplomatic relations between America and Spain for a generation, and stimulated Christian mission work in Africa.

Joseph Cinque, by Nathaniel Jocelyn, 1840. Cinque led the rebellion aboard La Amistad, *a Spanish ship carrying captive Africans along the coast of Cuba in 1839. They commandeered the ship and sailed it north toward New England, where they were rescued off the coast of Connecticut. Cinque, celebrated as a great leader, sat for the painting while he and his people awaited trial. They were freed by a decision of the U.S. Supreme Court in 1841 and returned to their homeland in Sierra Leone in West Africa.*

AP Photo/New Haven Colony Historical Society

Natchez and New Orleans. As the United States expanded westward, white Americans promoted their assimilation through education and conversion to Christianity. In 1819, in response to missionary lobbying, Congress appropriated $10,000 annually for "civilization of the tribes adjoining the frontier settlements."

Within five years, thirty-two boarding schools run by Protestant missionaries enrolled Indian students. They substituted English for American Indian languages and taught agriculture alongside the Christian gospel. But settlers still eyed Indian land. Wherever native peoples lived, illegal settlers disrupted their lives. The federal government halfheartedly enforced treaties, as legitimate Indian land rights gave way to the advance of white civilization.

With loss of land came dependency. The Choctaws relied on white Americans for manufactured goods and even food. Disease further facilitated removal of American Indian peoples to western lands. While other groups increased rapidly, the Indian population fell, some nations declining by 50 percent in three decades. As many as one hundred thousand eastern and southern Indian peoples were removed between 1820 and 1850; about thirty thousand died in the process.

Removal had a profound impact on Shawnees, the people of the Prophet and Tecumseh (see pages 207–208). After giving up 17 million acres in Ohio in a 1795 treaty, the Shawnees scattered to Indiana and eastern Missouri. Others moved to the Kansas Territory in 1825. By 1854, Kansas was open to white settlement, and the Shawnees had ceded seven-eighths of their land, or 1.4 million acres. Men lost their traditional role as providers; their skills hunting woodland animals were useless on the Kansas prairies. As grain became the tribe's dietary staple, Shawnee women played a greater role as providers, supplemented by government aid under treaty provisions. Remarkably, the Shawnees preserved their language and culture despite these devastating dislocations.

Indian Removal as Federal Policy

Cherokees, Creeks, Choctaws, Chickasaws, and Seminoles aggressively resisted white encroachment after the War of 1812. In his last annual message to Congress in late 1824, President James Monroe proposed that all Indians be moved beyond the Mississippi River. Monroe considered this an "honorable" proposal that would protect Indians from invasion and provide them with independence for "improvement and civilization." He believed force would be unnecessary. But all five tribes unanimously rejected Monroe's proposition. Between 1789 and 1825, the five nations negotiated thirty treaties with the United States, and they reached their limit. Most wished to remain on what little was left of their ancestral land.

Pressure from Georgia prompted Monroe's policy. In the 1820s, the state accused the federal government of not fulfilling its 1802 promise to remove the Cherokees and Creeks from northwestern Georgia in return for the state's renunciation of its claim to western lands. In 1826, under federal pressure, the Creek nation ceded all but a small strip of its Georgia acreage, but for Georgians only their complete removal would resolve the conflict. In an unsuccessful attempt to retain the remainder of their traditional lands in Alabama, the Creeks radically altered their political structure. In 1829, they centralized tribal authority and forbade any chief from ceding land.

Indian Removal Act
Legislation authorizing Andrew Jackson to exchange public lands in the West for Indian territories in the East and appropriated federal funds to cover the expenses of removal.

Link to President Jackson Reports on Indian Removal, 1830

In 1830, after a narrow vote, Congress passed the **Indian Removal Act** authorizing the president to negotiate removal treaties with all tribes living east of the Mississippi. The bill, which provided federal funds for such relocations, would likely not have passed the House without the additional representation afforded slave states due to the Constitution's three-fifths clause.

Cherokees

No people met the challenge of assimilating to American standards more than the Cherokees, whose traditional home centered on eastern Tennessee and northern Alabama and Georgia. Between 1819 and 1829, the tribe became economically self-sufficient and politically self-governing; during this Cherokee renaissance the nearly fifteen thousand adult Cherokees regarded themselves as a nation, not a collection of villages. In 1821 and 1822, Sequoyah, a self-educated Cherokee, devised an eighty-six-character phonetic alphabet that made possible a Cherokee-language Bible and a bilingual tribal newspaper, *Cherokee Phoenix* (1828). Between 1820 and 1823, the Cherokees created a formal government with a bicameral legislature, a court system, and in 1827 they adopted a written constitution modeled after that of the United States. They transformed their economy from hunting, gathering, and subsistence agriculture to commodity trade based on barter, cash, and credit. The Cherokee nation, however, collectively owned all tribal land and forbade land sales to outsiders. Nonetheless, many became individual farmers and slaveholders; by 1833, they held fifteen hundred black slaves, and over time Cherokee racial identity became very complex.

But Cherokee transformations failed to win respect or acceptance from white southerners. In the 1820s, Georgia pressed them to sell the 7,200 square miles they held in the state. Congress appropriated $30,000 in 1822 to buy the Georgia land, but the Cherokees resisted. Impatient, Georgia annulled the Cherokees' constitution, extended the state's sovereignty over them, prohibited the Cherokee National Council from meeting except to cede land, and ordered their lands seized. The discovery of gold on Cherokee land in 1829 further whetted Georgia's appetite for Cherokee territory.

Cherokee Nation v. Georgia

The Cherokees under Chief John Ross turned to the federal courts to defend their treaty with the United States. In *Cherokee Nation v. Georgia* (1831), Chief Justice John Marshall ruled that under the Constitution an Indian tribe was neither a foreign nation nor a state and therefore had no standing in federal courts. Indians were deemed "domestic, dependent nations." Legally, they were in but not of the United States. Nonetheless, said Marshall, the Indians had a right to their lands; they could lose title only by voluntarily giving it up.

A year later, in *Worcester v. Georgia*, Marshall declared that the Cherokee nation was a distinct political community in which "the laws of Georgia can have no force" and into which Georgians could not enter without permission or treaty. The Cherokees celebrated. Jackson, however, whose reputation was built as an Indian fighter, tried to usurp the Court's action. Newspapers reported that Jackson had said, "John Marshall has made his decision: now let him enforce it." To open up new lands for settlement, Jackson favored expelling the Cherokees.

Georgians, too, refused to comply; they would not tolerate a sovereign Cherokee nation within their borders. A Cherokee census indicated that they owned thirty-three grist mills, thirteen sawmills, one powder mill, sixty-nine blacksmith shops, two tanneries, 762 looms, 2,486 spinning wheels, 172 wagons, 2,923 plows, 7,683 horses, 22,531 cattle, 46,732 pigs, and 2,566 sheep. "You asked us to…form a republican government," declared the Cherokee leader John Ridge in 1832. "We did so—adopting your own as a model. You asked us to cultivate the earth, and learn the mechanic arts: We did so. You asked us to learn to read: We did so. You asked us to cast away our idols, and worship your God: We did so." But neither the plow nor the Bible earned the Cherokees respect in the face of the economic, imperial, and racial quests of fellow southerners (see Map 9.2).

MAP 9.2
Removal of Native Americans from the South, 1820–1840

Over a twenty-year period, the federal government and southern states forced Native Americans to exchange their traditional homes for western land. Some tribal groups remained in the South, but most settled in the alien western environment.

Source: Copyright © Cengage Learning 2015

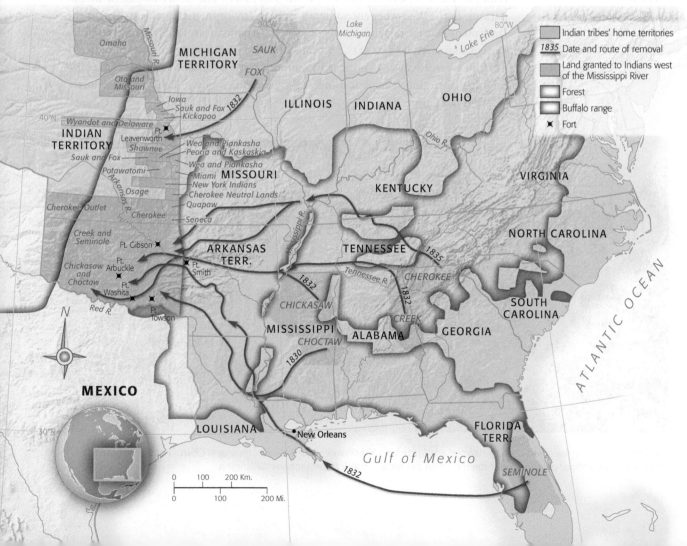

Trail of Tears

The Choctaws made the forced journey from Mississippi and Alabama to the West in the winter of 1831 and 1832. Alexis de Tocqueville was visiting Memphis when they passed through: "The wounded, the sick, newborn babies, and the old men on the point of death…. the sight will never fade from my memory," he wrote. The Creeks in Alabama resisted removal until 1836, when the army pushed them westward. A year later, the Chickasaws followed.

Some Cherokees believed that further resistance was hopeless and accepted removal, agreeing in 1835 to exchange their southern home for western land, in the Treaty of New Echota. Most wanted to stand firm. John Ross, with petitions signed by fifteen thousand Cherokees, lobbied the Senate against ratification of the treaty. He lost. But when the time for evacuation came in 1838, most Cherokees refused to move. President Martin Van Buren sent federal troops; about twenty thousand Cherokees were evicted, held in detention camps, and marched under military escort to Indian Territory in present-day Oklahoma. Nearly one-quarter died of disease and exhaustion on what came to be known as the **Trail of Tears**.

When the forced march ended, the Indians had traded about 100 million acres east of the Mississippi for 32 million acres west of the river plus $68 million. Forced removal had a disastrous impact on the Cherokees and other displaced Indian nations. In the West, they encountered an alien environment. Unable to live off the land, many became dependent on government payments. In 1839, followers of John Ross assassinated leaders of the protreaty faction. Violence continued sporadically until a new treaty in 1846 imposed a temporary truce. In time, the Cherokees reestablished their political institutions and a governing body in Tahlequah, in northeastern Oklahoma.

Trail of Tears Forced migration in 1838 of Cherokee Indians from their homelands in the southeast to what is now Oklahoma.

The Trail of Tears, *by twentieth-century Pawnee artist Brummet Echohawk. About twenty thousand Cherokees were evicted in 1838–1839, and about one-quarter of them died on the forced march to present-day Oklahoma.*

GILCREASE MUSEUM, TULSA OK

Seminole Wars

In Florida, some Seminole leaders agreed in the 1832 Treaty of Payne's Landing to relocate to the West within three years, but others opposed the treaty. A minority under Osceola, a charismatic leader, fought the protreaty group. When federal troops were sent to impose removal in 1835, Osceola waged a guerrilla war against them.

Florida Indians were a varied group that included many Creeks and mixed Indian–African Americans (ex-slaves or descendants of runaway slaves). The U.S. Army, however, considered them all Seminoles. General Thomas Jesup believed that the runaway slave population was the key to the war. "And if it be not speedily put down," he wrote a friend in 1836, "the South will feel the effects of it on their slave population before the end of the next season."

Osceola was captured and died in an army prison in 1838, but the Seminoles fought on under Chief Coacoochee (Wild Cat). In 1842, the United States abandoned removal. Most of Osceola's followers agreed to move west to Indian Territory after another war in 1858, but some remained in the Florida Everglades.

Social Pyramid in the Old South

What class tensions emerged in the antebellum South?

A large majority of white southern families (three-quarters in 1860) were yeoman farmers who owned land but no slaves. The social distance between poorer whites and the planter class could be great; still greater was the distance between whites and free blacks. White yeomen, landless whites, and free blacks occupied the broad base of the social pyramid in the Old South.

Yeoman Farmers

After the War of 1812, white farmers moved in waves down the southern Appalachians into the Gulf lands or through the Cumberland Gap into Kentucky and Tennessee. In large sections of the South, especially inland from the coast and away from large rivers, small, self-sufficient farms were the norm. Lured by stories of good land, many men repeatedly uprooted their wives and children.

Their status as a numerical majority did not mean they set the political or economic direction of the larger society. Self-reliant and often isolated, they operated both apart from and within the slave-based staple-crop economy.

On the southern frontier, men cleared fields, built log cabins, and established farms while their wives labored in the household economy and patiently re-created the social ties—to relatives, neighbors, fellow churchgoers—that enriched everyone's experience. Women dreaded the isolation and loneliness of the frontier.

Some yeomen acquired large tracts of land, purchased slaves, and became planters. They forged part of the new wealth of the cotton boom states of Mississippi and Louisiana, where mobility into the slave-owning class was possible. Others clung to familiar mountainous areas or sought self-sufficiency. As one historian has written, though they owned no slaves, yeomen were jealous of their independence, and "the household grounded their own claims to masterhood."

Yeoman Folk Culture

Yeomen enjoyed a folk culture based on family, church, and local region. Their speech patterns recalled their

Scots-Irish and Irish backgrounds. They flocked to religious revivals called camp meetings, and in between got together for house-raisings, logrollings, quilting bees, corn-shuckings, and hunting. Such occasions combined work with fun and fellowship, offering food and liquor in abundance.

Demanding work and family responsibilities shaped women's lives in the home. They worked in the fields but food preparation consumed much of women's time. Household tasks continued during frequent pregnancies and child care. Nursing and medical care also fell to mothers, who relied on folk wisdom. Women, too, wanted to be masters of their household, although with such heavy workloads, it often came at the price of their health.

Yeomen's Livelihoods   Probably typical of southern yeomen, Ferdinand L. Steel moved as a young man from North Carolina to Tennessee to work as a river boatman but eventually took up farming in Mississippi. Steel and his family raised corn and wheat, though cotton was their cash product: they sold five or six bales a year to obtain money for sugar, coffee, salt, calico, gunpowder, and other store-bought goods.

Thus, Steel entered the market economy as a small farmer, but with mixed results. He picked his own cotton and complained that it was brutal work and unprofitable. He felt like a serf in cotton's kingdom. When cotton prices fell, a small farmer like Steel could be driven into debt or lose his farm.

Steel's family in Mississippi in the 1840s retained much of the flavor of the frontier, and he survived on a household economy. He made all the family's shoes; his wife and sister sewed dresses, shirts, and "pantaloons." The Steel women rendered their own soap and spun and wove cotton into cloth; the men hunted game. Steel doctored his illnesses with boneset tea and herbs. As the nation fell deeper into crisis over slave labor and the planter class strove more aggressively to preserve its slave society, this independent farmer never came close to owning a slave.

The focus of Steel's life was family and religion. Family members prayed together daily, and he studied Scripture for an hour after lunch. "My Faith increases, & I enjoy much of that peace which the world cannot give," he wrote in 1841. Seeking to prepare himself for Judgment Day, Steel borrowed histories, Latin and Greek grammars, and religious books from his church. Eventually, he became a traveling Methodist minister. "My life is one of toil," he reflected, "but blessed be God that it is as well with me as it is."

Landless Whites   Roughly 25 to 40 percent of white southerners were hired hands who owned no land and worked for others. Their property consisted of a few household items and some animals—usually pigs. The landless included some immigrants, especially Irish, who did heavy and dangerous work, such as building railroads and digging ditches.

In the countryside, white farm laborers struggled to purchase land in the face of low wages or, if they rented, unpredictable market prices for their crops. Scrimping, some climbed yeoman ranks. When James and Nancy Bennitt of North Carolina succeeded in their ten-year struggle to buy land, they avoided the unstable cotton market and raised extra corn and wheat for cash. People like the Bennitts were both participants in and victims of an economy dominated by cotton producers who relied on slave labor.

Herdsmen with pigs and other livestock faced a desperate struggle. By 1860, as the South anticipated war to preserve its society, between 300,000 and 400,000 white people in Virginia, North and South Carolina, and Georgia—approximately one-fifth of the total white population—lived in poverty. Land and slaves determined wealth in the Old South, and many whites possessed neither.

Yeomen's Demands and White Class Relations

Class tensions emerged in the western, nonslaveholding parts of the seaboard states by the 1830s. There, yeoman farmers resented their underrepresentation in state legislatures and the corruption in local government. Voters in the more recently settled states of the Old Southwest adopted white manhood suffrage and other electoral reforms, including popular election of governors, legislative apportionment based on white population only, and locally chosen county government. Slave owners with new wealth, however, were determined to hold the reins of power.

Historians have offered several explanations why tensions between slaveholders and nonslaveholders did not fuel greater conflict. One of the most important factors was race. The South's racial ideology stressed the superiority of all whites to blacks. Thus, slavery became the basis of equality among whites, and white privilege inflated the status of poor whites, giving them a common interest with the rich. The dream of upward mobility blunted some class conflict.

Most important, before the Civil War yeomen worked their farms and avoided debt, largely unhindered by slaveholding planters. Likewise, slaveholders pursued their goals independently of yeomen. Suppression of dissent also played an increasing role. After 1830, white southerners who criticized the slave system were intimidated, attacked, or rendered politically powerless in a society held together partly by white racial solidarity.

Still, there were signs of class conflict. As cotton lands filled up, nonslaveholders faced narrower economic prospects; meanwhile, wealthy planters enjoyed expanding profits. The risks of entering cotton production were becoming too great and the cost of slaves too high for many yeomen to rise in society. From 1830 to 1860, the percentage of white southern families holding slaves declined steadily, from 36 to 25 percent. Although slave owners were a minority in the white population, planters' share of the South's agricultural wealth remained between 90 and 95 percent.

Anticipating possible secession, slave owners stood secure. In the 1850s, they occupied from 50 to 85 percent of the seats in state legislatures and a similarly high percentage of the South's congressional seats. And planters' interests controlled all other major social institutions, such as churches and colleges.

Free Blacks

The nearly quarter-million free blacks in the South in 1860 often fared little better than slaves. Upper South free blacks were usually descendants of people manumitted by their owners in the 1780s and 1790s. A remarkable number of slaveholders in Virginia and the Chesapeake had freed their slaves because of religious principles and revolutionary ideals in the wake of American independence (see Chapter 7). Many free blacks also became free as runaways, especially by the 1830s. A small number purchased their own freedom.

Some free blacks worked in towns or cities, but most lived in rural areas and struggled to survive. They usually did not own land and labored in someone else's fields, often alongside slaves. By law, free blacks could not own a gun, buy liquor, violate curfew, assemble except in church, testify in court, or (throughout the South after 1835) vote. Despite these obstacles, a minority bought land, and others found jobs as skilled craftsmen, especially in cities.

A few free blacks prospered and bought slaves. In 1830, there were 3,775 free black slaveholders in the South; 80 percent lived in Louisiana, South Carolina, Virginia, and Maryland, and half of the total lived in New Orleans and Charleston. Most purchased their own wives and children, whom they could not free because laws required newly emancipated blacks to leave their state. To free family members they had purchased, hundreds of black slaveholders petitioned for exemption from anti-manumission laws. At the same time, a few mulattos in New Orleans were active slave traders. Although rare in the United States, the greed and the tragic quest for power that lay at the root of slavery could cross racial or ethnic barriers.

Free Black Communities

In the cotton belt and Gulf regions, a large proportion of free blacks were mulattos, the privileged offspring of wealthy white planters. Not all planters freed their mixed-race offspring, but those who did often gave their children a good education and financial backing. In cities like New Orleans, Charleston, and Mobile, extensive interracial sex, as well as migrations from the Caribbean, produced a mulatto population that was recognized as a distinct class.

In many southern cities by the 1840s, free black communities formed, especially around churches. By the late 1850s, Baltimore had fifteen such churches, Louisville nine, and Nashville and St. Louis four each—most of them African Methodist Episcopal. In 1840, Baltimore contained 17,967 free blacks and 3,199 slaves out of a total population of 102,313. These free people of color worked in menial jobs, from domestic servants to dockworkers and draymen, and they also suffered under a strict Black Code, denying civil or political rights and restricting their movements.

The Planters' World

How did cotton shape the lives of planters and their families?

At the top of the southern social pyramid were slaveholding planters. Most lived in comfortable farmhouses, not in the opulence that legend suggests. The grand plantation mansions with outlying slave quarters are an enduring symbol of the Old South. But in 1850, 50 percent of southern slaveholders had fewer than five slaves; 72 percent had fewer than ten; 88 percent had fewer than twenty. Thus, the average slaveholder was not a wealthy aristocrat but an aspiring farmer.

The Newly Rich

In the 1840s, newly rich Louisiana cotton planter Bennet Barrow was preoccupied with moneymaking. He worried about his cotton crop, and to overcome his worries, he hunted and had a passion for racing horses and raising hounds. He could report the loss of a slave without feeling, but became emotional when illness afflicted his sporting animals. His strongest feelings surfaced when his horse Jos Bell "broke down running a mile … ruined for Ever." The same day, Barrow gave his human property a "general Whipping."

The richest planters used their wealth to model genteel sophistication. Extended visits, parties, and balls to which women wore the latest fashions provided opportunities for friendship, courtship, and display. These entertainments were important diversions for plantation women, who relished social events to break the monotony of their domestic lives. Yet socializing also sustained a rigidly gendered society.

Most of the planters in the cotton-boom states of Alabama and Mississippi were newly rich by the 1840s. As one historian put it, "a number of men mounted from log cabin to plantation mansion on a stairway of cotton bales, accumulating slaves as they climbed." And many did not live like rich men. They put their new wealth into cotton acreage and slaves even as they sought refinement and high social status.

The cotton boom in the Mississippi Valley created one-generation aristocrats. A case in point is Greenwood Leflore, a Chocktaw chieftain who owned a plantation in Mississippi with four hundred slaves. After selling his cotton on the world market, he spent $10,000 in France to furnish a single room of his mansion with handwoven carpets, furniture upholstered with gold leaf, tables and cabinets ornamented with tortoiseshell inlay, a variety of mirrors and paintings, and a clock and candelabra of brass and ebony.

Social Status and Planters' Values

Slave ownership was the main determinant of wealth in the South. Slaves were a commodity and an investment, much like gold; people bought them on speculation, hoping for a rise in their market value. Many slaveholders mortgaged their slaves and used them as collateral. People who could not pay cash for slaves would ask the sellers to purchase the mortgage, just as banks give mortgages on houses today. The slaveholder would repay the loan in installments with interest.

The availability of slave labor tended to devalue free labor: where strenuous work under supervision was reserved for an enslaved race, few free people relished it. When Alexis de Tocqueville crossed from Ohio into Kentucky in his 1831 travels, he observed "On the right bank of the Ohio [River] everything is activity, industry; labor is honoured; there are no slaves. Pass to the left bank and the scene changes so suddenly… the enterprising spirit is gone. There, work is not only painful; it is shameful."

Aristocratic values—lineage, privilege, pride, honor, and refinement of person and manner—commanded respect throughout the South. Many of those qualities were in short supply, however, in the recently settled portions of the cotton kingdom, where frontier values of courage and self-reliance ruled during the 1820s and 1830s. By the 1850s, a settled aristocratic group of planters did rule, however, much of the Mississippi Valley.

Aristocratic planters expected to wield power and receive deference from poorer whites. But the independent yeoman class resented infringements of its rights, and many yeomen belonged to evangelical faiths that exalted simplicity and condemned the planters' wealth. Much of the planters' power and claims to leadership were, after all, built on their assumption of a monopoly on world cotton and a foundation of black slave labor.

King Cotton in a Global Economy

The American South so dominated the world's supply of cotton that southern planters gained enormous confidence that the cotton boom was permanent and that the industrializing nations of England and France would always bow to **King Cotton**.

King Cotton Term expressing the southern belief that the U.S. and British economies depended on cotton, making it "king."

American cotton production doubled in yield each decade after 1800 and provided three-fourths of the world's supply by the 1840s. Southern staple crops were three-fifths of American exports by 1850, and one of seven workers in England depended on American cotton for a job. Cotton production made slaves the most valuable financial asset in the United States—greater than banks, railroads, and manufacturing combined. In 1860 dollars, the slaves' total value as property equaled an estimated $3.5 billion (roughly $75 billion in early twenty-first-century dollars).

"Cotton is King," the *Southern Cultivator* declared in 1859. Until 1840, cotton furnished much of the export capital to finance northern economic growth. After that, the northern economy expanded without dependence on cotton profits. Nevertheless, southerners boasted of King Cotton's supremacy. "No power on earth dares…to make war on cotton," James Hammond lectured the U.S. Senate in 1858. Although the South produced 4.5 million bales in 1861, its greatest cotton crop ever, such world dominance was about to collapse.

Paternalism

Slaveholding men often embraced a paternalistic ideology that justified their dominance over black slaves and white women. They stressed their obligations, viewing themselves as custodians of society and of the black families they owned. The paternalistic planter saw himself not as an oppressor but as the benevolent guardian of an inferior race.

Paul Carrington Cameron, North Carolina's largest slaveholder, exemplifies this mentality. After a period of sickness among his one thousand North Carolina slaves (he had hundreds more in Alabama and Mississippi), Cameron wrote, "I fear the Negroes have suffered much from the want of proper attention and kindness under this late distemper no love of lucre shall ever induce me to be cruel." He later described to his sister his sense of responsibility: "Do you remember a cold & frosty morning, during [our mother's] illness, when she said to me Paul my son the people ought to be shod' this is ever in my ears, whenever I see any ones shoes in bad order; and in my ears it will be, so long as I am master."

This comforting self-image let rich planters obscure the harsh dimensions of slave treatment. And slaves—accommodating to the realities of power—encouraged masters to think that their benevolence was appreciated. Paternalism also served as a defense against abolitionist criticism. In reality, paternalism grew as a give-and-take relationship between masters and slaves—owners took labor from the bondsmen, while slaves sought to obligate masters to provide them a measure of autonomy and living space.

But Cameron's benevolence vanished with changed circumstances. After the Civil War, he bristled at African Americans' efforts to be free and made sweeping economic decisions without regard for their welfare. Writing on Christmas Day 1865, Cameron showed little Christian charity (but a healthy profit motive) when he declared, "I am convinced that the people who gets rid of the free negro first will be the first to advance in improved agriculture. Have made no effort to retain any of mine." He turned off his land nearly a thousand black people, rented his fields to several white farmers, and invested in industry.

Relations between men and women in the planter class were similarly defined by paternalism. The upper-class southern woman was raised to be a wife, mother, and subordinate companion to men. South Carolina's Mary Boykin Chesnut wrote of her husband, "He is master of the house....All the comfort of my life depends upon his being in a good humor." Women found it difficult to challenge society's rules on sexual or racial relations.

Planters' daughters usually attended one of the South's rapidly multiplying boarding schools. Typically, the young woman could entertain suitors whom her parents approved. But she quickly had to choose a husband and commit herself to a man whom she generally had known only briefly. Young women had to follow the wishes of their family, especially their father.

Upon marriage, a planter-class woman ceded to her husband most of her legal rights, becoming part of his family. She was isolated on a large plantation, where she supervised the cooking and preserving of food, managed the house, watched children, and attended sick slaves. These realities were more confining on the frontier, where isolation was greater. Men on plantations could occasionally escape into the public realm—to town, business, or politics. Women could retreat from rural plantation culture only into kinship and associations with other women.

Virginia Luxuries, *folk painting, artist unknown.* Abby Aldrich Rockefeller Folk Art Museum, the Colonial Williamsburg Foundation.

Abby Aldrich Rockefeller Folk Art Museum, The Colonial Williamsburg Foundation. Museum Purchase

Marriage and Family Among Planters

A perceptive young white woman approached marriage with anxiety. Lucy Breckinridge, a wealthy Virginia girl of twenty, lamented the autonomy she surrendered at the altar. In her diary, she recorded: "A woman's life after she is married, unless there is an immense amount of love, is nothing but suffering and hard work."

Childbearing often involved grief, poor health, and death. In 1840, the birth rate for white southern women was almost 30 percent higher than the national average. The average southern white woman would bear eight children in 1800; by 1860, the figure had decreased to only six. Childbirth complications were a major cause of death, occurring twice as often in the hot South as in the Northeast.

Sexual relations between planters and slaves were another problem that white women endured but were not supposed to notice. "Violations of the moral law ... made mulattos as common as blackberries," protested a woman in Georgia, but wives had to play "the ostrich game." Such habits produced a large mixed race population by the 1850s.

In the 1840s and 1850s, as abolitionist attacks on slavery increased, southern men published several articles stressing that women should restrict their concerns to the home. The *Southern Quarterly Review* declared, "The proper place for a woman is at home. One of her highest privileges is to be politically merged in the existence of her husband."

But a study of women in Petersburg, Virginia, a large tobacco-manufacturing town, revealed behavior that valued financial autonomy. Over several decades before 1860, the proportion of women who never married, or did not remarry after a spouse's death, grew to exceed 33 percent. Likewise, the number of women who worked for wages, controlled their own property, and ran dressmaking businesses increased.

Slave Life and Labor

What was the true nature of the master-slave relationship?

Slaves knew a life of poverty, coercion, toil, and resentment. They provided the strength and know-how to build an agricultural empire. But they embodied a fundamental contradiction: in the world's model republic, slaves were on the wrong side of a brutally unequal power relationship.

Slaves' Everyday Conditions

Southern slaves enjoyed few material comforts. Although they generally had enough to eat, their diet was monotonous and nonnutritious. Clothing was coarse and inexpensive. Few slaves received more than two changes of clothing for hot and cold seasons and one blanket each winter. Children of both sexes ran naked in hot weather and wore long cotton shirts in winter. Many slaves went without shoes until December. Conditions were better in cities, where slaves frequently lived in the same dwelling as their owners and were regularly hired out, enabling them to accumulate their own money.

On plantations, the average slave lived in a crude, one-room cabin. Each dwelling housed one or two families. Crowding and lack of sanitation spread infection and such contagious diseases as typhoid fever, malaria, and dysentery. White plantation doctors were hired to care for sick slaves, and some "slave doctors" attained a degree of power in the quarters and with masters by healing through herbalism and spiritualism.

Slave Work Routines

Long hours and large work gangs characterized Gulf Coast cotton districts. Overseers rang the morning bell before dawn, and black people, tools in hand, walked toward the fields. Slaves who cultivated tobacco in the Upper South worked long hours picking the sticky, sometimes noxious, leaves under harsh discipline. As one woman recalled when interviewed in the 1930s, "it was way after sundown fore they could stop that field work. Then they had to hustle to finish their night work [such as watering livestock or cleaning cotton] in time for supper, or go to bed without it."

Working "from sun to sun" became a norm in much of the South. Profit took precedence over paternalism. Slave women did heavy fieldwork, even during pregnancy. Old people cared for young children, doing light chores, or carding, ginning, and spinning cotton.

South Carolina and Georgia low country planters used a **task system** whereby slaves were assigned measured amounts of work to be performed in a given time period. So much cotton per day was to be picked from a designated field, so many rows hoed or plowed in a specified section. Upon completion, slaves' time was their own for working garden plots, tending hogs, even hiring out their own labor. From this experience, many slaves developed a sense of property ownership.

Of the 1860 population of 4 million slaves, fully half were under the age of sixteen. "A child raised every two years," wrote Thomas Jefferson, "is of more profit than the crop of the best laboring man." In 1858, a slave owner writing in an agricultural magazine calculated that a slave girl purchased in 1827 for $400 had borne three sons now worth $3,000 as field hands. Slave children gathered kindling, carried water to the fields, swept the yard, lifted cut sugar-cane stalks into carts, stacked wheat, chased birds away from sprouting rice plants, and labored in cotton and tobacco production.

As slave children matured, they faced psychological traumas including powerlessness and an awareness that their parents could not protect them. They had to fight to keep from internalizing what whites labeled their inferiority. Many former slaves resented their denial of education. And for girls reaching maturity, the potential trauma of sexual abuse loomed.

task system Labor system in which each slave had a daily or weekly quota of tasks to complete.

Link to *Twelve Years a Slave* by Solomon Northup, 1853

Violence and Intimidation Against Slaves

Whites throughout the South believed that slaves "can't be governed except with the whip." One South Carolinian explained to a northern journalist that he whipped his slaves regularly, because "the fear of the lash kept them in good order." Evidence suggests that whippings were less frequent on small farms than on large plantations. But beatings symbolized authority to the master and tyranny to the slaves, who used them to evaluate a master. Former slaves said a good owner was one who did not "whip too much," whereas a bad owner "whipped till he's bloodied you and blistered you."

The master wielded absolute authority on his plantation. Slaveholders rarely had to answer to the law or to the state. Yet physical cruelty may have been less prevalent in the United States than in other slaveholding parts of the New World. Especially in some of the Caribbean sugar islands, death rates from violence were so high that the heavily male slave population shrank. In the United States, the slave population experienced a steady natural increase, as births exceeded deaths.

The worst evil of American slavery was the nature of slavery itself: coercion, belonging to another person, and having virtually no hope for change. Recalling their time in bondage, some former slaves emphasized the physical abuse, memories focused on the tyranny of whipping as much as the pain. Delia Garlic made the point: "It's bad to belong to folks that own you soul an' body...you couldn't guess the awfulness of it." To be a slave was to be the object of another person's will and material gain, as the saying went, "from the cradle to the grave."

Most American slaves retained their mental independence and self-respect despite their bondage. They had to be subservient and speak honeyed words to their masters, but they talked and behaved differently among themselves. In *Narrative of the Life of Frederick Douglass, an American Slave, Written by Himself* (1845), **Frederick Douglass** wrote that most slaves, when asked about "their condition and the character of their masters, almost universally say they are contented, and that their masters are kind." Slaves did this, said Douglass, because they were governed by the maxim that "a still tongue makes a wise head."

Frederick Douglass
A former slave who was the leading black abolitionist during the antebellum period.

Slave-Master Relationships

Some former slaves remembered warm feelings between masters and slaves, but the prevailing attitudes were distrust and antagonism. One woman said her mistress was "a mighty good somebody to belong to" but only "'cause she was raisin' us to work for her."

Slaves were alert to the daily signs of their degraded status. One man recalled the general rule that slaves ate cornbread and owners ate biscuits. If blacks did get biscuits, "the flour that we made the biscuits out of was the third-grade sorts." If the owner took his slaves' garden produce to town to sell for them, slaves often suspected him of pocketing part of the profits.

Suspicion often grew into hatred. When a yellow fever epidemic struck in 1852, many slaves saw it as God's retribution. An elderly ex-slave named Minnie Fulkes cherished the conviction that God was going to punish white people for their cruelty to blacks. On the plantation, of course, slaves had to keep such thoughts to themselves and created many ways to survive and to sustain their humanity in this world of repression.

Slave Culture and Resistance

How did slaves adapt Christianity to make it their own?

The resource that enabled slaves to maintain defiance was their culture: beliefs, values, and practices born of their past and maintained in the present. As best they could, they built a community knitted together by stories, music, a religious worldview, leadership, the smells of their cooking, the sounds of their voices, and the tapping of their feet. "The values expressed in folklore," wrote African American poet Sterling Brown, provided a "wellspring to which slaves … could return in times of doubt to be refreshed."

African Cultural Survival

Slave culture changed significantly after 1808, when Congress banned further importation of slaves and the generations born in Africa died out. South Carolina illegally reopened the international slave trade, but by the 1830s, the majority of slaves in the South were native-born Americans.

Yet African influences remained strong. Some slave men plaited their hair into rows and designs; slave women often wore their hair tied in small bunches secured by a string or piece of cloth. A few men and many women wrapped their heads in kerchiefs of the styles and colors of West Africa.

Music, religion, and folktales were part of daily life for slaves. Borrowing from their African background and forging new American folkways, they developed what scholars have called a sacred worldview, which affected work, leisure, and self-understanding. Slaves made musical instruments with carved motifs that resembled African stringed instruments. One visitor to Georgia in the 1860s described an African ritual dance called the ring shout: "A ring of singers is formed.... They then utter a kind of melodious chant, which gradually increases in strength, and in noise, until it fairly shakes the house, and it can be heard for a long distance."

Many slaves continued to believe in spirit possession. While whites believed in ghosts and charms, slaves' belief resembled the African concept of the living dead—deceased relatives visiting the earth for years until the process of dying is complete. Slaves also practiced conjuration and quasi-magical root medicine. By the 1850s, noted conjurers and root doctors were reputed to live in South Carolina, Georgia, Louisiana, and other isolated coastal areas with high slave populations.

As they became African Americans, slaves increasingly developed a racial identity. In the colonial period, Africans arrived in America from many states and kingdoms, represented in distinctive languages and traditions. Africans landed in the New World with virtually no concept of "race;" by the antebellum era, their descendants had learned through bitter experience that race was the defining feature of their lives.

Slaves' Religion and Music

Over time, more and more slaves adopted Christianity, fashioning it into an instrument of support and resistance. Theirs was a religion of justice and deliverance, quite unlike their masters' religious propaganda. "You ought to have heard that preachin,'" said one man. "'Obey your master and mistress, don't steal chickens and eggs and meat,' but nary a word about havin' a soul to save." In slaves' interpretations of biblical stories, as one historian has said, they were "willing themselves reborn."

Devout slaves worshipped every day. Some slaves held secret prayer meetings that lasted into the night. Many nurtured the belief that God would end their bondage. This faith—and the emotional release that accompanied worship—sustained them.

Slaves also adapted Christianity to African practices. In West African belief, devotees are possessed by a god so thoroughly that the god's personality replaces the human personality. In the late antebellum era, Christian slaves experienced possession by the Protestant "Holy Spirit." The combination of shouting, singing, and dancing that seemed to overtake black worshippers formed the heart of their religious faith. "The old meeting house caught fire," recalled an ex-slave preacher. "The spirit was there.... God saw our need and came to us." In brush arbors or meetinghouses, slaves thrust their arms to heaven, made music with their feet, and sang away their woes.

Rhythm and physical movement were crucial to slaves' religious experience. In black preachers' chanted sermons, an American tradition was born. The chanted sermon was a scriptural message and patterned form that required audience response punctuated by "yes sirs!" and "amens!" But through song the slaves left their most sublime gift to American culture.

Through the spirituals, slaves tried to impose order on the chaos of their lives. Often referred to later as the "sorrow songs," lyrics covered many themes, including imminent rebirth. Sadness could give way to joy: "Oh, Oh, Freedom/Oh, Oh, Freedom over me—/But before I'll be a slave,/I'll be buried in my grave,/And go home to my Lord,/And Be Free!"

Many songs also express intimacy and closeness with God. Some display rebelliousness, such as the enduring "He said, and if I had my way/If I had my way, if I had my way,/I'd tear this building down!" And some spirituals reached for a collective sense of hope in the black community.

> O, gracious Lord! When shall it be,
> That we poor souls shall all be free;
> Lord, break them slavery powers—
> Will you go along with me?
> Lord break them slavery powers,
> Go sound the jubilee!

In many ways, American slaves converted the Christian God to themselves. They sought an alternative world—a home other than the earthly one fate had given them. With variations on the Br'er Rabbit folktales—in which the weak survive by wit and power is reversed—and in songs, they fashioned survival from their own cultural imagination.

The Black Family in Slavery

Although American law did not recognize slave families, slave owners *expected* slaves to form families and have children. As a result, there was a normal ratio of men to women, young to old. On some of the largest South Carolina cotton plantations, when masters allowed their slaves increased autonomy through the task system, the property accumulation in livestock, tools, and garden produce led to more stable and healthier families.

Following African kinship traditions, African Americans avoided marriage between cousins (commonplace among aristocratic slave owners). By naming their children after relatives of past generations, African Americans emphasized family histories. Kinship networks and extended families held life together in many slave communities.

For slave women, sexual abuse and rape by white masters were ever-present threats. By 1860, there were 405,751 mulattos in the United States, comprising 12.5 percent of the African American population. White planters were sometimes open with their behavior toward slave women, but not in the way they talked about it. Buying slaves for sex was common at the New Orleans slave market. In what was called the "fancy trade" (a "fancy" was a young, attractive slave girl), females were sold for prices as much as 300 percent higher than average. At such auctions, slaveholders exhibited some of the ugliest values of the slave system by paying $3,000 to $5,000 for female "companions."

Slave women like Harriet Jacobs spent years dodging their owners' sexual pursuit. In recollecting her desperate effort to protect her children, Jacobs asked a haunting question: "Why does the slave ever love? Why allow the tendrils of the heart to twine around objects which may at any moment be wrenched away by the hand of violence?"

The Domestic Slave Trade

Slave families most feared and hated separation by violence from those they loved, sexual appropriation, and sale. Many struggled to keep their children together and, after emancipation, to reestablish contact with loved ones lost by forced migration and sale. Between 1820 and 1860, roughly 2 million slaves were moved into the region from western Georgia to eastern Texas. When the Union army registered thousands of black marriages in Mississippi and Louisiana in 1864 and 1865, 25 percent of the men over age forty reported that they had been forcibly separated from a previous wife. Thousands of black families were disrupted annually to serve the expanding cotton economy.

Many antebellum white southerners made their living from the slave trade. In South Carolina by the 1850s, there were more than one hundred slave-trading firms selling approximately 6,500 slaves annually to southwestern states. One 1858 estimate indicated that slave sales in Richmond, Virginia, that year netted $4 million. A market guide to 1858 Richmond slave sales listed average prices for "likely ploughboys," ages twelve to fourteen, at $850 to $1,050; "extra number 1 fieldgirls" at $1,300 to $1,350; and "extra number 1 men" at $1,500.

At slave "pens" in cities like New Orleans, traders promoted "a large and commodious showroom … prepared to accommodate over 200 Negroes for sale." Traders made slaves appear young, healthy, and happy, cutting gray whiskers off men; using paddles as discipline to avoid scarring their merchandise; and forcing people to dance and sing as buyers arrived. When transported to the southwestern markets, slaves were often chained together, making journeys of 500 miles or more on foot.

Missouri Historical Museum

The complacent mixture of racism and business among traders is evident in their own language. "I refused a girl 20 year[s] old at 700 yesterday," one trader wrote in 1853. "She is very badly whipped but good teeth." Some sales were transacted at owners' requests, often for tragically inhumane reasons. "Bought a cook yesterday that was to go out of state," wrote a trader; "she just made the people mad that was all."

Strategies of Resistance

Slaves brought to their resistance the same common sense and determination that characterized their struggle to secure family lives. The scales weighed against overt revolution, but they seized opportunities to alter work conditions. They sometimes slacked off when they were not watched. Daily discontent and desperation were also manifest in equipment sabotage; carelessness about work; theft of food, livestock, or crops; or getting drunk on stolen liquor. A woman named Ellen, hired as a cook in Tennessee in 1856, put mercury poison into a roasted apple for her unsuspecting mistress. And some slave women

A bill of sale documents that this slave woman, Louisa, was owned by the young child whom she holds on her lap. In the future, Louisa's life would be subject to the child's wishes and decisions.

resisted by trying to control their own pregnancy, either by avoiding it or by seeking to improve their conditions.

Male, and some female, slaves sometimes violently attacked overseers or owners. Southern court records and newspapers contain accounts of these resistant slaves who contradicted the image of the docile bondsman. Rebels were customarily flogged, sold, or hanged. Many slaves attempted to run away to the North, and some received assistance from the loose network known as the Underground Railroad (see page 348). But it was more common for slaves to run off temporarily to hide in the woods. Approximately 80 percent of runaways were male; children prevented women from fleeing. Fear, disgruntlement over treatment, or family separation might motivate slaves to flee. Only a minority made it to freedom in the North, but these fugitives made slavery an insecure institution by the 1850s.

American slavery also produced fearless revolutionaries. Gabriel's Rebellion involved about a thousand slaves when it was discovered in 1800, before it would have exploded in Richmond, Virginia (see page 193). According to controversial court testimony, a similar conspiracy existed in Charleston in 1822, led by Denmark Vesey, a free black. Born a slave in the Caribbean, Vesey won a lottery of $1,500 in 1799, bought his freedom, and became a religious leader. According to one long-argued interpretation, Vesey was a heroic revolutionary determined to free his people. But in a recent challenge, historian Michael Johnson notes that the court testimony is the only reliable source on the alleged insurrection. Might the testimony reveal less of reality than of white South Carolina's fears of slave rebellion? The court, says Johnson, built its case on rumors and intimidated witnesses, and "conjured into being" an insurrection that was not truly about to occur. Nonetheless, thirty-seven "conspirators" were executed, and more than three dozen others were banished from the state.

Nat Turner A slave who led a bloody rebellion in Southampton County, Virginia, in 1831.

Nat Turner's Insurrection

The most famous rebel, **Nat Turner**, struck for freedom in Southampton County, Virginia, in 1831. The son of a woman who passionately hated her enslavement and a father who escaped to freedom, Turner learned to read as a child and was encouraged by his first owner to study the Bible. He enjoyed certain privileges but also endured hard work and changes of masters.

Young Nat became a preacher known for eloquence and mysticism. After planning for years, Turner led rebels from farm to farm in the predawn darkness of August 22, 1831. The group severed limbs and crushed skulls with axes or shot victims. Before planters stopped them, Nat Turner and his followers had in forty-eight hours slaughtered sixty whites. In retaliation whites randomly killed slaves across the region, and Turner was caught and hanged. As many as two hundred African Americans lost their lives as a result of the rebellion.

Nat Turner remains a haunting symbol in America's unresolved history of racial slavery and discrimination. While in jail, Turner was interviewed by Virginia lawyer and slaveholder, Thomas R. Gray. Their intriguing creation, *The Confessions of Nat Turner*, became a best seller within a month of Turner's hanging. Gray called the rebel a "gloomy fanatic," but in a manner that made him fascinating and produced one of the most remarkable documents of American slavery. After Turner's insurrection, many states passed stiffened legal codes against black education and religious practice.

Visualizing THE PAST

Imaging Nat Turner's Rebellion

Below is the title page from *The Confessions of Nat Turner,* by Thomas R. Gray, 1831. This nearly twenty-page document was published by the lawyer who recorded and likely refashioned Turner's lengthy statement during an interview in his jail cell before his execution. *The Confessions* became a widely sold and sensational documentation of Turner's identity and his motivations and methods during the rebellion. It portrayed Turner as a religious mystic and fanatic and allowed the public to imagine the mind of a religiously motivated slave rebel. Below and to the right is "Horrid Massacre in Virginia," 1831, woodcut. This composite of scenes depicts the slaughter of innocent women and children, as well as white men as victims and resistants. The fear, confusion, and retribution that dominated the aftermath of the Turner rebellion are on display here. Why was Nat Turner's insurrection such a shock to the nation as well as to the South? What kind of impact did Nat Turner's rebellion have on the South's evolving defense of slavery in the coming decades?

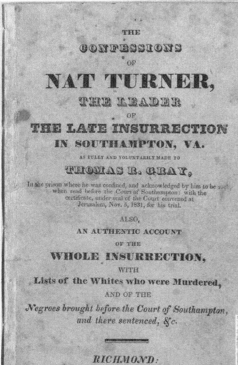

Everett Collection

Library of Congress

Reparations for Slavery

How should the United States come to terms with 250 years of racial slavery? Is this period best forgotten as a terrible passage, or does the nation owe a long-overdue debt to black people for their oppression? After emancipation in 1865, and rooted in vague federal promises, many former slaves believed they were entitled to "forty acres and a mule," but these never materialized.

In 1897, Callie House, a poor mother of four born in 1865 in a contraband camp for ex-slaves, organized the National Ex-Slave Pension and Bounty Association, modeled after soldiers' pension systems. House traveled throughout the South, recruiting 250,000 members at 10-cent dues. Her lobbying of the federal government for slave pensions failed; she was accused of mail fraud and imprisoned for one year in 1916.

More recently, widespread debate over "reparations" for slavery has emerged. In the rewriting of slavery's history since the 1960s, Americans have learned how slave labor created American wealth: how insurance companies insured slaves, how complicit the U.S. government was in slavery's expansion, and how slaves built the U.S. Capitol while their owners received $5 a month for their labor.

The debate is fueled by analogies: reparations paid to Japanese Americans interned during World War II; reparations paid to Native American tribes for stolen land; the reparations paid to Holocaust survivors; and a suit settled in 1999 that will pay an estimated $2 billion to some twenty thousand black farmers for discrimination by the Agriculture Department in the early twentieth century.

Some argue that, because there are no living former slaves or slaveholders, reparations can never take the form of money. But in 2002, a lawsuit was filed against three major corporations that allegedly profited from slavery, and the National Reparations Coordinating Committee promises a suit against the U.S. government. Some city councils have passed resolutions forcing companies in their jurisdictions to investigate possible past complicity with slave trading or ownership, prompting some firms to establish scholarship programs for African Americans.

Critics argue that resources would be better spent "making sure black kids have a credible education" and rebuilding inner cities. Advocates contend that, when "government participates in a crime against humanity," it is "obliged to make the victims whole." The movement for reparations has sparked broad public debate. The legacy of slavery for a people and a nation promises to become America's most traumatic test of how to reconcile its history with justice.

Most important, in 1832 a shocked Virginia held a legislative and public debate over gradual emancipation to rid itself of slavery and of blacks. The plan would not have freed any slaves until 1858 and provided that eventually all blacks would be colonized outside Virginia. When the House of Delegates voted, gradual abolition lost, 73 to 58. Virginia merely reinforced its defense of slavery. It was the last time white southerners would debate emancipation until war forced their hand.

Summary

During the four decades before the Civil War, the South grew in land, wealth, and power along with the rest of the country. Although southern states were enmeshed in the nation's heritage and political economy, they also developed as a distinctive region, ideologically and economically, because of slavery. More than the North, the antebellum South was a biracial society; whites grew up influenced by black folkways and culture; and blacks, the vast majority of whom were slaves, became cobuilders of a rural, agricultural society.

With the cotton boom and state and federal policies of Indian removal, the South became a huge slave society. The coercive influence of slavery affected southern life and politics and increasingly produced a leadership determined to preserve a hierarchical social and racial order. Despite their shared white supremacy, yeomen's democratic values often clashed with aristocratic planters' profit motives. Slaveholders' benevolent self-image and paternalistic ideology was tested by slaves' own judgments. African American slaves responded by fashioning a rich folk culture and a religion of deliverance. Their experiences could differ regionally and by labor type. Some blacks were crushed by bondage; others transcended it through survival and resistance.

By 1850, through their wits and on the backs of African labor, white southerners had aggressively built one of the last profitable, expanding slave societies on earth. North of them and deeply intertwined with them in the same nation, economy, constitutional system, and history, a different kind of society had grown even faster—driven by industrialism and free labor. The clash of these two deeply connected—yet mutually divided societies—would soon explode in political storms over the nation's future.

Chapter Review

The "Distinctive" South

What made the antebellum South different from the North?

Both regions were capitalist and Christian (largely Protestant) and embraced the heroes and causes of the American Revolution. They were also roughly the same physical size. But they differed in their economic development: because of its climate and longer growing season, the South's development was agricultural and rural, whereas the North became increasingly urban and industrial. With a comparatively low population density and people spread out from each other, the South had little income for developing its commercial, educational, and health-related institutions. The South was also slower to develop a regional transportation network and relied on slaves for labor and the North for banking and shipping of its products. The South had fewer urban areas, and those that existed were primarily port cities, such as Charleston, that provided a link for commerce and small manufacturing. With few labor opportunities, the South also did not attract as many immigrants as the North.

Southern Expansion, Indian Resistance, and Removal

How did Native Americans living in western territories respond to increasing migration by southern whites?

Indians dealt with white encroachment on their land in several ways. Some embraced accommodation, establishing trading posts to exchange supplies with settlers, often ultimately falling into heavy debt that could only be repaid by selling their land. Others resisted, rejecting removal/relocation plans that whites offered, and holding fast to their land. The Creeks and Cherokees assimilated to American standards—even changed their political structure to more closely resemble that of whites—in an effort to keep their land. When Congress narrowly passed the Indian Removal Act in 1830, which provided funds to relocate Indians to territory farther west, the Cherokees refused to leave and sued the state of Georgia in federal court. While the courts found them entitled to their land, President Andrew Jackson ignored the ruling and sent in troops to evacuate thousands of Cherokees and march them from Georgia to present-day

Oklahoma. Many refused to go and were imprisoned; others died of disease and exhaustion on the trek known as the Trail of Tears.

Social Pyramid in the Old South

What class tensions emerged in the antebellum South?

Although they were fewer in number, the slaveholding planter class occupied the highest rungs of southern society and dominated its political life (controlling up to 85 percent of legislative posts) as well as churches and colleges. Before the 1830s, the vast socioeconomic differences between rich planters and small, independent, nonslaveholding yeomen farmers were mediated by their shared racial status as white. However, tensions emerged as yeomen began to resent their underrepresentation in state government and the corruption of local governments. They sought universal manhood suffrage and other reforms, including popular election of governors and legislative apportionment based solely on the white population—all of which planters resisted. Moreover, as cotton farming made land less and less available, nonslaveholders faced fewer opportunities to improve their station, while planters enjoyed greater and greater profits.

The Planters' World

How did cotton shape the lives of planters and their families?

Cotton production touched every aspect of slave society; during the boom years, it made many families rich. Most, however, lived in farmhouses and not the mansions of legend. Wealth in the cotton south was measured in terms of slave ownership; planters typically put their profits back into slaves and land. Along with a racial hierarchy, the society was also organized in terms of class and gender. White elites expected deference from poorer whites (though many yeomen resisted). Elite women were to be wives, mothers and subordinate to men, who were masters of the entire household. When a woman married, her legal and property rights were ceded to her husband. Women often felt isolated, their relationships restricted to family and other women, while men could engage in the broader world of business and politics. Slaveholding men justified their dominance over black slaves and wives and children via an ideology of paternalism, viewing themselves as custodians of their families, which

included slaves. The truth of their treatment of slaves and wives often made a lie of such paternalism, however.

Slave Life and Labor

What was the true nature of the master-slave relationship?

Generally speaking, slaves' lives belied the paternalism white masters claimed. They enjoyed few material comforts, occupying one-room cabins, often with other families. They were worked long, arduous days into the night, and while they typically had enough to eat, their diet was not nutritious. Slaves in the task system could be hired out once they completed assigned chores and were sometimes allowed to keep a portion of what they earned. But instead of being truly treated as family members, most slaves were recognized as property upon which wealth for whites could be built. Profit was the primary definer of master-slave relationships. There was also much cruelty and brutality—rather than paternalism—on the part of many owners, including whippings and the rape of slave women. Slave families were often separated, as one or more members were sold away to other plantations. For slaves, the vulnerability and frustration of being owned and at the mercy of another human being, along with being used for harsh physical labor, sparked resentment, resistance, and sometimes outright rebellion.

Slave Culture and Resistance

How did slaves adapt Christianity to make it their own?

While many slaves maintained and adapted aspects of the African heritage to their new circumstances, they also embraced and remade Christianity as a form of resistance. In secret prayer meetings, slaves focused on justice and deliverance, believing God would liberate them from their servitude and exact retribution from those who unjustly enslaved or abused them. They also merged their Christianity with African practices, adding shouting, singing, dancing, and other rituals to their religious meetings, along with chanted sermons, which were regarded as vital for the conversion experience. Their religious rituals not only attempted to restore order and meaning to their lives but also to establish closeness with God and hope for the future. Finally, while prayer meetings were often held in secret, they helped forge relationships and community in slave quarters.

Suggestions for Further Reading

Ira Berlin, *Generations of Captivity: A History of African American Slaves* (2003)

David Brion Davis, *Inhuman Bondage: The Rise and Fall of Slavery in the New World* (2006)

Erskine Clarke, *Dwelling Place: A Plantation Epic* (2005)

Steven Deyle, *Carry Me Back: The Domestic Slave Trade in American Life* (2005)

Annette Gordon-Reed, *The Hemingses of Monticello: An American Family* (2008)

Walter Johnson, *Soul by Soul: Life Inside the Antebellum Slave Market* (1999)

Charles Joyner, *Down by the Riverside: A South Carolina Slave Community* (1984)

James D. Miller, *South by Southwest: Planter Emigration and Identity in the Slave South* (2002)

James Oakes, *Slavery and Freedom: An Interpretation of the Old South* (1991)

Michael O'Brien, *Conjectures of Order: Intellectual Life and the American South, 1810–1860*, 2 vols. (2004)

Seth Rockman, *Scraping By: Wage Labor, Slavery, and Survival in Early Baltimore* (2009)

Daniel H. Usner Jr., *American Indians in the Lower Mississippi Valley* (1998)

The Restless North

1815–1860

After 25 stormy days at sea, Mary Ann and James Archbald and their four children finally arrived in New York on April 17, 1807. The couple left their ancestral homeland in Scotland, envisioning a bright future in which their children would be beholden to no one—neither landlord nor employer. They were pursuing the Jeffersonian dream of republican independence.

The Archbalds bought a farm in central New York, along a Hudson River tributary, where they raised sheep, grew hay and vegetables, skinned rabbits for meat and fur—and then sold whatever they did not need. From the wool shorn by her husband and sons, Mary Ann and her daughters spun thread and wove cloth for their own use and for sale. They used the cash to pay their mortgage. Twenty-one years after leaving Scotland, Mary Ann, in anticipation of making their last payment, declared: "being out of debt is, in my estimation, being rich." By then, her sons were young adults with visions of wealth that centered on water, not land.

On April 17, 1817—a decade after the Archbalds reached American shores—the New York State legislature authorized construction of a canal connecting Lake Erie to the Hudson River, and surveyors mapped a route through the Archbalds' farm. The sons helped dig the canal, while Mary Ann and her daughters cooked and cleaned for the twenty Irish laborers whom the sons hired. The Archbald sons soon tried commercial speculation, borrowing money to buy wheat and lumber in western New York to resell it at substantial profits to merchants in Albany and New York City. As early as 1808, Mary Ann had reached an unpleasant conclusion about her new home: "We are a nation of traders in spite of all Mr. Jefferson can say or do."

After the War of 1812, the market economy took off in unanticipated ways. In the North, steamboats, canals, and then railroads remapped the young republic's geography and economy, setting off booms in westward migration, industry, commerce, and urban growth.

Chapter Outline

Or Was the North Distinctive?

The Transportation Revolution
 Roads | Steamboats | Canals | Railroads | Regional Connections | Ambivalence Toward Progress

Factories and Industrialization
 Factory Work | Textile Mills | Labor Protests | Labor Unions

LINKS TO THE WORLD *Internal Improvements*

Consumption and Commercialization
 The Garment Industry | Specialization of Commerce | Commercial Farming | Farm Women's Changing Labor | Rural Communities | Cycles of Boom and Bust

Families in Flux
 The "Ideal" Family | Shrinking Families | Women's Paid Labor

The Growth of Cities
 Urban Boom | Market-Related Development | Extremes of Wealth | Immigration | Ethnic Tensions | People of Color | Urban Culture | The Penny Press | Cities as Symbols of Progress

Revivals and Reform
 Revivals | Moral Reform | Penitentiaries and Asylums | Temperance | Public Schools | Engineering and Science

VISUALIZING THE PAST *Engaging Children*

Utopian Experiments
 Mormons | Shakers | Oneidans, Owenites, and Fourierists | American Renaissance

Still, even after the War of 1812, the United States' financial connections to Europe, particularly Britain, remained profound. When Europeans suffered hard times, so did American merchants, manufacturers, farmers, and workers. For wage-earning Americans, economic downturns meant unemployment and destitution.

The economy's rapid expansion following the War of 1812 inspired fears that, if not properly controlled, market growth would threaten the nation's moral fiber. It upset traditional family patterns and relied on unskilled workers—often immigrants and free African Americans—who seemed unfit for republican citizenship. Commercially minded Americans saw cities as exemplars of civilization and breeding grounds of depravity. Anxious about the era's rapid changes, many Americans turned to evangelical religion, which in turn inspired reform movements.

Only through faith in improvement, progress, and upward mobility could Americans remain hopeful that the nation's greatness lay with commercial expansion. They did so partly by articulating a free-labor ideology that rationalized the negative aspects of market expansion while promoting the northern labor system as superior to the South's.

As you read this chapter, keep the following questions in mind:

- **What factors contributed to the commercialization of northern society, and why did they have less of an influence on the South?**

- **How did the daily lives—work, family, leisure—of northerners (rural and urban) change between 1815 and 1860?**

- **In what ways did reformers try to preserve existing American ideals and in what ways did they try to change them?**

Abolitionism
  Evangelical Abolitionism | *The American Antislavery Society* | *African American Abolitionists* | *Opposition to Abolitionism* | *Moral Suasion Versus Political Action* | *Free-Labor Ideology*

LEGACY FOR A PEOPLE AND A NATION
P. T. Barnum's Publicity Stunts

SUMMARY

Or Was the North Distinctive?

What happened to the North and South economically after the War of 1812?

Historian James McPherson has proposed a new twist to the old question of southern distinctiveness: perhaps it was the *North*—New England, the Middle Atlantic, and the Old Northwest—that diverged from the norm. At the republic's birth, the two regions had much in common: slavery, ethnic homogeneity, a majority of the population engaged in agriculture, a small urban population. But that started to change with economic development after the War of 1812. State and local governments and private entrepreneurs engaged in

Chronology

1790s–1840s	Second Great Awakening
1820s	Model penitentiaries established
1820s–1840s	Utopian communities founded
1824	*Gibbons v. Ogden* prohibits steamboat monopolies
1825	Erie Canal completed
1826	American Society for Promotion of Temperance founded
1827	Construction begins on Baltimore and Ohio (B&O) Railroad
1830	First locomotive runs on B&O Railroad
	Joseph Smith organizes Mormon Church
1830s	Penny press emerges
1830s–50s	Urban riots commonplace
1833	American Antislavery Society founded
1834	Women workers strike at Lowell
1837–42	Croton Aqueduct constructed
1839–43	Hard times spread unemployment and deflation
1840	Split in abolitionist movement; Liberty Party founded
1840s	Female mill workers' publications appear
1844	Federal government sponsors first telegraph line
	Lowell Female Reform Association formed
1845	Massive Irish immigration begins
1846	Smithsonian Institute founded
1848	American Association for the Advancement of Science established
1850s	Free-labor ideology spreads

development, which happened faster and more extensively in the North. As the North embraced economic progress, it—rather than the South—diverged from the norm. The North, writes McPherson, "hurtled forward toward a future that many Southerners found distasteful if not frightening." With its continual quest for improvement, the North—much more so than the South—embodied what Frenchman Alexis de Tocqueville, who toured the United States in 1831–1832, called the nation's "restless spirit."

While the South expanded as a slave society, the North transformed, as one historian has put it, from a society with markets to a market society. In the colonial era, settlers lived in a society in which they engaged in long-distance trade—selling their surpluses to merchants, who in turn sent raw materials to Europe, using the proceeds to purchase finished goods for resale—but in which most settlers remained self-sufficient. During and after the War of 1812, the North became a market society in which participation in long-distance commerce altered individuals' aspirations and activities. With European trade largely halted during the war, entrepreneurs invested in domestic factories. More men, women, and children began working for others rather than on family farms, increasing domestic demand for foodstuffs. Farming became commercialized, with farmers abandoning self-sufficiency and specializing in crops that would yield cash on the market. Farmers then used the cash to buy goods they once made for themselves, such as cloth and soap along with some luxuries. Unlike the typical southern yeoman, they were not self-reliant, and isolation was rare. In the North, market expansion altered much of life. Some historians see these rapid changes as a market revolution.

The Transportation Revolution

How did the transportation revolution help lay the groundwork for a market economy?

To market goods far from where they were produced, Americans needed internal improvements. Before the War of 1812, natural waterways provided the most readily available and cheapest transportation routes for people and goods, but with limitations. Boatmen poled bateaux (cargo boats) down shallow rivers or floated flatboats down deep ones. Cargo generally moved downstream only, and most boats were destroyed for lumber at their destination. Upstream commerce was limited.

Roads

Overland transport was limited, too. Roads constructed during the colonial and revolutionary eras often became obstructed by fallen trees, soaked by mud, or clouded in dust. To reduce mud and dust, turnpike companies built "corduroy" roads, whose tightly lined-up logs resembled the ribbed cotton fabric. But the continual jolts caused nausea among passengers and discouraged merchants from shipping fragile wares. Land transportation was slow and expensive. In 1800, it cost as much to ship a ton of goods thirty miles into the interior as to ship it from New York to England. The lack of cheap, quick transportation impeded westward expansion and industrial growth.

Aside from the National Road (see Chapter 8), financing fell to states and private investors, and enthusiasm for building turnpikes greatly outpaced the money and manpower expended. Turnpike companies sometimes adopted improvements, such as laying hard surfaces made of crushed stone and gravel, but many of the newly built roads suffered from old problems.

Steamboats

In 1807, Robert Fulton's *Clermont* traveled between New York and Albany on the Hudson River in thirty-two hours, demonstrating the feasibility of using steam engines to power boats. After the Supreme Court's ruling against steamboat monopolies in *Gibbons v. Ogden* (1824), steamboat companies flourished on eastern rivers and, to a lesser extent, on the Great Lakes. They transported settlers to the Midwest, where they would grow grain and raise pigs that fed northeastern factory workers. Along western rivers like the Mississippi and the Ohio, steamboats carried midwestern timber and grain and southern cotton to New Orleans, where they were transferred to oceangoing vessels destined for northern and international ports. To travel between Ohio and New Orleans by flatboat in 1815 took several months; in 1840, the same trip by steamboat took just ten days. In the 1850s, steamboats became subject to federal regulations after deadly accidents in which boilers exploded, fires ignited, and boats collided.

Canals

In the late eighteenth and early nineteenth centuries, private companies (sometimes with state subsidies) built small canals to transport goods to and from interior locations. These projects rarely reaped substantial profits, discouraging future investment. In 1815, only three canals measured more than 2 miles long;

the longest was 27 miles. After Madison's veto of the Bonus Bill (see Chapter 8) dashed commercially minded New Yorkers' hopes for a canal connecting Lake Erie to the port of New York, Governor DeWitt Clinton pushed successfully for a state-sponsored initiative. What later became the **Erie Canal** was to run 363 miles between Buffalo and Albany, and was to be four feet deep.

Erie Canal Major canal that linked the Great Lakes to New York City, opening the upper Midwest to wider development.

Construction began on July 4, 1817. The canal, its promoters emphasized, would help demonstrate how American ingenuity and hard work could overcome obstacles, including the combined ascent and descent of 680 feet between Buffalo and Albany. By so doing, it would help unify the nation and secure its commercial independence from Europe.

Over the next eight years, nine thousand laborers felled forests, shoveled dirt, blasted rock, hauled boulders, rechanneled streams, and molded the canal bed. Stonemasons and carpenters built aqueducts and locks. The work was dangerous, sometimes fatal, with workers succumbing to malaria, rattlesnake bites, gunpowder explosions, and asphyxiation from collapsed canal beds.

The canal's promoters celebrated the waterway as the work of "republican free men," but few canal workers would have perceived their construction jobs as fulfilling Jefferson's notion of republican freedom. Once completed, the Erie Canal relied on child labor: Boys led the horses who pulled the canal boats between the canal's eighty-three locks, while girls cooked and cleaned on the boats. When the canal froze shut in winter, many workers lost their jobs.

Once completed in 1825, the Erie Canal proved immediately successful. Horse-drawn boats, stacked with bushels of wheat, barrels of oats, and piles of logs, streamed eastward from Lake Erie and western New York. Forty thousand passengers in 1825 alone traveled the new waterway. The canal shortened the journey between Buffalo and New York City from twenty to six days and reduced freight charges by nearly 95 percent—thus securing New York City's position as the nation's preeminent port. None of the other new canals enjoyed the Erie's financial success. As the cost of construction combined with an economic contraction, investment slumped in the 1830s. Several midwestern states could not repay their canal loans, leading them to bankruptcy or near-bankruptcy. By midcentury, the canal era had ended, though the Erie Canal (by then twice enlarged and rerouted) continued to prosper, still operates today (as the New York State Barge Canal), though primarily for leisure travel.

Railroads

The future belonged to railroads. Trains moved faster than canal boats and operated year-round. Railroads could connect remote locations to national and international markets. By 1860, the United States had 60,000 miles of track, mostly in the North. Railroads dramatically reduced the cost and the time involved in shipping goods.

The U.S. railroad era began in 1830 when Peter Cooper's locomotive, Tom Thumb, steamed along 13 miles of Baltimore and Ohio Railroad track. Not until the 1850s did railroads offer long-distance service at reasonable rates. Even then, lack of a common standard for track width thwarted development of a national system. A journey from Philadelphia to Charleston involved eight different gauges, requiring passengers and freight to change trains seven times. Only at Bowling Green, Kentucky, did northern and southern railroads connect. Despite the race to construct internal improvements, the nation's canals and railroads did little to unite the regions and promote nationalism, as proponents of government-sponsored internal improvements had hoped.

Northern governments and investors spent more on internal improvements than did southerners. Pennsylvania and New York together accounted for half of all state monies invested. Southern states invested in railroads, but—with smaller free populations—they collected fewer taxes and had less to spend.

The North and South laid roughly the same amount of railroad track per person before the Civil War, but when measured in mileage, the more populous North had tracks that stretched farther, forming an integrated system of local lines branching off major trunk lines. In the South, railroads remained local. Neither people nor goods moved easily across the South, unless they traveled via steamboat or flatboat along the Mississippi River system—and even then, flooded banks often disrupted passage.

Regional Connections

The North's frenzy of canal and railroad building expanded transportation networks far into the hinterlands. In 1815, nearly all produce from the Old Northwest floated down the Mississippi to New Orleans, tying that region's fortunes to the South. By the 1850s, though, canals and railroads strengthened the economic, cultural, and political links between the Old Northwest—particularly the more densely populated northern regions—and the Northeast. (See Map 10.1.)

Internal improvements hastened westward migration, making western settlement more appealing by providing easy access to eastern markets. News, visitors, and luxuries now traveled regularly to previously remote areas of the Northeast and Midwest. Delighted that the Erie Canal brought fresh seafood to central New York, Mary Archbald explained that "distance … is reduced to nothing here."

Samuel F. B. Morse's invention of the telegraph in 1844 allowed news to travel almost instantaneously along telegraph wires. By 1852, more than 23,000 miles of lines were strung nationwide. The telegraph enabled the birth of modern business practices involving the coordination of market conditions, production, and supply across great distances.

Ambivalence Toward Progress

Many northerners hailed internal improvements as symbols of progress. They proclaimed that, by building canals and railroads, they had completed God's design for the North American continent. Practically speaking, canals and railroads allowed them to seek opportunities in the West.

But even people who welcomed such opportunities could find much to lament. Mary Ann Archbald savored fresh seafood dinners but regretted that her sons turned to speculation. Others decried the Irish canal diggers and railroad track layers, whom they deemed depraved and racially inferior. Still others worried that, by promoting urban growth, transportation innovations fostered social ills.

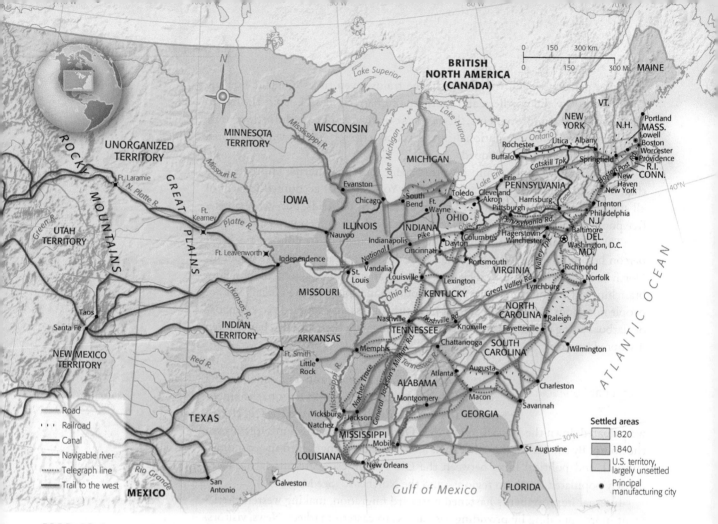

MAP 10.1

Major Roads, Canals, and Railroads, 1850

A transportation network linked the seaboard to the interior. Settlers followed those routes westward, and they sent back grain, grain products, and cotton to the port cities. Source: Copyright © Cengage Learning 2015

The degradation of the natural world proved worrisome, too. When streams were rerouted, swamps drained, and forests felled, natural habitats were disturbed, even destroyed. Deprived of waterpower, mills no longer ran. Without forests, wild animals—on which many rural people had relied for protein—sought homes elsewhere. Fishermen, too, found their sources of protein (and cash) dried up when natural waterways were dammed or rerouted to feed canals.

Factories and Industrialization

How was factory work different from the work life people previously knew?

By lowering transportation costs, internal improvements facilitated the Northeast's rapid manufacturing and commercial expansion. Western farmers supplied raw materials and foodstuffs for northeastern factories and workers. They also expanded the domestic market for northeastern manufactured goods. Focused on cultivating their lands, western settlers preferred to buy rather than make cloth, shoes, and other goods.

Factory Work

Much early industrialization involved processing raw materials—milling flour, turning hogs into packaged meat, sawing lumber. The pork-packing industry illustrates how specialization turned skilled craftsmen into laborers. Traditionally, each butcher carved an entire pig. Under the new industrial organization, each worker performed a particular task—such as cutting off the right front leg—as the pig traveled down a "disassembly line."

Factory work, with its impersonal and regimented nature, contrasted with more informal artisan shops and farm households. In large factories, laborers never saw owners, working instead under paid supervisors, nor did they see the final product. Factory workers lost their sense of autonomy, as the bell or steam whistle governed their day. Competition from cheaper, less-skilled workers—particularly after European immigration soared in the 1840s—created job insecurity and few opportunities for advancement.

Initially Americans imported or copied British machines that made mass production possible. Soon they built their own. The **American System of manufacturing** used machinery to produce interchangeable parts. Eli Whitney, the cotton gin's inventor, promoted interchangeable parts in 1798, when he contracted with the federal government to make ten thousand rifles in twenty-eight months. The American System quickly produced the machine-tool industry—the manufacture of machines for the purpose of mass production. The new system permitted large-scale production of inexpensive but high-quality household items.

American System of manufacturing System of manufacturing that used interchangeable parts.

Textile Mills

Mechanization was most dramatic in textiles, with production centered in New England, near water sources to power spinning machines and looms. After 1815, New England's rudimentary cotton mills developed into modern factories with mass-produced goods. Cotton cloth production rose from 4 million yards in 1817 to 323 million in 1840. In the mid-1840s, cotton mills employed approximately eighty thousand "operatives"; more than half were women.

With labor scarce near the mills, managers recruited New England farm daughters, whom they housed in dormitories in what became known as the **Waltham** or **Lowell** plan of industrialization. People who farmed were often suspicious of those who did not—particularly in the United States, where an agrarian lifestyle was associated with virtue. To ease such concerns, mill managers offered paternalistic oversight of mill girls; they enforced curfews and required church attendance.

Despite restrictions, the Waltham system offered farm girls opportunities to socialize and earn wages to help their families, save for their dowries or education, or spend on such items as clothing. Workers wrote literary pieces for the owner-subsidized *Lowell Offering* and attended educational lectures in the evenings. Working conditions in textile mills—the deafening roar of the power looms, the long hours, and regimentation—made young women cling to notions that their jobs were temporary. The average girl arrived at sixteen and stayed five years, usually leaving to get married.

Although the Waltham plan drew international attention, more common was the Rhode Island (or Fall River) plan employed by **Samuel Slater**, among others. Mills hired entire families, lodging them in boardinghouses. Men worked farm

Waltham, Lowell Sites of early textile mills in New England, which were precursors to modern factories. Nearly 80 percent of the workers in Waltham, Lowell, and similar mills were young, unmarried women who had been lured from farms by the promise of wages.

Link to "A Week in the Mill"
Lowell Offering,
October 1845

Samuel Slater British mechanic who carried plans for textile mills to the United States.

Links TO THE WORLD

Internal Improvements

On July 4, 1827, ninety-one-year-old Charles Carroll, the only surviving signer of the Declaration of Independence, shoveled the first spadeful of earth on the Baltimore and Ohio Railroad, the nation's first westward railroad. Internal improvements, he and others believed, would cement the United States' economic independence by supplying the nation's growing industrial centers with food and raw materials, while transporting manufactured goods back to its rural population.

Although boosters championed canals and railroads as the triumph of American republicanism, such projects depended on technology, funding, and labor from abroad. American engineers scrutinized canals and railroads in France, the Low Countries, and England. Railroad companies purchased locomotives from English manufacturers. Foreign investors financed significant portions of projects. Thousands of immigrants, mostly from Ireland, worked blasting boulders, draining malaria-filled swamps, picking at roots and rocks, and heaving dirt. After the Civil War, Chinese immigrants helped build the transcontinental railroad.

Internal improvements allowed people, raw materials, and goods to move inexpensively and quickly across the continent, spurring the nation's growth—but also strengthening ties to Europe. Cotton and grain moved eastward, with much of it sold overseas. Cotton fed European textile mills; grain fed their workers. Thus, whenever economic conditions constricted in Europe, reverberations were felt on cotton and wheat farmss across America.

Canals and railroads, hailed as symbols of American independence, linked American farmers to an increasingly complex and volatile international economy.

Workers repair a section of the Erie Canal, near Little Falls, in 1831. While hailed as a great achievement of human progress, the canal required frequent repairs, frustrating travelers, merchants, boat workers, and people living along its banks.

Erie Canal, NY, 1831 (graphite, w/c and gouache on paper), Hill, John William (1812–79)/
© Collection of the New-York Historical Society, USA/The Bridgeman Art Library

plots nearby while wives and children worked in the mills, though as the system developed, men worked in the factories supervising wives and children in family-based work units.

Labor Protests

Mill life grew more difficult, especially during the depression of 1837 to 1843, when demand for cloth declined and mills ran part time. To increase productivity, managers sped up machines and required each worker to operate more machines. To boost profits, owners lengthened hours, cut wages, and packed the boardinghouses.

Workers organized, and in 1834 (and again in 1836), reacting to a 25 percent wage cut, they unsuccessfully "turned out" (struck) against the Lowell mills. In 1844, Massachusetts mill women formed the Lowell Female Reform Association and joined other workers in pressing, unsuccessfully, for state legislation mandating a ten-instead of fourteen-hour day.

Women aired their complaints in worker-run newspapers: in 1842, the *Factory Girl* appeared in New Hampshire, the *Wampanoag and Operatives' Journal* in Massachusetts. Two years later, mill workers founded the *Factory Girl's Garland* and the *Voice of Industry*, nicknamed "the factory girl's voice." Even the owner-sponsored *Lowell Offering* faced controversy when workers charged its editors with suppressing articles criticizing working conditions.

Few militant native-born mill workers stayed to fight the managers and owners, and gradually, fewer New England daughters entered the mills. In the 1850s, Irish immigrant women replaced them. Technological improvements made the work less skilled, enabling mills to hire lower-paid laborers. Male workers, too, protested changes wrought by the **market economy**. As voters, they formed labor political parties first in Pennsylvania, New York, and Massachusetts in the 1820s, and then elsewhere. They advocated free public education and an end to imprisonment for debt, and opposed banks and monopolies. Aspiring to own land, some advocated for free homesteads.

market economy Newly developing commercial economy that depended on goods and crops produced for sale rather than for personal consumption.

Labor Unions

The courts provided organized labor's greatest victory: protection from conspiracy laws. When journeyman shoemakers organized during the early 1800s, employers accused them of criminal conspiracy. The cordwainers' (shoemakers') cases between 1806 and 1815 left labor organizations in an uncertain position. Although the courts acknowledged the journeymen's right to organize, judges viewed strikes as illegal until a Massachusetts case, **Commonwealth v. Hunt** (1842), ruled that Boston journeyman bootmakers could strike "to subserve their own interests."

The first unions represented journeymen in printing, woodworking, shoemaking, and tailoring. Locally organized, they sought protection against competition from inferior workmen by regulating apprenticeships and establishing minimum wages. Umbrella organizations of individual craft unions, like the National Trade Union (1834), arose in several cities in the 1820s and 1830s. But the movement disintegrated amid wage reductions and unemployment in the depression of 1839–1843.

Commonwealth v. Hunt A court case in 1842 where the Massachusetts Supreme Judicial Court ruled that labor unions were not illegal monopolies that restrained trade.

Permanent labor organizations were difficult to sustain. Skilled craftsmen disdained less skilled workers. Moreover, workers divided along ethnic, religious, racial, and gender lines.

Consumption and Commercialization

How did farm women's work change as the commercial economy expanded?

By producing inexpensive cloth, New England mills spawned the ready-made clothing industry. Before the 1820s, women sewed most clothing at home. Tailors and seamstresses made wealthy men's and women's clothing to order. By the 1820s and 1830s, much clothing was mass-produced for sale in clothing stores. A division of labor took hold: one worker cut patterns all day, another sewed hems, another affixed buttons. The sewing machine, invented in 1846 and widely available in the 1850s, accelerated the process. Many farm families still made their own clothing yet bought clothes when they could afford to, freeing time for raising both crops and children.

The Garment Industry

Market expansion created demand for mass-produced clothing. Girls working in factories no longer had time to sew clothes. Young immigrant men—separated from mothers and sisters—bought the crudely made, loose-fitting clothing. But the biggest market for ready-made clothes was in the cotton South. Planters bought ready-made shoes and clothes for slaves, in whose hands they would rather place a hoe than a needle and thread.

Retailers often bought goods wholesale, though many manufactured shirts and trousers in their own factories. Lewis and Hanford of New York City boasted of cutting more than 100,000 garments in winter 1848–1849. The New York firm did business mostly in the South and owned a retail outlet in New Orleans. While southerners and westerners engaged in the clothing trade, its center remained in New York.

The garment industry often took the form of what some historians call metropolitan industrialization, which relied on reorganization of labor, similar to the earlier putting-out system. Much production of ready-made clothing, for example, occurred in tenements throughout New York City, where thousands of women spent long hours sewing buttons onto a piece of ready-made clothing, while others sewed hem after hem.

Specialization of Commerce

Commercial specialization transformed some urban traders into merchant princes. After the Erie Canal opened, New York City became a stop on every major trade route from Europe, southern ports, and the West. Traders sometimes invested in factories, further stimulating urban manufacturing. Some cities specialized: Rochester became a milling center ("The Flour City"), and Cincinnati ("Porkopolis") became the first meatpacking center.

Merchants who engaged in complex commercial transactions required large, mostly male, office staffs. At the bottom were messenger boys, often preteens, who delivered documents. Above them were copyists, who hand-copied documents. Clerks processed documents and did translations. Above them were the bookkeeper and confidential chief clerk. Those seeking employment in such countinghouses took a course from a writing master. All hoped to rise to partner, although their chances grew increasingly slim.

Specialization lagged in small towns, where merchants continued to exchange goods with local farm women and craftsmen continued to sell finished goods, such as shoes and clothing. In some rural areas, peddlers were general merchants. But as transportation improved and towns grew, small-town merchants increasingly specialized.

Commercial Farming

Even amid commercial booms, agriculture remained the northern economy's backbone. But the **transportation revolution** and market expansion transformed semi-subsistence farms into commercial enterprises. Many families abandoned mixed agriculture for specialization in cash crops. By the 1820s, eastern farmers had cultivated nearly all available land, and their small farms, often with uneven terrains, were ill suited for the labor-saving farm implements introduced in the 1830s, such as mechanical sowers, reapers, and threshers. Many northern farmers thus either moved west or quit farming for jobs in merchants' houses and factories.

transportation revolution Rapid expansion of canals, steamships, and railroads.

In 1820, about one-third of northern produce was intended for the market, but by 1850 that amount surpassed 50 percent. As farmers shifted toward market-oriented production, they invested in additional land, new equipment, and new labor sources (hired hands). Many New England and Middle Atlantic farm families faced competition from midwestern farmers after the Erie Canal opened. They abandoned wheat and corn production, shifting to livestock and vegetable and fruit production. Much of what they produced fed the North's rapidly growing urban and manufacturing populations.

Farmers financed innovations through land sales and debts. Indeed, increasing land values promised the greatest profit. Farm families who owned land flourished, but it became harder to become a farmer. The number of tenant farmers and hired hands increased, and farmers who had previously employed unpaid family members and enslaved workers now leased portions of their farms or hired paid labor.

Farm Women's Changing Labor

As the commercial economy expanded, rural women assumed additional responsibilities. Some did outwork (see Chapter 8). Many increased production of eggs, dairy products, and garden produce for sale; others raised bees or silkworms.

With the New England textile mills producing more finished cloth, farm women and children often abandoned time-consuming spinning and weaving, bought factory-produced cloth, and produced more marketable products, such as butter and cheese. Some mixed-agriculture farms converted entirely to dairy production, with men taking over formerly female tasks. Canals and railroads carried cheese to eastern ports, where wholesalers sold it worldwide.

Rural Communities

Despite pressure to manage farms like time-efficient businesses, some farmers clung to old practices such as barn raisings and husking bees. But by the 1830s with young women working in textile mills and young men laboring as clerks or factory hands, there were fewer people at such events. While farmers continued to swap labor and socialize with neighbors, they increasingly reckoned debts in dollars and watched national and international markets more closely. When financial panics hit, cash shortages almost halted business activity, casting many farmers further into debt, sometimes bankruptcy. Faced with potentially losing their land, farmers called in neighbors' debts, sometimes rupturing long-established relationships.

Cycles of Boom and Bust

With market expansion came booms and busts that often hit the Northeast hardest. Prosperity stimulated demand for finished goods, such as clothing and furniture, which led to higher prices and still higher production and to land speculation. Investment money was plentiful as Americans saved and foreign, mostly British, investors bought U.S. bonds and securities. Then production surpassed demand. Prices and wages fell; land and stock values collapsed, and investment money left the United States.

Although the 1820s and 1830s were boom times, financial panic triggered a bust cycle in 1837, the year after the Second Bank of the United States closed. Economic contraction remained severe through 1843. Many banks could not repay depositors, and states, facing deficits, defaulted on their bonds. Because of the **Panic of 1837**, European, especially British, investors became suspicious of U.S. loans and withdrew money from the United States.

Panic of 1837 A severe depression that struck the United States beginning in May 1837.

Hard times had come. "The streets seemed deserted," Sidney George Fisher observed of Philadelphia in 1842. "The largest [merchant] houses are shut up and to rent, there is no business … no money, no confidence." The hungry formed lines at soup societies, and beggars crowded the sidewalks. Laborers demanding their deposits gathered at closed banks. Sheriffs sold seized property at one-quarter of former prices. Congress passed the Federal Bankruptcy Law of 1841; by the time the law was repealed two years later, 41,000 bankrupts had sought protection under its provisions.

Families in Flux

How were men's and women's roles within the family redefined in the new industrial era?

Anxieties about economic fluctuations reverberated into northern homes. Sweeping changes in the household economy led to new family ideals. In the preindustrial era, families were the primary economic units; now they became a moral and cultural institution, though in reality few families could live up to this ideal.

The "Ideal" Family

In the North, the market economy increasingly separated the home from the workplace, leading to a new middle-class ideal in which men functioned in the public sphere while women oversaw the private or domestic sphere. The home became, in theory, an emotional retreat from the competitive, selfish business world. Men provided and protected, while women nurtured and guarded the family's morality. Childhood expanded: children were to remain at home until their late teens or early twenties. This ideal became known as separate-spheres ideology, the cult of domesticity, or the cult of true womanhood. Although it rigidly separated the male and female spheres, this ideology elevated domestic responsibilities. In her widely read *Treatise on Domestic Economy* (1841), Catharine Beecher approached housekeeping as a science while trumpeting mothers' role as their family's moral guardian. Beecher maintained that women's natural superiority as moral, nurturing caregivers made them especially suited for teaching (when single) and parenting (once married).

Shrinking Families   These new domestic ideals depended on smaller families enabling parents, particularly mothers, to offer children greater attention, education, and financial help. With the market economy, parents could afford to have fewer children because children no longer played a vital economic role. Urban families produced fewer household goods, and commercial farmers, unlike self-sufficient ones, relied on hired laborers. Although smaller families resulted partly from first marriages' occurring at a later age, they also resulted from planning, made easier when cheap rubber condoms became available in the 1850s. Some women chose, too, to end accidental pregnancies with abortion.

In 1800, American women bore seven or eight children; by 1860, five or six. This decline occurred even though immigrants with large-family traditions were settling in the United States; thus, the birth rate among native-born women declined more sharply. Although rural families remained larger than urban ones, birth rates among both groups declined comparably.

Still, few northern women could fulfill the middle-class ideal of **separate spheres**. Most wage-earning women provided essential income for their families and could not stay home. They often saw domestic ideals as oppressive, as middle-class reformers mistook poverty for immorality, condemning working mothers for letting their children work or scavenge rather than attend school. Although most middle-class women stayed home, new standards of cleanliness proved time-consuming. Although their household contributions were generally assessed in moral terms, their economic contributions were significant. They provided, without remuneration, the labor for which wealthier women paid when they hired domestic servants to perform chores. Without servants, women could not devote themselves primarily to their children, making the ideals of the cult of domesticity impossible for many middle-class families.

separate spheres Middle-class ideology that emerged with the market revolution and divided men's and women's roles into distinct and separate categories based on their perceived gender differences, abilities, and social functions. Men were assigned the public realm of business and politics, while women were assigned to the private world of home and family.

Women's Paid Labor   In working-class families, girls left home as early as age twelve, earning wages most of their lives, with short respites for bearing and rearing children. Unmarried girls and women worked primarily as domestic servants or in factories; married and widowed women worked as laundresses, seamstresses, and cooks. Some hawked food and wares on city streets; others did piecework; and some became prostitutes. Few could support themselves or a family comfortably.

Middle-class Americans sought to keep daughters closer to home, except for brief stints as mill girls or teachers. In the 1830s, Catharine Beecher successfully campaigned for teacher-training schools for women. She argued both for women's moral superiority and their economic value; because these women would be single, she contended, they need not earn as much as their male counterparts, whom she presumed to be married (not all were). Unmarried women earned about half the salary of male teachers. By 1850, schoolteaching had become a woman's profession.

The proportion of single women in the population increased significantly in the nineteenth century. As more young men headed west, some eastern communities were disproportionately female. Other women chose to remain independent, seeking opportunities opened by the market economy and urban expansion. Because women's work generally paid poorly, those who forswore marriage faced serious challenges, leaving many single women dependent on charitable or family assistance.

The Growth of Cities

How could cities be seen at once as symbols of progress and of moral decay?

No period in American history saw more rapid urbanization than between 1820 and 1860. The percentage of people living in urban areas (defined by a population of 2,500 or more) grew from 7 percent in 1820 to nearly 20 percent in 1860. The greatest growth occurred in the Northeast and the Midwest. Although most northerners continued to live on farms or in small villages, cities boomed. Many urban residents were temporary, and many were immigrants.

Urban Boom

In 1820, the United States had thirteen places with a population greater than ten thousand; in 1860, it had ninety-three (see Map 10.2). New York City, already the nation's largest city in 1820, saw its population grow from 123,709 in that year to 813,669 in 1860. Philadelphia, the nation's second-largest city, saw its population multiply ninefold during that forty-year period. In 1815, Rochester, New York, had just 300 residents. By 1830, the Erie Canal turned the sleepy agricultural town into the nation's twenty-fifth-largest city, with a population of over 9,000.

Cities experienced geographic expansion too. In 1825, Fourteenth Street was New York City's northern boundary. By 1860, Forty-second Street was its northern limit. Public transit made city expansion possible. By the 1850s, all big cities had horse-drawn streetcars, allowing wealthier residents who could afford the fare to settle on the cities' outskirts.

Market-Related Development

The period between 1820 and 1860 saw the creation of many inland cities in the North—usually places that emerged with the creation of transportation lines or manufacturing establishments. The Boston Manufacturing Company, for example, selected the site for Lowell, Massachusetts, because of its proximity to the Merrimack River, which could power its textile mill. Incorporated in 1826, by the 1850s Lowell was the second-largest city in New England.

Northern cities developed elaborate municipal services but lacked taxing power to provide services for all. New services and basic sanitation depended on residents' ability to pay. Another solution was to charter private companies to sell basic services. Baltimore first chartered a private gas company in 1816. By midcentury, every major city had done so. Private firms lacked capital to build adequate water systems, and they laid pipe only in commercial and well-to-do residential areas. Supplying water ultimately fell to city governments.

Extremes of Wealth

Wealth was concentrating among a relatively small number of people. By 1860, the top 5 percent of

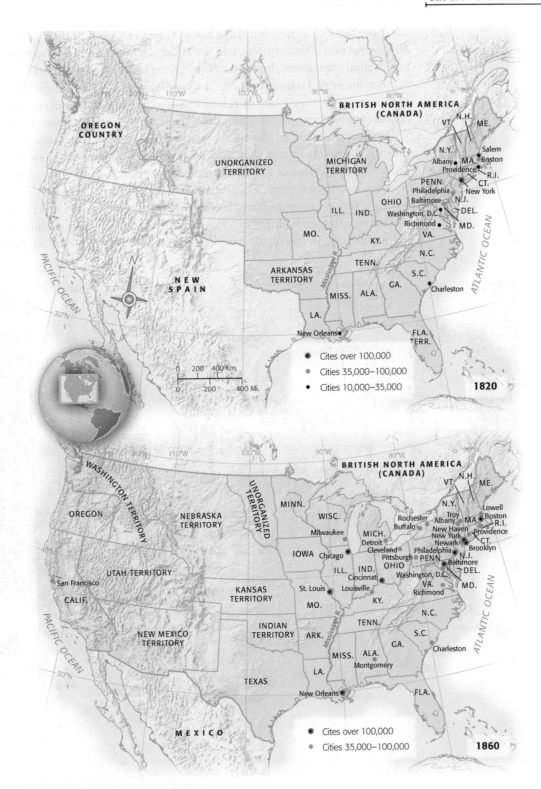

MAP 10.2

Major American Cities in 1820 and 1860

The number of Americans who lived in cities increased rapidly between 1820 and 1860, and the number of large cities grew as well. In 1820, only New York City had a population exceeding 100,000; forty years later, eight more cities had surpassed that level. Source: Copyright © Cengage Learning 2015

American families owned more than half of the nation's wealth, and the top 10 percent owned nearly three-quarters. In the South, income extremes were most apparent on rural plantations, but in the North, cities revealed economic inequities.

A number of factors contributed to widespread poverty in America's industrial cities: poor wages, lack of full-time employment, and the increasingly widespread employment of women and children, which drove down wages for everyone. Women and children, employers rationalized, did not need a living wage because they were dependent, meaning they relied on men to support them. In reality, though, not all women or children had men to support them, nor were men's wages always adequate to support a family comfortably.

New York provides an example of the extremes of wealth accompanying industrialization. Houses built for two families often held four. Some families took in lodgers to pay the rent; such crowding encouraged poorer New Yorkers to head

Visible signs of urban poverty in the 1850s were the homeless and orphaned children, most of them immigrants, who wandered the streets of New York City. The Home for the Friendless Orphanage, at Twenty-ninth Street and Madison Avenue, provided shelter for some of the orphan girls.

outdoors. But poor neighborhoods were filthy. Excess sewage from outhouses drained into ditches, carrying urine and fecal matter into the streets. People piled garbage into gutters, backyards, or alleys. Pigs, geese, dogs, and vultures scavenged the streets, while rats roamed under wooden sidewalks and through large buildings. Typhoid, dysentery, malaria, and tuberculosis thrived in such conditions, and cholera epidemics struck in 1831, 1849, and 1866.

Just beyond poverty-stricken neighborhoods were lavish mansions, whose residents escaped to country estates during the summer's heat or epidemics. Much of this wealth was inherited. Rich New Yorkers increased their fortunes by investing in commerce and manufacturing.

The middle class was larger than the wealthy elite but smaller than the working classes. They were businessmen, traders, and professionals, and the rapid turn toward industrialization and commercial specialization made them a larger presence in northern cities than in southern ones. Middle-class families enjoyed new consumer items: wool carpeting, fine wallpaper, and rooms full of furniture. Houses were large, from four to six rooms. By the 1840s and 1850s, middle-class families used indoor toilets that were mechanical, though not yet flushing. These families formed the backbone of urban clubs and societies, filled the family pews in church, and sent their sons to college.

Immigration

Many of the urban poor were immigrants. The 5 million immigrants to the United States between 1830 and 1860 outnumbered the country's entire population in 1790 (see Figure 10.1). During the peak period of pre–Civil War immigration (1847–1857), 3.3 million immigrants entered the United States, including 1.3 million Irish and 1.1 million Germans. By 1860, 15 percent of the white population was foreign born, with 90 percent of immigrants living in northern states.

Various factors "pushed" Europeans from their homes and "pulled" them to the northern United States. In Ireland, the potato famine (1845–1850)—a period of widespread starvation caused by a diseased potato crop—drove millions from their homeland. Although economic conditions pushed most Germans, some were political refugees—liberals, freethinkers, socialists, communists, and anarchists—who fled after the abortive revolutions of 1848. Employers, states, and shipping companies promoted opportunities in America with this message: work and prosper in America or starve in Europe. Once in the United States, immigrants soon saw the fallacy of promoters' promises of riches, and hundreds of thousands returned home.

Many early immigrants lived or worked in rural areas. Like the Archbalds, a few settled on farms and bought land. Others worked as hired farmhands, canal diggers, or railroad track layers—often hoping to buy land later. By the 1840s and 1850s—when immigration soared—the prospects of buying land became increasingly remote.

By 1860, most immigrants settled in cities, often near where they arrived. The most destitute could not afford the fare farther inland. Some had resources but fell victim to swindlers. Others liked the cities' ethnic flair. In 1855, 52 percent of New York's 623,000 inhabitants were immigrants, 28 percent from Ireland and 16 percent from the German states. Throughout the 1850s, about 35 percent of Boston was foreign born; more than two-thirds were Irish.

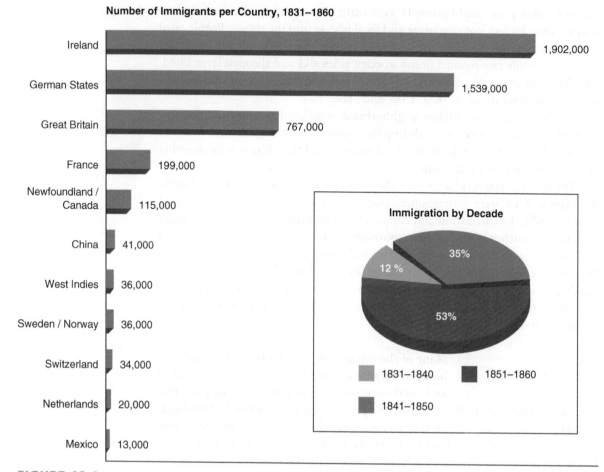

Number of Immigrants per Country, 1831–1860

Country	Number
Ireland	1,902,000
German States	1,539,000
Great Britain	767,000
France	199,000
Newfoundland / Canada	115,000
China	41,000
West Indies	36,000
Sweden / Norway	36,000
Switzerland	34,000
Netherlands	20,000
Mexico	13,000

Immigration by Decade

- 35% 1831–1840
- 53% 1841–1850
- 12% 1851–1860

FIGURE 10.1

Major Sources of Immigration to the United States, 1831–1860

Most immigrants came from two areas: Great Britain, of which Ireland was a part, and the German states. These two areas sent more immigrants between 1830 and 1860 than the inhabitants of the United States enumerated at the first census in 1790. By 1860, 15 percent of the white population was of foreign birth.

(Source: Data from Stephan Thernstrom, ed., *Harvard Encyclopedia of American Ethnic Groups* [Cambridge, Mass., and London: Harvard University Press, 1980], 1047.)

Most of the new Irish immigrants were young, poor, rural, and Roman Catholic. Women worked as domestic servants or mill hands, while men labored in construction or transportation. Most Germans came with enough resources to head to states such as Ohio, Illinois, Wisconsin, and Missouri. Although some southern cities like Charleston and Savannah had Irish immigrants, most European immigrants disliked slavery and semitropical heat and preferred the Northeast or Midwest.

Ethnic Tensions

Tension—often about the era's economic changes—characterized the relationship between native-born Americans and immigrants, particularly Irish Catholics. Native-born workers blamed immigrants for scarce job opportunities and low wages. Middle-class whites blamed them for poverty and crime. They believed immigrants' moral depravity—not poor wages—led to poverty.

White northerners often portrayed Irish immigrants as nonwhite, as African in appearance. But Irish and African Americans did not develop a sense of solidarity. Instead, some of the era's most virulent riots erupted between Irish immigrants and African Americans.

Anti-Catholicism became strident in the 1830s. In Boston, anti-Catholic riots occurred frequently. Nearby Charlestown, Massachusetts, saw a mob burn a convent in 1834. In Philadelphia, a crowd attacked priests and nuns and vandalized churches in 1844. Urban riots usually attracted more newspaper attention, fueling fears that cities were violent, depraved places.

Protestant German immigrants fared better than the Irish. Because Germans generally arrived with resources and skills, Americans stereotyped them as hardworking. But non-Protestant Germans—Catholics and Jews (whom white Americans considered a separate race) frequently encountered racial and religious prejudice.

Immigrants often lived in ethnic enclaves, setting up social clubs and mutual aid societies. Irish Catholics had their own neighborhoods, where they established Catholic churches and schools. In larger cities, immigrants from the same German states clustered together.

A Female Employment Office (oil on canvas), Burr, William Henry (1819–1908)/© Collection of the New-York Historical Society, USA/ The Bridgeman Art Library

Domestic servants await their fate at a hiring office. Because servants resided with their employers, concerns about honesty often topped an employer's list of priorities for a suitable servant.

People of Color

African Methodist Episcopal churches First American denomination established by and for African Americans.

African Americans also forged their own communities and culture. By 1860 nearly 250,000 (many of them refugees from southern slavery) lived in the urban North. **African Methodist Episcopal churches** and preachers helped forge communities. Ministers were political leaders; churches hosted political forums and protest meetings.

White racism impinged on northern African Americans' lives. Streetcars, hotels, restaurants, and theaters could turn away African Americans without legal penalty. City laws barred African Americans from public buildings. Even where laws were liberal, whites' attitudes constrained African Americans' opportunities. In Massachusetts, for example, African Americans enjoyed more legal rights than anywhere else. Still, whites often refused to shop at black businesses. African Americans were excluded from factory and clerical jobs. Women worked as house servants, cooks, washerwomen, and child nurses. Most African American men worked as construction workers, porters, longshoremen, or day laborers—all jobs subject to frequent unemployment. Others took lower-paying but stable jobs as servants, waiters, cooks, barbers, and janitors. Many African American men became sailors and merchant seamen, jobs offering regular employment and advancement, though not protection from racial taunts.

In cities, African Americans turned service occupations into businesses, opening restaurants, taverns, hotels, barbershops, and employment agencies for domestic servants. Some sold used clothing or were junk dealers. A few became wealthy, invested in real estate, and loaned money. With professionals—ministers, teachers, physicians, dentists, lawyers, and newspaper editors—they formed a small but growing African American middle class.

Still, African Americans became targets of urban violence. White rioters clubbed and stoned African Americans, destroying their houses, churches, and businesses—and sent many fleeing for their lives. Philadelphia experienced five major riots in the 1830s and 1840s. By 1860, hundreds of African Americans had died in urban riots.

Urban Culture

Living in cramped, squalid conditions, working-class families spent little time indoors. In the 1840s, a working-class youth culture developed on the Bowery, one of New York's entertainment strips. Lined with theaters, dance halls, and cafés, it became an urban midway. The Bowery boys' greased hair, distinctive clothing, and swaggering gait frightened many middle-class New Yorkers, as did Bowery girls' colorful costumes. Equally scandalous were the middle-class clerks who succumbed to urban temptations, notably prostitution.

Gangs of garishly dressed young men and women flaunting their sexuality and drinking excessively drove respectable citizenry to establish private clubs. Some men joined the Masonic order, which offered members an elaborate code of deference between ranks, while women organized literary clubs and benevolent societies.

Increasingly, urban recreation and sports became commodities. Horse racing, walking races, and, in the 1850s, baseball attracted urban men. Wall Street office workers formed the Knickerbocker Club in 1842 and in 1845 drew up rules for playing baseball. Large cities boasted two or more theaters catering to different

GREAT RIOT AT THE ASTOR PLACE OPERA HOUSE, NEW YORK.
ON THURSDAY EVENING MAY 10th 1849.

On May 10, 1849, a working-class protest at the elitist Astor Place Theater led to a clash with state militia, resulting in at least twenty-two deaths and over one hundred and fifty injuries.

classes. Some plays cut across class lines—Shakespeare was so widely performed that even illiterate theatergoers knew his plays.

In the 1840s, singing groups, theater troupes, and circuses traveled from city to city. Minstrel shows were popular, featuring white men (often Irish) in makeup imitating African Americans in song, dance, and patter. In the early 1830s, Thomas D. Rice of New York became famous for portraying Jim Crow, an old southern slave. In patched clothing and torn shoes, the blackface Rice danced and sang. Minstrel performers told jokes mocking economic and political elites, and evoked nostalgia for preindustrial work habits and morality. But blackface actors encouraged a racist stereotyping of African Americans as sensual and lazy.

The Penny Press

Accounts of urban culture peppered the penny press, which emerged in the 1830s, soon sweeping northern cities. Made possible by technological advances—the advent of the steam-powered press, improved methods for producing paper, and transportation innovations—the penny press (each newspaper cost one cent) differed from traditional (six-cent) newspapers. The older papers covered mostly commercial news and identified strongly with a political party; the penny press proclaimed political independence and hired reporters to cover local, national, and international stories. Where six-cent newspapers relied on subscriptions and political contributions, penny newspapers were sold by newsboys on the street. They earned money from advertising, and drew an economically diverse readership. Working-class people could now regularly afford newspapers.

Penny newspapers focused on daily life, giving one social class the opportunity to peer into the lives of other classes, ethnicities, and races. The penny press often sensationalized the news, thereby influencing urban dwellers' views of one another and of cities.

Cities as Symbols of Progress

To many northerners, cities symbolized progress and decay. Cities nurtured churches, schools, civil governments, and museums—signs of civilization and culture. As canals and railroads opened the West for mass settlement, many white northerners applauded the appearance of church steeples and public buildings in areas that had been "savage wilderness," or territory controlled by Native Americans.

Yet some middle-class Americans deplored the nation's largest cities, which they saw as havens of disease, poverty, crime, and vice—emblems of moral decline. They considered epidemics to be divine scourges, striking the filthy, intemperate, and immoral. Theft and prostitution provided evidence of moral vice, and wealthy observers perceived these crimes not as by-products of poverty but as proof of individual failing. They pushed city officials to establish the first police forces. Boston hired daytime policemen in 1838, and New York formed its police force in 1845.

Middle-class reformers focused on purifying cities of disease and vice. If disease was divine punishment, then Americans would have to become more godly. Reformers sought to convince the urban working classes that life would improve if they gave up alcohol, worked harder, and prayed frequently. This belief became central to northerners' ideas about progress.

Revivals and Reform

How did religious revival movements lead to social reform?

Second Great Awakening
Religious revival that swept the country and helped inspire reform movements.

Religious revivals in the late eighteenth and early nineteenth centuries—sometimes called the **Second Great Awakening** for their resemblance to the eighteenth-century Great Awakening—raised people's hopes for the Second Coming of the Christian messiah and the establishment of God's kingdom on earth. Revivalists created communities of believers resolved to speed the millennium, or the thousand years of peace that would accompany Christ's Second Coming, by combating sin. Some believed the United States had a special mission in God's design. If evil could be eliminated, individuals and society could be perfected, readying the earth for Christ's return.

Revivalists strove for large-scale conversions. Rural women, men, and children traveled long distances to camp meetings, where they heard fiery sermons preached day and night from hastily constructed platforms and tents in forests or fields. In cities, women in particular attended daily services and prayer meetings. Converts vowed to live sanctified lives and help others see the light.

Revivals

Northern revivalists emphasized social reform. The most prominent preachers were Lyman Beecher, who began in New England before moving to Cincinnati, and **Charles G. Finney**, who traveled the canals and roads linking the Northeast to the Midwest. Revivalist preachers argued that evil was avoidable, that Christians were not doomed by original sin, and that anyone could achieve salvation. Revivalism thrived among Methodists and Baptists, whose denominational structures maximized democratic participation and drew ministers from ordinary folk.

Finney achieved his greatest successes in sections of western New York experiencing rapid changes in transportation and industrialization—in what he called the "Burned-Over District" because of the region's intense evangelical fires. Rapid change raised fears of social disorder—family dissolution, drinking, swearing, and prostitution. Many individuals worried, too, about their economic fate during the era's booms and busts.

When northern revivalist preachers emphasized good works—good deeds—they helped ignite social reform movements, first in the Burned-Over District and then in New England, the Middle Atlantic, and the upper Midwest. Evangelically inspired reform associations constituted what historians call the "benevolent empire." They shared a commitment to human perfectibility and often turned to the same wealthy men for financial resources and advice.

Charles G. Finney A lawyer-turned-Presbyterian minister who conducted revivals in towns like Utica along the Erie Canal and who stressed individual responsibility.

Moral Reform

Those resources enabled reformers to use the era's new technologies—steam presses and railroads. By mass-producing pamphlets and newspapers for distribution into the country's interior, reformers spread their message widely. With canals and railroads making travel easier, reformers could attend conventions and host speakers from distant places. Most reform organizations sponsored weekly newspapers, creating a community of reformers.

While industrialists and merchants provided financial resources for evangelical reform, their wives and daughters solicited new members and circulated petitions. Reforms expanded the cult of domesticity's role for women—beyond moral guardians for the family—to the public realm. Women established reformatories for wayward youth or asylums for orphans. Participation in reform movements allowed women to exercise moral authority outside the household, giving them new influence.

Many female reformers had attended a female academy or seminary—which embraced women as men's intellectual equals—where the curriculum included arts of "refinement"—music, dance, penmanship—but focused on science and literature. By 1820, approximately equal numbers of men and women attended institutions of higher education. Women prepared themselves to influence public opinion even as many maintained substantial domestic responsibilities. A few women became prominent editors and writers, but most influenced society as educators and reformers.

The aftermath of an 1830 exposé of prostitution in New York City illustrates reformers' public influence and belief in moral uplift. Female reformers there organized a shelter and tried to secure respectable employment for prostitutes. They also publicized brothel clients' names to shame these men. Organizing as the Female Moral Reform Society, by 1840 this group had 555 affiliated chapters nationwide. It soon lobbied successfully for criminal sanctions in New York State against men who seduced women into prostitution.

Dorothea Dix Leader of movement to improve conditions for the insane.

Penitentiaries and Asylums

A similar belief in perfectibility led reformers to establish penitentiaries aimed to transform criminals into productive members of society through disciplined regimens. Other reformers sought to improve treatment of the mentally ill, who were often imprisoned alongside criminals, and put in cages or dark dungeons. **Dorothea Dix**, the movement's leader, exemplifies the reformer who started with a religious belief in human perfectibility and moved into social action. Investigating asylums, petitioning the Massachusetts legislature, and lobbying other states and Congress, Dix had encouraged twenty-eight states to build institutions for the mentally ill by 1860.

temperance Abstinence from alcohol; name of the movement against alcohol.

Temperance

Temperance reformers, who advocated partial or full abstinence from alcoholic beverages, likewise crossed into the political sphere. Drinking was widespread in the early nineteenth century, when men gathered in public houses and inns to drink, talk, and play cards. Contracts were sealed and celebrations commemorated with liquor.

Link to Reverend M'Ilvaine Denounces Intemperance, 1839

Evangelicals considered drinking sinful, and forsaking alcohol was often part of conversion. Preachers condemned Sunday drinkers of alcohol for violating the Sabbath—workers' one day off. Factory owners claimed alcohol made workers unreliable. Civic leaders connected alcohol with crime. Middle-class reformers, often women, condemned it for diverting men from family responsibilities and fostering abusive behavior. In the early 1840s, thousands of women formed Martha Washington societies to reform alcoholics, raise children as teetotalers, and spread the temperance message.

As the temperance movement grew, its goal shifted from moderation to abstinence to prohibition. By the mid-1830s, five thousand state and local temperance societies touted teetotalism, and more than a million people had pledged abstinence. Per capita consumption of alcohol fell from five gallons per year in 1800 to below two gallons in the 1840s. The American Society for the Promotion of Temperance, organized in 1826, pushed for legislation ending alcohol manufacture and sale. In 1851, Maine became the first state to ban alcohol except for medicinal purposes; by 1855, similar laws were passed throughout New England and in New York, Pennsylvania, and the Midwest.

The temperance campaign had an anti-immigrant and anti-Catholic strain to it. Along the nation's canals, reformers lamented taverns catering to Irish workers, and in the cities, they expressed outrage at the Sunday tradition of German families' gathering at beer gardens. Some Catholics heeded the message, pledging abstinence and forming organizations such as the St. Mary's Mutual Benevolence Total Abstinence Society in Boston.

But many workers—Protestants and Catholics—rejected reformers' imposition of their middle-class values. Workers agreed that poverty and crime were problems but blamed poor wages, not drinking habits. Even some who resisted alcohol opposed prohibition, believing that nondrinking should be about self-control, not state coercion.

Public Schools

Public education usually included religious education, but when teachers taught Protestant beliefs and used the King James Bible, Catholics established their own

Visualizing THE PAST

Engaging Children

Hundreds of thousands of children joined the temperance movement, often by enlisting in the so-called Cold Water Army. Like adult temperance societies, the Cold Water Army advocated for complete abstinence from alcoholic beverages. On holidays such as George Washington's birthday and the Fourth of July, they marched at public gatherings, singing temperance songs and carrying banners and fans such as the one pictured below. Reverend Thomas P. Hunt, a Presbyterian minister, founded the Cold Water Army because he believed

that by recruiting children, he stood a greater chance of eradicating alcohol consumption than if he aimed his temperance efforts directly at adults. What might have been his logic? Why might children have wanted to join a Cold Water Army? Do the images on the certificate and fan offer any clues? What were the benefits of participating in the movement? What were the implied consequences of failing to do so? Why might Hunt have chosen the term *army*, and what about that choice might have proved appealing to his young recruits?

Children who participated in a Cold Water Army often received a certificate that acknowledged their commitment to the cause while reiterating the pledge they had taken.

Children in Cold Water Army parades sometimes carried decorative fans, which they may have displayed in their homes as well, as reminders to themselves and their parents of temperance's virtues.

schools. Some Protestants feared that Catholics would never assimilate into American culture and charged Catholics with plotting to impose papal control. Still, public education touched more Americans than did any other reform movement. **Horace Mann**, a Massachusetts lawyer and reformer from humble beginnings advocated free, tax-supported education to replace church schools and private schools. Universal education, Mann proposed, would "prepare children to become good citizens," end crime and help Americanize immigrants.

During Mann's tenure as secretary of the Massachusetts Board of Education from 1837 to 1848, Massachusetts led the "common school" movement, establishing teacher training, lengthening the school year, and raising salaries to make teaching more attractive. Adhering to notions that women had special claims to morality and could be paid less as men's dependents, Mann envisioned a system in which women educated future clerks, farmers, and workers with a practical curriculum that emphasized geography, arithmetic, and science. Due partly to expanding public education in the North, by 1850 most native-born white Americans were literate.

Horace Mann First secretary of the newly created Massachusetts Board of Education who presided over sweeping reforms to transform schools into institutions that occupied most of a child's time and energy.

Engineering and Science

Public education's emphasis on science reflected a broader belief that engineering and science could help remedy the nation's problems. Scientists and doctors blamed not immorality but unclean, stagnant water for causing epidemics. After the devastating 1832 cholera epidemic, New York City planned a massive waterworks, and between 1837 and 1842 built the forty-one-mile Croton Aqueduct that brought water from upstate New York to Manhattan.

Several scientific institutions were also founded in this era. After James Smithson, a wealthy British scientist, left his estate to the United States government, Congress established the Smithsonian Institution (1846), which promoted scientific knowledge. Joseph Henry, the Smithsonian's director, was a renowned scientist; his experiments in electromagnetism helped make possible the telegraph and, later, the telephone. Like Henry, many nineteenth-century Americans considered religion and science compatible. They saw scientific discoveries as signs of progress, symbolizing that the millennium was approaching. God created the natural world, they believed, and it was their Christian duty to perfect it in preparation for God's return.

Utopian Experiments

What were the goals of utopian communities?

Some idealists dreamed of a new social order. They established dozens of utopian communities based on religious principles, a resistance to the market economy's excessive individualism, or both. Some groups, like the **Mormons**, arose during the Second Great Awakening. Utopian communities attempted to recapture what they perceived as the past's more communal nature, even while offering radical departures from marriage and child rearing.

Mormons Members of the Church of Jesus Christ of Latter-day Saints, the first major denomination founded in the United States; members were persecuted for many years.

Joseph Smith Founder of the Mormon Church.

Mormons

No utopian experiment was more enduring than the Church of Jesus Christ of Latter-day Saints, whose members were known as Mormons. During the 1820s religious ferment in western New York, **Joseph Smith**, a young farmer, reported that an angel called Moroni gave him divinely engraved gold plates. Smith published his revelations as the *Book of Mormon* and organized a church in 1830. The next year, the community moved to Ohio to build a "New Jerusalem" and await the Second Coming of Jesus.

After angry mobs drove the Mormons from Ohio, they settled in Missouri. Anti-Mormons charged that Mormonism was a scam created by Joseph Smith, and feared Mormon economic and political power. In 1838, Missouri's governor charged Smith with fomenting insurrection and worked to indict him and other leaders for treason.

Smith and his followers left for Nauvoo, Illinois. The state legislature gave them a city charter making them self-governing. But again the Mormons met antagonism, especially after Smith introduced polygamy in 1841, allowing men to have several wives at once. In 1844, after Smith and his brother were charged with treason and jailed, then murdered, the Mormons left Illinois to seek security in the western wilderness. Under Brigham Young's leadership, they established a cooperative community in the Great Salt Lake Valley.

Shakers

The **Shakers**, the largest communal utopian experiment, reached their peak between 1820 and 1860, with six thousand members in twenty settlements in eight states. Shaker communities emphasized agriculture and handcrafts, contrasting with the new factory regime. Founded in England in 1772 by Mother Ann Lee, their name derived from their worship service, which included shaking their entire bodies. Ann Lee's children died in infancy, and she saw their deaths as retribution for her sin of intercourse; thus, she advocated celibacy. After imprisonment in England in 1773–1774, she settled in America.

Shakers Utopian sect that stressed celibacy and emphasized agriculture and handcrafts; became known for furniture designs long after the community itself ceased to exist.

Shakers lived communally, with men and women in separate quarters; individual families were abolished. Men and women shared leadership equally. Many Shaker settlements became temporary refuges for orphans, widows, runaways, abused wives, and laid-off workers. Their settlements depended on new recruits, partly because celibacy meant no reproduction and because some members left, unsuited to communal living or the Shakers' spiritual message.

Oneidans, Owenites, and Fourierists

Other utopian communities joined in resisting social change. John Humphrey Noyes, a lawyer converted by Finney's revivals, established two perfectionist communities: in Putney, Vermont, in 1835, and—after being indicted for adultery—in Oneida, New York, in 1848. Noyes advocated communal property, communal child rearing, and "complex marriage," in which all the community's men were married to all its women, but a woman could reject a sexual proposition. Couples applied to Noyes for permission to have a child, or Noyes assigned two people to reproduce. Robert Dale Owen's community in **New Harmony**, Indiana (1825–1828), also abolished private property and advocated communal child rearing. The Fourierists, named after French philosopher Charles Fourier, established more than two dozen communities in the Northeast and Midwest that resisted individualism and promoted gender equality.

New Harmony An important and well-known utopian community, founded in Indiana by Robert Owen.

The most famous Fourier community was Brook Farm, in West Roxbury, Massachusetts. Inspired by **transcendentalism**—the belief that the physical world is secondary to the spiritual realm, which human beings can reach only by intuition—Brook Farm's rural communalism combined spirituality, manual labor, intellectual life, and

transcendentalism The belief that the physical world is secondary to the spiritual realm, which humans can reach only by intuition.

play. Founded in 1841 by Unitarian minister George Ripley, Brook Farm attracted farmers, craftsmen, and writers, including novelist Nathaniel Hawthorne. In 1845, Brook Farm's one hundred members organized themselves into phalanxes (working-living units), following Fourier's model. As regimentation replaced individualism, membership dropped. A year after a disastrous fire in 1846, the experiment collapsed.

American Renaissance

Ralph Waldo Emerson, a pillar of transcendentalism, was the prime inspiration for a literary outpouring now known as the American Renaissance. After quitting his Boston Unitarian ministry in 1831, he spent two years in Europe before returning to lecture and write, preaching self-reliance. Widely admired, he influenced Hawthorne, *Dial* editor Margaret Fuller, Herman Melville, and Henry David Thoreau. The American Renaissance was distinctively American and an outgrowth of the European romantic movement. It addressed universal themes using American settings and characters. Hawthorne, for instance, used Puritan New England as a backdrop.

Thoreau championed individualism. In his 1849 essay on "Resistance to Civil Government" (known after his death as "Civil Disobedience"), Thoreau advocated resistance to a government engaged in immoral acts. During the War with Mexico (see Chapter 13), Thoreau refused to pay his taxes, believing they would aid an immoral war to expand slavery, and was briefly jailed. Later, defying federal law, Thoreau helped escaped slaves on their way to freedom.

Abolitionism

How did evangelicalism transform the antislavery movement?

Thoreau joined evangelical abolitionists trying to eradicate slavery, which they deemed a sin. Their efforts built on an earlier generation of antislavery activism among blacks and whites.

William Lloyd Garrison
Founder of *The Liberator* and a controversial white advocate of abolition, he demanded an immediate end to slavery and embraced civil rights for blacks on par with those of whites.

Evangelical Abolitionism

In the early 1830s, a new group of radical white abolitionists—most prominently, **William Lloyd Garrison**—rejected earlier gradualism and colonization (see Chapter 8) and demanded immediate and uncompensated emancipation. Garrison began publishing his abolitionist newspaper *The Liberator* in 1831; in 1833, he founded the American Antislavery Society, the era's largest abolitionist organization.

Immediatists believed slavery was a sin needing eradication. They were influenced by African American abolitionist societies and evangelicals' notion that humans, not God, determined their spiritual fate by choosing good or evil. When all humans had chosen good, the millennium would come. Slavery, however, denied enslaved men and women the ability to act as what Finney called "moral free agents."

Garrison advocated "moral suasion," hoping to bring emancipation by winning over slave owners and others who supported or tolerated slavery. Evangelical abolitionism depended, then, on large numbers of ministers and laypeople spreading the word nationwide.

The American Antislavery Society

By 1838, at its peak, the society had two thousand local affiliates and over 300,000 members. Unlike earlier white abolitionists, the immediatists welcomed men and women of all races and classes. Lydia Maria Child, Maria Chapman, and Lucretia Mott served on its executive committee; Child edited its official paper, the *National Anti-Slavery Standard*, from 1841 to 1843, and the society sponsored black and female speakers.

With the "great postal campaign" in 1835, the society flooded the mails with antislavery tracts. Women went door to door collecting signatures on antislavery petitions; by 1838, more than 400,000 petitions were sent to Congress. Abolitionist-minded women met in "sewing circles," making clothes for escaped slaves while organizing activities, such as antislavery fairs at which they sold goods—often hand-made—donating the proceeds to antislavery causes.

African American Abolitionists

At the same time, African Americans continued independent efforts to end slavery and improve free African Americans' status. Former slaves—famously, Frederick Douglass, Henry Bibb, Harriet Tubman, and Sojourner Truth—fought slavery through speeches, publications, and participation in a secret network known as the Underground Railroad, which spirited enslaved men, women, and children to freedom. By the thousands, African Americans established churches, moral reform societies, newspapers, and schools and orphanages.

Opposition to Abolitionism

But abolitionists' visibility inspired virulent opposition among southerners and northerners who recognized cotton's vital economic role and feared that emancipation would prompt an influx of freed slaves into the North. They questioned the institution's morality but believed blacks to be inherently inferior and incapable of the virtue and diligence required of freedom and citizenship.

Opposition to abolitionism could become violent. In Boston, David Walker, a southern-born free black, died under mysterious circumstances in 1830, one year after advocating the violent overthrow of slavery in his *Appeal ... to the Colored Citizens*. Among northerners who despised abolitionists, most were elites with economic connections to the southern cotton economy and political connections to leading southerners. Northern gentlemen incited anti-abolitionist riots. Mob violence peaked in 1835, with more than fifty riots aimed at abolitionists or African Americans. In 1837, in Alton, Illinois, a mob murdered white abolitionist editor Elijah P. Lovejoy, and rioters sacked his printing office.

Moral Suasion Versus Political Action

Violence made some immediatists question moral suasion as a tactic. James G. Birney, the son of a Kentucky slave owner, believed abolition could be effected only through politics. Involving women violated the natural order and detracted from the ultimate goal: freedom for slaves. Thus, when William Lloyd Garrison, an ardent women's rights supporter, endorsed Abby Kelley's appointment to the American Antislavery Society's business committee in 1840, he provoked an irreparable split in the abolitionist movement. Arthur Tappan and Theodore Weld led a dissident group that established the American and Foreign Anti-Slavery Society. That society formed a new political party: the Liberty Party, which nominated Birney for president in 1840 and 1844.

Destruction by Fire of Pennsylvania Hall,
On the night of the 17th May, **1838**

The Burning of Pennsylvania Hall, 1838 (colour litho), American School, (19th century)/Library Company of Philadelphia, PA, USA/The Bridgeman Art Library

Three days after its dedication in 1838, Pennsylvania Hall—an abolitionist center in Philadelphia—was burned to the ground by anti-abolitionist rioters.

Although committed to immediate abolition, the Liberty Party thought only states had the jurisdiction to determine slavery's legality. They believed the federal government could act only in western territories; the party demanded that new territories prohibit slavery. Prominent black abolitionists, including Frederick Douglass, endorsed the party, whose leaders also emphasized combating northern prejudice.

Free-Labor Ideology

Secular and religious belief in progress—and upward mobility—coalesced into the notion of free labor (that, in a competitive marketplace, those who worked hard and lived virtuous lives could improve their status). Many laborers initially rejected free-labor ideology, seeing it as a veiled attempt to rationalize poor wages, denigrate Catholicism, and quell worker protest. But by the 1850s, with slavery's expansion into the West, more northerners embraced free-labor ideology and saw slavery as antithetical to it. This way of thinking especially made the North distinctive.

Legacy FOR A PEOPLE AND A NATION

P. T. Barnum's Publicity Stunts

Usually remembered for the Ringling Brothers and Barnum & Bailey Circus, P. T. Barnum (1810–1891) left another legacy: the publicity stunt. Using hoaxes and spectacles, Barnum's American Museum in New York City drew tens of millions of visitors between 1841 and 1868, making Barnum the era's second wealthiest American.

Barnum first gained widespread publicity in 1835 with his traveling exhibition of Joice Heth, whom he claimed was George Washington's 161-year-old former slave. When interest waned, Barnum planted a rumor that she was a machine made of leather and bones. The penny press reveled in the ensuing controversy, swelling admissions and earning Barnum enough to purchase the American Museum, whose "500,000 natural and artificial curiosities" he promoted through similar stunts. Barnum also hosted the nation's first beauty pageant in 1854. Offensive to middle-class sensibilities, it flopped, but Barnum persevered with pageants featuring dogs, babies, and chickens. The baby show alone attracted 61,000 visitors. Selling more than a million copies, Barnum's autobiography inspired generations of entrepreneurs.

Many cultural icons began as promotional gimmicks, including the Miss America Pageant (1921), the Macy's Thanksgiving Day parade (1924), and the Goodyear blimp (1925). Since 1916, Nathan's has hosted a Fourth of July hot dog–eating contest, now attracting forty thousand spectators and a television audience. The *Guinness Book of World Records*, begun as an Irish beer company's promotional brochure, inspires thousands each year to attempt to break records. Even failed attempts generate publicity.

By staging stunts for media exposure, today's entrepreneurs reveal the enduring legacy of P. T. Barnum, the self-proclaimed greatest showman on earth.

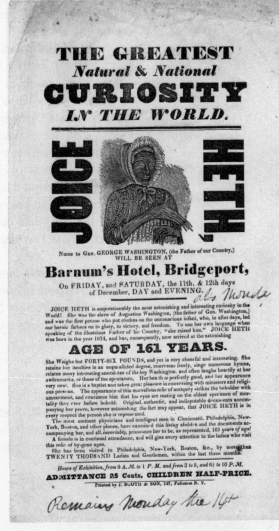

P. T. Barnum's first great success came in 1835 when he charged admission to see Joice Heth, whom he claimed was the 161-year-old former slave of George Washington.

Summary

During the first half of the nineteenth century, the North became enmeshed in commercial culture. Northern states and capitalists invested heavily in internal improvements, which lay the groundwork for market expansion. Most northerners shifted toward commercial farming or, in smaller numbers, toward industrial wage labor. Farmers specialized in cash crops, while their children worked in factories or countinghouses.

To many northerners, the market economy symbolized progress, bringing easier access to cheap western lands, employment for surplus farm laborers, and commercial availability of goods that had been time-consuming to produce. But the market economy also led to increased specialization, a depersonalized workplace, and a sharper divide between work and leisure. The market economy tied northerners to fluctuating national and international markets, and during economic downturns, many northern families experienced destitution.

With less need for children's labor, northerners began producing smaller families. Even as working-class children worked, middle-class families created a model of childhood that had parents shielding children from the world's dangers. Mothers, in theory, became moral guardians, keeping the home safe from the new economy's competitiveness. Few women, though, could devote themselves entirely to nurturing their families.

Immigrants and free African Americans performed the lowest-paying work, and many native-born whites blamed them for problems spurred by rapid economic change. Anti-immigrant (especially anti-Catholic) and antiblack riots became commonplace. Immigrants and African Americans responded by forming their own communities.

Cities came to symbolize the possibilities and limits of market expansion. Urban areas were marked by extremes of wealth, vibrant working-class cultures, as well as poverty, crime, and mob violence. To reconcile the seeming contradictions, middle-class northerners articulated free-labor ideology, touting the possibility for upward mobility in a competitive marketplace. This ideology would become increasingly central to northern regional identity.

Chapter Review

Or Was the North Distinctive?

What happened to the North and South economically after the War of 1812?

The South continued as an agricultural region and expanded its slave system, while the North transformed quickly into a market economy. With the war cutting off European trade, northern entrepreneurs invested in domestic production and factories. Commercial farming emerged in the North, with farmers shifting from producing just what they needed—with small amounts for trade—to specializing in crops that would generate cash, which they could use to buy goods they formerly made at home, such as soap and cloth.

The Transentation Revolution

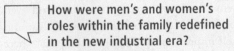
How did the transportation revolution help lay the groundwork for a market economy?

The lack of inexpensive, quick, and convenient transportation impeded westward expansion and industrial growth until the early nineteenth century. Beginning in the 1800s, however, several innovations—steamboats, canals, and railroads—dramatically reduced the cost and time to transport raw materials, goods, and people. Canals connected regions and shortened travel times, and steamboats reduced trips that previously took months to just days. Faster and less costly to build, railroads soon replaced canals, with transportation costs overall cut by as much as 95 percent. Goods that were previously unavailable in the nation's interior now could be had easily and cheaply. Westward migration expanded, creating new markets and cultural links between previously distant regions, as news, products, and people of various backgrounds fanned out from the Northeast to the Northwest.

Factories and Industrialization

How was factory work different from the work life people previously knew?

The artisan shops and family farms that predated factories had fewer formal rules and less structure than the factories that arose in the late eighteenth and early nineteenth centuries. Artisans traditionally saw themselves as producers, in charge of their labor and its outcome and working side by side with hired helpers. In factories, workers infrequently saw owners and worked for wages under the watchful eye of supervisors with strict rules and a clock governing their day. Instead of learning how to make something from start to finish, workers now specialized in only one part of the process and never saw the finished item. There was no job security, and employers often cut wages or eliminated jobs during economic downturns. Workers resisted by organizing strikes—as the mill girls did—or forming unions.

Consumption and Commercialization

How did farm women's work change as the commercial economy expanded?

Along with their regular farm and household duties, rural women took on new responsibilities to help pay for some of the items they now bought (such as

textiles) instead of bartering for or making on their own. Some took in outwork; others increased production of eggs, milk, butter, and produce and other items for sale in the market. Daughters often went to work in textile mills, sending part of their wages home to aid their families.

Families in Flux

How were men's and women's roles within the family redefined in the new industrial era?

Before the rise of the market economy, families were the center of production and economic activity. As industrialization took hold, however, new ideals transformed families into moral and cultural institutions. Men, particularly middle-class men, occupied the public sphere, providing for and protecting their families. In this new "separate spheres" ideology, women's roles were confined to the home, and they were charged with making it a retreat for husbands and children from the harshness of economic life. This ideology, which elevated women's domestic roles, was later dubbed *the cult of domesticity* or *the cult of true womanhood*. However, this ideology was rarely realized in practice.

The Growth of Cities

How could cities be seen at once as symbols of progress and of moral decay?

America experienced rapid urbanization between 1820 and 1860, particularly in the Northeast and Midwest, as some previously agricultural regions—such as Rochester near the Erie Canal—became cities and existing cities grew dramatically in population and size. People flocked to cities, seeking opportunities. On the one hand, cities served as transportation and industrial hubs and nurtured schools, churches, civil governments, and museums—all signs of progress. On the other hand, some middle-class Americans regarded them as centers of disease, poverty, crowding, crime, and vice—symbols of moral decline. Prostitution, vagrancy, and theft led reformers to seek to purify cities. They targeted the working class, who many saw as contributing to urban decay, with the promise of upward mobility and free-labor ideology—that those who worked hard, lived virtuous lives, and gave up alcohol would become successful. Workers initially rejected such notions as an imposition on their lives, but with slavery's potential expansion westward in the 1850s, many embraced free-labor ideology.

From Revival to Reform

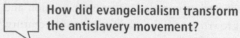

How did religious revival movements lead to social reform?

Ministers and preachers in the Second Great Awakening raised hope for their audiences that the second coming of Jesus Christ was at hand—as long as listeners were able to renounce sin and purge society of sinful behaviors such as drinking, swearing, and even slavery. Revivalists stressed human perfectibility and promoted self-improvement. They preached that there was a direct link between how people lived and whether they would enter God's Kingdom, and in so doing, inspired social and moral reform. Women were often a major force in reform movements, expanding their domestic roles in the home into efforts to counteract the evils of the market economy. Reform goals included reformatories for wayward youth, orphan asylums, rehabilitation for criminals, temperance, and improvements in education.

Utopian Experiments

What were the goals of utopian communities?

Often inspired by religious revivalism, the utopian movement sought to hold the line on the rapid social change that members found disturbing, in particular, the rising market economy's excessive individualism. Some dreamed of creating a new social order; others wanted to recapture the supposed communal nature of the past and at the same time reshape marriage, child rearing, and other social arrangements. The Shakers, for example, built a profitable community around agriculture and handcrafts, but also abolished individual families in favor of men and women living in separate quarters and sharing leadership. The Oneida community centered on communal property ownership, communal child rearing, and "complex marriage" in which all men were married to all women. The Fourierists included writers and intellectuals who inspired an American renaissance in literature and the arts, with Brook Farm in West Roxbury, Massachusetts, their most famous community. During its brief existence, the community

embraced transcendentalism, the notion that the physical world is secondary to the spiritual realm.

Abolitionism

How did evangelicalism transform the antislavery movement?

Abolitionism dates back to the nation's earliest days, when efforts to end slavery were initiated by both free blacks and elite whites. After 1830, however, evangelical abolitionists seeking to eradicate America's sins focused on slavery with renewed vigor. The activist and newspaper editor William Lloyd Garrison led a new, more radical strain of abolitionism known as "immediatism," which called for the immediate and complete end of slavery without compensating slave owners. Immediatists shared the evangelical belief that people determined their spiritual fate through good or evil acts and that by ending slavery, they could bring about the millennium, or Christ's return to earth. These abolitionists welcomed women and African Americans to the movement, inviting former slaves to serve as speakers and encouraging women to not only join but serve on executive committees, a controversial move that ultimately led to the split of the abolitionist movement in 1840.

Suggestions for Further Reading

Jeanne Boydston, *Home and Work: Housework, Wages, and the Ideology of Labor in the Early Republic* (1990)

Nancy Cott, *The Bonds of Womanhood: "Women's Sphere" in New England, 1780–1835* (1977)

Daniel Walker Howe, *What Hath God Wrought: The Transformation of America, 1815–1848* (2007)

Mary Kelley, *Learning to Stand and Speak: Women, Education, and Public Life in America's Republic* (2006)

Bruce Laurie, *Artisans into Workers: Labor in Nineteenth-Century America* (1989)

Steven Mintz, *Moralists and Modernizers: America's Pre–Civil War Reformers* (1995)

Carol Sheriff, *The Artificial River: The Erie Canal and the Paradox of Progress, 1817–1862* (1996)

Christine Stansell, *City of Women: Sex and Class in New York, 1789–1860* (1986)

Melvyn Stokes and Stephen Conway, eds., *The Market Revolution in America: Social, Political, and Religious Expressions, 1800–1880* (1996)

George Rogers Taylor, *The Transportation Revolution, 1815–1860* (1951)

11

The Contested West

1815–1860

To eight-year-old Henry Clay Bruce, moving west was an adventure. In April 1844, the Virginia boy began a 1,500-mile, two-month trip to his new home in Missouri. Henry marveled at the beautiful terrain, impressive towns, and steamboat ride from Louisville to St. Louis. Once in Missouri, Henry noticed how much the West differed from the East. Farms were farther apart, and the countryside abounded with wild fruits, game, and fish. Still, rattlesnakes, wolves, and vicious hogs kept Henry and his playmates close to home.

A slave, Henry made the trip with his mother and siblings after his owner, Pettis Perkinson, decided to seek a fresh start in the West. Perkinson and three other white Virginians crammed their families, slaves, and whatever belongings they could fit into three wagons. In Missouri, Pettis resided with his brother, who—according to Henry—readily yelled at and whipped his own slaves. Henry's first year in Missouri was as carefree as a slave child's life could be. The boy fished, hunted (with dogs, not guns), and gathered prairie chickens' eggs. But by age nine, Henry was hired out, first to a brickmaker, then to a tobacco factory. He worked sunup to sundown, and when he failed to satisfy his bosses, he was whipped.

Meanwhile, Pettis Perkinson, unenamored with Missouri, returned to Virginia, later summoning some of his slaves, including Henry. Slaves' work was less rigorous in Virginia, but that did not compensate for leaving loved ones behind in Missouri. Soon Pettis Perkinson again grew weary of Virginia and renewed his quest for opportunity in the West, this time in Mississippi, where his sister lived. But cotton plantation life suited neither Henry nor his master, who now decided—to his slaves' joy—to give Missouri another chance.

Two years later, Perkinson headed for Texas. Henry, now in his late teens, and his brothers refused to go. Although livid, Pettis Perkinson abandoned his plans rather than contend with recalcitrant slaves. Henry became the foreman on Perkinson's Missouri farm, where he remained until escaping during the Civil War to the free state of Kansas. Finally, Henry Clay Bruce found the opportunity and freedom that had led so many westward.

Chapter Outline

The West in the American Imagination
Defining the West | Frontier Literature | Western Art | Countering the Myths

Expansion and Resistance in the Trans-Appalachian West
Deciding Where to Move | Indian Removal and Resistance | Black Hawk War | Selling the West | Clearing the Land

The Federal Government and Westward Expansion
The Fur Trade | Transcontinental Exploration | A Military Presence | Public Lands

LINKS TO THE WORLD *Gold in California*

The Southwestern Borderlands
Southwestern Slavery | The New Mexican Frontier | The Texas Frontier | The Comanche Empire | American Empresarios | Texas Politics | The Lone Star Republic | "War of a Thousand Deserts" | Wartime Losses and Profits

VISUALIZING THE PAST *Paintings and Cultural Impressions*

Cultural Frontiers in the Far West
Western Missionaries | Mormons | Oregon and California Trails | Indian Treaties | Ecological Consequences of Cultural Contact | Gold Rush | Mining Settlements

LEGACY FOR A PEOPLE AND A NATION
Descendants of Early Latino Settlers

SUMMARY

299

In 1820, about 20 percent of the nation's population lived west of the Appalachian Mountains. By 1860, nearly 50 percent did. Most whites and free blacks moved west seeking better opportunities. Easterners envisioned in the West enormous tracts of fertile, uncultivated land, or, beginning in the late 1840s, gold or silver mines. Some saw opportunities for lumbering or ranching or for selling goods or services to farmers, miners, lumbermen, and cattlemen.

For some white Americans, mostly southerners, the ability to own slaves in the West signaled the epitome of their own freedom. For other northerners and southerners, slavery's westward expansion frustrated dreams for a new beginning in a region free from what they saw as slavery's degrading influence on white labor. Northerners often set their sights on the Oregon Territory, where they hoped to find agricultural prosperity in a land free from blacks, enslaved and free.

Men often decided to go west without consulting their wives and children, and slaves' wishes received less consideration. Nor did western settlers consider the impact of their migration on Indian peoples living there on lands they had occupied for generations, or since being relocated by the U.S. government.

Beyond removing Indians, the federal government made laws regulating settlement and the establishment of territorial governments, surveyed and fixed prices on public lands, sold those lands, invested in transportation routes, and established a military presence.

In the 1820s, the Mexican government, too, encouraged Anglo-American settlement in the West along its northern borderlands, which it would later regret. U.S. settlers vied with the region's other inhabitants—Indians, Hispanics, and people of mixed heritage—for land and natural resources. A decade later, Mexico's northern province of Texas declared its independence and sought annexation by the United States. Thus began heightened tensions between the United States and Mexico, and within the United States as Texas's future became entangled with slavery.

Human interactions in the West involved cooperation and conflict. But with each passing decade, conflict—between expectations and reality, between people with different aspirations and worldviews—would increasingly define daily life.

As you read this chapter, keep the following questions in mind:

- **How did conditions and tensions in the East influence western migration and settlement?**

- **How did public, private, and individual initiatives converge to shape the West's development?**

- **What motivated cooperation in the West, and what spurred conflict?**

The West in the American Imagination

What were the myths that helped shape white Americans' perceptions of the West?

For historian Frederick Jackson Turner, writing in the late nineteenth century, the western frontier, with its abundance of free land, was the "meeting point between savagery and civilization." It bred American democracy, shaped the American character, and made the United States exceptional. Modern historians generally eschew the notion of

Chronology

1812	General Land Office established
1820	Price lowered on public lands
1821	Santa Fe Trail charted
	Mexico's independence
1823	Mexico allows Stephen Austin to settle U.S. citizens
1824	Congressional General Survey Act
	Jedediah Smith's South Pass publicized
	Indian Office established
1825–32	*Empresario* contracts signed
1826	Fredonia rebellion fails
1830	Indian Removal Act (see Chapter 9)
1830–46	Comanche, Navajo, and Apache raiders devastate northern Mexican states
1832	Black Hawk War
1834	McCormick reaper patented
1836	Lone Star Republic founded
	U.S. Army Corps of Topographical Engineers established
1840–60	250,000 to 500,000 migrants travel overland
1841	Log Cabin Bill
	Texas annexed (See Chapter 12)
1846–48	War with Mexico (Chapter 12)
1847	Mormons settle Great Salt Lake valley
1848	California gold discovered
1849–50s	Migrants stream into Great Plains and Far West
1857–58	Mormons and U.S. Army in armed conflict
1862	Homestead Act

American exceptionalism, stressing instead the deep and complex connections between the United States and the rest of the world. Although today's scholars reject the racialist assumptions of Turner's definition of *frontier*, some see continued value in the term to signify a meeting place of different cultures. Others see the West as a place, not a process, though they disagree over what delineates it.

Defining the West

For early-nineteenth-century Americans of European descent, the West included anything west of the Appalachian Mountains. It represented the future— a place offering economic and social betterment, typically through landownership. The West's seeming abundance of land meant that anyone could hope to own a farm and achieve independence. Men who already owned land, like Pettis Perkinson, looked westward for cheaper, bigger, and more fertile landholdings. With the discovery of gold in California in 1848, the West became a place to strike it rich. Others went west by force, including slaves and Indians removed from their eastern homelands by the U.S. military under the Indian Removal Act of 1830.

To others, the notion of the West would have been baffling. Emigrants from Mexico and Central or South America traveled north to get to what European Americans called the West. Chinese nationals traveled eastward to California. Many Indians simply considered the West home. Other Indians and French Canadians journeyed southward to the West. All arrived in the western portion of the North American continent because of a combination of factors pushing and pulling them.

Frontier Literature

For European Americans, Daniel Boone became the archetypal frontiersman, whose daring individual-ism opened the Eden-like West for hardworking free-dom lovers. Through biographies, Boone became a familiar figure in American and European households. The mythical Boone lived in the wilderness and shrank from society. He overpowered bears and Indians and became the pathfinder for civilization. As a friend wrote, Boone "has been the instrument of opening the road to millions of the human family … to a Land flowing with milk and honey." By borrowing biblical language—the land of milk and honey denoting the Promised Land—Boone's friend suggested that Boone was Moses-like, leading his people to a land of abundance.

With the invention of the steam press in the early 1830s, western adventure stories became cheap and widely read. Davy Crockett, another real-life figure turned into mythical hero, was featured in many of them. Crockett first fought the Creeks under Andrew Jackson but later championed Indian rights. Still, after his death

MAP 11.1
Westward Expansion, 1800–1860

Through exploration, purchase, war, and treaty, the United States became a continental nation, stretching from the Atlantic to the Pacific. Source: Copyright © Cengage Learning 2015

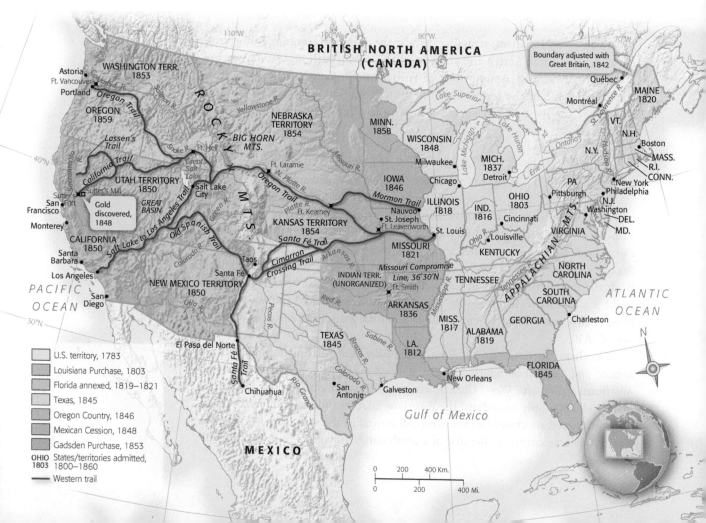

defending the Alamo mission during Texas's fight for independence (1836), Crockett nonetheless appeared in stories portraying the West as violent, a place where one escaped civilized society and fought Indians and Mexicans. But even in this myth, the American West symbolized what white Americans saw as their nation's core value: freedom.

Western Art

Artists' images often revealed more about white Americans' ideals than about the West itself. In these portrayals, the West was sometimes an untamed wilderness inhabited by savages (noble or otherwise), and sometimes a cultivated garden, a land of milk and honey where the Jeffersonian agrarian dream was realized.

The first Anglo-American artists to travel west were Samuel Seymour and Titian Ramsay Peale, whom the federal government hired to accompany explorer Stephen H. Long to the Rocky Mountains in 1830. They pioneered an influential art genre: facsimiles in government reports. Between 1840 and 1860, Congress published nearly sixty works on western exploration, featuring hundreds of lithographs and engravings of plants, animals, and people. Some reports became best sellers. The government distributed more than 53,000 copies of its popular twelve-volume Pacific Railway Survey (1855–1860), which helped easterners visualize the continent's western reaches.

In one of his most famous portraits, George Catlin painted Wi-Jun-Jon, an Assiniboine Indian, both before and after he had mingled with white men. In the "before" stance, the Indian is a dignified, peace-pipe-bearing warrior; in the "after" portrait, the "corrupted" Indian has abandoned dignity for vanity and his peace pipe for a cigar.

Smithsonian American Art Museum, Washington, DC/Art Resource, NY

Sometimes government reports made telling alterations to the paintings they included. When Richard Kern accompanied explorer James H. Simpson in 1849 to the Southwest, he painted a Navajo man in a submissive pose. The reproduction transformed the man's pose into a rebellious one. In other cases, the government reports changed artists' depictions of Indian-occupied landscapes into empty terrain free for the taking.

Artists' cultural assumptions colored their portrayals of the West, too, and commercial artists produced what they thought the public craved. When **George Catlin** traveled west immediately following the Indian Removal Act of 1830, he painted the region with a moral in mind. Indians came in two varieties—those who preserved their original, almost noble qualities of freedom and moderation, and those who, after coming in contact with whites, had become "dissolute." Indians, he implied, benefited from removal from white Americans' corrupting influence.

George Catlin American painter who traveled throughout the West and produced numerous portraits of Native Americans that reflected his fascination with and beliefs about them.

Countering the Myths

But western realities often clashed with promoters' promises, and disappointed settlers sometimes tried to clarify matters for future migrants. Rebecca Burlend and her son were lured to Illinois by a fellow Englishman's letters extolling "a land flowing with milk and honey." Later, Burlend and her son wrote *A True Picture of Emigration* (1831), which described Illinois' hardships—intemperate weather, difficult working conditions, and swindlers. Her account sought not to discourage emigration, but to substitute a realistic for a rosy description.

Expansion and Resistance in the Trans-Appalachian West

What made the Midwest especially appealing to white settlers?

In the 1820s and 1830s, settlers streamed into the Old Northwest and the Old Southwest by foot, horseback, wagon, canal boat, steamboat, or a combination of means. Many people, like Pettis Perkinson and his slaves, moved several times, and when opportunities failed to materialize, some returned home.

Both the Old Northwest and the Old Southwest saw population explosions during the early nineteenth century. While the Old Southwest grew by 50 percent each decade, the Northwest's population grew exponentially. In 1790, the Northwest region's white population numbered just a few hundred. By 1860, nearly 7 million people called it home. Between 1810 and 1830, Ohio's population more than quadrupled, while Indiana and Illinois grew fourteenfold and thirteenfold, respectively. Michigan's population multiplied fiftyfold between 1820 and 1850. Migration accounted for most of this growth. Once in the Old Northwest, people did not stay put. By the 1840s, more people left Ohio than moved into it. Geographic mobility, the search for better opportunities, and connections to the market economy defined the region that became known as the Midwest.

Deciding Where to Move

Moving west meant leaving behind worn-out soil and settled areas with little land available for purchase. The journey was arduous; the labor of clearing new lands, backbreaking. The West was a land of opportunity but also of uncertainty. What if the soil proved less fertile than anticipated? What if neighbors proved unfriendly, or worse? Like Pettis Perkinson, people often relocated where they had relatives or friends and traveled with acquaintances. They chose areas with familiar climates. Migrants also settled in ethnic communities or with people of similar religious affiliations. As a result, the Midwest was—in the words of two historians—"more like an ethnic and cultural checkerboard than the proverbial melting pot."

The legal status of slavery influenced where people settled. Some white southerners, tired of the planter elite's power, sought areas free from slavery—or at least where there were few plantations. Many others went west to improve their chances of owning slaves, or of purchasing additional slaves. White northerners hoped to distance themselves from slavery as well as from free blacks. In the 1850s, many midwestern states passed "black laws" prohibiting African Americans, free or enslaved, from living within their boundaries. Ironically, free blacks migrated west to free themselves from eastern prejudice. Enslaved people moved west in enormous numbers after 1815. Some traveled with their owners; others with slave traders. When white parents gave their westward-bound children slaves, they tore those slaves from their own spouses, children, or parents. For those traveling with slave traders, their first destination in the West was the slave pen, often in New Orleans, where they were auctioned to the highest bidder, who became their new owner and took them farther west. Nonetheless, some slaves took advantage of frontier conditions—vast forests, inconsistent law enforcement, and the proximity of Native American communities willing to harbor runaway slaves—to seize their freedom.

Between 1815 and 1860, few western migrants settled on the Great Plains, a region reserved for Indians until the 1850s, and few easterners risked the overland journey to California and Oregon before the transcontinental railroad's

MAP 11.2

Settlement in the Old Southwest and Old Northwest, 1820 and 1840

Removal of Indians and a growing transportation network opened up land to white and black settlers in the regions known as the Old Southwest and the Old Northwest, as the U.S. population grew from 9.6 million in 1820 to 17.1 million in 1840. Source: Copyright © Cengage Learning 2015

completion in 1869. At first the Southwest appealed most to settlers. But beginning in the 1820s, the Midwest drew more settlers with its better-developed transportation routes, democratic access to economic markets, smaller African American population, cheaper average landholding, and climatic similarity to New England and northern Europe. The Old Northwest's thriving transportation hubs also made good first stops for western migrants lacking cash to purchase land. They found work unloading canal boats, planting and harvesting wheat, grinding wheat into flour, sawing trees into lumber—or, more often, cobbling together a combination of seasonal jobs. With the Old Northwest's population growing quickly, white southerners worried increasingly about congressional representation and laws regarding slavery.

Indian Removal and Resistance

In the Midwest and the Southwest, white settlement depended on Indian removal. Even as the U.S. Army escorted Indians from the Old Southwest (see Chapter 9), the federal government arranged eighty-six treaties between 1829 and 1851 in which northeastern Indian nations relinquished land titles in exchange for lands west of the Mississippi River. Some northern Indians evaded removal, including the Miamis in Indiana, the Ottawas and Chippewas in the upper Midwest, and the Winnebagos in southern Wisconsin. In 1840, Miami chiefs acceded to pressure to exchange 500,000 acres in Indiana for equivalent

In 1834, Karl Bodmer painted a farm on the Illinois prairie, depicting the more permanent, if still modest, structures that farmers built after the initial urgency to clear fields for cultivation had subsided.

acreage in Indian Country. Under the treaty, their people had five years to move or be escorted out by federal troops. But about half of the Miami nation dodged the soldiers—and many of those who trekked to Indian Country later returned. In Wisconsin, some Winnebagos eluded removal or returned to Wisconsin after being escorted west by soldiers.

Black Hawk War

In a series of treaties between 1804 and 1830, Sauks (or "Sacs") and Fox leaders exchanged lands in north-western Illinois and southwestern Wisconsin for lands across the Mississippi River in Iowa Territory. Black Hawk, a Sauk warrior, disputed the treaties' validity and in 1832 led Sauk and Fox families to Illinois, panicking white settlers. The state's governor activated the militia, who were joined by militia from surrounding states and territories and U.S. Army regular soldiers. Over several months, hundreds of Indians and dozens of whites died under often gruesome circumstances in the Black Hawk War. As the Sauks and Fox tried to flee across the Mississippi River, American soldiers fired indiscriminately. Those who survived the river crossing met gunfire from Lakota (Sioux), now allied with the Americans.

Black Hawk surrendered, and U.S. officials impressed upon him and other leaders the futility of resistance. After being imprisoned, then sent to Washington, D.C., along a route meant to underscore the United States' immense size and population, and imprisoned again, the Indians were returned home. The Black Hawk War ended militant Indian uprisings in the Old Northwest.

Selling the West

Land speculators, developers of "paper towns" (ones existing on paper only), steamboat companies, and manufacturers of farming implements promoted the Midwest as a tranquil place of unbounded opportunity. Land proprietors emphasized the region's connections to eastern customs and markets. They knew that, when families moved west, they did not seek to escape civilization.

Western settlement generally followed connections to national and international markets. Eastern farmers, looking to shed tired soil or tenancy, sought fertile lands for commercial crops. Labor-saving devices, such as Cyrus McCormick's reaper (1834) and John Deere's steel plow (1837), made the West more alluring. McCormick, a Virginia inventor, patented a horse-drawn reaper that allowed two men to harvest the same number of acres of wheat that previously required between four and sixteen men. The reaper's efficiency achieved its greatest payoffs on the large, flat prairie lands, so McCormick relocated his factory to Chicago in 1847. Without John Deere's steel plow, which could break through tough grass and roots without constant cleaning, "breaking the plains" might not have been possible.

Clearing the Land

After locating a suitable land claim, settlers constructed a rudimentary cabin if none already existed. Time did not permit elaborate structures; settlers first had to clear the land. At the rate of five to ten acres a year, depending on a family's size, the average family needed ten years to fully clear a farm. Prairie land took less time.

Whereas farming attracted families, lumbering and, later, mining appealed to single young men (although employers regarded married men as the most stable workforce, they only wanted "good Families without children," whose wives would work as cooks or laundresses). By the 1840s, as eastern forests became depleted, northeastern lumber companies and laborers migrated to Wisconsin, Michigan, and Minnesota. Recently arrived Scandinavians and French Canadians also worked in the lumber industry. As the Great Lakes forests thinned, lumbermen moved again—some to the Gulf States' pine forests, some to Canada, and some to the Far West, where Mexicans in California and British in Canada had already established flourishing lumber industries. With the rapid growth of California's cities following the **Gold Rush** of 1849, timber's demand soared, drawing midwestern lumbermen farther west.

Gold Rush After an American carpenter discovered gold in the foothills of California's Sierra Nevada range in 1848, Americans and people from around the world moved to California to look for gold.

Midwestern cities nurtured the surrounding countryside's settlement. Steamboats turned river settlements like Louisville and Cincinnati into commercial centers, while Chicago, Detroit, and Cleveland grew up on the Great Lakes' banks. By the mid-nineteenth century, Chicago, with its railroads, stockyards, and grain elevators, dominated the region's economy; western farmers transported livestock and grain by rail to that city, where pigs became packed meat and grain became flour before being shipped east. The promise of future flour and pigs gave rise to commodities markets. Some of the world's most sophisticated and speculative economic practices took place in Chicago.

The Federal Government and Westward Expansion

How did the federal government sponsor and speed up westward expansion?

Few white Americans considered settling in the West before the region had been explored, surveyed, secured, and "civilized," which meant Indian removal and the establishment of churches, businesses, and American legal structures. Wide-scale settlement depended on the federal government's sponsorship.

The Fur Trade

Fur trappers were among the first white Americans in the trans-Appalachian West, but their lives bore faint resemblance to their mythical representation as mountain men who dared to go where whites never trod. Fur trappers lived among Indians, became multilingual, and often married Indian women. Indian women transformed animal carcasses into finished pelts, and they smoothed trade relations between husbands and their native communities. The offspring of such marriages—métis or mestizos (people of mixed Indian and European heritage)—added to the West's cultural complexity.

The fur trade was an international business, with pelts from America reaching Europe and Asia. Until the 1820s, British companies dominated the trade, but American ventures prospered in the 1820s and 1830s. The American Fur Company made John Jacob Astor—who managed his business from New York City—the nation's wealthiest man. Beginning in the 1820s, trappers and traders met annually for a "rendezvous"—a multiday gathering where they traded fur for guns, tobacco,

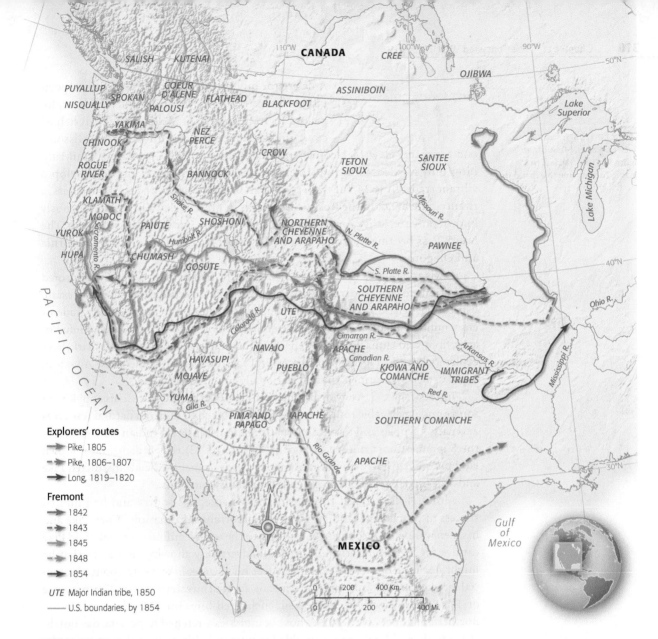

Explorers' routes

➤ Pike, 1805
➤ Pike, 1806–1807
➤ Long, 1819–1820

Fremont

➤ 1842
➤ 1843
➤ 1845
➤ 1848
➤ 1854

UTE Major Indian tribe, 1850
— U.S. boundaries, by 1854

MAP 11.3
Western Indians and Routes of Exploration

Although western explorers believed they were discovering new routes and places, Indians had long lived in most of the areas through which explorers traveled. Source: Robert Utley, *The Indian Frontier of the American West, 1846–1890*, University of New Mexico Press, 1984, p. 5. Reprinted by permission of the University of New Mexico Press. © Cengage Learning 2015

and beads that they could exchange with Indians. Modeled on Indian gatherings, the rendezvous united Americans, Indians, Mexicans, and people of mixed heritage to trade, gamble, and socialize.

By 1840, the American fur trade was fading. Beavers had been overhunted and fashions had shifted, with silk supplanting beaver fur for hats. The traders' legacy includes resource extraction and depletion, introducing native peoples to devastating diseases, and developing trails across the trans-Mississippi West.

Santa Fe Trail Trading route from St. Louis, Missouri, to Santa Fe, New Mexico, that enabled commerce to expand its reach farther west.

Transcontinental Exploration

A desire for quicker and safer routes for transporting goods to trading posts drove much early exploration. In 1821, merchant William Becknell helped chart the **Santa Fe Trail** running between Missouri and Santa Fe, New Mexico, where it connected to the Chihuahua Trail running into Mexico, allowing American and Mexican merchants to develop a vibrant trade. In 1824, fur trader Jedediah Smith rediscovered the South Pass, a twenty-mile break in the Rocky Mountains in present-day Wyoming previously known only to Native Americans and some Pacific Fur Company trappers. The South Pass became the route followed by most overland travelers to California and Oregon.

Lewis and Clark's Corps of Discovery was the first of many federally sponsored expeditions to chart the trans-Mississippi West. These expeditions sought to establish cordial relations with Indian groups with whom Americans might trade or enter military alliances. Some were scientific, exploring the region's native inhabitants, flora, and fauna. But they were always commercial. Like Lewis and Clark, later explorers hoped to locate land, water, and rail routes that would allow American businessmen and farmers to trade nationally and internationally.

In 1805, the U.S. Army dispatched Zebulon Pike to find the Mississippi River's source and a navigable route west. He was instructed to research natural resources and native peoples and foster diplomatic relationships with Indian leaders. Before the Supreme Court ruled in *Johnson v. M'Intosh* (1823) that Indians did not own land but merely had a "right of occupancy," government officials instructed Pike and other explorers to purchase lands for military garrisons.

Although Pike failed to identify the Mississippi's source and had limited success in purchasing land, he gathered important information. When Pike and his men wandered into Spanish territory to the south, military officials held Pike captive for several months in Mexico, inadvertently showing him areas that he might not have otherwise explored. After his release, Pike wrote about a potential market in furs and precious metals in southwestern cities. The province of Tejas (Texas), with its fertile soil, enchanted him. But Pike dismissed other northern provinces of Mexico, whose boundaries stretched to present-day northern Nevada and Utah, as unsuitable for human habitation. Although nomadic Indians might sustain themselves there, he explained, the region was unfit for civilized people.

In 1820, army explorer Stephen Long similarly deemed modern-day Oklahoma, Kansas, and Nebraska as "the Great American Desert," incapable of cultivation. Until the 1850s, when a transcontinental railroad was planned, this "desert" was reserved for Indian settlement. In 1838, Congress established the U.S. Army Corps of Topographical Engineers to systematically explore the West. As second lieutenant in that corps, **John C. Frémont** undertook three expeditions to the region between the upper Mississippi and Missouri rivers, the Rockies, the Great Basin, Oregon, and California. He helped survey the Oregon Trail. Aided by his wife, Jessie Benton Frémont, he published best-selling accounts of his explorations. The Corps of Topographical Engineers' most significant contributions came in the 1850s with its surveying of possible routes for a transcontinental railroad.

John C. Frémont Explorer who played a role in a California rebellion against Mexico; later a senator and presidential candidate and force in national politics.

Link to Frémont, The Exploring Expedition to the Rocky Mountains, Oregon, and California

A Military Presence

The army also helped ready the West for settlement. With the General Survey Act of 1824, Congress empowered the military to chart transportation improvements vital to military protection or commercial growth. Army engineers helped design state- and privately sponsored roads, canals, and railroads, and army soldiers cleared forests and laid roadbeds. A related bill, also in 1824, authorized the army to improve the Ohio and Mississippi rivers; a later amendment did the same for the Missouri.

By the 1850s, 90 percent of the U.S. military was stationed west of the Mississippi River. When Indians refused to relinquish their lands, the army escorted them westward; when they harmed whites, the army waged war. The army sometimes destroyed crops and buildings of white squatters refusing to vacate lands settled illegally. But, primarily, the army assisted overland migration. Army forts intimidated Indians, defended settlers from Indian attacks, and supplied information and provisions. In theory, the army was also supposed to protect Indians by driving settlers off Indian lands and enforcing laws prohibiting alcohol sales to Indians. Yet the army's small size relative to the territory made it virtually impossible to do so.

The Office of Indian Affairs handled the government's other Indian interactions, including treaty negotiations, school management, and trade oversight. Created in 1824 as part of the War Department, the Indian Office cooperated with the military in removing Indians from lands necessary for American expansion and in protecting citizens who relocated in the West. In 1849 the Indian Office became part of the newly established Department of the Interior, and soon shifted from removal to civilization, through a reservation system. Whereas some Indians accepted reservations as protection from white incursion, others rejected them, sometimes sparking deadly intratribal disagreements.

Public Lands

The federal government controlled vast tracts of land, procured either from the states' cessions of their western claims after the Revolution or through treaties with foreign powers, including Indian nations. The General Land Office, established in 1812 as part of the Treasury Department, handled those lands' distribution. Its earliest policies divided western lands into 640-acre tracts to be auctioned at a minimum of $2 an acre. These policies favored speculators—who bought up millions of acres—over individual, cash-poor farmers. Many settlers became squatters, prompting Congress in 1820 to lower land prices to $1.25 per acre and to sell tracts as small as 80 acres. Twelve years later, it sold 40-acre tracts. Yet it demanded that the land be bought outright; few would-be western settlers (particularly after the Panic of 1819) had enough cash to purchase government land. Because speculators sold land on credit, many small-time farmers bought from them at inflated prices.

Farmers pressed for a federal policy of preemption—that is, the right to settle on land without obtaining title, to improve it, and buy it later at the legal minimum price ($1.25 an acre). Some states offered lands through preemption, and Congress sometimes authorized preemption of federal lands in the 1820s and 1830s. But the first general preemption law, the so-called Log Cabin Bill, came in 1841, and it applied only to surveyed land. Preemption extended to unsurveyed

Gold in California

When James Marshall discovered gold in Sutter's Mill, California, in January 1848, word spread quickly worldwide. Within a year, tens of thousands of adventurers from other countries rushed to California, making it the most cosmopolitan place in North America.

In an era before the telegraph crossed the oceans, the news traveled surprisingly fast. Mexicans heard first. Next, word spread to Chile, Peru, and throughout South America; then across the Pacific to Hawai'i, China, and Australia; and then to Europe—Ireland, France, and the German states. Overland travelers brought the news south to Baja California and Sonora in Mexico. By spring 1849, some six thousand Mexicans were panning for gold. Many of the Mexicans came seasonally, spreading news of California on every trip home.

The newspaper *Honolulu Polynesian* announced California gold in the kingdom on June 24, 1848.

Regular steamship service between Hawai'i and California transported gold seekers as early as 1853.

A ship brought news of California gold discoveries to Valparaiso, Chile, in August 1848. People in Chile's cities talked feverishly about gold, and newspapers reported rumors of California's overnight riches. Before year's end, two thousand Chileans had left for California.

Word of gold and California reached Australia in December 1848, and by 1850 every ship in Sydney Harbour was California-bound. News reached China in mid-1848. Widespread poverty and gold's allure prompted many Chinese to migrate. By the mid-1850s, one in five gold miners was Chinese.

In 1850, the new state of California had nearly 40 percent foreign-born inhabitants, the majority non-European. Through word of mouth, rumor, letters home, and newspaper reports, the 1848 discovery of gold linked California to millions of ordinary people around the globe.

This 1855 Frank Marryat drawing of a San Francisco saloon dramatizes the international nature of the California gold rush. Like theater performers, the patrons of the saloon dress their parts as Yankees, Mexicans, Asians, and South Americans.

The Art Archive at Art Resource, NY

lands with the **Homestead Act** of 1862, which provided that land would be provided free to any U.S. citizen (or foreigner who declared the intention of becoming a citizen), after residing on it for five years and improving it. Alternatively, settlers could buy land outright at $1.25 an acre after six months of residency, which allowed them to use the land as collateral for loans for additional land, farming supplies, or machinery.

Homestead Act Passed in 1862, it embodied the Republican Party's ideal of "free soil, free labor, free men" by granting 160 acres of public land to settlers who resided on it for five years and improved it.

The Southwestern Borderlands

What factors led white Americans to settle in Texas?

Along the Louisiana Territory's southwestern border lay vast provinces controlled mostly by the Comanches and other Indians but claimed first by Spain and then—after 1821—by the newly independent nation of Mexico. **New Mexico**, with commercial centers in Albuquerque and Santa Fe, remained under Mexican control until the United States conquered the territory during its War with Mexico. Texas became an autonomous state in 1824, giving it greater independence from federal authorities than New Mexico enjoyed. This situation fostered Texas's struggle for national independence and then annexation to the United States, which returned slavery to the forefront of American political debate (see Chapter 12).

New Mexico Former Spanish colony in the upper Rio Grande Valley that became part of Mexico after 1821.

Southwestern Slavery

Slavery in the Southwest was centuries old. Yet as practiced by indigenous peoples—Comanches, Apaches, Kiowas, Navajos, Utes, and Pueblos—and by Spaniards, slavery centered on capturing women and children, who were then assimilated into their captors' communities, where they provided labor and status while fostering economic and diplomatic exchanges with their former communities.

This system was built on racial mixing—a practice anathema to most white Americans. As white slaveholders from the Southeast pushed into Mexican territory during the 1820s and 1830s, they often justified their conquest in racial terms. The region's Hispanic settlers, they reasoned, had been rendered lazy and barbarous by racial intermixing and were thus destined to be supplanted.

The New Mexican Frontier

When Mexico gained independence from Spain in 1821, New Mexico's Hispanic population outnumbered the indigenous Pueblo peoples by three to one. There were 28,000 Hispanics, including people born in Spain and *criollos*, people born in New Spain to parents of Spanish descent. Most New Mexicans engaged in irrigated agriculture, but to the south, larger farms and ranches predominated. Rancheros became wealthy selling wool and corn in distant markets, and from using unpaid laborers, often relatives, bound by debt. Threatened by the province's raiding Indian tribes—Apaches, Utes, Navajos, and Comanches—Hispanics, Pueblos, and mestizos sometimes united in defense. But their numerical superiority allowed Hispanics to seize many Pueblo villages and lands in the rich northern river valleys.

The Santa Fe Trail caused a commercial explosion in New Mexico, doubling the value of imports in two years. Whereas the Spanish tried to keep foreigners out, the Mexican government offered enormous land grants to Anglo-American and French entrepreneurs, hoping they would develop the region's industry and agriculture and strengthen commercial ties with the United States.

Although commercial relationships grew, few Americans settled in New Mexico during the 1820s and 1830s. The best lands were occupied by Indians and Hispanics. And Americans seeking cheap, fertile land could find it in Texas.

The Texas Frontier

In 1821, indigenous Indians remained the dominant group in Texas, though there were also Hispanics, Anglos, mestizos, and immigrant Indians. Of the thirty thousand indigenous people, most were Comanches. Texas was part of what one historian has called the Comanche Empire, an enormous territory from northern Mexico to Louisiana that the Comanches dominated through kinship, trade, diplomacy, and violence. People of European heritage were a small presence in Texas in 1821. Hispanic peoples had been there since the 1500s, establishing missions and presidios, but by 1820, they numbered only five thousand.

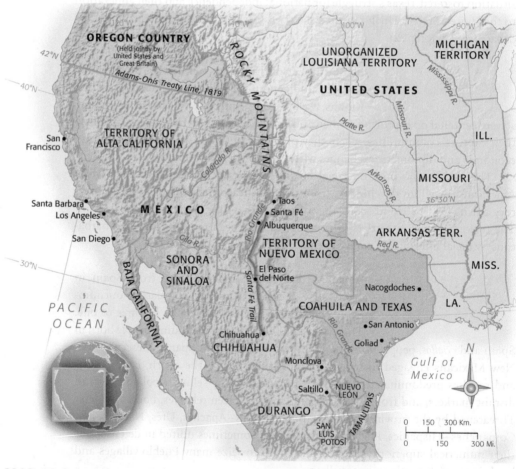

MAP 11.4
Mexico's Far North

What is now considered the American Southwest was made up of the northern provinces of Mexico until the United States conquered the territory during the Mexican War (1846–1848). Source: Copyright © Cengage Learning 2015

Most raised livestock on ranches, while others traded with Indians. They formed a distinctive identity as **Tejanos** (or Texans) rather than as Spaniards. Many inter-married with Indians.

Tejanos A native Texan of Mexican descent.

After the War of 1812, Anglo-Americans started entering Texas, where they sought furs, silver, or adventure. They traded manufactured goods—guns, ammunition, and kettles—for animal hides, horses, and mules, quickly supplanting the Tejanos as the Indians' trading partners. Although some Anglos settled in Texas, most traveled the Santa Fe and Chihuahua trails without settling.

The Comanche Empire

As Indians competed for resources, the southwestern borderlands experienced intermittent but brutal violence. Mounted on horses, the Comanches hunted bison, took captives, and stole horses, livestock, and crops from their enemies. Smaller Indian groups, such as the Wichitas and Caddos, grew corn, beans, squash, and pumpkin. When crops failed, farmers turned to bison hunting, sometimes causing conflict with the Comanches.

Tensions increased around the time of Mexican independence, when another ten thousand Indians migrated into the region. From the Old Northwest came Shawnees and Kickapoos—former members of Tecumseh's confederacy. From the Old Southwest came Cherokees, Creeks, Choctaws, Chickasaws, and Seminoles, some with African American slaves. Indian newcomers vied for land and animals, often clashing with established groups. Some immigrant Indians, having adopted Anglo clothing and racial ideologies, dismissed as "savage" the indigenous Indians who hunted buffalo, wore skins, and did not regard land as a commodity.

Smithsonian American Art Museum, Washington, DC/Art Resource, NY

The Comanche controlled a vast empire along the Louisiana Territory's southwestern border with Mexico. Here, in a George Catlin painting from 1834, Comanche women dress robes and dry meat.

Visualizing THE PAST

Paintings and Cultural Impressions

Although few people of Spanish descent settled in Texas, those who did developed a distinctive and proud cultural identity. Calling themselves Tejanos, they adapted their inherited culture—music, dances, and cuisine—to their new surroundings. In the painting below of an 1844 celebration in San Antonio, French-born painter Theodore Gentilz captures the mixture of cultural carryovers and frontier adaptations. Which elements of the scene seem reminiscent of life in Spain or in the colonial capital of Mexico City? Which elements seem to be adaptations to life along a cultural frontier and political borderland? Which elements of the painting seem to celebrate Tejano culture, and which, if any, seem critical of it? If you were using this painting as a source of information about Tejano culture and its influence on contemporary music and dance, what else would you want to know about the artist and the scene he has captured?

Although the musician in Gentilz's painting is playing the fiddle, other artistic depictions record the widespread use of the guitar, which helped give rise to the corrido, a folk ballad whose legacy is still apparent in today's country and western music.

bpk, Berlin/Art Resource, NY

Daughters of the Republic of Texas Library

Theodore Gentilz arrived in Texas in the 1840s and soon began portraying the region's culture with his paintbrush. Here, Tejano settlers perform the fandango, a Spanish dance.

Because violence threatened Indian removal and disrupted trade, the U.S. government brokered a treaty in 1835: the Comanches would allow immigrants onto their lands in exchange for trade opportunities. Trade soon boomed. Immigrant Indians swapped agricultural products and manufactured goods, such as rifles and ammunition, for the Comanches' meats, robes, and horses. That same year, the Comanches ended their longstanding war with the Osages. With peace came American traders. Meanwhile, the U.S. government's Indian removal continued, fueling Americans' commitment to cotton cultivation and expansionism.

American *Empresarios* A decade earlier, before Mexican independence, the Spanish worried about the security of Texas, which they considered a buffer between hostile Indians and the United States. Their solution was to populate the region. Thus when Missouri miner and trader Moses Austin approached Spanish authorities in January 1821 about settling Americans in Texas, they agreed as long as Austin brought Americans willing to assimilate into Texas society. In exchange for promising to bring three hundred Catholic families—and no slaves—Austin would receive two hundred thousand acres along the Brazos River. Before Austin could act, though, he died, and Mexico won its independence from Spain in September 1821.

Austin's son, Stephen, pursued his father's scheme, pressing the new Mexican government to honor the grant, which it did in 1823, provided that Austin renounce his American citizenship and become a Mexican national. By 1825, Stephen Austin had settled two thousand white people and four hundred "contract laborers" of African descent. With ninety-year contracts, these African Americans were essentially slaves. Austin later brought nine hundred additional families in exchange for more land.

Satisfied with the Austin experiment, in 1824 Mexico passed a Colonization Law providing land and tax incentives to future foreign settlers. The state of Coahuila y Texas specified that the head of a family could obtain up to 4,428 acres of grazing land or 177 acres of farming land. The land was cheap and could be paid for in installments over six years, with nothing due until the fourth year. Foreigners had to be upstanding Christians and permanent residents. To encourage settlers to assimilate into Mexican society, the Coahuila y Texas government provided additional land to those who married Mexican women.

Most U.S. citizens who settled in Mexico did so under an *empresario*, or immigration agent, who selected "moral" colonists, distributed lands, and enforced regulations. In exchange, he received nearly 25,000 acres of grazing land and 1,000 acres of farming land for every hundred families he settled. Between 1825 and 1832, approximately twenty-four empresario contracts (seventeen of which went to Anglo-Americans) were signed for eight thousand families. The land grants covered almost all of present-day Texas.

During the 1820s, some Anglo-Americans who emigrated to Texas felt pushed by the Panic of 1819 and pulled by cheap land and generous credit terms. Despite Mexican efforts to encourage assimilation, these Americans tended to settle in separate communities. Anglo-Americans outnumbered Tejanos two to one. Authorities worried that the transplanted Americans would try to make Texas part of the United States.

Texas Politics

In 1826, an empresario named Haden Edwards called for an independent Texas, the "Fredonia Republic." Other empresarios, seeing advantages in peaceful relations with the Mexican government, resisted Edwards's secessionist movement. Although the Fredonia revolt failed, Mexican authorities dreaded what it might foreshadow.

Consequently, in 1830 Mexican authorities terminated legal immigration from the United States while encouraging immigration from Europe and other parts of Mexico. They prohibited American slaves from entering Texas, which brought Texas in line with the rest of Mexico—where slavery had been outlawed the previous year. Yet these laws did not discourage Americans and their slaves from coming; soon they controlled most of the Texas coastline and its U.S. border. Mexican authorities repealed the anti-immigration law in 1833, reasoning that it discouraged upstanding settlers without deterring undesirables. By 1835, the non-Indian population of Texas was nearly thirty thousand, with Americans outnumbering Tejanos seven to one.

Among white Texans, some, like Stephen Austin, favored staying in Mexico but demanded more autonomy, the legalization of slavery, and free trade with the United States. Others pushed for Texas secession from Mexico and wanted annexation to the United States. In 1835, the secessionists overtook a Mexican military installation charged with collecting taxes at Galveston Bay. Austin advocated a peaceful resolution, but, suspicious, Mexican authorities jailed him for eighteen months, which converted him to the independence cause.

General Santa Anna Mexican president and dictator whose actions led Texans to revolt.

Sam Houston Military and political leader of Texas during and after the Texas Revolution.

The Lone Star Republic

With discontent over Texas increasing throughout Mexico, Mexican president **General Santa Anna** declared himself dictator and marched his army toward Texas. Fearing Santa Anna would free their slaves, Texans rebelled. After initial defeats at the Alamo mission in San Antonio and at Goliad in March 1836, the Texans easily triumphed by year's end. They declared themselves the Lone Star Republic and elected **Sam Houston** as president. Their constitution legalized slavery and banned free blacks.

Texas then faced the challenge of nation building, which to its leaders involved Indian removal. When the Indians refused to leave, Mirabeau Lamar, the nation's second president, mobilized the Texas Rangers—mounted nonuniformed militia—to drive them out through terror. The Rangers raided Indian villages, where they robbed, raped, and murdered. This "ethnic cleansing," as one historian has labeled it, ultimately cleared the land of native settlers to make room for white Americans and their African American slaves.

"War of a Thousand Deserts"

Since the early 1830s, Mexico's ten northern states had been wracked by raiding warfare perpetrated by Plains Indians—Comanches, Navajos, and Apaches. When Mexicans resisted by killing Comanches or their Kiowa allies, the Comanches escalated their violence ravishing the countryside and its inhabitants in what one historian has deemed vengeance killings. When additional Comanches fell in the course of avenging a killing, then another round of

Smithsonian American Art Museum, Washington, DC/Art Resource, NY

Plains Indians, including the Apaches portrayed here, frequently and brutally raided the northern provinces of Mexico beginning in the 1830s, leading to a cycle of vengeance killings that devastated the region and made it more vulnerable to invasion by the United States Army during the War with Mexico in the mid-1840s.

revenge killing ensued. The raiders devastated Mexican settlements, where once-thriving farms became man-made "deserts."

With the Mexican government's concerns focused on U.S. and French threats, individual Mexican states responded to the raids themselves, and often turned against one another, with Mexicans killing other Mexicans. The resulting carnage fed U.S. proponents of **manifest destiny**—those who believed that racially superior (white) Americans were destined to spread their culture westward to regions inhabited by inferior races (Indians and Mexicans). The United States would use manifest destiny to justify its war with Mexico from 1846 to 1848 (see Chapter 12). When American soldiers marched to Mexico's capital with seeming ease, they did so because they traversed huge swaths of Mexican territory that had been devastated or deserted by fifteen years of Indian raiding.

manifest destiny Coined by editor John L. O'Sullivan, it was the belief that the United States was endowed by God with a mission to spread its republican government and brand of freedom and Christianity to less fortunate and uncivilized peoples; it also justified U.S. territorial expansion.

Wartime Losses and Profits

After annexing Texas in 1845, the United States, seeking further territorial expansion, waged war against Mexico. In the borderlands, as in Mexico, civilians—Indians, Tejanos, Californios, and Mexicans—lost their lives, and many suffered wartime depredations. If they aided the Mexicans, the U.S. Army destroyed their homes; if they refused aid to the Mexicans, the Mexicans destroyed their homes. An 1847 U.S. Army report acknowledged that its "wild volunteers … committed … all sorts of atrocities on the persons and property of Mexicans." After the war ended in the borderlands, violence continued, with Texas Rangers slaughtering Indians from 1847 to 1848.

Some civilians profited from the war. Farmers sold provisions and mules to the armies, peddlers sold alcohol and food to soldiers, and others set up gambling and prostitution businesses near army camps.

Cultural Frontiers in the Far West

How did the gold rush influence the development of the Far West?

Even before the United States seized expansive territory during the War with Mexico, some Americans moved to the Far West, often to California, Utah, and other places Mexico controlled. Some sought religious freedom or to convert others to Christianity, but most wanted fertile farmland.

Western Missionaries

Catholic missionaries maintained a strong presence in the Far West. In Spanish missions, priests introduced Indians to Catholic sacraments; enforced rigid rules about prayer, sexual conduct, and work; and treated them as legal minors. Indians who did not measure up were subject to corporal punishment. When they ran away, they were forcibly returned. With few options, Indians often responded to abusive practices with armed uprisings, ultimately weakening the mission system.

A Mexican law secularized the California missions in 1833, using them to organize Indian labor. Some Indians stayed at the missions; others left to farm their own land or to find employment elsewhere, but for almost all, secularization brought enhanced personal freedom despite limited legal rights.

Still, Catholic missionaries—Americans, Europeans, and converted Indians—continued ministering to immigrants, working to convert Indians. Missionaries founded schools and colleges, introduced medical services, and aided in railroad explorations.

In the Pacific Northwest, Catholics vied directly with Protestants for Indian souls. Under the auspices of the American Board of Commissioners for Foreign Missions, two missionary couples—credited as being the first white migrants along the Oregon Trail—traveled to the Pacific Northwest in 1836. Narcissa and Marcus Whitman built a meetinghouse for Cayuse Indians in Waiilatpu, near present-day Walla Walla, Washington, while Eliza and Henry Spalding worked to convert the Nez Percé at Lapwai, in what is now Idaho. The Whitmans did little to endear themselves to the Cayuses, whom Narcissa deemed "insolent"; their dark skin, fitting of their "heathenism." The Cayuse, in turn, saw the Whitmans as "severe and hard," and none converted. The Whitmans turned their attention to white migrants flowing into Oregon in the 1840s.

These migrants' arrival escalated tensions with the Cayuses, and when a devastating measles epidemic struck in 1847, the Cayuses saw it as a calculated assault. They retaliated by murdering the Whitmans and twelve other missionaries. The Spaldings abandoned their successful mission, blamed Catholics for inciting the massacre, and became farmers in Oregon.

Mormons

Persecuted in Missouri and Illinois, the Mormons in 1847 followed Brigham Young to their "Promised Land" in the Great Salt Lake valley, still under Mexican control but soon to become part of the U.S. territory of Utah. As non-Mormons settled in Utah, Young diluted their influence by attracting new Mormon settlers to what he called the state of Deseret.

The Mormons' arrival in the Great Basin complicated relations among Indians. The Utes, for example, had long traded in stolen goods and captured people, particularly Paiutes. After Mormons tried to curtail the slave trade, Ute slavers tortured Paiute captives, particularly children, calculating that Mormons would buy them. The purchased children often worked as servants in Mormon homes. Although the Mormons tried to convert the Paiutes, their condescending treatment caused friction, even violence. Sharing the Utes as a common enemy, the Mormons and Paiutes formed an uneasy alliance in the early 1850s.

With their slave trade threatened and their economy in shambles, the Utes attacked Mormon and Paiute settlements. War erupted in 1853, and although an uneasy truce was reached in 1854, tensions continued between the Mormons and Indians.

And between Mormons and their white neighbors. Although Mormons prospered from providing services and supplies to California-bound settlers, Young discouraged "gentiles" (his term for non-Mormons) from settling in Deseret and advocated boycotts of gentile businesses. When in 1852 the Mormons openly sanctioned polygamy, anti-Mormon sentiment increased nationwide. In June 1857, President James Buchanan dispatched 2,500 federal troops to suppress an alleged Mormon rebellion. Anxious over their safety, some Mormons joined some Paiutes in attacking a passing wagon train of non-Mormon migrants. Approximately 120 men, women, and children died in the so-called Mountain Meadows Massacre in August 1857. In the next two years, the U.S. Army and the Mormons engaged in armed conflict, with property destruction but no fatalities.

Oregon and California Trails

From 1840 until 1860, between 250,000 and 500,000 people, including many children, walked across much of the continent, usually over seven months. Although they traveled armed, most of their encounters with Indians were peaceful, if tense.

The overland journeys began at one of the so-called jumping-off points—towns such as Independence, St. Joseph, and Westport Landing—along the Missouri River, where migrants bought supplies for the 2,000-mile trip. While miners frequently traveled alone or with fortune-seeking young men, farmers traveled with relatives, neighbors, church members, and other acquaintances.

They timed their departures to be late enough to find forage grass for their oxen and livestock, but not so late that they would encounter the treacherous snows of the Rockies and the Sierra Nevada. Not all were successful. From 1846 to 1847, the Donner Party took a wrong turn, got caught in a blizzard, and resorted to cannibalism. More fortunate overland migrants trudged alongside their wagons, averaging fifteen miles a day, in weather from freezing cold to blistering heat. Men generally tended livestock, while women set up camp, prepared meals, and tended small children. Indians were usually peaceful, if cautious. During the trails' early days, Indians provided food and information or ferried migrants across rivers. In exchange, migrants offered wool blankets, knives, metal pots, tobacco, ornamental beads, and other items. When exchanges went wrong—due to misunderstandings or conscious attempts to swindle—tensions escalated.

Indian Treaties

Still, the U.S. Indian Office negotiated treaties to keep Indians—and their intertribal conflicts—from interfering with western migration and commerce. The **Fort Laramie Treaty** of 1851 (or the Horse Creek Council Treaty) was signed by the United States and eight northern Plains tribes—the Lakotas, Cheyennes, Arapahos, Crows, Assiniboines, Gros-Ventres, Mandans, and Arrickaras—who occupied the Platte River valley through which the three great overland routes westward—the Oregon, California, and Mormon trails—all passed. Two years later, in 1853, the United States signed a treaty with three southwestern nations, the Comanches, Kiowas, and Apaches, who lived near the Sante Fe Trail. Under both treaties, the Indians agreed to maintain peace, recognize government-delineated tribal boundaries, allow the United States to construct roads and forts within those boundaries, refrain from depredations against western migrants, and issue restitution for any depredations nonetheless committed. In return, they would receive annual allotments from the U.S. government for ten years, paid with provisions, domestic animals, and agricultural implements.

Fort Laramie Treaty A treaty between the United States and eight northern Plains tribes in which the Indians agreed to maintain intertribal peace, accepted the U.S.-defined territorial regions for each tribe, and allowed the United States to construct roads. In exchange, they received annual payouts of provisions and agricultural necessities.

Contrary to U.S. expectations, Indian chiefs did not see such treaties as perpetually binding. Government officials, meanwhile, promised allotments but did little to ensure their timely arrival, often leaving Indians starving. Treaties did not end intertribal warfare, nor did they secure overlanders' safety. But they represented the U.S. government's efforts to promote expansion and protect westward-bound citizens.

Ecological Consequences of Cultural Contact

Armed conflict took relatively few lives compared to cholera, smallpox, and other maladies. The trails' jumping-off points bred disease, which migrants inadvertently carried to their Indian trading partners. Fearful of infection, Indians and migrants increasingly shied away from trading.

The disappearance of the buffalo (American bison) from the region further inflamed tensions. The buffalo provided protein to Plains Indians and held spiritual significance. Many Native Americans blamed the migrants for the buffalo's disappearance, even though most overlanders never saw a buffalo. By the time the overland migration peaked in the late 1840s and the 1850s, the herds were long overhunted, partly by Native Americans eager to trade their hides. The surviving buffalo scattered to where the grass was safe from the overlanders' livestock. On rare occasions when wagon trains stumbled upon bison herds, men rushed to fulfill their frontier fantasies and shot the animals. For sport, overlanders also hunted antelopes, wolves, bears, and birds—animals that held spiritual significance for many Native Americans.

Gold Rush

Migrants especially intruded on Indian life near the California gold strikes. In January 1848, John Wilson Marshall discovered gold on John Sutter's property along a shallow tributary to the American River near present-day Sacramento, California. During the next year, tens of thousands of "forty-niners" rushed to California, where they practiced placer mining, panning and dredging for gold, seeking instant riches.

Some did indeed make fortunes. Peter Brown, a black man from Ste. Genevieve, Missouri, wrote his wife in 1851 that "California is the best country in the world to make money. It is also the best place for black folks on the globe." Most forty-niners, however, never found enough gold to pay their expenses. With their dreams dashed, many forty-niners took wage-paying jobs with large mining companies that used dangerous machinery to cut deep into the earth's surface.

As a remote Mexican province, California had small settlements surrounded by military forts (presidios) and missions. It was inhabited mostly by Indians, along with some Mexican rancheros, who raised cattle and sheep on enormous landholdings worked by coerced Indian laborers. With gold strikes, new migrants—from South America, Asia, Australia, and Europe—rushed to California. Although a California Supreme Court ruling—*People v. Hall* (1854)—made it impossible to prevent violence against Chinese immigrants, Chinese citizens continued to seek their fortune in California; by 1859, approximately 35,000 of them worked in the goldfields.

With hungry gold miners to feed, California experienced an agricultural boom. Wheat became the preferred crop: it required minimal investment, was easily planted, and had a short growing season. California's large-scale wheat farming depended on bonded Indian laborers.

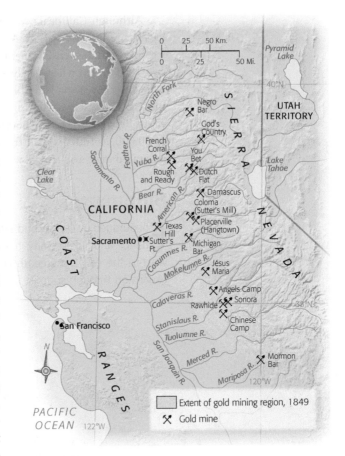

MAP 11.5
The California Gold Rush

Gold was discovered at Sutter's Mill in 1848, sparking the California gold rush that took place mostly along the western foothills of the Sierra Nevada Mountains. Source: Copyright © Cengage Learning 2015

Mining Settlements

Mining brought a commercial and industrial boom, too, as enterprising merchants rushed to supply new settlers. Among them was Levi Strauss, a German Jewish immigrant, whose tough mining pants found a ready market among prospectors. Because men greatly outnumbered women, women's skills (and company) were in demand. As men set up all-male households and performed traditionally female tasks, women received high fees for cooking, laundering, and sewing. Women also ran boardinghouses, hotels, and brothels.

Cities sprang up. In 1848, San Francisco was a small mission settlement of about 1,000 Mexicans, Anglos, soldiers, friars, and Indians. With the gold rush, it became a city, ballooning to 35,000 people in 1850. It was the West Coast gateway to the interior, and ships bringing people and supplies jammed the harbor.

Although California was admitted into the Union as a free state in 1850, its legislature soon passed "An Act for the Government and Protection of Indians" that legalized Indians' enslavement. Using enslaved Indians in the mines between 1849 and 1851 ended when newly arrived miners brutally attacked the Indian workers, believing they degraded white labor and gave an unfair advantage to established miners. Those slaves who survived the violence became field workers and house servants. Between 1821 and 1860, the Indian population of California fell from 200,000 to 30,000, as Indians died from disease, starvation, and violence. Because masters separated male and female workers, Indians failed to reproduce in large numbers.

Summary

Encouraged by literary and artistic images of the frontier as a place of natural abundance and opportunity, millions poured into the Old Southwest and Old Northwest in the early nineteenth century. The federal government promoted westward expansion through support for transportation improvements, surveying, cheap land,

Legacy FOR A PEOPLE AND A NATION

Descendants of Early Latino Settlers

Today, American news media frequently report on Latinos in the United States, for current census figures identify them as the nation's largest racial or ethnic minority. Stories focus on the growing number of documented and undocumented Latino immigrants, their increasing social impact, and their occasionally difficult relationships with African Americans. Yet all the attention to recent arrivals overlooks the sizable number of Latinos who are descended from people whose residency in North America predated the existence of the United States.

When the region stretching from eastern Texas to California was acquired by the United States in the 1840s, its population included indigenous Indian nations and thousands of people with at least partial European ancestry, primarily Spanish or Portuguese. Their descendants have included such U.S. congresspeople as Manuel Luján (1969–1988) and such senators as Kenneth Salazar (who served from 2004 to 2009, when he resigned to become secretary of the interior). Their families have resided in what is now U.S. territory for twelve or fourteen generations.

Persuasive evidence suggests that many of the early Iberian settlers in New Mexico were *conversos*, or of New Christian descent—that is, people whose Jewish ancestors converted to Catholicism in the fifteenth century to avoid religious persecution. After Jews were expelled from Spain and Portugal in 1492, many fled to the Spanish empire's far corners. Some participated in Juan de Oñate's 1598 expedition to New Mexico. There, some secretly maintained such Jewish customs as Sabbath observances and food restrictions. Today, some Latino residents of New Mexico have acknowledged their converso roots and reclaimed a Jewish identity.

These long-standing Latino citizens of the United States, not just those of converso descent, have given the nation and its people an important multicultural legacy.

and protection from Indians. Still, western migrants did not always find what they were seeking. Some returned home, some moved elsewhere, and some stayed in the West, abandoning their dreams of economic independence.

Large numbers of African American slaves were moved westward by owners or slave traders between 1820 and 1860. Native Americans saw their lands and livelihoods constrict, and their environments drastically altered, threatening their economic and spiritual lives. Some Indians responded to white incursion through accommodation and peaceful overtures; others resisted. For Indians in Texas and California, white incursions brought devastation, yet not before the Comanches and their allies ravaged farming settlements along the Mexico-U.S. border, paving the way for the U.S. Army to invade its southern neighbor from 1846 to 1848.

White beliefs about Native Americans' supposed inferiority allowed many to rationalize the Indians' fate; white attitudes toward black people and slavery drove where they settled in the West. Those who believed that slavery degraded white labor headed along a northern trajectory, whereas those who dreamed of slave ownership headed southward, where they clashed with yet another group they deemed racially inferior: Mexicans. When American settlers in Texas achieved independence from Mexico and legalized slavery, they triggered events that would bring the divisive issue of slavery's westward expansion forward in American politics.

Chapter Review

The West in the American Imagination

> What were the myths that helped shape white Americans' perceptions of the West?

In novels, artists' paintings, and materials recruiting settlers, the West was depicted as a place of cheap or free, abundant, and unoccupied land where anyone could seek to better himself or herself. They often neglected the reality that many of these lands were home to native peoples. Artists often depicted Indians as savages (sometimes noble savages) or as docile and easily conquered. Frontiersmen like Daniel Boone were portrayed as having the courage and independent spirit needed to tame the so-called uncivilized wilderness and open the West to freedom-loving white settlers. The West effectively symbolized core American values of freedom, independence, and opportunity.

Expansion and Resistance in the Trans-Appalachian West

> What made the Midwest especially appealing to white settlers?

Migrants who headed west in search of a better life often chose the Midwest because they wanted a region with a climate, features, and conveniences similar to those where they previously lived. The Midwest, compared to the Old Southwest, had better-developed transportation routes, easier access to markets, a smaller African American population, cheaper landholdings, and a climate similar to New England's. The region proved a good first stop for those who did not yet have enough cash to purchase land; in the Midwest, they could obtain jobs unloading canal boats or working in farms or mills, before moving on.

The Federal Government and Westward Expansion

How did the federal government sponsor and speed up westward expansion?

U.S. federal policies regarding Indians and land, particularly Indian removal from desirable lands, did much to encourage white movement into the West. Many whites, in fact, awaited government efforts to clear lands before moving there. The federal government funded expeditions to chart the trans-Mississippi West, including efforts to find the best location for a transcontinental railroad. Army engineers helped design roads, canals, and railroads, while soldiers cleared forests and did other work. The military also established forts that intimidated Indians, removed Indians from lands that whites desired, defended settlers from Indian attacks, or pushed squatters from land they did not own. Sales of government-controlled land also encouraged settlement.

The Southwestern Borderlands

What factors led white Americans to settle in Texas?

First, the Panic of 1819 pushed some Anglo-Americans to seek cheap land and a fresh start in the Texas territory controlled by Mexico. Beginning in 1824, officials in Mexico also encouraged settlement by offering tax incentives and land grants to foreigners. American Stephen Austin initially settled over two thousand whites, who, contrary to their agreement, brought four hundred slaves. He later brought another nine hundred families. Mexico required settlers be Christians willing to establish permanent residences and to assimilate. But early on, Mexican officials rightly feared that the transplanted Americans would seek to annex Texas to the United States. Beginning in 1826, there were calls for an independent Texas under the name "Fredonia Republic"; as the proportion of Americans to Tejanos reached seven to one in 1835, demand for secession heightened, culminating in battles and the eventual declaration of Texas as the Lone Star Republic in 1836.

Cultural Frontiers in the Far West

How did the gold rush influence the development of the Far West?

As miners flooded into California seeking gold, an agricultural boom emerged, with wheat becoming the main crop, often farmed by Indian slaves. Wherever mining areas sprung up, a commercial and industrial boom usually followed, as merchants provided necessities and other goods to new settlers. Cities also grew up fast; San Francisco went from one thousand people in 1848 to thirty-five thousand two years later. While California was admitted as a free state that year, it quickly legalized the enslavement of Indians, using them to work in the mines and later in fields or homes.

Suggestions for Further Reading

Gary Clayton Anderson, *The Conquest of Texas: Ethnic Cleansing in the Promised Land, 1820–1875* (2005)

Stuart Banner, *How the Indians Lost Their Land: Law and Power on the Frontier* (2005)

Ned Blackhawk, *Violence over the Land: Indians and Empires in the Early American West* (2006)

Andrew R. L. Cayton and Peter S. Onuf, *The Midwest and the Nation: Rethinking the History of an American Region* (1990)

William Cronon, *Nature's Metropolis: Chicago and the Great West* (1991)

Brian DeLay, *War of a Thousand Deserts: Indian Raids and the U.S.-Mexican War* (2008)

Pekka Hämäläinen, *The Comanche Empire* (2008)

Robert V. Hine and John Mack Faragher, *The American West: A New Interpretive History* (2000)

Albert L. Hurtado, *Indian Survival on the California Frontier* (1998)

Anne F. Hyde, *Empires, Nations & Families: A History of the North American West, 1800–1860* (2011)

Susan L. Johnson, *Roaring Camp: The Social World of the California Gold Rush* (2000)

Andrés Reséndez, *Changing National Identities at the Frontier: Texas and New Mexico, 1800–1850* (2005)

Michael L. Tate, *Indians and Emigrants: Encounters on the Overland Trails* (2006)

Politics and the Fate of the Union

12

1824–1859

Chapter Outline

Jacksonianism and Party Politics
Expanding Political Participation | Election of 1824 | Election of 1828 | Democrats | King Andrew

Federalism at Issue: The Nullification and Bank Controversies
Nullification | The Force Bill | Second Bank of the United States | Political Violence | Antimasonry | Election of 1832 | Jackson's Second Term | Specie Circular

The Second Party System
Democrats and Whigs | Political Coalitions | Election of 1836 | Van Buren and Hard Times | William Henry Harrison and the Election of 1840

Women's Rights
Legal Rights | Political Rights

The Politics of Territorial Expansion
President Tyler | Texas and "Manifest Destiny" | Fifty-Four Forty or Fight | Polk and the Election of 1844 | Annexation of Texas

The War with Mexico and Its Consequences
Oregon | "Mr. Polk's War" | Foreign War and the Popular Imagination | Conquest | Treaty of Guadalupe Hidalgo | "Slave Power Conspiracy" | Wilmot Proviso | The Election of 1848 and Popular Sovereignty

VISUALIZING THE PAST *The Mexican War in Popular Imagination*

1850: Compromise or Armistice?
Debate over Slavery in the Territories | Compromise of 1850 | Fugitive Slave Act | The Underground Railroad | Election of 1852 and the Collapse of Compromise

Never has a work of popular literature so caught the tide of politics as Harriet Beecher Stowe's **Uncle Tom's Cabin** (1852). While Stowe created many enduring scenes, especially powerful was that of the young slave Eliza, child in arms, escaping across the Ohio River, after her owner sold the infant to a slave trader. "Nerved with strength such as God gives only to the desperate," continued Stowe, "with one wild cry and flying leap, she [Eliza] vaulted clear over the turbid current … on to the raft of ice beyond.… she … felt nothing, till dimly, as in a dream, she saw the Ohio side, and a man helping her up the bank."

The daughter and sister of prominent preachers and theologians, Stowe saw her story first serialized in a Washington, D.C., newspaper in 1851, and published as a book in 1852. The novel captured the agonies of slave families broken apart and sold. Stowe spread the blame widely in her indictment of slavery. For example, the most evil slaveholder (Simon Legree) is a transplanted New Englander. The story's humane slaveholder, St. Clair, is southern bred, but almost too good for this corrupt world, and dies before he can reform it. In Eliza, Little Eva, Topsy, and Uncle Tom himself, a Christ-like figure whom the story ushers toward unforgettable martyrdom, the nation and the world vicariously experienced not only slavery's inhumanity, but its destruction of the human soul, as it also threatened the life of the republic.

By mid-1853, the book had sold over 1 million copies and was soon translated into numerous foreign languages. Its popularity alarmed white southerners, inspiring nearly twenty anti–Uncle Tom novels in the 1850s. Southern writers justified slavery as more humane than northern wage labor, and attacked Stowe for breaking gender conventions by engaging in a public critique of the South. In stories such as J. W. Page's *Uncle Robin in his Cabin and Tom Without One in Boston*, fiendish abolitionists induced slaves to run away, only to starve in northern cities. In these novels, masters are benevolent and slaves loyal as they perform roles dictated by nature and God. Many novels let slaves philosophize on slavery's behalf. In *Aunt Phillis's Cabin*, Phillis visits the North

Slavery Expansion and Collapse of the Party System

The Kansas-Nebraska Act |
Birth of the Republican Party |
Know-Nothings | *Party Realignment and the Republicans' Appeal* | *Republican Ideology* | *Southern Democrats* |
Bleeding Kansas | *Election of 1856*

LINKS TO THE WORLD *William Walker and Filibustering*

Slavery and the Nation's Future

Dred Scott Case | *Abraham Lincoln and the Slave Power* | *The Lecompton Constitution and Disharmony Among Democrats* | *John Brown's Raid on Harpers Ferry*

LEGACY FOR A PEOPLE AND A NATION
Coalition Politics

SUMMARY

Uncle Tom's Cabin Harriet Beecher Stowe's best-selling 1852 novel that aroused widespread northern sympathy for slaves (especially fugitives) and widespread southern anger.

with her owners, where abolitionists encourage her to escape. "I want none of your help," she declares; she refuses to "steal" herself, longing instead for her southern "home."

In *Uncle Tom's Cabin*, Stowe cast a feminist, abolitionist thunderbolt into the slavery debate. That debate had been largely submerged in the political system dominated, beginning in the 1830s, by the Jacksonian Democrats and Whigs.

Yet Democrats and Whigs varied on other issues. Democrats typically emphasized small government, whereas Whigs advocated an activist federal government to promote economic development. Democrats championed agricultural expansion into the West, while Whigs urged commercial growth in the East, via their "American System" of high protective tariffs, centralized banking, and federally funded internal improvements. Together, Whigs and Democrats forged the second party system.

Sectional conflict resurfaced after Texas's annexation in 1845. From 1846 to 1848, the United States went to war against Mexico, escalating the problem of slavery's expansion. The Compromise of 1850's fugitive slave law sent thousands of enslaved blacks fleeing into Canada, and prompted Stowe to write her novel. In Kansas Territory by 1855, open warfare exploded between proslavery and antislavery settlers. The following year, the Supreme Court issued a dramatic decision about slavery's constitutionality and the status of African American citizenship. And by 1858, abolitionist John Brown was planning a raid into Virginia to start a slave rebellion.

As the 1850s advanced, slavery divided Americans, North and South. The old nationwide political parties fractured, replaced by virulent sectionalism. People everywhere believed America's future was at stake. In 1855, the famous black leader Frederick Douglass spoke for the enslaved when he wrote that "the thought of only being a creature of the past and present, troubled me, and I longed to have a future – a future with hope in it."

As you read this chapter, keep the following questions in mind:

- **What were the main issues dividing Democrats and Whigs?**

- **After 1845, how and why did westward expansion become so intertwined with the future of slavery and freedom?**

- **During the 1850s, why did Americans (white males, virtually all of whom could vote, and blacks, few of whom had the franchise) care so deeply about electoral politics?**

Jacksonianism and Party Politics

How did changes in voting laws influence the outcome of the 1824 presidential election and the future of political parties?

Throughout the 1820s and 1830s, politicians sought to appeal to an increasingly broad-based electorate. Hotly contested elections helped make politics the great nineteenth-century American pastime among voters and nonvoters alike. But they also fueled bitter rivalries.

Expanding Political Participation

Property restrictions for voters remained in just seven of twenty-six states by 1840. Some even allowed foreign nationals who officially declared their intention of becoming American citizens to vote. Between 1824 and 1828 the number of votes cast in presidential elections tripled, from 360,000 to over 1.1 million. The proportion of eligible voters who cast ballots also grew, from about 27 percent in 1824 to more than 80 percent in 1840.

The selection of presidential electors also became more democratic. Previously, a caucus of party leaders typically picked them, but by 1824 eighteen out of twenty-four states chose electors by popular vote. Consequently, politicians augmented their appeals to voters, and the 1824 election saw the end of the congressional caucus, when House and Senate members of the same political party selected their candidate.

Election of 1824

As a result, five Democratic-Republican candidates entered the presidential campaign of 1824. The Republican caucus chose William H. Crawford of

Eliza crossing the ice floes of the Ohio river to freedom, illustration from 'Uncle Tom's Cabin' by Harriet Beecher Stowe, engraved by Charles Bour (1814–81) (litho) (see also 90903), Bayot, Adolphe Jean-Baptiste (1810–66) (after)/Private Collection/The Bridgeman Art Library

Eliza Crossing the Ice Flows of the Ohio River, depicting one of the most famous scenes in American literature, illustration from Uncle Tom's Cabin, *engraved by Charles Bour.*

Chronology

1824	No electoral college majority in presidential election
1825	House of Representatives elects Adams president
1828	Tariff of Abominations
	Jackson elected president
1830s–40s	Democratic-Whig competition gels in second party system
1831	Antimasons hold first national political convention
1832	Jackson vetoes rechartering Second Bank of the United States
	Jackson reelected president
1832–33	Nullification Crisis
1836	Specie Circular
	Van Buren elected president
1837	Financial panic ends boom of the 1830s
1839–43	Hard times spread unemployment and deflation
1840	Whigs win presidency under Harrison
1841	Tyler assumes presidency after Harrison's death
1845	Texas annexed
	"Manifest destiny" term coined
1846	War with Mexico begins
	Oregon Treaty negotiated
	Wilmot Proviso inflames sectional divisions
1847	Cass proposes idea of popular sovereignty
1848	Treaty of Guadalupe Hidalgo gives United States new territory in the Southwest
	Free-Soil Party formed
	Taylor elected president
	Gold discovered in California, which later applies for admission to Union as free state
	Seneca Falls Woman's Rights Convention
1850	Compromise of 1850 passes, containing controversial Fugitive Slave Act
1852	Stowe publishes *Uncle Tom's Cabin*
	Pierce elected president
1854	"Appeal of the Independent Democrats" published
	Kansas-Nebraska Act approved, igniting controversy
	Republican Party formed
	Fugitive Burns returned to slavery in Virginia
1856	Bleeding Kansas troubles nation
	Brooks attacks Sumner in Senate chamber
	Buchanan elected president, but Republican Frémont wins most northern states
1857	*Dred Scott v. Sanford* endorses white southern views on black citizenship and slavery in territories
	Economic panic and widespread unemployment begin
1858	Kansas voters reject Lecompton Constitution
	Lincoln-Douglas debates
	Douglas contends popular sovereignty prevails over *Dred Scott* decision in territories
1859	Brown raids Harpers Ferry

Georgia, secretary of the treasury. Instead of Congress, state legislatures now nominated candidates, offering the expanded electorate a slate of sectional candidates. John Quincy Adams drew support from New England, while westerners backed House Speaker Henry Clay of Kentucky. Some southerners initially supported Secretary of War John C. Calhoun, who later ran for the vice presidency instead. The Tennessee legislature nominated military hero Andrew Jackson.

Jackson led in electoral and popular votes, but no candidate received an electoral college majority. Adams finished second. Under the Constitution, the House of Representatives, voting by state delegation, one vote to a state, would select the next president from among the three electoral vote leaders. Clay, with the fewest votes, was dropped. Crawford, disabled from a stroke, never received consideration. Clay backed Adams, who won with thirteen of the twenty-four state delegations and became president (see Map 12.1). Adams named Clay secretary of state, the traditional stepping-stone to the presidency.

Angry Jacksonians denounced the election's outcome as a "corrupt bargain," claiming Adams had stolen the election by promising Clay a cabinet position for his votes. The Republican Party split. The Adams wing emerged as the National Republicans, and the Jacksonians became the **Democrats**.

As president, Adams proposed a strong nationalist policy incorporating Clay's American System of protective tariffs, a national bank, and internal improvements. Adams believed the federal government's active role should extend to education, science, and the arts. He proposed a national university in Washington, D.C. Brilliant as a diplomat and secretary of state, Adams fared less well as chief executive.

Election of 1828

The 1828 election pitted Adams against Jackson. Nicknamed "Old Hickory," Jackson was a tough, ambitious man. Born in South Carolina in 1767, he rose from humble beginnings to become a wealthy Tennessee planter and slaveholder. After leading the Tennessee militia to remove Creeks from the Alabama and Georgia frontier, Jackson garnered national acclaim in 1815 as the hero of the Battle of New Orleans; in 1818, his fame increased in an expedition against Seminoles in Spanish Florida. Jackson served as a congressman and senator from Tennessee and as the first territorial governor of Florida (1821).

Jackson's supporters accused Adams of stealing the 1824 election and, when he was envoy to Russia, of securing prostitutes for the czar. Adams supporters countered with reports that Jackson's wife, Rachel, married Jackson before divorcing her first husband. In 1806 while attempting to defend Rachel's integrity, Jackson killed a man during a duel, and the cry of "murderer!" reappeared in the election.

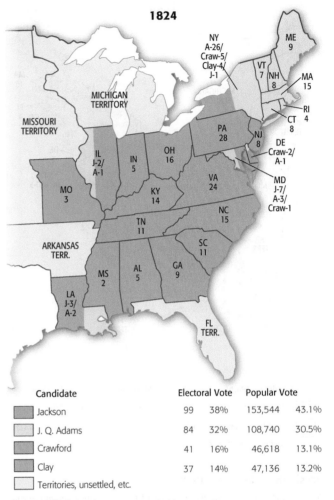

1824

Candidate		Electoral Vote		Popular Vote	
Jackson		99	38%	153,544	43.1%
J. Q. Adams		84	32%	108,740	30.5%
Crawford		41	16%	46,618	13.1%
Clay		37	14%	47,136	13.2%
Territories, unsettled, etc.					

MAP 12.1
Presidential Election, 1824
Andrew Jackson led in both electoral and popular votes but failed to win a majority of electoral college votes. The House elected John Quincy Adams president. Source: Copyright © Cengage Learning 2015

Democrats Members of the party that emerged from Jefferson's Republican Party as one of the two dominant parties in the second party system.

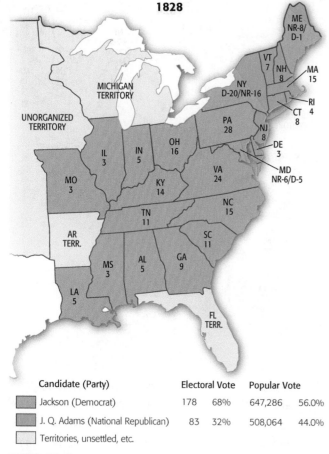

1828

Candidate (Party)		Electoral Vote		Popular Vote	
Jackson (Democrat)		178	68%	647,286	56.0%
J. Q. Adams (National Republican)		83	32%	508,064	44.0%
Territories, unsettled, etc.					

MAP 12.2

Presidential Election, 1828

Andrew Jackson avenged his 1824 loss of the presidency, sweeping the election in 1828. Source: Copyright © Cengage Learning 2015

spoils system Practice of rewarding political supporters with public office.

Although Adams kept the states he won in 1824, Jackson swamped him, polling 56 percent of the popular vote and winning in the electoral college by 178 to 83 votes (Map 12.2). Through a coalition of state parties, political leaders, and newspaper editors, a popular movement had elected the president. The Democrats became the first well-organized national party.

Democrats

Democrats shared a commitment to the Jeffersonian concept of an agrarian society. They viewed a strong central government as antithetical to individual liberty, and they condemned government intervention in the economy as favoring the rich. Jacksonians called for federal intervention in westward expansion, however, with Jackson initiating Indian removal despite northeastern reformers' protests.

Like Jefferson, Jackson strengthened the government's executive branch while advocating limited government. He centralized power in the White House and relied on political friends, his "Kitchen Cabinet," for advice, rarely consulting his official cabinet. He appointed loyal Democrats to offices, a practice his critics called the **spoils system**, in which the victor gives the spoils of victory to supporters. The spoils system, opponents charged, corrupted the government because it based appointments on loyalty, not competency.

King Andrew

Opponents mocked Jackson as "King Andrew I," charging him with abuse of power by ignoring the Supreme Court's ruling on Cherokee rights, sidestepping his cabinet, and replacing officeholders with his cronies. Jackson's critics especially disliked his frequent use of the veto to promote limited government. In 1830, he vetoed the Maysville Road bill, which would have funded construction of a sixty-mile turnpike from Maysville to Lexington, Kentucky. Constitutionally, he insisted, states bore responsibility for funding internal improvements within a single state. The veto undermined Clay's American System and underscored differences between the two parties.

The first six presidents vetoed nine bills; Jackson alone vetoed twelve. Previous presidents believed vetoes were justified only on constitutional grounds, but Jackson considered policy disagreements legitimate grounds. He made the veto an effective weapon for controlling Congress, which had to weigh the possibility of a veto as it deliberated.

Federalism at Issue: The Nullification and Bank Controversies

What was at issue in the Nullification Crisis?

The slave South feared federal power—especially South Carolina, where the planter class was strongest and slavery most concentrated. Southerners resented protectionist tariffs, which in 1824 and 1828 bolstered manufactures by imposing import duties on foreign cloth and iron. In protecting northern factories, the tariff raised the costs of manufactured goods to southerners, who labeled the high 1828 tariff the **Tariff of Abominations**.

Tariff of Abominations
Protective tariff of 1828 that infuriated southerners and spawned the Nullification Crisis.

Nullification

South Carolina's political leaders rejected the 1828 tariff, invoking the doctrine of nullification, maintaining that a state had the right to overrule, or nullify, federal legislation. Nullification borrowed from the 1798 Virginia and Kentucky Resolutions—that the states, representing the people, have a right to judge the constitutionality of federal actions. Jackson's vice president, John C. Calhoun of South Carolina, argued in his unsigned *Exposition and Protest* that, in disagreements between federal and state governments, a special state convention should decide the conflict by either nullifying or affirming the federal law.

As Jackson's running mate in 1828, Calhoun avoided endorsing nullification and embarrassing the Democratic ticket; he also sought Jackson's support as the Democratic presidential heir apparent. Thus, in early 1830, Calhoun presided silently over the Senate when Massachusetts Senator Daniel Webster and South Carolina Senator Robert Y. Hayne debated states' rights. The debate over the tariff soon focused on the nature of the Union, with nullification a subtext. Hayne charged the North with threatening to bring disunity. Webster defended New England and the republic.

Though sympathetic to states' rights and distrustful of the federal government, Jackson rejected state sovereignty and embraced the Union. The president articulated his position at a Jefferson Day dinner with the toast "Our Federal Union, it must and shall be preserved." Vice President Calhoun toasted "The Federal Union—next to our liberty the most dear," revealing his adherence to states' rights. Calhoun and Jackson grew apart, and Jackson eyed Secretary of State Martin Van Buren as his successor.

Tension resumed in 1832 when Congress passed a new tariff, reducing some duties but retaining high taxes on imported iron, cottons, and woolens. Although a majority of southern representatives supported the new tariff, South Carolinians did not. They feared the act could set a precedent for congressional legislation on slavery. In November 1832, a South Carolina state convention nullified the 1828 and 1832 tariffs, declaring it unlawful for federal officials to collect duties in the state.

The Force Bill

Jackson soon issued a proclamation opposing nullification. He moved troops to federal forts in South Carolina and prepared U.S. marshals to collect the duties. At Jackson's request, Congress passed the Force Bill, authorizing the president to call up troops but offering a way to avoid force by collecting duties before foreign ships reached Charleston's harbor. Jackson also extended an olive branch by recommending tariff reductions.

Calhoun resigned as vice president and won election to the U.S. Senate, where he worked with Henry Clay on the compromise Tariff of 1833. Quickly passed by Congress and signed by the president, the new tariff lengthened the list of duty-free items and reduced duties over nine years. Satisfied, South Carolina's convention repealed its nullification law.

Nullification became a debate on the principles of the republic. Each side believed it was upholding the Constitution. South Carolina opposed the tyranny of the federal government and manufacturing interests. Jackson fought the tyranny of South Carolina, whose actions threatened the republic. It took another crisis, over a central bank, to define the powers of the federal government more clearly.

Second Bank of the United States

At stake was the Second Bank of the United States, whose twenty-year charter would expire in 1836. The bank served as a depository for federal funds and provided business credit. Its bank notes circulated as currency nationwide and could be exchanged for gold. Through its twenty-five branch offices, the Second Bank acted as a clearinghouse for state banks, refusing notes lacking sufficient gold reserves. Most state banks saw the central bank's police role as potentially ruinous. Moreover, state banks could not compete with the Second Bank, which had more money in reserve.

Many states regarded the national bank as unresponsive to local needs. Western settlers and urban workers bitterly remembered the bank's conservative credit policies during the Panic of 1819. As a private, profit-making institution, its policies reflected its owners' interests, especially those of its president, Nicholas Biddle. An eastern patrician, Biddle symbolized what westerners resented about the bank, and what eastern workers disliked about the commercial elite.

Political Violence

Controversy over the Second Bank inflamed long-standing political animosities, igniting street violence. Elections often involved fraud, and with no secret ballot, political parties employed operatives to intimidate voters. New York City was home to the most powerful political machine, the Democrats' Tammany Hall, and thus in the midst of the Bank controversy, New York's mayoral election of 1834 sparked mayhem.

Three days of rioting began when Democratic operatives stormed Whig headquarters. After beating some **Whigs** unconscious, the Democrats attacked police; eight of them suffered severe wounds, and the mayor was also injured. Vowing revenge, more than five hundred Whigs stole weapons from the armory, but the state militia restored order.

Months later, an election-day riot in Philadelphia left two dead and five buildings burned to the ground. These two riots stood out for their intensity, but voter intimidation and fraud characterized the second party system.

Whigs Formerly called the National Republicans; a major political party in the 1830s.

Antimasonry

Violence was a catalyst for the formation of the Antimason Party, which started in upstate New York in the mid-1820s as a grassroots movement against Freemasonry, a secret male fraternity of prominent middle- and upper-class men. Antimasons claimed Masons colluded to bestow business and political favors on each other, and—in the incident that sparked the organized Antimasonry movement—Masons had obstructed justice in the investigation of the 1826 disappearance and presumed murder of a disgruntled former member who had written an exposé of the society. Evangelicals denounced Masonry, claiming its members neglected their families for alcohol and ribald entertainment. In the 1828 presidential election, the Antimasons opposed Jackson, a Mason. The Antimasons held the first national political convention in Baltimore in 1831, nominating William Wirt of Maryland for president and Amos Ellmaker of Pennsylvania for vice president.

Election of 1832

Democrats and National Republicans held conventions. Democrats reaffirmed Jackson for president and nominated Martin Van Buren of New York for vice president. The National Republican convention selected Clay and John Sergeant of Pennsylvania. The Independent Democrats ran John Floyd and Henry Lee of Virginia.

The Bank of the United States became the election's main issue. Jacksonians denounced it as a vehicle for special privilege, while the Republicans supported it. The bank's charter was valid until 1836, but Clay persuaded Biddle to ask Congress for an early rechartering. If Jackson signed the rechartering bill, then Clay could attack the president's inconsistency. If he vetoed it, Clay hoped voters would favor him. The plan backfired. The president vetoed the bill with a message appealing to voters who feared that rapid economic development spread advantages undemocratically. Jackson stood against special interests seeking to use the government to their own advantage and won 54 percent of the popular vote to Clay's 37 percent. He captured 76 percent of the electoral college. The Antimasons won only Vermont but galvanized anti-Jackson opposition.

Jackson's Second Term

Jackson began in 1833 dismantling the Second Bank and depositing federal funds in state-chartered banks. When its federal charter expired in 1836, it became just another Pennsylvania-chartered private bank, closing five years later. Congress passed the Deposit Act of 1836, authorizing the secretary of the treasury to designate one bank per state and territory to provide services formerly performed by the Bank of the United States. The act also provided that federal surplus exceeding $5 million—income derived from the sale of public lands to speculators, who gobbled it up to resell at a profit—be distributed to the states as interest-free loans beginning in 1837. Eager to use the money for state-funded internal improvements, Democrats joined Whigs in supporting the measure. Fearing that the act would

Whigs, who named themselves after the loyal opposition in Britain, delighted in portraying Andrew Jackson as a power-hungry leader eager to turn a republic into a monarchy.

fuel speculation, promote inflation, and thus undermine farmers' interests, Jackson opposed it. Because support was strong enough to override a veto, Jackson signed the bill but first insisted on a provision prohibiting state banks from issuing or accepting small-denomination paper money. Jackson hoped that by encouraging the use of coins, the provision would prevent unscrupulous businessmen from paying workers in devalued paper bills.

Specie Circular

The president then ordered treasury secretary Levi Woodbury to issue the Specie Circular, which provided that, after August 1836, only settlers could use paper money to buy land; speculators had to use specie (gold or silver). The policy proved disastrous, significantly reducing public land sales, which in turn reduced the federal government's surplus and its loans to the states. A banking crisis emerged. Fearful that bank notes would lose value, people redeemed them for specie, creating a shortage that forced the banks to suspend payment. In the waning days of Jackson's administration, Congress repealed the circular, but the president pocket-vetoed the bill by holding it unsigned until Congress adjourned. In May 1838, after Jackson had left office, a joint resolution of Congress overturned the circular.

The Second Party System

How did Whigs and Democrats differ ideologically?

In the 1830s, opponents of the Democrats, including remnants of the National Republican and Antimason parties, united as the Whig Party. From 1834 through the 1840s, Whigs and the Democrats competed on nearly equal footing, and each drew supporters from all regions. The era's political competition—the second party system— thrived on ideological rivalry.

Democrats and Whigs

The two parties differed about the route to national prosperity. Democrats embraced westward expansion's opportunities for independent landownership. Whigs were suspicious of rapid westward expansion, and instead pushed for commercial development within the nation's current boundaries.

The Whigs' economic vision demanded an activist government, while Democrats promoted limited government. Whigs supported corporate charters, a national bank, and paper currency; Democrats opposed all three. Whigs believed in progress and perfectibility, and they favored social reforms, including public schools, prison and asylum reform, and temperance. Jacksonians criticized reformers for undermining the people's will. Nor did Whigs object to helping special interests if it promoted the general welfare. The chartering of corporations, they argued, expanded opportunity for everyone. Whigs stressed a "harmony of interests" among all classes while Democrats saw society as divided into the "haves" and the "have nots." Whigs preferred to see society ruled from the top down; they believed in free-labor ideology and thought that society's wealthy had risen by merit. Democrats alleged that the wealthy had benefited from special favors.

Political Coalitions

Religion and ethnicity, as much as class, influenced party affiliation. The Whigs' support for moral reform appealed to evangelical Protestants along with free black voters. In many locales, membership rolls of reform societies overlapped those of the party. Whigs' rallies resembled camp meetings; their speeches employed pulpit rhetoric; their programs embodied reformers' perfectionist beliefs.

By appealing to evangelicals, Whigs alienated other faiths. The evangelicals' ideal Christian state had no room for nonevangelical Protestants, Catholics, Mormons, or religious freethinkers. Consequently, more than 95 percent of Irish Catholics, 90 percent of Reformed Dutch, and 80 percent of German Catholics voted Democratic.

The parties' platforms thus attracted seemingly odd coalitions of voters. Democrats' promises to open additional lands for settlement attracted yeoman farmers, wage earners, frontier slave owners, and immigrants. The Whigs' preference for slower, controlled settlement of western lands attracted groups as diverse as black New Englanders and slave owners in the Upper South; the former hoped to undercut slavery itself, and the latter wanted to protect their investments from cheap western competition. With broad voter coalitions, room existed within each party for a spectrum of beliefs, particularly regarding slavery.

Some politicians went to extremes to keep the potentially divisive issue of slavery out of national political debate. Responding to the American Antislavery Society's petitioning campaign, the House of Representatives in 1836 adopted what abolitionists labeled the "gag rule," which automatically tabled abolitionist petitions. Former president John Quincy Adams, now a representative from Massachusetts, defended the right to petition and spoke against the gag rule, which was repealed in 1844.

Election of 1836

Vice President Martin Van Buren headed the Democratic ticket in the 1836 presidential election. A career politician, Van Buren built a political machine—the Albany Regency—in New York and joined Jackson's cabinet in 1829, first as secretary of state and then as American minister to Great Britain.

Not yet a national party in 1836, Whigs entered three sectional candidates: Daniel Webster (New England), Hugh White (the South), and William Henry Harrison (the West). Van Buren captured the electoral college even though he had only a 25,000-vote lead. No vice presidential candidate received a majority of electoral votes, and for the only time in American history, the Senate decided a vice presidential race, selecting Democratic candidate Richard M. Johnson of Kentucky.

Van Buren and Hard Times

Weeks after Van Buren took office, the American credit system collapsed. With banks refusing to redeem paper currency with gold in response to the Specie Circular, a downward economic spiral curtailed bank loans. After a brief recovery, hard times persisted from 1839 until 1843.

Van Buren followed Jackson's hard-money, antibank policies, proposing the Independent Treasury Bill, which became law in 1840 but was repealed in 1841. The independent treasury created regional treasury branches that accepted and dispersed only gold and silver coin; they did not accept paper currency or checks drawn on state banks, and thus accelerated deflation. Whigs favored new banks, more paper currency, and readily available corporate and bank charters. As the party of hard money, Democrats favored eliminating paper currency; by the mid-1840s, most favored eliminating bank corporations.

William Henry Harrison and the Election of 1840

With the nation facing hard times, Whigs confidently approached the election of 1840 with a simple strategy: maintain loyal supporters and court independents by blaming hardship on Democrats. Whigs rallied behind military hero General William Henry Harrison, conqueror of the Shawnees at Tippecanoe Creek in 1811. The Democrats renominated President Van Buren, and the newly formed Liberty Party ran James Birney.

Harrison and his running mate, John Tyler of Virginia, ran a people's crusade against the aristocratic president in "the Palace." Although descended from a Virginia plantation family, Harrison presented himself as an ordinary farmer. Whigs wooed voters with rallies, parades, songs, posters, campaign mementos, and a party newspaper, *The Log Cabin*. They appealed to voters as well as nonvoters, including women, who attended rallies and actively promoted the Whig cause. Roughly 80 percent of eligible voters cast ballots. Narrowly winning the popular vote, Harrison swept the electoral college, 234 to 60.

Women's Rights

What inspired the rise of the women's movement in the mid-nineteenth century?

Although women participated in electoral campaigns, states denied them the right to vote, along with other rights afforded male citizens. The movement for women's rights gained steam with the 1830s religious revivalism and reform movements (see Chapter 10). While revivals emphasized human equality, reform movements brought middle-class women into the public sphere.

By the 1840s, female abolitionists took the lead in demanding women's legal and political rights. Committed to notions of human equality, they were frustrated by their subordinated status within the abolitionist movement. Dismayed that female abolitionists were denied seats in the main hall at the first World Anti-Slavery Convention in London in 1840, Lucretia Mott and Elizabeth Cady

Stanton united eight years later to organize the first American women's rights convention. **Angelina and Sarah Grimké**, sisters who were born into a South Carolina slaveholding family, became abolitionists in the North, where critics attacked them for speaking to audiences that included men. Some thought the next step was obvious: full citizenship rights for women.

Angelina and Sarah Grimké Southern-born sisters who were powerful antislavery speakers; later leaders of the women's rights movement.

Legal Rights

After independence, American states carried over traditional English marriage law, giving husbands control over the family. Husbands owned their wives' property and whatever they or their children produced or earned. Fathers were their children's legal guardians and could deny their daughters' choice of husband, though by 1800 few did.

Married women made modest gains in property and spousal rights after 1830. Arkansas in 1835 passed the first married women's property law, and by 1860 sixteen states allowed women to own and convey property and write wills. When a wife inherited property, it was hers, though money earned still belonged to her husband. Such laws were popular among wealthy Americans, hoping to protect family fortunes during economic downturns; property in a woman's name was safe from her husband's creditors. In the 1830s, states also added cruelty and desertion as grounds for divorce, but divorce remained rare.

Political Rights

The movement to secure women's political rights was launched in July 1848, with the first Woman's Rights Convention at **Seneca Falls**, New York. The three hundred women and men in attendance demanded women's social and economic equality. Their Declaration of Sentiments, modeled on the Declaration of Independence, broadcast the injustices suffered by women and proclaimed "all men and women are created equal." The similarities between abolitionism and women's rights led reformers, including former slaves like Sojourner Truth, to work for both movements in the 1850s. Abolitionists William Lloyd Garrison and Frederick Douglass supported women's right to vote, but most men opposed it. The Seneca Falls suffrage resolution passed only after Douglass passionately endorsed it. In 1851, **Elizabeth Cady Stanton** joined with temperance advocate **Susan B. Anthony** to become the most vocal suffrage activists. They won relatively few converts and many critics, however.

Seneca Falls The location of a women's rights convention in 1848.

Elizabeth Cady Stanton, Susan B. Anthony Vocal advocates of women's suffrage.

The Politics of Territorial Expansion

How did territorial expansion expose political fissures?

After taking office in 1841, President Harrison convened Congress in special session to pass the Whig program: repeal of the independent treasury system, a new national bank, and a higher protective tariff. But the sixty-eight-year-old Harrison caught pneumonia and died within a month of his inauguration. John Tyler, who left the Democratic Party to protest Jackson's nullification proclamation, became the first vice president to succeed to the presidency. Tyler assumed executive powers, setting a precedent that would not be codified in the Constitution until 1967 with the Twenty-fifth Amendment's ratification.

President Tyler

In office, Tyler became more Democrat than Whig. He vetoed Clay's protective tariffs, internal improvements, and bills to revive the Bank of the United States. After Tyler's second veto of a bank bill, the entire cabinet ultimately resigned. Tyler became a president without a party. Tyler's expansionist vision contained Whig elements, though: he eyed commercial markets in Hawai'i and China. During his presidency, the United States negotiated its first treaties with China, and Tyler expanded the Monroe Doctrine to include Hawai'i (or the Sandwich Islands). But Tyler fixed mostly on Texas and westward expansion.

Texas and "Manifest Destiny"

Soon after establishing the Lone Star Republic in 1836, Sam Houston approached American authorities to propose annexation as a state. But a new slave state would upset the balance of slave and free states in the Senate. Neither Whigs nor Democrats, wary of causing sectional divisions, wanted to address it. In the 1830s, Democratic presidents Andrew Jackson and Martin Van Buren—one a strong proponent of slavery, the other a mild opponent—sidestepped the issue. But by the mid-1840s—with cotton cultivation expanding rapidly—some Democratic politicians equated Texas's annexation with manifest destiny.

The belief that American expansion westward and southward was inevitable, just, and divinely ordained dated to the nation's founding but was first labeled "manifest destiny" in 1845 by John L. O'Sullivan, editor of the *United States Magazine and Democratic Review*. O'Sullivan claimed that Texas annexation would be "the fulfillment of our manifest destiny to overspread the continent allotted by Providence for the free development of our yearly multiplying millions." Manifest destiny implied that Americans had a God-given right, even obligation, to expand their republican and Christian institutions to less fortunate and less civilized peoples. Implicit in the idea of manifest destiny was the belief that American Indians and Hispanics, like people of African descent, were inferior peoples best controlled or conquered. Manifest destiny provided a political rationale for territorial expansion.

Link to John L. O'Sullivan, Annnexation (1845)

Fifty-Four Forty or Fight

To the north, Britain and the United States had jointly occupied the disputed Oregon Territory since 1818. Beginning with John Quincy Adams's administration, the United States tried to fix the boundary at the 49th parallel, but Britain wanted access to Puget Sound and the Columbia River. In the early 1840s, expansionists demanded the entire Oregon Country for the United States, up to its northernmost border at latitude 54°40'. Soon "fifty-four forty or fight" became their rallying cry.

President Tyler wanted Oregon and Texas, but was obsessed with Texas specifically. He argued that slavery's expansion would spread the nation's black population more thinly, causing the institution's gradual demise. But when word leaked out that Secretary of State John Calhoun had written to the British minister in Washington justifying Texas annexation to protect slavery, the Senate rejected annexation in 1844 by 35 to 16.

Polk and the Election of 1844

Worried southern Democrats persuaded their party's 1844 convention to require that the presidential nominee receive two-thirds of the convention votes, effectively allowing them to block the nomination of Martin Van Buren, who opposed annexation. Instead, the party ran House Speaker **James K. Polk**, an expansionist and slaveholding Tennessee cotton planter. The Democratic platform called for occupation of the entire Oregon Territory and annexation of Texas. The Whigs, who ran Henry Clay, argued that the Democrats' belligerent nationalism would trigger war with Great Britain or Mexico or both. Clay favored expansion through negotiation, whereas many northern Whigs opposed annexation altogether, fearful it would add slave states and strain relations with trading partners. Polk won the election by 170 electoral votes to 105, though with a margin of just 38,000 out of 2.7 million ballots cast.

James K. Polk President from 1845 to 1849; supporter of immediate annexation of Texas who wanted to gain California and Oregon for the United States as well.

Annexation of Texas

Interpreting Polk's victory as a mandate for annexation, President Tyler proposed that Texas be admitted by joint resolution of Congress. The usual method of annexation, by treaty negotiation, required a two-thirds majority in the Senate—which annexationists did not have. Joint resolution required a simple majority. On March 1, 1845, the resolution passed the House by 120 to 98 and the Senate by 27 to 25. Three days before leaving office, Tyler signed the measure. Mexico, which never recognized Texas independence, broke relations with the United States. In October, Texas citizens ratified annexation, and Texas joined the Union, with a constitution permitting slavery. The nation was on the brink of war with Mexico. That conflict would lay bare the inextricable relationships among westward expansion, slavery, and sectional discord.

The War with Mexico and Its Consequences

How did Polk's decisions push the United States toward war with Mexico?

The annexation of Texas did not make war with Mexico inevitable, but several of Polk's decisions did. During the annexation process, Polk urged Texans to seize all land to the Rio Grande and claim the river as their southern and western border. Mexico held that the Nueces River was the border; hence, the stage was set for conflict. Polk wanted Mexico's territory all the way to the Pacific, and all of Oregon Country as well. He and his expansionist cabinet achieved their goals, unaware of expansionism's impact on domestic harmony.

Oregon

During the 1844 campaign, Polk's supporters threatened war with Great Britain to gain Oregon. Polk, not wanting to fight Mexico and Great Britain simultaneously, sought diplomacy in the Northwest. In 1846, the Oregon Treaty gave the United States all of present-day Oregon, Washington, and Idaho, and parts of Wyoming and Montana (see Map 12.3). Thus, a new era of land acquisition and conquest had begun.

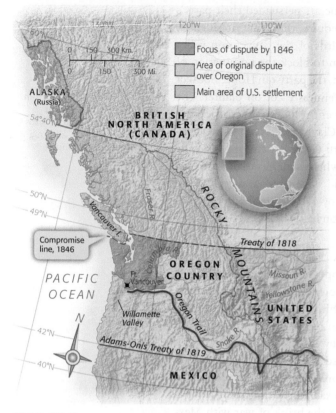

MAP 12.3
American Expansion in Oregon
The slogan of Polk's supporters had been "fifty-four forty or fight," but negotiation of a boundary at the forty-ninth parallel avoided the danger of war with Great Britain. Source: Copyright © Cengage Learning 2015

"Mr. Polk's War"

Toward Mexico, Polk was aggressive. In early 1846, he ordered American troops under General Zachary Taylor to defend the contested border of the Rio Grande. Polk saw California as the prize, and he attempted to buy from Mexico a huge tract extending to the Pacific. Failing that, Polk waited for war. After a three-week standoff, on April 24, 1846, Mexican cavalry ambushed a U.S. cavalry unit on the north side of the river; eleven Americans were killed, and sixty-three were captured. On April 26, Taylor sent a dispatch to Washington, D.C., announcing, "Hostilities may now be considered as commenced."

Polk then drafted a message to Congress: Mexico had "passed the boundary of the United States, had invaded our territory and shed American blood on American soil." Polk deceptively declared that "war exists by the act of Mexico itself." Two days later, on May 13, the House recognized a state of war with Mexico by a vote of 174 to 14, and the Senate, by 40 to 2. Because Polk withheld key facts, the full reality of what had happened on the distant Rio Grande was unknown.

Foreign War and the Popular Imagination

The idea of war unleashed public celebrations in southern and northern cities. After news came of General Taylor's first victories at Palo Alto and Resaca de la Palma, volunteers swarmed recruiting stations. In New York, writer Herman Melville remarked that "Nothing is talked of but the Halls of the Montezumas." Publishers rushed books about Mexican geography into print. New daily newspapers boosted sales by giving the war a romantic appeal.

Here was an adventurous war of conquest, the fulfillment of an Anglo-Saxon–Christian destiny to possess the North American continent and civilize the "semi-Indian" Mexicans. Racism fueled the expansionist spirit. In 1846, an Illinois newspaper justified the war by calling Mexicans "reptiles in the path of progressive democracy." War correspondents reported on battles, and ships from Vera Cruz on the Gulf Coast of Mexico carried news dispatches to New Orleans. Near war's end, news traveled by telegraph in only three days from New Orleans to Washington, D.C.

The war spawned poetry, song, drama, travel, literature, and lithographs that glorified the conflict. But not everyone cheered. Abolitionist James Russell Lowell considered the war a "national crime committed in behoof of slavery, our common sin." Even proslavery spokesman John C. Calhoun saw the perils of expansionism.

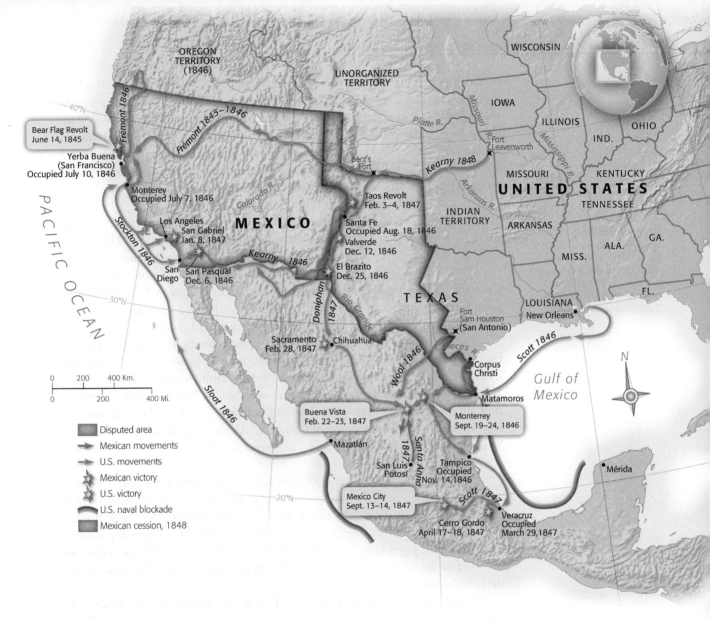

MAP 12.4

The War with Mexico

This map shows the territory disputed between the United States and Mexico. After U.S. gains in northeastern Mexico, in New Mexico, and in California, General Winfield Scott captured Mexico City in the decisive campaign of the war. Source: Copyright © Cengage Learning 2015

Conquest

Early in the war, U.S. forces made significant gains. In May 1846, Polk ordered Colonel Stephen Kearny to invade the remote provinces of New Mexico and California. General Zachary Taylor's forces attacked Monterrey, which surrendered in September, securing northeastern Mexico (see Map 12.4).

New Mexico proved more difficult to subdue, however. In January 1847, in Taos, northwest of Santa Fe, Hispanics and Indians led by Pablo Montoya and Tomas Romero rebelled against the Americans. In the Taos Revolt, some 500 Mexican and Indian insurgents laid siege to a mill in Arroyo Hondo, outside Taos. The U.S. command suppressed the revolt, and the insurgents retreated to a thick-walled church in Taos Pueblo. With cannon, the U.S. Army killed 150 and captured 400 rebels. Approximately 28 insurgent leaders were hanged in the Taos plaza, ending bloody resistance to U.S. occupation. Before the end of 1846, American forces also established dominion over California. General Winfield Scott then led fourteen thousand men toward Mexico City in what proved the war's decisive campaign. Outnumbered and threatened by yellow fever, Scott's men repeatedly discovered flanking routes around their foes. U.S. troops captured the Mexican capital.

Treaty of Guadalupe Hidalgo
Agreement that ended the U.S. War with Mexico, in which Mexico ceded vast amounts of its territory and was forced to recognize the Rio Grande as Texas's southern boundary.

Treaty of Guadalupe Hidalgo

Representatives of both countries signed the **Treaty of Guadalupe Hidalgo** in February 1848. The United States gained California and New Mexico (including present-day Nevada, Utah, and Arizona, and parts of Colorado and Wyoming), and recognition of the Rio Grande as Texas's southern boundary. The American government agreed to settle the $3.2 million in its citizens' claims against Mexico and to pay Mexico a mere $15 million.

The war's costs included the lives of thirteen thousand Americans (mostly from disease) and fifty thousand Mexicans. Enmity between Mexico and the United States endured into the twentieth century. Domestically, southwesterners and southern planters were enthusiastic about the war; New Englanders opposed it. Whigs in Congress charged that Polk, a Democrat, had "provoked" an unnecessary war and "usurped the power of Congress." Abolitionists and some antislavery Whigs charged that the war was a plot to extend slavery.

"Slave Power Conspiracy"

These charges fed northern fear of the "Slave Power." Abolitionists long warned of a slaveholding oligarchy that would dominate federal power. Slaveholders gained control of the South by suppressing dissent. They forced the gag rule on Congress in 1836. To many white northerners, this battle over free speech made the idea of a Slave Power credible. The War with Mexico deepened such fears.

Initially, some southern Whigs attacked the Democratic president for causing the war, and few southern congressmen saw slavery as the paramount issue. Many whites, North and South, feared that large land seizures would bring nonwhite Mexicans into the United States and upset the racial order. An Indiana politician did not want "any mixed races in our Union, nor men of any color except white, unless they be slaves." Despite their racism and exaggerations, many statesmen soon saw other potential outcomes of a war of conquest in the Southwest.

Wilmot Proviso

In August 1846, Pennsylvania Democrat David Wilmot proposed an amendment, or proviso, to a military appropriations bill: that "neither slavery nor involuntary servitude shall ever exist" in territories gained from Mexico. Although the proviso never passed, it transformed the debate over slavery's expansion. Southerners intensified efforts to protect slavery's future. Alexander H. Stephens declared that slavery was based on the Bible, and John C. Calhoun insisted that slaveholders had a constitutional right to take their slaves (as property) anywhere.

Visualizing THE PAST

The Mexican War in Popular Imagination

The War with Mexico was the first American foreign conflict to be covered by the press with actual correspondents and the first to stimulate the creation of widespread promotional popular art and commemorative objects. General Zachary Taylor, the American commander in Mexico, became the hero of the war, and in its wake was elected president in 1848 in a campaign that featured countless forms of this art. Why was the War with Mexico the first American foreign war to be covered by journalists and so widely depicted in political and military art? Do you think the artistic depictions of the War with Mexico increased or decreased the popularity of the war?

Presentation pitcher: ca. 1848–1850 (porcelain), French School (nineteenth century), Portrait of Zachary Taylor (1784–1850) on one side, twelfth president of the United States (1849–1850); landscape with battle on the other side, hero of the Mexican war (1846–1848), commemorates Taylor's triumph in the 1847 battle of Buena Vista.

The Bayou Bend Collection, gift of Miss Ima Hogg/Bridgeman Art Library

Chicago History Museum, USA/Bridgeman Art Library

Painting, General Zachary Taylor in command at the Battle of Buena Vista, in Mexico, 1847, oil on canvas, by William Henry Powell (1823–1879).

This position, often called "state sovereignty," was a radical reversal of history. In 1787, the Confederation Congress discouraged slavery in the Northwest Territory; Article IV of the U.S. Constitution authorized Congress to make "all needful rules and regulations" for the territories; and the Missouri Compromise barred slavery from most of the Louisiana Purchase. Now southern leaders demanded guarantees for slavery.

Wilmot Proviso A proposed amendment that would have prohibited slavery in territories acquired from Mexico; though it never passed, it transformed the national debate over slavery.

The **Wilmot Proviso** became a rallying cry for abolitionists. While fourteen northern states endorsed it, not all supporters were abolitionists. Wilmot was neither an abolitionist nor an antislavery Whig. Instead, his goal was to obtain California "for free white labor."

The majority of white northerners were not active abolitionists, and their desire to keep the West slavery free was often matched by their desire to keep blacks out. At stake was the free individual's access to social mobility by acquiring western land. Slave labor, thousands of northerners believed, would degrade the toil of free men and render them unemployable. The West must therefore ban slavery.

The Election of 1848 and Popular Sovereignty

The divisive slavery question infested national politics. After Polk renounced a second term as president, the Democrats nominated Senator Lewis Cass of Michigan for president and General William Butler of Kentucky for vice president. Cass devised in 1847 the idea of "popular sovereignty"—letting residents in the western territories decide the slavery question for themselves. His party's platform declared that Congress lacked the power to interfere with slavery's expansion. The Whigs nominated General Zachary Taylor, a southern slaveholder and war hero; New York Congressman Millard Fillmore was his running mate. The Whig convention similarly denied that Congress had power over slavery in the territories.

Free-Soil Party A political party that sprang from and represented the movement to prevent slavery in the western territories.

Many southern Democrats distrusted Cass and voted for Taylor because he was a slaveholder. New York Democrats committed to the Wilmot Proviso nominated former president Martin Van Buren. Antislavery Whigs and former supporters of the Liberty Party joined them to organize the **Free-Soil Party**, with Van Buren as its candidate (see Table 12.1). This party, which sought to restrict slavery's expansion in the West and whose slogan was "Free Soil, Free Speech, Free Labor, and Free Men," won almost 300,000 northern votes. Taylor polled 1.4 million votes to Cass's 1.2 million and won the White House, but the results were ominous.

TABLE 12.1   New Political Parties

Party	Period of Influence	Area of Influence	Outcome
Liberty Party	1839–1848	North	Merged with other antislavery groups to form Free-Soil Party
Free-Soil Party	1848–1854	North	Merged with Republican Party
Know-Nothings (American Party)	1853–1856	Nationwide	Disappeared, freeing most to join Republican Party
Republican Party	1854–present	North (later nationwide)	Became rival of Democratic Party and won presidency in 1860

Sectionalism and religion, too, severed into northern and southern wings. As the 1850s dawned, the legacies of the War with Mexico threatened the nature of the Union.

1850: Compromise or Armistice?

What were the two troubling issues inherent in the Compromise of 1850?

More than eighty thousand Americans flooded into California during the 1849 gold rush. With Congress unable to agree on how to govern the territories, President Taylor urged settlers to apply for admission to the Union. They did, proposing a state constitution that banned slavery. Because California's admission as a free state would upset the Senate's sectional balance of power (the ratio of slave to free states was fifteen to fifteen), southern politicians wanted to postpone admission and make California a slave territory, or extend the Missouri Compromise to the Pacific.

Debate over Slavery in the Territories

Twice before—in 1820 and 1833—Henry Clay, the Whig leader and "Great Pacificator," had shaped sectional compromise; now he struggled one last time to preserve the nation. In the winter of 1850, Clay and Senator Stephen A. Douglas of Illinois steered their compromise package through debate and amendment.

The problems were numerous. Would California become a free state? How should the territory acquired from Mexico be organized? Texas, which allowed slavery, claimed large portions as far west as Santa Fe. Southerners complained that fugitive slaves were not returned as the Constitution required, and northerners objected to slave auctions in the nation's capital. Most troublesome, however, was the status of slavery in the territories.

Clay and Douglas found in the idea of popular sovereignty what one historian called a "charm of ambiguity." Ultimately, Congress would have to approve statehood for a territory, but "in the meantime," said Lewis Cass, it should allow the people living there "to regulate their own concerns in their own way." To avoid dissension within their party, northern and southern Democrats explained Cass's statement to their constituents in two incompatible ways. Southerners claimed that neither Congress nor a territorial legislature could bar slavery. Northerners, however, insisted that Americans living in a territory were entitled to local self-government and thus could outlaw slavery.

The cause of compromise gained a powerful supporter when Senator Daniel Webster committed his prestige to Clay's bill. Webster urged northerners not to "taunt or reproach" the South with antislavery measures. He warned that disunion inevitably would cause violence and destruction. Many of Webster's former abolitionist friends in New England accused him of going over to the "Devil."

Three days earlier, Calhoun was carried from his sickbed to speak against the compromise. When Calhoun was unable to speak, Senator James Mason of Virginia read his address, which predicted disunion if southern demands went unanswered, frightening some into support of compromise.

With Clay sick, Douglas reintroduced the compromise measures one at a time. Douglas realized that because southerners favored some bills and northerners the rest, a small majority for compromise could be achieved on each distinct issue. The strategy worked, and the Compromise of 1850 became law.

Compromise of 1850

The compromise had five essential measures:

1. California became a free state.
2. The Texas boundary was set at its present limits (see Map 12.5), and the United States paid Texas $10 million in compensation for the loss of New Mexico Territory.
3. The territories of New Mexico and Utah were organized on a basis of popular sovereignty.
4. The fugitive slave law was strengthened.
5. The slave trade was abolished in the District of Columbia.

At best, the Compromise of 1850 was an artful evasion. Douglas found a way to pass the five proposals without convincing northerners and southerners to agree on fundamentals. The compromise bought time, but it did not resolve territorial questions.

Furthermore, the compromise had two flaws. The first concerned the ambiguity of popular sovereignty. Southerners insisted on no prohibition of slavery during the territorial stage, and northerners declared that settlers could bar slavery whenever they wished. The compromise allowed for the appeal of a territorial legislature's action to the Supreme Court.

Fugitive Slave Act Part of the Compromise of 1850, this controversial measure gave additional powers to slave owners to recapture slaves and angered northerners by requiring them to hunt so-called fugitive slaves.

Fugitive Slave Act

The second flaw lay in the **Fugitive Slave Act**, which gave new—and controversial—protection to slavery. The law empowered slave owners to legally claim that a slave had escaped. That claim would then serve as proof of a person's slave status, even in free states and territories. Specially appointed federal commissioners adjudicated the identity of alleged fugitives, and those commissioners were paid fees that favored slaveholders: $10 if the alleged fugitive was returned, and $5 if not. Abolitionist newspapers attacked the Fugitive Slave Act as a violation of American rights. Why would northerners be arrested if they harbored runaways? The "free" states, moreover, were no longer a safe haven for black folk. An estimated twenty thousand fled to Canada in the wake of the Fugitive Slave Act.

Between 1850 and 1854, protests and violent resistance to slave catchers occurred in northern towns. Many abolitionists became convinced that violence was a legitimate means of opposing slavery. In an 1854 column, Frederick Douglass said that the only way to make the fugitive slave law "dead letter" was to make a "few dead slave catchers."

Underground Railroad
A loosely organized route by which fugitive slaves, often of their own volition, escaped to freedom in the northern United States and Canada.

The Underground Railroad

By the 1850s, slaveholders were especially disturbed by the **Underground Railroad**, a loose, illegal network, spiriting runaways to freedom. Thousands of slaves escaped by these often disorganized routes, but largely through their own wits and courage with assistance from blacks in northern cities. Lewis Hayden in Boston, David Ruggles in New York, William Still in Philadelphia, and Jacob Gibbs in Washington, D.C., were among the many black abolitionists who managed fugitive slave escapes.

Harriet Tubman, herself an escapee in 1848, returned to her native Maryland and to Virginia at least a dozen times and secretly helped as many as three hundred slaves— some her family members—to freedom. Outraged Maryland planters offered a $40,000 reward for her capture.

In Ohio, white abolitionists, often Quakers, joined with blacks to help slaves cross the river to freedom. The Underground Railroad also had numerous maritime routes, as coastal slaves escaped aboard ships from Virginia, the Carolinas, or New Orleans, and ended up in northern port cities, the Caribbean, or England. Many fugitive slaves from the Lower South and Texas escaped to Mexico, which abolished slavery in 1829. Some joined Seminole communities in Florida, where they joined forces against the U.S. Army in the Seminole Wars of 1835–1842 and 1855–1858.

Slave escapes were a testament to human courage and the will for freedom. They never reached the scale believed by angry slaveholders or claimed by northern towns and local historical societies today. Nonetheless, the Underground Railroad applied pressure to the institution of slavery and gave slaves hope.

Election of 1852 and the Collapse of Compromise

The 1852 election had southern leaders optimistic that slavery would be secure under a new president. Franklin Pierce, a New Hampshire Democrat, won over Whig General Winfield Scott. Pierce supported the Compromise of 1850, where Scott's views on the compromise were unknown.

By 1852 sectionalism had essentially killed the Whig Party. President Pierce's enforcement of the Fugitive Slave Act provoked northern fear of the Slave Power, especially in the case of the fugitive slave Anthony Burns, who fled Virginia in 1852. In Boston, thinking he was safe, Burns began a new life. But in 1854, federal marshals placed him under guard in Boston's courthouse. An interracial crowd of abolitionists attacked the courthouse, killing a jailer while attempting to free Burns.

Pierce sent troops to Boston. Soldiers marched Burns to Boston harbor while his supporters, draped in black, hung American flags at half-mast. At a cost of $100,000, a single black man was returned to slavery.

This demonstration of federal support for slavery radicalized opinion, even among conservatives. Juries refused to convict the abolitionists who stormed the Boston courthouse. New England states passed personal liberty laws that blocked federal enforcement and absolved local judges from enforcing the Fugitive Slave Act, effectively nullifying federal authority. What northerners now saw as evidence of a dominating Slave Power, slaveholders saw as defense of their rights. Pierce constantly faced sectional conflict. His proposal for a transcontinental railroad derailed when congressmen disputed its location, through the North or South. An annexation treaty with Hawai'i failed because southern senators would not vote for another free state, and efforts to acquire slaveholding Cuba angered northerners.

Slavery Expansion and Collapse of the Party System

How did the Kansas-Nebraska Act lead to the collapse of existing political parties?

A greater controversy began in a surprising way. Stephen A. Douglas introduced a bill to establish the Kansas and Nebraska Territories. Ambitious for the presidency, Douglas did not view slavery as a fundamental problem, and was willing to risk controversy to economically aid his home state of Illinois. A transcontinental railroad would encourage Great Plains settlement and stimulate the Illinois economy. Thus, with these goals, Douglas further inflamed sectional passions.

Kansas-Nebraska Act
Effectively repealed the Missouri Compromise and inflamed sectional disputes around the expansion of slavery in the territories. The act left the decision of whether to allow slavery in the new territories of Kansas and Nebraska up to the people residing there (popular sovereignty).

The Kansas-Nebraska Act

The **Kansas-Nebraska Act** exposed conflicting interpretations of popular sovereignty. Douglas's bill left "all questions pertaining to slavery in the Territories ... to the people residing therein." Northerners and southerners, however, disagreed over what territorial settlers could constitutionally do. Moreover, the Kansas and Nebraska Territories lay within the Louisiana Purchase, and the Missouri Compromise prohibited slavery there from latitude 36°30' north to the Canadian border. If popular sovereignty were applied in Kansas and Nebraska, it would mean that the Missouri Compromise was no longer in effect.

Southern congressmen, anxious to establish slaveholders' right to take slaves into any territory, pressed Douglas for a repeal of the 36°30' limitation in exchange for their support. During a carriage ride with Kentucky senator Archibald Dixon, Douglas conceded: "I will incorporate it in my bill, though I know it will raise a hell of a storm."

Douglas believed that climate and soil conditions would keep slavery out of Kansas and Nebraska. Nevertheless, his bill allowed slavery on land from which it had been prohibited for thirty-four years. Many Free-Soilers and antislavery forces considered this a betrayal of trust. The bill became law in May 1854 by a vote that demonstrated the dangerous sectionalization of American politics (see Map 12.5 and Table 12.2).

Meanwhile, opposition to the Fugitive Slave Act grew dramatically; between 1855 and 1859, Connecticut, Rhode Island, Massachusetts, Michigan, Maine, Ohio, and Wisconsin passed personal-liberty laws. These laws enraged southerners by providing counsel for alleged fugitives and requiring trial by jury. The Kansas-Nebraska Act devastated political parties. The weakened Whig Party broke into northern and southern wings. Democrats survived, but their northern support plummeted in the 1854 elections. Northern Democrats lost sixty-six of their ninety-one congressional seats and lost control of all but two free-state legislatures.

Birth of the Republican Party

The beneficiary of northern voters' wrath was a new political party. During debate on the Kansas-Nebraska Act, six congressmen—most prominently, Joshua Giddings, Salmon Chase, and Charles Sumner—published

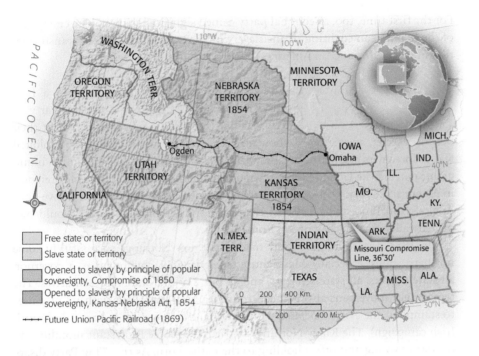

MAP 12.5
The Kansas-Nebraska Act and Slavery Expansion, 1854

The vote on the Kansas-Nebraska Act in the House of Representatives (see also Table 12.2) demonstrates the sectionalization of American politics due to the slavery question.

Source: Copyright © Cengage Learning 2015

an "Appeal of the Independent Democrats." In it they attacked Douglas's legislation as a "gross violation of a sacred pledge" (the Missouri Compromise) and a "criminal betrayal of precious rights" that would make free territory a "dreary region of despotism." Their appeal tapped a reservoir of northern concern, cogently expressed by Abraham Lincoln of Illinois.

Although Lincoln did not condemn southerners, he exposed the meaning of the Kansas-Nebraska Act. Lincoln argued that the founders, from love of liberty, banned slavery from the Northwest Territory, kept the word *slavery* out of the Constitution, and treated it as a "cancer" on the republic. The Kansas-Nebraska Act promised to extend slavery. America's future, Lincoln warned, was being mortgaged to slavery.

Thousands of white northerners agreed. During summer and fall 1854, antislavery Whigs and Democrats, Free-Soilers, and reformers throughout the Old Northwest formed the new Republican Party, dedicated to keeping slavery from the territories. Republicans' influence rapidly spread to the East. They won a stunning victory in the 1854 elections, capturing a majority of northern House seats and inspiring roughly a quarter of northern Democrats to desert their party.

TABLE 12.2   The Vote on the Kansas-Nebraska Act

The vote was 113 to 100 in favor.

	Aye	Nay
Northern Democrats	44	42
Southern Democrats	57	2
Northern Whigs	0	45
Southern Whigs	12	7
Northern Free-Soilers	0	4

For the first time, too, a sectional party gained significant power. The emergence of the Republican coalition of antislavery interests is the most rapid transformation in party allegiance in American history.

Know-Nothings

Know-Nothings Anti-Catholic and anti-immigrant party that enjoyed a brief surge of popularity in the early 1850s.

Republicans also drew into their coalition a fast-growing nativist movement, the American Party or **Know-Nothings** (because its first members kept their purposes secret, answering, "I know nothing" to questions). This group exploited fear of foreigners and Catholics. Between 1848 and 1860, nearly 3.5 million immigrants entered the United States—proportionally the heaviest inflow of foreigners in American history. Democrats courted these new citizens, but many native-born Anglo-Saxon Protestants believed that Irish and German Catholics would owe primary allegiance to the pope in Rome.

In 1854, anti-immigrant fears made the Know-Nothings successful in some northern states, especially Massachusetts, electing 11 congressmen, a governor, all state officers, all state senators, and all but 2 of 378 state representatives. The temperance movement also gained ground early in the 1850s with its promises to stamp out the evils associated with liquor and immigrants (a particularly anti-Irish campaign). The Know-Nothings strove to reinforce Protestant morality and to restrict voting and office holding to the native born. As the Whig Party disappeared, the Know-Nothings filled the void. But like the Whigs, the Know-Nothings could not keep their northern and southern wings together regarding slavery's expansion, and they dissolved after 1856. The growing Republican coalition wooed the nativists with temperance ordinances and laws postponing suffrage for naturalized citizens (see Table 12.1).

Party Realignment and the Republicans' Appeal

The Whig Party's demise ensured a major realignment of the political system. Immigration, temperance, homestead bills, the tariff, and internal improvements were crucial issues for voters during the 1850s. Commercial agriculture was booming in the Ohio–Mississippi–Great Lakes area, but residents desired more canals, roads, and river and harbor improvements. Because credit was scarce, a homestead program—the idea that western land should be free to individuals who would farm and make a home on it—attracted voters. Republicans appealed to those interested in the economic development of the West.

Partisan ideological appeals characterized the realigned political system. As Republicans preached, "Free Soil, Free Labor, Free Men," they captured many northerners' self-image. These phrases resonated with traditional ideals of equality, liberty, and opportunity under self-government—the heritage of republicanism. Invoking that heritage also undercut charges that the Republican Party was radical and abolitionist.

The northern economy was booming, and thousands of migrants moved west to establish farms and communities. Midwesterners multiplied their yields using new machines, such as mechanical reapers. Railroads were carrying their crops to urban markets. And industry was making available goods that recently had been unaffordable for most people.

Republican Ideology

Many people thought the key to progress was free labor—the dignity of work. Traditional republicanism hailed the virtuous common man as the nation's backbone. In Abraham Lincoln, a man of humble origins who became a successful lawyer and political leader, Republicans had a symbol of that tradition. They portrayed their party as the guardian of economic opportunity, giving individuals a chance to work, acquire land, and attain success. Republicans argued that the South, with little industry and slave labor, remained backward.

At stake in the crises of the 1850s were thus two competing definitions of "liberty:" southern planters' claims to protection of their liberty in the possession and transport of their slaves anywhere, and northern workers' and farmers' claims to protection of their liberty to seek a new start on free land, unimpeded by a system that defined labor as slave and black.

Opposition to slavery's extension helped create the Republican Party, but members broadened their appeal by adopting other causes. Their coalition ideology consisted of many elements: resentment of southern political power, devotion to unionism, antislavery sentiments based on free-labor arguments, moral revulsion to slavery, and racial prejudice. As *New York Tribune* editor Horace Greeley wrote in 1860, "an Anti-Slavery man per se cannot be elected." But, "a Tariff, River-and-Harbor, Pacific Railroad, Free Homestead man, may succeed although he is Anti-Slavery."

Southern Democrats

The disintegration of the Whig Party left many southerners at loose ends politically, including wealthy planters, smaller slaveholders, and urban businessmen. In the tense atmosphere of sectional crisis, these people were susceptible to states' rights positions and the defense of slavery. Hence, most formerly Whig slaveholders became Democratic.

Since Andrew Jackson's day, however, nonslaveholding yeomen had been the heart of the Democratic Party. Democratic politicians, though often slave owners, lauded the common man and claimed to advance his interests. According to the southern version of republicanism, white citizens in a slave society enjoyed liberty and equality because black people were enslaved. As Jefferson Davis explained in 1851, in the South, slavery elevated every white person to "stand upon the broad level of equality with the rich man." To retain support from ordinary whites, southern Democrats appealed to racism, asking, "Shall negroes govern white men, or white men govern negroes?"

Racial fears and traditional political loyalties kept the alliance between yeoman farmers and planters intact through the 1850s. Across class lines, white southerners united against what they perceived as the Republican Party's capacity to cause slave unrest. In the South, no viable party emerged to replace the Whigs, and political realignment sharpened sectional identities.

Political leaders of both sections used race in their arguments about opportunity. The *Montgomery* (Alabama) *Mail* warned southern whites in 1860 that the Republicans intended "to free the negroes and force amalgamation between them and the children of the poor men of the South." Republicans warned northern

William Walker and Filibustering

Between 1848 and 1861, the United States was at peace with foreign nations. But that did not stop private citizens, sometimes supported by politicians and businessmen, from launching adventurous attempts to take over foreign lands, especially in Mexico, Central America, and the Caribbean. The 1850s was the heyday of "filibustering," defined then as private military expeditions designed to destabilize or conquer foreign lands in the name of manifest destiny, commerce, the spread of slavery and white supremacy, or masculine daring.

At least a dozen filibustering schemes emerged in this era of expansion and sectional crises, all violations of the Neutrality Act of 1818. Such laws did not stop some senators, railroad and shipping entrepreneurs, or the self-styled soldier of fortune, William Walker, from seeking the "Southern dream" of a Latin American empire. They also did not stop several American presidents from attempting to annex Cuba.

Born in Tennessee, Walker studied in Europe in 1848 before returning to New Orleans for a stint editing a newspaper. He moved to California, practiced law, and courted conflict by fighting duels. After an ill-fated attempt in 1853 to forcibly create an American "colony" in Sonora and the Baja peninsula in Mexico, Walker turned to Nicaragua, whose isthmus was the fastest route to the California gold fields.

With a small army of mercenaries, Walker invaded Nicaragua in 1856, seized its government, declared himself president, and reintroduced slavery, which Nicaragua had banned. Defeated by a coalition of Nicaraguans and British in 1857, Walker returned to the United States and launched a fund-raising and speaking campaign on which he was often treated as a romantic hero. On his return to Nicaragua, he was arrested by a U.S. Navy squadron, brought to America, tried, and acquitted.

In 1860, Walker published an account of his exploits, *War in Nicaragua*. Famous for his swashbuckling character, Walker was regarded by some as a pirate serving the "Slave Power Conspiracy," and by others as the "grey-eyed man of destiny" advancing slavery and American hegemony. On Walker's third return to Central America in 1860, he was arrested and Honduran authorities executed him by firing squad. These filibustering adventures fired the imagination of manifest destiny and were small precursors of a larger United States exploitation and conquest of Latin America in the century to follow. Walker's legend, heroic and notorious, lives on today in Central America and in two American movies, *Burn* (1969), starring Marlon Brando, and *Walker* (1987), starring Ed Harris. Filibusters were links to the world that gave the United States a difficult legacy to overcome with its neighbors from Cuba to Hawai'i.

Library of Congress Prints and Photographs Division [LC-USZC4-10802]

Portrait of William Walker, Tennessee-born filibusterer, a self-styled soldier of fortune who attempted to create his own empire in Nicaragua, where he reinstituted slavery. To some, especially southerners, he was a romantic hero, but to others—especially northerners and the U.S. government—he was a notorious villain and arch proponent of the worst aspects of manifest destiny.

workers that, if slavery entered the territories, the great reservoir of opportunity for ordinary citizens would be poisoned.

Bleeding Kansas

The Kansas-Nebraska Act spawned violence as land-hungry partisans clashed in Kansas Territory. Abolitionists and religious groups sent armed Free-Soil settlers; southerners sent reinforcements to establish slavery and prevent "northern hordes" from stealing Kansas. Conflicts led to bloodshed, and soon the nation was talking about "Bleeding Kansas."

Politics in the territory resembled war more than democracy. During 1855 elections for a territorial legislature, thousands of proslavery Missourians—known as Border Ruffians—invaded the polls and ran up a fraudulent majority for proslavery candidates. They murdered and intimidated free state settlers. The resulting legislature legalized slavery. Free-Soilers responded with an unauthorized convention at which they created their own government and constitution.

In May, a proslavery posse sent to arrest the Free-Soil leaders sacked the town of Lawrence, Kansas, killing several people and destroying a hotel. In revenge, radical abolitionist John Brown and his followers murdered five proslavery settlers along Pottawatomie Creek. The victims' heads and limbs were hacked by heavy broadswords. Brown did not wield a sword, but he fired a fatal shot into the head of one foe. Soon, armed bands of guerrillas battled over land claims as well as slavery.

Violence reached the U.S. Senate in May 1856, when Charles Sumner of Massachusetts denounced "the Crime against Kansas." Radically opposed to slavery, Sumner assailed the president, the South, and Senator Andrew P. Butler of South Carolina. Butler's cousin, Representative Preston Brooks, approached Sumner, raised his cane in defense of his kin's honor, and beat Sumner on the head. The senator collapsed.

Shocked northerners recoiled from another seeming case of wanton southern violence and assault on free speech. William Cullen Bryant, editor of the *New York Evening Post,* asked, "Has it come to this, that we must speak with bated breath in the presence of our southern masters?" Popular opinion in Massachusetts supported Sumner; South Carolina voters reelected Brooks.

Election of 1856

The election of 1856 showed extreme polarization. Democrats chose James Buchanan of Pennsylvania, who, as ambassador to Britain for four years, was uninvolved in territorial controversies. Superior party organization helped Buchanan win 1.8 million votes and the election, but he owed his victory to southern support. Hence, he was labeled "a northern man with southern principles."

Eleven of sixteen free states voted against Buchanan, and Democrats did not regain those states for decades. The Republican candidate, John C. Frémont, won those eleven free states and 1.3 million votes; Republicans became the dominant party in the North after only two years of existence. The coming battle would pit a sectional Republican Party against an increasingly divided Democratic Party, with voter turnouts as high as 75 to 80 percent in many states.

Slavery and the Nation's Future

How did the issue of slavery—and the Dred Scott decision—further divide the nation?

For years, the issue of slavery in the territories convulsed Congress, and Congress tried to settle the issue. In 1857, the Supreme Court took up this emotionally charged issue and attempted to silence controversy with a definitive verdict.

Dred Scott Case

A Missouri slave named Dred Scott and his wife, Harriet Robinson Scott, sued for their freedom. Scott argued that his former owner, an army surgeon, had taken him for several years into Illinois, a free state, and to Fort Snelling in the Minnesota Territory, from which slavery was barred by the Missouri Compromise. Scott first won and then lost his case as it moved on appeal through the state courts, into the federal system, and after eleven years, to the Supreme Court.

The impetus for the lawsuit likely came as much from Harriet as from Dred Scott. They were legally married at Fort Snelling (free territory) in 1836 when Dred was forty and Harriet seventeen. She lived as a slave on free soil for about five years and had four children, also born on free soil: two sons who died in infancy and two daughters, Eliza and Lizzie, who lived. The quest for "freedom papers" through a lawsuit—begun in 1846 as two separate cases, one in his name and one in hers—possibly came as much from Harriet's desire to protect her teenage daughters from potential sale and sexual abuse. Her case for freedom may have been stronger than Dred's, but lawyers subsumed her case into his during the long appeal process.

After hesitation, the Supreme Court agreed to hear *Dred Scott v. Sanford* and decided to rule on the Missouri Compromise after all. The precedent before the court was this: Was a black person like Dred Scott a citizen of the United States and thus eligible to sue in federal court? Had residence in a free state or territory made him free? Did Congress have the power to prohibit or promote slavery in a territory? Two northern justices indicated they would dissent from the assigned opinion and argue for Scott's freedom and the constitutionality of the Missouri Compromise. This emboldened southerners on the Court, who were growing eager to declare the 1820 geographical restriction on slavery unconstitutional. In March 1857, Chief Justice Roger B. Taney of Maryland delivered the majority opinion of a divided Court (the vote was 7 to 2). Taney declared that Scott

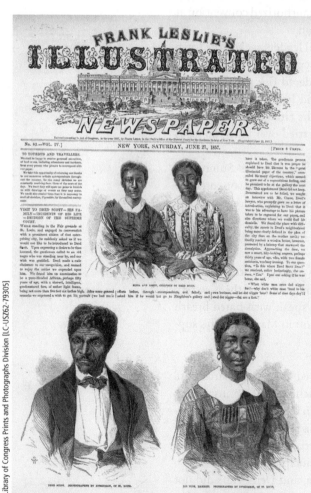

Library of Congress Prints and Photographs Division [LC-USZ62-79305]

Frank Leslie's Illustrated Newspaper, *June 27, 1857. Dred Scott and his wife, Harriet, below, and their two children, Eliza and Lizzie, above. Such dignified pictures and informative articles provided Americans broadly with images of the otherwise mysterious Dred Scott and his family in the landmark Supreme Court case.*

was not a citizen of the United States or Missouri, that residence in free territory did not make Scott free, and that Congress had no power to bar slavery from any territory. The decision not only overturned a thirty-seven-year-old compromise, it also invalidated the Wilmot Proviso and popular sovereignty.

The Slave Power seemed to have won a major constitutional victory. African Americans were dismayed, for Taney's decision asserted that the founders had never intended for blacks to be citizens. At the nation's founding, the chief justice wrote, blacks had been regarded "as beings of an inferior order" with "no rights which the white man was bound to respect." Taney was mistaken, however. African Americans had been citizens in several original states and had voted.

Nevertheless, the ruling seemed to shut the door permanently on black hopes for justice. In northern black communities, rage and despair prevailed. Many fugitive slaves sought refuge in Canada; others considered the Caribbean or Africa. One black abolitionist said that the **Dred Scott decision** made slavery "the supreme law of the land." In this state of social dislocation and fear, blacks contemplated whether they had any future in the United States.

Northern whites who rejected the decision were suspicious of the circumstances that produced it. Five of the nine justices were southerners; three northern justices dissented or refused to concur in parts of the decision. The only northerner who supported Taney's opinion, Justice Robert Grier of Pennsylvania, was close to President Buchanan.

Link to The Dred Scott Decision, 1857

Dred Scott decision
Controversial 1857 Supreme Court decision that stated that slaves were not U.S. citizens. It also deemed the Missouri Compromise unconstitutional because Congress lacked the authority to ban slavery in the territories.

Abraham Lincoln and the Slave Power

Republican politicians used these fears to strengthen their antislavery coalition. Abraham Lincoln declared as early as 1854 that the nation wanted the territories reserved as "homes of free white people. This they cannot be, to any considerable extent, if slavery shall be planted within them."

More important, Lincoln warned of slavery's increasing control over the nation. While the founders recognized slavery's existence, Lincoln argued in the "House Divided" speech of 1858, by which he launched his campaign against Stephen Douglas for the U.S. Senate from Illinois, the public believed that slavery would die naturally or by legislation. The next step in the unfolding Slave Power conspiracy, Lincoln alleged, would be a Supreme Court decision "declaring that the Constitution does not permit a State to exclude slavery from its limits." Indeed, lawsuits challenged state laws that freed slaves brought within their borders.

In the epic Lincoln-Douglas debates, staged before massive crowds in September-October, 1858, these two candidates squared off over the issues dividing the country: the westward expansion of slavery, abolitionism, federal power over property in slaves, whether the Declaration of Independence signaled racial equality, and ultimately, the American republic's future. Perhaps never before or since have Americans demonstrated such an appetite for democratic engagement.

As Lincoln showed in these debates, politically, Republicans were now locked in conflict with the *Dred Scott* decision. By endorsing the South's doctrine of state sovereignty, the Court had effectively declared that the Republican Party's central position—no extension of slavery—was unconstitutional. Republicans could only repudiate the decision, appealing to a "higher law," or hope to change the personnel of the Court.

The Lecompton Constitution and Disharmony Among Democrats

Northern voters were alarmed by the prospect that the territories would be opened to slavery. To retain their support, northern Democrats like Stephen Douglas had to reassure these voters. Yet, given his presidential ambitions, Douglas could not alienate southern Democrats.

Douglas chose to stand by popular sovereignty, even if the result angered southerners. In 1857, Kansans voted on a proslavery constitution drafted at Lecompton. It was defeated by more than ten thousand votes in a referendum boycotted by proslavery voters. Kansans overwhelmingly opposed slavery, yet President Buchanan tried to force the Lecompton Constitution through Congress to hastily organize the territory.

Never had the Slave Power's influence over the government seemed more blatant; the Buchanan administration and southerners demanded a proslavery outcome, contrary to majority will in Kansas. Douglas threw his weight against the Lecompton Constitution, infuriating southern Democrats like Senator Albert G. Brown of Mississippi. Increasingly, many southerners believed that their sectional rights and slavery would be safe only in a separate nation. And northern Democrats, led by Douglas, found it harder to support the territorial protection for slavery that southern Democrats insisted was a constitutional right.

John Brown's Raid on Harpers Ferry

Soon, the nation would be drawn to a new dimension of antislavery activism—armed rebellion. Born in Connecticut in 1800, John Brown was raised by religious antislavery parents. Between 1820 and 1855, he engaged in some twenty business ventures, nearly all failures. In his abolitionism, Brown relied on an Old Testament conception of justice—"an eye for an eye"—and he believed that slavery was an "unjustifiable" state of war. He also believed that violence in a righteous cause was a holy act. To Brown, the destruction of slavery in America required revolutionary acts.

On October 16, 1859, Brown led eighteen whites and blacks in an attack on the federal arsenal at Harpers Ferry, Virginia. Hoping to trigger a slave rebellion, Brown failed and was captured. In a celebrated trial in November and widely publicized execution in December, in Charles Town, Virginia, Brown became an enduring martyr, and villain, of American history.

White southerners were outraged when they learned that Brown received financial backing from prominent abolitionists and that such northern intellectuals as Ralph Waldo Emerson

The Metropolitan Museum of Art/Art Resource, NY

The Last Moments of John Brown, *depicting Brown's mythical kissing of the black child while leaving the jail for his journey to the gallows, by Thomas Hovenden, oil on canvas, 1882. Metropolitan Museum of Art, New York, Art Resource New York.*

Coalition Politics

In a democracy, constituencies with diverse interests often form coalition parties to win elections. In the 1830s and 1840s Democrats and Whigs held varied beliefs, particularly regarding slavery. From the Mexican War into the 1850s, when third parties (the Free-Soilers and nativists) threatened the two-party system, and with the triumph of the Republicans in forging a new antislavery alliance that destroyed the second party system, the antebellum era provided a model of coalition politics.

The most rapidly successful third-party movement in American history was the Republican Party, founded in 1854. Never before or since has a coalition of politicians and voters from long-standing parties coalesced so clearly around a single goal—stopping slavery's spread.

Northern Democrats bolted to the Republicans; by the 1856 election, they formed 25 percent of the new party's vote. Northern Whigs also joined the Republicans. Radical abolitionists of the old Liberty or Free-Soil parties now found leadership positions among the exclusively northern Republicans.

This antislavery coalition forged divergent outlooks into a new worldview: resentment of southern society and political power; an aggressive antislavery, pro- free-labor argument; fear of disunion; moral revulsion to slavery as inhumane; a racist urge to keep free blacks from the West; and finally, commitment to the northern social order as the model of progress. Such a multi-part ideology coalesced against the common foe of the "Slave Power Conspiracy," an alleged concentration of southern power determined to control the nation's future.

Whether in the rural and urban reformers who formed the Populist and Progressive movements of the late nineteenth and early twentieth centuries; the mixture of urban working classes, rural southern whites, African Americans, and intellectuals of the New Deal coalition from the Great Depression to the 1970s; or the modern conservative counterrevolution, with its antigovernment determination to dismantle the New Deal's social contract, all coalitions have drawn upon this enduring legacy of pre–Civil War American politics.

and Henry David Thoreau praised Brown as a holy warrior. The South interpreted Brown's attack at Harpers Ferry as an act of terrorism and the fulfillment of their dread of "abolition emissaries" who would infiltrate the region to incite slave rebellion.

When Brown went to the gallows, he handed a note to his jailer with the famous prediction "I John Brown am now quite certain that the crimes of this guilty land will never be purged away, but with blood."

Summary

During the 1820s, politicians broadened their appeal to an expanding electorate of white men, helping give birth to the second party system with its rivalry between the Democrats and Whigs. Both parties favored economic development but Whigs advocated centralized government, whereas Democrats advocated limited government and agricultural expansion. Controversies over the Second Bank of the United States and nullification exposed different interpretations of the nation's founding principles. Although women participated in political campaigns and sought equality, activists won few supporters. Instead, the nation was focused on economic development and westward expansion.

The War with Mexico fostered massive land acquisition, which forced an open debate about slavery in the West. The Compromise of 1850 attempted to settle the dispute but only exacerbated sectional tensions, leading to the fateful Kansas-Nebraska Act of 1854, which tore asunder the political party system and gave birth to an antislavery coalition. With Bleeding Kansas and the *Dred Scott* decision by 1857, Americans faced clear and dangerous choices about the future of labor and the meaning of liberty in an expanding society. Finally, by 1859, when radical abolitionist John Brown attacked Harpers Ferry to foment a slave insurrection, southerners and northerners regarded each other in conspiratorial terms. Meanwhile, African Americans, slave and free, feared slave catchers and expected violent resolutions to their dreams of freedom in America.

During the 1850s, every southern victory in territorial expansion increased fear of the Slave Power, and each new expression of Free-Soil sentiment prompted slaveholders to harden their demands. In the profoundest sense, slavery was the root of the war. As a people and a nation, Americans reached the most fateful turning point in their history. Resolution would now come from the battlefield.

Chapter Review

Jacksonianism and Party Politics

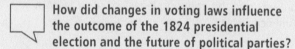

How did changes in voting laws influence the outcome of the 1824 presidential election and the future of political parties?

As suffrage laws changed to eliminate property requirements and allow immigrants to vote, the number of eligible voters tripled from 1824 to 1828. Politicians broadened their outreach to these new voters and successfully urged states to shift from appointing presidential electors to electing them by popular vote. That, combined with the end of candidate selection by congressional caucus, meant that five Democratic-Republican candidates ran for president in 1824. Although Andrew Jackson led in both electoral and popular vote, no one had a clear majority, leaving the House of Representatives to choose the president. Its members chose second-place John Quincy Adams, which led to charges of election-stealing and divided the party into the National Republicans (behind Adams) and the Democrats (behind Jackson). With two parties and only two candidates in the 1828 election, Jackson handily won the presidency, and the Democratic Party became the first well-organized national political party in the United States.

Federalism at Issue: The Nullification and Bank Controversies

What was at issue in the Nullification Crisis?

At the core of the Nullification Crisis were differing interpretations of the Constitution regarding federal power and states' rights. The doctrine of nullification—that states could overrule federal legislation—was based on the Virginia and Kentucky Resolutions of 1798, which argued that states could judge whether federal actions were constitutional, and ultimately nullify federal laws that did not pass the test. President Jackson rejected state sovereignty and saw nullification as leading to disunion. When South Carolina nullified a federal tariff, Jackson threatened force to collect the duties. As a compromise, the tariff was reduced and South Carolina withdrew its nullification. But the debate on the nature of the republic and of federal power continued.

The Second Party System

How did Whigs and Democrats differ ideologically?

Unlike the Democrats, Whigs advocated for economic growth via an activist federal government. They were for corporate charters, a national bank, and paper currency and promoted public schools and prison reform. Nor did Whigs worry about government aiding special interests; to them, as long as the public benefited, they saw no problem in it. Democrats believed in the Jefferson model of limited government and embraced unrestricted westward expansion. Democrats saw the world divided into "haves" and "have nots" and saw in the West an opportunity for greater equality and social mobility for hardworking, independent farmers. Whigs worried about rapid westward expansion, thought government should be ruled from the top down, and believed that the wealthy obtained their status through their hard work, not political favors.

Women's Rights

What inspired the rise of the women's movement in the mid-nineteenth century?

The religious revivals of the Second Great Awakening provided the first impetus for a later women's movement by encouraging women to see themselves as equal spiritually to men and encouraging them to help reform society. Women's growing participation in the antislavery movement—and their subordinated status within it—lay the groundwork for the women's rights movement. After 1830, married women made small gains in property and spousal rights. Traditional marriage law, borrowed from the English, gave husbands control over the family, including wives' property and earnings, but new married women's property acts—beginning with Arkansas in 1835—enabled them to own and control inherited property. Eight years after being denied a seat at the World Anti-Slavery Convention because of their sex, Elizabeth Cady Stanton and Lucretia Mott joined others in holding the first Woman's Rights Convention in 1848 at Seneca Falls, New York. There, three hundred participants outlined their demands for political and social equality, including the right to vote, in their Declaration of Sentiments, a document that paralleled the Declaration of Independence.

The Politics of Territorial Expansion

How did territorial expansion expose political fissures?

Efforts to expand the territorial holdings of the United States ultimately magnified sharp regional and political divisions and ended the second party system's cross-sectional alliances. While Democrats embraced westward expansion as part of their vision of a society of independent white farmers, Whigs preferred to focus on commercial development within the nation's existing boundaries. Initially, both parties were able to reach compromises with factions in the North and South, until the divisive issue of slavery's role in westward expansion became unavoidable. Those who embraced widening America's territory to the Pacific as its manifest destiny sought to annex Texas—formerly Mexico's holding—and Oregon, which the United States jointly occupied with Great Britain. Whigs feared annexation of Texas would widen slavery's reach, tip the balance of free and slave states, lead to war with Mexico, and strain trade relations. Southern Democrats, including President James Polk, wanted to extend slavery as part of westward expansion, and took the first step by annexing Texas in 1845 as a slave state. The move made regional divisions unavoidable and moved the nation toward a war with Mexico and its own sectional crisis.

The War with Mexico and Its Consequences

How did Polk's decisions push the United States toward war with Mexico?

President Polk wanted to expand America's borders to the Pacific during the 1840s and was not going to take no for an answer. He supported annexation of Texas—which angered the Mexican government—and contested the U.S. border with Mexico, urging Texans to claim territory to the Rio Grande despite Mexico's strong objections that the boundary lay at the Nueces River. While unsuccessfully attempting to buy California from Mexico, Polk also sent troops to defend the Rio Grande dividing line. There, they were met by Mexican cavalry. After a three-week standoff, the Mexican cavalry ambushed a U.S. unit, killing eleven Americans and taking sixty-three captive. Polk informed Congress that Mexico had crossed what he considered the U.S. boundary (the disputed area), and thereby deceptively claimed that Mexico had incited the conflict that would become the War with Mexico.

1850: Compromise or Armistice?

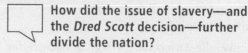

What were the two troubling issues inherent in the Compromise of 1850?

The Compromise of 1850 attempted to resolve the debate between the North and South over slavery in the territories. In the end, it only furthered the controversy. First, it left the definition of popular sovereignty unclear so that southerners could interpret it to mean that a region could not ban slavery during the territorial stage, whereas northerners believed it was up to the people to decide at any point. Second, the Fugitive Slave Act enabled slave owners to present evidence in state courts that a slave had escaped, which would then serve as proof of slave status even in free states and territories—and without investigation into its truth. Moreover, the fees paid to commissioners were twice as much if a person were deemed to be a slave. Northerners could be arrested if they hid escaped slaves in their homes, which further angered northerners who saw this as a violation of their rights, thereby aggravating regional tensions.

Slavery Expansion and Collapse of the Party System

How did the Kansas-Nebraska Act lead to the collapse of existing political parties?

The Kansas-Nebraska Act, which ultimately eroded the 1850 Compromise, prompted sectional divisions within the political parties that led to each party's breakdown. The act established the Kansas and Nebraska Territories, but it applied popular sovereignty to let the territories decide what to do about slavery. Northerners argued that since the territories were within the Louisiana Purchase, they were subject to the Missouri Compromise (which prohibited slavery from latitude 36°30' north to the Canadian border). When the act was passed in 1854, sectional divisions intensified. The weakened Whig Party split into northern and southern wings. Democrats' support in the North plummeted, costing them most of their congressional seats and control of all but two state legislatures. In late 1854, antislavery Whigs and Democrats, Free-Soilers, and reformers throughout the Old Northwest formed the new Republican Party to keep slavery from the territories.

Slavery and the Nation's Future

How did the issue of slavery—and the *Dred Scott* decision—further divide the nation?

The *Dred Scott* decision validated northern fears of a southern Slave Power, and inspired new fears about the territories being open to slavery. The Supreme Court was ultimately stacked in favor of the southern position on slavery and its extension into the new territories. Five of the nine justices were southerners, which had northerners fearing conspiracy. The court's decision in the *Dred Scott* case—that Scott was a slave despite the fact that he had lived in the free state of Illinois and the free territory of Missouri and that Congress could not make any laws that barred slavery from the territories—invalidated the Missouri Compromise. African Americans were devastated by the court's opinion that the nation's founders had never intended them to be citizens, while white northerners saw the decision as proof of the Slave Power's growing reach.

Suggestions for Further Reading

Edward L. Ayers and Carolyn R. Martin, eds., *America on the Eve of the Civil War* (2010)

Donald B. Cole, *Vindicating Andrew Jackson: The 1828 Election and the Rise of the Two-Party System* (2009)

Marc Egnal, *Clash of Extremes: The Economic Origins of the Civil War* (2009)

Nicole Etcheson, *Bleeding Kansas: Contested Liberty in the Civil War Era* (2004)

Don E. Fehrenbacher, *The Slaveholding Republic: An Account of the United States Government's Relations to Slavery* (2001)

Joan D. Hedrick, *Harriet Beecher Stowe: A Life* (1994)

Daniel Walker Howe, *What Hath God Wrought: The Transformation of America, 1815–1848* (2007)

Robert W. Johannsen, *To the Halls of the Montezumas: The Mexican War and the American Imagination* (1985)

Bruce Levine, *Half Slave and Half Free: The Roots of the Civil War* (2005)

Lynn Hudson Parsons, *The Birth of Modern Politics: Andrew Jackson, John Quincy Adams, and the Election of 1828* (2009)

Elizabeth R. Varon, *Disunion! The Coming of the American Civil War, 1789–1859* (2008)

Harry L. Watson, *Liberty and Power: The Politics of Jacksonian America* (2006)

Susan Zaeske, *Signatures of Citizenship: Petitioning, Antislavery, and Women's Political Identity* (2003)

13

Transforming Fire: The Civil War,

1860–1865

Slave pens were the ugly crossroads of American history. Wallace Turnage, a seventeen-year-old slave from a cotton plantation in Pickens County, Alabama, entered wartime Mobile in December 1862 through the slave traders' yard; he would leave Mobile from that same yard twenty months later.

Turnage was born in 1846 on a tobacco farm near Snow Hill, North Carolina. In mid-1860, as the nation teetered toward disunion, he was sold to a Richmond, Virginia, slave trader named Hector Davis. Turnage worked in Davis's three-story slave jail, organizing auctions until he was sold for $1,000 in early 1861 to a cotton planter from Pickens County, Alabama. Frequently whipped, the desperate teenager tried four times over the next two years to escape to the Union army in Mississippi. He was captured each time and returned to his owner.

Frustrated, his owner sold Turnage for $2,000 at the Mobile slave traders' yard to a wealthy merchant in the port city. During 1864, as Mobile came under siege, its slaves were enlisted to build trenchworks. Turnage did many urban tasks for his new owner's family, including driving their carriage on errands.

In early August, Turnage crashed the carriage on a Mobile street. Furious, his owner took him to the slave pen, hiring the jailer to administer thirty lashes in the "whipping house." Stripped naked, his hands tied, Turnage was hoisted up on a hook. When it was over, his owner instructed Wallace to walk home. Instead, Turnage "took courage," as he wrote in his postwar narrative, and walked southwest through the Confederate encampment. The soldiers mistook the bloodied and tattered black teenager for one among hundreds of slaves who did camp labor.

For three weeks, Turnage crawled and waded twenty-five miles through the snake-infested swamps of the Foul River estuary, down the west edge of Mobile Bay. Nearly starved and narrowly escaping Confederate patrols, Turnage reached Cedar Point, where he could see Dauphin Island, now occupied by Union forces. Alligators swam nearby, as Turnage hid from

Chapter Outline

Election of 1860 and Secession Crisis
Secession and the Confederate States of America | Fort Sumter and Outbreak of War | Causation

America Goes to War, 1861–1862
First Battle of Bull Run | Grand Strategy | Union Naval Campaign | War in the Far West | Grant's Tennessee Campaign and the Battle of Shiloh | McClellan and the Peninsula Campaign | Confederate Offensive in Maryland and Kentucky

War Transforms the South
The Confederacy and Centralization | Confederate Nationalism | Southern Cities and Industry | Changing Roles of Women | Human Suffering, Hoarding, and Inflation | Inequities of the Confederate Draft

Wartime Northern Economy and Society
Northern Business, Industry, and Agriculture | The Quartermaster and Military-Government Mobilization | Northern Workers' Militancy | Economic Nationalism and Government-Business Partnership | The Union Cause | Northern Women on Home Front and Battlefront | Walt Whitman's War

The Advent of Emancipation
Lincoln and Emancipation | Confiscation Acts | Emancipation Proclamations | African American Recruits | Who Freed the Slaves? | A Confederate Plan of Emancipation

The Soldiers' War
Ordinary Soldiers and Ideology | Hospitals and Camp Life | The Rifled Musket | The Black Soldier's Fight for Manhood

VISUALIZING THE PAST *Black Soldiers in the Civil War*

1863: The Tide of Battle Turns
Battle of Chancellorsville | Siege of Vicksburg | Battle of Gettysburg

Disunity: South, North, and West
Union Occupation Zones | Disintegration of Confederate Unity | Food Riots in Southern Cities | Desertions from the Confederate Army | Antiwar Sentiment, South and North | Peace Democrats | New York City Draft Riots | War Against Indians in the Far West | Election of 1864

1864–1865: The Final Test of Wills
Northern Diplomatic Strategy | Battlefield Stalemate and a Union Strategy for Victory | Fall of Atlanta | Sherman's March to the Sea | Virginia's Bloody Soil | Surrender at Appomattox | Financial Tally | Death Toll and Its Impact

LINKS TO THE WORLD *The Civil War in Britain*

LEGACY FOR A PEOPLE AND A NATION
Abraham Lincoln's Second Inaugural Address

SUMMARY

Confederates. He remembered: "It was death to go back and it was death to stay there and freedom was before me."

Then, Turnage noticed an old rowboat. He began to row out into the bay. Suddenly, he "heard the crash of oars and behold there was eight Yankees in a boat." Turnage jumped into the Union gunboat. For a few moments, the oarsmen in blue "were struck with silence" by the frail young black man crouched before them. Turnage looked back at Confederate soldiers on the shore and took his first breaths of freedom.

The Civil War brought astonishing changes to daily life, North and South. Millions of men were swept into training camps and regiments. Armies numbering in the hundreds of thousands marched over the South, devastating the countryside. Families struggled to survive without men; businesses coped with fewer workers. Women took on extra responsibilities and moved into new workforce jobs, including nurses and hospital workers.

But southerners also experienced defeat. For most, wealth changed to poverty as farms were ruined. Late in the war, many southerners yearned only for an end to inflation, shortages, slave escapes, and the death that visited most families. Southern slaves did not always encounter sympathetic liberators like those who aided Turnage, fed and clothed him, and took him before a Union general, where the freedman could either join a black regiment or become a white officer's camp servant. Until war's end, Turnage cooked for a Maryland captain.

In the North, farm boys and mechanics would be asked for heretofore unimagined sacrifices. The conflict ensured vast government expenditures and lucrative federal contracts. Businessmen found war profitable. "The battle of Bull Run," predicted an eminent financier in *Harper's Monthly*, "makes the fortune of every man in Wall Street who is not a natural idiot."

Change was most drastic in the South, where secessionists launched a conservative revolution for their section's independence. Born of states' rights doctrine, the Confederacy had to be transformed into a centralized nation to fight the war. Southern whites feared that a peacetime government of Republicans would interfere with slavery and ruin plantation life. Instead, their actions led to a war that turned southern society upside down and imperiled slavery's existence.

The war created social strains in North and South. Disaffection was strongest, though, in the Confederacy, where poverty and class resentment threatened the South from within. In the North, dissent also flourished, and antiwar sentiment occasionally erupted into violence.

The Civil War forced a social and political revolution regarding race. It compelled leaders and citizens to finally face the question of slavery. And blacks embraced the most fundamental turning point in their experience as Americans.

As you read this chapter, keep the following questions in mind:

- **How and why did the Civil War bring social transformations to both South and North?**

- **How did the war to preserve the Union or for southern independence become the war to free the slaves?**

- **By 1865, when Americans on all sides searched for the *meaning* of the war they had just fought, what might some of their answers have been?**

Election of 1860 and Secession Crisis

What were the issues leading to secession and the dissolution of the Union?

Many Americans believed the election of 1860 would decide the Union's fate. The Democratic Party was the only party that was truly national in scope. But at its 1860 convention in Charleston, South Carolina, the Democratic Party split.

Stephen Douglas wanted his party's presidential nomination, but he feared alienating northern voters by accepting the southern position on the territories. Southern Democrats, however, insisted on recognition of their rights—as defined by the *Dred Scott* decision. When Douglas obtained a majority for his version of the platform, delegates from the Deep South walked out. The Democrats presented two nominees: Douglas for the northern wing, and Vice President John C. Breckinridge of Kentucky for the southern.

Republicans nominated Abraham Lincoln, a reflection of the Midwest's growing power. Lincoln was perceived as more moderate on slavery than the early front-runner, Senator William H. Seward of New York. A Constitutional Union Party nominated John Bell of Tennessee.

Bell's only issue in the ensuing campaign was preserving the Union. Douglas sought to unite his northern and southern supporters, while Breckinridge backed away from the appearance of extremism, and his supporters in several states stressed his unionism. Although Lincoln and the Republicans denied any intent to interfere with slavery where it existed, they rejected its extension into the territories.

The 1860 election was sectional, and the only one in American history in which the losers refused to accept the result. Lincoln won, but Douglas, Breckinridge, and Bell together received a majority of the votes. Douglas had broad-based support but won few states. Breckinridge carried nine states in the Deep South. Bell won pluralities in Virginia, Kentucky, and Tennessee. Lincoln prevailed in the North, but in the four slave states that remained loyal to the Union (Missouri, Kentucky, Maryland, and Delaware—the border states) he gained only a plurality (see Table 13.1). Lincoln's victory was won in the electoral college. He polled only 40 percent of the total vote and was not on the ballot in ten slave states.

Chronology

1860	Election of Lincoln
	Secession of South Carolina
1861	Firing on Fort Sumter
	Battle of Bull Run
	McClellan organizes Union army
	Union blockade begins
	U.S. Congress passes first confiscation act
	Trent affair
1862	Union captures Fort Henry and Fort Donelson
	U.S. Navy captures New Orleans
	Battle of Shiloh shows the war's destructiveness
	Confederacy enacts conscription
	McClellan's peninsula campaign fails to take Richmond
	U.S. Congress passes second confiscation act, initiating emancipation
	Battle of Antietam ends Lee's drive into Maryland in September
	British intervention in the war on Confederate side is averted
1863	Emancipation Proclamation takes effect
	U.S. Congress passes National Banking Act
	Union enacts conscription

	African American soldiers join Union army
	Food riots occur in southern cities
	Battle of Chancellorsville ends in Confederate victory but Jackson's death
	Union wins key victories at Vicksburg and Gettysburg
	Draft riots take place in New York City
1864	Battles of the Wilderness and Spotsylvania produce heavy casualties on both sides
	Battle of Cold Harbor continues carnage in Virginia
	Sherman captures Atlanta
	Confederacy begins to collapse on home front
	Lincoln wins reelection, eliminating any Confederate hopes for negotiated end to war
	Jefferson Davis proposes arming slaves
	Sherman marches through Georgia to the sea
1865	Sherman marches through Carolinas
	U.S. Congress approves Thirteenth Amendment
	Lee surrenders at Appomattox Court House
	Lincoln assassinated
	Death toll in war reaches more than 700,000

Opposition to slavery's extension was the core issue for Lincoln and the Republican Party. Meanwhile, in the South, proslavery advocates and secessionists whipped up public opinion and demanded that state conventions assemble to consider secession.

Lincoln did not soften his party's position on the territories. Although many conservative Republicans—eastern businessmen and former Whigs who did not feel

TABLE 13.1   Presidential Vote in 1860

Lincoln (Republican)*	Carried all northern states and all electoral votes except 3 in New Jersey
Breckinridge (Southern Democrat)	Carried all slave states except Virginia, Kentucky, Tennessee, Missouri
Bell (Constitutional Union)	Carried Virginia, Kentucky, Tennessee
Douglas (Northern Democrat)	Carried only Missouri

*Lincoln received only 26,000 votes in the entire South and was not even on the ballot in ten slave states. Breckinridge was not on the ballot in three northern states.

strongly about slavery—hoped for a compromise, the original and most committed Republicans—old Free-Soilers and antislavery Whigs—held firm on slavery expansion.

In winter of 1860–1861, numerous compromise proposals were floated in Washington, including resurrecting the Missouri Compromise line, 36°30', and initiating a "plural presidency," with one president from each section. When Lincoln rejected concessions on the territorial issue, these peacemaking efforts collapsed.

Secession and the Confederate States of America

Meanwhile, on December 20, 1860, South Carolina passed an ordinance of secession. The Union was broken. Secessionists urged other states to follow South Carolina, believing that those favoring compromise could make a better deal outside the Union than in it.

Southern extremists called separate state conventions and passed secession ordinances in Mississippi, Florida, Alabama, Georgia, Louisiana, and Texas. By February 1861, these states joined South Carolina to form a new government in Montgomery, Alabama: the Confederate States of America. The delegates at Montgomery chose Jefferson Davis of Mississippi as their president.

Many southerners—perhaps even 40 percent in the Deep South—opposed immediate secession. In some state conventions, the secession vote was close and decided by overrepresentation of plantation districts. Four states in the Upper South—Virginia, North Carolina, Tennessee, and Arkansas—rejected secession and did not join the Confederacy until after fighting commenced. In border states, popular sentiment was divided; minorities in Kentucky and Missouri tried to secede, but these slave states ultimately came under Union control, along with Maryland and Delaware (see Map 13.1).

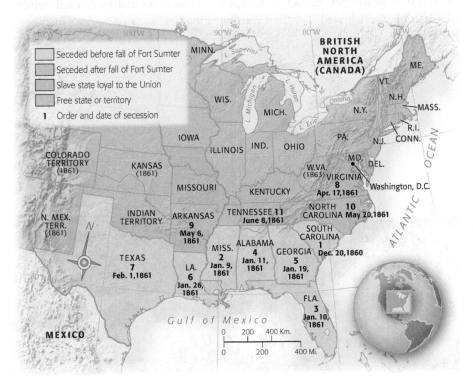

MAP 13.1

The Divided Nation—Slave and Free Areas, 1861

After fighting began, the Upper South joined the Deep South in the Confederacy. How does the nation's pattern of division correspond to the distribution of slavery and the percentage of blacks in the population? Source: Copyright © Cengage Learning 2015

Secession posed new challenges for southerners. Analysis of election returns from 1860 and 1861 indicates that slaveholders and nonslaveholders were beginning to part company politically. Slaveholding counties strongly supported secession. But nonslaveholding areas proved less willing to support secession. With war looming, yeomen were beginning to consider their class interests and how far they would go to support slavery and slave owners.

As for why the Deep South bolted, the speeches and writings of the secession advocates prove revealing. Repeatedly, they stressed independence as the only way to preserve white racial security and the slave system. Only secession, said Alabama commissioner Stephen Hale to the Kentucky legislature, could sustain the "heaven-ordained superiority of the white over the black race."

Fort Sumter and Outbreak of War

President Lincoln's dilemma on Inauguration Day in March 1861 was how to maintain the authority of the federal government without provoking war. By holding onto forts in the states that had left the Union, he could assert federal sovereignty while awaiting restoration. But Jefferson Davis could not claim to lead a sovereign nation if the Confederate ports were under foreign (that is, U.S.) control.

The two sides collided early on April 12, 1861, at **Fort Sumter** in Charleston harbor. A federal garrison there ran low on food, and Lincoln notified the South Carolinians that he was sending a supply ship. For the Montgomery government, the alternatives were to attack the fort or acquiesce to Lincoln's authority. The Confederate secretary of war ordered local commanders to obtain a surrender or attack the fort. After two days of heavy bombardment, the federal garrison surrendered. Confederates permitted U.S. troops to sail away on unarmed vessels while Charlestonians celebrated. The Civil War—the bloodiest war in America's history—had begun.

Fort Sumter Federal fort in Charleston harbor, South Carolina where the first shots of the Civil War were fired when the Union attempted to resupply troops.

Photograph of interior of Fort Sumter, in Charleston harbor, April 14, 1861, the day Major Robert Anderson and his troops surrendered and the Civil War began.

National Archives

Causation

Historians have debated the causes of the Civil War. Some have interpreted it as a clash of two civilizations on divergent historical trajectories. But the issues dividing Americans in 1861 were fundamental to the republic's future. Republican ideology tended toward abolishing slavery, even though Republicans denied such intention. Southern ideology led to establishing slavery everywhere, though southern leaders, too, denied such motives.

Lincoln put these facts succinctly. In a postelection letter to his old congressional colleague, Alexander Stephens of Georgia, soon to be vice president of the Confederacy, Lincoln stated, "You think slavery is right and ought to be expanded; while we think it is wrong and ought to be restricted. That I suppose is the rub."

Without slavery, there would have been no war. But the significance of states' rights, then as now, is always in the cause in which it is employed. If secession was an exercise in states' rights—then, to what end?

America goes to War, 1861–1862

The onset of hostilities sparked patriotic sentiments, speeches, and ceremonies in both North and South. Northern communities raised companies of volunteers eager to save the Union. Southern recruits boasted of whipping the Yankees and returning home before Christmas. Southern women sewed dashing uniforms for men who would soon be lucky to wear drab gray or butternut homespun. Americans went to war in 1861 with romantic notions.

What was the impact of the North's naval victories along the southern coast?

First Battle of Bull Run

Through the spring of 1861, both sides scrambled to organize and train their undisciplined armies. On July 21, 1861, the first battle took place outside Manassas Junction, Virginia, near a stream called **Bull Run**. General Irvin McDowell and thirty thousand Union troops attacked General P. G. T. Beauregard's twenty-two thousand southerners (see Map 13.2). Federal forces gained ground until they ran into a line of Virginia troops under General Thomas "Stonewall" Jackson. Jackson's line held, and the arrival of nine thousand Confederate reinforcements won the day for the South. Union troops fled to Washington.

Bull Run The location of the first major land battle in the Civil War.

The unexpected rout at Bull Run proved that although the United States enjoyed an advantage in resources, victory would not be easy. Pro-Union feeling was growing in western Virginia, and loyalties were divided in the four border slave states—Missouri, Kentucky, Maryland, and Delaware. But the rest of the Upper South—North Carolina, Virginia, Tennessee, and Arkansas—joined the Confederacy after Fort Sumter. Half a million southerners volunteered to fight—so many that the Confederate government could hardly arm them all. The United States therefore undertook a massive mobilization of troops around Washington, D.C.

Lincoln gave command of the army to General **George B. McClellan**, who proved better at organization and training than fighting. McClellan devoted fall and winter of 1861 to readying a force of a quarter-million men to take Richmond, the Confederate capital.

George B. McClellan Union general very popular with troops who proved better at organization and training than at fighting.

MAP 13.2
McClellan's Campaign

This map shows the water route chosen by McClellan to threaten Richmond during the peninsular campaign.

Source: Copyright © Cengage Learning 2015

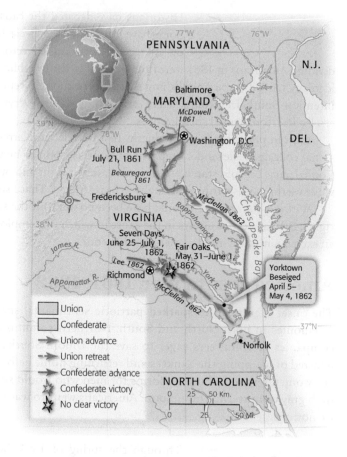

"Anaconda plan" Called for the Union to blockade southern ports, capture the Mississippi River, and, like a snake, strangle the Confederacy.

Grand Strategy

While McClellan prepared, the Union began to implement other parts of its strategy, which called for a blockade of southern ports and capture of the Mississippi River. Like a constricting snake, this **"Anaconda plan"** would strangle the Confederacy. The Union navy had too few ships to patrol 3,550 miles of the southern coastline. Gradually, the navy increased the blockade's effectiveness, though it never stopped southern commerce completely.

The Confederate strategy was essentially defensive, given the South's claim of independence and the North's advantage in resources (see Figure 13.1). But Jefferson Davis called the southern strategy an "offensive defensive," maximizing opportunities to attack and using its transportation interior lines to concentrate troops at crucial points. The Confederacy did not need to conquer the North; the Union effort, however, required conquest of the South.

Both sides slighted the importance of the West, the expanse between Virginia and the Mississippi River and beyond. Guerrilla warfare broke out in 1861 in politically divided Missouri, and key locations along the Mississippi and other western rivers would prove crucial prizes in the North's victory. Beyond the Mississippi, the Confederacy hoped to gain an advantage by negotiating treaties with the Creeks, Choctaws, Chickasaws, Cherokees, Seminoles, and smaller groups of Plains Indians. Meanwhile, the Republican U.S. Congress carved the West into territories

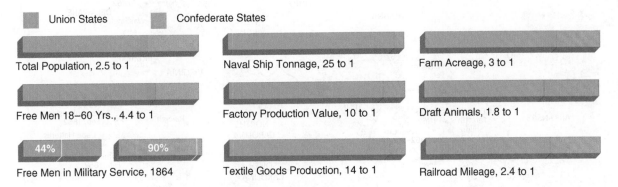

FIGURE 13.1
Comparative Resources, Union and Confederate States, 1861
The North had vastly superior resources. Although the North's advantages in manpower and industrial capacity proved very important, the South still had to be conquered, its society and its will crushed.

in anticipation of state making. For most Indians west of the Mississippi, the Civil War was nearly three decades of an enveloping strategy of conquest, relocation, and slaughter.

Union Naval Campaign The last half of 1861 brought no major land battles, but in late summer, Union naval forces captured Cape Hatteras and Hilton Head, one of the Sea Islands off Port Royal, South Carolina. A few months later, federal naval operations established significant beachheads along the Confederate coastline, including vital points in North Carolina, as well as Fort Pulaski, which defended Savannah (see Map 13.3).

The coastal victories off South Carolina foreshadowed a revolution in slave society. As federal gunboats approached, planters abandoned their land and fled. The Confederate cavalry tried to round up slaves and move them to the interior. But thousands of slaves greeted what they hoped to be freedom with rejoicing and broke the hated cotton gins. Some entered their masters' homes and took clothing and furniture. Many runaways poured into Union lines. Unwilling at first to wage a war against slavery, the federal government did not acknowledge the slaves' freedom—though it used their labor. These emancipated slaves, defined by Union officers as war "contraband" (confiscated enemy property), forced first a bitter debate within the Union army and government over how to treat the freedmen, and then an attempt to harness their labor and military power.

Spring 1862 brought stronger evidence of the war's gravity. In March, two iron-clad ships—the *Monitor* (a Union warship) and the *Merrimack* (a Union ship that had been seized by the Confederacy)—fought off the coast of Virginia. Their battle, though indecisive, ushered in a new era in naval design. In April, Union ships commanded by Admiral David Farragut smashed through log booms blocking the Mississippi River and moved upstream to capture New Orleans. The South's greatest seaport and slave-trading center was now in federal hands.

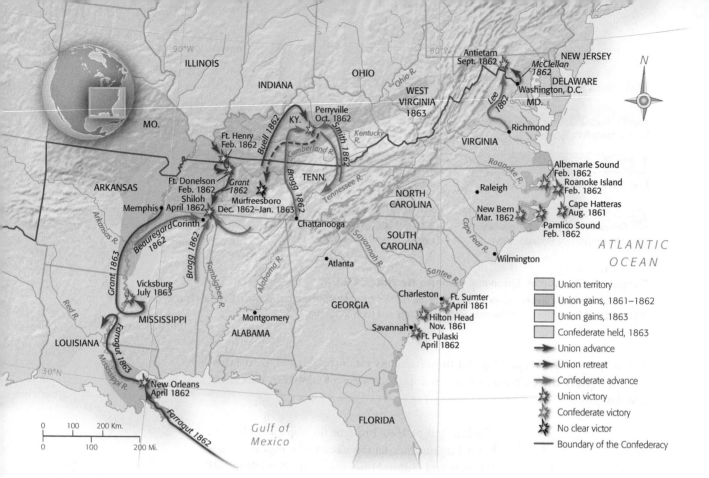

MAP 13.3
The War in the West

Here is an overview of the Union's successful campaigns in the West and its seizure of the key points on the Mississippi River, as well as along the Atlantic coast in 1862 and 1863. These actions were decisive in paving the way for ultimate northern victory.

Source: Copyright © Cengage Learning 2015

War in the Far West

Farther west, three Confederate regiments were organized, mostly of Cherokees, but a Union victory at Elkhorn Tavern, Arkansas, shattered southern control of the region. Thereafter, Confederate operations in Indian Territory amounted to guerrilla raids.

In the westernmost campaign of the war, from February to May 1862, some three thousand Confederate and four thousand Union forces fought for control of New Mexico Territory. The Confederate invasion had aimed to access the trade riches of the Santa Fe Trail and seize gold mines in Colorado and California. But Colorado and New Mexico Unionists fought back, and in a series of battles at Glorieta Pass, twenty miles east of Santa Fe, on March 26 through 28, they blocked the Confederates. By May 1, Confederate forces straggled down the Rio Grande River into Texas, ending efforts to take New Mexico.

Grant's Tennessee Campaign and the Battle of Shiloh

Meanwhile, in February 1862, forces in northern Tennessee won significant Union victories. Union commander **Ulysses S Grant** saw the strategic importance of Fort Henry and Fort Donelson, the Confederate

Ulysses S Grant Commander of the Union army.

outposts guarding the Tennessee and Cumberland rivers. Over ten days, he seized the forts—cutting off the Confederates and demanding "unconditional surrender" of Fort Donelson. A path into Tennessee, Alabama, and Mississippi now lay open before the Union army.

Grant moved on into southern Tennessee and the first of the war's shockingly bloody encounters, the **Battle of Shiloh** (see Map 13.3). On April 6, Confederate general Albert Sidney Johnston caught federal troops with their backs to the Tennessee River, awaiting reinforcements. The Confederates attacked and inflicted heavy damage. Close to victory, General Johnston was killed. Union reinforcements arrived that night. The next day, the battle turned and, after ten hours of combat, the Confederates withdrew.

Battle of Shiloh The bloodiest battle in American history to that date (April 6–7, 1862).

Neither side won a decisive victory at Shiloh, yet losses were staggering, and Confederates were forced to retreat into northern Mississippi. Northern troops lost thirteen thousand men (killed, wounded, or captured) out of sixty-three thousand; southerners sacrificed eleven thousand out of forty thousand. Total casualties in this single battle exceeded those in all three of America's previous wars combined. Before Shiloh, Grant hoped that southerners would soon tire of the conflict. After Shiloh, he recalled, "I gave up all idea of saving the Union except by complete conquest." Memories of the Shiloh battlefield would haunt surviving soldiers for the rest of their lives.

McClellan and the Peninsula Campaign

On the Virginia front, President Lincoln had problems with General McClellan. Only thirty-six, McClellan had achieved success as an army officer and railroad president. Habitually overestimating the size of enemy forces, he called for reinforcements and ignored Lincoln's directions to advance. McClellan advocated a war of limited aims to ensure a quick reunion. He intended neither disruption of slavery nor war on noncombatants. McClellan finally sailed his troops down the Chesapeake, landing on the peninsula between the York and James rivers, and advanced on Richmond (see Map 13.2).

After a bloody battle at Fair Oaks on May 31 through June 1, the federal armies moved to within seven miles of the Confederate capital. The Confederate commanding general, Joseph E. Johnston, was wounded at Fair Oaks, and President **Jefferson Davis** placed his chief military adviser, **Robert E. Lee**, in command. The fifty-five-year-old Lee was an aristocratic Virginian, a lifelong military officer, and a veteran of the War with Mexico. Although he initially opposed secession, Lee gave his allegiance to his state and became a staunch Confederate. He soon foiled McClellan's legions.

Jefferson Davis President of the Confederacy.

Robert E. Lee Commander of the Confederate army.

First, Lee sent Stonewall Jackson's corps of seventeen thousand northwest into the Shenandoah Valley behind Union forces, where they threatened Washington, D.C., and drew some troops from Richmond to protect their own capital. Further, in mid-June, in an extraordinary four-day ride around the entire Union army, Confederate cavalry under J. E. B. Stuart confirmed the exposed position of McClellan's army north of the Chickahominy River. Then, in the Seven Days Battles, from June 26 through July 1, Lee struck at McClellan's army. Lee's daring move of taking the majority of his army northeast and attacking the Union right flank, while leaving only a small force to defend Richmond, forced McClellan to retreat toward the James River.

During the sustained fighting of the Seven Days, the Union forces suffered 20,614 casualties and the Confederates, 15,849. By August 3, McClellan withdrew his army to the environs of Washington. Richmond remained safe for almost two more years.

Confederate Offensive in Maryland and Kentucky

Buoyed by these results, Jefferson Davis conceived an ambitious plan to gain military advantage and recognition of the Confederacy by European nations. He ordered a general offensive, sending Lee north into Maryland and Generals Kirby Smith and Braxton Bragg into Kentucky. Calling on residents of Maryland and Kentucky, still slave states, to make peace with his government, Davis also invited northwestern states like Indiana, which sent much of their trade down the Mississippi to New Orleans, to leave the Union. This was an effort to take the war to the North and force a military and political turning point.

The plan was promising, but the offensive ultimately failed. Lee's forces achieved a striking success at the battle of Second Bull Run, August 29 through 30. The entire Union army retreated to the federal capital. Thousands of wounded occupied schools and churches, and two thousand suffered on cots in the U.S. Capitol rotunda.

But in the bloodiest day of the war, September 17, 1862, McClellan turned Lee back from Sharpsburg, Maryland. In the **Battle of Antietam**, five thousand men died, and another eighteen thousand were wounded. McClellan intercepted a battle order, wrapped around cigars for each Confederate corps commander and lost by a courier. But McClellan moved slowly, failed to use his larger forces in simultaneous attacks, and allowed Lee's stricken army to retreat to across the Potomac. Lincoln removed McClellan from command.

In Kentucky, Generals Smith and Bragg secured Lexington and Frankfort, but their effort to force the Yankees back to the Ohio River was stopped at the Battle of Perryville on October 8. Bragg's army retreated back into Tennessee, where from December 31, 1862, to January 2, 1863, it fought an indecisive but bloody battle at Murfreesboro. Casualties exceeded even those of Shiloh.

Outnumbered and disadvantaged in resources, the South could not continue the offensive. Davis admitted to Confederate representatives that southerners were entering "the darkest and most dangerous period we have yet had."

But 1862 also brought painful lessons to the North. On December 13, Union general Ambrose Burnside, now in command of the Army of the Potomac, unwisely ordered his soldiers to attack Lee's army, which held fortified positions at

Battle of Antietam First major battle on northern soil.

Library of Congress

Photograph of "Sunken Road," Antietam battlefield, taken shortly after the battle, September 1862, often called "The Harvest of Battle."

Fredericksburg, Virginia. Lee's men performed so efficiently in killing northerners that Lee was moved to say, "It is well that war is so terrible. We should grow too fond of it." Burnside's repeated assaults up Marye's Heights shocked his opponents, with thirteen hundred dead and ninety-six hundred wounded Union soldiers. The scale of carnage now challenged people on both sides to question the meaning of such a war.

War Transforms the South

What happened to the South's embrace of state sovereignty during the war?

War disrupted civilian life. One of the first traditions to fall was the southern preference for local and limited government. States' rights had been a formative ideology for the Confederacy, but state governments were weak. To withstand the North's massive power, the South needed to centralize; like the colonial revolutionaries, southerners could unite or die separately.

The Confederacy and Centralization

Jefferson Davis brought arms, supplies, and troops under centralized control. But by early 1862, the scope and duration of the conflict required more recruits. Tens of thousands of Confederate soldiers volunteered for one year, planning to return home in the spring to plant crops. Faced with a critical troop shortage, in April 1862 the Confederate government enacted the first national conscription (draft) law in American history.

Davis adopted a firm leadership role toward the Confederate Congress, which raised taxes and later passed a tax-in-kind—paid in farm products. Nearly forty-five hundred agents dispersed to collect the tax. Where opposition arose, the government suspended the writ of habeas corpus (which prevented individuals from being held without trial) and imposed martial law. Still, this tax system proved inadequate for the South's war effort.

To replace the food that men in uniform would have grown, Davis exhorted state governments to require farmers to switch from cash crops to food crops. But shortages continued. The War Department impressed slaves to work on fortifications, and after 1861 officers raided farms and carted away grain, meat, wagons, and draft animals to feed the troops. Such raids caused increased hardship and resentment for women managing farms without husbands and sons.

Soon, the Confederate administration gained control over the southern economy. The Confederate Congress also gave the central government almost complete control of the railroads. A large bureaucracy of over seventy thousand civilians administered Confederate operations. By the war's end, the southern bureaucracy was larger in proportion to population than its northern counterpart.

Confederate Nationalism

Historians have long argued over whether the Confederacy itself was a "rebellion," a "revolution," or the creation of a genuine "nation." Whatever label, Confederates created a culture and ideology of nationalism. In flags, songs, language, seals, school readers, and other national characteristics, Confederates crafted their own story.

Southerners believed the Confederacy was the true legacy of the American Revolution—a bulwark against centralized power that was in keeping with the war. To southerners, theirs was a continuing revolution against the excesses of Yankee democracy, and George Washington (a Virginian) on horseback formed the center of the Confederacy's official seal.

Also central to Confederate nationalism was a refurbished defense of slavery as a benign, protective institution, complete with the image of the "faithful slave." In wartime schoolbooks, children were instructed in the divinely inspired, paternalistic character of slavery. A poem popular among whites captured an old slave's rejection of the Emancipation Proclamation:

> Now, Massa, dis is berry fine, dese words
> You've spoke to me,
> No doubt you mean it kindly, but ole Dinah
> Won't be free …
> Ole Massa's berry good to me—and though I am
> His slave,
> He treats me like I'se kin to him—and I would
> Rather have
> A home in Massa's cabin, and eat his black
> Bread too,
> Dan leave ole Massa's children and go and
> Lib wid you.

Southern Cities and Industry

Clerks and subordinate officials crowded the cities where Confederate departments established offices. The sudden urban migration overwhelmed the housing supply and stimulated new construction. Richmond's population increased 250 percent. Mobile's population jumped from 29,000 to 41,000, and 10,000 people poured into war-related industries in little Selma, Alabama.

As the Union blockade disrupted imports, the traditionally agricultural South forged new industries. Many planters shared Davis's hope that industrialization would bring "deliverance … from all commercial dependence" on the North or the world. Indeed, the Confederacy achieved tremendous industrial development. Chief of Ordnance Josiah Gorgas increased the capacity of Richmond's Tredegar Iron Works and other factories so that by 1865 his Ordnance Bureau was supplying all Confederate small arms and ammunition. The government constructed new railroad lines and ironworks, using slaves relocated from farms and plantations.

Changing Roles of Women

White women, restricted to narrow roles in antebellum society, gained new responsibilities in wartime. The wives and mothers of soldiers now headed households and performed men's work, including raising crops and tending animals. Women in nonslaveholding families cultivated fields, while wealthier women acted as overseers. In the cities, white women—who had been largely excluded from the labor force—found respectable paying jobs, often in the Confederate bureaucracy. Female schoolteachers appeared in the South for the first time.

Patriotic sacrifice appealed to some women; others resented their new burdens. A Texas woman who had struggled to discipline slaves pronounced herself "sick of trying to do a man's business." Others grew angry over shortages, scornful of the war, and demanded that their men return to provide for their families.

Human Suffering, Hoarding, and Inflation

For millions of southerners, the war brought privation and suffering. Mass poverty descended on a large minority of the white population. Many yeoman families lost their breadwinners to the army. Women sought help from relatives, neighbors, friends, anyone. Sometimes they pleaded with the Confederate government to discharge their husbands.

The South was in many places so sparsely populated that the conscription of one craftsman could wreak hardship on an entire county. Often people begged together for the exemption or discharge of the local miller, neighborhood tanner, or wheelwright. Most serious, however, was the loss of a blacksmith, who could repair farming tools.

The blockade of Confederate shipping created shortages of important supplies—salt, sugar, coffee, nails—and speculation and hoarding made shortages worse. Greedy businessmen cornered the supply of some commodities; prosperous citizens stocked up on food. Inflation skyrocketed, fueled by the Confederate government's heavy borrowing and inadequate taxes, until prices increased almost 7,000 percent. Inflation particularly imperiled urban dwellers without their own food sources. As early as 1862, officials predicted that "women and children are bound to come to suffering if not starvation." A rudimentary relief program organized by the Confederacy failed to meet the need.

Inequities of the Confederate Draft

The Confederate government's policies decidedly favored the upper class. Until the war's last year, for example, prosperous southerners could avoid military service by hiring substitutes. Well over fifty thousand upper-class southerners purchased such substitutes, despite skyrocketing prices that reached $5,000 or $6,000 per man. Mary Boykin Chesnut knew of one aristocrat who "spent a fortune in substitutes.... He is at the end of his row now, for all able-bodied men are ordered to the front."

Anger at such discrimination exploded in October 1862, when the Confederate Congress exempted from military duty anyone who was supervising at least twenty slaves. Protests poured in from across the Confederacy, and North Carolina's legislators condemned the law. Its defenders argued, however, that exemption preserved order and aided food production, and the statute remained on the books.

This "twenty Negro" law is indicative of the racial fears many Confederates felt as the war threatened to overturn southern society. But it also fueled desertion and stimulated Unionism in nonslaveholding regions of the South. In Jones County, Mississippi, a wooded area with few slaves or plantations, Newt Knight, a Confederate soldier, led renegades who took over the county, declared their allegiance to the Union, and called their district the "Free State of Jones." They held out for the remainder of the war as an enclave of Union sympathizers.

The bitterness of letters to Confederate officials suggests the depth of the dissension and class anger. "If I and my little children suffer [and] die while there Father is in service," threatened one woman, "I invoke God Almighty that our blood rest upon the South." War magnified social tensions in the Confederacy.

Wartime Northern Economy and Society

How did the war affect workers in the North?

War dramatically altered northern society as well. Factories and citizens' associations geared up to support the war, and the federal government and its executive branch gained new powers. Idealism and greed flourished together, and the northern economy proved its awesome productivity.

Northern Business, Industry, and Agriculture

At first, the war was a shock to business. Northern firms lost their southern markets, and southern debts became uncollectible, jeopardizing northern merchants and western banks. Farm families struggled with a labor shortage caused by army enlistments. Cotton mills lacked cotton; construction declined; shoe manufacturers sold few of the cheap shoes that planters bought for slaves.

Certain entrepreneurs, such as wool producers, benefited from shortages of competing products, and soaring demand for war-related goods swept some businesses to new success. The U.S. Treasury issued $3.2 billion in bonds and paper money called "greenbacks," and the War Department spent over $360 million in revenues from new taxes, including the nation's first income tax.

War-related spending and government contracts revived business in many northern states. The northern economy also grew because of a complementary relationship between agriculture and industry. Mechanization of agriculture began before the war. Wartime recruitment and conscription gave western farmers an added incentive to purchase laborsaving machinery. Cyrus and William McCormick built an industrial empire in Chicago from the sale of their reapers. Between 1862 and 1864, the manufacture of mowers and reapers doubled to 70,000 yearly; by war's end, 375,000 reapers were in use, triple the number in 1861. Thus northern farm families whose breadwinners went to war did not suffer as much as did their counterparts in the South.

The Quartermaster and Military-Government Mobilization

This government-business marriage emerged from a greatly empowered Quartermaster Department, which became the single largest employer in the United States, issuing thousands of manufacturing contracts to hundreds of firms. Secretary of War Edwin M. Stanton's list of the weapons supplies needed by the Ordnance Department indicates the scope of the demand for government and business cooperation: "7,892 cannon, 11,787 artillery carriages, 4,022,130 small-arms, … 1,022,176,474 cartridges for small-arms, 1,220,555,435 percussion caps, … 26,440,054 pounds of gunpowder, … and 90,416,295 pounds of lead." The government also purchased huge quantities of uniforms, boots, food, camp equipment, saddles, horses, ships, and other necessities. By 1865, the government had purchased some 640,000 horses and 300,000 mules at a cost exceeding $100 million.

Two-thirds of U.S. war spending went to supply troops, and President Lincoln appointed West Point–trained engineer Montgomery Meigs to command that process. Meigs spent $1.8 billion to wage the war, more than all previous U.S. government expenditures since independence combined. His efforts, argued one historian, made the Union army "the best fed, most lavishly supplied army that had ever existed." The success of such military mobilization left an indelible mark on American political-economic history and provided perhaps the oldest root of the modern American "military-industrial state."

The story of Jay Cooke, a wealthy New York financier, best illustrates the wartime partnership between business and government. Cooke earned hefty commissions marketing government bonds to finance the war. But the financier's profit served the Union cause, as the interests of capitalism and government merged in American history's first era of "big government."

Northern Workers' Militancy

Northern industrial and urban workers did not fare as well. After the initial slump, jobs became plentiful, but inflation ate up much of a worker's paycheck. The price of coffee tripled; rice and sugar doubled; and between 1860 and 1864, consumer prices rose at least 76 percent, while daily wages rose only 42 percent. Workers' families consequently suffered a substantial decline in their standard of living.

Industrial workers also lost job security. To increase production, some employers replaced workers with laborsaving machines. Others urged the government to promote immigration to secure cheap labor. Workers responded by forming unions and sometimes by striking. Indeed, thirteen occupational groups—including tailors, coal miners, and railway engineers—formed national unions during the Civil War, and the number of strikes climbed.

Manufacturers viewed labor activism as a threat and formed statewide or craft-based associations to pool information. They shared blacklists of union members and required new workers to sign "yellow dog" contracts (promises not to join a union). To put down strikes, they hired strikebreakers, and sometimes used federal troops.

Labor militancy, however, did not keep employers from profiting or profiteering on government contracts. With immense demand for army supplies, unscrupulous businessmen sold clothing and blankets made of "shoddy"—wool fibers reclaimed from rags or worn cloth. Shoddy goods often came apart in the rain. Contractors sold inferior guns for double the usual price and passed off tainted meat as good. Rampant corruption led to a yearlong investigation by the House of Representatives.

Economic Nationalism and Government-Business Partnership

Legitimate enterprises also made healthy profits. The output of woolen mills increased so dramatically that industry dividends nearly tripled. Some cotton mills made record profits, even while reducing output. Brokerage houses earned unheard-of commissions. Railroads increased their business so much that railroad stocks skyrocketed.

Railroads were also a leading beneficiary of government largesse. With southern representatives absent from Congress, the northern route of the transcontinental railroad prevailed. In 1862 and 1864, Congress chartered two corporations—the Union Pacific Railroad and the Central Pacific Railroad—and assisted them financially in connecting Omaha, Nebraska, with Sacramento, California. For each mile of track laid, the railroads received a loan of $16,000 to $48,000 in government bonds plus 20 square miles of land along a free 400-foot-wide right of way. Overall, the two corporations gained approximately 20 million acres of land and nearly $60 million in loans.

Morrill Land Grant Act
Law in which Congress granted land to states to establish colleges focusing on agriculture, engineering, and military science.

Other businessmen benefited handsomely from the **Morrill Land Grant Act** (1862). To promote public education in agriculture, engineering, and military science, Congress granted each state thirty thousand acres of federal land for each of its congressional districts. The law eventually fostered sixty-nine colleges and universities as it also enriched a few prominent speculators. Similarly, the Homestead Act of 1862 offered cheap, and sometimes free, land to people who would settle the West and improve their property.

Before the war, banks operating under state charters issued seven thousand different kinds of currency notes. During the war, Congress and the Treasury Department established a national banking system to issue national bank notes, and by 1865 most state banks were forced by a prohibitive tax to join the national system. This created sounder currency but also inflexibility in the money supply and an eastern-oriented financial structure.

In the excitement of wartime moneymaking, an eagerness to display one's wealth flourished in the largest cities. The *New York Herald* noted: "This war has entirely changed the American character.… The individual who makes the most money—no matter how—and spends the most—no matter for what—is considered the greatest man."

The Union Cause

In the first two years of the war, northern morale remained high for a cause that today may seem abstract—the Union—but at the time meant the preservation of a social and political order that people cherished.

Secular and church leaders supported the cause, and even ministers who preferred to separate politics and pulpit denounced "the iniquity of causeless rebellion." Abolitionists campaigned to turn the war into a crusade against slavery. Free black communities and churches, both black and white, sent clothing, ministers, and teachers to aid the freedpeople. Indeed, thousands of northern blacks volunteered to join the war effort in spite of the initial rejection they received from the Lincoln administration. Thus, in wartime northern society, materialism and greed flourished alongside idealism, religious conviction, and self-sacrifice.

Northern Women on Home Front and Battlefront

U.S. Sanitary Commission
Civilian organization in the North staffed by large numbers of women that was a major source of medical and nutritional aid for soldiers.

Northern women, like their southern counterparts, took on new roles. They organized over ten thousand soldiers' aid societies, rolled bandages, and raised $3 million to aid injured troops. Women pressed for the first trained ambulance corps in the Union army, and they formed the backbone of the **U.S. Sanitary Commission**, a civilian agency recognized by the War Department in 1861, which provided nutritional and medical aid to soldiers. Although most of its officers were men, the volunteers who ran its seven thousand auxiliaries were primarily women. Women organized elaborate "Sanitary Fairs" to raise money and awareness for soldiers' health and hygiene.

Approximately thirty-two hundred women also served as nurses in front-line hospitals. Yet women had to fight to serve; the professionalization of medicine since the Revolution created a medical system dominated by men who resisted women's assistance. Even **Clara Barton**, famous for working in the worst hospitals at the front, was ousted from her post in 1863. But women such as Dorothea Dix, who sought to reform asylums for the insane, and Illinois widow Mary Ann Bickerdyke, who served in Sherman's army in the West, established a heroic tradition for Civil War nurses. They also advanced the professionalization of nursing, as several schools of nursing were established in northern cities during or after the war.

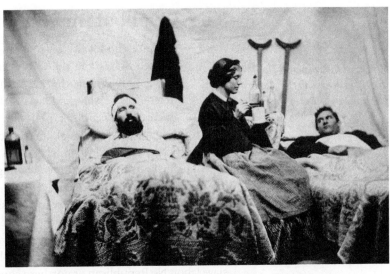

Nurse Anne Bell tending to wounded soldiers in a federal hospital, Nashville, Tennessee, ca. 1863. The distant gaze of the man on the left and the grateful gaze of the one on the right realistically represent the agonies of military hospitals.

Clara Barton Nurse who worked for the Sanitary Commission and later founded the Red Cross.

Women also wrote sentimental war poetry, short stories, novels, and songs that reached thousands of readers in illustrated weeklies, monthly periodicals, and special "story papers." In many stories, female characters seek recognition for their loyalty and Union service, while others probe the suffering and death of loved ones. Louisa May Alcott arrived at her job as a nurse in Washington, D.C., after the horrific Union defeat at Fredericksburg, in December 1862. She later immortalized her experience in *Hospital Sketches* (1863), providing northern readers a view of the hospitals where loved ones agonized and perished. By 1863, many women found slaves' liberation an inspiring subject, as Julia Ward Howe did in her "Battle Hymn of the Republic":

> As He died to make men holy
> Let us die to make men free.

Walt Whitman's War

The poet **Walt Whitman** recorded his experiences as a volunteer nurse in Washington, D.C. As he dressed wounds and comforted suffering men, Whitman found "the marrow of the tragedy concentrated in those Army Hospitals." But he also found inspiration and a deepening faith in American democracy. In "The Wound Dresser," Whitman meditated unforgettably on the deaths he witnessed:

Walt Whitman Well-known poet and author of *Leaves of Grass*; Whitman wrote about his experiences as a nurse and his renewed faith in democracy.

> The crush'd head I dress, (poor crazed hand tear not the bandage away,)
> The neck of the cavalry-man with the bullet through and through I examine,
> Hard the breathing rattles, quite glazed already the eye, yet life struggles hard, (Come
> sweet death! be persuaded O beautiful death! In mercy come quickly.)

Indeed, the scale of death in this war shocked many Americans into believing that the conflict had to be for purposes larger than themselves.

The Advent of Emancipation

Why did Lincoln and Davis both avoid addressing the slavery issue in the early days of the war?

Despite the loyalty of soldiers and civilians, the governments of the United States and the Confederacy lacked clarity about the war's purpose. Throughout the war's early months, Davis and Lincoln avoided references to slavery. Davis realized that emphasis on the issue could increase class conflict in the South. Instead, he told southerners that they were fighting for constitutional liberty: northerners betrayed the founders' legacy, and southerners seceded to preserve it.

Lincoln had his reasons for avoiding slavery. It was crucial at first not to antagonize the Union's border slave states, whose loyalty was tenuous. Lincoln also hoped that a pro-Union majority would assert itself in the South and help coax the South back into the Union. And there were powerful political considerations. Some Republicans burned with moral outrage over slavery; others were frankly racist, dedicated to protecting free whites from the Slave Power and the competition of cheap slave labor. No Republican or northern consensus on slavery existed early in the war.

Lincoln and Emancipation

Lincoln's compassion, humility, and moral anguish during the war were evident in his speeches and writings. But as a politician, Lincoln distinguished between his convictions and his official acts. The latter were calculated for maximum advantage.

Many blacks attacked Lincoln during the first year of the war for his refusal to convert the struggle into an "abolition war." When Lincoln countermanded General John C. Frémont's order of liberation for slaves owned by disloyal masters in Missouri in September 1861, the *Anglo-African* declared that the president, by his actions, "hurls back into the hell of slavery thousands … rightfully set free." As late as July 1862, Frederick Douglass characterized administration policy as reconstruction of "the old union on the old and corrupting basis of compromise, by which slavery shall retain all the power that it ever had." Douglass wanted the old Union destroyed and the Constitution rewritten in the name of human equality. Within a year, just such a profound result began to take place.

Lincoln first substantively broached the subject of slavery in March 1862, when he proposed that states consider emancipation. He asked Congress to promise aid to any state that emancipated, appealing especially to border state representatives. What Lincoln proposed was gradual emancipation, with compensation for slaveholders and colonization of the freed slaves outside the United States.

Until well into 1864, Lincoln's administration promoted an impractical scheme to colonize 4.2 million freed slaves in Central America or the Caribbean. He was as yet unconvinced that America could become a biracial society, and he feared that white northerners might not support a war for black freedom. Black abolitionists vehemently opposed the Lincoln administration's machinations.

Radical Republicans A group of Republicans who assailed the U.S. president early in the war for failing to make emancipation a war goal and, later, for making it too easy for defeated rebel states to return to the Union.

A group of congressional Republicans, known as the **Radical Republicans** and led by George Julian, Charles Sumner, and Thaddeus Stevens, dedicated themselves to a war for emancipation. They were instrumental in creating a special House-Senate committee on the conduct of the war, which investigated Union reverses, sought to improve military efficiency, and prodded the president to take stronger measures against slavery.

Library of Congress Prints and Photographs [LC-DIG-stereo-1s02760]

A group of "contrabands" (liberated slaves), photographed at Cumberland Landing, Virginia, May 14, 1862, at a sensitive point in the war when their legal status was still not fully determined. The faces and generations of the women, men, and children represent the human drama of emancipation.

Confiscation Acts

In August 1861, at the Radicals' instigation, Congress passed its first confiscation act. Designed to punish the Confederates, the law confiscated all property used for "insurrectionary purposes." A second confiscation act (July 1862) confiscated the property of anyone who supported the rebellion, even those who resided in the South and paid Confederate taxes. Their slaves were declared "forever free of their servitude."

In summer 1862, Lincoln stood by his proposal of voluntary gradual emancipation. In protest, Horace Greeley, editor of the powerful *New York Tribune*, published an open letter to the president entitled "The Prayer of Twenty Millions." Greeley declared, "Mr. President, there is not one … intelligent champion of the Union cause who does not feel that all attempts to put down the Rebellion and at the same time uphold its inciting cause are preposterous and futile." Lincoln offered a calculated reply. He disagreed with those who would make slavery the paramount issue of the war and said, "If I could save the Union without freeing any slave I would do it, and if I could save it by freeing all the slaves I would do it; and if I could save it by freeing some and leaving others alone I would also do that. What I do about slavery, and the colored race, I do because I believe it helps to save the Union."

But Lincoln had already decided to boldly issue a presidential **Emancipation Proclamation**. He was waiting for a Union victory so that it would not appear an act of desperation. Yet the letter to Greeley represents Lincoln's concern with conditioning public opinion for the coming social revolution.

Emancipation Proclamation
Lincoln's decree freeing all slaves in Confederate-held territories. It exempted border slave states that remained within the Union.

Emancipation Proclamations

On September 22, 1862, shortly after Union success at the Battle of Antietam, Lincoln issued the first of his two-part proclamation. Invoking his powers as commander-in-chief, he announced that on January 1, 1863, he would emancipate the slaves in the states "in rebellion" (those lacking legitimate representatives in the U.S. Congress by January). Thus, his September 1862 proclamation was less a declaration of the right of slaves to be free than a threat to southerners: unless they put down their arms and returned to Congress, they would lose their slaves. Lincoln had little expectation that southerners would give up, but he wanted a response.

Link to the Emancipation Proclamation, 1863

In the fateful January 1, 1863, proclamation, Lincoln declared that "all persons held as slaves" in areas in rebellion "shall be then, thenceforward, and forever free." But he excepted every Confederate county or city that had fallen under Union control. Those areas, he declared, "are, for the present, left precisely as if this proclamation were not issued." Nor did Lincoln liberate slaves in the border slave states that remained in the Union. "The President has … proclaimed emancipation only where he has notoriously no power to execute it," charged the anti-administration *New York World.*

But Lincoln was worried about the constitutionality of his acts, and he anticipated that after the war southerners might sue for restoration of their "property." Making the liberation of the slaves "a fit and necessary war measure" raised a variety of legal questions: Would it expire with the suppression of a rebellion? The proclamation did little to clarify the status or citizenship of the freed slaves, although it did open the possibility of military service for blacks. How, indeed, would this change the character and purpose of the war?

If the Emancipation Proclamation was legally ambiguous, as a moral and political document it had great meaning. Because the proclamation defined the war as a war against slavery, congressional Radicals could applaud it. Yet it also protected Lincoln's position with conservatives, enabling him to retreat and forcing no immediate changes on the border slave states. Most important, though, thousands of slaves had already reached Union lines across the South. They had "voted with their feet" for emancipation well before the proclamation. And now, every advance of federal forces into slave society was a liberating step.

Across the North and in Union-occupied sections of the South, blacks and their white allies celebrated the Emancipation Proclamation. At a large "contraband camp" in Washington, D.C., some six hundred black men, women, and children gathered at the superintendent's headquarters on New Year's Eve and sang through the night. In chorus after chorus of "Go Down, Moses" they announced the magnitude of their painful but beautiful exodus.

African American Recruits

The need for men soon convinced the administration to recruit northern and southern blacks for the Union army. By spring 1863, African American troops were answering the call of a dozen or more black recruiters in northern cities and towns. Lincoln came to see black soldiers as "the great available and yet unavailed of force for restoring the Union."

African American leaders hoped that military service would secure equal rights for their people. Once the black soldier had fought for the Union, wrote Frederick Douglass, "there is no power on earth which can deny that he has earned the right of citizenship in the United States."

In June 1864, with thousands of black former slaves in blue uniforms, Lincoln gave his support to a constitutional ban on slavery. On the eve of the Republican national convention, Lincoln called on the party to "put into the platform as the keystone, the amendment of the Constitution abolishing and prohibiting slavery forever." The party promptly called for the **Thirteenth Amendment**, which passed in early 1865 and was sent to the states for ratification. The war to save the Union had become the war to free the slaves.

Thirteenth Amendment
Ended slavery in all U.S. territory.

Who Freed the Slaves? It has long been debated whether Abraham Lincoln deserved the label (one he never claimed for himself) of "Great Emancipator." Was Lincoln ultimately a reluctant emancipator, following rather than leading Congress and public opinion? Or did Lincoln provide essential presidential leadership by going slow but, once moving, never backpedaling on black freedom? Once he focused on the unconditional surrender of the Confederates, Lincoln made slavery's destruction central to the war's purpose.

Others have argued, however, that the slaves were central in achieving their own freedom. When they were in proximity to war zones, slaves fled by the thousands. Some worked as camp laborers for the Union armies, and eventually more than 180,000 black men served in the Union army and navy. Some found freedom as individuals in 1861, and some not until 1865, as refugees trekking to contraband camps.

Nevertheless, emancipation was a historical confluence of a policy directed by and dependent on the military authority of the president and the will and courage of African Americans for self-emancipation. Wallace Turnage's escape in Mobile Bay in 1864 demonstrates that emancipation could result from both a slave's own heroism and Union forces. Most blacks comprehended their freedom as given and taken, but also as their human right. "I could now speak my opinion," Turnage concluded, "to men of all grades and colors."

A Confederate Plan of Emancipation Before the war was over, the Confederacy, too, addressed emancipation. Late in the war, Jefferson Davis was willing to sacrifice slavery to achieve independence. He proposed that the Confederate government purchase forty thousand slaves to work as army laborers, with a promise of freedom at the end of their service. He then called for the recruitment and arming of slaves as soldiers, who likewise would gain their freedom at war's end, as would their wives and children.

Bitter debate over Davis's plan resounded throughout the Confederacy. When the Confederate Congress finally approved slave enlistments in March 1865, owners had to comply only on a voluntary basis. With manpower shortages, General Lee supported the idea of slave soldiers, while most Confederate slaveholders vehemently opposed the enlistment plan. Supporters hoped to fight to a stalemate, achieve independence, and control the postwar racial order through their limited wartime emancipation schemes, but it was too late. By contrast, Lincoln's Emancipation Proclamation stimulated a vital infusion of forces into the Union armies: 134,000 former slaves (and 52,000 free blacks) fought for freedom and the Union. Their participation was pivotal in northern victory.

The Soldiers' War

What led previously reluctant white military leaders to accept black soldiers?

Military service completely altered soldiers' lives. Enlistment submerged young men in large organizations whose military discipline ignored their individuality. Army life meant tedium, physical hardship, and separation from loved ones. Yet it also had powerful attractions.

Ordinary Soldiers and Ideology

The old idea that Civil War soldiers fought largely because of unit cohesion and the devotion of fellow recruits is no longer an adequate explanation of why so many endured hardship for so long. Comradeship, duty, and honor were powerful motivators, as were "union," "home," "the government," "freedom," "flag," "liberty," and "states' rights." But according to recent studies, men on both sides were committed to the ideological purposes of the war. Literate soldiers left testimony in letters and regional newspapers of how they saw slavery at the heart of the matter. Members of Morgan's Confederate Brigade from Virginia declared: "any man who pretends to believe that this is not a war for the emancipation of the blacks … is either a fool or a liar."

Hospitals and Camp Life

The soldiers' lot was often misery. They benefited from new products, such as canned condensed milk, but blankets, clothing, and arms were often poor quality. Hospitals were badly managed at first. Rules of hygiene in large camps were scarcely enforced. Water supplies were unsafe and typhoid epidemics common. About 57,000 men died from dysentery and diarrhea; 224,000 Union troops died from disease or accidents, double the 110,100 who died from battle. Confederate troops were less well supplied. Still, an extensive network of hospitals, aided by white female volunteers and black female slaves, sprang up.

On both sides, troops quickly learned that soldiering was far from glorious. Fighting, wrote a North Carolina volunteer in 1862, taught him "the realities of a soldier's life.… Without time to wash our clothes or our persons … the whole army became lousy more or less with body lice." Union troops "skirmished" against lice by boiling their clothes, but to little avail.

War soon exposed them to the blasted bodies of friends and comrades. "It is a sad sight to see the dead and if possible more sad to see the wounded—shot in every possible way you can imagine," wrote one Confederate.

Still, as campaigns dragged on, soldiers who did not desert grew determined to see the struggle through. "We now, like true Soldiers go determined not to yield one inch," wrote a New York corporal. When the war was over, "it seemed like breaking up a family to separate," one man observed.

The Rifled Musket

Advances in technology made the Civil War particularly deadly. The most important were the rifle and the "minie ball." Bullets fired from a smoothbore musket were not accurate at distances over eighty yards. Cutting spiraled grooves inside the barrel gave the projectile greater accuracy, but rifles remained difficult to load and use until the Frenchman Claude Minie and the American James Burton developed a new kind of bullet that expanded on firing and flew accurately. With these bullets, rifles were deadly at four hundred yards.

This meant that soldiers assaulting a position defended by riflemen were in greater peril. While artillery now fired from a safe distance, there was no substitute for the infantry assault or the popular turning movements aimed at an enemy's flank. Thus, advancing soldiers exposed themselves repeatedly to accurate rifle fire. Because medical knowledge was rudimentary, even minor wounds often led to amputation and death through infection. Never before in Europe or America had such massive forces pummeled each other with weapons of such destructive power.

The Black Soldier's Fight for Manhood

At the outset of the war, racism in the Union army was strong. Most white soldiers wanted nothing to do with black people and regarded them as inferior. For many, acceptance of black troops grew only because they could do heavy labor and "stop Bullets as well as white people." A popular song celebrated "Sambo's Right to Be Kilt" as the only justification for black enlistments.

But white officers who volunteered to lead segregated black units to gain promotion found that experience altered their opinions. After one month with black troops, a white captain informed his wife, "I have a more elevated opinion of their abilities than I ever had before. I know that many of them are vastly the superiors of those … who would condemn them all to a life of brutal degradation."

Black troops had a mission to destroy slavery and demonstrate their equality. "When Rebellion is crushed," wrote a black volunteer from Connecticut, "who will be more proud than I to say, I was one of the first of the despised race to leave the free North with a rifle on my shoulder.…" Corporal James Henry Gooding of Massachusetts's black Fifty-fourth Regiment explained that his unit intended "to live down all prejudice against its color, by a determination to do well in any position it is put."

Indeed, blacks and whites of the Fifty-fourth Massachusetts forged deep bonds. Just before the regiment launched its costly assault on Fort Wagner in Charleston harbor, in July 1863, a black soldier called out to abolitionist Colonel Robert Gould Shaw, who would perish that day, "Colonel, I will stay by you till I die." "And he kept his word," noted a survivor of the attack. "He has never been seen since." The Fort Wagner assault was celebrated for demonstrating the valor of black men, but this bloody chapter in the history of American racism also proved that black men had to die in battle to be acknowledged as men.

Such valor emerged despite persistent discrimination. The Union government paid white privates $13 per month plus a clothing allowance of $3.50, whereas black privates earned only $10 per month less $3 for clothing. Outraged, several regiments refused to accept any pay, and Congress eventually remedied the inequity.

1863: The Tide of Battle Turns

What turned the tide of war toward Union victory?

The fighting in spring and summer 1863 did not settle the war, but it suggested the outcome. The campaigns began in a deceptively positive way for Confederates, as Lee's army performed brilliantly in battles in central Virginia.

Battle of Chancellorsville

On May 2 and 3, west of Fredericksburg, Virginia, some 130,000 members of the Union Army of the Potomac bore down on fewer than 60,000 Confederates. Boldly, Lee and Stonewall Jackson divided their forces, ordering 30,000 men under Jackson on a daylong march westward to prepare a flank attack.

Arriving at their position in late afternoon, Jackson's seasoned "foot cavalry" found unprepared Union troops laughing, smoking, and playing cards. The Confederate attack drove the entire right side of the Union army back. Eager to

Visualizing THE PAST

Black Soldiers in the Civil War

The image below is of the storming of Fort Wagner in July 1863 by the Fifty-fourth Massachusetts Regiment in Charleston, South Carolina, by Chicago printmakers Kurtz and Allison. Kurtz and Allison issued vivid and colorful chromolithographs in the 1880s, celebrating the military valor of African Americans. This scene depicts the most famous combat action of black troops in the Civil War; the Fifty-fourth was the first northern-recruited black unit, and their bravery and sacrifice served as a measure of African American devotion to the Union cause. At right is a medal for valor won by a member of the Fifty-fourth Massachusetts Regiment. Why was this regiment such a symbolic test case for the military ability and political meaning of black soldiers in the Civil War? Why did black men have to die on battlefields for many Americans in the Civil War era to consider them fully men and citizens?

STORMING FORT WAGNER.

Library of Congress

Picture Research Consultants & Archives

press his advantage, Jackson rode forward with a few officers to study the ground. As Jackson and his team returned at twilight, southern troops mistook them for federals and fired, fatally wounding their commander. The next day, Union forces left in defeat. Southern forces won at Chancellorsville, but it cost them Stonewall Jackson, who would remain a legend in Confederate memory.

Siege of Vicksburg

July brought crushing defeats for the Confederacy in two critical battles—**Vicksburg** and **Gettysburg**— that damaged Confederate hopes for independence. Vicksburg was the last major fortification on the Mississippi River in southern hands (see Map 13.3). General Ulysses S. Grant laid siege to Vicksburg in May, bottling up the defending army of General John Pemberton. If Vicksburg fell, Union forces would control the river, cutting the Confederacy in two and gaining an open path into its interior. To stave off such results, Jefferson Davis put General Joseph E. Johnston in charge and beseeched him to aid Pemberton. Meanwhile, General Robert E. Lee proposed a Confederate invasion of the North, which, though it would not relieve Vicksburg directly, could stun the North and possibly lead to peace. By invading the North a second time, Lee hoped to move away from war-weary Virginia, garner civilian support in Maryland, win a major victory on northern soil, threaten major cities, and thereby force a Union capitulation.

As Lee's emboldened army advanced through western Maryland and into Pennsylvania, Confederate prospects along the Mississippi darkened. Davis repeatedly wired General Johnston, urging him to attack Grant's army. Johnston, however, considered "saving Vicksburg hopeless." Grant's men, meanwhile, were supplying themselves from the abundant crops of the Mississippi River valley and could continue their siege indefinitely.

Battle of Gettysburg

On July 4, 1863, Vicksburg's commander surrendered. The same day, a battle that had been raging for three days concluded at Gettysburg, Pennsylvania (see Map 13.4). On July 1, Confederate forces hunting for a supply of shoes collided with the Union army. Heavy fighting on the second day left federal forces in possession of high ground along Cemetery Ridge, where they were shielded by a stone wall and had a clear view of their foe across almost a mile of open field.

Undaunted, Lee believed his reinforced troops could break the Union line, and on July 3 he ordered an assault. Virginians under General George E. Pickett and North Carolinians under General James Pettigrew marched up the slope in a doomed assault known as Pickett's Charge.

Vicksburg Union victory that gave the North complete control of the Mississippi River.

Gettysburg Union victory that halted the Confederate invasion of Pennsylvania; turning point in the war in the East.

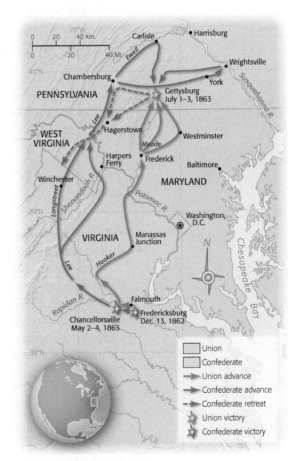

MAP 13.4
Battle of Gettysburg

In the war's greatest battle, fought around a small market town in southern Pennsylvania, Lee's invasion of the North was repulsed. Union forces had the advantage of the high ground, shorter lines, and superior numbers. The casualties for the two armies—dead, wounded, and missing—exceeded 50,000 men.

Source: Copyright © Cengage Learning 2015

They breached the enemy's line, but most fell in heavy slaughter. On July 4, Lee had to withdraw, having suffered almost four thousand dead and about twenty-four thousand missing and wounded. The Confederate general blamed himself and offered to resign, but President Davis refused. The Confederacy had reached what many consider its high-water mark at Gettysburg. Southern troops displayed unforgettable courage and dedication at Gettysburg, and under General George G. Meade, the Union army, which suffered 23,000 casualties (nearly one-quarter of the force), exhibited the same bravery in stopping the Confederate invasion.

After Gettysburg and Vicksburg, the Confederacy was split; west of the Mississippi, General E. Kirby Smith had to operate on his own, virtually independent of Richmond. Moreover, the heartland of Louisiana, Tennessee, and Mississippi lay exposed to invasion. Lee's northern defeat spelled the end of major southern offensive actions. By wearing down northern morale, the South might yet win, but its prospects were darker than before.

Disunity: South, North, and West

What were the causes of wartime dissent in the South?

Northern and southern governments waged the final two years of the war with increasing opposition at home. The gigantic costs of a civil war fed the unrest. But protest also arose from stresses in the region's social structures.

Union Occupation Zones

Wherever Union forces invaded, they imposed a military occupation consisting of three zones: garrisoned towns, with many troops controlling civilian and economic life; the Confederate frontier, areas still under southern control but with some federal military penetration; and "no man's land," regions between the two armies, beyond Confederate authority and under frequent Union patrols.

Roughly one hundred southern towns were garrisoned, causing severe social disruption. Large parts of Tennessee, Virginia, Louisiana, Mississippi, and Georgia were occupied and suffered food shortages, crop and property destruction, disease, roadway banditry, guerrilla warfare, summary executions, and the random flow of escaped slaves. After two years of occupation, a southern white woman wrote to a kinsman about their native Clarksville, Tennessee: "it is nothing but a dirty hole filled … with niggers and Yankees."

Disintegration of Confederate Unity

Vastly disadvantaged in industrial capacity, natural resources, and labor, southerners felt the cost of war more painfully than northerners. And internally, the southern class system threatened the Confederate cause.

Planters were increasingly opposed to their own government. Along with new taxation, Confederate military authorities impressed slaves to build fortifications. And when Union forces advanced, Confederate commanders burned cotton stores that lay in the enemy's path, enraging planters about such interference with their agricultural production and finances.

Years of opposition to the federal government within the Union had frozen southerners in a defensive posture. Now they erected the barrier of states' rights as a defense against change. Nor were the centralizing policies of the Davis administration popular. The Confederate constitution granted substantial powers to the central government, especially in wartime. But many planters took the position articulated by R. B. Rhett, editor of the *Charleston Mercury*, that the Confederate constitution "leaves the States untouched in their Sovereignty, and commits to the Confederate Government only a few simple objects, and a few simple powers to enforce them."

Confused and embittered planters struck out at Jefferson Davis. Conscription, thundered Governor Brown, was "subversive of [Georgia's] sovereignty, and at war with all the principles for the support of which Georgia entered into this revolution." To frustrate the law, Brown ordered local enrollment officials not to cooperate with the Confederacy.

Food Riots in Southern Cities

Widespread hunger and suffering sparked food riots in spring 1863 in Atlanta, Macon, Columbus, and Augusta, Georgia, and in Salisbury and High Point, North Carolina. On April 2, a crowd assembled in Richmond to demand relief. Responding to a passerby's questions about the group, a young girl replied, "We are starving. We are going to the bakeries and each of us will take a loaf of bread." That action fueled a riot that Davis ordered quelled at gunpoint.

Throughout the rural South, ordinary people resisted more quietly—by refusing to cooperate with conscription, tax collection, and impressments of food. Farmers who did provide food for the army refused to accept payment in certificates of credit or government bonds, as required by law. Conscription officers increasingly found no one to draft. In some areas, tax agents were killed.

Austere and private, Jefferson Davis was ill equipped to deal with such discontent. His class perspective also distanced him from common people's suffering. While his social circle in Richmond dined on duck and oysters, ordinary southerners went hungry.

Desertions from the Confederate Army

Such discontent affected the Confederate armies. Worried about their loved ones and resentful of what they saw as a rich man's war, large numbers of men abandoned the army, supported by friends and neighbors. Mary Chesnut observed a man being dragged back to the army as his wife looked on. "Desert agin, Jake!" she cried.

Desertion did not become a serious problem for the Confederacy until mid-1862, and stiffer policing solved the problem that year. But from 1863 on, the number of men on duty fell rapidly. By mid-1863, John A. Campbell, the South's assistant secretary of war, estimated that 40,000 to 50,000 troops were absent without leave and that 100,000 were evading duty. By November 1863, one-third of the army could not be accounted for.

The defeats at Gettysburg and Vicksburg dealt a heavy blow to Confederate morale. Desperate, President Davis and several state governors resorted to racial scare tactics to drive southern whites to further sacrifice. Defeat, Davis warned, would mean "extermination of yourselves, your wives, and children." Mississippi Governor Charles Clark predicted "elevation of the black race to a position of equality—aye, of superiority, that will make them your masters and rulers."

Internal disintegration of the Confederacy quickened. Confederate leaders realized they were losing the people's support. It is remarkable how long and effectively the Confederacy sustained a military effort while facing internal division.

Antiwar Sentiment, South and North

In North Carolina, William W. Holden, a popular Democratic politician and editor, led a growing peace movement. Over one hundred public meetings supporting peace negotiations took place during summer 1863. In Georgia early in 1864, Governor Brown and Alexander H. Stephens, vice president of the Confederacy, led a similar effort. Ultimately, the lack of a two-party system made questionable the legitimacy of any government criticism.

In the 1863 congressional elections, secessionists and supporters of the administration lost seats to men not identified with the government. In the war's last years, Davis's support in the Confederate Congress dwindled. Some newspaper editors and soldiers, especially in Lee's Army of Northern Virginia, kept the Confederacy alive despite disintegrating popular support.

By 1864, southerners were giving up the struggle. Deserters dominated some whole towns and counties. Active dissent was particularly common in upland and mountain regions, where Union support always held fast. Opposition to the war, though less severe, also existed in the North. Alarm intensified over the growing centralization of government. The draft sparked protest, especially among poor citizens, and the Union army struggled with a troubling desertion rate. But with greater human resources, the Union government's effectiveness was never threatened.

Moreover, unlike Davis, Lincoln knew how to stay in touch with the ordinary citizen. Through public letters to newspapers and private ones to soldiers' families, he reached the common people. The battlefield carnage, political problems, and criticism weighed on him, but his administration never lost control of the war effort.

Peace Democrats

Much of the wartime protest in the North was political. The Democratic Party fought to regain power by blaming Lincoln for the war's death toll, the expansion of federal powers, inflation and the high tariff, and the emancipation of blacks. Its leaders called for an end to the war and reunion on the basis of "the Constitution as it is and the Union as it was." Democrats denounced conscription and martial law and defended states' rights. They charged that Republican policies were designed to flood the North with blacks, threatening white men's privileges. In the 1862 congressional elections, Democrats made a strong comeback, with peace Democrats wielding influence in New York State and majorities in the legislatures of Illinois and Indiana.

Led by outspoken men like Representative Clement L. Vallandigham of Ohio, the peace Democrats became highly visible. Vallandigham criticized Lincoln as a "dictator" who suspended the writ of habeas corpus without congressional authority, arrested thousands of innocent citizens, and shut down opposition newspapers (charges that were true). He urged voters to depose "King Abraham." Vallandigham's attacks seemed so damaging that military authorities arrested him for treason. Lincoln wisely decided against punishment—and martyr's status—for the Ohioan and exiled him to the Confederacy. (Eventually, Vallandigham returned to the North through Canada.)

Some antiwar Democrats did encourage draft resistance, sabotage communications, and plot to aid the Confederacy. Republicans sometimes branded them— and by extension the peace Democrats—as **"Copperheads"**, after the poisonous snake. Although some Confederate agents were active in the North and Canada, they never genuinely threatened the Union war effort.

"Copperheads" Poisonous snakes; also the Republican nickname for antiwar northern Democrats. Some were pacifists, while others were activists who encouraged draft resistance, sabotage, and efforts to aid the Confederacy.

New York City Draft Riots

More violent opposition to the government arose from citizens facing the draft, which became law in 1863. Although many soldiers risked their lives willingly, others openly sought to avoid service.

Urban poor and immigrants in strongly Democratic areas were especially hostile to conscription. The North's poor viewed the system as discriminatory, and many immigrants suspected (wrongly, on the whole) that they were disproportionately called. (Approximately 200,000 men born in Germany and 150,000 born in Ireland served in the Union army.)

As a result, enrolling officers received rough treatment in many northern areas, and riots occurred in New Jersey, Ohio, Indiana, Pennsylvania, Illinois, and Wisconsin. The most serious violence occurred in New York City in July 1863. The war was unpopular there, and racial, ethnic, and class tensions ran high. Shippers had recently broken a longshoremen's strike by hiring black strikebreakers. Working-class New Yorkers feared an inflow of black labor from the South and regarded blacks as the cause of the war. Poor Irish workers resented being forced to serve in the place of others who could afford to avoid the draft.

Military police officers were attacked first, and then mobs crying, "Down with the rich" looted wealthy homes and stores. But blacks became the special target. Mobs rampaged through African American neighborhoods, beating and murdering people in the streets, and burning an orphan asylum. At least seventy-four people died during three days of violence. Army units directly from Gettysburg ended this tragic episode.

War Against Indians in the Far West

A civil war of another kind raged on the Great Plains and in the Southwest. By 1864, U.S. troops commanded by Colonel John Chivington waged full-scale war against the Sioux, Arapahos, and Cheyennes to eradicate Indian title to eastern Colorado. Indian chiefs sought peace, but American commanders had orders to "burn villages and kill Cheyennes." A Cheyenne chief, Lean Bear, was shot from his horse as he rode toward U.S. troops, holding papers given him by President Lincoln during a visit to Washington, D.C. Another chief, Black Kettle, was told by the U.S. command that his people would find a safe haven in Sand Creek, Colorado. Instead, on November 29, 1864, 700 cavalrymen, many drunk, attacked the Cheyenne village. With most men away hunting, the slaughter at the Sand Creek Massacre included 105 Cheyenne women and children and 28 men. American soldiers scalped and mutilated their victims, carrying women's body parts on their saddles or hats back to Denver.

In New Mexico and Arizona Territories, an authoritarian and brutal commander, General James Carleton, waged

THE RIOTS IN NEW YORK: DESTRUCTION OF THE COLOURED ORPHAN ASYLUM.

A contemporary wood engraving of the destruction of the Colored Orphan Asylum during the New York City draft riots, July 13–16, 1863.

The Granger Collection, NYC

war on the Apaches and the Navajos. For generations both tribes raided the Pueblo and Hispanic peoples of the region to maintain their security and economy. During the Civil War years, Anglo-American farms also became Indian targets. In 1863, the New Mexico Volunteers, commanded by former mountain man Kit Carson, defeated the Mescalero Apaches and forced them onto a reservation at Bosque Redondo in the Pecos River valley.

But the Navajos resisted. Carson destroyed their livestock, orchards, and crops, causing the starving Navajos to surrender for food in January 1864. Three-quarters of the 12,000 Navajos were forced to march 400 miles (the "Long Walk") to the Bosque Redondo Reservation, suffering malnutrition and death en route. Permitted to return to a fraction of their homelands later that year, the Navajos never forgot the federal government's ruthless policies of removal and eradication of Indian peoples.

Election of 1864

Back east, war weariness reached a peak in summer of 1864, when the Democratic Party nominated popular general George B. McClellan for president and inserted a peace plank into its platform. Written by Vallandigham, it called for an armistice and spoke vaguely about preserving the Union. Democrats made racist appeals to white insecurity, calling Lincoln "Abe the nigger-lover." No incumbent president had been reelected since 1832, and some Republicans worked to dump Lincoln from their ticket for Salmon P. Chase or John C. Frémont, although little came of either effort.

With the fall of Atlanta and Union victories in the Shenandoah Valley by early September, Lincoln's prospects rose. A decisive factor: eighteen states allowed troops to vote at the front. Lincoln won 78 percent of the soldier vote. With 55 percent of the popular vote, Lincoln's reelection—a referendum on the war and emancipation—devastated southern morale. Without this political outcome, a Union military victory and a redefined nation might never have happened.

1864–1865: The Final Test of Wills

Why was it so crucial to northern military strategy that Europe remain neutral during the Civil War?

The Confederates could still have won their version of victory in the war's last year if military stalemate and northern antiwar sentiment had forced a negotiated settlement. But northern determination prevailed.

Northern Diplomatic Strategy

From the outset, the North had pursued one paramount goal: to prevent recognition of the Confederacy by European nations. Foreign recognition would belie Lincoln's claim that the United States was fighting an illegal rebellion and might lead to the financial and military aid that could ensure Confederate independence. Both England and France stood to benefit from a divided and weakened America. Thus, Lincoln and Secretary of State Seward needed to avoid serious military defeats and controversies with European powers.

Since the textile industry employed one-fifth of the British population, southerners banked on British recognition of the Confederacy. But at the war's start, British mills had a 50 percent surplus of cotton, and they later found new supplies in India, Egypt, and Brazil. The British government flirted with recognition of the Confederacy but awaited southern battlefield successes. France was unwilling to act without Britain. Confederate agents purchased arms and supplies in Europe and obtained loans from European financiers, but they never achieved a diplomatic breakthrough.

An acute crisis occurred in 1861 when the overzealous commander of an American frigate stopped the British steamer *Trent* and removed two Confederate ambassadors, James Mason and John Slidell, to a Boston prison. The British interpreted the capture as a violation of freedom of the seas and demanded the prisoners' release. Lincoln and Seward waited until northern public opinion cooled before releasing them. The incident strained U.S.-British relations.

Then the sale to the Confederacy of warships constructed in England sparked protest from U.S. ambassador Charles Francis Adams. Over twenty-two months, the English-built ship, the *Alabama,* destroyed or captured more than sixty U.S. ships.

Battlefield Stalemate and a Union Strategy for Victory

On the battlefield, northern victory was far from won in 1864. General Nathaniel Banks's Red River campaign to capture more of Louisiana and Texas fell apart, and the capture of Mobile Bay in August did not cause the fall of Mobile. Union general William Tecumseh Sherman soon brought total war to the southern heartland. On the eastern front during winter 1863–1864, the two armies in Virginia settled into a stalemate, awaiting another northern spring offensive.

Military authorities have historically agreed that deep invasion is risky: the farther an army penetrates enemy territory, the more vulnerable its communications and supply lines become. Moreover, observed the Prussian expert Karl von Clausewitz, if the invader encounters a "truly national" resistance, his troops will be "everywhere exposed to attacks by an insurgent population."

General Grant, by now in command of the entire federal army, tested southern will with massive raids. Grant proposed to use armies to destroy Confederate railroads, thus ruining the enemy's transportation and economy. Union troops would live off the land while destroying resources useful to the Confederate military and to the civilian population. After General George H. Thomas's troops won the Battle of Chattanooga in November 1863, Georgia's heartland lay open. Grant entrusted General Sherman with 100,000 men for an invasion toward Atlanta's rail center.

Fall of Atlanta

Jefferson Davis positioned General Joseph E. Johnston's army in Sherman's path. Davis hoped for Lincoln's political defeat and the election of a president who would bring peace. When General Johnston fell silent and continued to retreat, Davis replaced him with the one-legged General John Hood, who knew his job was to fight and preserve Atlanta.

Hood attacked but was beaten, and Sherman's army occupied Atlanta on September 2, 1864. The victory buoyed northern spirits and ensured Lincoln's reelection. Davis exhorted southerners to fight on. Hood's army marched north to cut Sherman's supply lines and force him to withdraw, but Sherman marched sixty thousand of his marauding men to the sea, destroying Confederate resources as he went (see Map 13.5).

The Civil War in Britain

Because of the direct reliance of the British textile industry on southern cotton (cut off by the war), the American war was significant in Britain's economy and domestic politics. The British aristocracy and most cotton mill owners were pro-Confederate and proslavery, whereas clergymen, shopkeepers, artisans, and radical politicians worked for the Union and emancipation. Most British workers saw their future at stake in a war for slave emancipation. "Freedom" to the huge British working class (who could not vote) meant basic political and civil rights as well as jobs in an industrializing economy.

English aristocrats and conservatives believed in the superiority of the British system of government and looked askance at America's leveling tendencies. And some aristocratic British Liberals sympathized with the Confederacy's demand for independence. English racism also intensified, exemplified by the popularity of minstrelsy and the employment of science in racial theory.

The British propaganda war over the American conflict was widespread: public meetings organized by both sides were huge affairs, with competing banners, carts and floats, orators and resolutions. In a press war, the British argued over when rebellion is justified, whether secession was right or legal, whether slavery was at the heart of the conflict, and especially over the democratic image of America. This bitter debate became a test of reform in Britain: those eager for a broadened franchise and increased democracy were pro-Union, and those who preferred Britain's class-ridden political system favored the Confederacy.

The nature of the internal British debate was symbolized by the dozens of African Americans who served as pro-Union agents in England. The most popular was William Andrew Jackson, Confederate president Jefferson Davis's former coachman, who escaped from Richmond in September 1862. At British public meetings, Jackson countered pro-Confederate arguments that the war was not about slavery.

In the end, the British government did not recognize the Confederacy and, by 1864, English cotton lords found new sources in Egypt and India. But in this link between America and its English roots at its time of greatest travail, we can see the Civil War's international significance.

The Granger Collection, NYC

Some southern leaders pronounced that cotton was king and would bring Britain to their cause. This British cartoon shows King Cotton brought down in chains by the American eagle, anticipating the cotton famine to follow and the intense debate in Great Britain over the nature and meaning of the American Civil War.

Sherman's March to the Sea

Sherman's army was formidable, composed almost entirely of battle-tested veterans and officers who rose through the ranks from the midwestern states. Before the march, army doctors weeded out men who were weak or sick. Although many harbored racist attitudes, most now supported emancipation because, as one said, "Slavery stands in the way of putting down the rebellion."

As Sherman's men moved across Georgia, they cut a path 50 to 60 miles wide and more than 200 miles long. The massive destruction they caused later prompted historians to deem this the first modern "total war." A Georgia woman described the "Burnt Country" this way: "The fields were trampled down and the road was lined with carcasses of horses, hogs, and cattle that the invaders, unable either to consume or to carry with them, had wantonly shot down to starve our people."

After reaching Savannah in December, Sherman marched his armies into the Carolinas. To his soldiers, South Carolina was "the root of secession." They burned and destroyed as they marched, encountering little resistance. The opposing army of General Johnston was small, but Sherman's men should have faced guerrilla raids and attacks by local defense units. The absence of both led South Carolina's James Chesnut Jr. (a politician and Mary Chesnut's husband) to write that his state "was shamefully and unnecessarily lost." Southerners lost the will to continue.

In Georgia alone, nearly twenty thousand slaves followed the marauding Union troops. Others remained on plantations to await war's end because of either wariness of whites or negative experiences with federal soldiers. The destruction of food harmed slaves and white rebels, and many blacks lost livestock, crops, and other valuables to their liberators.

MAP 13.5
Sherman's March to the Sea

The Deep South proved a decisive theater at the end of the war. From Chattanooga, Union forces drove into Georgia, capturing Atlanta. Following the fall of Atlanta, General Sherman embarked on his march of destruction through Georgia to the coast and then northward through the Carolinas. Source: Copyright © Cengage Learning 2015

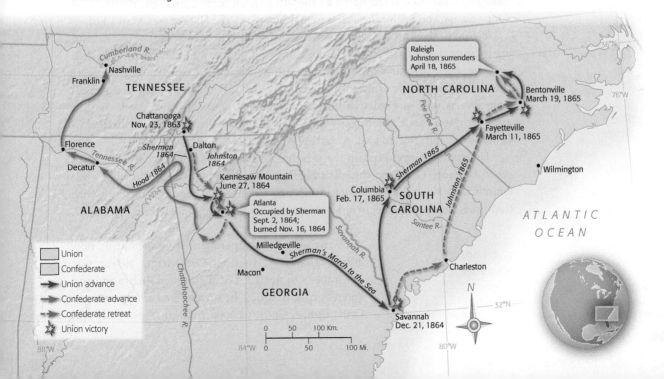

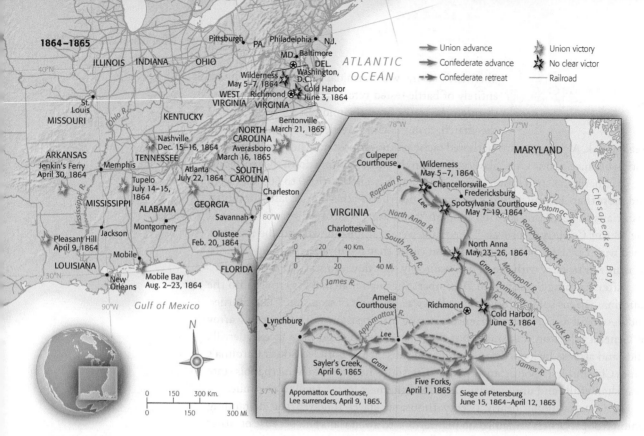

MAP 13.6
The War in Virginia

At great cost, Grant hammered away at Lee's army until the weakened southern forces finally surrendered at Appomattox Court House.

Source: Copyright © Cengage Learning 2015

Virginia's Bloody Soil

Intent on capturing Richmond, throughout spring and summer 1864, Grant hurled his troops at Lee's army and suffered appalling losses: almost eighteen thousand casualties in the Battle of the Wilderness; more than eight thousand at Spotsylvania; and twelve thousand in just hours at Cold Harbor (see Map 13.6).

Before the assault at Cold Harbor, Union troops pinned scraps of paper bearing their names to their backs, certain they would be mowed down as they rushed Lee's trenches. In four weeks in May and June, Grant lost as many men as were enrolled in Lee's entire army. From early May until July, when Union forces fought from forests west of Fredericksburg to Petersburg, south of Richmond, the two armies engaged each other nearly every day. Wagon trains carrying thousands of Union wounded crawled back toward Washington.

Undaunted, Grant kept up the pressure. Although costly, these battles enabled eventual victory: Lee's army shrank until offensive action was no longer possible, while Grant's army kept replenishing itself with new recruits. The siege of Petersburg, with the armies facing each other in miles of trenches, lasted throughout winter 1864–1865.

Surrender at Appomattox

With the numerical superiority of Grant's army now greater than two to one, Confederate defeat was inevitable. On April 2, Lee abandoned Richmond and Petersburg. On April 9, he surrendered at **Appomattox Court House**. Grant treated his rival respectfully and

Appomattox Court House
Site of Lee's surrender to Grant, marking the end of the Civil War.

paroled the defeated troops, allowing cavalrymen to keep their horses. Within weeks, Johnston surrendered to Sherman in North Carolina, and Davis, who fled Richmond, was captured in Georgia. The war was over. The North rejoiced, and most southerners fell into despair.

Lincoln lived to see but a few days of the war's aftermath. On the evening of April 14, he accompanied his wife to Ford's Theatre in Washington. There John Wilkes Booth, an embittered southern sympathizer, shot the president in the head at point-blank range. Lincoln died the next day. Twelve days later, troops tracked and killed Booth. Relief at the war's end mingled with a renewed sense of loss and anxiety about the future.

Financial Tally

Property damage and financial costs were enormous, though difficult to tally. U.S. loans and taxes during the conflict totaled almost $3 billion, and interest on the war debt was $2.8 billion. The Confederacy borrowed over $2 billion but lost far more in the destruction of homes, crops, livestock, and other property. Union troops looted factories and put two-thirds of the South's railroad system out of service.

Estimates of the war's total cost exceed $20 billion—five times the total expenditures of the federal government from its creation until 1861. By 1865, the federal government's spending soared to twenty times the prewar level and accounted for over 26 percent of the gross national product. Many changes were more or less permanent, as wartime measures left the government more deeply involved in manufacturing, banking, and transportation.

Death Toll and Its Impact

More men died in the Civil War than in all other American wars combined until Vietnam. The total number of casualties exceeded 1 million—frightfully high for a nation of 31 million people. Using microdata samples from the 1850, 1860, 1870, and 1880 censuses, a recent study has raised the official count of 620,000 dead in the Civil War to approximately 750,000. Scholarship also shows that we have never been able to carefully account for civilian casualties in the war, nor for the possibly one in four freed people who died in the process of achieving their own freedom. Not all died on the battlefield: 30,218 northerners died in southern prisons, and 25,976 Confederates died in Union prisons.

The scale and the anonymous nature of death overwhelmed American culture and led to the establishment of national cemeteries, where the large majority of the fallen were buried without identification. The desperate urge to memorialize individual soldiers in this war, writes historian Drew Faust, stemmed from "the anguish of wives, parents, siblings, and children who found undocumented, unconfirmed, and unrecognizable loss intolerable."

Summary

The Civil War altered American society forever. Although precise figures on enlistments are unavailable, it appears that 700,000 to 800,000 men served in the Confederate armies. Possibly 2.3 million served in the Union armies. All were taken from home, family; their lives, if they survived, were permanently altered. During the war, northern and southern women took on new roles to manage the hardships of the home front and support the war.

Abraham Lincoln's Second Inaugural Address

Historian Don Fehrenbacher wrote that "some of Lincoln's words have acquired transcendent meaning as contributions to the permanent literary treasure of the nation." How is this so with the short oration Lincoln delivered at the Capitol on March 4, 1865?

In a 701-word prose poem at his second inauguration, Lincoln probed the tragedy of the Civil War and interpreted its ultimate meanings. The first paragraph acknowledges the "progress of our arms" over four years of war. In the second paragraph, Lincoln entwines North and South in a mutual fate, but suggests responsibility for which side "would make war," and which side "would accept war," and leaves it to posterity: "And the war came."

Then, Lincoln offers a theological-historical explanation of the war that still resonates today in how Americans interpret this historical turning point. Lincoln declares that "all knew ... somehow" slavery was the "cause" of the conflict. Both sides appealed to the "same God." But Lincoln imagined slavery as an "offence" that came "in the providence of God," and brought "this mighty scourge of war" as its awful price.

Suddenly, in rhetoric unusual for presidential inaugurals, Lincoln assumed the prophet's mantle: "Yet if God wills that it [the war] continue, until all the wealth piled by the bond-man's two hundred and fifty years of unrequited toil shall be sunk, and until every drop of blood drawn by the lash, shall be paid by another drawn with the sword, as was said three thousand years ago, so still it must be said the judgments of the Lord are true and righteous altogether."

Famously, Lincoln ended by declaring "malice toward none ... charity for all" the healing balm for the "nation's wounds." Whether Lincoln was the nation's healer or its war maker who would demand any sacrifice to restore the Union and destroy slavery has animated the study of his personal story. The legacy of the Civil War, and Lincoln's place in it, are forever enmeshed in interpretations of this oratorical masterpiece.

Link to the text of Abraham Lincoln's Second Inaugural Address

Industrialization and economic enterprises grew exponentially with the war. Ordinary citizens' futures were increasingly tied to huge organizations. Under Republican leadership, the federal government expanded its power to preserve the Union and extend freedom. A social revolution and government authority emancipated the slaves. It was unclear at war's end how or whether the nation would use its power to protect former slaves' rights. The war left many unanswered questions: How would white southerners, embittered and impoverished, respond to efforts to reconstruct the nation? How would the country care for the maimed, the orphans, the widows? What would be the place of black men and women in American life?

In the West, a second civil war resulted in conquest of southwestern Indians by U.S. troops and land-hungry settlers. On the diplomatic front, the Union government managed to keep Great Britain and other foreign powers out of the war. Dissent played a crucial role in the Confederacy's collapse.

In the Civil War, Americans experienced a dramatic transformation. White southerners experienced a defeat that few other Americans ever faced. Blacks were moving proudly but anxiously from slavery to freedom. White northerners were self-conscious victors in a massive war for the nation's existence and for new definitions of freedom. The war would leave a compelling memory in American hearts and minds for generations.

Chapter Review

Election of 1860 and Secession Crisis

What were the issues leading to secession and the dissolution of the Union?

Abraham Lincoln's contested election in 1860, in which voters divided along regional lines, along with the inability to reach a compromise on the extension of slavery in the territories, ultimately fueled the movement to secede. Lincoln, the Republican candidate, won by carrying the North and winning in the electoral college, but for the first time in American history, the losing side (with its large southern base) refused to accept an election result. When President Lincoln rejected a compromise that would divide the territories into slave and free at the Missouri Compromise line (36°30′), hopes for preventing secession collapsed. South Carolina passed the first secession ordinance in December 1860; Mississippi, Florida, Alabama, Georgia, Louisiana, and Texas followed. A month after Lincoln's inauguration, these states established their own national capitol in Montgomery, Alabama, dubbing themselves the Confederate States of America.

America Goes to War, 1861–1862

What was the impact of the North's naval victories for enslaved peoples along the southern coast?

In essence, they triggered a revolution in slave society. As federal gunboats drew near the South Carolina coast, planters fled their land. Confederate soldiers tried to round up slaves, who saw the arrival of the Union navy as a possible door to their freedom. Thousands of slaves celebrating by rebelling against the symbols of slavery: they broke cotton gins and stole clothing and furniture from masters' homes. Many ran away to join the Union army. While the Union initially did not acknowledge the slaves as free—and instead labeled them war "contraband"—it did put them to work for the Union army.

War Transforms the South

What happened to the South's embrace of state sovereignty during the war?

The state power that had been so sacred to the South before the war was forced—by the need to mobilize—to yield to a central authority. To maintain the war effort, the Confederacy centralized its operations, troops, and supplies, seeing the efforts of individual states as likely to fragment the greater cause. President Jefferson Davis took a firm leadership role toward the Confederate Congress and urged state governments to require farmers to switch from cash crops to food production. The central government assumed control of the southern economy and nearly complete control of the railroads. Much to the dismay of many secessionists, the southern bureaucracy ironically became larger than its northern counterpart and provided new employment opportunities for women.

Wartime Northern Economy and Society

How did the war affect workers in the North?

Northern urban and industrial workers did not fare as well as business owners and merchants during the war. While they enjoyed more job opportunities and higher wages as the wartime economy grew, inflation devoured much of their earnings. Consumer prices rose at nearly twice the rate of workers' salary increases, and workers' families saw their standard of living decline. They also lost job security as employers replaced workers with new laborsaving machines or cheap immigrant workers. Workers in several industries responded by starting unions or going out on strike, but manufacturers fought back with blacklists or by requiring workers to sign "yellow dog" contracts promising not to join a union.

The Advent of Emancipation

Why did Lincoln and Davis both avoid addressing the slavery issue in the early days of the war?

Davis feared the issue would increase class conflict between slaveless yeoman farmers and slave-owning plantation owners in the South. Instead, he preferred to say that southerners were fighting to preserve their constitutional liberties against northerners and for their independence. Lincoln avoided the topic of slavery to keep from antagonizing the Union's border states, whose loyalty he sought to preserve. He also hoped to inspire a pro-Union majority in the South that might push the region back to the national fold. Avoiding the topic was also politically expedient, since no consensus on slavery existed among Republicans or northerners early in the war—some were strident abolitionists, while others were racists who wanted to protect whites from both the southern Slave Power and the competition of slave labor.

The Soldiers' War

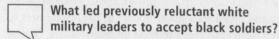
What led previously reluctant white military leaders to accept black soldiers?

At the beginning of the war, the Union army was racist, and many soldiers did not want to fight with blacks, whom they considered inferior. They tolerated them only as black recruits who would do the jobs white soldiers disliked. White officers' opinions changed when they witnessed the bravery and determination of the segregated black units they led. Black soldiers, too, felt they were fighting prejudice through their military successes, thereby proving their manhood and legitimate claim to freedom. Black soldiers' willingness to die in battle also earned the respect of white men. Many black soldiers who fought for white officers did forge deep ties, especially members of the ill-fated Fifty-fourth Massachusetts Regiment.

1863: The Tide of Battle Turns

What turned the tide of war toward Union victory?

Battles at Vicksburg and Gettysburg changed the course of war from a possible Confederate victory to assured victory for the Union. Vicksburg was the last major fortification on the Mississippi River in southern hands, while Gettysburg marked Lee's attempts to break the Union line and invade the North. Both battles produced heavy losses but also left the Confederate army divided, so that west of the Mississippi General E. Kirby Smith operated alone, while Louisiana, Tennessee, and Mississippi were vulnerable to invasions. After Gettysburg, there were no more Confederate offensive moves; severely weakened, the Confederate army could only act defensively.

Disunity: South, North, and West

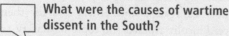
What were the causes of wartime dissent in the South?

People across class lines increasingly disliked the actions taken by their government. Planters opposed new taxation and the impressments of their slaves to build fortifications. They also resented that Confederate commanders burned planters' cotton stores as Union soldiers

advanced. People universally rejected the increasing size and power of the central government in Richmond and conscription for military service. Many people faced food shortages and refused to comply with conscription, taxation, or the demand to provide food for soldiers. The ability of wealthy people to buy their way out of military service by hiring substitutes fueled resentment among soldiers, some of whom abandoned the army.

1864–1865: The Final Test of Wills

Why was it so crucial to northern military strategy that Europe remain neutral during the Civil War?

Lincoln believed that if foreign countries recognized the Confederacy, that action would legitimize what Lincoln considered an illegal rebellion. He also feared that foreign recognition could lead to military and financial aid that would facilitate a Confederate victory and ultimate independence. The president knew that both England and France would gain by a divided America, but France would not act without Britain, and Britain was not making a move until there were major southern battlefield successes. While England's relationship with southern textile mills made the Confederacy hopeful for an alliance, Britain's large cotton surplus and new supplies in India, Egypt, and Brazil kept it from doing more than selling arms and supplies or offering loans.

Suggestions for Further Reading

Stephen V. Ash, *When the Yankees Came: Conflict and Chaos in the Occupied South* (1995)

Edward L. Ayers, *In the Presence of Mine Enemies: War in the Heart of America, 1859–1863* (2002)

Ira Berlin et al., eds., *Freedom: A Documentary History of Emancipation, 1861–1867,* 3 vols. (1979–1982)

David W. Blight, *Frederick Douglass' Civil War: Keeping Faith in Jubilee* (1989)

Alice Fahs, *The Imagined Civil War: Popular Literature of the North and South* (2001)

Drew G. Faust, *This Republic of Suffering: Death and the American Civil War* (2008)

Gary W. Gallagher, *The Confederate War* (1997)

J. David Hacker, "A Census-Based Count of the Civil War Dead," *Civil War History,* (Dec. 2011).

Chandra Manning, *What This Cruel War Was Over: Soldiers, Slavery, and the Civil War* (2007)

James M. McPherson, *Battle Cry of Freedom: The Civil War Era* (1987)

Philip S. Paludan, *"A People's Contest": The Union and the Civil War* (1989)

Mark R. Wilson, *The Business of Civil War: Military Mobilization and the State, 1861–1865* (2006)

Reconstruction: An Unfinished Revolution

14

1865–1877

The lower half of secession's seedbed, Charleston, South Carolina, lay in ruin when most of the white population evacuated on February 18, 1865. A bombardment by Union forces around Charleston harbor destroyed many lovely, low-country planters' homes. Fires broke out everywhere. To many observers, the flames were the funeral pyres of a dying civilization.

Among the first Union troops to enter Charleston, the Twenty-first U.S. Colored Regiment received the city's surrender from its mayor. For black Charlestonians, who were mostly former slaves, this was a time to celebrate their freedom. Charleston's freedpeople converted Confederate ruin into a vision of Reconstruction based on Union victory and black liberation.

During the war's final year, Confederates transformed the planters' Race Course, a horse-racing track, and its famed Washington Jockey Club, into a prison. Kept outdoors in the interior of the track, 257 Union soldiers died of exposure and disease and were buried in a mass grave behind the grandstand. After the city fell, more than twenty black workmen reinterred the dead in marked graves. On the archway over the cemetery's entrance they painted the inscription "Martyrs of the Race Course."

On the morning of May 1, 1865, ten thousand people marched around the planters' Race Course, led by three thousand children carrying roses and singing "John Brown's Body." Black women with flowers and wreaths came next, followed by black men. The parade concluded with black and white Union regiments and white missionaries and teachers. At the gravesite, five black ministers read from scripture, and a black children's choir sang "America," "The Star-Spangled Banner," and Negro spirituals. After the ceremony, the crowd retired to the Race Course for speeches, picnics, and military festivities.

African Americans founded this "Decoration Day"—now Memorial Day—to remember those lost in battle. In their vision, they were creating the Independence Day of a Second American Revolution.

Chapter Outline

Wartime Reconstruction
Lincoln's 10 Percent Plan | Congress and the Wade-Davis Bill | Thirteenth Amendment | Freedmen's Bureau | Ruins and Enmity

The Meanings of Freedom
The Feel of Freedom | Reunion of African American Families | Blacks' Search for Independence | Freedpeople's Desire for Land | Black Embrace of Education | Growth of Black Churches | Rise of the Sharecropping System

VISUALIZING THE PAST *Sharecropping: Enslaved to Debt*

Johnson's Reconstruction Plan
Andrew Johnson of Tennessee | Johnson's Racial Views | Johnson's Pardon Policy | Presidential Reconstruction | Black Codes

The Congressional Reconstruction Plan
The Radicals | Congress Versus Johnson | Fourteenth Amendment | The South's and Johnson's Defiance | Reconstruction Acts of 1867–1868 | Failure of Land Redistribution | Constitutional Crisis | Impeachment of President Johnson | Election of 1868 | Fifteenth Amendment

Politics and Reconstruction in the South
White Resistance | Black Voters and the Southern Republican Party | Triumph of Republican Governments | Industrialization and Mill Towns | Republicans and Racial Equality | Myth of "Negro Rule" |

Carpetbaggers and Scalawags |
*Tax Policy and Corruption as Political
Wedges* | *Ku Klux Klan*

Retreat from Reconstruction
Political Implications of Klan Terrorism |
*Industrial Expansion and Reconstruction
in the North* | *Liberal Republican Revolt* |
General Amnesty | *The West, Race, and
Reconstruction* | *Foreign Expansion* |
Judicial Retreat from Reconstruction |
*Disputed Election of 1876 and
Compromise of 1877*

LINKS TO THE WORLD *The "Back to Africa"
Movement*

LEGACY FOR A PEOPLE AND A NATION
The Lost Cause

SUMMARY

The Civil War and its aftermath wrought unprecedented changes in American society, law, and politics, but economic power, racism, and judicial conservatism limited Reconstruction's revolutionary potential. The nation had to determine the nature of federal-state relations, whether confiscated land could be redistributed, and how to bring justice to freedpeople and aggrieved white southerners. Americans also had to heal psychologically from a bloody fratricidal war. How they would negotiate the relationship between healing and justice would determine the fate of Reconstruction.

The turmoil of Reconstruction was most evident in national politics. Lincoln's successor, Andrew Johnson, fought with Congress over Reconstruction policies. Although a southerner, Johnson disliked the South's wealthy planters, and his first acts suggested that he would be tough on "traitors." Before late 1865, however, Johnson became the protector of white southern interests.

Johnson imagined a lenient and rapid "restoration" of the South to the Union rather than the fundamental "reconstruction" that Republican congressmen favored. Between 1866 and 1868, the president and Republican congressional leadership disagreed. Before it ended, Congress impeached the president, enfranchised freedmen, and gave them a role in reconstructing the South. The nation also adopted the Fourteenth and Fifteenth Amendments, ensuring equal protection of the law, citizenship, and universal manhood suffrage. But the cause of equal rights for African Americans fell almost as fast as it had risen.

By 1869, the Ku Klux Klan employed violence to thwart Reconstruction and undermine black freedom. As white Democrats in the South took over state governments, they encountered little opposition. Moreover, the wartime industrial boom created new opportunities and priorities. The West drew American resources like never before. Political corruption became a nationwide scandal, and bribery part of business.

The white South's desire to reclaim control of its states and of race relations overwhelmed the national interest in stopping it. Thus, Reconstruction became a revolution eclipsed, leaving legacies with which the nation has struggled ever since.

As you read this chapter, keep the following questions in mind:

• **Should the Reconstruction era be considered the Second American Revolution? By what criteria should we make such a judgment?**

• **What were the origins and meanings of the Fourteenth Amendment in the 1860s? What is its significance today?**

• **Reconstruction is judged to have "ended" in 1877. Over the course of the 1870s, what caused its end?**

Chronology

1865	Johnson begins rapid and lenient Reconstruction
	White southern governments pass restrictive black codes
	Congress refuses to seat southern representatives
	Thirteenth Amendment ratified, abolishing slavery
1866	Congress passes Civil Rights Act and renewal of Freedmen's Bureau over Johnson's veto
	Congress approves Fourteenth Amendment
	In *Ex parte Milligan*, the Supreme Court reasserts its influence
1867	Congress passes First Reconstruction Act and Tenure of Office Act
	Constitutional conventions called in southern states
1868	House impeaches and Senate acquits Johnson
	Most southern states readmitted to Union under Radical plan
	Fourteenth Amendment ratified
	Grant elected president
1869	Congress approves Fifteenth Amendment (ratified in 1870)
	Sharecropping takes hold across a cash-poor southern economy
1871	Congress passes second Enforcement Act and Ku Klux Klan Act
	Treaty with England settles *Alabama* claims
1872	Amnesty Act frees almost all remaining Confederates from restrictions on holding office
	Grant reelected
1873	*Slaughter-House* cases limit power of Fourteenth Amendment
	Panic of 1873 leads to widespread unemployment and labor strife
1874	Democrats win majority in House of Representatives
1875	Several Grant appointees indicted for corruption
	Congress passes weak Civil Rights Act
	Democratic Party increases control of southern states with white supremacy campaigns
1876	*U.S. v. Cruikshank* further weakens Fourteenth Amendment
	Presidential election disputed
1877	Congress elects Hayes president

Wartime Reconstruction

Which two political acts recognized the centrality of slavery to the war?

How best to reconstruct the Union was an issue as early as 1863, well before the war ended. Four vexing problems compelled early thinking and would haunt the Reconstruction era. One, who would rule in the South once it was defeated? Two, who would rule in the federal government—Congress or the president? Three, what were the dimensions of black freedom, and what rights under law would freedmen enjoy? And four, would Reconstruction be a preservation of the old republic or a second Revolution, reinventing a new republic?

Lincoln's 10 Percent Plan

Abraham Lincoln had never been anti-southern. His fear was that the war would collapse into guerrilla warfare by surviving Confederates. Lincoln insisted on leniency for southern soldiers once they surrendered. In his Second Inaugural Address, delivered a month before his assassination, Lincoln promised "malice toward none; with charity for all."

Lincoln planned early for a swift and moderate Reconstruction process. In his December 1863 "Proclamation of Amnesty and Reconstruction," he proposed replacing majority rule with "loyal rule" to reconstruct southern state governments.

He suggested pardons for ex-Confederates except the highest-ranking military and civilian officers. Once 10 percent of a given state's voting population in the 1860 general election had taken an oath to the United States and established a government, the new state would be recognized. Lincoln did not consult Congress in these plans, and "loyal" assemblies were created in Louisiana, Tennessee, and Arkansas in 1864, states largely occupied by Union troops on which they depended for survival.

Congress and the Wade-Davis Bill

Congress was hostile toward Lincoln's moves to readmit southern states prematurely. Radical Republicans, proponents of emancipation and of aggressively defeating the South, regarded the 10 percent plan a "mere mockery" of democracy. Led by Pennsylvania congressman Thaddeus Stevens and Massachusetts senator Charles Sumner, congressional Republicans proposed a harsher approach. Stevens advocated a "conquered provinces" theory, arguing that southerners organized as a foreign nation to war on the United States and, by secession, destroyed their statehood status. They therefore must be treated as "conquered foreign lands" and returned to the status of "unorganized territories" before applying for readmission.

In July 1864, the Wade-Davis bill, sponsored by Ohio senator Benjamin Wade and Maryland congressman Henry W. Davis, emerged from Congress with three specific conditions for southern readmission.

1. It demanded a "majority" of white male citizens participate in the creation of a new government.
2. To vote or be a delegate to constitutional conventions, men had to take an "iron-clad" oath (declaring that they had never aided the Confederate war effort).
3. All officers above the rank of lieutenant and all civil officials in the Confederacy would be disfranchised and deemed "not a citizen of the United States."

Lincoln pocket-vetoed the bill and issued a conciliatory proclamation that he would not commit to any "one plan" of Reconstruction.

This exchange occurred when the outcome of the war and Lincoln's reelection were still in doubt. On August 5, Radical Republicans issued the "Wade-Davis Manifesto" to newspapers. It accused Lincoln of usurpation of presidential powers and disgraceful leniency toward an eventually conquered South. Lincoln saw Reconstruction as a means of weakening the Confederacy and winning the war; the Radicals saw it as a transformation of the nation's political and racial order.

Thirteenth Amendment

In early 1865, Congress and Lincoln joined in two important measures that recognized slavery's centrality to the war. On January 31, Congress passed the **Thirteenth Amendment**, which abolished involuntary servitude and declared that Congress shall have the power to enforce this outcome by "appropriate legislation." When the measure passed by 119 to 56, just 2 votes more than the necessary two-thirds, supporters in Congress rejoiced.

Thirteenth Amendment The constitutional amendment that abolished slavery; passed by Congress in 1865.

The Thirteenth Amendment emerged from a congressional debate and considerable petitioning and public advocacy. One of the first and most remarkable petitions for a constitutional amendment abolishing slavery was submitted in 1864 by Elizabeth Cady Stanton, Susan B. Anthony, and the Women's Loyal National League. Women throughout the Union accumulated thousands of signatures, even venturing into staunchly pro-Confederate regions of Kentucky and Missouri to secure supporters. It was a long road from the Emancipation Proclamation to the Thirteenth Amendment—through treacherous constitutional theory about individual "property rights," beliefs that the sacred document ought never to be altered, and partisan politics. But the logic of winning the war by crushing slavery, and securing a new beginning for the nation, prevailed. This story again gained attention in the 2012 movie, *Lincoln,* directed by Steven Spielberg.

Freedmen's Bureau

On March 3, 1865, Congress created the Bureau of Refugees, Freedmen, and Abandoned Lands—the **Freedmen's Bureau**, an unprecedented agency of social uplift. With thousands of refugees in the South, the government continued what private freedmen's aid societies started in 1862. In its four-year existence, the Freedmen's Bureau supplied food and medical services, built several thousand schools and some colleges, negotiated several hundred thousand employment contracts between freedmen and former masters, and managed confiscated land.

Freedmen's Bureau Created by Congress in March 1865, this agency had responsibility for the relief, education, and employment of former slaves as well as white refugees.

Link to the congressional act establishing the Freedmen's Bureau

The bureau was a controversial aspect of Reconstruction. Southern whites hated it, and politicians divided over its constitutionality. Some bureau agents were devoted to freedmen's rights; others exploited the chaos of the postwar South. The war prompted an eternal question of republics: what are the social welfare obligations of the state toward its people, and what do people owe their governments in return? Apart from conquest and displacement of the eastern Indians, Americans were inexperienced at the Freedmen's Bureau's task—social reform through military occupation.

Ruins and Enmity

In 1865, America was a land with ruins from the war. Some cities lay in rubble, large stretches of the southern countryside were depopulated and defoliated, and thousands of people, white and black, were refugees. Of the approximately 18,300,000 rations distributed across the South in the Freedmen's Bureau's first three years, 5,230,000 went to destitute whites.

In October 1865, after a five-month imprisonment in Boston, former Confederate vice president Alexander H. Stephens rode a train southward. When he reached northern Georgia, his native state, he expressed shock: "War has left a terrible impression…. Fences gone, fields all a-waste, houses burnt." Every northern traveler encountered hatred among white southerners. A North Carolina innkeeper told a journalist that Yankees had killed his sons, burned his house, and stolen his slaves, and left him "one inestimable privilege…to hate'em."

The Meanings of Freedom

How did blacks exert their newfound freedom?

Black southerners entered life after slavery with hope and circumspection. A Texas man recalled his father's words, "Our forever was going to be spent living among the Southerners, after they got licked." Often the changes people valued most were personal—alterations in employer or living arrangements.

The Feel of Freedom

For former slaves, Reconstruction meant a chance to explore freedom. Former slaves remembered singing into the night after federal troops, who confirmed rumors of their emancipation, reached their plantations. One angry grandmother dropped her hoe and confronted her mistress. "I'm free!" she yelled. "Yes, I'm free! Ain't got to work for you no more!" Another man recalled that he and others "started on the move," either to search for family members or just to move on.

As slaves, they learned to expect hostility from white people; they did not presume it would instantly disappear. Many freedpeople evaluated potential employers cautiously. After searching for better circumstances, a majority of blacks eventually settled as agricultural workers back on their former farms or plantations. But they relocated their houses and tried to control the conditions of their labor.

Reunion of African American Families

Throughout the South, former slaves focused on reuniting their families, separated during slavery by sale or hardship, and during the war by dislocation. By relying on the black community for help and by placing ads in black newspapers into the 1880s, some succeeded, while others searched in vain.

Husbands and wives who belonged to different masters established homes together to raise their own children. When her old master claimed a right to whip her children, a mother replied, "he warn't goin' to brush none of her chilluns no more."

Blacks' Search for Independence

Many black people wanted to minimize contact with whites because, as Reverend Garrison Frazier told General Sherman in January 1865, "There is a prejudice against us...that will take years to get over." Blacks abandoned slave quarters and fanned out to distant corners of the land they worked. Some described moving "across the creek." Other rural dwellers established small, all-black settlements that still exist along the South's back roads.

Freedpeople's Desire for Land

In addition to a fair employer, freedpeople most wanted to own land, which represented self-sufficiency and compensation for generations of bondage. General Sherman's special Field Order Number 15, issued in February 1865, set aside 400,000 acres of land in the Sea Islands for settlement of freedpeople. Hope swelled among ex-slaves as forty-acre plots and mules were promised to them. But President Johnson ordered them removed in October and the land returned to its original owners under army enforcement. Most members of both political parties opposed land redistribution to the freedmen. Even northern reformers who administered the Sea Islands during the war showed little sympathy for black aspirations. The former Sea Island slaves wanted small, self-sufficient farms. Northern soldiers, officials, and missionaries brought education and aid to the freedmen but insisted that they grow cotton for the competitive market. The U.S. government eventually sold thousands of acres in the Sea Islands, 90 percent of which went to wealthy investors from the North.

Black Embrace of Education

Blacks hungered for education that previously belonged only to whites. With freedom, they started schools and filled dirt-floor classrooms day and night. Children brought infants to school with them, and adults attended at night or after "the crops were laid by." Despite their poverty, many blacks paid tuition, typically $1 or $1.50 a month, which constituted major portions of a person's agricultural wages and totaled more than $1 million by 1870.

In its brief life, the Freedmen's Bureau founded over four thousand schools, and northern reformers established others funded by private philanthropy. The Yankee schoolmarm—dedicated, selfless, and religious—became an agent of progress in many southern communities. More than 600,000 African Americans were enrolled in elementary school by 1877.

Blacks and their white allies also established colleges and universities. The American Missionary Association founded seven colleges, including Fisk University and Atlanta University, between 1866 and 1869. The Freedmen's Bureau helped establish Howard University in Washington, D.C., and northern religious groups, such as the Methodists, Baptists, and Congregationalists, supported seminaries and teachers' colleges.

During Reconstruction, African American leaders often were highly educated members of the prewar elite of free people of color. Francis Cardozo, who held various offices in South Carolina, attended universities in Scotland and England. P. B. S. Pinchback, who became lieutenant governor of Louisiana, was the son of a planter who sent him to school in Cincinnati.

Growth of Black Churches

Freed from slavery's restrictions, blacks could build their own institutions. Slavery's secret churches became visible; in communities throughout the South, ex-slaves "started a brush arbor," which was "a sort of…shelter with leaves for a roof," where freed men and women worshipped.

Within a few years, branches of the Methodist and Baptist denominations attracted most southern black Christians. By 1877, in South Carolina, the African Methodist Episcopal (A.M.E.) Church had a thousand ministers, forty-four thousand members, and a school of theology, while the A.M.E. Zion Church had forty-five thousand members. In these churches, some of which became the wealthiest

Churches became a center of African American life, both social and political, during and after Reconstruction. Churches large and small, like this one, Faith Memorial Church in Hagley Landing, South Carolina, became the first black-owned institutions for the postfreedom generation.

Private Collection/Picture Research Consultants & Archives

and most autonomous institutions in black life, the freedpeople created enduring communities.

Rise of the
Sharecropping System

Since former slaves lacked money to buy land, they preferred the next best thing: renting it. But the South had few sources of credit, and few whites would rent to blacks. Black farmers and white landowners therefore turned to **sharecropping**, a system in which the landlord or a merchant "furnished" food and supplies, such as draft animals and seed to farmers, and received as payment a portion of the crop. White landowners and black farmers bargained with one another. As the system matured during the 1870s and 1880s, most sharecroppers worked "on halves"—half for the owner and half for themselves.

sharecropping A system where landowners and former slaves managed a new arrangement, with tenants paying landowners a portion of their crops for the use of the land on which they farmed, thereby usually ending up in permanent debt.

Sharecropping, which materialized by 1868, originated as a compromise between former slaves and landowners. It eased landowners' problems with cash and credit, and provided a permanent, dependent labor force; blacks accepted it because it freed them from supervision. But sharecropping proved disastrous. Owners and merchants developed a monopoly of control over the agricultural economy, as sharecroppers faced ever-increasing debt.

The fundamental problem was that southern farmers still concentrated on cotton. At the same time, freed black women valued making independent choices about gender roles and family and preferred domestic chores over picking cotton. Even as the South recovered its prewar share of British cotton purchases, cotton prices began a long decline, as world demand declined.

Thus, southern agriculture slipped into depression. Black sharecroppers struggled under growing debt that bound them to landowners and merchants almost as oppressively as slavery. Many white farmers gradually lost their land and became sharecroppers. By Reconstruction's end, over one-third of southern farms were worked by sharecropping tenants, white and black.

Johnson's Reconstruction Plan

What was Johnson's vision for Reconstruction?

Many people expected Reconstruction under President Andrew Johnson to be harsh. Throughout his career in Tennessee, he criticized wealthy planters and championed the small farmers. When an assassin's bullet thrust Johnson into the presidency, former slave owners feared Johnson would deal sternly with the South. When northern Radicals suggested the exile or execution of ten or twelve leading rebels, Johnson replied, "How are you going to pick out so small a number?"

Andrew Johnson
of Tennessee

Like Lincoln, Johnson moved from obscurity to power. With no education, he became a tailor's apprentice. But from 1829, while in his early twenties, he held nearly every office in Tennessee politics: alderman, state representative, congressman, two terms as governor, and U.S. senator by 1857. Although elected as a Democrat, Johnson was the only senator from a seceded state who refused to leave the Union. Lincoln appointed him war governor of Tennessee in 1862; hence his symbolic place on the ticket in the president's 1864 bid for reelection.

Visualizing THE PAST

Sharecropping: Enslaved to Debt

Sharecropping became an oppressive system in the postwar South. A new labor structure that began as a compromise between freedmen who wanted independence and landowners who wanted a stable workforce evolved into a method of working on "halves," where tenants owed endless debts to the furnishing merchants, who owned plantation stores like this one, photographed in Mississippi in 1868. Merchants recorded in ledger books, like the one at right, the debts that few sharecroppers were able to repay. Why did both former slaves and former slave owners initially find sharecropping an agreeable, if difficult, new labor arrangement? What were the short- and long-term consequences of the sharecropping system for the freedpeople and for the southern economy?

This Mississippi plantation store, shown in 1868, is a typical example of the new institution of the furnishing merchant and its power over postslavery agriculture in the South.

Furnishing merchants kept ledger books such as this for decades; they became the record of how sharecroppers fell deeper in debt from year to year, and "owed their soul" to the country store.

Although a Unionist, Johnson's political beliefs made him an old Jacksonian Democrat. Before the war, he supported tax-funded public schools and homestead legislation, fashioning himself as a champion of the common man. Johnson advocated limited government. His philosophy toward Reconstruction? "The Constitution as it is, and the Union as it was."

Through 1865, Johnson alone controlled Reconstruction policy, for Congress recessed shortly before he became president and did not reconvene until December. Johnson formed new state governments in the South by using his power to grant pardons and offered terms to former Confederates.

Johnson's Racial Views

Johnson had owned house slaves, although he was never a planter. He accepted emancipation, but believed that black suffrage could never be imposed on southern states by the federal government. This set him on a collision course with the Radicals. On race, Johnson was a white supremacist. He declared in his 1867 annual message that blacks possessed less "capacity for government than any other race of people...wherever they have been left to their own devices they have shown a constant tendency to relapse into barbarism."

Such racial views influenced Johnson's policies. Where whites were concerned, however, Johnson proposed rules that would keep the wealthy planter class at least temporarily out of power.

Johnson's Pardon Policy

To gain amnesty or pardon, white southerners were required to swear an oath of loyalty, but Johnson refused this option to former federal officials, high-ranking Confederate officers, and political leaders or graduates of West Point or Annapolis who joined the Confederacy. He also barred ex-Confederates whose taxable property was worth more than $20,000. These individuals had to apply personally to the president for pardon. The president, it seemed, wanted revenge on the old planter elite and to promote a new yeoman leadership.

Johnson appointed provisional governors, who began Reconstruction by calling state constitutional conventions. The delegates had to draft new constitutions that eliminated slavery and invalidated secession. After ratification, new governments could be elected, and the states restored to the Union. But only southerners who had taken the oath of amnesty and were eligible voters when the state seceded could participate. Thus, unpardoned whites and former slaves were ineligible.

Presidential Reconstruction

The old white leadership proved resilient; prominent Confederates won elections and secured appointive offices. Then Johnson started pardoning planters and leading rebels. By September 1865, hundreds were issued in a single day. These pardons, plus the return of planters' abandoned lands, restored the old elite to power and made Johnson seem the South's champion.

Why did Johnson allow the planters to regain power? He may have enjoyed turning proud planters into pardon seekers. He also sought rapid Reconstruction to deny the Radicals any opportunity for thorough racial and political changes in the South. Johnson needed southern support in the 1866 elections; hence, he declared Reconstruction complete only eight months after Appomattox. In December 1865, many Confederate congressmen claimed seats in the U.S. Congress, including former Confederate vice president Alexander Stephens, who was now Georgia's senator-elect.

Black Codes

To define the status of freed men and women and control their labor, some legislatures revised the slave codes by substituting the word *freedmen* for *slaves*. The new black codes compelled former slaves to carry passes, observe a curfew, and live in housing provided by a landowner. Stiff vagrancy laws and restrictive labor contracts bound freedpeople to plantations, and "anti-enticement" laws punished anyone luring these workers to other employment. State-supported schools and orphanages excluded blacks.

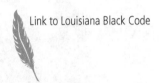

Link to Louisiana Black Code

It seemed to northerners that the South was intent on returning African Americans to servility and that Johnson's Reconstruction policy held no one responsible for the war. Thus, the Republican majority in Congress halted Johnson's plan. The House and Senate refused to admit newly elected southern representatives. Instead, they bluntly challenged the president's authority and established a joint committee to study a new direction for Reconstruction.

The Congressional Reconstruction Plan

What made Radical Reconstruction different from Johnson's plan?

The Constitution mentioned neither secession nor reunion, but it gave Congress the primary role in admitting states. Moreover, the Constitution declared that the United States shall guarantee to each state a "republican form of government." This provision, legislators believed, gave them the authority to devise Reconstruction policies.

The key question: What had rebellion done to the relationship between southern states and the Union? Congressmen who favored vigorous Reconstruction measures argued that the war had broken the Union and that the South was subject to the victor's will. Moderate congressmen held that the states forfeited their rights through rebellion and thus came under congressional supervision.

The Radicals

Northern Democrats, weakened by their opposition to the war in its final year, denounced racial equality and supported Johnson's policies. Conservative Republicans, despite their party loyalty, favored a limited federal role in Reconstruction. Although a minority, Radical Republicans, led by Thaddeus Stevens, Charles Sumner, and George Julian, wanted to democratize the South, establish public education, and ensure freedpeople's rights. They favored black suffrage, supported some land confiscation and redistribution, and were willing to exclude the South from the Union for years to achieve their goals.

The Radicals brought a new civic vision; they wanted to create an activist federal government and the beginnings of racial equality. Many moderate Republicans,

Library of Congress

Photograph of Thaddeus Stevens, Republican congressman and staunch abolitionist from Pennsylvania, and leader of the "Radicals" during the creation of Reconstruction policies, from 1866 to 1868.

led by Lyman Trumbull, opposed Johnson's leniency but wanted to restrain the Radicals. They were, however, committed to federalizing the enforcement of civil, if not political, rights for freedmen.

With the 1866 elections looming, Johnson and the Democrats sabotaged the possibility of a conservative coalition by refusing to cooperate with conservative or moderate Republicans. They insisted that Reconstruction was over, that the new state governments were legitimate, and that southern representatives should be admitted to Congress. The Radicals' influence grew in proportion to Johnson's intransigence.

Congress Versus Johnson

Republicans believed they reached a compromise with Johnson in spring 1866. Under its terms, Johnson would modify his program by extending the Freedmen's Bureau for another year and passing a civil rights bill to counteract the black codes. This would force southern courts to practice equality under the scrutiny of the federal judiciary. Its provisions applied to public, not private, acts of discrimination. The Civil Rights Bill of 1866 was the first statutory definition of the rights of American citizens.

Johnson, however, destroyed the compromise by vetoing both bills (they became law when Congress overrode his veto). Because the civil rights bill defined U.S. citizens as native-born persons who were taxed, Johnson claimed it operated "in favor of the colored and against the white race."

Hope of presidential-congressional cooperation was dead. In 1866, newspapers reported daily violations of blacks' rights in the South and carried alarming accounts of antiblack violence. In Memphis, forty blacks were killed and twelve schools burned by white mobs, and in New Orleans, the toll was thirty-four African Americans dead and two hundred wounded. Violence convinced Republicans, and the northern public, that more needed to be done. A new Republican plan focused on the **Fourteenth Amendment** to the Constitution.

Fourteenth Amendment
Defined U.S. citizens as anyone born or naturalized in the United States, barred states from interfering with citizens' constitutional rights, and stated for the first time that voters must be male.

Fourteenth Amendment

Of the five sections of the Fourteenth Amendment, the first would have the greatest legal significance. It conferred citizenship on "all persons born or naturalized in the United States" and prohibited states from abridging their constitutional "privileges and immunities" (see the Appendix for the Constitution and all amendments). It also barred states from taking a person's life, liberty, or property "without due process of law" and from denying any person "equal protection of the laws." These phrases have become powerful guarantees of African Americans' civil rights—indeed, of the rights of all citizens, except for Indians, who were not granted citizenship rights until 1924.

Republicans almost universally agreed on the amendment's second and third sections. The fourth declared the Confederate debt null and void, and guaranteed the United States' war debt. Northerners rejected paying taxes to reimburse those who financed a rebellion, and business groups agreed on the necessity of upholding the U.S. government's credit, an element of the Fourteenth Amendment invoked in debates between congressional Republicans and the Obama administration over raising the federal "debt ceiling" in 2011 and 2013. The second and third sections barred Confederate leaders from holding state and federal office. Only Congress, by a two-thirds vote of each house, could remove the penalty. The amendment thus guaranteed some punishment for Confederate leaders.

The second section of the amendment also dealt with representation and embodied the compromises that produced the Constitution. Northerners disagreed about whether blacks should have the right to vote. Public will, North and South, lagged behind the egalitarianism of enactments that became new constitutional cornerstones. Many northern states still maintained black disfranchisement laws during Reconstruction.

Emancipation ended the three-fifths clause for the purpose of counting blacks, which would increase southern representation. Thus, the postwar South stood to gain power in Congress, and if white southerners did not allow blacks to vote, former secessionists would derive the political benefit from emancipation. So Republicans determined that, if a southern state did not grant black men the vote, their representation would be reduced proportionally and vice versa.

The Fourteenth Amendment specified for the first time that voters were "male." As such, it frustrated the women's rights movement. Advocates of women's equality worked with abolitionists for decades, often subordinating their cause to the slaves'. During the drafting of the Fourteenth Amendment, however, female activists such as Elizabeth Cady Stanton and Susan B. Anthony ended their alliance with abolitionists and fought for women, infusing new life into the women's rights movement. Other female activists, however, argued that it was "the Negro's hour." Many male former abolitionists were willing to delay woman suffrage to secure freedmen the vote in the South.

The South's and Johnson's Defiance

Johnson tried to block the Fourteenth Amendment. The president urged state legislatures in the South to vote against ratification, and all but Tennessee rejected the amendment by a wide margin.

To present his case to northerners, Johnson organized a National Union Convention. He boarded a special train for a "swing around the circle" that carried his message into the Northeast, Midwest, and back to Washington. Increasingly, audiences rejected his views, jeering at him. Johnson handed out American flags with thirty-six rather than twenty-five stars, declaring the Union restored. And, he labeled the Radicals "traitors" for attempting to take over Reconstruction.

MAP 14.1

The Reconstruction Act of 1867

This map shows the five military districts established when Congress passed the Reconstruction Act of 1867. As the dates within each state indicate, conservative Democratic forces quickly regained control of government in four southern states. So-called Radical Reconstruction was curtailed in most of the others as factions within the weakened Republican Party began to cooperate with conservative Democrats. Source: Copyright © Cengage Learning 2015

In the 1866 elections, Radicals and moderates whom Johnson denounced won reelection by large margins, and the Republican majority grew to two-thirds of both congressional houses. The North was clear: Johnson's policies of states' rights and white supremacy were giving the advantage to rebels and traitors. Thus Republican congressional leaders won a mandate to pursue their Reconstruction plan.

But nothing could be accomplished as long as the "Johnson governments" existed and the southern electorate remained exclusively white. Republicans resolved to form new state governments in the South and enfranchise the freedmen.

Reconstruction Acts of 1867–1868

After debate, the First Reconstruction Act passed in March 1867. This plan, under which the southern states were readmitted to the Union, incorporated part of the Radical program. Union generals, commanding small garrisons and charged with supervising elections, assumed control in five military districts in the South (see Map 14.1). Confederate leaders designated in the Fourteenth Amendment were barred from voting until new state constitutions were ratified. The act guaranteed freedmen the right to vote and serve in state constitutional conventions. In addition, each southern state was required to ratify the Fourteenth Amendment and its new constitution by majority vote, then submit it to Congress for approval (see Table 14.1).

TABLE 14.1   Plans for Reconstruction Compared

	Johnson's Plan	Radicals' Plan	Fourteenth Amendment	Reconstruction Act of 1867
Voting	Whites only; high-ranking Confederate leaders must seek pardons	Give vote to black males	Southern whites may decide but can lose representation if they deny black suffrage	Black men gain vote; whites barred from office by Fourteenth Amendment cannot vote while new state governments are being formed
Office holding	Many prominent Confederates regain power	Only loyal white and black males eligible	Confederate leaders barred until Congress votes amnesty	Fourteenth Amendment in effect
Time out of Union	Brief	Several years; until South is thoroughly democratized	Brief	3–5 years after war
Other change in southern society	Little; gain of power by yeomen not realized; emancipation grudgingly accepted, but no black civil or political rights	Expand education; confiscate land and provide farms for freedmen; expansion of activist federal government	Probably slight, depending on enforcement	Considerable, depending on action of new state governments

The Second, Third, and Fourth Reconstruction Acts, passed between March 1867 and March 1868, provided the details for voter registration boards, the adoption of constitutions, and the administration of "good faith" oaths by white southerners.

Failure of Land Redistribution

The Radicals blocked Johnson, but they had hoped Congress could do much more. Thaddeus Stevens, for example, argued that economic opportunity was essential to the freedmen. He drew up a plan for extensive confiscation and redistribution of land, but it was never realized.

Racial fears and an American obsession with the sanctity of private property made land redistribution unpopular. Thus, black farmers had to seek work in a hostile environment in which landowners opposed their acquisition of land.

Constitutional Crisis

To restrict Johnson's influence and safeguard its plan, Congress passed several controversial laws. First, it limited Johnson's power over the army by requiring the president to issue military orders through the general of the army, Ulysses S Grant. Then Congress passed the Tenure of Office Act, which gave the Senate power to approve changes in the president's cabinet. Designed to protect Secretary of War Stanton, a Radical sympathizer, this law violated the tradition of presidents controlling cabinet appointments. These measures, along with the Reconstruction Acts, were passed by a two-thirds override of presidential vetoes.

In response, Johnson limited the military's power in the South, increasing the powers of the civil governments he created in 1865. Then he removed military officers who were enforcing Congress's new law, preferring commanders who allowed disqualified Confederates to vote. Finally, he tried to remove Secretary of War Stanton, pushing the confrontation to its climax.

Impeachment Process to remove a president from office; attempted but failed in case of Andrew Johnson.

Impeachment of President Johnson

Impeachment is a political procedure provided for in the Constitution as a remedy for crimes or serious abuses of power by presidents, federal judges, and other high government officials. Those impeached (politically indicted) in the House are then tried in the Senate. Historically, this power was not used to investigate and judge the private lives of presidents, although more recently it was used this way against President Bill Clinton.

Twice in 1867, the House Judiciary Committee considered impeachment of Johnson, first rejecting it and then recommending it by a 5-to-4 vote, which was defeated by the House. After Johnson tried to remove Stanton, however, a third attempt to impeach him carried in early 1868. The indictment concentrated on his violation of the Tenure of Office Act, though modern scholars regard his efforts to obstruct enforcement of the Reconstruction Act of 1867 as a more serious offense.

Johnson's trial in the Senate lasted more than three months. The prosecution, led by Radicals, attempted to prove that Johnson was guilty of "high crimes and misdemeanors." But they also argued that the trial was a means to judge Johnson's performance. The Senate rejected such reasoning, which could have made removal from office a political weapon against any chief executive who disagreed with Congress. The prosecution fell one vote short of the necessary two-thirds majority. Johnson remained in office, politically weakened.

Election of 1868

In the 1868 presidential election, Ulysses S. Grant, running as a Republican, defeated Horatio Seymour, a New York Democrat. Grant was not a Radical, but his

congressional Reconstruction The process by which the Republican-controlled Congress sought to make the Reconstruction of the ex-Confederate states longer, harsher, and under greater congressional control.

platform supported **congressional Reconstruction** and endorsed black suffrage in the South. (Significantly, Republicans stopped short of endorsing black suffrage in the North.) Democrats, meanwhile, denounced Reconstruction and preached white supremacy, conducting the most openly racist campaign to that point in American history. Both sides waved the "bloody shirt," blaming each other for the war's sacrifices. By associating with rebellion and Johnson's repudiated program, Democrats were defeated in all but eight states, though the popular vote was close. Blacks voted en masse for General Grant.

In office, Grant vacillated in dealings with the southern states, sometimes defending Republican regimes and sometimes currying favor with Democrats. On occasion, Grant called out federal troops to stop violence or enforce acts of Congress. But he never imposed a military occupation on the South. Rapid demobilization reduced a federal army of more than 1 million to 57,000 within a year of the Appomattox surrender. Thereafter, the number of troops in the South declined, until in 1874 there were only 4,000 in the southern states outside Texas. The legend of "military rule," so important to southern claims of victimization during Reconstruction, was steeped in myth.

Fifteenth Amendment

In 1869, the Radicals pushed through the **Fifteenth Amendment**, the final major measure in Reconstruction's constitutional revolution. It forbade states to deny the vote "on account of race, color, or previous condition of servitude." Such wording did not guarantee the right to vote. It left states free to restrict suffrage on other grounds so that northern states could continue to deny suffrage to women and certain men—Chinese immigrants, illiterates, and those too poor to pay poll taxes.

Fifteenth Amendment
Prohibited states from denying the vote to any citizen on account of "race, color, or previous condition of servitude."

The Fifteenth Amendment became law in 1870. Although African Americans rejoiced, it left open the possibility for states to create countless qualification tests to obstruct voting.

Politics and Reconstruction in the South

How did black voters in the early days of Reconstruction transform the South?

From the start, white southerners resisted Reconstruction and opposed emancipation, as evident in the black codes. The former planter class proved especially unbending because of its tremendous financial loss in slaves. For many poor whites who never owned slaves and yet sacrificed during the war, destitution, plummeting agricultural prices, disease, and the uncertainties of a growing urban industrialization drove them off land, toward cities, and into hatred of black equality.

White Resistance

Some planters attempted to postpone freeing slaves by denying or misrepresenting events. Former slaves reported that their owners "didn't tell them it was freedom" or "wouldn't let [them] go." To retain workers, some landowners claimed control over black children and used guardianship and apprentice laws to bind black families to the plantation.

Adamant resistance by whites soon manifested itself in other ways, including violence. A local North Carolina magistrate clubbed a black man on a public street, and in several states bands of "Regulators" terrorized blacks who displayed independence. And after President Johnson encouraged the South to resist congressional Reconstruction, many white conservatives captured the new state governments, while others boycotted the polls to defeat Congress's plans.

Black Voters and the Southern Republican Party

Enthusiastically, blacks went to the polls, voting Republican, as one man said, to "stick to the end with the party that freed me." Illiteracy did not prohibit blacks (or uneducated whites) from making intelligent choices. Mississippi's William Henry could read only "a little," but he said, "We saw D. Sledge vote; he owned half the county. We knowed he voted Democratic so we voted the other ticket so it would be Republican." Women, who could not vote, encouraged their husbands and sons, and preachers exhorted their congregations to use the franchise.

Thanks to a large black turnout and the restrictions on prominent Confederates, a new southern Republican Party came to power in the 1868–1870 constitutional conventions. Republican delegates consisted of a sizable black contingent

(265 out of the total of just over 1,000 delegates throughout the South), northerners who had moved to the South, and native southern whites seeking change. The new constitutions they drafted were more democratic than anything previously adopted in the South. They eliminated property qualifications for voting and holding office, turned many appointed offices into elective posts, and provided for public schools and institutions to care for the mentally ill, the blind, the deaf, the destitute, and the orphaned.

The conventions broadened women's rights in property holding and divorce. Usually the goal was not gender equality but providing relief to thousands of suffering debtors. Since husbands typically contracted the debts, giving women legal control over their own property provided some protection for families.

Triumph of Republican Governments

Under these new constitutions, southern states elected Republican-controlled governments. For the first time, state legislators in 1868 included black southerners. Contrary to what white southerners later claimed, Republican state governments did not disfranchise ex-Confederates as a group. James Lynch, a leading black politician from Mississippi, saw disfranchising whites as foolish. Landless former slaves "must be in friendly relations with the great body of the whites in the state," he explained. "Otherwise…peace can be maintained only by a standing army." Despised and lacking power, southern Republicans strove for safe ways to gain a foothold in a depressed economy.

Far from vindictive toward the race that enslaved them, most southern blacks appealed to white southerners to embrace fairness. Hence, the South's Republican Party condemned itself to defeat if white voters would not cooperate. Within a few years, most fledgling Republican parties in southern states would be struggling for survival against violent white hostility.

Industrialization and Mill Towns

Reconstruction governments promoted industry via loans, subsidies, and short-term exemptions from taxation. The southern railroad system was rebuilt and expanded, and coal and iron mining made possible Birmingham's steel plants. Between 1860 and 1880, the number of manufacturing establishments in the South nearly doubled.

This emphasis on big business, however, produced higher state debts and taxes, drew money

The Queen of Industry, Or, The New South.

The Queen of Industry, or the New South, *cartoon by Thomas Nast, 1882, contrasting the pre–Civil War plantation economy with the more industrialized economy of the 1880s.*

The Granger Collection, NYC

from schools and other programs, and multiplied possibilities for corruption. The alliance between business and government often operated at the expense of farmers and laborers. This conservative strategy also doomed Republicans' chances with poorer whites.

Poverty remained the lot of many southern whites. The war caused a massive onetime loss of income-producing wealth, such as livestock, and a steep decline in land values. In many regions, the old planter class still ruled the best land and access to credit or markets.

As poor whites and blacks found farming less tenable, they moved to cities and mill towns. Industrialization did not sweep the South as it did the North, but it laid deep roots. Attracting textile mills to southern towns became a competitive crusade. In 1860, the South counted some 10,000 mill workers; by 1880, the number grew to 16,741 and by century's end to 97,559. Many poor southerners moved from farmer to mill worker and other low-income wage work.

Republicans and Racial Equality

Whites who controlled the southern Republican Party were reluctant to allow blacks a share of offices proportionate to their electoral strength. Aware of their weakness, black leaders did not push hard for revolutionary change. Instead, they led efforts to establish public schools, although without pressing for integrated facilities. In 1870, South Carolina passed the first comprehensive school law in the South. By 1875, 50 percent of black school-age children were enrolled in school there, and approximately one-third of the three thousand teachers were black.

African American politicians who did fight for civil rights and integration were typically from cities such as New Orleans or Mobile, where large populations of light-skinned free blacks existed before the war. Their experience made them sensitive to status issues. Laws requiring equal accommodations won passage but often went unenforced.

Economic progress, particularly landownership, was a major concern for most freedpeople. Land reform failed because in most states whites were the majority, and former slave owners controlled the best land and financial resources. Much land did fall into state hands for nonpayment of taxes. Such land was sold in small lots. But most freedmen had too little cash to bid against investors or speculators. Any widespread land redistribution had to arise from Congress, which never supported such action.

Myth of "Negro Rule"

Within a few years, white hostility to congressional Reconstruction increasingly dominated. Conservatives, who had always wanted to fight Reconstruction through pressure and racist propaganda, began to do so. Charging that the South had been turned over to ignorant blacks, conservatives used "black domination" as a rallying cry for a return to white supremacy.

Such attacks were inflammatory propaganda and part of the growing myth of "Negro rule," which would become a central theme in battles over the memory of Reconstruction. African Americans participated in politics but hardly dominated. They were a majority in only two out of ten state constitutional conventions.

In state legislatures, only in South Carolina's lower house did blacks constitute a majority. Sixteen blacks won seats in Congress before Reconstruction was over. Only eighteen served in a high state office, such as lieutenant governor, treasurer, superintendent of education, or secretary of state.

Some four hundred blacks served in political office during Reconstruction, an enormous achievement. Elected officials, such as Robert Smalls in South Carolina, labored for cheaper land prices, better health care, access to schools, and the enforcement of civil rights. For too long, the black politicians of Reconstruction were forgotten heroes of this seedtime of America's long civil rights movement.

Carpetbaggers and Scalawags

"carpetbaggers" Derogatory nickname southerners gave to northerners who moved south after the Civil War, perceiving them as greedy opportunists who hoped to cash in on the South's plight.

Conservatives also assailed the allies of black Republicans. Their propaganda denounced northern whites as **"carpetbaggers,"** greedy crooks planning to pour stolen tax revenues into their luggage made of carpet material. In fact, most northerners who settled in the South had come seeking business opportunities, as schoolteachers, or to find a warmer climate; most never entered politics. Those who entered politics generally wanted to democratize the South and to introduce northern ways, such as industry and public education.

Carpetbaggers' real actions never matched the sensational stereotypes, although by the mid-1870s even some northerners who soured on Reconstruction endorsed the images. Thomas Wentworth Higginson, a Union officer and commander of an African American regiment during the Civil War, suggested that any Yankee politician still in the South by 1874 was a "mean man," a "scoundrel."

"scalawag" Term used by conservative southerners to describe other white southerners who were perceived as aiding or benefiting from Reconstruction.

Conservatives also invented the term **"scalawag"** to discredit white southerners cooperating with Republicans, as many wealthy men did. Most scalawags were yeoman farmers from mountain areas and nonslaveholding districts who were Unionists under the Confederacy. They hoped to benefit from the education and opportunities Republicans promoted. Sometimes banding with freedmen, they pursued common class interests to make headway against long-dominant planters. Ove time, however, most black-white coalitions floundered due to racism.

Tax Policy and Corruption as Political Wedges

Republicans wanted to repair the war's destruction, stimulate industry, and support such new ventures as public schools. But the Civil War damaged the South's tax base. One category of valuable property—slaves—had disappeared. Hundreds of thousands of citizens lost much of their property—money, livestock, fences, and buildings—to the war. Tax increases (sales, excise, and property) were necessary even to maintain traditional services. Inevitably, Republican tax policies aroused strong opposition, especially among yeomen.

Corruption charges also plagued Republicans. Many carpetbaggers and black politicians engaged in fraudulent schemes or sold their votes, participating in what scholars recognize was a nationwide surge of corruption in an age ruled by "spoilsmen" (see pages xxx). Corruption crossed party lines, but Democrats successfully blamed unqualified blacks and greedy carpetbaggers among southern Republicans.

Ku Klux Klan

Republican leaders also allowed factionalism along racial and class lines to undermine party unity. But in many southern states, the deathblow came through violence. The **Ku Klux Klan**, a secret veterans' club that began in Tennessee in 1866, spread through the South, rapidly becoming a terrorist organization. Klansmen sought to frustrate Reconstruction and keep the freedmen in subjection with nighttime harassment, whippings, beatings, rapes, and murders.

Although the Klan tormented blacks, its main purpose was political. Lawless night riders targeted Republicans, killing leading whites and blacks in several states. After freedmen who worked for a South Carolina scalawag started voting, terrorists visited the plantation and, as one victim noted, "whipped every...[black] man they could lay their hands on." Klansmen also attacked Union League clubs—Republican organizations that mobilized the black vote—and schoolteachers who aided freedmen.

Specific social forces shaped and directed Klan violence, with Alamance and Caswell Counties in North Carolina receiving the worst Klan violence. Slim Republican majorities there rested on cooperation between black voters and white yeomen. Together, these black and white Republicans ousted long-entrenched officials. The wealthy and powerful men who lost their accustomed political control were the Klan's county officers and local chieftains. By intimidation and murder, the Klan weakened the Republican coalition and restored a Democratic majority.

Klan violence ultimately destroyed Republicans across the South. One of every ten black delegates to the 1867–1868 state constitutional conventions was attacked, seven fatally. In one North Carolina judicial district, the Ku Klux Klan was responsible for twelve murders, over seven hundred beatings, rape, and arson. A single attack on Alabama Republicans in Eutaw left four blacks dead and fifty-four wounded. According to historian Eric Foner, the Klan "made it virtually impossible for Republicans to campaign or vote in large parts of Georgia."

Thus, Republican mistakes, racial hostility, and terror brought down the Republican regimes. In most southern states, Radical Reconstruction lasted only a few years (see Map 14.1). Its most enduring failure, however, was its inability to alter the South's social structure or its distribution of wealth and power.

Ku Klux Klan A terrorist organization established by six Confederate war veterans that sought to reestablish white supremacy in the South, suppress black voting, and topple Reconstruction governments.

Two members of the Ku Klux Klan, photographed in regalia, circa 1870. Dallas Historical Society,

Dallas Historical Society, Texas, USA/The Bridgeman Art Library

Retreat from Reconstruction

What led the North to lose interest in reconstructing the South?

During the 1870s, northerners lost the will to sustain Reconstruction, as they faced economic and social transformations in their region and the West. Radical Republicans like Albion Tourgée, a former Union soldier who moved to North Carolina and was elected a judge, condemned Congress's timidity. He, and many African Americans, believed that during Reconstruction, the North "threw all the Negroes on the world without any way of getting along." As the North lost interest in the South, Reconstruction collapsed.

Political Implications of Klan Terrorism

Whites in the old Confederacy referred to this decline of Reconstruction as "southern redemption." During the 1870s, "redeemer" Democrats claimed to be the South's saviors from alleged "black domination" and "carpetbag rule." Violence and terror emerged as tactics in politics.

In 1870 and 1871, the Ku Klux Klan's violent campaigns forced Congress to pass two **Enforcement Acts** and an anti-Klan law. These laws made actions by individuals against the civil and political rights of others a federal criminal offense. They also provided for election supervisors and permitted martial law and suspension of the writ of habeas corpus to combat murders, beatings, and Klan threats. In 1872 and 1873, Mississippi and the Carolinas saw many prosecutions; but in other states, the laws were ignored. Southern juries sometimes refused to convict Klansmen; less than half of the 3,310 cases ended in convictions. Although many Klansmen fled their state to avoid prosecution, and the Klan officially disbanded, paramilitary organizations known as Rifle Clubs and Red Shirts often took the Klan's place.

Enforcement Acts Laws that sought to protect black voters, made violations of civil and political rights a federal offense, and sought to end Ku Klux Klan violence.

Still, there were ominous signs that the North's commitment to racial justice was fading, as some influential Republicans opposed the anti-Klan laws. Rejecting other Republicans' arguments that the Thirteenth, Fourteenth, and Fifteenth Amendments made the federal government the protector of citizens' rights, dissenters charged that Congress was infringing on states' rights. This foreshadowed a general revolt within Republican ranks in 1872.

Industrial Expansion and Reconstruction in the North

Immigration and industrialization surged in the North. Between 1865 and 1873, 3 million immigrants entered the country, most settling in the industrial cities of the North and West. Within only eight years, industrial production increased by 75 percent. For the first time, nonagricultural workers outnumbered farmers, and wage earners outnumbered independent craftsmen. Government policies encouraged this rapid growth. Low taxes on investment and high tariffs on manufactured goods helped create a new class of powerful industrialists, especially railroad entrepreneurs.

From 1865 to 1873, thirty-five thousand miles of new track were laid, which fueled the banking industry and made Wall Street the center of American capitalism. Eastern railroad magnates, such as Thomas Scott of the Pennsylvania Railroad, created economic empires with the assistance of huge government subsidies of cash and land. Railroad corporations also bought up mining operations, granaries, and lumber companies. Big business now employed lobbyists to curry favor with government. Corruption ran rampant; some congressmen and legislators were paid annual retainers by major companies. The railroads brought modernity to the United States like almost nothing else; but they also taught the nation sordid lessons about the perils of monopoly and corruption, and by the late nineteenth century railroad entrepreneurs were the most hated men in the West.

As captains of industry amassed unprecedented fortunes in an age with no income tax, gross economic inequality polarized American society. The workforce, worried a prominent Massachusetts business leader, was in a "transition state…living in boarding houses" and becoming a "permanent factory population." In New York or Philadelphia, workers increasingly lived in unhealthy tenement housing. Thousands would list themselves on the census as "common laborer." In 1868, Republicans passed an eight-hour workday bill for federal workers. The "labor question" (see Chapter 16) now preoccupied northerners far more than the "southern" or the "freedmen" question.

Then the Panic of 1873 ushered in more than five years of economic contraction. Three million people lost their jobs, especially in large cities. Debtors and the unemployed sought easy-money policies to spur expansion (workers and farmers desperately needed cash). Businessmen, disturbed by the strikes and industrial violence that accompanied the panic, defended property rights and demanded "sound money" policies. The chasm between farmers and workers and wealthy industrialists widened.

Liberal Republican Revolt

Disenchanted with Reconstruction, a largely northern group calling itself the Liberal Republicans bolted the party in 1872 and nominated Horace Greeley, editor of the *New York Tribune,* for president. A varied group, Liberal Republicans included foes of corruption and advocates of a lower tariff. Two popular attitudes united them: distaste for federal intervention in the South and an elitist desire to let market forces and the "best men" determine policy.

Democrats also nominated Greeley in 1872, but it was not enough to stop Grant's reelection. Greeley's campaign for North-South reunion was a harbinger of the future in American politics. Organized Blue-Gray fraternalism (gatherings of Union and Confederate veterans) began in 1874. Grant continued to use military force sparingly and in 1875 refused a desperate request from Mississippi's governor for troops to quell racial and political terrorism there.

Grant made a series of poor appointments that fueled public dissatisfaction. His secretary of war, his private secretary, and officials in the treasury department and navy were involved in bribery or tax-cheating scandals. Instead of exposing the corruption, Grant defended the culprits. In 1874, Democrats recaptured the House of Representatives, signaling the end of the Radical Republican vision of Reconstruction.

General Amnesty

Democratic gains in Congress weakened legislative resolve on southern issues. Congress had already lifted the political disabilities of the Fourteenth Amendment from many former Confederates. In 1872, it adopted an Amnesty Act, which pardoned most of the remaining rebels. In 1875, Congress passed a **Civil Rights Act**,

Civil Rights Act An act designed to desegregate public places that lacked enforcement provisions.

partly in tribute to the recently deceased Charles Sumner, purporting to guarantee black people equal accommodations in public places, such as inns and theaters, but the bill was watered down and contained no enforcement provisions. (The Supreme Court later struck down this law; see page xxx.)

Democrats regained control of four state governments before 1872 and eight by late January 1876 (see Map 14.1). In the North, Democrats successfully stressed the failure and scandals of Reconstruction governments. Sectional reconciliation now seemed crucial for commerce. The nation was expanding westward, and the South was a new frontier for investment.

The West, Race, and Reconstruction

As the Fourteenth Amendment and other enactments granted blacks the beginnings of citizenship, other nonwhite peoples faced continued persecution. Across the West, the federal government pursued a containment policy against Native Americans. In California, where white farmers and ranchers often forced Indians into captive labor, some civilians practiced "Indian hunting." By 1880, thirty years of violence left an estimated forty-five hundred California Indians dead at the hands of white settlers.

In Texas and the Southwest, expansionists still deemed Mexicans and other mixed-race Hispanics to be "lazy," and incapable of self-government. In California and the Far West, initially few whites objected to Chinese immigrants who did the dangerous work of building railroads through the Rocky Mountains. But when the Chinese competed for urban, industrial jobs, conflict emerged. Anti-coolie clubs appeared in California in the 1870s, seeking laws against Chinese labor, fanning the racism flames, and organizing vigilante attacks on Chinese workers and the factories that employed them. Western politicians sought white votes by pandering to prejudice, and in 1879 the new California constitution denied Chinese the vote.

Viewing America from coast to coast, the Civil War and Reconstruction years dismantled racial slavery and fostered a volatile new racial complexity, especially in the West. Some African Americans asserted that they were more like whites than "uncivilized" Indians, while others, like the Creek freedmen of Indian Territory, sought an Indian identity. In Texas, whites, Indians, blacks, and Hispanics had mixed for decades, and by the 1870s forced reconsideration in law and custom of exactly who was "white."

America was undergoing what one historian has called a reconstruction of the concept of *race* itself. The turbulence of the expanding West reinforced the new nationalism and the reconciliation of North and South based on a resurgent white supremacy.

Foreign Expansion

In 1867, new expansion pressures led Secretary of State William H. Seward to purchase Alaska from Russia (see Chapter 19). Opponents ridiculed Seward's $7.2 million venture, but Seward convinced congressmen of Alaska's economic potential, and other lawmakers favored potential friendship with Russia.

Also in 1867, the United States took control of the Midway Islands, a thousand miles northwest of Hawai'i. Through diplomacy, Seward and his successor

The "Back to Africa" Movement

In the wake of the Civil War, and especially after the despairing end of Reconstruction, some African Americans sought to leave the South for the American West or North, but also to relocate to Africa. Liberia had been founded in the 1820s by the white-led American Colonization Society (ACS), an organization dedicated to relocating blacks "back" to Africa. Some eleven thousand African Americans had emigrated voluntarily to Liberia by 1860, with largely disastrous results. Many died of disease, and others felt disoriented in the strange new land and ultimately returned to the United States.

Reconstruction reinvigorated the emigration impulse, especially in cotton-growing districts where blacks had achieved political power before 1870 but were crushed by violence and intimidation in the following decade. When blacks felt confident in their future, the idea of leaving America fell quiet; but when threatened or under assault, whole black communities dreamed of a place where they could become an independent "race," a "people," or a "nation" as their appeals often announced. Often that dream, more imagined than realized, lay in West Africa.

Before the Civil War, most blacks denounced the ACS for its racism and hostility to their sense of American birthright. But letters of inquiry flooded the organization's headquarters after 1875. Wherever blacks felt the reversal of the promise of emancipation the keenest, they formed local groups such as the Liberia Exodus Association of Pinesville, Florida; or the Liberian Exodus Arkansas Colony; and many others.

At emigration conventions, and especially in churches, blacks penned letters to the ACS asking for maps or information about a new African homeland. Some local organizers would announce eighty or a hundred recruits "widawake for Liberia," although

such enthusiasm rarely converted into an Atlantic voyage. The impulse was genuine, however. "We wants to be a People," wrote the leader of a Mississippi emigration committee; "we can't be it heare and find that we ar compel to leve this Cuntry." Henry Adams, a former Louisiana slave, Union soldier, and itinerant emigration organizer, advocated Liberia, but also supported "Kansas fever" with both biblical and natural rights arguments. "God . . . has a place and a land for all his people," he wrote in 1879. "It . . . is the idea that pervades our breast 'that at last we will be free,' free from oppression, free from tyranny, free from bulldozing, murderous southern whites."

By the 1890s, Henry McNeal Turner, a freeborn former Georgia Reconstruction politician, and now bishop of the African Methodist Episcopal Church, made three trips to Africa and campaigned through press and pulpit for blacks to "Christianize" and "civilize" Africa. Two shiploads of African Americans sailed to Liberia, although most returned disillusioned or ill. Turner's plan of "Africa for the Africans" was as much a religious vision as an emigration system, but like all such efforts then and since, it reflected the despair of racial conditions in America more than realities in Africa. The numbers do not demonstrate the depth of the impulse in this link to the world: in 1879–1880, approximately twenty-five thousand southern blacks moved to Kansas, whereas from 1865 to 1900, just under four thousand emigrated to West Africa.

Departure of African American emigrants to Liberia aboard the Laurada, *Savannah, Georgia, March 1896. The large crowd bidding farewell to the much smaller group aboard the ship may indicate both the fascination with and the ambivalence about this issue among blacks in the South.*

Illustrated American/Historical/Corbis

Hamilton Fish arranged a financial settlement of claims on Britain for damage done by the *Alabama* and other cruisers built in England and sold to the Confederacy. Sectional reconciliation in Reconstruction America would serve new ambitions for world commerce and expansion.

Judicial Retreat from Reconstruction

Meanwhile, the Supreme Court played its part in the northern retreat from Reconstruction. During the Civil War, the Court was cautious and inactive. Reaction to the *Dred Scott* decision (1857) was so vehement, and the Union's wartime emergency so great, that the Court had avoided interference with government actions. But that changed in 1866 when *Ex parte Milligan* reached the Court.

Lambdin P. Milligan of Indiana had plotted to free Confederate prisoners of war and overthrow state governments. Consequently, a military court sentenced Milligan, a civilian, to death. Milligan challenged the military tribunal's authority, claiming he was entitled to a civil trial. The Supreme Court declared that military trials were illegal when civil courts were functioning.

In the 1870s, the Court successfully renewed its challenge to Congress's actions when it narrowed the meaning of the Fourteenth Amendment. The *Slaughter-House* cases (1873) began in 1869, when the Louisiana legislature granted one company a monopoly on livestock slaughtering in New Orleans. Rival butchers sued. Their attorney, former Supreme Court justice John A. Campbell, argued that Louisiana had violated the rights of some citizens in favor of others. The Fourteenth Amendment, Campbell contended, had brought individual rights under federal protection.

But in the *Slaughter-House* decision, the Supreme Court dealt a blow to the scope of the Fourteenth Amendment. It declared state citizenship and national citizenship separate. National citizenship involved only matters such as the right to travel freely from state to state, and only such narrow rights, held the Court, were protected by the Fourteenth Amendment.

Shrinking from a role as "perpetual censor" for civil rights, the Court's majority declared that the framers of recent amendments had not intended to "destroy" the federal system, in which the states exercised "powers for domestic and local government, including the regulation of civil rights." Thus, the justices severely limited the amendment's potential for protecting the rights of black citizens—its original intent.

The next day, the Court decided *Bradwell v. Illinois,* a case in which Myra Bradwell, a female attorney, was denied the right to practice law in Illinois because she was a married woman, and hence not a free agent. Using the Fourteenth Amendment, Bradwell's attorneys contended that the state had unconstitutionally abridged her "privileges and immunities" as a citizen. The Supreme Court disagreed, declaring a woman's "paramount destiny…to fulfill the noble and benign offices of wife and mother."

In 1876, the Court further weakened the Reconstruction era amendments. In *U.S. v. Cruikshank,* the Court overruled the conviction under the 1870 Enforcement Act of Louisiana whites who had attacked a meeting of blacks and conspired to deprive them of their rights. The justices ruled that the Fourteenth Amendment did not give the federal government power to act against these whites. The duty of protecting citizens' equal rights, the Court said, "rests alone with the States."

Such judicial conservatism blunted the revolutionary potential of the Civil War amendments.

Disputed Election of 1876 and Compromise of 1877

As the 1876 presidential election approached, the nation was focused on economic issues, and the North lost interest in Reconstruction. Samuel J. Tilden, the Democratic governor of New York, ran strongly in the South and needed one electoral vote to beat Rutherford B. Hayes, the Republican nominee. Nineteen electoral votes from Louisiana, South Carolina, and Florida (the only southern states not yet under Democratic rule) were disputed; both Democrats and Republicans claimed to have won those states despite fraud committed by their opponents (see Map 14.2).

To resolve this unprecedented situation, Congress established a fifteen-member electoral commission, balanced between Democrats and Republicans. Because Republicans held the majority in Congress, they prevailed, 8 to 7, on every attempt to count the returns, with commission members voting along party lines. Hayes would become president if Congress accepted the commission's findings.

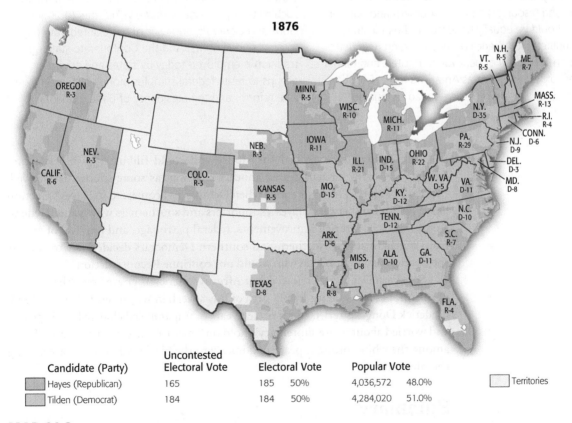

Candidate (Party)	Uncontested Electoral Vote	Electoral Vote		Popular Vote	
Hayes (Republican)	165	185	50%	4,036,572	48.0%
Tilden (Democrat)	184	184	50%	4,284,020	51.0%

Territories

MAP 14.2
Presidential Election of 1876 and the Compromise of 1877

In 1876, a combination of solid southern support and Democratic gains in the North gave Samuel Tilden the majority of popular votes, but Rutherford B. Hayes won the disputed election in the electoral college, after a deal satisfied Democratic wishes for an end to Reconstruction. Source: Copyright © Cengage Learning 2015

The Lost Cause

All major wars compel a struggle over their memory. After the Civil War, white southerners and their northern allies constructed a "Lost Cause" tradition, a racially exclusive version of the war and Reconstruction that persists today.

For ex-Confederates, the Lost Cause served as a psychological response to the trauma of defeat. Over time it also included reinterpretations of the war's causes; southern resistance to Reconstruction; doctrines of white supremacy; and a mythic popular culture enjoyed by northerners and southerners. Lost Cause advocates—from officers to soldiers to women leading memorial associations—argued that the war was never about slavery; that the Confederates lost due to Yankee numbers and resources; and that southern and northern sacrifice should be equally honored. In the industrial, urban, multiethnic America of the emerging twentieth century, an Old South of benevolent masters and faithful slaves, of Robert E. Lee as America's truest Christian soldier, provided a sentimentalized road to reunion.

By the 1890s, elite southern white women—among them the United Daughters of the Confederacy—built monuments, lobbied congressmen, delivered lectures, ran contests for schoolchildren, and strove to control the content of history textbooks, to exalt the South. Above all, Lost Causers advocated what one historian has called a "victory narrative" of the nation's triumph over Reconstruction's racial revolution and constitutional transformations. In his 1881 memoir, Jefferson Davis declared the Lost Cause not lost: "Well may we rejoice in the regained possession of self-government.... This is the great victory...a total noninterference by the Federal government in the domestic affairs of the States." These stories endure in Civil War memorabilia, such as the epic *Gone with the Wind,* the 2003 film *Gods and Generals*, and uses of the Confederate flag to oppose civil rights. And the Confederate state rights tradition is employed today by states and advocacy groups to resist federal stimulus money, national health care reform, and the presidency of Barack Obama.

But Democrats controlled the House and could filibuster to block action on the vote. Many citizens feared another civil war, as some southerners vowed, "Tilden or Fight!" The crisis ended when Democrats acquiesced in Hayes's election based on a "deal" between Hayes's supporters and southerners who wanted federal aid to railroads, internal improvements, federal patronage, and removal of troops from southern states. Northern and southern Democrats decided not to contest the election of a Republican who would not continue Reconstruction.

Southern Democrats rejoiced, but African Americans grieved over the betrayal of their hopes for equality. In a Fourth of July speech in Washington, D.C., in 1875, Frederick Douglass reflected on fifteen years of unparalleled change for his people and worried about white supremacy's hold on America's historical memory: "If war among the whites brought peace and liberty to the blacks, what will peace among the whites bring?"

Summary

Reconstruction left a contradictory record. It was an era of tragic aspirations and failures but also of unprecedented legal, political, and social change. The Union victory brought increased federal power, stronger nationalism, sweeping federal intervention in the southern states, and landmark constitutional amendments. It also sparked a revolution in how people would see the role of the state in their lives. But northern commitment to impose lasting change eroded, leaving the revolution unfinished. The promise for new lives and liberties among the freedpeople was tarnished, although not dead, by 1877.

The North embraced emancipation, black suffrage, and constitutional alterations strengthening the central government, primarily to defeat the rebellion. As wartime pressure declined, Americans, especially northerners, retreated from Reconstruction. The people and the courts maintained a preference for state authority and a distrust of federal power. Free-labor ideology stressed respect for property and individual self-reliance. Racism transformed into Klan terror and theories of black degeneration.

New challenges began to overwhelm the aims of Reconstruction. Industrialization promised prosperity but also wrought labor exploitation. Moreover, industry increased the nation's power and laid the foundation for an enlarged American role in international affairs.

In the wake of the Civil War, Americans faced two profound tasks—healing and dispensing justice. Making sectional reunion compatible with black freedom and equality overwhelmed American politics, and the nation still faced this ongoing dilemma more than a century later.

Chapter Review

Wartime Reconstruction

Which two political acts recognized the centrality of slavery to the war?

Passage of the Thirteenth Amendment and establishment of the Freedmen's Bureau in early 1865 sent a clear signal that slavery was a major cause for the Civil War. The Thirteenth Amendment first abolished slavery ("involuntary servitude") and, second, gave Congress the power to enforce it. Then, a few months later, Congress established the Bureau of Refugees, Freedmen and Abandoned Lands, known as the Freedmen's Bureau, to help former slaves. During its four years as a federal agency, it supplied food and medical services, built thousands of schools and colleges, negotiated job contracts between former slaves and masters, and managed confiscated lands.

The Meanings of Freedom

How did blacks exert their newfound freedom?

With emancipation, former slaves sought to reunite families broken apart through slave sales. Community also became important, as they built their own

churches that ultimately served to strengthen racial ties. Seeking greater control over their work lives, African Americans wanted fairer employers and hoped to own land; when that was not possible, they rented land from former masters under the sharecropping system, in which they paid for supplies and rent by giving owners half their crops on average. Former slaves also embraced the education that had been denied them under slavery and started schools, colleges, and universities throughout the South or attended those launched by the Freedmen's Bureau.

Johnson's Reconstruction Plan

What was Johnson's vision for Reconstruction?

Johnson's approach to Reconstruction could be summed up in a single quote: "The Constitution as it is, and the Union as it was." As president, he controlled Reconstruction policy through 1865, pardoning former Confederates and reestablishing state governments in the South. Despising the planter class, he initially insisted that ex-Confederates with property worth more than $20,000 apply directly to him for pardons. Gradually, Johnson pardoned planters, too, which restored the former elite to power, possibly because he wanted to block

Radical Republicans from implementing extensive racial and political changes in the South. Deeply racist, Johnson remained silent when southern states implemented black codes to restrict former slaves' freedom by requiring them to carry passes, obey curfew laws, and live in housing provided by a landowner. Nonetheless, after just eight months, Johnson declared Reconstruction was completed.

The Congressional Reconstruction Plan

What made Radical Reconstruction different from Johnson's plan?

Radical Republicans in Congress were upset at Johnson's moderate approach, which seemed to hold no one responsible for the war and reestablished racial hierarchies and the southern elite. Initially a minority, the Radicals' popularity grew as Johnson increasingly dug in his heels. Radicals wanted to democratize the South through black suffrage, civil rights, and land confiscation and redistribution. They secured passage of the Fourteenth Amendment, which conferred citizenship on "all persons born or naturalized in the United States." They also passed four strident Reconstruction acts with strict and detailed plans for readmitting southern states to the Union. They barred ex-Confederates from voting until freedmen could and outlined the rules for voter registration boards and the adoption of state constitutions. Unpopular, land redistribution never materialized, but in 1869, Radicals pushed through their final measure, the Fifteenth Amendment, which prohibited states from denying the vote based on "race, color, or previous condition of servitude."

Politics and Reconstruction in the South

How did black voters in the early days of Reconstruction transform the South?

With a large black voter turnout and prominent Confederates barred from the polls and political positions, a new southern variant on the Republican Party came to power during the 1868 to 1870 state constitutional conventions. These constitutions were highly democratic, eliminating property qualifications for voting and political office, shifting some appointed offices to elected ones, and establishing public schools. They also gave women greater rights in terms of property holding and divorce. Blacks became state legislators for the first time in 1868. Angry whites charged they were being ruled by Negroes, and some resorted to violent resistance. In truth, while blacks did play a greater role in government, they remained a minority.

Retreat from Reconstruction

What led the North to lose interest in reconstructing the South?

During the 1870s, northerners faced economic and social transformations at home and became increasingly disillusioned with Reconstruction. Some northerners thought federal expansion had cut too far into states' rights. Second, while immigration and industrialization made northern economies boom from 1865 to 1873, it also widened the gap between the richest and the poorest and created a powerful new class of industrialists. When the Panic of 1873 brought hard times and job losses, interest in Reconstruction faded beside regional economic concerns. The Supreme Court also played a role, challenging congressional Reconstruction in several decisions. The Court ultimately narrowed the meaning of the Fourteenth Amendment by declaring state and national citizenship as distinguishable and limited the amendment's ability to safeguard black citizens, as it was intended to do.

Suggestions for Further Reading

David W. Blight, *Race and Reunion: The Civil War in American Memory* (2001)

Gregory P. Downs, *Declarations of Dependence: The Long Reconstruction of Popular Politics in the South, 1861–1908* (2011)

W. E. B. Du Bois, *Black Reconstruction in America* (1935)

Eric Foner, *Reconstruction: America's Unfinished Revolution, 1863–1877* (1988)

William Gillette, *Retreat from Reconstruction, 1869–1879* (1980)

Gerald Jaynes, *Branches Without Roots: The Genesis of the Black Working Class in the American South, 1862–1882* (1986)

George Rable, *But There Was No Peace* (1984)

Heather Richardson, *West from Appomattox: The Reconstruction of America after the Civil War* (2007)

Elliot West, "Reconstructing Race," *Western Historical Quarterly* (Spring 2003)

Richard White, *Railroaded: The Transcontinentals and the Making of Modern America* (2011)

Declaration of Independence in Congress, July 4, 1776

When, in the course of human events, it becomes necessary for one people to dissolve the political bonds which have connected them with another, and to assume, among the powers of the earth, the separate and equal station to which the laws of nature and of nature's God entitle them, a decent respect to the opinions of mankind requires that they should declare the causes which impel them to the separation.

We hold these truths to be self-evident: That all men are created equal; that they are endowed by their Creator with certain unalienable rights; that among these are life, liberty, and the pursuit of happiness; that, to secure these rights, governments are instituted among men, deriving their just powers from the consent of the governed; that whenever any form of government becomes destructive of these ends, it is the right of the people to alter or to abolish it, and to institute new government, laying its foundation on such principles, and organizing its powers in such form, as to them shall seem most likely to effect their safety and happiness. Prudence, indeed, will dictate that governments long established should not be changed for light and transient causes; and accordingly all experience hath shown that mankind are more disposed to suffer, while evils are sufferable, than to right themselves by abolishing the forms to which they are accustomed. But when a long train of abuses and usurpations, pursuing invariably the same object, evinces a design to reduce them under absolute despotism, it is their right, it is their duty, to throw off such government, and to provide new guards for their future security. Such has been the patient sufferance of these colonies; and such is now the necessity which constrains them to alter their former systems of government. The history of the present King of Great Britain is a history of repeated injuries and usurpations, all having in direct object the establishment of an absolute tyranny over these states. To prove this, let facts be submitted to a candid world.

He has refused his assent to laws, the most wholesome and necessary for the public good.

He has forbidden his governors to pass laws of immediate and pressing importance, unless suspended in their operation till his assent should be obtained; and, when so suspended, he has utterly neglected to attend to them.

He has refused to pass other laws for the accommodation of large districts of people, unless those people would relinquish the right of representation in the legislature, a right inestimable to them, and formidable to tyrants only.

He has called together legislative bodies at places unusual, uncomfortable, and distant from the depository of their public records, for the sole purpose of fatiguing them into compliance with his measures.

He has dissolved representative houses repeatedly, for opposing, with manly firmness, his invasions on the rights of the people.

He has refused for a long time, after such dissolutions, to cause others to be elected; whereby the legislative powers, incapable of annihilation, have returned to the people at large for their exercise; the state remaining, in the mean time, exposed to all the dangers of invasions from without and convulsions within.

He has endeavored to prevent the population of these states; for that purpose obstructing the laws for naturalization of foreigners; refusing to pass others to encourage their migration hither, and raising the conditions of new appropriations of lands.

He has obstructed the administration of justice, by refusing his assent to laws for establishing judiciary powers.

He has made judges dependent on his will alone, for the tenure of their offices, and the amount and payment of their salaries.

He has erected a multitude of new offices, and sent hither swarms of officers to harass our people and eat out their substance.

He has kept among us, in times of peace, standing armies, without the consent of our legislatures.

He has affected to render the military independent of, and superior to, the civil power.

He has combined with others to subject us to a jurisdiction foreign to our constitution, and unacknowledged by our laws, giving his assent to their acts of pretended legislation:

For quartering large bodies of armed troops among us;

For protecting them, by a mock trial, from punishment for any murders which they should commit on the inhabitants of these states;

For cutting off our trade with all parts of the world;

For imposing taxes on us without our consent;

For depriving us, in many cases, of the benefits of trial by jury;

For transporting us beyond seas, to be tried for pretended offenses;

For abolishing the free system of English laws in a neighboring province, establishing therein an arbitrary government, and enlarging its boundaries, so as to render it at once an example and fit instrument for introducing the same absolute rule into these colonies;

For taking away our charters, abolishing our most valuable laws, and altering fundamentally the forms of our governments;

For suspending our own legislatures, and declaring themselves invested with power to legislate for us in all cases whatsoever.

He has abdicated government here, by declaring us out of his protection and waging war against us.

He has plundered our seas, ravaged our coasts, burned our towns, and destroyed the lives of our people.

He is at this time transporting large armies of foreign mercenaries to complete the works of death, desolation, and tyranny already begun with circumstances of cruelty and perfidy scarcely paralleled in the most barbarous ages, and totally unworthy the head of a civilized nation.

He has constrained our fellow-citizens, taken captive on the high seas, to bear arms against their country, to become the executioners of their friends and brethren, or to fall themselves by their hands.

He has excited domestic insurrection among us, and has endeavored to bring on the inhabitants of our frontiers the merciless Indian savages, whose known rule of warfare is an undistinguished destruction of all ages, sexes, and conditions.

In every stage of these oppressions we have petitioned for redress in the most humble terms; our repeated petitions have been answered only by repeated injury. A prince, whose character is thus marked by every act which may define a tyrant, is unfit to be the ruler of a free people.

Nor have we been wanting in our attentions to our British brethren. We have warned them, from time to time, of attempts by their legislature to extend an unwarrantable jurisdiction over us. We have reminded them of the circumstances of our emigration and settlement here. We have appealed to their native justice and magnanimity; and we have conjured them, by the ties of our common kindred, to disavow these usurpations, which would inevitably interrupt our connections and correspondence. They, too, have been deaf to the voice of justice and of consanguinity. We must, therefore, acquiesce in the necessity which denounces our separation, and hold them, as we hold the rest of mankind, enemies in war, in peace friends.

We, therefore, the representatives of the United States of America, in General Congress assembled, appealing to the Supreme Judge of the world for the rectitude of our intentions, do, in the name and by the authority of the good people of these colonies, solemnly publish and declare, that these United Colonies are, and of right ought to be, FREE AND INDEPENDENT STATES; that they are absolved from all allegiance to the British crown, and that all political connection between them and the state of Great Britain is, and ought to be, totally dissolved; and that, as free and independent states, they have full power to levy war, conclude peace, contract alliances, establish commerce, and do all other acts and things which independent states may of right do. And for the support of this declaration, with a firm reliance on the protection of Divine Providence, we mutually pledge to each other our lives, our fortunes, and our sacred honor.

Articles of Confederation

Whereas the Delegates of the United States of America in Congress assembled did on the fifteenth day of November in the Year of our Lord One Thousand Seven Hundred and Seventy seven, and in the Second Year of the Independence of America agree to certain articles of Confederation and perpetual Union between the States of Newhampshire, Massachusetts Bay, Rhode Island and Providence Plantations, Connecticut, New York, New Jersey, Pennsylvania, Delaware, Maryland, Virginia, North Carolina, South Carolina and Georgia in the Words following, viz. "Articles of Confederation and perpetual Union between the states of Newhampshire, Massachusetts Bay, Rhode Island and Providence Plantations, Connecticut, New York, New Jersey, Pennsylvania, Delaware, Maryland, Virginia, North Carolina, South Carolina and Georgia.

Article I The Stile of this confederacy shall be "The United States of America."

Article II Each state retains its sovereignty, freedom and independence, and every Power, Jurisdiction and right, which is not by this confederation expressly delegated to the United States, in Congress assembled.

Article III The said states hereby severally enter into a firm league of friendship with each other, for their common defence, the security of their Liberties, and their mutual and general welfare, binding themselves to assist each other, against all force offered to, or attacks made upon them, or any of them, on account of religion, sovereignty, trade, or any other pretence whatever.

Article IV The better to secure and perpetuate mutual friendship and intercourse among the people of the different states in this union, the free inhabitants of each of these states, paupers, vagabonds and fugitives from Justice excepted, shall be entitled to all privileges and immunities of free citizens in the several states; and the people of each state shall have free ingress and regress to and from any other state, and shall enjoy therein all the privileges of trade and commerce, subject to the same duties, impositions and restrictions as the inhabitants thereof respectively, provided that such restriction shall not extend so far as to prevent the removal of property imported into any state, to any other state of which the Owner is an inhabitant; provided also that no imposition, duties or restriction shall be laid by any state, on the property of the united states, or either of them.

If any Person guilty of, or charged with treason, felony, or other high misdemeanor in any state, shall flee from Justice, and be found in any of the united states, he shall upon demand of the Governor or executive power, of the state from which he fled, be delivered up and removed to the state having jurisdiction of his offence.

Full faith and credit shall be given in each of these states to the records, acts and judicial proceedings of the courts and magistrates of every other state.

Article V For the more convenient management of the general interests of the united states, delegates shall be annually appointed in such manner as the legislature of each state shall direct, to meet in Congress on the first Monday in November, in every year, with a power reserved to each state, to recall its delegates, or any of them, at any time within the year, and to send others in their stead, for the remainder of the Year.

No state shall be represented in Congress by less than two, nor by more than seven Members; and no person shall be capable of being a delegate for more than three years in any term of six years; nor shall any person, being a delegate, be capable of holding any office under the united states, for which he, or another for his benefit receives any salary, fees or emolument of any kind.

Each state shall maintain its own delegates in a meeting of the states, and while they act as members of the committee of the states.

In determining questions in the united states, in Congress assembled, each state shall have one vote.

Freedom of speech and debate in Congress shall not be impeached or questioned in any Court, or place out of Congress, and the members of congress shall be protected in their persons from arrests and imprisonments, during the time of their going to and from, and attendance on congress, except for treason, felony, or breach of the peace.

Article VI No state without the Consent of the united states in congress assembled, shall send any embassy to, or receive any embassy from, or enter into any conference, agreement, or alliance or treaty with any King, prince or state; nor shall any person holding any office of profit or trust under the united states, or any of them, accept of any present, emolument, office or title of any kind whatever from any king, prince or foreign state; nor shall the united states in congress assembled, or any of them, grant any title of nobility.

No two or more states shall enter into any treaty, confederation or alliance whatever between them, without the consent of the united states in congress assembled, specifying accurately the purposes for which the same is to be entered into, and how long it shall continue.

No state shall lay any imposts or duties, which may interfere with any stipulations in treaties, entered into by the united states in congress assembled, with any king, prince or state, in pursuance of any treaties already proposed by congress, to the courts of France and Spain.

No vessels of war shall be kept up in time of peace by any state, except such number only, as shall be deemed necessary by the united states in congress assembled, for the defence of such state, or its trade; nor shall any body of forces be kept up by any state, in time of peace, except such number only, as in the judgment of the united states, in congress assembled, shall be deemed requisite to garrison the forts necessary for the defence of such state; but every state shall always keep up a well regulated and disciplined militia, sufficiently armed and accoutred, and shall provide and constantly have ready for use, in public stores, a due number of field pieces and tents, and a proper quantity of arms, ammunition and camp equipage.

No state shall engage in any war without the consent of the united states in congress assembled, unless such state be actually invaded by enemies, or shall have received certain advice of a resolution being formed by some nation of Indians to invade such state, and the danger is so imminent as not to admit of a delay, till the united states in congress assembled can be consulted: nor shall any state grant commissions to any ships or vessels of war, nor letters of marque or reprisal, except it be after a declaration of war by the united states in congress assembled, and then only against the kingdom or state and the subjects thereof, against which war has been so declared, and under such regulations as shall be established by the united states in congress assembled, unless such state be infested by pirates, in which case vessels of war may be fitted out for that occasion, and kept so long as the danger shall continue, or until the united states in congress assembled shall determine otherwise.

Article VII When land-forces are raised by any state for the common defence, all officers of or under the rank of colonel, shall be appointed by the legislature of each state respectively by whom such forces shall be raised, or in such manner as such state shall direct, and all vacancies shall be filled up by the state which first made the appointment.

Article VIII All charges of war, and all other expences that shall be incurred for the common defence or general welfare, and allowed by the united states in congress assembled, shall be defrayed out of a common treasury, which shall be supplied by the several states, in proportion to the value of all land within each state, granted to or surveyed for any Person, as such land and the buildings and improvements thereon shall be estimated according to such mode as the united states in congress assembled, shall from time to time direct and appoint. The taxes for paying that proportion shall be laid and levied by the authority and direction of the legislatures of the several states within the time agreed upon by the united states in congress assembled.

Article IX The united states in congress assembled, shall have the sole and exclusive right and power of determining on peace and war, except in the cases mentioned in the sixth article—of sending and receiving ambassadors—entering into treaties and alliances, provided that no treaty of commerce shall be made whereby the legislative power of the respective states shall be restrained from imposing such imposts and duties on foreigners, as their own people are subjected to, or from prohibiting the exportation or importation of any species of goods or commodities whatsoever—of establishing rules for deciding in all cases, what captures on land or water shall be legal, and in what manner prizes taken by land or naval forces in the service of the united states shall be divided or appropriated—of granting letters of marque and reprisal in times of peace—appointing courts for the trial of piracies and felonies committed on the high seas and establishing courts for receiving and determining final appeals in all cases of captures, provided that no member of congress shall be appointed a judge of any of the said courts.

The united states in congress assembled shall also be the last resort on appeal in all disputes and differences now subsisting or that hereafter may arise between two or more states concerning boundary, jurisdiction or any other cause whatever; which authority shall always be exercised in the manner following. Whenever the legislative or executive authority or lawful agent of any state in controversy with another shall present a petition to congress, stating the matter in question and praying for a hearing, notice thereof shall be given by order of congress to the legislative or executive authority of the other state in controversy, and a day assigned for the appearance of the parties by their lawful agents, who shall then be directed to appoint by joint consent, commissioners or judges to constitute a court for hearing and determining the matter in question: but if they cannot agree, congress shall name three persons out of each of the united states, and from the list of such persons each party shall alternately strike out one, the petitioners beginning, until the number shall be reduced to thirteen; and from that number not less than seven, nor more than nine names as congress shall direct, shall in the presence of congress be drawn out by lot, and the persons whose names shall be so drawn or any five of them, shall be commissioners or judges, to hear and finally determine the controversy, so always as a major part of the judges who shall hear the cause shall agree in the determination: and if either party shall neglect to attend at the day appointed, without showing reasons, which congress shall judge sufficient, or being present shall refuse to strike, the congress shall proceed to nominate three persons out of each state, and the secretary of congress shall strike in behalf of such party absent or refusing; and the judgment and sentence of the court to be appointed, in the manner before prescribed, shall be final and conclusive; and if any of the parties shall refuse to submit to the authority of such court, or to appear to defend their claim or cause, the court shall nevertheless proceed to pronounce sentence, or judgment, which shall in like manner be final and decisive, the judgment or sentence and other proceedings being in either case transmitted to congress, and lodged among the acts of congress for the security of the parties concerned: provided that every commissioner, before he sits in judgment,

shall take an oath to be administered by one of the judges of the supreme or superior court of the state, where the cause shall be tried, "well and truly to hear and determine the matter in question, according to the best of his judgment, without favour, affection or hope of reward:" provided also that no state shall be deprived of territory for the benefit of the united states.

All controversies concerning the private right of soil claimed under different grants of two or more states, whose jurisdictions as they may respect such lands, and the states which passed such grants are adjusted, the said grants or either of them being at the same time claimed to have originated antecedent to such settlement of jurisdiction, shall on the petition of either party to the congress of the united states, be finally determined as near as may be in the same manner as is before prescribed for deciding disputes respecting territorial jurisdiction between different states.

The united states in congress assembled shall also have the sole and exclusive right and power of regulating the alloy and value of coin struck by their own authority, or by that of the respective states—fixing the standard of weights and measures throughout the united states—regulating the trade and managing all affairs with the Indians, not members of any of the states, provided that the legislative right of any state within its own limits be not infringed or violated—establishing and regulating post-offices from one state to another, throughout all the united states, and exacting such postage on the papers passing thro' the same as may be requisite to defray the expences of the said office—appointing all officers of the land forces, in the service of the united states, excepting regimental officers—appointing all the officers of the naval forces, and commissioning all officers whatever in the service of the united states—making rules for the government and regulation of the said land and naval forces, and directing their operations.

The united states in congress assembled shall have authority to appoint a committee, to sit in the recess of congress, to be denominated "A Committee of the States," and to consist of one delegate from each state; and to appoint such other committees and civil officers as may be

necessary for managing the general affairs of the united states under their direction—to appoint one of their number to preside, provided that no person be allowed to serve in the office of president more than one year in any term of three years; to ascertain the necessary sums of Money to be raised for the service of the united states, and to appropriate and apply the same for defraying the public expences—to borrow money, or emit bills on the credit of the united states, transmitting every half year to the respective states an account of the sums of money so borrowed or emitted—to build and equip a navy—to agree upon the number of land forces, and to make requisitions from each state for its quota, in proportion to the number of white inhabitants in such state; which requisition shall be binding, and thereupon the legislature of each state shall appoint the regimental officers, raise the men and cloath, arm and equip them in a soldier like manner, at the expence of the united states, and the officers and men so cloathed, armed and equipped shall march to the place appointed, and within the time agreed on by the united states in congress assembled: But if the united states in congress assembled shall, on consideration of circumstances judge proper that any state should not raise men, or should raise a smaller number than its quota, and that any other state should raise a greater number of men than the quota thereof, such extra number shall be raised, officered, cloathed, armed and equipped in the same manner as the quota of such state, unless the legislature of such state shall judge that such extra number cannot be safely spared out of the same, in which case they shall raise, officer, cloath, arm and equip as many of such extra number as they judge can be safely spared. And the officers and men so cloathed, armed and equipped, shall march to the place appointed, and within the time agreed on by the united states in congress assembled.

The united states in congress assembled shall never engage in a war, nor grant letters of marque and reprisal in time of peace, nor enter into any treaties or alliances, nor coin money, nor regulate the value thereof, nor ascertain the sums and expences necessary for the defence and welfare of the united states, or any of them, nor emit bills, nor borrow money on the credit of the united states, nor appropriate money, nor agree upon the number of vessels of war, to be built or purchased, or the number of land or sea forces to be raised, nor appoint a commander in chief of the army or navy, unless nine states assent to the same: nor shall a question on any other point, except for adjourning from day to day be determined, unless by the votes of a majority of the united states in congress assembled.

The congress of the united states shall have power to adjourn to any time within the year, and to any place within the united states, so that no period of adjournment be for a longer duration than the space of six Months, and shall publish the Journal of their proceedings monthly, except such parts thereof relating to treaties, alliances or military operations as in their judgment require secresy; and the yeas and nays of the delegates of each state on any question shall be entered on the Journal, when it is desired by any delegate; and the delegates of a state, or any of them, at his or their request shall be furnished with a transcript of the said Journal, except such parts as are above excepted, to lay before the legislatures of the several states.

Article X The committee of the states, or any nine of them, shall be authorised to execute, in the recess of congress, such of the powers of congress as the united states in congress assembled, by the consent of nine states, shall from time to time think expedient to vest them with; provided that no power be delegated to the said committee, for the exercise of which, by the articles of confederation, the voice of nine states in the congress of the united states assembled is requisite.

Article XI Canada acceding to this confederation, and joining in the measures of the united states, shall be admitted into, and entitled to all the advantages of this union: but no other colony shall be admitted into the same, unless such admission be agreed to by nine states.

Article XII All bills of credit emitted, monies borrowed and debts contracted by, or under the authority of congress, before the assembling of the united states, in pursuance of the present confederation, shall be deemed and considered as a charge against the united states, for payment and satisfaction whereof the said united states, and the public faith are hereby solemnly pledged.

Article XIII Every state shall abide by the determinations of the united states in congress assembled, on all questions which by this confederation are submitted to them. And the Articles of this confederation shall be inviolably observed by every state, and the union shall be perpetual; nor shall any alteration at any time hereafter be made in any of them; unless such alteration be agreed to in a congress of the united states, and be afterwards confirmed by the legislatures of every state.

AND WHEREAS it hath pleased the Great Governor of the World to incline the hearts of the legislatures we respectively represent in congress, to approve of, and to authorize us to ratify the said articles of confederation and perpetual union. Know Ye that we the under-signed delegates, by virtue of the power and authority to us given for that purpose, do by these presents, in the name and in behalf of our respective constituents, fully and entirely ratify and confirm each and every of the said articles of confederation and perpetual union, and all and singular the matters and things therein contained: And we do further solemnly plight and engage the faith of our respective constituents, that they shall abide by the determinations of the united states in congress assembled, on all questions, which by the said confederation are submitted to them. And that the articles thereof shall be inviolably observed by the states we respectively represent, and that the union shall be perpetual. In Witness whereof we have hereunto set our hands in Congress. Done at Philadelphia in the state of Pennsylvania the ninth Day of July in the Year of our Lord one Thousand seven Hundred and Seventy-eight, and in the third year of the independence of America.

Constitution of the United States of America and Amendments*

Preamble

We the people of the United States, in order to form a more perfect union, establish justice, insure domestic tranquillity, provide for the common defense, promote the general welfare, and secure the blessings of liberty to ourselves and our posterity, do ordain and establish this Constitution for the United States of America.

Article I

Section 1 All legislative powers herein granted shall be vested in a Congress of the United States, which shall consist of a Senate and a House of Representatives.

Section 2 The House of Representatives shall be composed of members chosen every second year by the people of the several States, and the electors in each State shall have the qualifications requisite for electors of the most numerous branch of the State Legislature.

No person shall be a Representative who shall not have attained to the age of twenty-five years, and been seven years a citizen of the United States, and who shall not, when elected, be an inhabitant of that State in which he shall be chosen.

Representatives and direct taxes shall be apportioned among the several States which may be included within this Union,

---

* Passages no longer in effect are printed in italic type.

according to their respective numbers, *which shall be determined by adding to the whole number of free persons, including those bound to service for a term of years and excluding Indians not taxed, three-fifths of all other persons.* The actual enumeration shall be made within three years after the first meeting of the Congress of the United States, and within every subsequent term of ten years, in such manner as they shall by law direct. The number of Representatives shall not exceed one for every thirty thousand, but each State shall have at least one Representative; *and until such enumeration shall be made, the State of New Hampshire shall be entitled to choose three, Massachusetts eight, Rhode Island and Providence Plantations one, Connecticut five, New York six, New Jersey four, Pennsylvania eight, Delaware one, Maryland six, Virginia ten, North Carolina five, South Carolina five, and Georgia three.*

When vacancies happen in the representation from any State, the Executive authority thereof shall issue writs of election to fill such vacancies.

The House of Representatives shall choose their Speaker and other officers; and shall have the sole power of impeachment.

Section 3 The Senate of the United States shall be composed of two Senators from each State, *chosen by the legislature thereof,* for six years; and each Senator shall have one vote.

Immediately after they shall be assembled in consequence of the first election, they shall be divided as equally as may be into three classes. The seats of the Senators of the first class shall be vacated at the expiration of the second year, of the second class at the expiration of the fourth year, and of the third class at the expiration of the sixth year, so that one-third may be chosen every second year; and if vacancies happen by resignation or otherwise, during the recess of the legislature of any State, the Executive thereof may make temporary appointments until the next meeting of the legislature, which shall then fill such vacancies.

No person shall be a Senator who shall not have attained to the age of thirty years, and been nine years a citizen of the United States, and who shall not, when elected, be an inhabitant of that State for which he shall be chosen.

The Vice-President of the United States shall be President of the Senate, but shall have no vote, unless they be equally divided.

The Senate shall choose their other officers, and also a President *pro tempore,* in the absence of the Vice-President, or when he shall exercise the office of President of the United States.

The Senate shall have the sole power to try all impeachments. When sitting for that purpose, they shall be on oath or affirmation. When the President of the United States is tried, the Chief Justice shall preside: and no person shall be convicted without the concurrence of two-thirds of the members present.

Judgment in cases of impeachment shall not extend further than to removal from the office, and disqualification to hold and enjoy any office of honor, trust or profit under the United States: but the party convicted shall nevertheless be liable and subject to indictment, trial, judgment and punishment, according to law.

Section 4 The times, places and manner of holding elections for Senators and Representatives shall be prescribed in each State by the legislature thereof; but the Congress may at any time by law make or alter such regulations, except as to the places of choosing Senators.

The Congress shall assemble at least once in every year, and such meeting *shall be on the first Monday in December, unless they shall by law appoint a different day.*

Section 5 Each house shall be the judge of the elections, returns and qualifications of its own members, and a majority of each shall constitute a quorum to do business; but a smaller number may adjourn from day to day, and may be authorized to compel the attendance of absent members, in such manner, and under such penalties, as each house may provide.

Each house may determine the rules of its proceedings, punish its members for disorderly behavior, and with the concurrence of two-thirds, expel a member.

Each house shall keep a journal of its proceedings, and from time to time publish the same, excepting such parts as may in their judgment require secrecy; and the yeas and nays of the members of either house on any question shall, at the desire of one-fifth of those present, be entered on the journal.

Neither house, during the session of Congress, shall, without the consent of the other, adjourn for more than three days, nor to any other place than that in which the two houses shall be sitting.

Section 6 The Senators and Representatives shall receive a compensation for their services, to be ascertained by law and paid out of the treasury of the United States. They shall in all cases except treason, felony and breach of the peace, be privileged from arrest during their attendance at the session of their respective houses, and in going to and returning from the same; and for any speech or debate in either house, they shall not be questioned in any other place.

No Senator or Representative shall, during the time for which he was elected, be appointed to any civil office under the authority of the United States, which shall have been created, or the emoluments whereof shall have been increased, during such time; and no person holding any office under the United States shall be a member of either house during his continuance in office.

Section 7 All bills for raising revenue shall originate in the House of Representatives; but the Senate may propose or concur with amendments as on other bills.

Every bill which shall have passed the House of Representatives and the Senate, shall, before it become a law, be presented to the President of the United States; if he approve he shall sign it, but if not he shall return it with objections to that house in which it originated, who shall enter the objections at large on their journal, and proceed to reconsider it. If after such reconsideration two-thirds of that house shall agree to pass the bill, it shall be sent, together with the objections, to the other house, by which it shall likewise be reconsidered, and, if approved by two-thirds of that house, it shall become a law. But in all such cases the votes of both houses shall be determined by yeas and nays, and the names of the persons voting for and against the bill shall be entered on the journal of each house respectively. If any bill shall not be returned by the President within ten days (Sundays excepted) after it shall have been presented to him, the same shall be a law, in like manner as if he had signed it, unless the Congress by their adjournment prevent its return, in which case it shall not be a law.

Every order, resolution, or vote to which the concurrence of the Senate and House of Representatives may be necessary (except on a question of adjournment) shall be presented to the President of the United States; and before the same shall take effect, shall be approved by him, or being disapproved by him, shall be repassed by two-thirds of the Senate and House of Representatives, according to the rules and limitations prescribed in the case of a bill.

Section 8   The Congress shall have power

To lay and collect taxes, duties, imposts, and excises, to pay the debts and provide for the common defense and general welfare of the United States; but all duties, imposts and excises shall be uniform throughout the United States;

To borrow money on the credit of the United States;

To regulate commerce with foreign nations, and among the several States, and with the Indian tribes;

To establish an uniform rule of naturalization, and uniform laws on the subject of bankruptcies throughout the United States;

To coin money, regulate the value thereof, and of foreign coin, and fix the standard of weights and measures;

To provide for the punishment of counterfeiting the securities and current coin of the United States;

To establish post offices and post roads;

To promote the progress of science and useful arts by securing for limited times to authors and inventors the exclusive right to their respective writings and discoveries;

To constitute tribunals inferior to the Supreme Court;

To define and punish piracies and felonies committed on the high seas and offenses against the law of nations;

To declare war, grant letters of marque and reprisal, and make rules concerning captures on land and water;

To raise and support armies, but no appropriation of money to that use shall be for a longer term than two years;

To provide and maintain a navy;

To make rules for the government and regulation of the land and naval forces;

To provide for calling forth the militia to execute the laws of the Union, suppress insurrections, and repel invasions;

To provide for organizing, arming, and disciplining the militia, and for governing such part of them as may be employed in the service of the United States, reserving to the States respectively the appointment of the officers, and the authority of training the militia according to the discipline prescribed by Congress;

To exercise exclusive legislation in all cases whatsoever, over such district (not exceeding ten miles square) as may, by cession of particular States, and the acceptance of Congress, become the seat of government of the United States, and to exercise like authority over all places purchased by the consent of the legislature of the State, in which the same shall be, for erection of forts, magazines, arsenals, dockyards, and other needful buildings; —and

To make all laws which shall be necessary and proper for carrying into execution the foregoing powers, and all other powers vested by this Constitution in the government of the United States, or in any department or officer thereof.

Section 9   *The migration or importation of such persons as any of the States now existing shall think proper to admit shall not be prohibited by the Congress prior to the year 1808; but a tax or duty may be imposed on such importation, not exceeding $10 for each person.*

The privilege of the writ of habeas corpus shall not be suspended, unless when in cases of rebellion or invasion the public safety may require it.

No bill of attainder or ex post facto law shall be passed.

No capitation, or other direct, tax shall be laid, unless in proportion to the census or enumeration herein before directed to be taken.

No tax or duty shall be laid on articles exported from any State.

No preference shall be given by any regulation of commerce or revenue to the ports of one State over those of another; nor shall vessels bound to, or from, one State, be obliged to enter, clear, or pay duties in another.

No money shall be drawn from the treasury, but in consequence of appropriations made by law; and a regular statement and account of the receipts and expenditures of all public money shall be published from time to time.

No title of nobility shall be granted by the United States: and no person holding any office of profit or trust under them, shall, without the consent of the Congress, accept of any present, emolument, office, or title, of any kind whatever, from any king, prince, or foreign state.

Section 10   No State shall enter into any treaty, alliance, or confederation; grant letters of marque and reprisal; coin money; emit bills of credit; make anything but gold and silver coin a tender in payment of debts; pass any bill of attainder, ex post facto law, or law impairing the obligation of contracts, or grant any title of nobility.

No State shall, without the consent of Congress, lay any imposts or duties on imports or exports, except what may be absolutely necessary for executing its inspection laws: and the net produce of all duties and imposts, laid by any State on imports or exports, shall be for the use of the treasury of the United States; and all such laws shall be subject to the revision and control of the Congress.

No State shall, without the consent of Congress, lay any duty of tonnage, keep troops or ships of war in time of peace, enter into any agreement or compact with another State, or with a foreign power, or engage in war, unless actually invaded, or in such imminent danger as will not admit of delay.

Article II

Section 1   The executive power shall be vested in a President of the United States of America. He shall hold his office during the term of four years, and, together with the Vice-President, chosen for the same term, be elected as follows:

Each State shall appoint, in such manner as the legislature thereof may direct, a number of electors, equal to the whole number of Senators and Representatives to which the State may be entitled in the Congress; but no Senator or Representative, or person holding an office of trust or profit under the United States, shall be appointed an elector.

The electors shall meet in their respective States, and vote by ballot for two persons, of

whom one at least shall not be an inhabitant of the same State with themselves. And they shall make a list of all the persons voted for, and of the number of votes for each; which list they shall sign and certify, and transmit sealed to the seat of government of the United States, directed to the President of the Senate. The President of the Senate shall, in the presence of the Senate and House of Representatives, open all the certificates, and the votes shall then be counted. The person having the greatest number of votes shall be the President, if such number be a majority of the whole number of electors appointed; and if there be more than one who have such majority, and have an equal number of votes, then the House of Representatives shall immediately choose by ballot one of them for President; and if no person have a majority, then from the five highest on the list said house shall in like manner choose the President. But in choosing the President the votes shall be taken by States, the representation from each State having one vote; a quorum for this purpose shall consist of a member or members from two-thirds of the States, and a majority of all the States shall be necessary to a choice. In every case, after the choice of the President, the person having the greatest number of votes of the electors shall be the Vice-President. But if there should remain two or more who have equal votes, the Senate shall choose from them by ballot the Vice-President.

The Congress may determine the time of choosing the electors and the day on which they shall give their votes; which day shall be the same throughout the United States.

No person except a natural-born citizen, *or a citizen of the United States at the time of the adoption of this Constitution,* shall be eligible to the office of President; neither shall any person be eligible to that office who shall not have attained to the age of thirty-five years, and been fourteen years a resident within the United States.

In cases of the removal of the President from office or of his death, resignation, or inability to discharge the powers and duties of the said office, the same shall devolve on the Vice-President, and the Congress may by law provide for the case of removal, death, resignation, or inability, both of the President and Vice-President, declaring what officer shall then act as President, and such officer shall act accordingly, until the disability be removed, or a President shall be elected.

The President shall, at stated times, receive for his services a compensation, which shall neither be increased nor diminished during the period for which he shall have been elected, and he shall not receive within that period any other emolument from the United States, or any of them.

Before he enter on the execution of his office, he shall take the following oath or affirmation:—"I do solemnly swear (or affirm) that I will faithfully execute the office of the President of the United States, and will to the best of my ability preserve, protect and defend the Constitution of the United States."

Section 2 The President shall be commander in chief of the army and navy of the United States, and of the militia of the several States, when called into the actual service of the United States; he may require the opinion, in writing, of the principal officer in each of the executive departments, upon any subject relating to the duties of their respective offices, and he shall have power to grant reprieves and pardons for offenses against the United States, except in cases of impeachment.

He shall have power, by and with the advice and consent of the Senate, to make treaties, provided two-thirds of the Senators present concur; and he shall nominate, and by and with the advice and consent of the Senate, shall appoint ambassadors, other public ministers and consuls, judges of the Supreme Court, and all other officers of the United States, whose appointments are not herein otherwise provided for, and which shall be established by law: but Congress may by law vest the appointment of such inferior officers, as they think proper, in the President alone, in the courts of law, or in the heads of departments.

The President shall have power to fill up all vacancies that may happen during the recess of the Senate, by granting commissions which shall expire at the end of their next session.

Section 3 He shall from time to time give to the Congress information of the state of the Union, and recommend to their consideration such measures as he shall judge necessary and expedient; he may, on extraordinary occasions, convene both houses, or either of them, and in case of disagreement between them, with respect to the time of adjournment, he may

adjourn them to such time as he shall think proper; he shall receive ambassadors and other public ministers; he shall take care that the laws be faithfully executed, and shall commission all the officers of the United States.

Section 4 The President, Vice-President and all civil officers of the United States shall be removed from office on impeachment for, and on conviction of, treason, bribery, or other high crimes and misdemeanors.

Article III

Section 1 The judicial power of the United States shall be vested in one Supreme Court, and in such inferior courts as the Congress may from time to time ordain and establish. The judges, both of the Supreme and inferior courts, shall hold their offices during good behavior, and shall, at stated times, receive for their services a compensation which shall not be diminished during their continuance in office.

Section 2 The judicial power shall extend to all cases, in law and equity, arising under this Constitution, the laws of the United States, and treaties made, or which shall be made, under their authority;—to all cases affecting ambassadors, other public ministers and consuls;—to all cases of admiralty and maritime jurisdiction;—to controversies to which the United States shall be a party;—to controversies between two or more States;— *between a State and citizens of another State;*—between citizens of different States;—between citizens of the same State claiming lands under grants of different States, and between a State, or the citizens thereof, and foreign states, citizens or subjects.

In all cases affecting ambassadors, other public ministers and consuls, and those in which a State shall be party, the Supreme Court shall have original jurisdiction. In all the other cases before mentioned, the Supreme Court shall have appellate jurisdiction, both as to law and fact, with such exceptions, and under such regulations, as the Congress shall make.

The trial of all crimes, except in cases of impeachment, shall be by jury; and such trial shall be held in the State where said crimes shall have been committed; but when not committed within any State, the trial shall be at such place or places as the Congress may by law have directed.

Section 3 Treason against the United States shall consist only in levying war against them, or in adhering to their enemies, giving them aid and comfort. No person shall be convicted of treason unless on the testimony of two witnesses to the same overt act, or on confession in open court.

The Congress shall have power to declare the punishment of treason, but no attainder of treason shall work corruption of blood, or forfeiture except during the life of the person attainted.

Article IV

Section 1 Full faith and credit shall be given in each State to the public acts, records, and judicial proceedings of every other State. And the Congress may by general laws prescribe the manner in which such acts, records, and proceedings shall be proved, and the effect thereof.

Section 2 The citizens of each State shall be entitled to all privileges and immunities of citizens in the several States.

A person charged in any State with treason, felony, or other crime, who shall flee from justice, and be found in another State, shall on demand of the executive authority of the State from which he fled, be delivered up, to be removed to the State having jurisdiction of the crime.

No person held to service or labor in one State, under the laws thereof, escaping into another, shall, in consequence of any law or regulation therein, be discharged from such service or labor, but shall be delivered up on claim of the party to whom such service or labor may be due.

Section 3 New States may be admitted by the Congress into this Union; but no new State shall be formed or erected within the jurisdiction of any other State; nor any State be formed by the junction of two or more States, or parts of States, without the consent of the legislatures of the States concerned as well as of the Congress.

The Congress shall have power to dispose of and make all needful rules and regulations respecting the territory or other property belonging to the United States; and nothing in this Constitution shall be so construed as to prejudice any claims of the United States, or of any particular State.

Section 4 The United States shall guarantee to every State in this Union a republican form of government, and shall protect each of them against invasion; and on application of the legislature, or of the executive (when the legislature cannot be convened), against domestic violence.

Article V

The Congress, whenever two-thirds of both houses shall deem it necessary, shall propose amendments to this Constitution, or, on the application of the legislatures of two-thirds of the several States, shall call a convention for proposing amendments, which, in either case, shall be valid to all intents and purposes, as part of this Constitution, when ratified by the legislatures of three-fourths of the several States, or by conventions in three-fourths thereof, as the one or the other mode of ratification may be proposed by the Congress; provided *that no amendments which may be made prior to the year one thousand eight hundred and eight shall in any manner affect the first and fourth clauses in the ninth section of the first article;* and that no State,

without its consent, shall be deprived of its equal suffrage in the Senate.

Article VI

All debts contracted and engagements entered into, before the adoption of this Constitution, shall be as valid against the United States under this Constitution, as under the Confederation.

This Constitution, and the laws of the United States which shall be made in pursuance thereof; and all treaties made, or which shall be made, under the authority of the United States, shall be the supreme law of the land; and the judges in every State shall be bound thereby, anything in the Constitution or laws of any State to the contrary notwithstanding.

The Senators and Representatives before mentioned, and the members of the several State legislatures, and all executive and judicial officers, both of the United States and of the several States, shall be bound by oath or affirmation to support this Constitution; but no religious test shall ever be required as a qualification to any office or public trust under the United States.

Article VII

The ratification of the conventions of nine States shall be sufficient for the establishment of this Constitution between the States so ratifying the same.

Done in Convention by the unanimous consent of the States present, the seventeenth day of September in the year of our Lord one thousand seven hundred and eighty-seven and of the Independence of the United States of America the twelfth. In witness whereof we have hereunto subscribed our names.

Amendments to the Constitution*

Amendment I

Congress shall make no law respecting an establishment of religion, or prohibiting the free exercise thereof; or abridging the freedom of speech, or of the press; or the right of the people peaceably to assemble, and to petition the government for a redress of grievances.

Amendment II

A well-regulated militia being necessary to the security of a free State, the right of the people to keep and bear arms shall not be infringed.

Amendment III

No soldier shall, in time of peace, be quartered in any house without the consent of the owner, nor in time of war, but in a manner to be prescribed by law.

Amendment IV

The right of the people to be secure in their persons, houses, papers, and effects, against unreasonable searches and seizures, shall not be violated, and no warrants shall issue but upon probable cause, supported by

*The first ten Amendments (the Bill of Rights) were adopted in 1791.

oath or affirmation, and particularly describing the place to be searched, and the persons or things to be seized.

Amendment V

No person shall be held to answer for a capital, or otherwise infamous crime, unless on a presentment or indictment of a grand jury, except in cases arising in the land or naval forces, or in the militia, when in actual service in time of war or public danger; nor shall any person be subject for the same offense to be twice put in jeopardy of life or limb; nor shall be compelled in any criminal case to be a witness against himself, nor be deprived of life, liberty, or property, without due process of law; nor shall private property be taken for public use without just compensation.

Amendment VI

In all criminal prosecutions, the accused shall enjoy the right to a speedy and public trial, by an impartial jury of the State and district wherein the crime shall have been committed, which district shall have been previously ascertained by law, and to be informed of the nature and cause of the accusation; to be confronted with the witnesses against him; to have compulsory process for obtaining witnesses in his favor, and to have the assistance of counsel for his defense.

Amendment VII

In suits at common law, where the value in controversy shall exceed twenty dollars, the right of trial by jury shall be preserved, and no fact tried by a jury shall be otherwise reexamined in any court of the United States, than according to the rules of the common law.

Amendment VIII

Excessive bail shall not be required, nor excessive fines imposed, nor cruel and unusual punishments inflicted.

Amendment IX

The enumeration in the Constitution, of certain rights, shall not be construed to deny or disparage others retained by the people.

Amendment X

The powers not delegated to the United States by the Constitution, nor prohibited by it to the States, are reserved to the States respectively, or to the people.

Amendment XI

[Adopted 1798]

The judicial power of the United States shall not be construed to extend to any suit in law or equity, commenced or prosecuted against one of the United States by citizens of another State, or by citizens or subjects of any foreign state.

Amendment XII

[Adopted 1804]

The electors shall meet in their respective States, and vote by ballot for President and Vice-President, one of whom, at least, shall not be an inhabitant of the same State with themselves; they shall name in their ballots the person voted for as President, and in distinct ballots the person voted for as Vice-President, and they shall make distinct lists of all persons voted for as President, and of all persons voted for as Vice-President, and of the number of votes for each, which lists they shall sign and certify, and transmit sealed to the seat of government of the United States, directed to the President of the Senate;— the President of the Senate shall, in the presence of the Senate and House of Representatives, open all the certificates and the votes shall then be counted;—the person having the greatest number of votes for President shall be the President, if such number be a majority of the whole number of electors appointed; and if no person have such majority, then from the persons having the highest numbers not exceeding three on the list of those voted for as President, the House of Representatives shall choose immediately, by ballot, the President. But in choosing the President, the votes shall be taken by States, the representation from each State having one vote; a quorum for this purpose shall consist of a member or members from two-thirds of the States, and a majority of all the States shall be necessary to a choice. And if the House of Representatives shall not choose a President whenever the right of choice shall devolve upon them, before *the fourth day of March* next following, then the Vice-President shall act as President, as in the case of the death or other constitutional disability of the President.

The person having the greatest number of votes as Vice-President shall be the Vice-President, if such number be a majority of the whole number of electors appointed; and if no person have a majority, then from the two highest numbers on the list the Senate shall choose the Vice-President; a quorum for the purpose shall consist of two-thirds of the whole number of Senators, and a majority of the whole number shall be necessary to a choice. But no person constitutionally ineligible to the office of President shall be eligible to that of Vice-President of the United States.

Amendment XIII

[Adopted 1865]

Section 1 Neither slavery nor involuntary servitude, except as a punishment for crime whereof the party shall have been duly convicted, shall exist within the United States, or any place subject to their jurisdiction.

Section 2 Congress shall have power to enforce this article by appropriate legislation.

Amendment XIV

[Adopted 1868]

Section 1 All persons born or naturalized in the United States, and subject to the jurisdiction thereof, are citizens of the United States and of the State wherein they reside. No State shall make or enforce any law which shall abridge the privileges or immunities of citizens of the United States; nor shall any State deprive any person of life, liberty, or property, without due process of law; nor deny to any person within its jurisdiction the equal protection of the laws.

Section 2 Representatives shall be apportioned among the several States according to their respective numbers, counting the whole number of persons in each State, excluding Indians not taxed. But when the right to vote at any election for the choice of Electors for President and Vice-President of the United States, Representatives in Congress, the executive and judicial officers of a State, or the members of the legislature thereof, is denied to any of the male inhabitants of such State, being twenty-one years of age and citizens of the United States, or in any way abridged, except for participation in rebellion, or other crime, the basis of representation therein shall be reduced in the proportion which the number of such male citizens shall bear to the whole number of male citizens twenty-one years of age in such State.

Section 3 No person shall be a Senator or Representative in Congress, or Elector of President and Vice-President, or hold any office, civil or military, under the United States, or under any State, who, having previously taken an oath, as a member of Congress, or as an officer of the United States, or as a member of any State legislature, or as an executive or judicial officer of any State, to support the Constitution of the United States, shall have engaged in insurrection or rebellion against the same, or given aid or comfort to the enemies thereof. Congress may, by a vote of two-thirds of each house, remove such disability.

Section 4 The validity of the public debt of the United States, authorized by law, including debts incurred for payment of pensions and bounties for services in suppressing insurrection or rebellion, shall not be questioned. But neither the United States nor any State shall assume or pay any debt or obligation incurred in aid of insurrection or rebellion against the United States, or any claim for the loss of emancipation of any slave; but all such debts, obligations, and claims shall be held illegal and void.

Section 5 The Congress shall have power to enforce, by appropriate legislation, the provisions of this article.

Amendment XV
[Adopted 1870]

Section 1 The right of citizens of the United States to vote shall not be denied or abridged by the United States or by any State on account of race, color, or previous condition of servitude.

Section 2 The Congress shall have power to enforce this article by appropriate legislation.

Amendment XVI
[Adopted 1913]

The Congress shall have power to lay and collect taxes on incomes, from whatever source derived, without apportionment among the several States, and without regard to any census or enumeration.

Amendment XVII
[Adopted 1913]

Section 1 The Senate of the United States shall be composed of two Senators from each State, elected by the people thereof, for six years; and each Senator shall have one vote. The electors in each State shall have the qualifications requisite for electors of [voters for] the most numerous branch of the State legislatures.

Section 2 When vacancies happen in the representation of any State in the Senate, the executive authority of such State shall issue writs of election to fill such vacancies: Provided, that the Legislature of any State may empower the executive thereof to make temporary appointments until the people fill the vacancies by election as the Legislature may direct.

Section 3 This amendment shall not be so construed as to affect the election or term of any Senator chosen before it becomes valid as part of the Constitution.

Amendment XVIII
[Adopted 1919; Repealed 1933]

Section 1 After one year from the ratification of this article the manufacture, sale, or transportation of intoxicating liquors within, the importation thereof into, or the exportation thereof from the United States and all territory subject to the jurisdiction thereof, for beverage purposes, is hereby prohibited.

Section 2 The Congress and the several States shall have concurrent power to enforce this article by appropriate legislation.

Section 3 This article shall be inoperative unless it shall have been ratified as an amendment to the Constitution by the legislatures of the several States, as provided by the Constitution, within seven years from the date of the submission thereof to the States by the Congress.

Amendment XIX
[Adopted 1920]

Section 1 The right of citizens of the United States to vote shall not be denied or abridged by the United States or by any State on account of sex.

Section 2 The Congress shall have power to enforce this article by appropriate legislation.

Amendment XX
[Adopted 1933]

Section 1 The terms of the President and Vice-President shall end at noon on the 20th day of January, and the terms of Senators and Representatives at noon on the 3rd day of January, of the years in which such terms would have ended if this article had not been ratified; and the terms of their successors shall then begin.

Section 2 The Congress shall assemble at least once in every year, and such meeting shall begin at noon on the 3rd day of January, unless they shall by law appoint a different day.

Section 3 If, at the time fixed for the beginning of the term of the President, the President-elect shall have died, the Vice-President-elect shall become President. If a President shall not have been chosen before the time fixed for the beginning of his term, or if the President-elect shall have failed to qualify, then the Vice-President-elect shall act as President until a President shall have qualified; and the Congress may by law provide for the case wherein neither a President-elect nor a Vice-President-elect shall have qualified, declaring who shall then act as President, or the manner in which one who is to act shall be selected, and such persons shall act accordingly until a President or Vice-President shall have qualified.

Section 4 The Congress may by law provide for the case of the death of any of the persons from whom the House of Representatives may choose a President whenever the right of choice shall have devolved upon them, and for the case of the death of any of the persons from whom the Senate may choose a Vice-President whenever the right of choice shall have devolved upon them.

Section 5 Sections 1 and 2 shall take effect on the 15th day of October following the ratification of this article.

Section 6 This article shall be inoperative unless it shall have been ratified as an amendment to the Constitution by the Legislatures of three-fourths of the several States within seven years from the date of its submission.

Amendment XXI

[Adopted 1933]

Section 1 The eighteenth article of amendment to the Constitution of the United States is hereby repealed.

Section 2 The transportation or importation into any State, Territory, or Possession of the United States for delivery or use therein of intoxicating liquors, in violation of the laws thereof, is hereby prohibited.

Section 3 This article shall be inoperative unless it shall have been ratified as an amendment to the Constitution by conventions in the several States, as provided in the Constitution, within seven years from the date of submission thereof to the States by the Congress.

Amendment XXII

[Adopted 1951]

Section 1 No person shall be elected to the office of President more than twice, and no person who has held the office of President, or acted as President, for more than two years of a term to which some other person was elected President shall be elected to the office of President more than once. But this article shall not apply to any person holding the office of President when this article was proposed by the Congress, and shall not prevent any person who may be holding the office of President, or acting as President, during the term within which this article becomes operative from holding the office of President or acting as President during the remainder of such term.

Section 2 This article shall be inoperative unless it shall have been ratified as an amendment to the Constitution by the legislatures of three-fourths of the several States within seven years from the date of its submission to the States by the Congress.

Amendment XXIII

[Adopted 1961]

Section 1 The District constituting the seat of Government of the United States shall appoint in such manner as the Congress may direct:

A number of electors of President and Vice-President equal to the whole number of Senators and Representatives in Congress to which the District would be entitled if it were a State, but in no event more than the least populous State; they shall be in addition to those appointed by the States, but they shall be considered for the purposes of the election of President and Vice-President, to be electors appointed by a State; and they shall meet in the District and perform such duties as provided by the twelfth article of amendment.

Section 2 The Congress shall have the power to enforce this article by appropriate legislation.

Amendment XXIV

[Adopted 1964]

Section 1 The right of citizens of the United States to vote in any primary or other election for President or Vice-President, for electors for President or Vice-President, or for Senator or Representative in Congress, shall not be denied or abridged by the United States or any State by reason of failure to pay any poll tax or other tax.

Section 2 The Congress shall have the power to enforce this article by appropriate legislation.

Amendment XXV

[Adopted 1967]

Section 1 In case of the removal of the President from office or of his death or resignation, the Vice-President shall become President.

Section 2 Whenever there is a vacancy in the office of the Vice-President, the President shall nominate a Vice-President who shall take office upon confirmation by a majority vote of both Houses of Congress.

Section 3 Whenever the President transmits to the President pro tempore of the Senate and the Speaker of the House of Representatives his written declaration that he is unable to discharge the powers and duties of his office, and until he transmits to them a written declaration to the contrary, such powers and duties shall be discharged by the Vice-President as Acting President.

Section 4 Whenever the Vice-President and a majority of either the principal officers of the executive departments or of such other body as Congress may by law provide, transmit to the President pro tempore of the Senate and the Speaker of the House of Representatives their written declaration that the President is unable to discharge the powers and duties of his office, the Vice-President shall immediately assume the powers and duties of the office as Acting President.

Thereafter, when the President transmits to the President pro tempore of the Senate and the Speaker of the House of Representatives his written declaration that no inability exists, he shall resume the powers and duties of his office unless the Vice-President and a majority of either the principal officers of the executive department[s] or of such other body as Congress may by law provide, transmit within four days to the President pro tempore of the Senate and the Speaker of the House of Representatives their written declaration that the President is unable to discharge the powers and duties of his office. Thereupon Congress shall decide the issue, assembling within forty-eight hours for that purpose if not in session. If the Congress, within twenty-one days after receipt of the latter written declaration, or, if Congress is not in session, within twenty-one days after Congress is required to assemble, determines by two-thirds vote of both Houses that the President is unable to discharge the powers and duties of his office, the Vice-President shall continue to discharge the same as Acting President; otherwise, the President shall resume the powers and duties of his office.

Amendment XXVI

[Adopted 1971]

Section 1 The right of citizens of the United States, who are eighteen years of age or older, to vote shall not be denied or abridged by the United States or by any State on account of age.

Section 2 The Congress shall have power to enforce this article by appropriate legislation.

Amendment XXVII

[Adopted 1992]

No law, varying the compensation for the services of the Senators and Representatives, shall take effect, until an election of Representatives shall have intervened.

Presidential Elections

Year	Number of States	Candidates	Parties	Popular Vote	% of Popular Vote	Electoral Vote	% Voter Participation[a]
1789	10	GEORGE WASHINGTON	No party designations			69	
		John Adams				34	
		Other candidates				35	
1792	15	GEORGE WASHINGTON	No party designations			132	
		John Adams				77	
		George Clinton				50	
		Other candidates				5	
1796	16	JOHN ADAMS	Federalist			71	
		Thomas Jefferson	Democratic-Republican			68	
		Thomas Pinckney	Federalist			59	
		Aaron Burr	Democratic-Republican			30	
		Other candidates				48	
1800	16	THOMAS JEFFERSON	Democratic-Republican			73	
		Aaron Burr	Democratic-Republican			73	
		John Adams	Federalist			65	
		Charles C. Pinckney	Federalist			64	
		John Jay	Federalist			1	
1804	17	THOMAS JEFFERSON	Democratic-Republican			162	
		Charles C. Pinckney	Federalist			14	
1808	17	JAMES MADISON	Democratic-Republican			122	
		Charles C. Pinckney	Federalist			47	
		George Clinton	Democratic-Republican			6	
1812	18	JAMES MADISON	Democratic-Republican			128	
		DeWitt Clinton	Federalist			89	
1816	19	JAMES MONROE	Democratic-Republican			183	
		Rufus King	Federalist			34	
1820	24	JAMES MONROE	Democratic-Republican			231	
		John Quincy Adams	Independent Republican			1	
1824	24	JOHN QUINCY ADAMS	Democratic-Republican	108,740	30.5	84	26.9
		Andrew Jackson	Democratic-Republican	153,544	43.1	99	
		Henry Clay	Democratic-Republican	47,136	13.2	37	
		William H. Crawford	Democratic-Republican	46,618	13.1	41	
1828	24	ANDREW JACKSON	Democratic	647,286	56.0	178	57.6
		John Quincy Adams	National Republican	508,064	44.0	83	
1832	24	ANDREW JACKSON	Democratic	701,780	54.2	219	55.4
		Henry Clay	National Republican	484,205	37.4	49	
		Other candidates		107,988	8.0	18	
1836	26	MARTIN VAN BUREN	Democratic	764,176	50.8	170	57.8
		William H. Harrison	Whig	550,816	36.6	73	
		Hugh L. White	Whig	146,107	9.7	26	
1840	26	WILLIAM H. HARRISON	Whig	1,274,624	53.1	234	80.2
		Martin Van Buren	Democratic	1,127,781	46.9	60	
1844	26	JAMES K. POLK	Democratic	1,338,464	49.6	170	78.9
		Henry Clay	Whig	1,300,097	48.1	105	
		James G. Birney	Liberty	62,300	2.3		

Presidential Elections (continued)

Year	Number of States	Candidates	Parties	Popular Vote	% of Popular Vote	Electoral Vote	% Voter Participation[a]
1848	30	ZACHARY TAYLOR	Whig	1,360,967	47.4	163	72.7
		Lewis Cass	Democratic	1,222,342	42.5	127	
		Martin Van Buren	Free Soil	291,263	10.1		
1852	31	FRANKLIN PIERCE	Democratic	1,601,117	50.9	254	69.6
		Winfield Scott	Whig	1,385,453	44.1	42	
		John P. Hale	Free Soil	155,825	5.0		
1856	31	JAMES BUCHANAN	Democratic	1,832,955	45.3	174	78.9
		John C. Frémont	Republican	1,339,932	33.1	114	
		Millard Fillmore	American	871,731	21.6		
1860	33	ABRAHAM LINCOLN	Republican	1,865,593	39.8	180	81.2
		Stephen A. Douglas	Democratic	1,382,713	29.5	12	
		John C. Breckinridge	Democratic	848,356	18.1	72	
		John Bell	Constitutional Union	592,906	12.6	39	
1864	36	ABRAHAM LINCOLN	Republican	2,206,938	55.0	212	73.8
		George B. McClellan	Democratic	1,803,787	45.0	21	
1868	37	ULYSSES S. GRANT	Republican	3,013,421	52.7	214	78.1
		Horatio Seymour	Democratic	2,706,829	47.3	80	
1872	37	ULYSSES S. GRANT	Republican	3,596,745	55.6	286	71.3
		Horace Greeley[b]	Democratic	2,843,446	43.9		
1876	38	RUTHERFORD B. HAYES	Republican	4,036,572	48.0	185	81.8
		Samuel J. Tilden	Democratic	4,284,020	51.0	184	
1880	38	JAMES A. GARFIELD	Republican	4,453,295	48.5	214	79.4
		Winfield S. Hancock	Democratic	4,414,082	48.1	155	
		James B. Weaver	Greenback-Labor	308,578	3.4		
1884	38	GROVER CLEVELAND	Democratic	4,879,507	48.5	219	77.5
		James G. Blaine	Republican	4,850,293	48.2	182	
		Benjamin F. Butler	Greenback-Labor	175,370	1.8		
		John P. St. John	Prohibition	150,369	1.5		
1888	38	BENJAMIN HARRISON	Republican	5,447,129	47.9	233	79.3
		Grover Cleveland	Democratic	5,537,857	48.6	168	
		Clinton B. Fisk	Prohibition	249,506	2.2		
		Anson J. Streeter	Union Labor	146,935	1.3		
1892	44	GROVER CLEVELAND	Democratic	5,555,426	46.1	277	74.7
		Benjamin Harrison	Republican	5,182,690	43.0	145	
		James B. Weaver	People's	1,029,846	8.5	22	
		John Bidwell	Prohibition	264,133	2.2		
1896	45	WILLIAM MCKINLEY	Republican	7,102,246	51.1	271	79.3
		William J. Bryan	Democratic	6,492,559	47.7	176	
1900	45	WILLIAM MCKINLEY	Republican	7,218,491	51.7	292	73.2
		William J. Bryan	Democratic; Populist	6,356,734	45.5	155	
		John C. Wooley	Prohibition	208,914	1.5		
1904	45	THEODORE ROOSEVELT	Republican	7,628,461	57.4	336	65.2
		Alton B. Parker	Democratic	5,084,223	37.6	140	
		Eugene V. Debs	Socialist	402,283	3.0		
		Silas C. Swallow	Prohibition	258,536	1.9		

Year	Number of States	Candidates	Parties	Popular Vote	% of Popular Vote	Electoral Vote	% Voter Participation[a]
1908	46	WILLIAM H. TAFT	Republican	7,675,320	51.6	321	65.4
		William J. Bryan	Democratic	6,412,294	43.1	162	
		Eugene V. Debs	Socialist	420,793	2.8		
		Eugene W. Chafin	Prohibition	253,840	1.7		
1912	48	WOODROW WILSON	Democratic	6,296,547	41.9	435	58.8
		Theodore Roosevelt	Progressive	4,118,571	27.4	88	
		William H. Taft	Republican	3,486,720	23.2	8	
		Eugene V. Debs	Socialist	900,672	6.0		
		Eugene W. Chafin	Prohibition	206,275	1.4		
1916	48	WOODROW WILSON	Democratic	9,127,695	49.4	277	61.6
		Charles E. Hughes	Republican	8,533,507	46.2	254	
		A. L. Benson	Socialist	585,113	3.2		
		J. Frank Hanly	Prohibition	220,506	1.2		
1920	48	WARREN G. HARDING	Republican	16,143,407	60.4	404	49.2
		James M. Cox	Democratic	9,130,328	34.2	127	
		Eugene V. Debs	Socialist	919,799	3.4		
		P. P. Christensen	Farmer-Labor	265,411	1.0		
1924	48	CALVIN COOLIDGE	Republican	15,718,211	54.0	382	48.9
		John W. Davis	Democratic	8,385,283	28.8	136	
		Robert M. La Follette	Progressive	4,831,289	16.6	13	
1928	48	HERBERT C. HOOVER	Republican	21,391,993	58.2	444	56.9
		Alfred E. Smith	Democratic	15,016,169	40.9	87	
1932	48	FRANKLIN D. ROOSEVELT	Democratic	22,821,857	57.4	472	56.9
		Herbert C. Hoover	Republican	15,761,841	39.7	59	
		Norman Thomas	Socialist	884,781	2.2		
1936	48	FRANKLIN D. ROOSEVELT	Democratic	27,752,869	60.8	523	61.0
		Alfred M. Landon	Republican	16,674,665	36.5	8	
		William Lemke	Union	882,479	1.9		
1940	48	FRANKLIN D. ROOSEVELT	Democratic	27,307,819	54.8	449	62.5
		Wendell L. Willkie	Republican	22,321,018	44.8	82	
1944	48	FRANKLIN D. ROOSEVELT	Democratic	25,606,585	53.5	432	55.9
		Thomas E. Dewey	Republican	22,014,745	46.0	99	
1948	48	HARRY S TRUMAN	Democratic	24,179,345	49.6	303	53.0
		Thomas E. Dewey	Republican	21,991,291	45.1	189	
		J. Strom Thurmond	States' Rights	1,176,125	2.4	39	
		Henry A. Wallace	Progressive	1,157,326	2.4		
1952	48	DWIGHT D. EISENHOWER	Republican	33,936,234	55.1	442	63.3
		Adlai E. Stevenson	Democratic	27,314,992	44.4	89	
1956	48	DWIGHT D. EISENHOWER	Republican	35,590,472	57.6	457	60.6
		Adlai E. Stevenson	Democratic	26,022,752	42.1	73	
1960	50	JOHN F. KENNEDY	Democratic	34,226,731	49.7	303	62.8
		Richard M. Nixon	Republican	34,108,157	49.5	219	
1964	50	LYNDON B. JOHNSON	Democratic	43,129,566	61.1	486	61.7
		Barry M. Goldwater	Republican	27,178,188	38.5	52	

Presidential Elections (continued)

Year	Number of States	Candidates	Parties	Popular Vote	% of Popular Vote	Electoral Vote	% Voter Participation[a]
1968	50	RICHARD M. NIXON	Republican	33,045,480	43.4	301	60.6
		Hubert H. Humphrey	Democratic	31,850,140	42.7	191	
		George C. Wallace	American Independent	171,422	13.5	46	
1972	50	RICHARD M. NIXON	Republican	47,169,911	60.7	520	55.2
		George S. McGovern	Democratic	29,170,383	37.5	17	
		John G. Schmitz	American	1,099,482	1.4		
1976	50	JAMES E. CARTER	Democratic	40,830,763	50.1	297	53.5
		Gerald R. Ford	Republican	39,147,793	48.0	240	
1980	50	RONALD W. REAGAN	Republican	43,904,153	50.7	489	52.6
		James E. Carter	Democratic	35,483,883	41.0	49	
		John B. Anderson	Independent	5,720,060	6.6		
		Ed Clark	Libertarian	921,299	1.1		
1984	50	RONALD W. REAGAN	Republican	54,455,075	58.8	525	53.3
		Walter F. Mondale	Democratic	37,577,185	40.6	13	
1988	50	GEORGE H. W. BUSH	Republican	48,886,097	53.4	426	50.1
		Michael S. Dukakis	Democratic	41,809,074	45.6	111[c]	
1992	50	WILLIAM J. CLINTON	Democratic	44,909,326	43.0	370	55.2
		George H. W. Bush	Republican	39,103,882	37.4	168	
		H. Ross Perot	Independent	19,741,048	18.9		
1996	50	WILLIAM J. CLINTON	Democratic	47,402,357	49.2	379	49.1
		Robert J. Dole	Republican	39,196,755	40.7	159	
		H. Ross Perot	Reform	8,085,402	8.4		
		Ralph Nader	Green	684,902	0.7		
2000	50	GEORGE W. BUSH	Republican	50,456,169	47.9	271	51.2
		Albert Gore	Democratic	50,996,116	48.4	266	
		Ralph Nader	Green	2,783,728	2.7		
2004	50	GEORGE W. BUSH	Republican	62,039,073	50.7	286	55.3
		John F. Kerry	Democratic	59,027,478	48.2	251	
		Ralph Nader	Independent	240,896	0.2		
2008	50	BARACK OBAMA	Democratic	69,498,459	53.0	365	61.7
		John McCain	Republican	59,948,283	46.0	173	
		Ralph Nader	Independent	739,165	0.55		
2012	50	BARACK OBAMA	Democratic	65,907,213	51.07	332	
		Mitt Romney	Republican	60,931,767	47.21	206	
		Gary Johnson	Independent	1,275,804	0.99		

Candidates receiving less than 1 percent of the popular vote have been omitted. Thus the percentage of popular vote given for any election year may not total 100 percent.

  Before the passage of the Twelfth Amendment in 1804, the electoral college voted for two presidential candidates; the runner-up became vice president.
  Before 1824, most presidential electors were chosen by state legislatures, not by popular vote.

[a]Percent of voting-age population casting ballots.
[b]Greeley died shortly after the election; the electors supporting him then divided their votes among minor candidates.
[c]One elector from West Virginia cast her electoral college presidential ballot for Lloyd Bentsen, the Democratic Party's vice-presidential candidate.

Presidents and Vice Presidents

1. *President* George Washington 1789–1797
   Vice President John Adams 1789–1797

2. *President* John Adams 1797–1801
   Vice President Thomas Jefferson 1797–1801

3. *President* Thomas Jefferson 1801–1809
   Vice President Aaron Burr 1801–1805
   Vice President George Clinton 1805–1809

4. *President* James Madison 1809–1817
   Vice President George Clinton 1809–1813
   Vice President Elbridge Gerry 1813–1817

5. *President* James Monroe 1817–1825
   Vice Priesident Daniel Tompkins 1817–1825

6. *President* John Quincy Adams 1825–1829
   Vice President John C. Calhoun 1825–1829

7. *President* Andrew Jackson 1829–1837
   Vice President John C. Calhoun 1829–1833
   Vice President Martin Van Buren 1833–1837

8. *President* Martin Van Buren 1837–1841
   Vice President Richard M. Johnson 1837–1841

9. *President* William H. Harrison 1841
   Vice President John Tyler 1841

10. *President* John Tyler 1841–1845
    Vice President None

11. *President* James K. Polk 1845–1849
    Vice President George M. Dallas 1845–1849

12. *President* Zachary Taylor 1849–1850
    Vice President Millard Fillmore 1849–1850

13. *President* Millard Fillmore 1850–1853
    Vice President None

14. *President* Franklin Pierce 1853–1857
    Vice President William R. King 1853–1857

15. *President* James Buchanan 1857–1861
    Vice President John C. Breckinridge 1857–1861

16. *President* Abraham Lincoln 1861–1865
    Vice President Hannibal Hamlin 1861–1865
    Vice President Andrew Johnson 1865

17. *President* Andrew Johnson 1865–1869
    Vice President None

18. *President* Ulysses S. Grant 1869–1877
    Vice President Schuyler Colfax 1869–1873
    Vice President Henry Wilson 1873–1877

19. *President* Rutherford B. Hayes 1877–1881
    Vice President William A. Wheeler 1877–1881

20. *President* James A. Garfield 1881
    Vice President Chester A. Arthur 1881

21. *President* Chester A. Arthur 1881–1885
    Vice President None

22. *President* Grover Cleveland 1885–1889
    Vice President Thomas A. Hendricks 1885–1889

23. *President* Benjamin Harrison 1889–1893
    Vice President Levi P. Morton 1889–1893

24. *President* Grover Cleveland 1893–1897
    Vice President Adlai E. Stevenson 1893–1897

25. *President* William McKinley 1897–1901
    Vice President Garret A. Hobart 1897–1901
    Vice President Theodore Roosevelt 1901

26. *President* Theodore Roosevelt 1901–1909
    Vice President Charles Fairbanks 1905–1909

27. *President* William H. Taft 1909–1913
    Vice President James S. Sherman 1909–1913

28. *President* Woodrow Wilson 1913–1921
    Vice President Thomas R. Marshall 1913–1921

29. *President* Warren G. Harding 1921–1923
    Vice President Calvin Coolidge 1921–1923

30. *President* Calvin Coolidge 1923–1929
    Vice President Charles G. Dawes 1925–1929

31. *President* Herbert C. Hoover 1929–1933
    Vice President Charles Curtis 1929–1933

32. *President* Franklin D. Roosevelt 1933–1945
    Vice President John N. Garner 1933–1941
    Vice President Henry A. Wallace 1941–1945
    Vice President Harry S Truman 1945

33. *President* Harry S Truman 1945–1953
    Vice President Alben W. Barkley 1949–1953

34. *President* Dwight D. Eisenhower 1953–1961
    Vice President Richard M. Nixon 1953–1961

35. *President* John F. Kennedy 1961–1963
    Vice President Lyndon B. Johnson 1961–1963

36. *President* Lyndon B. Johnson 1963–1969
    Vice President Hubert H. Humphrey 1965–1969

37. *President* Richard M. Nixon 1969–1974
    Vice President Spiro T. Agnew 1969–1973
    Vice President Gerald R. Ford 1973–1974

38. *President* Gerald R. Ford 1974–1977
    Vice President Nelson A. Rockefeller 1974–1977

39. *President* James E. Carter 1977–1981
    Vice President Walter F. Mondale 1977–1981

40. *President* Ronald W. Reagan 1981–1989
    Vice President George H. W. Bush 1981–1989

41. *President* George H. W. Bush 1989–1993
    Vice President J. Danforth Quayle 1989–1993

42. *President* William J. Clinton 1993–2001
    Vice President Albert Gore 1993–2001

43. *President* George W. Bush 2001–2009
    Vice President Richard B. Cheney 2001–2009

44. *President* Barack H. Obama 2009–2017
    Vice President Joseph R. Biden 2009–2017

Justices of the Supreme Court

	Term of Service	Years of Service	Life Span		Term of Service	Years of Service	Life Span
John Jay	1789–1795	5	1745–1829	Noah H. Swayne	1862–1881	18	1804–1884
John Rutledge	1789–1791	1	1739–1800	Samuel F. Miller	1862–1890	28	1816–1890
William Cushing	1789–1810	20	1732–1810	David Davis	1862–1877	14	1815–1886
James Wilson	1789–1798	8	1742–1798	Stephen J. Field	1863–1897	34	1816–1899
John Blair	1789–1796	6	1732–1800	Salmon P. Chase	1864–1873	8	1808–1873
Robert H. Harrison	1789–1790	–	1745–1790	William Strong	1870–1880	10	1808–1895
James Iredell	1790–1799	9	1751–1799	Joseph P. Bradley	1870–1892	22	1813–1892
Thomas Johnson	1791–1793	1	1732–1819	Ward Hunt	1873–1882	9	1810–1886
William Paterson	1793–1806	13	1745–1806	Morrison R. Waite	1874–1888	14	1816–1888
John Rutledge*	1795	–	1739–1800	John M. Harlan	1877–1911	34	1833–1911
Samuel Chase	1796–1811	15	1741–1811	William B. Woods	1880–1887	7	1824–1887
Oliver Ellsworth	1796–1800	4	1745–1807	Stanley Mathews	1881–1889	7	1824–1889
Bushrod Washington	1798–1829	31	1762–1829	Horace Gray	1882–1902	20	1828–1902
Alfred Moore	1799–1804	4	1755–1810	Samuel Blatchford	1882–1893	11	1820–1893
John Marshall	1801–1835	34	1755–1835	Lucius Q. C. Lamar	1888–1893	5	1825–1893
William Johnson	1804–1834	30	1771–1834	Melville W. Fuller	1888–1910	21	1833–1910
H. Brockholst Livingston	1806–1823	16	1757–1823	David J. Brewer	1890–1910	20	1837–1910
Thomas Todd	1807–1826	18	1765–1826	Henry B. Brown	1890–1906	16	1836–1913
Joseph Story	1811–1845	33	1779–1845	George Shiras Jr.	1892–1903	10	1832–1924
Gabriel Duval	1811–1835	24	1752–1844	Howell E. Jackson	1893–1895	2	1832–1895
Smith Thompson	1823–1843	20	1768–1843	Edward D. White	1894–1910	16	1845–1921
Robert Trimble	1826–1828	2	1777–1828	Rufus W. Peckham	1895–1909	14	1838–1909
John McLean	1829–1861	32	1785–1861	Joseph McKenna	1898–1925	26	1843–1926
Henry Baldwin	1830–1844	14	1780–1844	Oliver W. Holmes	1902–1932	30	1841–1935
James M. Wayne	1835–1867	32	1790–1867	William D. Day	1903–1922	19	1849–1923
Roger B. Taney	1836–1864	28	1777–1864	William H. Moody	1906–1910	3	1853–1917
Philip P. Barbour	1836–1841	4	1783–1841	Horace H. Lurton	1910–1914	4	1844–1914
John Catron	1837–1865	28	1786–1865	Charles E. Hughes	1910–1916	5	1862–1948
John McKinley	1837–1852	15	1780–1852	Willis Van Devanter	1911–1937	26	1859–1941
Peter V. Daniel	1841–1860	19	1784–1860	Joseph R. Lamar	1911–1916	5	1857–1916
Samuel Nelson	1845–1872	27	1792–1873	Edward D. White	1910–1921	11	1845–1921
Levi Woodbury	1845–1851	5	1789–1851	Mahlon Pitney	1912–1922	10	1858–1924
Robert C. Grier	1846–1870	23	1794–1870	James C. McReynolds	1914–1941	26	1862–1946
Benjamin R. Curtis	1851–1857	6	1809–1874	Louis D. Brandeis	1916–1939	22	1856–1941
John A. Campbell	1853–1861	8	1811–1889	John H. Clarke	1916–1922	6	1857–1945
Nathan Clifford	1858–1881	23	1803–1881	William H. Taft	1921–1930	8	1857–1930

	Term of Service	Years of Service	Life Span
George Sutherland	1922–1938	15	1862–1942
Pierce Butler	1922–1939	16	1866–1939
Edward T. Sanford	1923–1930	7	1865–1930
Harlan F. Stone	1925–1941	16	1872–1946
Charles E. Hughes	1930–1941	11	1862–1948
Owen J. Roberts	1930–1945	15	1875–1955
Benjamin N. Cardozo	1932–1938	6	1870–1938
Hugo L. Black	1937–1971	34	1886–1971
Stanley F. Reed	1938–1957	19	1884–1980
Felix Frankfurter	1939–1962	23	1882–1965
William O. Douglas	1939–1975	36	1898–1980
Frank Murphy	1940–1949	9	1890–1949
Harlan F. Stone	1941–1946	5	1872–1946
James F. Byrnes	1941–1942	1	1879–1972
Robert H. Jackson	1941–1954	13	1892–1954
Wiley B. Rutledge	1943–1949	6	1894–1949
Harold H. Burton	1945–1958	13	1888–1964
Fred M. Vinson	1946–1953	7	1890–1953
Tom C. Clark	1949–1967	18	1899–1977
Sherman Minton	1949–1956	7	1890–1965
Earl Warren	1953–1969	16	1891–1974
John Marshall Harlan	1955–1971	16	1899–1971
William J. Brennan Jr.	1956–1990	34	1906–1997
Charles E. Whittaker	1957–1962	5	1901–1973
Potter Stewart	1958–1981	23	1915–1985
Byron R. White	1962–1993	31	1917–
Arthur J. Goldberg	1962–1965	3	1908–1990
Abe Fortas	1965–1969	4	1910–1982
Thurgood Marshall	1967–1991	24	1908–1993
Warren C. Burger	1969–1986	17	1907–1995
Harry A. Blackmun	1970–1994	24	1908–1998
Lewis F. Powell Jr.	1972–1987	15	1907–1998
William H. Rehnquist	1972–2005	33	1924–2005
John P. Stevens III	1975–2010	35	1920–
Sandra Day O'Connor	1981–2006	25	1930–
Antonin Scalia	1986–	—	1936–
Anthony M. Kennedy	1988–	—	1936–
David H. Souter	1990–2009	19	1939–
Clarence Thomas	1991–	—	1948–
Ruth Bader Ginsburg	1993–	—	1933–
Stephen Breyer	1994–	—	1938–
John G. Roberts	2005–	—	1955–
Samuel A. Alito, Jr.	2006–	—	1950–
Sonia Sotomayor	2009–	—	1954–
Elena Kagan	2010–	—	1960–

Note: Chief justices are in italics.

*Appointed and served one term, but not confirmed by the Senate.

Index

Abenakis, 67–68
Abolitionism, 292–294, 296, 298
  African American abolitionists, 293
  American Antislavery Society, 292–293
  early efforts, 210–211
  evangelical, 292
  immediatism, 292–293
  opposition to, 293
  Quakers and, 349
  Wilmot Proviso and, 346
Abortion, 277
Accused persons, rights of, 177
Acoma Pueblo, 35
Act of Religious Toleration (1649), 40
Adams, Abigail, 187–188
Adams, Charles Francis, 395
Adams, Henry, 427
Adams, John, 98, 109, 131, 141–142, 162, 194
  defense of British soldiers, 127
  election of 1796, 183–184
  election of 1800, 193–194
  presidency of, 183–185
Adams, John Quincy
  Amistad case and, 240
  in election of 1824, 329–331, 360
  as representative, 337
  as secretary of state, 226
Adams, Samuel, 127–129, 132, 174
Adams-Onís Treaty, 226
Advertising, for slaves, 75
Afghanistan, criticism of war in, 194
Africa
  corn production, 22
  slaves and Anglo-American economy, 58, 64
"Africa for the Africans," 427
African Americans
  abolitionists, 293–294
  American Revolution and, 147, 149, 153, 156, 163
  Back to Africa movement and, 427
  in Civil War, 383–388, 402
  early colonization movement and, 211–212
  education of, after emancipation, 409
  families in colonial times, 94
  free black population, 190–191, 196, 247–248
  genealogy of, 79
  growth of black churches, 409
  proportion of total population (map), 191
  Reconstruction and reunion of families, 408
  revolutionary ideology and, 189–190
  in Sierra Leone, 147

  voting rights of, 201
  westward expansion by, 304–305, 325
African Methodist Episcopal (AME) church, 191, 284, 409
African societies, 8–10
  characteristics of, 8–9, 26–27
  complementary gender roles, 9–10
  Portuguese trading posts, 13
  slavery in Guinea, 10
  West Africa (Guinea), 9
Agriculture
  in central Mexico, 3–4
  in Civil War north, 378
  commercial, 275
  preindustrial farming, 219
  and rise of North American civilizations, 21
  sharecropping, 410–411
Alabama, 224
Alamo, 318
Alaska, purchase of, 426, 428
Albany Congress, 112–113
Albany Regency, 337–338
Alcohol abuse, temperance movement and, 288–289
Alcott, Louisa May, 381
Alexander VI (Pope), 15
Algonquians, 6–8, 39, 67–68
Alien and Sedition Acts, 184–185, 194–196, 202
A.M.E. Zion Church, 409
America, 16
American and Foreign Anti-Slavery Society, 293–294
American Antislavery Society, 292–293
American Board of Customs Commissioners, 122
American Colonization Society, 211–212, 427
American Fur Company, 308–309
American Protestantism, 101
American Renaissance, 292
American Revolution
  African Americans and, 147
  alliance with France, 152
  battlefield and home front, 153–154
  British strategy, 151
  campaign of 1777, 151
  choosing sides, 146, 148–149
  colonial government, 131–133
  Continental Army and Navy, 141
  first year of war, 140
  formation of independent republic, 141–147
  Greene and the Southern campaign, 156–157
  hardship and disease, 154

  Indian neutrality and hostility, 137–138
  Lexington and Concord, 139
  loyalists, 137–138
  neutrals, 138
  northern struggle, 150–152
  prisoners of war, 154
  siege of Boston, 140
  surrender at Yorktown, 156, 158
  symbolism, 160
  victory in the south, 156–158, 162
American societies
  ancient America, 2–5, 26
  Aztecs, 5
  Cahokia, 4–5
  chronology, 3
  Mesoamerican civilizations, 4
  Pueblos and Mississippians, 4–5
American System, 221–222, 230
American System of manufacturing, 271
Amistad case, 240
Anaconda plan, 370
Ancient America, 3–4
Andros, Sir Edmund, 77
Anglo-Dutch wars, 65
Angola, 69–70
Animals, 10
Annapolis Convention, 170
Anthony, Susan B., 339, 407, 415
Antietam, Battle of, 374
Antifederalists, 173–174, 176, 194–195
Antimason Party, 335
Antislavery. *See* Abolitionism
Apaches, 67, 313
Appeal...to the Colored Citizens (Walker), 293
Appellate courts, 177
Appomattox Court House, 398–399
Archibald, Mary Ann and James, 264–265
Architecture, 204
Arms, right to keep and bear, 177
Arnold, Benedict, 158
Art, 303, 315–317. *See also* Literature
Articles of Confederation, 165–170
  economic depression and, 170
  failure of, 165–170
  financial affairs, 178–179
  foreign affairs, 165
Artisans, preindustrial, 219–220
Assembly, freedom of, 177
Astor, John Jacob, 308
Astronomy, 4
Asylums, 288
Athletics. *See* Sports
Atlanta Missionary Association, 409
Atlanta University, 409

Atlantic trading system
　African slavery and, 68–71, 73
　exotic beverages, 72
　New England and the Caribbean, 71, 73
　slaving voyages, 71, 73
　trade routes (map), 70
Attorney General, 177
Attucks, Crispus, 127
Austin, Moses, 317
Austin, Stephen, 317
Australia, 147
Autocratic rule, 77–78
Aztecs, 1–2, 4, 5, 18

Back to Africa movement, 427
Bacon, Nathaniel, 68, 80
Bacon's Rebellion, 68
Baird, Jessie Little Doe, 25
Balboa, Vasco Núñez de, 17–18
Banking system
　bank controversies, 334
　collapse of, and Panic of 1819, 222–223
Banneker, Benjamin, 191
Bantu-speaking peoples, 9
Baptists, 198
Barbados, 54, 68
Barbary Wars, 209, 218, 229
　First, 209
　Second, 218
Barnum, P.T., 295
Barrow, Bennet, 248–249
Bartering, 96–97
Barton, Clara, 381
Baseball, 284–285
Battle at Yorktown, 156, 158
"Battle Hymn of the Republic" (Howe),
　381
Battle of Antietam, 374
Battle of Bunker Hill, 140
Battle of Chancellorsville, 387, 389
Battle of Concord, 139, 150
Battle of Fallen Timbers, 186
Battle of Gettysburg, 389–391
Battle of Lexington, 139
Battle of New Orleans, 216
Battle of Put-in-Bay, 215
Battle of Shiloh, 373
Battle of the Thames, 215
Battles of Bull Run, 369, 374
"Bear Flag Rebellion," 343
Beaver Wars, 66–67
Becknell, William, 310
Beecher, Catharine, 277
Beecher, Lyman, 287
Bell, John, 365
Bennitt, James and Nancy, 246–247
Berbers, 8
Beringia, 2
Berkeley, John Lord, 62
Berkeley, William, 68
Berlin, Ira, 64

Bernard, Francis, 124
Bibb, Henry, 293
Bicameral legislature, 171–172
Bickerdyke, Mary Ann, 381
Biddle, Nicholas, 334–335
Bill of Rights, 173–177, 194, 195
Biloxi Bay, 85
Birney, James G., 293–294, 338
Black codes, 413–414
Black Death epidemic, 11
Black Hawk War, 307
Black Kettle, 393
"Black laws," 304
Blacks. See African Americans
"Bleeding Kansas," 355, 360
Blue laws, 50
Board of Trade and Plantations, 78
Boleyn, Anne, 36
Bonaparte, Napoleon, 185
Bondsmen, 149
"Book of Negroes," 163
Boone, Daniel, 302
Booth, John Wilkes, 399
Border Ruffians, 355
Boston, siege of, 141
Boston Manufacturing Company, 220–221
Boston Massacre, 127–128
Bour, Charles, 329
Boycotts
　Continental Congress and, 132–133
　of Stamp Act, 125
Boylston, Zabdiel, 99
Braddock, Edward, 113
Bradwell, Myra, 428
Bradwell v. Illinois, 428
Brady, Matthew (photograph by), 374
Brant, Mary and Joseph, 152
Brant, Molly, 137
Brazil, colonization and sugar cultivation
　in, 52–53
Breckinridge, John C., 365
Breed's Hill, 140
*A Briefe and True Report of the New Found
　Land of Virginia* (Harriot), 24
British colonies
　colonial assemblies, 102–103
　colonial cultures, 95–100
　commerce and manufacturing in, 90, 107
　European rivalries and, 104
　politics in, 97–98, 102–103, 107–108
　regional economies, 92–93
　rioters and regulators, 131
　slave rebellions, 103–104
　wealth and poverty, 91
British troops
　Boston Massacre, 127–128
　stationing of, in Boston, 127
　withdrawal from colonies of, 163–164
Brook Farm, 291–292
Brooks, Preston, 355
Brown, Albert G., 338

Brown, James E., 391, 392
Brown, John, 355, 358–361
Brown, Noah, 215
Brown, Peter, 323
Brown, William Hill, 175
Bruce, Henry Clay, 299
Bryant, William Cullen, 355
Buchanan, James, 321, 355
Buffalo hunting, 21, 27–28, 322–323
Bull Run
　first battle of, 369
　second battle of, 374
Bunker Hill, Battle of, 140
Buren, Martin Van, 333, 337–338, 346
Burgoyne, John, 151–152
Burlend, Rebecca, 304
Burned-Over District, 287
Burns, Anthony, 349
Burr, Aaron, 183, 193, 196, 203–204
Burr Conspiracy, 203–204
Burton, James, 386
Business
　in Civil War north, 378
　government cooperation wity, 378–380,
　　584–585
Butler, Andrew P., 355
Butler, William, 346

Cabboto, Zuan. See Cabot, John
Cabot, John, 14, 23, 39
Cabot, Sebastian, 17
Cabral, Pedro Álvares, 17
Cahokia (City of the Sun), **4–5**
Calendar, development of, 4
Calhoun, John C., 213, 222, 330–331,
　　333–334, 340, 344, 347
California
　admitted to the Union, 324, 347
　Gold Rush, 308, 312, 322–324
California Trail, 321–322
Calumet (pipe), 5–6
Calvert, Cecilius, 40
Calvert, George (Lord Baltimore), 40
Calvin, John, 37
Calvinists, 100
Cameron, Paul Carrington, 250–251
Campaign of 1777, 151
Campbell, John A., 237, 391, 428
Canada, 147
　U.S.-Canadian boundary settlement, 224
　in War of 1812, 215
Canals, 267–270, 272
　and trade, 222
Caniba (Caribs), 15
Capitalism, 424
Cardozo, Francis, 409
Caribbean
　during American Revolution, 156, 158
　slavery in, 71, 73
　trade and, 71, 73
Caribbean colonies, 50–54

Carleton, James, 393–394
Carnegie, Andrew, 106
Carolina colony, 62–63
Carpetbaggers, 422
Carretta, Vincent, 106
Carroll, Charles, 272
Carson, Kit, 394
Carteret, George, 61–62
Cartier, Jacques, 17, 32
Cass, Lewis, 346, 347
Castillo, Bernal Díaz del, 1, 18
Catherine of Aragón, 36
Catholic Church
    conversion of "heathens" by, 10–11
    in European societies, 11
    Spanish colonization and, 18–19
Catholicism, 130
    anti-Catholicism, 281–283
    Jesuit missions in New France, 33
Catlin, George, 303
Census, 172
Chaco Canyon, 5
Champlain, Samuel de, 32
Chancellorsville, Battle of, 387, 389
Chapman, Maria, 293
Charles I, king of England, 50, 58
Charles II, king of England, 59, 65
Charles River Bridge v. Warren Bridge (1837),
    225–226
Charleston, South Carolina, 403
Charles Town, 89–90
Chase, Salmon, 350–351, 394
Chase, Samuel, 202
Checks and balances, 173
Cherokee Nation v. Georgia (1831), 242–243
Cherokee Phoenix (newspaper), 242
Cherokees, 115, 241–245, 315
Chesapeake colony, 40–43, 64
    civic rituals, 96
    families, 42
    politics, 42–43
    slavery and, 73
    standard of living, 41–42
Chesapeake (USS), 210
Cheshire Baptists, 198–200
Chesnut, James Jr., 397
Chesnut, Mary Boykin, 251, 377, 391, 397
Cheyennes, 393–394
Chicago, Illinois, 308
Chickasaws, 315
Child, Lydia Maria, 293
Childbearing, 251–252
Children
    in Chesapeake colonies, 42
    child labor, 266, 268, 273
    infant mortality, 42
    in temperance movement, 289
China, corn production, 22
Chinese immigrants, 272
    in California, 323
    as railroad workers, 426

Chinooks, 5
Chippewas, 116
Chivington, John, 393
Chocolate trade, 72
Choctaws, 244, 315
Christianity, as motive for exploration, 12, 19
Church attendance, 100–101
Church of England, 36–37
Cinque, Joseph, 240
Cities. See also Urbanization
    colonial era, 91
City of the Sun (Cahokia), 4–5
"City upon a hill," 78
Civic rituals, 95–96
Civil Rights Act (1875), 425–426
Civil Rights Bill of 1866, 414
Civil War. See also Confederate States of
    America; Union Army; specific
    battles
    African American recruits, 384, 402
    antiwar sentiment, 392
    battlefield stalemate, 395
    Bull Run
        first battle, 369
        second battle, 374
    causation, 369
    comparative resources of Union
        and Confederacy, 371
    Confederate offensives, Maryland
        and Kentucky, 374–375
    death toll and impact, 399
    fall of Atlanta, 395–397
    in the far west, 372
    final stage of, 394–399
    financial cost of, 399
    Fort Sumter and outbreak of, 368
    hospitals and camp life, 386
    Northern diplomatic strategy, 394–395
    Northern women during, 380–381
    NYC draft riots and, 393
    Peninsula Campaign, 373–374
    political disunity of governments
        during, 390–394
    Sherman's March to the Sea, 397
    soldiers in, 385–387
    strategies, 370–371
    surrender at Appomattox, 398–399
    Tennessee Campaign and Battle
        of Shiloh, 372–373
    tide of battle in, 387, 389–390
    Union cause in, 380
    Union naval campaign, 371
    in Virginia, 398
    weapons, 386
Clark, Charles, 391
Clark, William, 206–207
Class inequities, 281–282, 284–286,
    296–297, 543
Clausewitz, Karl von, 395
Clay, Henry, 213, 221, 330–331, 334–335,
    341, 347

    Liberia and, 212
    and Missouri Compromise, 224
Clermont, 267
Cleveland, OH, 308
Clinton, Bill, impeachment of, 418
Clinton, DeWitt, 213
Clinton, George, 203, 211
Clinton, Hillary Rodham, 133
Clinton, Sir Henry, 156
Coacoochee (Chief), 245
Coal, 420
Codex Azcatitlan, 19
Coercive Acts, 129–130
Coffee trade, 72
Cold Harbor, Battle of, 398
Cold Water Army, 289
Collet, John (painting by), 101
Colonial cultures, 95–100
    Algonquian and English differences, 39
    chronology of, 84
    diversity in, 82–83
    the Enlightenment, 98–100
    genteel culture, 95–97
    life in New England, 48–50
    "middle ground" rituals, 95
    oral cultures, 95
    religious and civic rituals, 95–96
    rituals of consumption, 96–97
    tea and madeira, 97
Colonial families, 93–95
    African American, 94
    city life and, 91
    European American, 93–94
    Indian and mixed-race, 93, 137
    of New England, 48–49
Colonies and colonization. See also British
    colonies; specific colonies
    American Revolution and end of,
        109–110
    Anglo-American, 58–66, 80
    Anglo-American 18th century colonies
        (map), 60
    Carolina, 62–63
    Chesapeake, 40–43, 64
    chronology, 31
    chronology of Anglo-American
        expansion, 59
    chronology of end of, 111
    chronology of founding of (1565-1640),
        32
    diversity in, 82–83
    Dutch, 34
    English interest in, 36–44
    failures, 23–24, 28
    French, 30–36
    Jamaica, 63–64
    Jesuit missions in New France, 33
    labor demand in, 41
    lessons learned, 13–14
    mercantilism and, 76–77
    missionary activities, 47–48

New England, 64, 66
New Jersey, 61–62
New Mexico, 30–31
New Netherland, 33, 36
New York, 61
Pennsylvania, 62–63
political autonomy challenged, 76–79
political structures, 66
Quebec and Montreal, 32–33
settlements and Indian tribes (map), 34
Spanish, 17–20, 30–33
sugar cultivation, 63–64
Columbian Exchange, 20–21, 27
major items in (map), 20
smallpox and other diseases, 19–20
sugar, horses, and tobacco, 21
Columbus, Christopher, **14**–15
Comanche Empire, 315–316
Comanches, 83, 313, 315–316
Commerce
in British colonies, 90
pine tree shilling and, 65
regulation of, 173
specialization of, 274–276
Committees of Correspondence, 127–128, 130
Committees of observation and inspection, 132–133
Commodities markets, 308
"Common school" movement, 290
Common Sense (Paine), 142–143, 161
Commonwealth period, 58–59
Commonwealth v. Hunt, 273
Communal ideal, 46–47
Compromise of 1850, 328, 348, 362
Compromise of 1877, 429–430
Concord, Battle of, 140, 150
Confederate States of America, 367–368
army desertions in, 391
centralization and, 375
disunity in, 390–391
draft inequities in army of, 379
Emancipation plan in, 385
food riots, 391
Great Britain and, 394–396
human and economic hardship in, 377
nationalist ideology, 375–376
transformation of the south, 375–378
women's roles in, 376–377
Confederation Congress, 165, 169–172
Confiscation Acts, 383
Congregationalists, 49–50, 101
Congressional reconstruction, 418
Conquistadors, **17**–**18**
Constantinople, 11
Constitution, U. S. *See also* Bill of Rights
congressional and presidential powers, 173
Madison and, 171
national bank established under, 178–179

opposition and ratification, 164–165, 170–175
slavery and, 164–165, 172–173
Constitutional Convention, 171
Consumption
colonial rituals of, 96–97
commercialization and, 274–276
Continental Army, 141
officer corps, 153–154
staffing of, 153, 161–162
Continental Association, 132
Continental Association agreement, 132
Continental Congress, 130–132
Committees of observation, 132–133
First, 131–132
Second, 140–141, 165
Convention of 1800, 193–194
Convention of 1818, 226
Cooke, Jay, 379
Cooper, Peter, 268
Copley, John Singleton (painting by), 96, 176
Copperheads, 392
Corn, 2–4, 22
Cornwallis, Lord, 156, 158
Coronado, Francisco Vásquez de, 18
Corporate growth, 225–226
Corps of Discovery, 206–208, 229, 310
Corps of Topographical Engineers, 310
Cortés, Hernán, 1, 18
Cosmographiae Introductio (Introduction to Cosmography), 16
Cotton, 204
cotton kingdom, 233, 239, 250
demand for, after War of 1812, 218–220, 222
in global economy, 250
mills, 210
Southern dependence on, 222–223, 262
Cotton gin, 204
Coureurs de bois, 83
Covenant Chain, 67
Covey, James, 240
Crawford, William H., 329–331
Creeks, 75, 115, 168, 315
Crime, 96
Crockett, Davy, 302–303
Cromwell, Oliver, 58
Crosby, Alfred, 20
Cruel and unusual punishment, 177
Crusades, 11
Cuba, exploration of, 14
Cult of domesticity, 276–277
Cult of true womanhood, 276–277
Culture, nationalism and, 204
Culture areas, 5–6
Cumberland Road, 222
Currency Act, 118
Currency problems, pine tree shilling, 65
Custis, Martha, 141

da Gama, Vasco, 13
Daughters of Liberty, 125, 133
Davis, Henry W., 406
Davis, Jefferson, 353, 367–368, 373, 375, 382, 385, 389, 391, 395, 430
Dawes, William, 139
Declaration of Independence, 143
Declaration of Rights and Grievances, 132
Declaratory Act, 122
Decoration Day, 403
Deere, John, 307
Defense of the Constitutionality of the Bank (Hamilton), 179
Democratic Party, 352–353
Reconstruction and, 413–414
Democratic societies, 182
Democrats, 328, 331–332
election of 1860, 365–369
Lecompton Constitution and, 358
Whigs and, 336–337, 361
Department of the Interior, 311
Deposit Act of 1836, 335
de Soto, Hernán, 18
de Tocqueville, Alexis, 244, 249, 266
Detroit, MI
as frontier, 116, 155
settlement of, 308
Dew, Thomas R., 237
Dias, Bartholomew, 13
Dickinson, John, 172
Dinwiddie, Robert, 112
Disarmament treaties, 226
Diseases, 27–28
in Civil War, 386
Columbian Exchange, 19–20
in Continental Army, 154
Indians and, 66
measles epidemic, 320
smallpox, 18, 99
syphilis, 21
urbanization and, 280–281
in western territories, 322
Dissenters, 194
District courts, 177
Division of labor, 5–7, 26
Divorce, 339
Dix, Dorothea, 288
Doegs, 68
Dominion of New England, 77
Donner Party, 322
Douglas, Stephen A., 347–348
in election of 1860, 358, 365
Kansas-Nebraska Act and, 350
Lincoln-Douglas debates, 357
Douglass, Frederick, 254, 293–294, 328, 348, 382, 384, 430
Drake, Sir Francis, 23
Dred Scott decision, 356–357, 360, 362, 365, 428
Dual-sex principle, 9–10
The Duke's Laws, 61

Dunmore, Lord, 131, 149, 153
Dutch colonization, 33, 36
Dutch West India Company, 17, 33, 36, 61
Dysentery, 154

East Indian Company, 129
Echohawk, Brummet (painting by), 244
Economic crises, Van Buren and, 338
Economic expansion, 264–265, 601–606
Economies, regional colonial
    bartering, 96–97
    families, production, and reproduction
        in, 93–95, 107
    Georgia, 93
    New England, 92
    South Carolina, 92–93
Economy
    cycles of boom and bust, 276
    sectionalism and, 221–227
Education
    of blacks, 409
    public schools, 288, 290
    reform, 175–176
    of women, 175–176
Edwards, Haden, 318
Edwards, Jonathan, 100
Egalitarianism, 191
Election of 1786, 183–184
Election of 1800, 193–194
Election of 1804, 203–204
Election of 1808, 211
Election of 1824, 329–331
Election of 1828, 331–332
Election of 1832, 335
Election of 1844, 341
Election of 1848, 346
Election of 1852, 349
Election of 1856, 355
Election of 1860, 365–369
Election of 1864, 394
Election of 1868, 418
Election of 1876, 429–430
Elections
    colonial ritual and, 97–98
    fraud, 334
Electoral college, 173
Eliot, John, 47
Elizabeth I, queen of England, 10–11, 23,
    36–37
Emancipation, 188–189, 401–402
    advent of, 382–385
    Confederate plan for, 385
    Lincoln's role in, 382
    manumission and, 190–191
Emancipation Proclamation, 383–384
Embargo Act of 1807, 210
Emerson, Ralph Waldo, 292, 358–359
Empresarios, 317
Encomienda system, **18**, 32
Enforcement Acts, 424
England

Civil War in, 58–59, 64
    imports from, 123
    social and economic change, 36
    Stuart monarchs, 37–38
English monarchs
    Anne, 57–59
    Charles I, 37–38, 58–59
    Charles II, 58–59, 62
    Elizabeth I, 36–37
    Henry VIII, 36
    James I, 37–38, 40
    James II, 59, 61, 77
    Mary, 59, 77–78
    William, 59, 77–78
English reformation, 36–37
Enlightenment, 98–100
Equiano, Olaudah, 106
Era of Good Feelings, 224–225
Ericsson, Leif, 17
Erie Canal, 222, 267–268, 272
Essay Concerning Human Understanding
    (Locke), 98
Ethnic diversity
    geographic expansion and, 84–90
    maintaining ethnic identities, 90
Ethnic tension, 282–283
Etowaucum (Nicholas) (Indian convert
    and go-between), 57–58
Europe, deportation of "undesirables" to
    new world, 87–88
European-Indian warfare, 105–106
    Iroquois neutrality, 105–106
Europeans in North America
    contest between Spain and England,
        23–24
    Indians and, 113–115
    Roanoke, 24
    trade among Indians and Europeans, 23
European societies, 10–12
    effects of plague and warfare, 11
    gender, work, politics, and religion, 10–11
    male dominance of, 10–11
    motives for exploration, 12
    political and technological change,
        11–12
Evangelists, 100, 287
Executive branch, 177
Ex parte Milligan, 428
Experiments and Observations on Electricity
    (Franklin), 99
Exploration
    Christopher Columbus, 14–15
    early European, 12–14
    Hernán Cortés, 18
    John Cabot, 17
    map, 15
    in Mediterranean Atlantic, 13
    motives for, 12, 27–28
    Norse and other northern voyagers, 17
    Portuguese trading posts in Africa, 13
    Spanish conquests, 17–20

Factions, 163–164, 171, 180–182, 184,
    194–196
Factories, 270–274. *See also* Industrial
    development
    early factories, 220–221
    labor protests, 273
Fallen Timbers, Battle of, 186
Fall River plan, 271, 273
Families
    Chesapeake, 42
    in colonial New England, 48–49, 53
    "ideal," 53, 276–277
    shrinking size of, 277
    slave families, 256
    southern planters and, 251–252
"Fancy trade," 256
Farms and farming. *See also* Agriculture
    commercial, 264–265, 275
    labor-saving equipment, 275, 307, 357
    preemption policy, 311, 313
    preindustrial farms, 264–265
    rural communities, 275–276
    sharecropping, 410–411
Faust, Drew, 399
Federalism, 173–174, 360
Federalists, 173–174
    Hamilton and, 180
The Federalist Papers, 175
Fehrenbacher, Don, 400
Ferdinand and Isabella of Spain, 12, 14
Field Order Number 15, 408
Fifteenth Amendment, 419
Fifty-four Forty or fight, 340
Fifty-Fourth Massachusetts Regiment,
    387–388
Filibustering, 354
Fillmore, Millard, 346
Finance
    Articles of Confederation and, 178–179
    depreciation of Continental currency,
        179, 196
Finney, Charles G., 287
First Amendment, 177
First Bank of the United States, 178–179
First Congress, 176
First Continental Congress, 131–132
Fish, Hamilton, 428
Fish and fishing, 23, 208–209
Fisk University, 409
Florida, Adams-Onis Treaty and, 226
Folk culture, 245–246
Food crops. *See* Agriculture
Force Bill, 333–334
Foreign affairs, 165–166, 177
Foreign Anti-Slavery Society, 293
Forest clearing (controlled burning), 3–4
Fort Detroit, 116, 155
Fort Laramie Treaty, 322
Fort Mims massacre, 217
Fort Orange, 33
Fort Stanwix treaty, 166

Fort Sumter, 368
Fort Ticonderoga, 141, 151
Fort Wagner, 387
"Forty-niners," 323
Fossett, Joseph, 232
Fourier, Charles, 291
Fourierists, 291–292
Four Indian Kings, 57–58
Fourteenth Amendment, 414–415, 424–426
Fourth Amendment, 177
Fox Indians, 307
France
    North American colonies, 23, 80
    posts along the Mississippi, 85–86
    Quasi-War, 184
    territorial expansion, 84–85
    XYZ affair and, 184
Franklin, Benjamin, 99, 106, 112, 116, 142, 152, 162, 176
Frazier, Garrison, 408
"Fredonia Republic," 318
Free black communities, 247–248
Freedmen's Bureau, 407, 409, 414, 431
Freedom of the seas, 209
Freeholders, 41
Free-labor ideology, 294
Freemasonry, 335
Free press, 102–103
Free Soil Party, 346, 355
"Free State of Jones," 377
Frémont, Jessie Benton, 310
Frémont, John C., 310, 355, 394
French and Indian War, 105–106
French Revolution, 180, 195
Fries, John, 192–193
Fries's Rebellion, 192–193, 196
Frontenac, Louise de Buade, 66
Frontier hostilities, 155
Fugitive Slave Act, 328, 348–349
Fugitive slave laws, 169, 172–173
Fulkes, Minnie, 254
Fuller, Margaret, 292
Fulton, Robert, 225
Fundamental Orders of Connecticut, 46
Fur trade, 22, 32–33, 66–67, 80, 308–309

Gabriel's Rebellion, 193, 196
Gag rule, 337
Gallatin, Albert, 202
Galloway, Joseph, 132
Garlic, Delia, 253–254
Garment industry, 274
Garrison, William Lloyd, 292–293, 298
Gates, Horatio, 156
The Gazette of the United States, 181
Gender roles, 5–7, 9–10, 26. See also Women
    in Indian nations, 84–85
General Land Office, 311
General Survey Act of 1824, 311
Genêt, Edmond, 180

Genizaros, 93
Genteel culture, 95–97
Gentilz, Theodore, 316
Geography (Ptolemy), 12
George III, king of England, 116–117
Georgia
    in American Revolution, 156
    settlement of, 93
Germain, Lord George, 140
German immigrants, 89, 283
Gettysburg, Battle of, 389–391
Gibbons v. Ogden (1824), 225
Gibbs, Josiah, 240
Giddings, Joshua, 350–351
Glorious Revolution, 77–78, 103
Gold, Spanish colonial expansion and, 19–20
Gold Rush, 308, 312, 322–323, 326
Gooding, James Henry, 387
Government
    Articles of Confederation, 165–170
    business cooperation with, 378–380, 584–585
    colonial assemblies, 102–103
    First Continental Congress, 131–132
    state constitutions, 143
Grain Coast, 9
Grain exports, 92
Grant, Ulysses S., 372–373
    in Civil War, 372–373, 389, 395
    election of, 418
    in Reconstruction, 417
Gray, Thomas R., 258
Great Awakening, 100–102, 108
Great Britain
    Anglo-American relations, 182–183
    and U.S. Civil War, 394–396
    War of 1812, 214–219
Great Lakes, 116
Great Plains, horses and, 21
"Great postal campaign," 293
Greeley, Horace, 353, 383
Greenville, Indiana, 207
Grenville, George, 117
Grier, Robert, 357
Grimké, Angelina and Sarah, 339
Guanche people, 13
Gullah dialect, 74

Haiti, establishment of, 192
Haitian refugees, 192
Hakluyt, Richard, 23
Hale, Stephen, 368
Hamilton, Alexander, 82, 112, 195–196
    death of, 203
    The Federalist Papers and, 175
    financial plan of, 178–179
    First Bank of the United States and, 178–179
    on industrial development, 179
    and New York Evening Post, 202

Republicans and, 180
    as Treasury secretary, 177–179
    Washington's Farewell Address, 183
Hammond, James, 250
Hammond, James Henry, 237
Hancock, John, 127
Handsome Lake, 186
Harmar, Josiah, 186
Harpers Ferry, 358–359, 361
Harriot, Thomas, 24, 45
Harrison, William Henry, 337–339
    battle of Tippecanoe, 208
    election of 1840, 338
    in War of 1812, 215–217
Hartford Convention of 1814, 218–219
Harvard University, 98
Haudenosaunee, 7
Hawkins, Benjamin, 187
Hawkins, John, 23
Hawthorne, Nathaniel, 292
Hayden, Lewis, 348
Hayes, Rutherford B., election of, 429–430, 499
Hayne, Robert Y., 333
Hemings, Sally, 232
Henry, Joseph, 290
Henry, Patrick, 116, 118–119, 132, 174
Henry, William, 419
Henry the Navigator, 13
Henry VII, king of England, 12, 17
Henry VIII, king of England, 36
Hispaniola, 14
Hohokam, 4
Holden, William W., 392
Homestead Act, 313
Hood, John, 395, 397
Hooker, Thomas, 47
Horses, 21
    Spanish colonization and, 21
Horsmanden, Daniel, 103
Hospital Sketches (Alcott), 381
House, Callie, 260
House of Burgesses, 42, 105, 117
House of Delegates, 43
Houston, Sam, 318
Howe, Julia Ward, 381
Howe, William, 141, 150
Hudson, Henry, 17, 33
Huguenots, 31, 90
Huitzilopochtli, 5
Hull, John, 65
Hull, William, 215
Hundred Years' War, 11
Hunt, Thomas P., 289
Hutchinson, Anne, 50
Hutchinson, Thomas, 120, 129

Illinois, 224, 304
Illuminated manuscripts, 11
Immediatism, 292–293

Immigrants/immigration
    Chinese, 272, 323
    fear of, 352
    Haitian, 192
    Scots-Irish, Scots, and Germans, 89–90
    urbanization and, 281–282
Impeachment, 418
Impeachment powers, 173
Imperial crises, American colonization
        and, 66–68
Incas, 18
Indentured servants, 30, **41–42,** 53, 73
Indiana, 224
Indian Removal Act, 241–245, 306–307
Indians. *See also* Native cultures; specific
        tribes
    accommodation of, 239, 241
    of California, 323–324
    Cherokee Nation v. Georgia, 242–243
    Civil War and, 370, 372, 393–394
    confederacy of, 166
    conversion of, 57–58
    divisions among, 207
    enslavement in the Carolinas, 74–75
    European-Indian warfare, 105–106
    expansion of European settlement and,
        82–83, 114–115
    frontier hostilities, 155
    hostilities in Virginia, 39–40
    Indian families, 93
    languages of, revitalization efforts, 25
    and mixed-race families, 93, 137
    negotiations with, 166
    racial mixing among, 93, 313–314
    in Reconstruction era, 426
    removal of, 241–245, 304
    reservation system, 311
    Seminole wars, 245
    trade with Europeans, 23, 80
    Trail of Tears, 244
    treaties with, 239, 322
    westward expansion and, 238–239,
        241–245, 308–309, 325
Indian sovereignty, 186
Indian Trade and Intercourse Act of 1793,
        186–187
Indigo, slavery and, 74
Individualism, 290–292, 298
Individual liberty, 202
Industrial development and industrializa-
        tion. *See also* specific industry
    in Civil War north, 378
    in Civil War South, 376
    early industrialization, 219–221
    early industry, 265–266
    factories and, 270–274
    federal support for, 179
    garment industry, 274
    in the North, 220
    putting-out and early factories, 220
    in Reconstruction South, 420–421

Infant mortality, 42
Inflation, during American Revolution, 154
Intercultural rituals, 95
Interesting Narrative (Equiano), 106
Interior, Department of, 311
Interracial marriage, 79
Intolerable Acts, 129–130
Iraq, criticism of war in, 194
Ireland, 281–282
Iron, 420
Iron manufacturing, 90
Iroquois Confederacy, 7, 66–67, 80, 112,
        152, 186
    Fort Stanwix treaty and, 166
    neutrality policy, 105–106, 137–138
    New France and, 66–67, 80
    political structures, 8
Islam
    in 15th-Century Africa, 8
    influence on West Africa, 8–9
Itinerarium (Hamilton), 82

Jackson, Andrew, 217–218
    elected president in 1828, 330–332
    election of 1832, 335
    in election of 1824, 329–331, 360
    Indian removal and, 332
    opponents, 330–332
    second presidential term, 335
    on westward expansion and Indians, 239
Jackson, Stonewall, 373, 387, 389
Jackson, William Andrew, 396
Jacobs, Harriet, 256
Jamaica, colonization of, 63–64
James I, king of England, 21, 40
James II, king of England, 77
James the Duke of York, 61, 80
Jamestown, **38–39,** 68
Jay, John, 132, 162, 182–183
    The Federalist Papers and, 175
Jay Treaty, 182–184, 209
Jefferson, Martha, 232
Jefferson, Thomas, 164–165, 195
    Bank of United States and, 179
    on bill of rights, 174
    children of, 232
    death of, 232
    Declaration of Independence, 143
    election as president (1800), 193–194,
        229–230
    election of 1796, 182–183
    Indian relations, 207–208
    Kentucky and Virginia Resolutions, 228
    and Louisiana Purchase, 205–206
    political visions, 195–204
    on race, 164–165
    as Secretary of State, 177
    slave trade and, 210
    Virginia and Kentucky Resolutions
        and, 184
Jesuit missions, 33, 54

Jesup, Thomas, 245
Jim Crow, portrayal of, 285
Jocelyn, Nathaniel (painting by), 240
Johnson, Andrew
    and Fourteenth Amendment, 414–415
    impeachment of, 418
    pardon policy, 412
    racial views of, 412, 415
    Reconstruction plan, 410, 412, 431–432
Johnson, Richard M., 338
Johnson, William (Sir), 137
Johnson v. M'Intosh (1823), 310
Johnston, Joseph E., 389, 395
"Join or Die" cartoon, 112
Joint-stock companies, **38,** 44
Jolliet, Louis, 66
Judicial politics, 202
Judicial review, 203
Judiciary Act of 1789, 177
Judiciary branch, 177
Julian, George, 413
Justice Act, 129–130

Kansas-Nebraska Act, 350–351, 355, 362
Kansas Territory, 328, 355
Kearny, Stephen, 343
Kelley, Abby, 293
Kentucky Resolution, 185, 228, 360
Kern, Richard, 303
Key, Francis Scott, 217
Kickapoo, 315
King, Rufus, 203, 211, 224
King Cotton, 250
King George's War, 100, 104
King Philip's War, 67–68
King William's War, 104
Kiowas, 313
Kitchen Cabinet, 332
Knight, Newt, 377
Know-Nothings, 352
Knox, Henry, 177, 186
Ku Klux Klan, 404, 423–424

Labor. *See also* Labor unions; Work force
    in colonial New England, 49
    conditions of servitude, 41–42
    demand for, in Chesapeake colonies, 41
    division of, in families, 94
    eight-hour workday bill, 425
    protests, 273
    women in workforce, 277–278
Labor unions, 273–274
Ladies Association, 156
Lafayette, Marquis de, 152
Lakotas, 322
Lamar, Mirabeau, 318
Land claims (western claims and cessions),
        167
Land Ordinance of 1785, 167–168
Land riots, 130
Land sales, 167–168

L'Anse aux Meadows, Newfoundland, 17
La Salle, René-Robert Cavelier de, 66
las Casas, Bartolomé de, 18
Lasselle, Marie-Therese (self-portrait by), 155
Latin America, and the Monroe Doctrine, 226–227
Latino settlers, early descendants, 324
Lean Bear, 393
Lecompton Constitution, 358
Lee, Richard Henry, 132, 143, 174
Lee, Robert E., 373, 387, 389–390
Leflore, Greenwood, 249
Leisler, Jacob, 77
Le Moyne, Jacques (painting by), 7
L'Enfant, Pierre Charles, 204
Lewis, Meriwether, 206–207
Lewis and Clark Expedition, 206–207, 310
Lexington, Battle of, 140
Liberia, 212, 296, 427
Liberty Party, 294
Libyan Desert, 9
Life of Washington (Weems), 175
Limited government, Jefferson's concept of, 202
Lincoln, Abraham
    assassination of, 399
    election of, 357, 359, 365–369
    Emancipation Proclamations and, 382–385
    "House Divided" speech, 357
    on Kansas-Nebraska Act, 351
    Lincoln-Douglas debates, 357
    reconstruction plan, 405–407
    reelection of, 394
    second Inaugural Address, 400
Lincoln, Benjamin, 156
Literature
    of American Renaissance, 292
    frontier literature, 302–303
Little Turtle, 186
Living standards, in British colonies, 91
Livingston, Robert, 205, 225
Lobbyists, 424
Locke, John, 62–63, 98–100
Log Cabin, The (newspaper), 338
Log Cabin BIll, 311
Long, Stephen H., 303, 310
Long houses, 7
Lord Dunmore's War, 131
Los Adaes, 85
"Lost Cause" tradition, 430
Louisbourg (Nova Scotia), 104
Louisiana, 224
    function of, as French colony, 86
    map ca. 1720, 85
Louisiana Purchase, 205–207, 224, 226, 230
Louis XIV, king of France, 78
L'Ouverture, Toussaint, 192
Lovejoy, Elijah P., 293

Lowell, Francis Cabot, 220
Lowell, James Russell, 342
Lowell industrial village (Massachusetts), 220
Lowell Offering (journal), 271
Lowell plan of industrialization, 271
Loyalists, 119–120, 141, 148
Loyal Nine, 120
Lumber industry, 308
Luther, Martin, 37

Machine-tool industry, 271
Madeira wine, 97
Madison, Dolley, 213, 217
Madison, James
    on economic growth, 221–222
    election of, 211
    failed policies, 213
    The Federalist and, 175
    government building and, 178–180, 183, 185, 196
    Hamilton and, 179, 188–189
    on state debt, 178
    Virginia and Kentucky Resolutions and, 185, 227
    Virginia and New Jersey plans and, 171–172
    War of 1812 and, 213
Maize, 2–4, 22, 30, 54
Malinche, La, 1–2, 18
"Mammoth cheese," 198
Manifest destiny, 319, 340, 354, 361
Mann, Horace, 290
Mansur, Ustand (painting by), 45
Manufacturing
    in British colonies, 90
    in post-revolution era, 210
Manumission, 190
Marbury, William, 203
Marbury v. Madison, 203
Marco Polo, 12
Marina, Doña, 1–2, 18
Market economy, 273
Marquette, Jacques, 66
Marriage, among planters, 251–252
Marryat, Frank (drawing by), 312
Marshall, James, 312
Marshall, John, 202–203, 224–225, 229
Martha Washington Societies, 288
Mary, queen of England, 59, 77–78
Maryland, 40–43
    Glorious Revolution in, 77–78
    House of Delegates, 43
Mason, James, 347, 395
Massachusetts, as royal colony, 77–78
Massachusetts Bay Company, 44
Massachusetts Government Act, 129–130
Massasoit, 44
Mass production, 271
Mather, Cotton, 99
Matrilineal descent, 7–8

Mayas, 4
Mayflower, 44
Mayflower Compact, 44, 46
Mayhew, Thomas, 47
McClellan, George B., 369–370, 373–374, 394
McCormick, Cyrus, 307, 378
McCormick, William, 378
McCormick's reaper, 307
McCulloch v. Maryland (1819), 224–225
McPherson, James, 265
Meatpacking, 274
Meigs, Montgomery, 379
Melville, Herman, 292, 342
Memorial Day, 403
Menendez, Francisco, 69
Menéndez de Avilés, Pedro, 31
Mental institutions, 288
Mercantilism, 76–77 81
Mesoamerican civilizations, 4, 19, 22
Mestizos, 31, 93, 308
Metacom (King Philip), 67–68
Methodists, 200
Metis, 93, 308
Mexico
    far north of (map), 314
    independence of, 315
    Mesoamerican civilizations, 4
    Tenochtitlán site in, 18
    war with U.S., 318–319, 341–347, 360
Miami Confederacy, 186
Miami Indians, 306
Michigan lumber industry, 308
Middle class, ideal, 276–277
"Middle ground" rituals, 95
Middle passage, 71, 73
Midway Islands, 426
Midwest settlement, 303–304, 326
Military, westward expansion and, 311
Militia units (American Revolution), 153
Milligan, Lambdin P., 428
Minie, Claude, 386
Mining, 308
Mining settlements, 323–324
Minkisi, 88
Minnesota lumber industry, 308
Missionaries, 47–48, 320
Missions, 85
Mississippi, 224
Mississippians, 4–5
Mississippi River exploration, 310
Missouri Compromise, 224–225, 229
Mixed-race families, 93, 137
"Model of Christian Charity, A" (Winthrop), 46
Mogollon, 4
Mohawks, 66–68, 137
Molasses, 118
Money, Currency act and, 118
Monitor and Merrimack, battle of, 371
Monks Mound, 5

Monroe, James, 205
 election of, 224
 and "Era of Good Feelings," 224–225
 Liberia established under, 212
 Non Importation Act and, 210
Monroe Doctrine, 226–227
Montoya, Pablo, 343
Montreal, 32–33
Moral reform, 287
Morgan, Daniel, 158
Mormons, 290–291, 320–321
Morrill Land Grant Act, 380
Morse, Samuel F.B., 269
Motecuhzoma II, 1, 6
Mott, Lucretia, 293, 338–339, 361
Mountain Meadows Massacre, 321
Moveable type, **12**
Muguet, Peter, 72
Mulattos, 248
Multiracial Americans, 79
Murray, Elizabeth (portrait of), 96
Murray, Judith Sargent, 176, 195
Murray, William Vans, 185
Muskogeans, 7
Muslims. *See also* Islam
 African slaves as, 86

Narragansetts, 44
Narrative of the Life of Frederick Douglass
 (Douglass), 254
Narváez, Pánfilo de, 17–18
Natchitoches, 85
National debt, after War for Independence,
 178
National Ex-Slave Pension and Bounty
 Association, 260
National Intelligencer, 202
Nationalism, 221–228
 American System, 221–222
 of Confederacy, 375–376
Nationalist program, 230
 boundary settlements, 226
 early internal improvements, 222
 Era of Good Feelings, 224–225
 market expansion, 225
 Monroe Doctrine, 226, 228
National Road, 222
National Trade Union, 273–274
Native American Graves Protection and
 Repatriation Act (NAGPRA), 24
Native Americans. *See* Indians
Native cultures, 5–8
 gendered division of labor, 5–7
 map, 6
 religion, 8
 social organization, 7–8
 war and politics, 8
Native language revitalization movement, 25
Naturalization Act, 184, 202
Navajos, 313, 394
Navigation Acts, 76–78

"Negro rule" myth, 421–422
Neolin (Indian shaman), 116
Neutrality acts, 354
New Amsterdam, **33**
New England
 colonization of, 64, 66
 contrasting religious patterns, 43
 families in, 48–49
 founding of, 43–48, 55
 impact of religion in, 49–50
 labor in, 49
 regional demographics in, 43
 religious and civic rituals, 95–96
 towns, 47
 trade and, 71
Newfoundland, 17
New France
 Iroquois and, 66–67
 Jesuit missions in, 33
 Quebec and Montreal, 32–33
New Hampshire, 77
New Harmony, 291
New Jersey
 in American Revolution, 151
 colonization of, 61–62
New Jersey Plan, 171–172
"New Lights," 101
New Mexico, 31–32, 313
 colonial population, 85
 frontier, 313
 Mexican rebellion in, 343
 Pueblo Revolt of 1680 in, 67
 in U.S.-Mexican war, 344
New Mexico Volunteers, 394
New Netherland, **33**
New Orleans, 204–205
 establishment of, 85
 in War of 1812, 216–217
New Orleans, Battle of, 217
Newspapers
 in colonial era, 91–92, 98
 of the early republic, 181
 partisan press, 201–202
 penny press, 285–286
New Sweden, 36
New York
 in American Revolution, 151
 colonial revolt in, 77
 colonization of, 61, 77, 80
 slave rebellion, 103–104
New York City, 278
 draft riots, 393
 evacuation of British troops from,
 163–164
 migrants to, 90
 slave uprising, 103–104
The New-York Journal, 181
Nicaragua, 354
Nine Years' War, 78
Nomadic peoples
 of early North America, 5–6

Paleo-Indians, 3–4
Non Importation Act, 210
Non-Intercourse Act (1809), 213
Norse, **17**
North
 business, industry, and agriculture in,
 378
 Civil War economy in, 378–381
 draft riots in NYC, 393
 economic expansion in, 265–266
 economic nationalism, 379–380
 industrial expansion and reconstruction
 in, 424–425
 South-North comparisons, 234–237
 workers' militancy during Civil War, 379
North, Lord, 125, 140
North America, European rivalries in, 104
North Carolina, 63
 Indian enslavement in, 74–75
Northwest Ordinance, 169
Northwest Passage, 17
Northwest Territory, 168–169, 186
Nova Scotia, 147
Noyes, John Humphrey, 291
Nullification, 228, 333–334, 360

Office of Indian Affairs, 311
Oglethorpe, James, 93
Ohio Country, 104–105, 111, *172
"Old Lights," 101
Oliver, Andrew, 120
Olmecs, 4
Oñate, Juan de, 31–32
Oneida Colony, 291–292
Onigoheriago (John) (Indian convert
 and go-between), 57–58
Onix, Don Luis de, 226
Opechancanough, 40
Oral cultures, 95
Ordinance of 1785, 167–168
Oregon Trail, 310, 321–322
Oregon Treaty, 341
Organized labor. *See* Labor unions
Oriskany, New York, battle at, 152
Osages, 85
Osceola, 245
O'Sullivan, John L., 319, 340
Otis, James Jr., 118–119
Ottawas, 116
Owen, Robert Dale, 291
Owenites, 291–292

Paine, Thomas, 142–143, 161, 188
Paiutes, 85
Panic of 1819, 222–223
Panic of 1837, 276
"Paper towns," 307
Partisan press, 201–292
Partisanship, 180, 183, 195
Party politics, 329–332, 346, 359, 360
Party system, collapse of, 350–355

Patent laws, 226
Paternalism, 250–251
Paterson, William, 171–172
Patriotic Register, 181
Patriots, 137–138, 146–147
Patriot War, 217
Paxton Boys, 116
Peace Democrats, 392
Peace of Ryswick, 78
Peale, Charles Wilson, 175, 207
Peale, Titian Ramsay, 303
Pelosi, Nancy, 133
Pelts, trade in. *See* Fur trade
Pemberton, John, 389
Penitentiaries and reform, 288
Penn, William, 62–63
Pennsylvania
    colonization of, 62
    German immigrants to, 89–90
Pennsylvania Gazette, 112
Penny press, 285–286
People v. Hall (1854), 323
Pequot War, 47
Perkinson, Jack, 299
Perkinson, Pettis, 299
Perry, Oliver Hazard, 215
Perry, Rick, 228
Petition, freedom of, 177
Pettigrew, James, 389–390
Philadelphia, Pennsylvania, 62, 278
Pickering, John, 202
Pickett, George E., 389–390
Pickett's Charge, 389–390
Pierce, Franklin, 349
Pike, Zebulon, 310
Pilgrims, 44
Pinchback, P.B.S., 409
Pinckney, Charles Cotesworth, 193, 203, 211
Pinckney, Thomas, 183
Pinckney's Treaty, 182, 205
Pine tree shilling, 65
Pinkney, William, 209
Pitt, William, 113, 119, 122
Pizarro, Francisco, 18
Plague, 11
Plantation, 233
    model of plantation slavery, 13
    sugar and, 21
Planters, in southern states/territories, 248–252
    cotton in global economy, 250
    marriage and family among, 251–252
    newly rich, 248–249
    paternalism of, 250–251
    social status and values of, 249–250
Plymouth (Massachusetts), **44**
Pocahontas, 39
Poems on Various Subjects (Wheatley), 126
Pokanokets, 44, 45
Political parties, 346, 360
Politics

mobilization of, 201
party politics, 329–332
pre-Columbian America, 8
religion and, 339
territorial expansion, 339–341
women and, 213
Polk, James K., 341, 361
    Mexican war and, 342–344
    Oregon Treaty and, 341
Polygamy, 321–322
Ponce de León, Juan, 17
Pontiac, 116
Popé (Pueblo shaman), 67
Population growth
    agricultural improvements and, 18–19
    free blacks and, 190
    geographic expansion and, 84–90
    in North American colonies, 84–90
Port Royal, 32, 64
Portugal and Portuguese
    in the Azores, 13
    colonization in North America, 24, 52–53
    daily life in, illustration of, 11
    slavery and, 13, 68–70
    trading posts in Africa, 13
    Treaty of Tordesillas, 17
"Positive good," 237–238
Postmaster General, 177
Post offices, 226
Potato famine, 281–282
Potawatomis, 116
Powderly, Terence V., 47
Powell, William Henry (painting by), 345
Power of Sympathy, The (Brown), 175
Powhatan, 38–39
Preemption policy, 311
Prejudice, 282–283
Presbyterianism, 37
Presbyterians, 101
Prescott, Samuel, 139
Presidential powers, in Constitution, 173
Press, freedom of, 177
Princeton University, 98
Printing press, **12**
Proclamation of 1763, 116–117
Prophetstown, Indiana, 207
Prostitution, 284–285
Protective tariffs, 221–222
Protestant Reformation, **37**
Providence, Rhode Island, 50
Providence Island, 29–30
Provincial conventions, 133–134
Provincial cultures, 95–100
Ptolemy, 12
Publicity stunts, 295
Public schools, 288, 290
Pueblo Revolt of 1680, 67
Pueblos, 4–5, 7–9, 327
Puritans, 37
    covenant ideal, 46–47

migration to New England, 44, 64, 66
Pequot War and aftermath, 47
Put-in-Bay, Battle of, 215
Putting-out manufacturing systems, 220

Quakers, 62, 148, 211, 349
Quartering Act, 129–130
Quartermaster Department (Civil War), 378–379
Quasi-War, 184–185, 193–194
Quebec, 32–33
Quebec Act, 129–130
Queen Anne's War, 57, 78, 104. *See also* War of the Spanish Succession
Quetzalcoatl, temple of, 4
Quincy, Josiah Jr., 127

Racism, 187–192
    development of racist theory, 191
    manumission and, 190–191
    against Mexicans, 342
    stereotyping, 284
Radical Republicans, 382, 406
Railroads, 268–269, 420
Raleigh, Sir Walter, 23–24
Randolph, Edmund, 171
Real Whigs, 117
Reconstruction
    black codes, 413
    black voters and, 419–420
    carpetbaggers and scalawags, 422
    comparison of plans, 417
    Congressional plan for, 413–419
    Constitutional crisis, 417–418
    failure of land redistribution, 417
    foreign expansion and, 426, 428
    general amnesty, 425–426
    industrialization and mill towns, 420–421
    Johnson's plan for, 410, 412, 417, 431–432
    judicial retreat from, 428
    Liberal Republican revolt, 425
    military districts (map), 416
    myth of "Negro rule," 421–422
    in the North, 424–425
    Radicals and, 413–414, 417, 432
    Republicans and racial equality, 421
    Republican state governments, 420
    retreat from, 424–426, 428–430, 432
    Southern politics and, 419–423
    tax policy and corruption, 422
    in the West, 426
    white resistance, 419
Reconstruction Acts of 1867–1868, 416–417
Reconstruction era, 405–407
Red Stick Creeks, 217
Reform movements, 286–290. *See also* Abolitionism
    engineering/science and, 290
    moral reform, 287–288
    public schools, 288, 290

"Regulators," 131, 419
Religion
  black churches, 409
  Catholicism, 11
  Christianity, 11
  Congregationalism, 49–50
  European societies, 10–11
  evangelical, 287
  freedom of, 40, 177
  Great Awakening, 100–102
  maintaining religious identity, 90
  in Mesoamerica, 19
  Native American culture, 8
  in New England, 43–44, 55
  politics and, 339
  Quebec Act, 129–130
  religious revivalism, 200, 286–287
  religious rituals, 100
  Second Great Awakening, 286
  slavery and, 10, 255–256
  syncretism, 19
  traditional African, 9–10
Report on Manufactures (Hamilton), 179
Report on Public Credit, 178
Representation
  proposal for colonial represenation, 116
  theories of, 117
  virtual, 134
Republicanism, 180
  educational reform, 175–176
  government design, 173, 178, 180
  varieties of, 141–142, 173–174
Republican Party
  appeal of, 352–353
  birth of, 350–351
  election of 1860, 365–369
  ideology of, 353
  racial equality in Reconstruction and,
    430
  Reconstruction and, 413–414
  Southern Reconstruction politics and,
    419–420
Restoration colonies, 59, 61
Revenue Act, 118
Revenue Act of 1789, 176
Revere, Paul, 124, 128, 139
Revivalism, 101, 286–287
Revolutionary War. *See* American
    Revolution
Rhode Island, 50
Rhode Island plan, 271, 273
Rice, 74
Rice, Thomas D., 285
Rice Coast, 9
Ridge, John, 243
Rights, statement of colonial, 128
*Rights of the British Colonies Asserted and
    Proved* (Otis), 118–119
Ripley, George, 292
Roads, 267
Roanoke Island, 24

Rochester, NY, 278
Rockefeller, John D., 106
Rockingham, Lord, 122
Rolfe, John, 39
Romero, Tomas, 343
Ross, John, 244
Rowlandson, Thomas (sketch by), 147
Royal African Company, 69
Rudyerd, William, 29
Ruggles, David, 348–349
Rum trade, 71–72, 118
Rural communties, 275–276
Rush-Bagot Treaty, 226
Russell, Charles M, 208

Sacagawea, 206
Sagayenkwaraton (Brant) (Indian convert
    and go-between), 57–58
Saharan Desert, 9
"Sailing around the wind," 13, 27
Salem witchcraft trials, 78
San Antonio, 85
San Diego, 85
San Francisco, 323
Santa Anna, General Antonio Lopez de,
    318
Santa Fe Trail, 310, 321–322
São Tomé, 13
Saratoga, 152
Sauks, 307
Scot immigrants, 89–90
Scots-Irish immigrants, 89
Scott, Dred, 356–357
Scott, Harriet Robinson, 356
Scott, Thomas, 424
Scott, Winfield, 344, 349
Secession
  crisis of, 365–369
  states' rights and nullification, 228
Second Amendment, 177
Second Bank of the United States,
    222–225, 334
Second Barbary War, 218
Second Continental Congress, 140–141,
    148, 165
Second Great Awakening, 286, 298
Second party system, 336–338
Sectionalism, 221–227
Secularism, 102
Sedition Act, 184–185, 194, 195
Seditious libel, 102
Self-interest, 178
"Self-made men," 106
Seminoles, 315
Seminole wars, 245
Seneca Falls, 339, 361
Separate spheres, 277
Separation of church and state, 199–200
Separation of powers, 173
Separatists, 37, 43–44
Serra, Father Junipero, 85

Seven Years' War, 104, 113–116, 134, 136
Seward, William H., 365, 426, 428
Seymour, Horatio, 418
Seymour, Samuel, 303
Shakers, 291
Sharecropping, 410–411, 456
Shareholders, 226
Shaw, Robert Gould, 387
Shawnees, 131, 207, 315
Shays, Daniel, 170–171
Shay's Rebellion, 170–171
Sherman, William Tecumseh, 395
  Field Order Number 15, 408
  March to the Sea, 397
Shiloh, Battle of, 373
Shipbuilding, 76–77
Shirley, William, 104
Sierra Leone, 147
Silk Road, 9
Silver
  colonial currency and, 65
  Spanish colonial expansion and,
    19–20
Simpson, James H., 303
Slater, John, 220
Slater, Samuel, 220, 271, 273
Slaughter House cases, 428
Slave culture and resistance, 254–258, 260.
    See also Slaves and slavery
  African cultural survival, 254–255
  black family and, 256
  in British colonies, 94–95
  early examples, 75–76
  Gabriel's Rebellion, 193, 196
  Nat Turner's insurrection, 258, 260
  rebellions in South Carolina and New
    York, 103–104
  religion and music, 255–256
  resistance strategies, 257–260
  symbolic resistance, 88
  Wheatley's poetry and, 126
Slave Power Conspiracy, 344, 349,
    356–357, 360
Slaves and slavery. *See also* Slave culture
    and resistance
  advertising for, 75
  Anglo-American colonization and, 58,
    61, 64
  Atlantic trading system and, 53, 68–70,
    73, 80–81
  in the Caribbean, 53, 68–72, 81
  and the Constitution, 172–173
  Continental Association agreement,
    132–133
  domestic slave trade, 257
  Dred Scott case, 356–357
  in 18th century, 86
  emancipation of, 382–385
  everyday conditions, 252
  expansion of, 350–355
  families and, 94

freedom from, 407–410
fugitive slave laws, 169
by Indians, 85–86
international slave trade, 210
involuntary migrants from Africa, 86
in Latin America, 18
life and labor for, 252–254
middle passage, 71
model of plantation slavery, 13
in the North, 75
Northwest Ordinance and, 169
origins and destinations (map), 87
proslavery arguments, 237–238
reparations for, 260
Republican opposition to, 353
rice and indigo and, 74
secession crisis and, 365–369
sexual relations between masters and slaves, 251–252, 256
slave-master relationships, 254
"slave power conspiracy," 344
slave-trading practice, 86
South as slave society, 238
in southwest, 313
violence/intimidation against, 253–254
West Africa and, 10, 69–70
westward expansion and, 304–305
work routines, 252–253
Slidell, John, 395
Smallpox, 19–20
  in Continental Army, 154
  inoculation, 99, 154
Smith, E. Kirby, 390
Smith, John, **38**
Smith, Joseph, 290–291
Smithson, James, 290
Smithsonian Institution, 290
Smuggling, 76–77
Society of Friends (Quakers), 62
Society of Jesus (Jesuits), 33
Sons of Liberty, 121–122
Sotomayor, Sonia, 133
South. See also Confederate States of America
  Civil War and transformation of, 375–378
  distinctive characteristics of, 233–238
  industrialization and urbanization in, 376, 464–465
  proslavery arguments, 237–238
  Reconstruction politics in, 415–416, 419–423
  South-North comparisons, 234–237
South Carolina
  African enslavement and, 73–74
  in American Revolution, 156
  claim of right of secession, 228
  colonial economy, 92–93
  Indian enslavement and, 74–75
  rice cultivation and slavery, 86

secession and, 360
slave rebellion, 103–104
slave trade, 210
Southern Cultivator (journal), 250
Southern states and territories
  characteristics, 233–238
  landless whites, 246–247
  planters in, 248–252
  slave society in, 238
  social pyramid in, 245–248
  westward expansion, 238–239, 241–245
  world-view and proslavery argument, 237–238
  yeoman farmers, 245–246
South Pass, 310
Sovereignty, threats to, 209–210
Spain
  conquest and colonization, 17–20, 23–24, 27, 52–54
  gold and silver and decline of, 19–20
  Pinckney's Treaty, 182
  territorial expansion, 84–85
Spalding, Eliza and Henry, 320
Spanish Armada, 23
Specie Circular, 336, 338
Speech, freedom of, 177, 194
Spice Route, 8–9
Spices, 12
Spinning, 125
Spinning mill, 220
Spirituals, 256
Spoils system, 332
Sports, 284–285
Squanto. See Tisquantum
St. Augustine, 31–32
St. Clair, Arthur, 186
Stamp Act, 118–122
  demonstrations against, 118–122, 135
  opposition and repeal, 120–122
Stanton, Edwin M., 378, 417–418
Stanton, Elizabeth Cady, 338–339, 361, 407, 415
"The Star-Spangled Banner," 217
State debts, 178
State Department, 177
State governments, 195
  Constitution ratification, 174, 188–189
  limiting, 167
  Northwest Ordinance and, 169
Statement of colonial rights, 128
State's rights, Tenth Amendment, 228
Steamboats, 267, 308
Steam power, 222, 225
Steel, Ferdinand L., 246
Steel plow, 307
Stephens, Alexander H., 344, 369, 392, 407, 413
Stereotyping, of blacks, 284
Stevens, Thaddeus, 406, 413–414
Still, William, 348–349

Stono Rebellion, 103–104
Stowe, Harriet Beecher, 327
Strauss, Levi, 323
Strouds, 95
Stuart, Gilbert, 175
Stuart, J. E. B., 373
Stuart monarchs of England, 59
Suffrage, 339, 415. See also Women's rights
Sugar, 13–14, 21, 52–53, 63–64, 76–77, 135
Sugar Act, 118
Sumner, Charles, 350–351, 355, 406, 413–414
Supreme Court, U.S. See also specific rulings
  establishment of, 177
  under John Marshall, 202–203
Susquehannocks, 68
Sutter's Mill, 312, 323
Swahili language and culture, 8
Switzerland, 89
Syncretism, 19
Syphilis, 21

Taíno people, 14–15
Talleyrand, 184
Tallmadge, James Jr., 224
Taney, Roger, 356–357
Taos Revolt, 343
Tappan, Arthur, 293
Tariff of Abominations, 333
Tariffs
  protective tariffs, 221–222
  Tariff of 1816, 222
Task system, 74, 253
Taxes and taxation
  authority of national government for, 173
  Fries's Rebellion, 193
  issues leading to Constitution, 170–171
  Real Whig ideology and, 117
  Reconstruction policy and corruption, 422
Taylor, Zachary, 215, 343, 345, 346
Tea, 72, 97
Tea Act, 129
Teaching profession, 277–278
Tea party movement, 160
Tea tax, 122–125, 129
Tecumseh, 207–208, 215, 217, 218
Tejanos, 315
Tejonihokawara (Hendrick) (Indian convert and go-between), 57–58
Telegraph, 269
Temperance, 288–289, 352
Tenement housing, 425
Tenochtitlán, 1, 4, 5
Tenskwatawa, 207–208
Tenth Amendment, 228
Tenure of Office Act, 417
Teotihuacán, 4

Territorial expansion
ethnic diversity and, 84–90
slavery politics and, 361, 365–366
Spanish and French, 84–85
Texas
annexation of, 318–320, 326, 328, 341, 361
colonial population, 85
frontier, 314
as Lone Star Republic, 318
Manifest Destiny, 340
Mexican control of, 317
politics of, 318
Spanish settlement in, 85
Texas Rangers, 318
Textile industry, 271, 463–464
Thames, Battle of the, 215
Theaters, 284–285
Theyanoguin, Hendrick, 82, 111–112
Third Amendment, 177
Thirteenth Amendment, 384, 406–407, 431
Thomas, George H., 395
Thoreau, Henry David, 292, 359
Three-fifths clause, 172, 415
Tilden, Samuel J., 429
Tippecanoe, Battle of, 208
Tisquantum (Squanto), 44
Tobacco, 21, 39, 68–69, 74, 76, 90
Tompkins, Daniel, 224
Tom Thumb (locomotive), 268
Tourgée, Albion, 424
Townshend, Charles, 122
Townshend Acts
passage of, 122–125
repeal of, 125
resistance to, 122–125
tea tax, 122–123, 129
Township and range system, 168
Trade, 80–81
among Indians and Europeans, 23
Atlantic system of, 68–70, 73, 80–81
canals and, 221–224
fur trade, 23
with Indians, 95, 317
network of, in British colonies, 90
pine tree shilling and, 65
in pre-Columbian North America, 5–6
between states, 170–171
Trail of Tears, 244
Transcendentalism, 291–292
Transcontinental Railroad, 310
Transportation
canals, 267–270, 272
funding of, 221–224
government and, 268–269
railroads, 268–269, 420
regional connections, 269
roads, 267, 269–270
steamboats, 267, 269–270
urbanization and, 278
Transportation revolution, 275

Travels (Marco Polo), 12
Treasury Department, 177, 178
Treasury notes, as national currency, 179
Treaty of Alliance, 152, 180
Treaty of Amity and Commerce, 152
Treaty of Fort Jackson, 217
Treaty of Ghent, 217–218, 229
Treaty of Greenville, 186, 196, 207–208
Treaty of Guadalupe and Hidalgo, 344
Treaty of New Echota, 244
Treaty of Paris, 115, 159
Indian negotiations and, 166–168
opposition to provisions of, 166
Treaty of Payne's Landing, 245
Treaty of Tordesillas, 15, 17
Trenton, 151
Tripoli, 209
A True Picture of Emigration (Burlend), 304
Trumbull, John, 204
Trumbull, Lyman, 414
Truth, Sojourner, 293
Tsenacommacah, 38–39
Tubman, Harriet, 293, 349
Tudor dynasty, 12
Turkeys, 45
Turnage, Wallace, 363–364
Turner, Frederick Jackson, 300–301
Turner, Henry McNeal, 427
Turner, Nat, 237, 258–260
Tuscarora War, 75
Twelfth Amendment, 193, 203
"Twenty Negro" law, 377
Two Treatises of Government (Locke), 99–100
Tyler, John, 340

Uncle Robin in his Cabin and Tom Without One in Boston, 327–328
Uncle Tom's Cabin (Stowe), 327–328
Underground Railroad, 293, 348–349
Unilateralism, 182
Union Army, 387, 389–390. *See also* Civil War
occupation zones, 390
racism in, 387
United Daughters of the Confederacy, 430
United Provinces of Rio de la Plata, 226
United States, corn production, 22
Unreasonable search and seizure, 177
Urbanization, 278–286. *See also* Cities
cities as symbols, 286
ethnic tensions, 282–283
extremes of wealth, 278, 280–281
immigration and, 281–282
major 19th c. cities (map), 279
market-related development, 278
migration of poor blacks and whites, 420–421
racism and, 284
urban boom, 278
urban culture, 284–285
U.S. Military Academy at West Point, 215

U.S. Sanitary Commission, 380–381
U.S. v. Cruikshank, 428
USA PATRIOT Act, 194
Utes, 85, 313
Utopian communities, 290–292, 298
Utopian experiments, 290–292
Mormons, 290–291
Oneidans, Owenites, and Fourierists, 291–292
Shakers, 291

Vallandigham, Clement L., 394
Van Buren, Martin, 240, 244, 335
election of 1836, 337–338
Vassa, Gustavus, 106
Verrazzano, Giovanni da, 17
Vespucci, Amerigo, 15
Vetos, 332
Vice-admiralty courts, 77
Vicksburg, 389, 391, 402
Vinland, **17**
Violence, against slaves, 253–254, 256
Virginia
Algonquian and English cultural differences, 39
Baptists in, 101–102
Civil War in, 398
founding of, 38–40, 55
House of Burgesses, 42
Indian assaults, 39–40
Jamestown and Tsenacommacah, 38–39
population, 1625, 42
tobacco cultivation, 39
Virginia Company, 38, 40
Virginia Plan, 171–172
Virginia Resolution, 185, 228, 360
Virginia Stamp Act Resolves, 119
Virtual representation, 117, 134
Virtue, 175
Voting
state regulation of, 201
voter intimidation, 334
Voting rights, 415, 417–418

Wade, Benjamin, 406
Wade-Davis bill, 406
Waldseemüller, Martin, 16
Walker, David, 293
Walker, William, 354
Walking Purchase, 104–105
Waltham-Lowell Mills, 220–221
Waltham plan of industrialization, 271
Wampanoags, 67–68
War Department, 177
Warfare
in the Caribbean, 34–35
Colonial wars (1689-1763) chronology, 104
Europeans and Indians, 105–106
frontier hostilities, 155
War Hawks, 213

War of 1812, 213–219, 228–230
  American sovereignty reasserted, 218
  burning capitals, 215
  domestic consequences, 218–219
  invasion of Canada, 215
  naval battles, 215
  recruitment, 215–216
  selling of, 216
  in the south, 217
  Treaty of Ghent, 217–218
War of Austrian Succession, 92, 104
War of the Spanish Succession, 78, 104. *See also* Queen Anne's War
Washington, George, 132, 141, 151, 163, 175
  Annapolis Convention and, 170
  Farewell Address, 182
  France and, 180
  Jay Treaty debate, 182
  presidency of, 177, 195
  and Whiskey Rebellion, 179
Washington, Harry, 163
Wayne, Anthony, 186
Webster, Daniel, 337–338, 347
Webster, Noah, 204
Weems, Mason Locke, 175
Weld, Theodore, 293
West, concept of, 301
West Africa (Guinea), 9–10
  Atlantic slave trade and, 69–70
  slavery in, 10
Westos Indian tribe, 74–75
West Point, 215
Westward expansion, 185–187, 196, 204–208 307–308, 322
  in American imagination, 300–304, 325
  chronology, 301
  cultural frontiers, 320–324, 326
  federal government and, 308–311, 313, 326
  Indians and, 238–239, 241–245, 306–307
  land speculation, 222–223, 307–308
  Lewis and Clark Expedition, 206–207

Louisiana Purchase, 205–206
  maps, 302, 305
  military and, 311
  Missouri Compromise, 224
  motivations for, 304
  New Orleans, 204–205
  public lands, 311
  slavery debate, 347–348
  southwestern borderlands, 313–320, 326
  trans-Appalachian resistance, 304–308
  transcontinental exploration, 310
Wheatley, Phyllis, 126
Whigs, 328, 334–335
  demise of, 352–353
  Democrats and, 336–337, 361
  economic crisis and, 338
  election of 1840 and, 338
Whiskey Rebellion, 179, 182
White, Hugh, 337–338
White, John (watercolor by), 24
Whitefield, George, 100–101
Whitman, Narcissa and Marcus, 320
Whitman, Walt, 381
Whitney, Eli, 204, 271
Wilderness, Battle of the, 398
Wilkinson, James, 203–204
William, king of England, 59, 77–78
William and Mary College, 98
Williams, Roger, 50
Wilmot, David, 344
Wilmot Proviso, 344, 346, 357
Winnebagos, 304, 306
Winthrop, John, **45**, 46, 55
Wisconsin
  early settlement of, 306
  lumber industry, 308
Witchcraft trials, 66, 78
Women. *See also* Gender roles; Women's rights
  in agricultural societies, 7–8
  childbearing and, 251–252
  in Civil War, 376–377, 380–381
  education of, 98, 175–176

  on farms, 275
  in "ideal" family, 276–277
  in labor protests, 273
  moral reform and, 287–288
  political activism of, 133
  political leadership in pre-Columbian America, 8
  and politics, 213
  and the Republic, 187–188, 191–192
  rights of, 338–339, 361
  voting rights of, 201, 524, 534–535
  in workforce, 277–278
Women's Loyal National League, 407
Women's rights, 298
  property and spousal rights, 420
  suffrage, 415
Woodbury, Levi, 336
Woods, William, 46
Woolen mills, 210
Wôpanâak Language Reclamation Project, 25
Worcester v. Georgia (1832), 242
Workday, eight-hour workday bill, 425
Workforce, women in, 277–278
Working conditions, eight-hour workday, 425, 471
"The Wound Dresser" (Whitman), 381
Writ of mandamus, 203

XYZ Affair, 184

Yale University, 98
Yamasees, 75
Yeoman farmers, 238, 245–246
  class tensions and, 247
  folk culture of, 245–246
  livelihoods of, 245
York (slave), 206
Yorktown, Battle at, 156, 158
Young, Brigham, 321–322
Yucatan Peninsula, 4

Zenger, John Peter, 102